Teaching the Learning Disabled

A Cognitive Developmental Approach

D. Kim Reid
University of Texas, Dallas

Evelyn B. Block
University of Texas, Dallas

Gina Conti-Ramsden
University of Manchester, England

Carol Sue Englert
Michigan State University

George W. Fair
University of Texas, Dallas

Paula C. Grinnell
Carrollton–Farmers Branch Independent
School District, Texas

Sandy Friel-Patti
University of Texas, Dallas

Wayne P. Hresko
North Texas State University

Gaye McNutt
Resource-room teacher of LD children,
Houston, Texas

Annemarie Sullivan Palincsar
Michigan State University

Michael E. Pullis
University of Missouri, Columbia

Nancy Nelson Spivey
Carnegie-Mellon University, Pittsburgh

Allyn and Bacon, Inc.
Boston   London   Sydney   Toronto

Copyright © 1988 by Allyn and Bacon, Inc.
A Division of Simon & Schuster
160 Gould Street
Needham, Massachusetts 02194

Library of Congress Cataloging-in-Publication Data

Reid, D. Kim.
  Teaching the learning disabled.

  Bibliography: p.
  Includes index.
  1. Learning disabled children—Education—United
States. I. Title.
LC4705.F45 1988   371.92   87-33262
ISBN 0-205-10522-X

Acknowledgment is gratefully made for permission to reprint from the following source on pp. 234 and 300:

Brown Bear, Brown Bear, What Do You See? by Bill Martin, Jr. Copyright © 1967, 1983 by Holt, Rinehart & Winston. Reprinted by permission of Henry Holt and Co., Inc.

Production coordinator: Helyn Pultz
Editorial-production service: P. M. Gordon Associates
Cover administrator: Linda K. Dickinson

Printed in the United States of America

10 9 8 7 6 5 4   93

To Mom and John

Brief Contents

Complete Contents

Preface

This book is about teaching. It provides practical, research-based methods of instruction for teaching the learning disabled (LD). It is offered as a state-of-the-art approach to instruction. All of the interventions suggested are data-based (controlled studies and systematic classroom analyses provided the data) and theoretically sound. We fully expect the next few years of research to further our knowledge, and, as with all applications derived from ongoing research, teachers will need to stay abreast of important developments and revise their intervention practices accordingly.

Most textbooks designed to teach prospective and in-service teachers methods for instructing the LD adhere to either an underlying abilities or behavioral model of intervention. The first advocates the remediation of fundamental processes thought crucial to effective learning (e.g., memory, attention, perception), while the second focuses on the direct instruction of academic skills without regard for psychological processes.

Our cognitive developmental approach, in contrast, is based on information processing theory (rather than specific abilities or behavioral models) and has the advantage of being able to treat the processes of learning as a fundamental concern without changing the instructional goals of learning to read, write, problem solve, and calculate.

The cognitive developmental approach of this book is unique in that it treats learning problems as representative of a point on a continuum of learning abilities and disabilities. One impact of this approach is that the content area chapters, whenever appropriate, begin with a section on development prior to schooling, which discusses what children usually learn about the topic (e.g., language, reading, writing, or mathematics) before coming to school. This information is central to a cognitive approach for two reasons. First, since the cognitive orientation to instruction advocates that teachers build on children's strengths, background knowledge, and experience, teachers must learn what children already know. Second, many children will not have had (or will not have learned from) experiences commensurate with those of their peers. In such cases, the teacher may need to provide similar experiences. Additionally, these sections provide information for those teachers interested in the development of preschool children who may later exhibit achievement difficulties.

The competencies and characteristics with which a child comes to school, however, may not be the major sources of information that teachers need when planning instructional negotiations. There has recently been a movement toward examining instructional episodes from an *interactive perspective*, which minimizes the effects of typically unchangeable learner characteristics and focuses teachers' attention on factors—learners' activities, the materials to be learned, and the criterion task—that can be manipulated to maximize the impact of instruction. This book reflects that movement.

The first chapter of this book discusses the theoretical foundation from which the interactive perspective has been derived. The second chapter examines the effects that each and all of those factors are likely to have both on learning and on learning how to learn. The third chapter, which completes Part I, is devoted to an analysis of how learning interacts with teaching. It includes discussions of (1) what generally happens in resource room instruction where LD students are most often served, (2) what the recent research on teaching has revealed as criteria for effective instruction, and (3) what research-based interventions used with the LD appear to meet the established criteria. Continuous data-based assessment is advocated as the basis for evaluating both the pace of instruction and the effects of various interventions.

In addition to the documented benefits of direct instruction, the cognitive developmental approach described here advocates the use of scaffolding techniques which support students in activities they cannot perform alone. Together with direct instruction on strategic behaviors within the context of academic tasks, scaffolding has provided a powerful approach to instruction of LD students.

Because these students exhibit significant problems in social and emotional development, Part II of this book deals with affective issues. What is unique about this presentation is that, like the instruction of strategic behaviors, instruction in social and emotional skills is most often transparent, that is, it is the means to effective learning rather than an instructional objective per se. Part III contains specific instructional recommendations as they are related to the material to be learned and various criterion tasks, and addresses questions such as: What develops prior to schooling? What is an appropriate instructional model? What is to be learned? How will successful learning be demonstrated? What problems do LD students frequently have? What learner activities are appropriate? How will each student's strengths and weaknesses be assessed? What recovery procedures can be used for persistent problems? And, finally, how should students be matched to tasks and performance monitored? The majority of the content chapters cover oral and written language (reading, spelling and handwriting, and composition) and study skills, since these are currently the top priorities among resource-room teachers. Additional chapters on children's literature, mathematics, and computer instruction have been included to round out the curriculum.

In sum, Part I provides the framework for the book and reviews the research literature on guiding students' learning how to learn, that is, teaching. Part II functions almost as an overlay to Part I, mapping social-emotional considerations onto teaching functions related to achievement gains, and Part III is a compilation of content-specific theory and research reviews evaluated for their respective contributions to the art/science of teaching.

In addition to its theory and research-based approach to instruction, this book has several other features worthy of note. First, each chapter begins with a graphic display of its content, designed to provide students with an advance organizer. Numerous tables and figures are also included. Some are used to highlight information, some are used to provide handy reference guides to assessment or instructional procedures, and still others act as summary devices. Boxes have also been used to offset step-by-step descriptions of instructional activities so that they can be easily followed. Finally, each chapter begins with a set of questions that direct students' attention to the important concepts covered. The text is comprehensive with respect to instruction of the school-age child but is presented in simple language. When technical terms have been used, they have been defined and italicized.

A word of thanks is due to the people who contributed to this volume for keeping the faith when many persons would have abandoned hope. The writing was plagued by a series of catastrophes that included a divorce, the death of a loved one, a house razed by fire, and serious personal illnesses. Four writers, who joined this effort only months before the text went to press, submitted excellent work within very exacting deadlines. These kinds of superhuman efforts can never be sufficiently repaid.

As with any project so extensive, there are those wonderfully supportive persons whose names do not appear on the cover or chapter headings but without whose dedicated efforts the book would not have become a reality. Foremost among the people to whom this book owes a debt of appreciation are Drs. George Hay and Roberta Berger. Many a wide-eyed stare made it clear that George and Bobbi agreed to become involved when they were still innocent of the complexities of preparing a book-length manuscript for publication. Their indefatigable efforts have rapidly converted them into experts in managing the typing pool; drafting the myriad lists of tables, figures, contents, permissions, indices, and the like that publishers require, and checking headings and references. On behalf of all the contributors I offer George and Bobbi sincere thanks.

Many others worked closely with George, and these people too deserve recognition: Julie Herrick, Natalie Holley, Ginny Pitre, Marilyn Herrick, Patrick Pitre, and Leon Pitre. Finally, Lee White the program secretary in Special Education at the University of Texas at Dallas (now retired), encouraged us and even went so far as to try typing on a word processor—an impressive gesture, since she approached the machine with more than a little fear.

We sincerely appreciate the contributions our reviewers—Drs. Kay Butler, Carol Sue Englert, and Bernice Wong—made to this book. There are also two individuals who do not necessarily share the vision articulated in this text but who have served me well as friends and mentors, Drs. Jeanette McCarthy Gallagher and Donald D. Hammill. Their jaundiced eyes have sometimes spurred me on and sometimes made me pull up short, but in either case have encouraged me to be a better scholar.

The people closest to me, my friends and students and especially my energetic nine-year-old son, John, sustained me through this effort with a level of enthusiasm, sacrifice, and support that I shall always cherish. To them my deepest gratitude.

D.K.R.

About the Authors

Evelyn B. Block is a doctoral candidate in Human Development and Communication Sciences at the University of Texas at Dallas. She serves part time as psychiatric counselor for learning disabled and attention-deficit disordered children in Mt. Kisco, New York.

Gina Conti-Ramsden received a Ph.D. in Communication Disorders from the University of Texas at Dallas. She is currently a lecturer in the Department of Education at the University of Manchester, England, and is also doing postdoctoral research with Dr. Catherine Snow at Harvard University. Her major research interest is linguistic characterization of child-directed speech to language-impaired children.

Carol Sue Englert received a Ph.D. in Special Education from Indiana University and is now an Associate Professor of Special Education at Michigan State University, where she participates in the Institute for Research in Teaching. She is currently studying strategy instruction in reading and writing and the factors that make teachers effective change agents.

George W. Fair is both Program Head in Special Education and Deputy Acting Director of the Callier Center for Communication Disorders at the University of Texas at Dallas. His research and writing address issues in mathematics instruction for mildly handicapped children.

Sandy Friel-Patti received a Ph.D. from Purdue University and is an Associate Professor of Communication Disorders at the University of Texas at Dallas. She is well-known for her research in language and the interactive parameters of mothers and their language-impaired children. She is the Principal Investigator of an NIH project examining relations among speech, language, and early middle-ear disease.

Paula C. Grinnell received a Ph.D. in Reading from Texas Woman's University. She later undertook postdoctoral study with Professor Robert Sternberg in the Department of Psychology at Yale University. She is currently Test Development Coordinator in the Carrollton–Farmers Branch Independent School District in Texas. She is perhaps best known for her IRA micromonograph, "How can I prepare my young child for reading?"

Wayne P. Hresko is an Associate Professor in Special Education at North Texas State University. He is interested in applications of computer technology to teaching special-needs children and is the author of several nationally standardized tests for young children.

Gaye McNutt received a Ph.D. in Special Education from the University of Texas at Austin. She has long been a proponent of the whole-language orientation in literacy instruction. She is currently a resource-room teacher of LD children in Houston, Texas.

Annemarie Sullivan Palincsar received a Ph.D. in Special Education at the University of Illinois at Champaign–Urbana, where she was associated with the Center for the Study of Reading. She is currently an Associate Professor of Special Education at Michigan State University. Her research interests concern instructional strategies to improve listening and reading-comprehension skills.

Michael E. Pullis, currently at the University of Missouri at Columbia, was an Associate Professor of Special Education and College Master in the School of Human Development at the University of Texas at Dallas. His research focuses on developmental issues in psychopathology, especially temperamental effects.

D. Kim Reid is President of Education, Inc. of Dallas, TX. During the writing of this book she was an Associate Professor in the School of Human Development at the University of Texas at Dallas. Her research and writing bear directly on the explication and application of a cognitive developmental instructional model for LD children.

Nancy Nelson Spivey earned her doctorate at University of Texas–Austin and later taught at Texas Woman's University. Nancy is now in the English Department at Carnegie-Mellon University in Pittsburgh.

PART I

A Cognitive Developmental Approach
to Learning Disabilities: Cognition

During the late 1950s and early 1960s it became increasingly evident that a group of children were, for no apparent reason, failing one or more subjects in school. They were neither emotionally disturbed nor mentally retarded. Furthermore, they did not show clear evidence of either brain damage or physical disability. They looked and behaved like other children in most important respects. The preponderance of the group came from middle to upper income families who provided adequate care and schooling. Dr. Samuel Kirk coined the term *learning disability* (LD) to describe the problems of these children.

At first, it was thought that LD children could be "cured" during the early school years by training them in the basic perceptual or motor skills and abilities they were thought to be lacking. Only gradually was it recognized that LD is not an early and middle childhood problem but rather persists into adolescence and adulthood. Consequently, there has been increasing pressure to provide both educational and counseling services for LD secondary students and adults. (National Joint Committee on Learning Disabilities, 1985. See Box 1.1 for a listing of the member organizations.)

Until very recently there was little concern for the provision of programs for the preschool LD child. Typically, LD children have not been identified until they have failed in school—sometimes struggling for three or four years before being referred for testing and remediation. In 1985, however, the National Joint Committee on Learning Disabilities (NJCLD) issued a position paper calling for greater emphasis on identification, assessment, planning, and intervention for children from birth through kindergarten who demonstrate specific developmental delays or deficits that often foreshadow later learning disabilities.

Specific indicators of children at risk may vary with respect to the particular area of deficit or delay; for example, children who exhibit early delays in spoken language may later exhibit sustained oral or written language difficulties or both, or no difficulties at all. LD children who manifest problems in mathematics may or may not have exhibited early

1

Box 1.1 Member Organizations of the National Joint Committee on Learning Disabilities as of February 1985

Association for Children and Adults with Learning Disabilities

American Speech-Language-Hearing Association

Council for Learning Disabilities

Division for Children with Communication Disorders, Council for Exceptional Children

Division for Learning Disabilities, Council for Exceptional Children

International Reading Association

National Association for School Psychologists

The Orton Dyslexia Society

---

language difficulties. In short, there is presently no clearly identified relationship between early at-risk indicators and later learning outcomes. Consequently, the NJCLD recommends systematic observation and intervention whenever delay appears likely.

In this book chapters that address teaching in the content areas begin with sections that identify the abilities and skills that young children are likely to develop prior to school entrance. There is a burgeoning literature to testify that children develop literacy behaviors well before school entrance. The same is true for early mathematics learning. Consequently, rather than looking for potential predictors (or at-risk indicators), we are becoming increasingly better able to examine the progress preschoolers make in spontaneous development within specific domains. Because we now have information about normal developmental patterns, we can use this knowledge as a guideline for determining the amount of variability that constitutes an important difference in development among preschool children. In short, rather than examine at-risk indicators, we can measure the acquisition of domain-specific knowledge directly during the preschool years.

New understandings of both the development and importance of domain-specific knowledge have also had an impact on our thinking about school-age LD children. We used to think of LD children as disabled in the sense of a damaged or dysfunctional organism along the lines of a medical model (this is often referred to as the specific abilities approach), but we now know that human abilities are dynamic and mutable. Consequently, we try to determine the extent to which a child can operate efficiently while performing a particular academic task and to teach that child the remaining domain-specific knowledge requisite to successful performance (Brown & Campione, 1986; Campione & Armbruster, 1986; Derry & Murphy, 1986). As we will see in Chapter 1, our approach differs from the traditional behavioral approach in that it avoids the lack of transfer problem that results from learning skills in isolation by teaching new knowledge and procedures in the context in which they will be used. Obviously, this new approach requires that teachers have some knowledge of how learning occurs both generally and within specific domains. Consequently, the first chapter will describe how children learn and learn to learn so that we may understand why some children fail to do so.

Another recent trend has been to identify LD children with respect to both the severity of their disorders and the particular nature of the problem, that is, as functional subtypes. Poplin (1981) argued that LD children with severe disorders had been virtually neglected by special education professionals and that LD was becoming synonymous with "mildly handicapped." She pointed out the importance of subtype distinctions in understanding severe LD. Our approach is consistent with Poplin's view in that it defines children's problems with respect to the particular tasks they have trouble performing. But our approach labels the children with respect to the behaviors they need to acquire (e.g., a child with problems detecting reading errors), rather than as dysfunctional organisms (e.g., a reading disabled child). "The change in focus, from implicating a general, all pervading, intellectual weakness in the child to assessing partial or incomplete knowledge—could have important social and educational consequences" (Brown & Campione, 1986, p. 1062).

It is difficult to ascertain precisely how many children and adults fit current definitions of LD. Prevalence figures are influenced by a number of variables, including the definition used, the demographics of the population under study, and the levels of performance required on individual tests. As a result, estimates of the incidence of LD have ranged from 1 percent to 30 percent of the school-age population, depending on what criteria have been implemented. The National Advisory Committee on Handicapped Children (1968) has estimated that between 1 percent and 3 percent of school children are LD. This figure is conservative. McNutt (1986) determined from a national survey conducted among state education agencies that only 14.9 percent of the states identified so few children as LD. About two million children were receiving educational services for LD in 1980 (Werner & Smith, 1980). No one knows how many adults with LD exist.

We do not address the issue of the identification of LD children or adults because such a wide variety of operational definitions, tests, formulas and cut-off scores can be used (McNutt, 1986). Furthermore, teachers are typically not responsible for labeling people, except when they serve on committees whose standards and tests have been prespecified. It is fair to say, however, that in general children and adolescents are identified as LD if they (1) are of normal intelligence or above (they sometimes score slightly below the average range on intelligence tests, but there is reason to believe that the learning problem itself affects the test score); (2) are having difficulties in a few academic areas, but do not show a learning deficiency in others (although by high school development in all academic areas may be affected); and (3) are not suffering from a condition or disorder that can explain their learning problems. It is important to note that there has been a trend toward recognizing that LD and other handicapping conditions may coexist. It must not be the case, however, that the concomitant disorder alone can account for the problems in learning.

Thus, when we refer to LD children, adolescents, or adults, we do not mean to suggest that the *person* is deficient as an organism, but rather that this person's performance vis-à-vis some particular task or set of tasks is problematic. Knowing how people who perform well accomplish a particular task can sometimes (but not always) give guidance with respect to the kinds of behaviors the LD individual needs to learn. Our approach, therefore, is both cognitive (i.e., it focuses on the process of learning that goes on in the learner's mind) and developmental (i.e., it addresses the changes that occur over time).

Chapter 1

Learning and Learning to Learn

D. Kim Reid

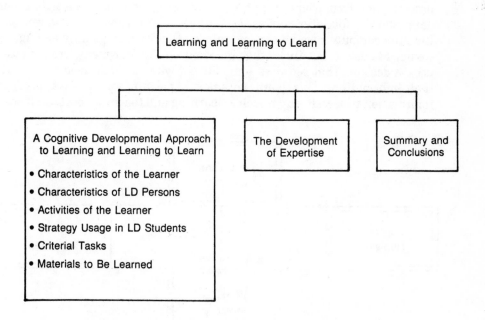

Questions to Consider

1. What contributions has the study of information processing made to our understanding of learning and teaching?
2. Why is it important for LD students to have access to a normalized (rather than a "bottom-up") curriculum?
3. What variables interact during learning?
4. What specific kinds of interactions are typical of LD students?
5. How does knowledge of the "development of expertise" enhance our understanding of LD?

Siegler (1983) has argued that the leading approach to the study of cognitive development is information processing. Scientists using this approach think of the human mind as similar in many respects to a digital computer (see Figure 1.1). This analogy provides us with a way of thinking about what happens in the human brain. It should be clear, however, that the brain is a far more powerful and wondrous instrument than a computer. Although the analogy should not be interpreted as a literal explanation of what happens when people learn and solve problems, some concepts about how computers work are extremely useful in understanding how our brains function. Like the computer, information stored in our brains, for example, is decoded (i.e., interpreted), encoded (i.e., represented by a code), and sometimes even recoded (i.e., represented in a different way). The complex cognitive system in our minds is able to process the informational input (e.g., compare it or combine it with other data, store it for later retrieval, or bring it into conscious awareness). Like the computer, we keep some information in storage only as long as we need to use it, but tuck other information into our memories for later use—a decision that requires some idea of what we will need to do with that information. This point becomes important when we apply the information-processing approach to learning and teaching, because it sug-

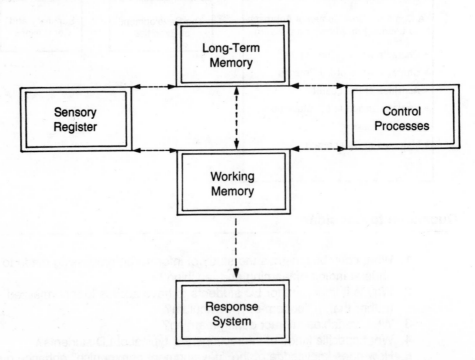

FIGURE 1.1 A Simplified Model of a Computer-like Information Processing System.

gests that learners must know at the outset what they will do with information if they are to know how to code it. (We will return to this idea in Chapter 3, when we discuss planning instruction for generalization.)

Different types of knowledge are stored in differently sized units and at various levels of complexity. The three types of knowledge are: (1) *declarative knowledge,* or facts, word meanings, and other data; (2) *procedural knowledge,* or information about how to carry out various activities; and (3) *conditional knowledge,* or information about when and why to perform various activities. This distinction is important to teachers because it shows that we can no longer be satisfied teaching content alone. We must also instruct students in how, when, and why to perform the tasks we assign—concerns currently addressed only infrequently.

Levels of size and complexity of knowledge range from small and elementary units (e.g., the perceptual features that enable us to recognize a letter of the alphabet) to larger wholes that encompass several elementary units and are at higher levels of abstraction (e.g., sentence meanings) to the higher order units that define knowledge structures (e.g., schemata, plans, strategies, and rules used in thinking and problem solving) (Flavell, 1985). Much of the instruction provided for LD students under both the specific abilities and behavioral approaches is directed toward helping them acquire elementary units of knowledge. When these units are not sufficiently well learned, teachers assume that they must be practiced over and over until they are mastered. Consequently, some students continue in a basic skills curriculum even in high school. This is frequently referred to as the "bottom-up" approach to learning, that is, learning proceeds from the smallest units to higher ones. The problem is that many LD students never acquire these elementary units or, if they acquire them, fail to use them in contexts in which they are needed.

If teachers use bottom-up procedures exclusively, LD persons are robbed of important opportunities to learn. Learning to read, for example, requires considerably more than accuracy in identifying words: It requires the ability to monitor comprehension, to detect errors, to determine the main idea of each paragraph, and to link information to understand the essential concepts. When children spend their time and effort learning words, they do not have an opportunity to learn these higher order skills. Continued emphasis on isolated skills thus contributes to a tendency among special needs children to grow farther and farther behind their normally achieving peers over time.

Schema theory provides us with a way of thinking about higher-order units of information. Schank and Abelson (1977) were among the earliest writers to describe schemata, or what they called *scripts.* Schemata are hierarchically organized descriptions of classes of concepts and their interrelations. In the schema for going to a restaurant depicted in Figure 1.2, for example, the highest and most abstract level is a stereotype that

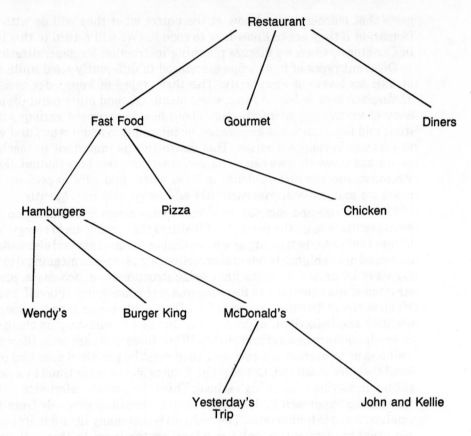

FIGURE 1.2 Restaurant Schema.

encompasses everything we know about going to restaurants, including that they are commercial establishments, that each person can choose from the array of items on the menu, that restaurants have tables or counters and people who wait on you, that a check is provided and must be paid before leaving, and that diners do not need to do their own dishes. Embedded within this highest level of organization are more specific schemata that organize information about gourmet restaurants, diners, outdoor stands, and fast food chains. As one moves down the hierarchy, the number of embedded schemata increases at each level, but each becomes more narrow in scope. At the lowest level are specific perceptual events, such as yesterday's trip to McDonald's. Schemata also provide sets of critical attributes that outline the structure of the schema. Restaurants, for example, can be described in terms of how expensive they are, how fancy they are, whether there are people to serve or just sell the food, what kind of food they offer, and so on. In short, *schemata are abstract knowledge structures that organize familiar experiences and provide a framework for making inferences* (Schank and Abelson, 1977).

Thinking, however, can also proceed from the top of the hierarchy to the bottom, which is called "top-down" processing. Some scholars of the reading process (e.g., Goodman, 1976; Smith, 1971) even argued that making sense of print proceeded in a "top-down" fashion, with readers using their highest level schemata to hypothesize about what the text was likely to say, thus enabling them to "short circuit" the need to process information in the text in a bottom-up fashion. Reading, however, requires the simultaneous coordination of schemata at all levels (Rumelhart, 1976). Bottom-up processes (from letters, to words to phrases to sentences and so on) occur at *the same time* that higher level schemata are evoked by information from the print. These higher level schemata structure readers' expectations and enable them to fill in the stereotype (from which the specifics are lacking) in a top-down manner. This process will be more fully described in Chapter 8. For now it is sufficient to note that reading and other forms of thinking, reasoning, and problem solving do not occur in a fixed sequence from top to bottom or bottom to top. Rather, top-down and bottom-up processes are *interactive*. When there are gaps at one level, information can frequently be supplied from another. Stanovitch (1980), for example, has shown that children who have difficulty with decoding skills often use their higher level knowledge to compensate, making guesses about unknown words on the basis of their prior knowledge and context clues.

This relatively new understanding of how knowledge sources interact suggests that teaching should not always proceed from the most elementary units to more complex ones. Indeed, higher level information (e.g., background knowledge) can be used to make lower level information more salient. Consequently, LD students need not practice phonics or word recognition skills in isolation until mastery before reading connected text. Neither must they master all the skills associated with a particular story in a basal reading series before moving to another story, especially one at a similar level of difficulty and interest. Difficult words can actually be easier to recognize in context and can be practiced in one story as well as another. Adams and Collins (1977) have concluded that the principles of schema theory "challenge the wisdom of bottom-up instructional strategies, and . . . all but nullify the generality of empirical findings based on 'isolated' processes" (p. 3).

The concept of levels of knowledge described by schema theory together with different types of knowledge provides us with a more flexible model for decision making in teaching. This approach underscores the importance of teaching and practicing in context rather than in isolation, since an important part of learning is acquiring the ability to process information from a variety of knowledge sources simultaneously and interactively.

However, information processing has other important characteristics of interest to teachers. Farnham-Diggory (1977) pointed out, tongue in cheek, that behaviorism (stimulus-response theory) assumes that "a stimulus goes in, a response comes out, and what happens in between is summarized by a hyphen" (p. 128). Information processing, in contrast, has as its primary objective an explicit, detailed understanding of how the learner's cognitive system actually operates when dealing with some task or problem. This specification includes processing limitations of the human mind, such as the number of units of information that can be attended to at one time (referred to as *capacity*) and what kinds of activities can be carried out simultaneously under what conditions and which need to be accomplished serially. Consequently, when we plan an instructional negotiation or try to analyze a student's problems in carrying out particular tasks, we have some idea about how to conceptualize the problem and therefore what to observe and how to intervene at different points (e.g., during decoding or retrieval). For example, what were once considered LD children's problems of visual perceptual encoding in the specific abilities model, when we considered only input and output, were found to be problems that occurred later in the learning process, that is, problems in storing and retrieving the labels for visual symbols (Vellutino, 1979) from an information processing perspective. In an important study, Morrison, Giordani, and Nagy (1977) found that recognition accuracy for visually presented symbols did not differ for delay intervals between zero and three hundred milliseconds—the duration of the perceptual information store. When delays were increased to include the time during which information undergoes active coding and transfer to short-term memory (i.e., from 300 to 2000 milliseconds), normally achieving children outperformed their LD peers. "*Working,* or short-term *memory, is a hypothetical buffer in the information processing system* [see Figure 1.2] *where incoming stimuli* [e.g., visual symbols] *are held momentarily for purposes of decoding* [retrieval and assignment of phonological and/or semantic representations] *and further processing* [necessary for storage in long-term memory]" (Worden, 1983, p. 134 [italics added]). Working memory is limited in size, and information therein undergoes rapid decay unless processed further. Such data have shown that what we thought for years were perceptual processing problems are more accurately classified as problems processing information *after* initial perceptual processing. Consequently, severe reading problems, often called dyslexia, are problems not in confused perceptions, but rather in handling and interpreting information properly perceived.

The study of information processing has, furthermore, led to an analysis of the kinds of programs (e.g., plans, strategies, and other *control processes*) the human mind uses to regulate learning. Moreover, information processing theorists have increased our understanding of *meta-*

cognition, that is, what learners know about how they learn and the important role such awareness plays in the acquisition of knowledge. Some researchers actually test their theories by trying to specify what happens in the human mind so thoroughly that they can program a computer to carry out the same functions within the same time constraints as humans. Others, especially psychologists from a developmental tradition, study (1) learners' verbal reports of what they do during problem solving, (2) eye movement data that reflect attentional patterns, (3) patterns of remembering and forgetting, and (4) analyses of correct answers and error patterns. Currently, most psychologists and educational researchers are studying learning within contexts relevant to schooling, that is, reading and mathematics. The following summary of these studies will help clarify what information processing theory has taught us about learning and learning how to learn in both LD and normally achieving children.

A Cognitive Developmental Approach to Learning and Learning to Learn

The ten years between 1970 and 1980 produced a new approach to the study of learning. The vast majority of the work conducted prior to 1970 was based on the premise that humans were essentially passive organisms responding to environmental influences. Much of the data base from which learning theories were derived was collected using rats and pigeons as subjects. Behaviorists such as Skinner, Hull, and Tolman believed that laws of learning could be applied to all types of learning and across species. Their theories addressed neither developmental issues nor what the learner contributed to the process of learning. Children were thought to learn in the same ways as adults, that is, in small increments that were the result of accumulated associations. In a review of this research White (1970) lamented, "No learning theory has ever been constructed from studies of children or been specifically directed toward them. Strictly speaking, there is no learning theory in child psychology" (p. 667).

Changes during the 1970s (Brown, Bransford, Ferrara, & Campione, 1983) provided the basis for the assumptions underlying the cognitive developmental instructional approach. First, there was a shift in our understanding of what the learner contributes to the act of learning. Gradually, researchers began to view children as *active learners who defined the environment through their own activities.* They started to ask questions about what activities children engaged in and what strategies they used to accomplish learning tasks. Second, researchers began to recognize that the specific materials children were asked to learn had an effect on what was learned. This led to a reconsideration of knowledge factors such as whether children's prior knowledge was sufficient for the task and whether they had access to and utilized this prior knowledge. Third, because developmental concerns were now emphasized, researchers set about uncovering growth patterns and the mechanisms of change that produced them. Finally, the boundaries that separated learning as a topic for study from experimental and developmental psychology became blurred. Researchers from a wide variety of fields became interested in how children acquired knowledge. This new approach to learning is both *cognitive*, in that it is primarily concerned with the process of learning that goes on inside the learner's head, and *developmental*, in that its focus is on how children change over time.

This cognitive developmental approach to learning and instruction can be represented by the tetrahedral model adapted from Jenkins (1979) and Bransford (1979) (see Figure 1.3), which identifies the four factors that must be considered in any instructional negotiation: the characteristics of learners, the learning activities, the criterial tasks, and the materials to be learned. The model is interactive, because all four factors influence what is learned, and dynamic, because it seeks to understand the processes in learning rather than only the products or outcomes of learning. It is important to realize at the outset, however, that there is seldom one strategy for one task, for there are typically many routes to learning.

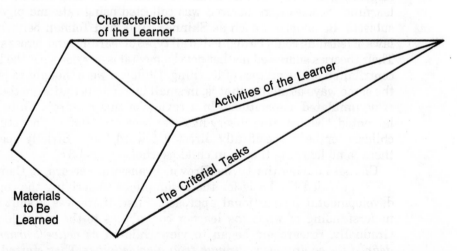

FIGURE 1.3 Tetrahedral Model of Learning.

Note. Adapted from "Four Points to Remember: A Tetraherdral Model and Memory Experiments" by J. J. Jenkins, 1979, in L. S. Cermak and F. I. M. Craik (Eds.), *Levels of Processing in Human Memory,* Hillsdale, NJ: Lawrence Erlbaum Associates; and *Human Cognition: Learning, Understanding, and Remembering* by J. D. Bransford, 1979, Belmont, CA: Wadsworth.

Characteristics of the Learner

Learners bring four basic sets of characteristics to the learning negotiation: strategies, knowledge of the world, metacognition, and capacity.

Strategies

Strategies are deliberate, planned activities used to acquire knowledge, such as rehearsing information that needs to be remembered or rereading a portion of text that is confusing. They were first studied when Flavell, Beach, and Chinsky (1966) asked questions about how children remember. Although it is important to know what strategies children have developed, one cannot be certain that they will be able to use these strategies in a variety of situations and under a variety of conditions. The term *production deficiency* is used to describe the situation in which a person fails to use an available strategy. Initially strategies are welded (Brown, 1974) to domains, that is, they are learned in a specific context and may be used in that context only. Rozin (1979) noted that one important aspect of development is the process of gradually extending the use of strategies to other appropriate situations. Eventually, children are able to think about the strategies they use and to select from them when working on a task. This "conscious access to the routines available to the system is the highest form of mature human intelligence" (Brown et al., 1983). Strategies will be discussed at length in the section below on learning activities.

Knowledge of the World

What learners are able to learn is dependent to a large extent upon what they already know. Consequently, behaviorists assessed learners' factual knowledge. Cognitive theorists, however, view the lack of an adequate knowledge base as both a *cause* and a *symptom* of the learners' inability to access, or utilize spontaneously, available information. Consequently, we assess the *processes* of learning as well as the outcomes.

The findings of a study by Bransford, Stein, Shelton, and Owings (1981) illustrate how children with learning problems fail to access information in relevant situations. They asked fifth graders to read a passage about robots that described the properties of the robots (e.g., suction-cup feet) and their function (e.g., washing the windows of high-rise buildings). One group of academically able students read a version of the text that explained explicitly how the robots' properties enabled them to perform their job (i.e., the suction-cup feet allowed them to climb high-rise buildings to wash the windows). Another group of academically able students read a version of the passage in which the relations between the robots' properties and functions were not explicitly stated. Both groups of students were equally able to remember the properties and to explain their significance.

Problem learners, on the other hand, showed different results. They did better when the relations between the properties and functions were explicitly stated. Although the group of problem learners who read the version of the text in which the relations were implied had all the information they needed, they failed to ask themselves how the information they read about the robots' properties was significant to their functions. They did not access the available information spontaneously, but they were able to see the relations when prompted to do so.

This study also demonstrated that problem learners' performances can be improved through the use of prompts, leading questions, and direct instruction. (See also the descriptions of work with LD children carried out by Wong and her colleagues.) The children's problem lies in their failure to *use* their knowledge spontaneously, that is, in learning how to learn. Efficiency and independence in learning depend on the learners' ability to access available knowledge and to apply it appropriately. Students vary not only in the knowledge base they bring to the instructional negotiation but also in whether and how they use that knowledge. Knowledge is thus necessary but not sufficient for performance. It is the efficiency with which a learner uses whatever information is available that defines intelligence (Brown et al., 1983). It appears that this inability to utilize knowledge accounts at least in part for LD students' sustained learning problems (Keogh & Hall, 1983).

Metacognition

Metacognition refers to both the knowledge about cognition and the regulation of cognition. The ability to reflect on one's cognition, that is, knowledge about cognition, develops during adolescence. It requires learners to step back and think about their cognitive processes, which, once conscious, can be discussed. Although this form of knowledge is stable, it can be wrong. Common sense notions about one's reasoning may not be supportable when observed scientifically.

The second type of metacognition, regulation of learning, is generally acquired quite early. Even children younger than two have been shown to prepare planfully for tests of memory. DeLoache and Brown (1983), for example, asked children between nineteen and twenty-three months to find, after a delay, a toy they had seen hidden behind a chair, under a pillow, or in a similar location. Videotaped evidence collected during the delay indicated that the children used a variety of procedures to remember where the toy was hidden. Some verbalized about the toy or the hiding place. Others gazed at or pointed to the hiding place. Some peeked at the toy, while others walked over to and stood near the hiding place. Some even tried to retrieve the toy. It was clear that these children were using a plan to help them do what they were asked to do. *Planning* is one aspect of regulating learning, which includes predicting outcomes, scheduling strategies, and imagining forms of trial and error.

Another aspect of regulating cognition is *monitoring* one's activities during learning, which includes testing, revising, and rescheduling the strategies that were planned. After reading a paragraph, for example, a child might realize that it was not well understood. Certain sentences may then be reread more slowly and carefully.

The final characteristic of self-regulation is *checking outcomes* to determine whether one's actions are effective and efficient. One example would be rereading questions to determine whether enough has been understood to answer them.

Capacity[1]

The functional *capacity* of human beings has been shown to increase with development. Chi and Gallagher (1982), for example, have argued that slow processing speed may be the source of children's limitations, causing inferior performances in memory and problem-solving tasks when compared to adults. They parsed the time it took children to react to a problem into four stages: encoding, manipulation, response selection, and response execution. They tentatively determined that the major retardation in the speed of processing occurred at the point of response selection. They found also that task complexity hindered children's performances, as did a lack of familiarity with the stimulus materials. Chi and Gallagher also speculated that the lesser density and strength of a child's knowledge base affected the rapidity with which information could be activated. Although these problems could be construed as structural limitations, Chi and Gallagher preferred to interpret them as evidence of *functional* limitations, since they can be overcome with greater experience.

Brown et al. (1983) go even further to argue that there is little evidence to suggest that total processing capacity per se changes after four years of age. Instead, developmental increases in span are due to the interactions among three other factors that change during childhood—the structure of the knowledge base, the use of strategies, and the efficiency of basic processes. Which factor is most responsible for different performances across age groups depends on the task, the materials, and the age of the learner. How children operate within capacity limitations, rather than capacity limitations per se, is what appears to undergo systematic and profound changes.

At least one other characteristic of cognition affects apparent capacity limitations: *automatic processing,* which Schneider and Shiffrin (1977) describe as a fast, parallel process that is not limited by working memory.

It requires little effort and demands little direct control from the learner. Controlled processing, on the other hand, is comparatively slow. It occurs serially, one thought at a time, and is limited by constraints on working memory. It requires both intensive effort and a high degree of control.

Initial learning requires controlled processing. When learning to write, for example, children consume their attentional capacity by forming letters, if they are required to make them as adults do. That is why there has been a shift toward emphasizing the message children are encoding and allowing letter formation to develop gradually. It has also been argued (LaBerge & Samuels, 1974) that beginning readers who rely on decoding as a primary word identification strategy put a great deal of effort into that task. It is not until, with repeated practice, they develop more automatic word recognition skills that their attentional resources are freed to derive meaning. Consequently, many teachers utilize familiar stories and songs as the first reading experiences to give children contextual support for predicting and checking on specific words.

In sum, learners bring varied repertoires of strategies to any learning task. They may fail to use available strategies, however, because they do not recognize that two tasks are sufficiently similar so that a strategy appropriate for one is also appropriate for the other. The same is true of knowledge of the world. Learners may fail to utilize their knowledge, unless specifically instructed to do so. Although even very young children are able to self-regulate their learning behaviors through planning, monitoring, and checking, learners do not consciously understand their learning processes until adolescence. Initial learning is both effortful and conscious. Activities that have been mastered, however, become automatic. Finally, although attentional capacity may not increase after age four, the ability to use one's capacity increases substantially.

Characteristics of LD Persons

LD children bring a configuration of skills and abilities to instructional negotiations that is more like that of younger normally achieving children than that of their peers. As we shall repeatedly see in subsequent chapters, LD students often fail to develop efficient and effective strategies for learning. They may also evidence production deficiencies, that is, fail to use the knowledge and strategies they do have (Keogh & Hall, 1983). Similarly, LD children may not have developed as rich a knowledge base as their more academically successful peers. Inadequacies in the knowledge base may be both a cause of subsequent learning problems and a symptom of LD students' failure to access existing knowledge. It should be noted, however, that the knowledge base itself (i.e., long-term memory) appears to be as well structured in LD people as in normally achieving persons (Worden, Malgren, & Gabourie, 1982), even though the amount of information in long-term store may be seriously depressed. Furthermore, many LD children fail to develop age-appropriate abilities with respect to planning, monitoring, and checking their behaviors during learning. Finally, capacity limitations may accrue from inadequate automatization of skills (Sternberg & Wagner, 1987). (For an extensive review of this issue, see Wong, in press.)

Since learning is an interactive process dependent on the learner's characteristics and activities as well as the criterial tasks and the nature of the materials, instruction of LD children must take into account their delayed acquisition of strategy usage, knowledge, metacognition, and capacity. Brown and Palincsar (1982) have recommended that teachers explicitly instruct LD students in specific task-appropriate strategies (declarative knowledge); contextualized practice in the orchestration, overseeing, and monitoring of those strategies (procedural knowledge); and concomitant explanations of the significance of such activities and the range of their utility (conditional knowledge). *Strategic behaviors, however, should not become the goal of instruction. Rather, they should be taught transparently, that is, as they are needed as methods to solve problems.*

Activities of the Learner

The activities learners choose to engage in are prime determinants of their learning efficiency. Deliberate plans for learning, or strategies, are called into play when children recognize that they are aids to remembering, learning, or problem solving. Repertoires of strategies become part of the knowledge base. Activity, however, is not synonymous with the strategies available. The earliest strategies are acquired as isolated, task-dependent actions. In skilled learners, these strategies evolve into flexible and generalizable skills. With considerable practice, strategy usage even becomes automatic.

Until the last decade, preschool children were thought to lack strategic behaviors. Recently, however, they have been found to be more competent than was supposed (see Flavell, 1985, for an excellent review). The development of rehearsal strategies in children serves as a prototype to explain the development of many other acquisition and retrieval strategies:

> Preschoolers make sporadic attempts to maintain information in memory through naming, pointing, or eye fixation. By age 5, children label some items sometimes. During the early school years, labeling becomes well established starting with maintainance rehearsal (the rote repetition of single items) and gradually developing into cumulative rehearsal (adding more items to the rehearsal sets). Continued refinement of cumulative rehearsal strategies through high school consists of (1) the planning of both acquisition and retrieval components and (2) increased attention to the size and composition of the set. Chil-

dren also gradually begin to use elaborated rehearsal which enables them to capitalize on the inherent conceptual organization in the list of items to be remembered. High school students and adults are active, systematic, and elaborative rehearsers, but their strategies continue to be refined even through the adult years. Rehearsal, like other strategies, is related to both knowledge and capacity factors. (Brown et al., 1983, p. 87).

In short, strategy development begins with the early, sporadic emergence of an appropriate activity. Over time the strategy becomes stable and may be applied across a variety of situations. Gradually, strategic behaviors become systematized and consolidated into patterns. Production deficiencies occur from time to time and result in performance decrements. Mature learning is both the result of the strategic application of rules and principles and the suppression of serviceable but less efficient habits, as the following example illustrates.

Brown and Day (1983) studied the ability of fifth, seventh, and tenth graders as well as college students to use the following summarizing rules: (1) delete trivia, (2) delete redundancy, (3) substitute a superordinate term when items are listed, and (4) select explicitly stated topic sentences or (5) invent topic sentences when they are implied. Even the youngest children were able to use the two deletion rules with more than 90 percent accuracy. Increasingly, students became adept at selecting the topic sentence. Not even the college students, however, invented topic sentences when it was appropriate to do so. Brown and Day explained the failure to use this strategy as a function of the subjects' preference for and persistence in using the copy-delete strategy, which worked quite well and was so generally applicable. It was thus difficult to convince students to abandon it for a more sophisticated approach. Consequently, the copy-delete strategy becomes an impediment to attaining more expert behaviors (such as combining information across paragraphs, rearranging information by topic, and formulating descriptions of the main idea in the students' own words).

Rather than being an issue of whether a strategy is present or absent, development involves the organization and refinement of strategic behaviors. It also requires the abandonment of partially effective and often preferred strategies in favor of more efficient ones. It is the coherence, sturdiness, and resistance of countersuggestions that distinguishes strategy usage in younger (and LD) students from that in older (and normally achieving) ones. Like characteristics of the learner, strategy usage is dependent on the nature of the criterial tasks and the materials.

Strategy Usage in LD Students[2]

A wide range of studies of LD students provides evidence of their failure to use age-appropriate knowledge-acquisition strategies (Sternberg, 1987).

This problem has been so very well documented, in fact, that its reme- diation has become the major focus of the University of Kansas Institute for Research in Learning Disabilities (Deshler & Schumaker, in press) and of Cawley's (1985) work in mathematics.[3] Three important lines of research that are illustrative of such delays are discussed here: (1) en- gagement in active semantic processing (Ceci, 1982; Gerber, 1981; Swan- son, 1978); (2) organization of input stimuli (Bauer, 1979; Wong, Wong, & Foth, 1977); and (3) initiation of mnemonic strategies (Torgesen, 1982a; Torgesen and Kail, 1980).

One researcher working in semantic processing, Ceci (1982), found in a series of studies that LD ten year olds were equivalent to their peers in automatic semantic processing, but performed more like younger, non- disabled children in purposive (i.e., strategic) processing. Ceci explained that children respond more quickly to semantically related (as opposed to nonrelated) words, because, through a process called spreading acti- vation, recognition of one word leads to a state of excitation in central nervous system pathways that facilitates recognition of a second word sharing some of the same pathways. When, however, LD children were asked to name pictures in slides that were cued by nonrelated words (meaning there was no automatic spreading activation), they, like younger children, failed to activate appropriate semantic processing strategies.

LD students have also been found to be inefficient in categorizing input stimuli into groups, although they do benefit from training that teaches them to do so (Hall, 1980; Torgesen & Houck, 1980). They also perform simple coding tasks, but have difficulty when elaboration is required (Bauer, 1979). Finally, Hallahan and his colleagues (Hallahan & Reeve, 1980) have found consistent difficulties among LD students in attending selectively to tasks. As mentioned above, the interpretation of these find- ings has recently, however, come under fire. Douglas and Peters (1979), for example, reviewed the literature on selective attention and distrac- tibility and concluded that LD students are *not* more distractible. Their specific learning deficits appear to be more strategic than attentional in nature (Worden, 1983).

Finally, LD students appear to lack an awareness that planned and strategic behaviors are needed and beneficial (Torgesen, 1980)—a problem of metacognition. Keogh and Hall (1983) report that LD students may have a repertoire of strategies, but fail to combine and recombine them into an overall plan of organization. Since the use of incentives without instruction can sometimes increase the use of rehearsal strategies in LD children (Haines & Torgesen, 1979), Keogh and Hall's suggestion that part of the problem may result from production deficiencies may well be accurate. Fortunately, however, unlike their mildly retarded peers, LD students appear to be able to maintain and generalize strategies they have learned when specific instructional techniques have been designed to foster such generalization (Brown & Palincsar, 1982; Conner, 1983; Schumaker, Deshler, Alley, & Warner, 1983).

In sum, LD students appear to experience a host of problems acquiring and utilizing age-appropriate strategies related to semantic processing, the organization of input stimuli, and rehearsal. It should be noted, however, that they appear able to learn such strategies when they are taught and even to maintain and generalize their use when specifically instructed to do so. In Chapter 3 we will further discuss the ideas of maintainence and generalization and will give specific recommendations for teaching for generalization.

Criterial Tasks

Learners tailor their learning activities to suit their understanding of what they will have to do with information. Skilled learners, for example, study in one way if they expect an essay examination and another way if they expect a multiple-choice test. One thus cannot ask whether learning activities are appropriate until one discusses their purpose. Anderson and Armbruster (1984) have argued that the more knowledge the student has of the demands of the criterial task, the better the outcomes of reading and studying will be.

Furthermore, the ability to judge whether mastery has been attained is dependent on knowledge of the criterial task. Nitsch (1977), for example, taught students several concepts. Some were taught in the same context, while others were taught in varied contexts. Both groups rated their learning as effective. Nitsch then gave a test in which students were required to identify examples of the concepts in novel contexts. A second assessment of their mastery levels taken after that test led the same-context group to lower their estimates of their mastery. The criterial task thus influenced their assessment of their own learning.

Ineffective or immature learners often fail to modify their activities in response to changes in the criterial task (Belmont & Butterfield, 1977). Teaching such children about the tetrahedral model described in Figure 1.3 can help them understand the importance of such modifications in their behaviors, for learning how to learn is a function of being able to tailor one's activities to the competing demands of the four factors shown by the model.

LD Students and the Criterial Task

One of the few studies that directly examined the impact of knowledge of the criterial task on LD students' learning was conducted by Wong, Wong, and LeMare (1982). In two experiments, they investigated the hypotheses that (1) LD readers' poor comprehension and recall might be due in part to their vague perception of the criterial task and (2) clarifying their perception would enhance the performance. In the first study, prereading questions corresponding to postreading questions led LD students to perform better than a control group on the questions and consider the comprehension questions as easier than a recall test for which the criterial task was only vaguely specified. In a follow-up study, these investigators found that when both LD and normally achieving children were explicitly told to attend to certain important information while studying for a recall test, both groups recalled substantially more of the passages than their respective control groups.

Materials to Be Learned

Because the third part of this text addresses LD students' problems vis-à-vis specific curriculum materials, only a few general comments are made here. Meaningful materials enable learners to construct images. Familiar materials facilitate learning and remembering. Moreover, these characteristics tend to be correlated with each other, that is, words with high meaning values also tend to be rich in imagery and to be frequently encountered (Bransford, 1979).

Memory for sentences is not equivalent to memory for the words in the sentence (see the above discussion of levels of knowledge). Children retain the essential meaning and not the words per se. In fact, if asked to recognize previously observed sentences, children will select not the exact sentences they have seen, but rather the sentence that best expresses the meaning of the earlier sentences *combined*. Consequently, an analysis of the nature of learning materials must look beyond individual words and sentences.

Word properties, such as their meaningfulness and potential for imagery, can therefore be used to facilitate learning. So too can the simplification of the materials, if the simplification does not impose greater conceptual loads. Flavell's (1985) summary of the research findings with young children suggests two ways to make a problem easier: (1) stripping away all but the problem's most essential elements, and (2) making the problem's elements and setting as familiar and meaningful as possible.

Text, however, may become inadvertently more difficult as an unwanted by-product of an attempt at simplification. Changing the sentence, "The tube exploded, because it was filled with highly flammable gases," into two simple sentences: "The tube exploded," and "It was filled with highly flammable gases," for example, can make the passage more difficult to read. In the complex sentence the relation between the explosion and the gases is explicitly mentioned. Once that conjunction is deleted, however, the relation must be inferred.

In sum, a cognitive developmental approach to learning and teaching recognizes the mutual interactions among learners' characteristics, activities, and understanding of the criterial task and the nature of the materials. Over the last decade research has advanced our knowledge of each of these factors of learning and substantially changed our approach to and understanding of learning. Conceptions of the learner as a passive organism at the mercy of the environment have been replaced by images of an active, environment-defining learner. Focus has shifted from a preoccupation with materials and criterial tasks to the other side of the equation—to learners and their activities. LD children may evidence deficiencies in any or all aspects of learner characteristics—strategy acquisition, world knowledge, metacognition, and capacity. Furthermore, they demonstrate a much higher proportion of production deficiencies than do their normally achieving peers. What appears to differentiate LD from normally achieving students is the formers' lack of spontaneous access to their knowledge base and strategies as well as their inability to coordinate their strategies (Hall, 1980).

Using the tetrahedral model as a means of examining the dynamic interactions that take place within the learner's mind enables us to see that learner characteristics do not in and of themselves account for learning—as most current approaches to special education have tended to assume. It is not enough to acquire knowledge, for children must learn how and when to utilize it. What they do in an instructional negotiation will be controlled by what they think about doing, by their understanding of the goal, and by what they know of the material to be learned and the most efficient ways to operate on it. As the knowledge base develops and children acquire greater levels of domain-specific expertise, their understanding of the problem and the appropriate strategies for solving it continually change.

Because the development of expertise, or the lack of it, may help both to explain learning problems in LD students and suggest ways to ameliorate those problems, we will pursue this topic further. As we have noted, becoming an expert in any domain of knowledge changes the nature and the quality of performance in that domain. Children's performances, therefore, need to be continually evaluated and reevaluated, so that learning and learning problems can be understood with respect to what children do and do not do vis-à-vis a given task, rather than in terms of characteristics that have been thought to be, but are not in fact, immutable. Furthermore, knowledge of expert performance can provide insight into how criterial tasks may be performed efficiently and consequently guide us in deciding on procedures for task solution to teach children.

The Development of Expertise

As children grow older and accumulate learning experiences in a given domain of knowledge, they gradually acquire performance characteristics more reminiscent of experts than novices. Learning, however, is not synonymous with performance. Although expert performance in reading or tennis, for example, requires considerable knowledge, having that knowledge does not ensure that one will be able to perform either activity skillfully. Thus is not sufficient to know something; instead that knowledge must be available at the proper time, must be represented in a form that is specific to the needs of the task, and must be so well practiced that the performer need not think consciously about how to perform.

Imagine trying to play tennis after having read a book about the rules of the game. Although it is important to know exactly how to hold the racquet, where the ball is allowed to land, and how to judge from an opponent's position where the ball is likely to land when it is hit back, such declarative knowledge will not enable you to win the game. Procedural knowledge, such as practice in swinging the racquet and judging the position of the ball, is also required. Furthermore, you will need to acquire the conditional knowledge that will tell you when to hit a lob over your opponent's head and when to rush the net. Analogous situations obtain with other complex skills, such as reading and writing, and will be addressed in greater depth in subsequent chapters. Our purpose here is to clarify the impact of the development of expertise on performance and subsequent learning. In a physical skill like tennis that impact is more easily described than it is in academic tasks. Tennis will, therefore, be used as an illustrative example here.

Five characteristics distinguish skilled performance (Norman, 1982): smoothness, automaticity, mental effort, stress, and point of view. *Smoothness* refers to the apparent ease with which good tennis players (or good readers) perform. Anyone who has seen Martina Navratilova play tennis is aware that she makes the game look easy. In contrast to many less skilled players, she seems to have more time and move more gracefully from one action to the next. Although her opponents appear to work harder, Martina—who does not seem to be doing anything special—consistently wins. Her performance not only has smoothness but also *automaticity*. She has practiced so long and so consistently that she does not have to think about how to hold her racquet or where the ball will land. The *mental effort* required to win the game is therefore reduced. The game seems easier, there is less mental fatigue, and less need to monitor each action with care. While her opponents concentrate solely on the game, Martina often jokes with the crowd, displaying her dismay with a referee's call or voicing her approval of an opponent's well-placed ball. She seems to have mental capacity to spare. Furthermore, even after a poor or failed return, she seldom shows *stress,* which robs a player of mental resources and causes performance to deteriorate. Martina, however, can lose several points in a row, a game, or even a set, and still play cooly and well. She seems to have at her disposal a wide variety of potential strategies. When one proves ineffective, she simply tries another and another until she starts making points again. In similar situations lesser players become befuddled and start making costly mistakes. Finally, expert performance is characterized by a shift in *point of view*. Where the novice worries about the serve, the forehand, the backhand, the volley, the return, and the like, Martina just plays tennis—just as the skilled walker goes to the store (without thinking of walking) and the skilled driver just drives.

Chi and Glaser (1980) have summarized the differences they detected between experts and novices in physics into two components: (1) content knowledge and (2) available strategies for performing cognitive actions on that content. Not only do experts know a greater number of domain-specific concepts than novices, they also have richer associations for each concept. These richer interconnections increase the probability that one concept will evoke another and that concepts will be recalled in chunks. With respect to the strategies they use, experts are more planful and more likely to analyze and categorize a problem before attempting to answer it. Because they have stored both large chunks of interrelated concepts and a variety of strategies, experts can frequently solve problems by recognizing their similarities to previous problems and using one of their ready-made solutions. "Thus, if one benefit of expertise is the ability to think better in the area of one's expertise, another is the ability to solve many problems in that area without having to think much at all" (Flavell, 1985, p. 90). The effect of becoming an expert is the ability to transform solution by creative problem solving into solution by the simple retrieval of stored answers (T. Anderson, cited in Flavell, 1985). Many aspects of a problem that require creative solutions from novices are routine to experts. Since their behavior is less error prone, experts can focus more attention on those aspects of the problem that cannot be routinized. Because all relevant concepts and the words that refer to those concepts are well learned and because the problems likely to be encountered are already familiar, processing capacity seems to be increased.

A similar situation exists when we compare the performances of LD and normally achieving students. Normally achieving students appear to have considerably more processing capacity than their LD peers (who have slower processing speeds and an increased rate of stimulus decay in working memory), but whether that difference is functional or structural is still open to debate. (For an in-depth treatment of this controversy, see Swanson, 1982.)

However, it is important for teachers of LD students to ask how *functional* capacity can be increased. Several possibilities have been suggested: First, less attentional energy might be expended in each cognitive operation, such as recognizing an item or comparing it with others. Research indicates that one way to use less attentional energy is to increase processing speed. Case, Kurland, and Goldberg (1982), for example, have shown consistent, positive correlations between the number of digits one is able to remember after a brief presentation and the speed of processing, that is, the faster the speed, the larger the span that can be remembered. The speed of processing is increased through the automaticity that results from repeated practice and experience. Schneider and Shiffrin (1977), for example, have argued that cognitive operations can become so familiar and well learned that they require virtually no attentional outlay. One way, then, to help LD students increase their functional capacity is to help them practice until their performances become automatic and rapid.

A second means of increasing functional capacity is to employ efficient information-processing strategies or other high-level executive maneuvers. One possibility would be to allocate one's resources more efficiently: For example, rather than study all aspects of a text equally carefully, efficient learners determine what is likely to be asked on a test as well as what they already know, and then study the remaining, important information. Considerable evidence indicates that LD students and other underachieving learners typically fail either to acquire appropriate strategies or to utilize the strategies they have acquired even when they would be both appropriate and beneficial. Teaching learners to employ strategic behaviors may thus increase their functional capacity.

Finally, functional capacity can be increased through the judicious use of external attentional and memory aids, such as procedure sheets and other paper and pencil aids, library books, computers, and other people's minds. *Procedure sheets* are lists of procedures that help organize behaviors. They may, for example, help students remember what to look for when editing their own stories (e.g., Are my ideas clearly stated? Does the order make sense? Have I started each sentence with a capital letter?) or follow appropriate problem-solving procedures (e.g., Do I understand what the problem is asking? What information do I need to solve this problem? Is all that information here or do I need additional resources?).

In sum, studies of the development of expertise suggest that differences between capacity limitations in LD and normally achieving students may be reduced, at least functionally, by having LD students: (1) achieve automaticity in their performances (Sternberg and Wagner, 1982, describe automatization failure as the hallmark of learning disabilities), (2) learn appropriate control processes for managing learning efficiently, and (3) utilize appropriate attentional and mnemonic aids.

Summary and Conclusions

Our first goal in this chapter was to describe aspects of information-processing theory that are important to understanding current LD research literature and that offer some new alternatives in teaching LD students. For a more in-depth accounting, the Lachman, Lachman, and Butterfield (1979) text on cognitive psychology and information processing is still a useful overview. The critical points of the theory for teachers of LD students are that (1) it uses the analogy of a computer to structure the study of human learning; (2) it acknowledges both different types of knowledge (declarative, procedural, and conditional) and different levels of information storage (elementary through organized structures); and (3) it seeks to specify exactly what happens in the human mind during cognitive activity.

Several specific suggestions for teaching were addressed: (1) broadening the scope of instruction to include procedural and conditional as well as declarative knowledge; (2) using various levels of schemata to support learning rather than limiting instruction to bottom-up arrangements; and (3) demonstrating and praticing complex skills (e.g., communicating orally, reading, writing) in context to enable students to utilize information from a variety of sources simultaneously and interactively. The last two points need clarification. There are times when it is appropriate to teach and practice both content (e.g., state capitals) and simple operations (e.g., multiplication) in isolation and in a bottom-up manner. Such practices, however, should be far more rare than they currently are and should be used only when rote learning is effective and when meaningful understanding has already been demonstrated. Furthermore, complex processes, such as reading, require the simultaneous integration of information from several knowledge sources and therefore cannot be practiced in exercises and drills, for when decomposed into its components the essential nature of the process changes. Finally, bottom-up instruction should not continue to prevent LD students from having access to a normalized curriculum in which literature as well as basal readers are read and measurement and probability as well as basic numerical operations are taught. Continued focus on word-level instruction in reading, for example, deprives problem learners of equal educational opportunity, since their nondisabled peers are also receiving sentence and text-level instruction—all of which are crucial to progress in reading ability.

The second section of this chapter was an overview of selected research in learning and learning how to learn. Learning was presented as an interaction among the characteristics of the learner, the learner's activities, the criterial task, and the materials to be learned. This tetrahedral model of learning will be advocated as the cornerstone of instructional decision making throughout this text.

LD students have a unique set of characteristics. They may acquire neither strategies nor knowledge at a rate consistent with that of their nondisabled peers. Even when they have an adequate repertoire of strategies or sufficient knowledge, they may fail to acess them appropriately because they may be unaware of the benefits of doing so. Finally, there is some evidence that LD students have severe capacity limitations, but these are most likely functional rather than structural.

Having knowledge and strategies available is no assurance that they are so well learned and organized that they will be used. Consequently, learners' activities in any given situation may differ substantially from what their characteristics would lead us to believe they *could* do. LD students appear to be "inactive learners" (Torgesen, 1977) in that they respond as well as their normally achieving peers on tasks for which processing is automatic, but perform like much younger nondisabled children when purposeful activity is required.

This does not mean, however, that LD students do nothing, for humans are inherently and spontaneously active (von Bertalanffy, 1981). But LD students often do not act in the most efficient way or do whatever else it is that helps successful learners accomplish a task. Research has shown, for example, that they rely on perceptual cues long after their normally achieving peers have switched to more productive strategies (Mason and Au, 1986). As another example, I recently asked an LD student to read a passage and try to remember what he read, so that he could answer some questions when he finished. The intention, of course, was to have the student remember the meaning. However, what he reported trying to remember were the author's exact words. In this case, the problem was that the child did not understand the criterial task in the same way as I did.

Scant attention has been paid in this chapter to the way LD students respond to the nature of the criterial task simply because so little research has directly examined the question. However, not only does the single direct study confirm the importance of a clearly specified criterial task, but it also suggests that LD students profit from such clarity on tasks involving both comprehension and recall.

Similarly, little attention has been given in this chapter to the effects the nature of the materials have on learning. Unlike the criterial task, however, the effects of materials have been so well documented that there was just too much to report. Specific content will be addressed throughout this text as we introduce instructional recommendations, the vast majority of which must necessarily be task-specific.

The final section of this chapter discussed the development of expertise, because it both provides insight into the types of problems LD students might be experiencing (in comparison to their peers) and gives some direction for remediation, for example, enlarging functional capacity. The implications for teaching are: (1) practice should continue until performances are automatic and rapid, (2) strategic behaviors should be taught, and (3) attentional and memory supports could, at least temporarily, be used to increase the levels of capacity available for other components of tasks.

Finally, it is safe if oversimplified to conclude with Worden (1983) that working memory is the locus of the problem for LD students. Perceptual information seems to be intact, as does the organization of semantic, long-term memory at the other end of the information-processing chain. Problems, whether strategic and metacognitive or structural, appear instead to be related to inefficient and incomplete processing in working memory.

Before the chapter ends, a caveat is in order. This chapter has addressed cognitive processing as if it were divorced from affect. Such is obviously not the case. Human beings are not machines. What is described above is the computerlike functioning of the brain that is unaffected by values, feelings, and fears. When children are threatened by fear of failure or bored by meaningless repetitions of an essentially meaningless drill, for example, the human machine operates at less than full strength or, at worst, shuts down completely. I have separated our discussion of affect from that of cognition for convenience only. Every instructional negotiation is affected in important ways by values, feelings, and a host of other personal, interpersonal, and situational variables. Part II is devoted to their discussion.

Endnotes

1. This term will be more fully explained in the section on the development of expertise.

2. Although we will be discussing some examples of problems in strategy usage here and throughout this text, the interested reader is directed to Wong (1983) and *Exceptional Education Quarterly,* vol. 4, no. 1, for more comprehensive treatments.

3. Their work will be reviewed in Chapter 3, when we discuss instructional concerns.

Chapter 2

Learning Disabilities and the
Cognitive Developmental Approach

D. Kim Reid

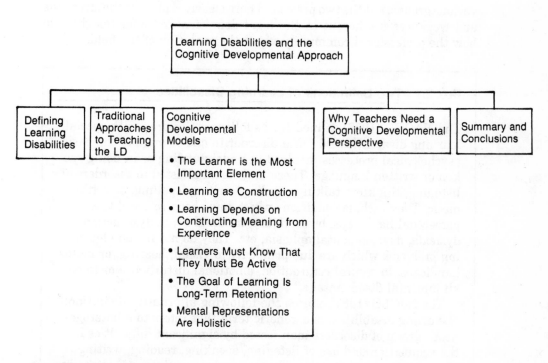

Learning Disabilities and the Cognitive Developmental Approach

Defining Learning Disabilities

Traditional Approaches to Teaching the LD

Cognitive Developmental Models

- The Learner is the Most Important Element
- Learning as Construction
- Learning Depends on Constructing Meaning from Experience
- Learners Must Know That They Must Be Active
- The Goal of Learning Is Long-Term Retention
- Mental Representations Are Holistic

Why Teachers Need a Cognitive Developmental Perspective

Summary and Conclusions

Questions to Consider

1. In what ways was the NJCLD definition of LD meant to improve on the current legal definition?
2. What assumptions about learning underlie the cognitive developmental approach to instruction?
3. What are the advantages to teachers of a cognitive developmental approach?

Defining Learning Disabilities

Now that we know how learning occurs and have some idea about the kinds of issues we need to consider in teaching LD persons, it is appropriate to discuss current definitions of LD and the assumptions underlying the cognitive developmental model.

The most widely used LD definition was drafted by the National Advisory Committee on Handicapped Children (NACHC) (1968). It continues to be the definition used for legal purposes, such as government funding. Recently, however, the National Joint Committee on Learning Disabilities (NJCLD) has challenged the 1968 definition on several grounds and has offered a new one. Each of these definitions is presented in Box 2.1 and will be evaluated below. Other definitions have been devised by various groups, but the two presented here clearly represent the strengths and weaknesses inherent in the legal definition and offer insight into how the professional community views the evolution of the field.

Box 2.1   Two Definitions of Learning Disabilities

The NACHC (1968) defined LD as follows: "Children with special learning disabilities exhibit a disorder in one or more of the basic psychological processes involved in understanding or in using spoken or written language. These may be manifested in disorders of listening, thinking, talking, reading, writing, spelling, or arithmetic. They include conditions which have been referred to as perceptual handicaps, brain injury, minimal brain dysfunction, dyslexia, developmental aphasia, etc. They do not include learning problems which are due primarily to visual, hearing, or motor handicaps, to mental retardation, emotional disturbance or to environmental disadvantage."

The NJCLD (1981) offered the following alternative definition: "Learning disabilities is a generic term that refers to a heterogeneous group of disorders manifested by significant difficulties in the acquisition and use of listening, speaking, reading, writing, reasoning, or mathematics. These disorders are intrinsic to the individual and presumed to be due to central nervous system dysfunction. Even though a learning disability may occur concomitantly with other handicapping conditions (e.g., sensory impairment, mental retardation, social and emotional disturbance) or environmental influences (e.g., cultural differences, insufficient/inappropriate instruction, psychogenic factors), it is not the direct result of those conditions or influences.

The earlier and currently legal definition of LD has had nearly two decades of use. The difficulties that it has spawned are readily identifiable. The most serious is that it is a definition by exclusion, that is, it lists conditions that are *not* LD but does not explain in any substantive way what LD *is*. Consequently, students, their parents, and their teachers often feel thwarted in their attempts to understand what is troubling the child. An exclusionary definition also hampers communication among professionals. Each discipline concerned with LD seems to have its own idea of what the disabilities are. As a result, each uses different tests, standards, and criteria to define this exceptionality.

These important differences exist not only among various disciplines but also among school systems. Because one school system uses a certain set of tests and another system employs a different set, a child may be labeled as LD, and therefore eligible for services, in one place but not in another. A more extensive analysis of the problems inherent in this definition is presented in Box 2.2

The 1981 definition proposed by the NJCLD differs from the earlier one of the NACHC in several important ways: First, it recognizes that LD can affect youth and adults as well as children and that LD encompasses a variety of disorders that can range from mild to severe. Second, it establishes that the disorder is at least presumably the result of problems associated with the operation of the central nervous system. Finally, it clarifies the possible relationship between LD and other handicapping conditions. Box 2.3 offers a line-by-line interpretation of the definition.

Subsequent to its approval by the NJCLD, the definition was embraced by the membership of most of the professional organizations represented on the Committee. The new definition does not solve all of the problems of the old one, but it has generated widespread awareness of the types of difficulties that exist and offers an alternative way of thinking about LD that is more compatible with the state of knowledge in the field. Perhaps its most important contribution for educators will be to focus both assessment and remediation more directly on the acquisition and use of listening, speaking, reading, writing, reasoning, and mathematics. Although there has been a reawakening of interest in various forms of "basic psychological processing," especially vision (see Keogh, 1985), the emphasis in instructional programing continues to be on academic skills (McNutt, 1986).

Traditional Approaches to Teaching the LD

As indicated in the introduction to Part I, two instructional models have dominated the LD field since its inception. The first, an outgrowth of the significant impact of the parent disciplines of neurology and psychology

Box 2.2   Problems with the NACHC's 1968 Definition of LD

Hammill, Leigh, McNutt, and Larsen (1981) have developed the following summary of difficulties with the NACHC's 1968 definition of LD:

1. The use of the term *children* is inappropriate and unnecessarily restrictive, since learning disabilities occur in persons of all ages. Indeed, a major trend in the field has been the recent extension of services to secondary school and adult populations.

2. The term *basic psychological processes* was originally intended to describe the intrinsic nature of learning disabilities, while shifting the emphasis away from a predominantly neurological orientation. The term, however, has become so strongly associated with the specific abilities model (the basis for training mentalistic processes and perceptual-motor skills) that it led to a polarization among professionals: those who supported such training programs and those who questioned their validity. Although the intention for including the term was legitimate, the controversies that resulted from its use were more closely related to curriculum preferences, rather than strictly definitional terms.

3. In 1977, the U.S. Office of Education acknowledged that although spelling was part of the 1968 definition, spelling had not become a part of the legal definition adopted for PL 94-142 (The Education for All Handicapped Children Act of 1975). The reason for its ommission was that spelling is subsumed under writing.

4. The term *learning disabilities* could neither be defined nor clarified by equating it with such terms as *perceptual handicap, brain injury, minimal brain dysfunction, dyslexia,* and *developmental aphasia,* since those terms themselves are ill-defined and have invited bitter controversy among members of the professional community.

5. The final clause, which states that LD does not include children who have learning problems which are primarily the result of visual, hearing, or motor handicaps, of mental retardation, of emotional disturbance, or environmental, cultural, or economic disadvantage, has led to the widespread assumption that learning disabilities could not co-exist with other handicapping conditions. The original intent, that it was not *primarily the result of those conditions,* had been lost.

Box 2.3   Interpretation of the NJCLD's 1981 Definition of LD

The NJCLD's intentions in its 1981 definition of LD, as articulated by Hammill, Leigh, McNutt, and Larsen (1981), were as follows:

1. *Learning disabilities is a generic term*
   A variety of distinct disorders could be appropriately grouped under the label.
2. *that refers to a heterogeneous group of disorders*
   The disorders subsumed under the label are different in nature and can be manifestations of a variety of causes and conditions.
3. *manifested by significant difficulties*
   Learning disabilities are typically regarded as a mildly handicapping condition. The Committee wished to underscore the fact that learning disabilities can be severe and equally as debilitating as what are often thought to be more serious conditions, such as cerebral palsy, mental defect, blindness, etc.
4. *in the acquisition and use of listening, speaking, reading, writing, reasoning, or mathematical abilities.*
   The handicapping condition must result in severe impairment of one or more of these abilities.
5. *These disorders are intrinsic to the individual*
   The source of the disorder is within the affected person. It is not imposed by the consequences of such factors as economic deprivation, poor child-rearing practices, faulty school instruction, societal pressures, and cultural differences.
6. *and presumed to be due to central nervous system dysfunction.*
   This phrase was intended to explain the intrinsic nature of the disorder. Central nervous system dysfunction may be the consequence of traumatic damage to tissue, inherited factors, biochemical insufficiencies or imbalances, or other similar conditions. Although organicity is frequently provable in cases of trauma, the vast majority of cases of learning disability are developmental. The Committee agreed, therefore, that substantiating claims of organicity was not necessary to diagnosis. The diagnosis of a learning disability is inappropriate, however, when the cause is known or thought to be something other than central nervous system dysfunction.

(continued)

Box 2.3 *(continued)*

---

7. *Even though a learning disability may occur concomitantly with other handicapping conditions (e.g., sensory impairment, mental retardation, social and emotional disturbance) or environmental influences (e.g., cultural differences, insufficient/inappropriate instruction, psychogenic factors),*

    Learning disabilities may be found among all populations, including the retarded and the disadvantaged.

8. *it is not the direct result of those conditions or influences.*

    Learning disabilities comprise a unique entity different from other handicapping conditions. Learning disabilities do not arise from the presence of other handicapping conditions nor from environmental influences.

(see Wiederholt, 1974), is frequently referred to as the *specific abilities model*. Primary emphasis, probably because of the state of the art when the LD field was emerging, was given to perceptual-motor skills and so-called psycholinguistic abilities. It was thought that children needed to acquire a sufficient level of competence within both areas *before* they could be successful in their academic efforts (reference was made to these processes in the NACHC's 1968 definition).

The impact of the specific abilities model on instructional programs was to divert time and effort from instruction in the academic skills with which the children were having difficulty to the amelioration of underlying deficits. Children were tested to determine their levels of perceptual-motor and psycholinguistic competence and then were asked to perform exercises designed to improve their performances.

It was not long before educators began raising questions about whether perceptual-motor and psycholinguistic processes could, in fact, be trained and whether such training eased LD children's difficulties learning academic subjects. Although there is still some controversy regarding the efficacy of such interventions (see, for example, Kavale & Glass, 1984; Kavale & Mattson, 1983), the preponderance of evidence suggests that the direct teaching of academic skills leads to better results. (For a review of the early LD literature, see Reid & Hresko, 1981).

The specific-abilities model is also suspect on theoretical grounds. Both the perceptual-motor and psycholinguistic models treated basic psychological processes as if they were separate and unitary entities that could be defective (almost in the sense of a machine's broken part). This approach is not at all surprising when one considers that such notions were widespread at the time these models were advanced. Recent work in both neurology and psychology, however, has documented that perception and what were called in these models psycholinguistic abilities (i.e., perception, memory, and attention) are actually *interactive processes*. The weight of the evidence today suggests that it is the activation and utilization of these processes rather than a structural or physical deficit that inhibits learning in most LD children.

An example will help to illustrate. Suppose an LD child were tested to determine visual and auditory memory strengths and weaknesses. From the perspective of the specific abilities model, a poor score on a subtest designed to measure visual memory was thought to indicate a visual memory disability. The child was then given exercises to remediate the problem. One such exercise was to have the child examine a series of pictures of familiar items. One item was then removed and the child was asked to name that item.

Modern conceptions define memory as a set of *capacities* that enable us to interact with incoming information to make sense of our environments. Memory encompasses both experienced and verbal knowledge and both the content of the memory store (roughly information) and procedures for behaving. If a child could not perform well on a task such as identifying a missing item, we would want to know whether the child had recognized the item and was trying to remember it. We would also ask whether he had a plan to help him retrieve that information, what strategies he used to code the information, how he integrated the information with his current knowledge, and the like. In sum, rather than assume that the memory store itself was defective, we would inquire about the behaviors he used in his efforts to remember. Any valid attempts to assess or train basic psychological processes in LD children would need to take this difference in perspective into account. Most importantly, practice trying to identify the missing item would not lead teachers to expect that the child's performance on academic tasks would improve. Modern teachers would want to have him practice reading, not some "underlying" ability, such as finding missing items.

The *behaviorists* would agree that the appropriate intervention, if reading is the goal, would be instruction in reading. Behavioral objectives specify what the child needs to do to demonstrate mastery of a particular content, for example, identifying the main idea of a paragraph. They also specify an acceptable level of performance, such as 80 percent, 90 percent, or 100 percent accuracy. Behavioral objectives are always observable and must be so well specified that they are both testable and teachable. They are also typically ordered hierarchically, so that the simplest behaviors can be incorporated into more complex behaviors—the behavioral interpretation of the importance of the knowledge base.

Aulls (1982), in his critique of objectives-based reading programs, has identified three assumptions that underlie behavioral programs. These assumptions are useful here both as a description and a critique of the behavioral approach. First, behavioral programs assume that reading (or any other curriculum area) is a composite of separate and measurable skills and that success with enough of these skills will lead to proficiency. Second, they assume that instruction will be improved if teachers know exactly what is to be learned, if they know what skills have and have not been learned by each child, and if they use work sheets or exercises to teach each missing skill. The third assumption is that objectives-based programs that correct weaknesses rather than build on strengths are more successful. We will examine each of these assumptions.

First, there is no empirical evidence that most skills, such as reading comprehension, can be hierarchically ordered from simple subskills to more complex skills (Athey, 1974). Furthermore, many skills, such as identification of the main idea of a passage, are neither present nor absent in children; instead, they are gradually refined over long periods of time (Brown & Smiley, 1977). Finally, there is no evidence that meeting criteria for mastery ensures that the skill considered to have been learned will be utilized in situations in which it is needed.

With respect to the second assumption, the teacher who tries to pinpoint children's competence vis-à-vis each possible subskill becomes a manager who tests and prescribes work sheets rather than a teacher (Durkin, 1978–79). Whenever a test is given, teaching time is decreased by the amount of time it takes to complete the examination. It is important to remember that monitoring and checking cannot be equated with proficient teaching. There are so many complexities to instruction that teachers rather than practice with materials must be considered the most critical factor in what and how well children will learn (Brophy, 1979; McDonald & Elias, 1976; Rutter, Maugham, Martimore, Ouston, & Smith, 1979). Furthermore, nonobservable aspects of children's performances (for example, self-monitoring behaviors) are lost, so teachers may not be able to become aware of them or help children remedy self-imposed obstacles to learning.

Finally, teaching to children's weaknesses rather than their strengths means that they will miss many of the instructional experiences that will benefit their peers. Consequently, they will be deprived of opportunities to learn. When there is no evidence that skills can be hierarchically ordered, there is no need to assume that children cannot make progress if they go on to subsequent lessons. In addition, children might spend so much time on a few difficult skills that their program becomes essentially different from that of their peers and fails to teach them the skills that good readers (or mathematicians or computer operators or whatever) are supposed to know. Repeated practice on a few skills, for example, may result in a child's failure to acquire the abilities needed to read the content area books. It may also have more intangible effects on reading instruction, such as a desire to read or the ability to derive pleasure from reading.

We are arguing for a cognitive developmental approach to instruction that utilizes direct, contextualized teaching in academic subjects, recognizes that very important learning skills are self-directed and unobservable, focuses on student strengths, and advocates a single curriculum for all students. It is important to understand, however, that by "single curriculum" we do not mean that all children must complete the same work sheets or read the same books. What is important is that each child has the opportunity to build on strengths and be exposed to all different levels of knowledge. Most elementary school teachers of reading, for example, believe that instruction during the first three grades involves "learning to read," while instruction during the remaining years of elementary school focuses on "reading to learn." Mason (1984), however, has shown through observational studies that instruction for any individual child tends to be stable throughout the six years of elementary school: children in the lowest reading groups consistently receive word-level instruction, those in the middle or so-called average groups receive sentence-level instruction, while only the children in the highest groups receive text-level instruction. Since reading requires the acquisition of text-level skills, those children who do not receive such instruction are deprived of a significant and important opportunity to learn.

Cognitive Developmental Models

In many respects, cognitive developmental models of teaching resemble approaches currently in vogue in special education. Strategies to ensure initial comprehension as well as drill and practice are often indistinguishable from more traditional orientations. Perhaps the three most important differences are:

1. Traditional approaches emphasize accuracy nearly exclusively, while cognitive developmental perspectives focus on speed and procedures and conditional knowledge as well.
2. Traditional approaches tend to emphasize practice of subskills (e.g., exercises designed to teach the short *a*), while practice is more likely to be on higher level, more complex, and contextualized performances (e.g., reading-connected text) in teaching that is inspired by cognitive developmental principles.
3. The knowledge children *bring to* any given task has been redefined in cognitive developmental models, because they recognize that children must not only have knowledge but also access to it and strategies for employing it. To understand a story, for example, it is not sufficient to be able to pronounce and understand the meaning of each word. To understand a story about cashing a check, for ex-

ample, a child must have some concept of how banks operate and must use that knowledge to make sense of the text.

It is the overall framework for learning rather than the specifics of daily instructional activities that becomes increasingly salient in cognitive developmental models. As a consequence, there is considerably more emphasis on teaching children procedures for learning, that is, learning how to learn. The basic assumptions of this model (Reid & Hresko, 1981), which draw on the information presented in Chapter 1, are listed in Box 2.4 and are explained below.

Instead of thinking about the learner as a passive responder who can be manipulated by the instructional environment, educators now recognize that learners *select* what they attend to and consequently what they

---

Box 2.4   Basic Assumptions of a Cognitive Developmental Model of Learning

The term *cognitive developmental* model is used to refer to explanations of learning and knowing that have the following characteristics (Reid & Hresko, 1981):

1. They take into account what is happening *internally* to the person who is knowing or learning.
2. They consider the learner—not books, lessons, machines, teachers, or other aspects of the learner's environment—as the most important element in the teaching-learning negotiation.
3. They regard learning as the learner's *construction* rather than as the internalization of an external model of some aspect of reality.
4. They view learning as the result of the learner's propensity and ability to construct meaning from experience.
5. They hold that learners must comprehend that they must be *active* in the learning process, a notion that is new to many learning disabled people.
6. They focus on methods of learning that lead to long-term retention of the material, rather than day-by-day acquisitions that may be easily forgotten in a week or a month.
7. Finally, they recognize that mental representations used during perception and comprehension (as well as the representations that result from perception and comprehension) have a holistic character; that is, they cannot be accounted for as the simple result of the functioning of constituent learnings or processes (Anderson, 1977).

learn. Furthermore, what is learned in any given situation is interpreted in light of what was already known. In a lesson on tropical fruits, for example, children who have never eaten them might have difficulty remembering the names of kiwi fruit or mangoes. Perhaps these children have little interest in such fruit or no way of understanding what they are like. Children who have eaten them, however, have a rich background of information to draw on: their color, taste, smell, juiciness, weight, and the like. Because children come to the instructional negotiation with different backgrounds, they take different information away from the lesson.

Prior knowledge, however, is only one variable that effects what is learned. What children see as the goal and relevance of learning and how they go about the process of learning also have an impact. All learning is thus the result of an *interaction* between what the learner brings to the instructional negotiation, including values, feelings, and past history, and what events transpire there. The most important point is that the learner engages in activities that are not visible, audible, or otherwise observable. Teachers can observe the materials and techniques used to present information and they can view the results in terms of answers to questions or test performances, but what actually happens between the input and the outcome occurs covertly inside the learner's head.

The Learner Is the Most Important Element

In any instructional negotiation, the learner is responsible for a number of activities that occur internally. First, the learner must change physical energy into nerve impulses and impose a preliminary organization (interpretation) on them. The learner must also recognize similarities and differences between incoming patterns of nervous activity and information stored in memory. If necessary, memory may be altered or enriched. Finally, alternative courses of action to deal with that information must be constructed and evaluated for their propriety and efficiency. What we observe as the child's behavior is the result of these covert activities.

Human learners are adaptive. They can change or nullify the effects of the environment. A dynamic, "elastic" fit exists between what learners already know or think and how they *interpret* events in their world. One might, for example, interpret a teacher's comment as criticism or as friendly advice depending upon the learner's relationship with a particular teacher, or response to certain situational variables. On the other hand, sustained support from one teacher may lead the learner to interpret all comments as friendly and helpful.

Some learning, such as the characteristics of tropical fruits, is dependent upon experience. Other learning, generated internally, is often the product of thought. The Swiss epistemologist Piaget has described many instances of learning derived from thought (see Gallagher and Reid, 1983). One of Piaget's (1970) frequently cited examples is of a little boy on the beach playing with pebbles. The boy learns from direct experience that the pebbles are smooth, cool, and heavy. After playing with them for some time, however, he discovers another, unobservable property—that he can arrange the pebbles in any configuration without changing their number. If he puts them in a line and counts from top to bottom, he has ten pebbles. If he counts from bottom to top, he still has ten. If he puts them in a circle, there are still ten. If he makes a heap of them, there are still ten. His new knowledge thus derives from *thinking about* his activity with the pebbles, not from their characteristics.

Since the learner has so many responsibilities in the instructional negotiation, it is difficult to avoid the conclusion that the learner rather than the particular materials or intervention techniques is the most critical variable. This is not to say that the materials and techniques are not important. It only affirms the supreme importance of the learner: "The most important single factor influencing learning is what the learner already knows. Ascertain this and teach him accordingly" (Ausabel, Noavk, and Hansian, 1979, p. iv).

Learning as Construction

Very often the conception of teaching and learning that dominates instruction is that the teacher (or the textbook or the computer) has some information that is to be imparted to the student. In other words, learning is thought to be a way of storing a "copy of reality" in one's mind. The teacher has mastered this internal representation and wants to share it with the learners. This view, however, negates the importance of interrelations. Knowledge is *not* the sum of individual learning experiences. It requires organization. It is not possible, for example, to learn about numbers by simply understanding oneness, twoness, and threeness. One must also understand that two is related to one and to three in that it is one more than one and one less than three. Numerosity is useful only when numbers are viewed as a system. The same is true of other basic concepts. Trucks, for example, cannot be understood in any but a superficial way unless their relation to cars, planes, and other means of transportation is also comprehended. To understand trucks, children must be able to determine when their use is appropriate. Although teachers can relate experiences with cars and trucks and discuss the uses of each, until the children can deduce appropriate uses from their own learnings—that is, until they can construct their own responses—their learnings are not useful. Whereas traditional models of learning stress learning about cars and trucks to mastery, cognitive models emphasize the ability to *use* the knowledge acquired as well. Learning is not considered adequate until children can *construct* and *control* information for themselves, that is, until they can draw relationships among the concepts learned and use that information to make inferences about yet other relationships.

Learning Depends on Constructing Meaning from Experience

Another way of highlighting the importance of the learner's contribution to the instructional negotiation is to consider the role of *meaning* in the learning process. People learn through many activities in which they appear to be passive, for example, while watching television, listening to a lecture, or observing others; they sometimes do this without any practice, reinforcement, or overt, observable activity. Cognitive elaborations such as inferences, images, memories, and analogies influence their understanding. Learners construct their own reality from these types of experiences instead of responding predictably to the sensory qualities of their environments. My own child once complained that he did not want to eat his meat. When I cut it for him, he burst into tears explaining that he didn't want to eat even one piece: Now he had many pieces to eat! The meaning I had attributed to this experience as an adult was that it would be easier for him to eat the meat in small pieces. The meaning he had attributed as a four year old was that he now had a lot more of the dreaded meat to consume. His level of understanding made his reality different from the reality I was experiencing.

Learners Must Know That They Must Be Active

A considerable body of research indicates that those children who possess an awareness that they must be responsible for their own learning by taking an active role in that process are the most successful students. Bransford, Stein, Shelton, and Owings (1981) have published one such study that demonstrates the importance of active construction during a learning task. In their research, several fifth graders who were reading on or above grade level were compared to less successful readers. Both groups were asked to read passages about boomerangs and then study for a comprehension test. After the tests were administered, the children were asked to explain how they studied. The competent readers explained that they first read the passage and then looked at the picture of a boomerang. Most attempted to determine which of the boomerangs described in the passage was pictured and how it differed from the other boomerang described. The less successful readers reported that they had read the passage, then read it again, and, if there was time, reread the passage one more time. (This is a good example of how LD students may be active without engaging in productive behaviors.)

The successful learners had studied by posing problems and questions to answer for themselves. They took an active role in their learning. The less successful readers read the passage repeatedly as if the text rather than their own minds held the key to success. A cognitive developmental perspective recognizes the impact that covert activity can have on learning. It does not leave these covert strategies to chance. A lesson planned from a cognitive developmental perspective would thus include explicit instruction on how one might study for such a test to increase the probability that all the children would be covertly active in profitable ways.

The Goal of Learning Is Long-Term Retention

If learning is to conform to the assumptions made by our system of education, information and skills acquired early must be available for later use. That assumption necessitates long-term retention. However, instructional techniques currently employed in special education, such as explanation, demonstration, drill, practice, and rehearsal, foster understanding and short-term retention. Teachers frequently voice concerns about children's forgetting what they have learned. A major thrust in cognitive developmental models is increasing the likelihood of long-term retention through the transformation or *elaboration* of the material. Elaboration requires drawing relationships, organizing information, and integrating new with prior knowledge.

The kinds of assignments that foster elaboration and long-term retention, which are rare in special education classrooms, include participating in discussions, writing summaries, generating topic sentences, recalling previous experiences, making inferences, drawing or interpreting diagrams or illustrations, and deriving analogies, metaphors, or rule statements. Such activities may be either inductive or deductive, but they must always be *child centered,* for they are designed to assist the children in drawing relations between new knowledge and past experience and in making judgments about the interrelations among items and topics of current learning. Thoughtful and accurate exploration of new material can powerfully improve the likelihood of information being stored in ways which facilitate its coding and retention.

Mental Representations Are Holistic

Learning is not usually accomplished by acquiring bits of knowledge to be added together, especially when a process is involved. In skiing instruction, for example, aspects of the sport are taught while the skier is in motion. A more sophisticated turn may be incorporated into the previous performance or perhaps a change may be made in the position of the skis. The point is that all but the initial learning is an elaboration or transformation of what is already known.

The same is true in mental representation. As the mind encounters more and more experiences, long-standing notions are revised and enriched. Reid (Reid & Hresko, 1981) has likened this process to that of a bit of clay being added to a clay ball. The newly added element is not just stuck to one side but rather is incorporated into the existing ball, thereby expanding and revising it.

Consider, for example, the concept of a city as it is enriched and revised throughout the life span. This idea may begin with the experience of visiting one particular city. Perhaps images of tall buildings, a lot of traffic, and loud noises are all that is remembered from that visit. With subsequent visits and with continued learning in other domains, the conception of cities may gradually evolve into one that incorporates an understanding of the social and economic reasons for their growth, the blight of many urban settings, the interrelations among world, national, and local concerns, and their impact on the life of the city. The original, naive notion has thus been continually enhanced until its initial character is nearly obscured—much as expert skiing bears almost no relation to the efforts of a novice.

In sum, children learn by constructing images of reality that come closer and closer to shared adult viewpoints. These viewpoints are built by the transformation and elaboration of more primitive notions. The change is an holistic one, that is, the human mind operates as a system; a change in one part may well lead to sweeping changes throughout (see also Gallagher and Reid, 1983).

Why Teachers Need a Cognitive Developmental Perspective

Because they struggle day after day with the difficulties of teaching children who have serious problems learning, teachers of LD students frequently begin to emphasize the inabilities of their pupils rather than their strengths. Teachers, for example, appear to be very cognizant of the differences in the reading performance of normally achieving learners and their LD students, but often overlook important similarities that can serve as the basis for instructional planning. The Individual Educational Plan (IEP) (Federal Register, 1977), which was at least partially intended to articulate weaknesses that require remediation, has served to institutionalize this orientation. The consequence has been that many LD children and adolescents continue to be denied the "adequate, appropriate and timely" (Airasian & Madaus, 1983) education they have been guaranteed by law. Cognitive developmental models can help focus teachers' attention on principles of learning so that similarities as well as differences in the performances of competent and problem learners are highlighted.

We know how to teach LD students to become productive and effective members of our society. When they are born into wealthy and caring families, for example, they are rarely relegated to the ranks of the cognitively incompetent. Instead the family resources are mobilized to provide the tutors, small classes, and individualized coaching that allow problem learners to achieve at levels commensurate with the expectations dictated by their social status. In the public school setting, however, LD children and adolescents are often placed in "basic skills" classes for prolonged periods, for approximately half of these children even through the middle and secondary school years (Deshler, Lowrey, & Alley, 1979). Only about one-quarter of the secondary school classes for LD adolescents provide the tutorial services necessary to support pupils in their content area classes and hence provide a normalized curriculum—the only route to equal educational opportunity (Adler, 1982). When we consider that LD students are by definition of near-normal or normal intelligence and make normal progress in most aspects of their development and learning, it becomes clear that a distinct curriculum is not only unwarranted but also runs counter to the basic principles upon which this country was founded.

We must look to the instructional environment as a major catalyst for remediating learning difficulties. As Allington (1984) has so cogently argued, the problems faced by LD children in mainstreamed classes, where they study side-by-side with their normally achieving peers, are most frequently a matter of degree rather than type. All students occasionally have problems with new vocabulary, word recognition, lack of appropriate background, poorly written textbooks, and the like. LD students display these same problems but in significantly greater quantity. Rather than look to specialized curricula to remediate learning problems, teachers of LD students must study the *learner* to determine what kinds of instruction would be most beneficial for that particular task. Often this requires determining what children do and do not know as well as the strategies with which they approach instructional tasks. The training of teachers of LD students must, therefore, focus on developing their competence in understanding and applying principles of learning. Furthermore, the teacher decision-making process must be influenced in such a way that issues related to learning take precedence over the current preoccupation with classroom management (Doyle, 1979).

Finally, as preschool and postsecondary programs are more and more frequently advocated or required by law, the need for life-span programing for LD persons is becoming increasingly evident (Wiederholt, 1982). A life-span approach would require teachers to become familiar with children's spontaneous development prior to schooling and with instructional techniques that would afford learning opportunities to pupils well beyond the traditional school program—in other words, procedures for learning how to learn. To date, however, no such perspective for the instruction of LD students has benefited from a consistent, well-integrated theory of learning and development. As the tenets of behaviorism continue to be challenged by a wide variety of disciplines (among them psychology, linguistics, and cognitive science), cognitive orientations that recognize the learner as an active participant and learning as the incorporation of new knowledge into existing frameworks seem more and more likely to foster a change in educational practice. Certainly a life-span perspective that is other than developmental would be a contradiction in terms. Yet both the majority of the research in the LD field and the objectives upon which curricula are based tend to remain focused on single age groups and on the outcomes rather than the processes of learning. The cognitive developmental approach, with its emphasis on the self-control of learning and developmental changes over time, may well be useful in providing the macrostructure for educational planning through the life spans of LD individuals.

In sum, a cognitive developmental approach to the instruction of LD children and adolescents is the only existing orientation that promises to enable educators to provide the equal educational opportunity to which LD students are entitled. This orientation can focus attention on pupil strengths as well as those aspects of learning and development that are normal or near-normal. The consequence should be a more balanced view of the LD person and a lessened tendency to underutilize whatever learning strengths these people do have available. Finally, this approach places LD students into the larger perspective of the goals of a democratic society in which public education strives to provide an adequate, appropriate, and timely learning environment for those who cannot be supported through family wealth.

Summary and Conclusions

The legal definition of LD has been challenged by the NJCLD, which collectively offered a substitute. This newer definition is an improvement over the legal one in several respects. First, it includes adolescents and adults. Second, it eliminates a reference to the "basic psychological processes" notion that polarized the field. Third, it does away with references to other ill-defined disorders. Fourth, it recognizes that LD can coexist with other handicapping conditions.

Two models of instruction have dominated educational interventions—the specific abilities and behavioral approaches. However, neither reflects recent advances in neurology, psychology, or education. We are advocating instead the adoption of a more realistic cognitive developmental approach to instruction that is based on the following assumptions:

1. Learning efforts are basically internal to the learner.
2. The learner is the most important element in the learning process.
3. Learning is a construction.
4. Learning depends on constructing meaning from experience.
5. Learners must know that they must be active in their own learning.
6. The goal of instruction is long-term retention.
7. Mental representations are holistic.

This model has several advantages for teachers: (1) it emphasizes the person's strengths; (2) it proposes a normalized curriculum; (3) it recognizes that normal and LD students learn in fundamentally the same ways; and (4) it provides a well-integrated framework for a life-span perspective.

Chapter 3

Guiding Learning so That Students Learn How to Learn

D. Kim Reid

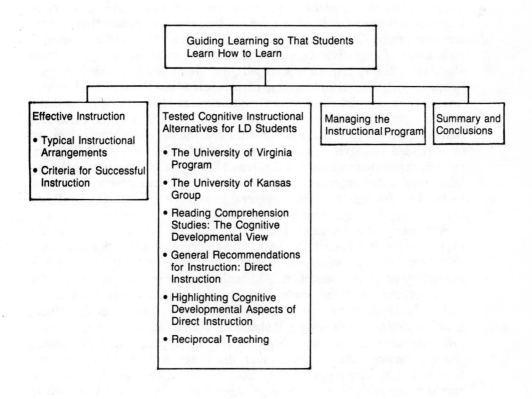

Questions to Consider

1. How do most current instructional arrangements for LD students fall short of our expectations?
2. What two methods of instruction meet the criteria for appropriate instructional outcomes?
3. What six functions of teaching are incorporated in the direct instruction approach?
4. When is reciprocal teaching a useful instructional procedure? What are its components, and why does it work so well?
5. Why is adequate assessment necessarily ongoing and data based?

More research about basic processes in LD persons and appropriate instructional practices has been packed into the last decade than in any previous period. This period has seen: (1) a proliferation of studies by a wide array of cognitive, developmental, and instructional psychologists elucidating the information-processing problems of LD youngsters, particularly with respect to learning; (2) an increase in theory-based, causal (rather than correlational) intervention studies in academic content domains, especially reading; (3) the funding of five LD research institutes that have produced a rich store of data specific to educational concerns; (4) extended research on the long-term effects of teaching methods, especially direct instruction; and (5) an awakening of interest in translating laboratory-tested interventions into actual classroom studies conducted by teachers (rather than investigators) to explore the ecological validity of laboratory findings. And these are merely the highlights!

Fortunately, this increased knowledge base has enabled us to evaluate even if somewhat cautiously, basic knowledge and instructional alternatives from both theoretical and pragmatic perspectives for the first time in the history of special education. Although this text is meant to capture the "state of the art," the reader must realize that how we think about children's development and how our theories are reflected in the educational treatments we provide will change as both basic and applied research grant us new insights and disprove current hypotheses. Furthermore, research findings are filtered through the biases and prejudices of those who articulate their applications. Consequently, we urge the reader to compare our analyses with those of other writers in the LD field and to discover the subtle distinctions among adaptations of the basic model presented in this chapter as they are articulated by the authors of the subsequent sections of this book (a rare opportunity since so few textbooks are edited compilations).

The goals of this chapter are to: (1) delineate characteristics of effective instruction, (2) compare and contrast selected data-based instructional alternatives that have been advocated for LD students and are labeled as cognitive, (3) generate from this analysis specific recommendations for a comprehensive teaching model applicable to a variety of content domains, and (4) surround this model with a variety of instructional management concerns.

Effective Instruction

This section will deal with typical instructional arrangements for LD students, the criteria that should be used to gauge successful instruction, and general recommendations for teacher behavior. In addition to the papers cited in the text, this chapter has been informed by four recent sets of reviews: Brophy and Good (1986); Deshler, Schumaker, Lenz, and Ellis (1984); Glaser and Takanishi (1986); and Rosenshine and Stevens (1984, 1986). It covers, however, only those teacher behaviors and instructional decisions related to achievement gains. Because we recognize the supreme importance of motivation and other affective variables for instruction of LD students, the entire second part of this text is devoted to their discussion.

Typical Instructional Arrangements

Contrary to the common opinion that LD students have one specific disability, they typically achieve at low levels in all content subjects by the time they are in high school (Ysseldyke, Thurlow, Graden, Wesson, Algozzine, and Deno, 1983). Most, whether mildly or severely handicapped, are served in resource rooms, where the four types of instruction usually offered are basic skills remediation, tutoring, circumvention of normal instructional demands, and, more recently, learning strategy instruction.

Most elementary and approximately 51 percent of secondary resource rooms are devoted to basic skills instruction, whether developmental or remedial. Deshler et al. (1984) attribute this predominance to LD students' sustained problems with the acquisition of such skills, the current emphasis on the skills, and the training of the majority of resource room teachers with an elementary focus. The large numbers of LD children whose problems in basic skills continue past their secondary school years is testimony that this type of instruction has been seriously unsuccessful. Gains made during elementary school are so modest that they leave the vast majority of LD students ill-equipped to cope with the demands of secondary and postsecondary education: By the upper junior high grades LD students tend to plateau at about the fifth-grade level in reading, writing, and arithmetic. The drop-out rate among such students is staggering.

The goal of tutoring, the second instructional approach, is to facilitate progress through the regular curriculum. Consequently, unlike the remedial approach, grade-level materials are generally used and the content of the instruction is dictated by minimal competency testing. Unfortunately, the student is not taught how to learn without tutorial assistance. Conversely, passive, dependent behaviors are reinforced. Achievement gains tend to be minimal.

Some programs have been designed to circumvent traditional curriculum demands. Bryant, Fayne, and Gettinger (1980), for example, successfully adjusted a basic reading and spelling curriculum to limit the size of the unit of information presented at any one time, provide strict teacher-directed focus, reduce response competition, teach skills to mastery, include distributive practice and review, and train specifically for transfer. Others have adjusted the rate or mode of presentation (i.e., listening to audiotapes or watching films rather than reading), but with few exceptions (see, for example, Schumaker, Deshler, Alley, Warner, & Denton, 1982) have failed to raise achievement scores substantially (in fact, some declines have been documented after such interventions). Students thus appear to respond to compensatory interventions inattentively and passively rather than actively.

Strategy instruction's purpose has been to teach LD students how to learn (i.e., how to employ cognitive and metacognitive strategies), rather than to master content per se, although substantial content gains have been a consistent ancillary outcome. A more comprehensive discussion of strategy instruction will be provided below. For now it is sufficient to point out that it has often increased LD students' performance to levels equivalent to those of their normally achieving peers, but has not always generalized across tasks or instructional settings such as mainstream classes.

Wong's (1985) review of the research on self-questioning is typical of the findings regarding strategy instruction. It indicates that: (1) Informed training that makes explicit the rationale behind the use of the strategy and the direct relationship between use of the strategy and improvements in learning is superior to blind training in which only the teacher (or experimenter) knows why the strategy is being taught. (2) Self-control training, however, is the most effective intervention because it is informed and has at its goal teaching students to learn how to learn and to behave like successful learners. In self-control training, direct instruction in the skills of planning, monitoring, and checking one's behavior is coupled with the coordination of a specific task. Students might, for example, be taught to discover the most important information in a passage by asking themselves questions like, "What is the main idea?" while monitoring their comprehension by asking, "Is there anything that I don't understand?"

Criteria for Successful Instruction

Recommendations for effective instruction must be based on what we know of the learning process. The assumptions of a cognitive developmental approach to instruction articulated in Chapter 2—respect for the central importance of an active learner who assumes personal responsibility for internally constructing meaning from experience in a manner that modifies holistic processes so that they remain available for the long-term—must certainly be met. Consequently, declarative, procedural, and conditional knowledge all need to be addressed in flexibly changing units so that all aspects of interactive processes may be learned. Emphasis is on alerting learners to the variety of processes that successful learners use in task performance in such a way that these processes neither divert attention from the goal nor fail to be spontaneously utilized when they are appropriate; in other words, the problem of transfer must be minimized.

Our discussion of resource room instruction above has also implied several important criteria against which the success of instructional techniques should be judged. One obvious criterion is substantial academic gains. With traditional instruction such gains have been elusive. The major promise of cognitive developmental approaches is that consistent gains have been demonstrated in both laboratory and classroom research, often with LD students performing as well as (and in a few cases even better than) their normally achieving peers.

A second criterion is the ability to help the student to meet the increased demands of mainstream classes, secondary and postsecondary instruction, and independent, adult living (Wang, 1987). Although no approach has successfully prepared students for all of these outcomes, generic problem-solving programs designed to provide LD adolescents with some important skills for independent living have been successfully taught (e.g., Hazel, Schumaker, Sherman, & Shelton, 1982). In addition, the characteristics of adaptive instruction, that is, instruction that allows all students to perform well in the mainstream, are becoming the concern of an increasing number of researchers (e.g., Walberg, 1984; Wang & Baker, 1985–1986; Waxman, Wang, Anderson, & Walberg, 1985). The findings of these studies that specify important characteristics of instruction very closely resemble the criteria specified here. Furthermore, the instructional models described below have demonstrated significant gains in grades or relative standing or both for resource room students in their mainstream classes as well as independent functioning and generalization across settings.

Since learning is the interaction of learner characteristics (including social, emotional, and motivational factors as well as ability) and activities, the criterial task, and the nature of the materials to be learned, any instructional format must lend itself to the manipulation of each of these variables. The approaches described above, with the exception of informed, self-control training, fail to differentiate between the learner's characteristics and task-specific activities—an oversight that severely limits their effectiveness. Any defensible instructional system must deal with the information-processing deficits that apparently define the LD population and not cite them as reasons (some might even say excuses) for why these children fail to learn.

As Rosenshine and Stevens (1986) have pointed out, there is generally good consensus between the results of the research on information processing and effective teaching. Three areas of overlap include: (1) the limits of working memory, (2) the importance of elaboration and practice, and (3) the importance of continuing practice until students are fluent.

Because humans have a limited capacity for processing information, good teaching must allow for the presentation of new, and especially difficult, data in manageable units and with sufficient practice. Working memory becomes swamped when meaningless or too much information is presented, and learners become confused, omit or skim material, and fail to complete processing correctly (Tobias, 1982). Teachers can help avoid this problem by providing or reviewing relevant knowledge and thus providing accessible cognitive structure for students to encode the new material. Activities that are useful in this regard include allowing students to select what and how they will learn, previewing lessons, telling students explicitly what they are about to learn, relating new to previously learned information, and providing lesson organizers and outlines. Three other suggestions for increasing functional capacity were suggested in Chapter 2: using procedure sheets, teaching children a wide variety of strategic behaviors, and practicing to overlearning.

Since information needs to be elaborated, reviewed, rehearsed, summarized, or otherwise enhanced to be retained for any length of time, teachers must actively engage students in practice. Appropriate activities include asking and having students ask and answer questions, having students paraphrase and summarize, assisting students in drawing relations between new and old information, having students tutor each other, supervising and coaching students as they practice new steps, and providing ongoing feedback.

Independence also requires active processing on the part of the student. One of the difficulties with the programs that circumvent typical instructional demands is that they do not, as a whole, foster active participation. Furthermore, the students who are taught in such programs never seem to learn the skills needed to benefit from the wide variety of instructional opportunities that are and will become available to them throughout their lives. Students must thus not only acquire information but also learn how to learn.

Finally, effective instructional programs must be capable of being implemented by teachers in a wide variety of settings. Gains that are demonstrated only under highly controlled laboratory conditions, typically decrease considerably when translated to day-to-day instructional settings. Powerful interventions must be flexible and able to be adapted to individual teachers' and students' personalities and goals. The following, therefore, is a partial list of our criteria for labeling any approach as successful:

1. It must respect the role of the learner.
2. It must address declarative, procedural, and conditional aspects of knowledge.
3. It must lead to substantial academic gains.
4. It must prepare the student for future increased demands by enabling independent functioning and generalization across time and settings (i.e., informed, self-control training).
5. It must cover information in manageable, meaningful units, provide instruction and practice in which students are actively engaged, and in the case of facts and procedures, lead to the rapid, effortless use of the learned material.
6. It must be effective in natural school settings (see MacMillan, Keogh, & Jones, 1986).

The ultimate goal, of course, is to come as close as possible to fostering expertlike performance in the individual student. Intervening subgoals are defined by increasingly higher levels of expertise. One must not forget, however, that the social and emotional outcomes described in Part II of this text must receive equal consideration in instructional planning. These are best addressed in the same way that effective strategies are taught: transparently as a means to an academic goal.

Tested Cognitive Instructional Alternatives for LD Students

Researchers concerned with instructional design for LD students have been actively studying teaching approaches derived from cognitive perspectives for the past ten or more years. Some of the more productive lines of research will be reviewed here. (Although numerous researchers and curriculum designers have used direct instruction to teach informed, self-control of various skills, only those that have included classroom applications will be presented here.) Other studies will be addressed in subsequent sections as content-specific instructional recommendations are made.

The University Of Virginia Program

The earliest of the attempts to employ cognitive instructional models with LD students was that of Hallahan and his colleagues at the University of Virginia's Learning Disabilities Research Institute (LDRI) in Charlottesville. Cognitive Behavior Modification (CBM) was originally developed by Meichenbaum (Meichenbaum and Goodman, 1969, 1971; Meichenbaum, 1977, 1979) to help impulsive children develop self-control by talking themselves through tasks. It seemed a particularly promising technique for teaching attention-monitoring strategies and academic routines to LD children who were thought to have attentional problems (Hallahan & Reeve, 1980; Kauffman & Hallahan, 1979).[1] As the work of the LDRI progressed, the focus shifted increasingly to information processing and both carefully controlled laboratory research and ecologically valid classroom techniques were studied. Some important findings of the LDRI were that: (1) instruction dispensed at a constant rate might exceed the processing capacity of LD children who are slow to encode and decode information; (2) the problem solving of LD children produces errors that are systematic and logical, suggesting *developmental delays rather than aberrant learning patterns*; and (3) training in self-monitoring skills is effective with such LD children (Gerber & Hall, 1983).

In their overview of the LDRI findings with respect to intervention strategies, Hallahan et al. (1983) describe the directions for the implementation of their CBM self-monitoring techniques. The following hypothetical teacher-student exchange captures the essence of their approach:

> John, you know how you have problems attending to your work? Teachers have to remind you, "John, pay attention," or ask you, "What are you supposed to be doing?" Well, we are going to help you learn to help yourself pay attention better. First, let's make sure that you know what paying attention means. [Teacher models attentive and inattentive behaviors and child is asked to categorize the teacher's behavior.] Now, let me show you what we are going to do to help you. While you are working, we will keep this tape recorder on. [Teacher plays tone on tape]. When you hear that sound, ask yourself, "Was I paying attention?" If you answer "yes," check this box. If you answer "no," check this one instead. [Teacher models entire procedure.] Now, I'll bet you can do this by yourself. I'll start the tape and you mark the paper. [Teacher observes, praises, corrects, and gradually withdraws.]

After this exercise, not only did the student's time-on-task improve but so did his performance in math and handwriting. Hallahan et al. note that their procedure is most effective when the child (rather than the teacher) does the assessment and when the child's major difficulty is continuously working on the tasks. It works for both group and individual seatwork instruction.

Academic strategy training, a second facet of the LDRI's work, was used to teach children routines for sounding out words, solving long division problems, and studying with the SQ3R method of learning—survey, question, read, recite, review (Robinson, 1962). This instruction (Lloyd

& de Bettencourt, 1982) followed principles of direct instruction: Teachers demonstrated multiple examples of appropriate and inappropriate applications of the strategy. Guided practice with reinforcements, corrections, and, when necessary, reteachings followed. Practice continued, while supervision was faded out, until the strategy was used independently with any similar item (e.g., math problem). Students were judged to have learned the strategy when they could consistently apply it accurately on trained and novel items.

This academic strategy training is like CBM, except that it relies on self-verbalization only incidentally. In CBM the technique is modeled by an instructor who also verbalizes important aspects of the task. The student then performs the task while the instructor verbalizes. Next, the student both performs and verbalizes the task. Then, the student performs the task while whispering the instructions. Finally, the task is performed with completely covert monitoring. Hallahan's group found that verbal rehearsal may not be an important component of such self-instruction.

If we arrange the interventions we are discussing along a behavioral-cognitive continuum (Keogh & Glover, 1980), this approach lies very close to the behavioral side. It is clearly molecular in focus and tested generalization as the application of appropriate strategies to novel items, rather than across time or settings. Furthermore, it is difficult to ascertain the flexibility of such routines because they are so task specific and molecular. As we will see, some strategies, such as paraphrasing, are useful in a variety of settings and with a variety of materials. Routines for solving long division problems are not widely applicable. Such interventions are, however, clearly useful for these tasks and may be employed productively, if learning to solve such problems is the goal.

The University of Kansas Group

One outgrowth of the LD Research Institute at the University of Kansas, Lawrence, was the development of a Learning Strategies Curriculum (LSC). In their efforts to help LD and other underachieving adolescents become independent learners, the Kansas research team (Deshler, et al., 1984) set out to design a comprehensive instructional program that would remedy some of the problems previously associated with cognitive skills training. Their considerations included: (1) whether means could be found for ensuring that students would use their knowledge of appropriate strategies—either cognitive (e.g., paraphrasing) or metacognitive (e.g., monitoring study behaviors to make certain learning is occurring)—spontaneously in appropriate situations and settings; (2) whether such training could be relevant to day-to-day schooling; (3) how individual differences (e.g., level of motivation) would affect the effectiveness of trained behaviors; and (4) whether cognitive strategy training was relevant to basic skills acquisition (e.g., reading comprehension). Consequently, they have field tested their program extensively and with very promising results.

The LSC curriculum is divided into three strands: The first strand is entitled *Acquisition* and includes strategy instruction in word identification, paraphrasing, self-questioning, visual imagery, interpreting visual aids, multipass (survey, identify key information, and study), and SOS (a simplified version of multipass). The second strand, *Storage,* encompasses first-letter mnemonic, paired associates, listening, and note taking. These strategies are designed to help adolescents transfer information to long-term storage. The third LSC strand is *Expression and Demonstration of Competence* and includes strategy training in writing sentences, paragraphs, and themes; monitoring errors; completing assignments; and taking tests. A consistent, step-by-step procedure (see Figure 3.1) has been designed to teach any of the strategies in succession. Tests, progress charts, and cue cards (similar to procedure sheets) as well as highly detailed explanations are available to teachers who undergo a brief training program, which is currently in use in a number of school districts.

As Figure 3.1 indicates, the first step in instruction is to determine who needs training. Assessment is accomplished by selecting a possible target strategy, such as paraphrasing, and determining whether a student uses it. Because all instruction is geared toward survival in the regular classroom, the resource room teacher, who usually carries out strategy instruction in small groups, uses grade-level, mainstream materials for the test. Following assessment, students are informed of their strengths and weaknesses vis-à-vis the task and asked to make a verbal commitment to improve their skills.

In the second step, the teacher explains the strategy and its costs and benefits. The third step involves the teacher's "thinking aloud" so students can observe the cognitive processes as well as the overt behaviors involved. Students are encouraged to ask questions and to try to apply the strategy themselves as checks on their understanding.

Before using the strategy, students learn to rehearse the steps of the procedure verbally to a level of automatic recitation. Practice sessions include pointing rapidly to members of the group in succession and requiring each to state the next step of the procedure. Individual testing is the last step in the check on verbal rehearsal.

Next the strategy is practiced with controlled materials (i.e., at the student's instructional level) until confidence and fluency are acquired. Feedback is liberally given throughout this phase, especially just after one attempt and just prior to another. To induce transfer to the criterion environment—the mainstream—students apply their learning to grade-level materials, with which they had been unable to cope on the initial assessment. Cues and prompts from the teacher are gradually faded to

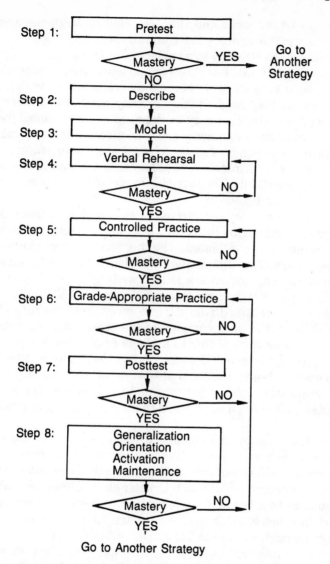

Step 1: Pretest

Mastery — YES → Go to Another Strategy

NO

Step 2: Describe

Step 3: Model

Step 4: Verbal Rehearsal

Mastery — NO

YES

Step 5: Controlled Practice

Mastery — NO

YES

Step 6: Grade-Appropriate Practice

Mastery — NO

YES

Step 7: Posttest

Mastery — NO

YES

Step 8: Generalization
Orientation
Activation
Maintenance

Mastery — NO

YES

Go to Another Strategy

FIGURE 3.1 Instructional Model for the University of Kansas Learning Strategies Curriculum.

Note. From *The Paraphrasing Strategy* (p. 4) by J. B. Schumaker, P. H. Denton, and D. D. Deshler, 1984, Lawrence, KS: The University of Kansas. Reprinted by permission.

ensure that the student is a responsible and active learner. Feedback now takes the form of asking the student to analyze problems in performance.

Step 7 repeats the assessment with similar materials and is used to analyze student progress. As with Steps 4, 5, and 6, students who need more practice can be retaught and then recycled through the system. Students who master the strategy are congratulated and asked to make a commitment to use the strategy in a variety of settings. The final phase of instruction, generalization, has three components. Discussions during an orientation phase help students become aware of situations and circumstances in which they might use the newly acquired strategy and some possible modifications that may be required as it is adapted for use in other settings. Specific assignments are then given so students can use the strategy in other settings. Finally, checks are conducted during a maintenance phase to determine whether students are continuing to apply the strategy appropriately. The curriculum specifically reminds teachers of the "use it or lose it" adage.

This program has some very real strengths. Schumaker, Deshler, Alley, and Warner (1983) summarized the results of their research with strategy training. Each strategy was validated as having an impact on adolescents' learning. Prior to training, LD students evidence very little strategy usage. Their reading comprehension is low, writing ability is poor, and lecture notes are sparse and incomprehensible. In over 80 studies, only a few students were identified who did not profit from training. With mastery of multipass, the most complex of the strategies, students improved their test scores from failing to average or above-average (Schumaker, Deshler, Alley, Warner, & Denton, 1982), thus changing their rank order in mainstream classes. Students also wrote at a level acceptable to a high school minimal competency board and used note taking and listening strategies well enough to improve their test scores and grades in regular classes.

The program's one sustained problem is with generalization, especially with durability of the training over time—an important criterion for LD students who are in high school and need to make the transition to more complex adult environments. Although Deshler et al. (1984) are probably correct in assuming that "generalization might be better conceptualized as a framework in which to couch the entire instructional sequence, rather than as a stage through which the LD adolescent must pass after acquisition has been accomplished" (p. 115), it seems that generalization would also be helped by *welding strategies to the tasks for which they are relevant*. That is, rather than have learning a generic strategy as the instructional goal, the student could be taught to, for example, study from text. A variety of strategies could be taught under such conditions simply as a part of the task itself (see below).

Reading Comprehension Studies: The Cognitive Developmental View

Much of the cognitively and metacognitively oriented work in reading comprehension was parented by research conducted at the Center for the Study of

Reading or one or more of the various instructional departments at the University of Illinois at Champaign—or some combination thereof. Although much of the research is investigator-directed, several clinic and classroom studies have been reported as well (see, for example, Idol-Maestas, 1987, in press). Because several excellent reviews of this work are available, including a large proportion of Chapter 9, only a few comments will be made here. As Pearson and Gallagher (1983) have noted, "much of the research about metacognitive awareness and comprehension monitoring cannot be separated from research about explicit comprehension monitoring" (p. 328). The traditions have been welded, just as initial strategy acquisition is welded to specific tasks in natural learning. Results suggest that such interventions are typically *more effective with problem learners* but contribute to gains among normally achieving students as well.

Most of this work utilizes some variation of a direct instructional model, such as explanation, guided practice, independent practice, and the like. It also relies heavily on consistent, well-timed feedback. Pearson and Gallagher note, however, that it differs from traditional direct instruction in that there is *no assumption that complex strategies must be broken down into separate, sequentially ordered subskills. Rather, explicit instruction is conceived in holistic phases. Neither is there any assumption that there is one right answer or one best way to apply a strategy. Instead, students are asked to justify their responses and assume responsibility for monitoring them. Feedback is more suggestive than corrective, praising students for effective applications and asking them to consider alternative ways of attacking a problem.* On the behavioral-cognitive continuum, this research clearly rests on the cognitive side and is developmentally oriented as well. An especially outstanding example of this approach, reciprocal teaching, will be discussed at length below.

General Recommendations for Instruction: Direct Instruction

This general model of effective instruction has been borrowed unabashedly from Rosenshine and Stevens's (1986) excellent review and detailed in Table 3.1. The six fundamental instructional functions are:

1. Review and check the previous day's work. Reteach, if necessary.
2. Present new content or skills. This should include clarifying goals and main points: step-by-step presentation of the information; modeling, explaining, and/or giving examples of specific procedures; and checking continuously for student understanding.
3. Guide student practice. Initial practice should always be guided, errors should be corrected, and reteaching should occur whenever necessary; practice should be continued until students can work independently.

Table 3.1 A General Model of Effective Instruction

1. Daily Review and Checking Homework
Checking homework (routines for students to check each other's papers)
Reteaching when necessary
Reviewing relevant past learning (may include questioning)
Review prerequisite skills (if applicable)

2. Presentation
Provide short statement of objectives
Provide overview and structuring
Proceed in small steps but at a rapid pace
Intersperse questions within the demonstration to check for understanding
Highlight main points
Provide sufficient illustrations and concrete examples
Provide demonstrations and models
When necessary, give detailed and redundant instructions and examples

3. Guided Practice
Initial student practice takes place with teacher guidance
High frequency of questions and overt student practice (from teacher and/or
    materials)
Questions are directly relevant to the new content or skill
Teacher checks for understanding (CFU) by evaluating student responses
During CFU teacher gives additional explanation, process feedback, or repeats
    explanation—where necessary
All students have a chance to respond and receive feedback; teacher ensures
    that all students participate
Prompts are provided during guided practice (where appropriate)
Initial student practice is *sufficient* so that students can work independently
Guided practice continues until students are firm
Guided practice is continued (usually) until a success
    rate of 80% is achieved

4. Correctives and Feedback
Quick, firm, and correct responses can be followed by another question or a
    short acknowledgment of correctness (i.e., "That's right").

Note. With older, more mature learners, or learners with more knowledge of the subject, the
following adjustments can be made: (1) the size of the step in presentation can be larger (more
material is presented at one time), (2) there is less time spent on teacher-guided practice and (3)
the amount of overt practice can be decreased, replacing it with covert rehearsal, restating and
reviewing.

Table 3.1 (*continued*)

Hesitant correct answers might be followed by process feedback (i.e., "Yes, Linda, that's right because . . .").

Student errors indicate need for more practice.

Monitor students for systematic errors.

Try to obtain a substantive response to each question.

Corrections can include sustaining feedback (i.e., simplifying the question, giving clues), explaining or reviewing steps, giving process feedback, or reteaching the last steps.

Try to elicit an improved response when the first one is incorrect.

Guided practice and corrections continue until the teacher feels that the group can meet the objectives of the lesson.

Praise should be used in moderation, and specific praise is more effective than general praise.

5. Independent Practice (Seatwork)

Sufficient practice

Practice is directly relevant to skills/content taught

Practice to overlearning

Practice until responses are firm, quick, and automatic

Ninety-five percent correct rate during independent practice

Students alerted that seatwork will be checked

Student held accountable for seatwork

Actively supervise students, when possible

6. Weekly and Monthly Reviews

Systematic review of previously learned material

Include review in homework

Frequent tests

Reteaching of material missed in tests

Reprinted with permission of Macmillan Publishing Company from "Teaching Functions" (p. 379) by B. Rosenshine and R. Stevens. In *Handbook of Research on Teaching*, edited by M.C. Wittrock. Copyright © 1983 by American Educational Research Association.

4. Provide feedback and correctives and, if necessary, reteaching. Student responses must be carefully monitored.

5. Students practice independently. Independent practice is facilitated when the teacher spends considerable time in demonstration and guided practice, students achieve mastery levels of 80 percent or better before working alone, independent activity relates to and immediately follows guided practice, and the teacher guides the

student through the first few problems. Cooperative student practice, in which students collaborate on a single assignment, often leads to higher achievement levels than individual work sheets, assignments, and the like.

6. Review weekly and monthly. These ensure that the material has actually been learned and provide a check on the teacher's pace. Reteaching may be necessary.

For nearly all of the activities listed above, small-group (and sometimes large-group) instruction seems preferable to individual instruction (Brophy & Good, 1986; Rosenshine & Stevens, 1984) for several reasons: First, it is more efficient. Second, students receive more modeling and demonstration from the teacher as well as other students. Third, it enables the teacher to monitor individual responses and provide feedback and correction, thus keeping students actively engaged (computers may function similarly). Rosenshine and Stevens (1984) have noted in their survey of classroom research in reading that three general instructional procedures have generally been highly correlated with achievement: teacher-directed instruction, group instruction, and an efficient, task-oriented academic emphasis.

The instructional model presented in Figure 3.2, adapted freely from an original sketch by Campione (Pearson & Gallagher, 1983), summarizes the important points presented in this section. First, instruction should gradually lead from teacher direction to informed self-control. Second, instruction should proceed from modeling and explanation to guided practice to individual practice and applications. Third, initial groups should give way to more individualized practice. Fourth, the students' level of learning determines when such shifts are made. In this figure, student learning is characterized as progressing from initial acquisition to advanced acquisition to initial proficiency to proficiency—a framework developed by Lovitt (1977) and discussed more fully in Chapter 6.

Highlighting Cognitive Developmental Aspects of Direct Instruction

The teacher behaviors described above are familiar to most special educators as elements of direct instruction. What differentiates a cognitive developmental approach from a behavioral one is attention to three activities: (1) teaching procedural and conditional knowledge in context as well as declarative knowledge, (2) practicing ongoing negotiation, and (3) using students' self-control as the overriding criterion.

Cognitive developmental orientations to instruction are nearly always carried out in context and utilize higher order, meaningful information.

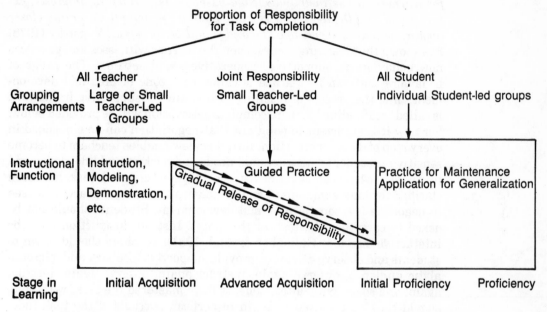

FIGURE 3.2 A Framework for Teaching.

Note. Based on a schematic from "Learning, academic achievement and instruction" by J. Campione, "The instruction of reading comprehension," paper presented at the Second Annual Conference on Reading Research of the Study of Reading, New Orleans, April, 1981, found in P. D. Pearson and N. C. Gallagher, 1983, *Contemporary Educational Psychology, 8.*

Reading is taught with text that incorporates examples of whatever is to be learned rather than with word cards or exercise sheets. Handwriting and spelling are taught in the context of meaningful writing experiences—such as essays, reports, and letters—rather than as repetitive, copying assignments. Arithmetic is practiced using real-world problems rather than isolated facts. It is only when the information is both meaningful and contextualized that the procedural and conditional aspects of knowledge can be acquired. Literally mounds of research studies have indicated that transfer is difficult for LD persons. Consequently, one cannot teach procedures for learning and then expect LD persons to recognize how and when to use them. Such learning must initially be welded to tasks—that is simply how development occurs! As Brown and Campione (1986) have pointed out, teaching in context "finesses the transfer problem" (p. 1062). Such teaching is usually accomplished by giving explicit directions and using think alouds.

Ongoing negotiation also contributes to direct instruction that is derived from the cognitive developmental perspective. Instruction is not viewed as imparting knowledge but rather as providing an opportunity *for learners to use their knowledge base, skills, strategies, interests, ex-pectations, and the like as the starting point for moving to closer and closer approximations of expert-like knowledge and performance.* Vygotsky (1978) has shown that learning occurs when the learner witnesses and practices new behaviors in supportive, cooperative social settings. The range of behaviors that can be learned is called the "zone of proximal develop-ment," and the process of teaching in this kind of supportive framework is called "scaffolding." A more complete description will be provided below. For now it is sufficient to point out that negotiation can be embedded in every step of direct instruction. Initial review enables teachers to become sensitive to students' instructional needs and background knowledge and to reteach whatever is needed. Once the new criterial task has been clarified through explanation and demonstration, guided practice is used to negotiate the zone of proximal development. Students should not be asked to carry out the task at this point. Instead, instruction must be interactive (see also Gallagher & Reid, 1981): Teachers should listen to students and observe attempts, provide supportive feedback and microan-alytic guidance, observe again, instruct again, observe again, instruct again, and so on. Only after students have mastered the task, with help, should they be required to begin to perform portions of the task inde-pendently. Consequently, practice should be delayed until proficiency has been reached. A child's failure thus demonstrates poor teaching, not poor learning!

Finally, because of its requirements that the learner assume an active and constructive role in learning and that learning should lead to the ability to continue to learn, the cognitive developmental approach defines *self-direction as the most pressing instructional goal.* In fact, the degree to which this goal is attained is a measure of the success of instruction directed toward procedural and conditional learning, the outcomes of negotiation.

This teaching model has been tested in both controlled laboratory and natural classroom settings (including resource rooms) and has met all of the criteria of good teaching. It uses primarily direct instructional tech-niques and relies heavily on ongoing teacher-student negotiation in context.

Scaffolding

Because the steps in reciprocal teaching, probably the best studied and well developed approach to scaffolding are described in Chapter 9, here we will only highlight what is unique and exciting about this technique and elaborate on the research that documents its effectiveness.

By reviewing the traditional reading education literature as well as theoretical treatments of reading instruction, Brown, Palincsar, and Armbruster (1984) identified six functions integral to comprehension success:

1. understanding both the explicit and implicit purposes of reading;
2. activating background knowledge;
3. allocating attention to major points rather than trivia;
4. evaluating content for consistency and compatibility with prior knowledge and common sense;
5. monitoring ongoing activity to ensure that comprehension is occurring; and
6. drawing and testing inferences (e.g., interpretations, predictions, and conclusions).

In their study, Palincsar and Brown (1984) selected four activities—summarizing, questioning, clarifying, and predicting—that were suitable for novice readers and collectively addressed all six functions. They held that the purpose of instruction is to answer questions about the text. Although clarifying and predicting were used only as they were appropriate, relevant background knowledge was discussed at the beginning of each instructional period.

The teaching methodology was designed to ameliorate previously reported difficulties with training strategies in isolation (as noted above, although they are mastered, they are typically used only fleetingly and there is very little evidence of transfer).

Consequently, Palincsar and Brown constructed their teaching to ensure that: (1) students could participate at whatever level they were capable, (2) processing activities would be observable, and (3) the strategies were taught in an actual reading context in which their goal would be transparent—that is, *the purpose for instruction is to answer questions not to learn to use strategies;* the strategies are merely a means to an end and are learned as they are needed.

This teaching methodology was also based on the notions of expert scaffolding and proleptic (meaning "in anticipation of competence") teaching (Rogoff & Gardner, in press; Wertsch & Stone, 1979):

> First, an expert (parent, teacher, master craftsman, etc.) guides the child's activity, doing most of the cognitive work herself. The child participates first as a spectator, then as a novice responsible for very little of the actual work. As the child becomes more experienced and capable of performing more complex aspects of the task, aspects that she has seen modeled by adults time and time again, the adult gradually cedes her greater responsibility. The adult and child come to share the cognitive work, with the child taking initiative and the adult correcting and guiding where she falters. Finally, the adult allows the child to take over the major thinking

role and adopts the stance of a supportive and sympathetic audience (Palincsar & Brown, 1984, p. 213).

This method uses a teacher (or another supportive person with expertise) as a model, critic, and interrogator who helps the child (novice) use more powerful strategies and apply them increasingly widely. As the novice becomes more adept, the critical role of the interrogator is slowly internalized and monitored through self-regulation and self-interrogation. The strategic behaviors, however, are welded to a task for which they are appropriate and used flexibly. Furthermore, rather than shift responsibility for performance of the behaviors from the teacher to the child with expectations of 80 percent mastery, the teacher remains an active participant who scaffolds the instructional negotiation by supporting the efforts of children as they become increasingly expert at performing the target behaviors. (Recall that the most effective instruction occurs when the teacher spends considerable time in demonstration and guided practice.) Rather than have children practice on independent or small-group assignments, they demonstrate competence by assuming the role of the teacher or expert.

In short, the children are immersed in an instructional environment that makes the strategic behaviors they are to acquire salient, necessary, and hence meaningful; supports them as they attempt—at whatever rate they can—to practice those behaviors; uses student teacher- or expert-like performance as the criterial task, and highlights the requirements of processing the specific material to be learned in a self-directed and flexible but welded manner. This approach deserves the label *interactive* for two reasons. First, the teacher continually interacts with the students and they with each other, and second, all the elements of the tetrahedral model of the learning process are manipulated.

A sample protocol from the Palincsar and Brown (1984) research, showing the reciprocal teaching of questioning, will illustrate (see Table 3.2). Charles was a seventh-grade minority student with an IQ of 70 and a reading comprehension grade-equivalent of third grade. The teacher, realizing that he was unable to formulate a question at the beginning of training, began by stating the main idea of the text. She continued to lead him, asking him to construct a *why* question, but when he was unable to respond, she provided him with a model to imitate. On Day 4, she gave Charles the opportunity to formulate the question, gradually increasing her demands by probing for rather than stating the main idea. On Day 7 she asked him to modify a question he had generated. When she received two well-formed questions on Day 11 (Charles had obviously learned to form questions for himself), she made him stick to the rules by asking him to ask one at a time. Finally, on Day 15, Charles could perform independently.

Table 3.2   Reciprocal Teaching of Questioning

The Acquisition of Question-Asking by a Weak Seventh-Grade Student (Charles)

Day 1:

TEXT: The water moccasin, somewhat longer than the copperhead, is found in the southeastern states. It lives in swampy regions. It belongs, as do also the copperhead and the rattlesnakes, to a group of poisonous snakes called pit vipers. They have pits between their eyes and their nostrils which, because they are sensitive to heat, help the snakes tell when they are near a warm-blooded animal. Another name for the water moccasin is "cottonmouth." This name comes from the white lining of the snake's mouth.

1. C: What is found in the southeastern snakes, also the copperhead, rattlesnakes, vipers—they have. I'm not doing this right.
2. T: All right. Do you want to know about the pit vipers?
3. C: Yeah.
4. T: What would be a good question about the pit vipers that starts with the word "why?"
5. C: (No response)
6. T: How about, "Why are the snakes called pit vipers?"
7. C: Why do they want to know that they are called pit vipers?
8. T: Try it again.
9. C: Why do they, pit vipers in a pit?
10. T: How about, "Why do they call the snakes pit vipers?"
11. C: Why do they call the snakes pit vipers?
12. T: There you go! Good for you.

Day 4:

TEXT: Spinner's mate is much smaller than she, and his body is dull brown. He spends most of his time sitting at one side of her web.

13. C: (No question)
14. T: What's this paragraph about?
15. C: Spinners mate. How do spinner's mate . . .
16. T: That's good. Keep going.
17. C: How do spinner's mate is smaller than . . . How am I going to say that?
18. T: Take your time with it. You want to ask a question about spinner's mate and what he does, beginning with the word "how."
19. C: How do you spend most of his time sitting?

(continued)

Note. T = teacher, C = student (Charles).

From "Reciprocal Teaching of Comprehension-fostering and Comprehension-monitoring Activities." By A. S. Palinscar and A. L. Brown, 1984, *Cognition and Instruction, 1,* pp. 138–139. Reprinted by permission of Lawrence Erlbaum Associates.

Table 3.2   (*continued*)

20. T: You're very close. The question would be, "How does spinner's mate spend most of his time?" Now, you ask it.

21. C: How does spinner's mate spend most of his time?

Day 7:

TEXT: Perhaps you are wondering where the lava and other volcanic products come from. Deep within our earth there are pockets of molten rock called *magma.* Forced upward in part by gas pressure, this molten rock continually tries to reach the surface. Eventually— by means of cracks in the crustal rocks or some similar zone of weakness—the magma may break out of the ground. It then flows from the vent as lava, or spews skyward as dense clouds of lava particles.

22. C: How does the pressure from below push the mass of hot rock against the opening? Is that it?

23. T: Not quite. Start your question with, "What happens when?"

24. C: What happens when the pressure from below pushes the mass of hot rock against the opening?

25. T: Good for you! Good job.

Day 11:

TEXT: One of the most interesting of the insect-eating plants is the Venus's flytrap. This plant lives in only one small area of the world—the coastal marshes of North and South Carolina. The Venus's flytrap doesn't look unusual. Its habits, however, make it truly a plant wonder.

26. C: What is the most interesting of the insect eating plants, and where do the plants live at?

27. T: Two excellent questions! They are both clear and important questions. Ask us one at a time now.

Day 15:

TEXT: Scientists also come to the South Pole to study the strange lights that glow overhead during the Antarctic night. (It's a cold and lonely world for the few hardy people who "winter over" the polar night.) These "southern lights" are caused by the Earth acting like a magnet on electrical particles in the air. They are clues that may help us understand the Earth's core and the upper edges of its blanket of air.

28. C: Why do scientists come to the south pole to study?

29. T: Excellent question! That is what this paragraph is all about.

This method was used in pilot work with LD students (Brown & Palincsar, 1982) and in two subsequent studies (Palincsar & Brown, 1984) with Palincsar and then resource room teachers instructing. The subjects were seventh-grade resource room students who closely resembled LD students (their IQs ranged from 67 to 99, their standardized reading scores were two or more years below grade-level expectations, and their scores on the initial assessment task were 40 percent or fewer correct answers), but were not so labeled. These students were adequate decoders but poor comprehenders, which may very well have been the reason for their not having been labeled LD, given the central importance accorded decoding skills in resource rooms. Expository instructional passages were on grade level and represented a range of topics. The intervention continued for twenty days and compared results across four groups. A control group took the base-line, maintenance, and pre- and post-tests, but attended no instructional sessions. A second control group both took the tests and practiced reading and answering questions on the daily assessment passages. A third group received instruction in locating information in prose passages, a skill previously found to improve reading comprehension. The intervention followed the same sequence as for the reciprocal teaching group: variable base line, intervention, maintenance (five days of testing at the termination of training), and long-term follow-up (three days of testing eight weeks later).

The results indicated that the students gradually became more like the adult model and were able to take turns as the dialogue leader. Main idea questions and summaries gradually replaced references to details and verbatim reiterations. Ill-formed and unclear responses disappeared. The teacher encouraged better performances by gradually demanding better responses. The students improved dramatically in twelve days on their daily assessments (70–80 percent correct), and improved their ranking to average or above in mainstream classes in social studies and science when the entire class was given tests by their regular teachers with absolutely no reference to the special project in which some of the students were enrolled. Finally, transfer to similar tasks was demonstrated by the students' ability to use condensation rules for summarizing, to predict questions a teacher might ask, and to detect sentence-level incongruities in prose passages. The same kinds of spectacular gains resulted when regular classroom teachers were trained in just a few sessions (and incidentally by very much the same method).

This method has met all of the criteria for effective teaching in a cognitive developmental framework and represents an important alternative to more traditional direct instructional techniques. Together these two forms of direct instruction (described by Rosenshine and Stevens, 1986 and Palincsar and Brown, 1984) should provide teachers with effective alternatives to enhance the quality of instruction for LD students.

Of course, careful daily monitoring of these and any techniques is the only acceptable acid test of their value. The description of this method in Chapter 9 provides more guidance in why and how to carry out this type of instruction. We will turn our attention to the management of the instructional program.

Managing the Instructional Program

We have chosen not to address assessment practices because: (1) a variety of professionals other than classroom or resource room teachers are typically responsible for carrying out the assessment that leads to IEP development; (2) many excellent sources *do* address this issue; and (3) we agree with Ysseldyke et al. (1983) that too much attention has been paid to assessment rather than to the careful monitoring of the ongoing instructional program. Consequently, we will limit our discussion to the data-based management of the daily instructional program. By definition LD students take longer to learn than their normally achieving peers. They thus need more rather than less instructional time. Teachers must be careful not to spend time testing at the expense of teaching. Nevertheless, the effectiveness of instructional practices for each student needs to be monitored regularly and carefully.

One impact of information-processing models that has been noted throughout the first three chapters is that knowledge is organized at different levels and that information is interactively derived from various levels in the performance of academic tasks. We have therefore seen changes in both initial instruction and practice (guided as well as individual) that document the efficacy of interventions focused on higher levels of processing: Pearson and Gallagher's (1983) description of phases of instruction, practice reading at the level of connected discourse to allow readers to become adept at integrating information from various sources simultaneously, and welding strategic instruction to specific high-level tasks (e.g., reading for meaning). Assessment can also be directed toward different levels of performance. Appropriate target behaviors include responding to comprehension questions and solving complex problems as well as the more traditional low-level behaviors such as applying phonics analyses.

Second, we recommend that, as much as possible, assessment be carried out during the presentation of new material and guided practice and as a review of individual practice sessions. Such assessment should involve analyzing students' products and processes rather than administering tests. When assessment is conducted as an integral part of the ongoing instructional process instead of after instruction has been completed, teachers can reteach or correct students on the spot and will not waste valuable time collecting assessment information or having students practice skills incorrectly. Furthermore, teachers will be better able to determine where in the instructional interaction problems are occurring: Are the characteristics of the learner affecting performance? Does the learner have knowledge or abilities that are not being accessed at appropriate times or in appropriate situations? Is the material too easy, too difficult, or otherwise inappropriate? Content-specific recommendations for assessment are presented throughout Part III. Our only purpose here is to describe a recording procedure.

We strongly recommend that student progress be continually documented. Examples of products can be saved and progress charted in some way that makes gains or plateaus (or even decrements) in performance easily comprehensible to the students, their parents, and other professionals interested in their work. Because we are painfully aware of the severe paperwork demands on teachers, we suggest that students be taught to record their own scores whenever possible. Examples of appropriate data to chart would include the number of questions answered during class discussion (a simple check sheet can be used); the number of addition, subtraction, or measurement problems solved correctly (products can be scored); the number of complete sentences or test answers written accurately (test data can be charted); and the number of words per minute read orally (a simple tally will suffice).

Whatever the nature of the data, base-line assessments must be taken (teachers typically omit this step and simply begin instructional procedures or carry out extensive testing). However, base-line data are quickly collected, reveal the student's initial level of performance, and determine whether instruction is warranted. Interventions can then be instituted and their impact on performance evaluated. As interventions change, they should be labeled on the chart. Finally, when mastery has been achieved and instruction ceases, maintenance performances can be checked and repeatedly spot checked. Generalization probes to other materials or settings as well transfer effects to similar tasks can also be charted. Changes in instruction can then be made as warranted. Figure 3.3 presents an example of a progress chart adapted from Smith (1981).

In sum, assessment must be carried out throughout the initial teaching phase, and during guided and independent practice. It can and should be conducted as an integral part of instruction, not as an adjunct or substitute (see Durkin, 1978–89, for documentation that reading comprehension testing often supplants comprehension instruction). Having students chart their progress contributes to their clear understanding of the criterial task and the results of their efforts at learning.

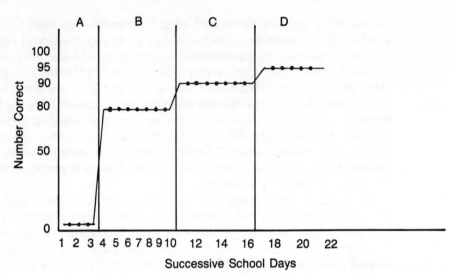

FIGURE 3.3 Sample Graph of Student Performance. A, Base line; B, During demonstration and teaching; C, Guided instruction; D, Group work.

Note. Adapted from Deborah Deutsch Smith, *Teaching the Learning Disabled,* © 1981, p. 50. Reprinted by permission of Prentice-Hall, Inc. Englewood Cliffs, New Jersey.

Summary and Conclusions

So much research has been conducted within the last decade on the nature of LD and the ecological validity of instructional techniques and programs that, for first time in the history of special education, we can judge interventions from both theoretical and practical frames of reference. Undoubtedly, as time progresses even better knowledge of individual functioning and instructional techniques will eclipse the integrity of the interventions recommended here. They are meant not as a panacea but rather as a description of the state of the art.

This substantial data base has suggested that most of the current, widely used interventions employed with LD students need modification. They are not producing adequate gains; do not prepare students for independent learning by including informed, self-control as a goal; do not directly address important processing difficulties; fail to present information in meaningful units; and do not ensure active practice to automaticity. Two instructional models that do meet these criteria are traditional direct instruction at its best and reciprocal teaching, the second being a unique and promising subtype of the first.

Research on direct instruction has delineated six important teaching functions: reviews and checks of the previous day's work, presentation of new content or skills, guided practice, feedback and correction, independent practice, and weekly and monthly reviews. As Rosenshine and Stevens (1968) have pointed out, this type of direct instruction is better suited to the mastery of content or skills that are well structured (e.g., mathematics or decoding procedures) and is least applicable to the content that is ill structured (e.g., reading comprehension or composition writing). The models proposed by the Virginia, Kansas, and Illinois research groups all contributed to our understanding of how to conduct effective direct instruction.

Reciprocal teaching, on the other hand, appears to be eminently well suited to ill structured tasks. It represents only one possible utilization of the learning principles formulated by Vygotsky (1978). We expect that other important applications of his analysis of the sociocultural aspects of learning will be forthcoming. Reciprocal teaching is powerful because it offers sustained modeling and guided practice, welds strategies to tasks so that the role of strategies becomes transparent, and provides expert support so that student novices can experience success at whatever level of functioning they are capable. Reciprocal teaching has been effective in: (1) promoting substantial academic gains that have actually enabled LD and other poorly achieving students to perform as well as their normally achieving peers, (2) enabling these students to execute expert behaviors appropriately and consistently, and (3) leading to impressive transfer and generalization effects.

Finally, aware that any instructional methodology must be filtered through individual teachers' goals and styles and students' learning interactions (including social-emotional factors), we argue that the data-based management of instructional programs is indispensable. One caveat, however, is that data-based assessment should not be equated with testing and take valuable time away from an already overburdened instructional day.

Endnote

1. Recall from earlier discussions that it has subsequently been agreed that specific deficits in learning are more strategic than attentional (Bauer, 1977, 1979; Douglas & Peters, 1979; Pehlam, 1979; Tarver, 1981).

PART II

A Cognitive Developmental Approach to Learning Disabilities: Affect

Every teacher's major responsibility is to implement the school curriculum. What and whether children learn, however, is dependent on a wide variety of factors that have little to do with methods of presentation, appropriate levels of curriculum interventions, and the like. Primary among these noncognitive factors is affect. Effective teaching requires a sound blending of systematic instructional practices and warm, enthusiastic interpersonal skills.

Devoting three chapters to the discussion of affect testifies to the importance of providing not only rigorous but also motivating and supportive instruction for LD students. As Pullis points out, anxious, depressed, or embarrassed children are not active learners. They instead tend to avoid painful instructional encounters just as well when they are sitting in the classroom and ostensibly participating in lessons as when they are physically absent.

The chapters in this section are both interrelated and incremental. Chapter 4 describes affective and motivational characteristics that influence classroom learning. Chapter 5 focuses on approaches to managing both affective and academic concerns simultaneously. Chapter 6 is devoted to the presentation of ideas for fostering independence in LD learners, including the use of Lovitt's (1976) description of the phases of knowledge and skill acquisition (see Figure 3.2) as a decision-making framework.

Several elements should be noted in the instructional approaches advocated by Pullis. First, like the treatment of strategic behavior in the reading comprehension and reciprocal teaching models presented in Chapter 3, Pullis views *affective knowledge and skills as transparent and welded to specific tasks; the goal of instruction is thus academic achievement, not social behavior.* He utilizes three instructional tactics: structure, direct instruction, and scaffolding. Structure acts as a preventive measure. When the classroom is highly organized and when students and the teacher all know and agree on the rules, positive behavior is invited. When there are few disruptions, both students and the teacher are free to concentrate on learning. With respect to curriculum materials per se, structure relates to instruction at appropriate levels, that is, where students can *succeed with effort*. Pullis advocates the use of direct instruction when affective problems are related to information. If students do not know what behavior is expected of them—and this often changes from class to class and teacher to teacher—they need to be taught those expectations. Similarly, when they do not know how to read cues in social situations and find it difficult to participate acceptably in group activities, they need to be taught how to do so. Our tendency as special education teachers has been to avoid social or group activities and to carry out instruction on a one-to-one basis using overwhelming numbers of worksheets and individual assignments. However, this kind of instruction is often both inefficient and ineffective, for not only does it undermine instructional efforts by isolating individual students, but it also fails to teach them the social knowledge and skills that will enable them to join in group settings outside of school. Surveys indicate that LD students participate very little in clubs or organizations (e.g., Boy Scouts) and other leisure activities (e.g., sports) in their communities. It is no wonder. Normally achieving students practice group behaviors consistently, while LD students work alone. Limited group experience represents just one more example of how LD students are systematically deprived of important learning opportunities.

Pullis does not label his recommendations as scaffolding, but consistently suggests that teachers use scaffolding behaviors. Whenever students need to acquire complex, ill-structured, flexible behaviors (e.g., new academic tasks or group activities), he argues that teachers should initially provide strong direction and support and gradually require students to accept responsibility for their behaviors.

In sum, these three chapters map affective concerns onto the cognitive considerations presented in Part I. Although the presentations are separate, cognition and affect are not. They jointly fuel all behavior, both in and out of school. Students respond best, both academically and interpersonally, to teachers who attend to their emotional and social needs in the context of positive expectations for learning. There is no other way to engender effective, independent learning.

Chapter 4

Affective and Motivational Aspects of Learning Disabilities

Michael E. Pullis

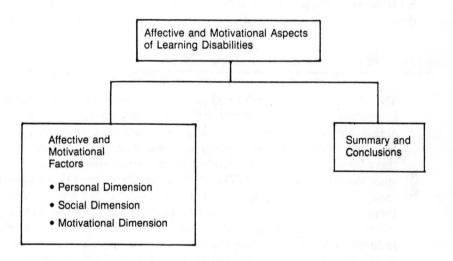

Questions to Consider

1. Why are affective concerns central to teaching?
2. What kinds of affective problems are LD students likely to bring into the classroom? How do they influence classroom behavior?
3. What must teachers be sensitive to in order to minimize the effects of affective problems?

It is becoming increasingly clear that many LD students experience significant affective and motivational problems (Meyer, 1983). Each LD child comes to the classroom with a complex and unique set of personal and educational experiences. Further, each student has interpreted and adapted to life experiences such as a disability and the reactions and behavior of parents, peers, and teachers with varying degrees of success and health. Each LD student, by definition, has experienced significant and often prolonged academic failure. This history of failure can have significant negative influences on both general development (Athey, 1976) and ongoing school performance. This chapter is devoted to those children who come to LD settings having been damaged by their experiences and who enter classrooms with personal, social, or motivational difficulties. The goals are to increase knowledge about affective and motivational problems and to enhance teachers' understanding of how such problems can manifest themselves in the classroom as nonproductive or even extremely disruptive behaviors.

Affective and Motivational Factors

The affective domain is defined as the nonintellective or emotional characteristics of a learner. Many different models describe the components of this domain. The one chosen as an organizer for this chapter is adapted from the work of Morse et al. (1981) (see Figure 4.1). Their model has three broad dimensions, each made up of several specific components that span the affective domain. The three dimensions are: (1) the personal, or "self," dimension, which deals with students' ideas and feelings about themselves as well as their ability to regulate their behavior; (2) the social dimension, which involves students' abilities in interpersonal relationships with both adults and peers; and (3) the attitudinal/dispositional dimension, which characterizes factors that underlie students' motivation or achievement strivings in classroom situations. Presumably each child could be characterized along some continuum ranging from very positive to very negative on each of the dimensions.

Before discussing the specific factors in the domains, three important points must be made. First, the factors or characteristics are considered separately only for the sake of presentation: All are quite complexly interrelated. Thus, each LD student has a unique profile of strengths and weaknesses in the affective domain. Second, these characteristics are developmental. Self-concept, for example, emerges over time and is far more multifaceted in adolescence than during the primary years. These factors are therefore also dynamic, or changing. At any given time they represent the results of a complex interaction that includes students' levels of development as well as their experience. Teachers can influence

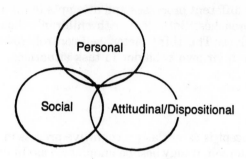

Personal: Ideas and feelings about self; ability to
   regulate behavior

Social: Interpersonal attributes of peers and adults

Attitudinal/Dispositional: Motivation or achievement
   strivings in school

FIGURE 4.1 The Affective Domain.

Note. Adapted from *Affective Education for Exceptional Children and Youth* by W. Morse et al., 1981, Reston, VA: CEC Publications.

these characteristics but only to the extent that students are developmentally ready. One may, for example, want to help students learn more appropriate social behavior. Assuming that optimal social learning experiences were provided, students will learn to use the social tactics only to the extent that they really can understand when, where, and how to use them. Thus, their social performance is constrained by their level of social cognitive development. Finally, the affective domain should not be considered as a distinct or competing area of concern compared to academic needs. Rather, it should be acknowledged as interrelated with the cognitive domain, for affect has an important influence on children's overall progress in special education and mainstream settings (Campos, Barrett, Lamb, Goldsmith, and Sternberg, 1983; Cowan, 1978).

Personal Dimension

The personal dimension has three major components of factors—self-concept, self-regard, and self-control. The first two terms are often used interchangeably in the literature, but, while they are certainly closely related, they are somewhat different processes and attempts to influence them require different approaches. Both deal with children's thoughts and feelings about themselves. The third factor, self-control, refers to students' ability to regulate their own behavior in task situations.

Self-Concept

The development of self-concept is essentially a cognitive process involving the child's definition of the self. It may best be understood as children's gradual awareness of the various roles they play—such as boy or girl, son or daughter, friend or playmate, student or LD student—which is achieved through the process of watching and imitating others (modeling) as well as from direct feedback from adults and peers (Bandura, 1977). When children are acting within a certain role, such as that of the student, teachers, classmates, and parents react to their behavior and inform them about its appropriateness or success. Many such instances of feedback help the children form ideas or construct predictions about what they are expected to do in the various roles.[1] Thus, behavior within a role is consistent with and can be predicted by a child's understanding of that role. As children mature cognitively and add to their experiences, their ideas about various roles become more complex and differentiated. Thus, the student role behavior of an adolescent will be more sophisticated than that of a younger child. Even elementary school children have several roles for which they have developed personal definitions that guide their behavior (Harter, 1983).

Classroom Problems   Children are often characterized as having either good or poor self-concepts. Given the explanation above, these are not appropriate assessments. Instead, when trying to diagnose reasons for classroom misbehavior, teachers should consider the possibility that a child's self-concept or role definition is inaccurate, is not as sophisticated as that of other children of the same age, or is inconsistent with the teacher's expectations. If any of these are true, the child's poor classroom performance is mainly a function of either (1) general cognitive developmental delays compared with peers or (2) lack of specific information and feedback from the teacher concerning expected academic performance and social behavior.

Teacher Sensitivity   Students with such problems in self-concept or role definition can be assisted in becoming more comfortable and more productive in the classroom. One technique teachers can use is to develop classroom rules (expectations concerning behavior), routines, and academic performance standards (regarding, for example, length of tasks, accuracy, and neatness). This is a challenge, since LD resource or self-contained classes typically serve students who vary considerably in age, academic needs, and affective strengths and weaknesses. One solution is to plan general rules and then individualize their administration. The important concept here is knowing what students are capable of (based on assessment), to accept them at this level, and to exert expectations for improvement gradually across the various areas of academic and behavioral skills. Thus, the first self-concept technique involves adequate planning and sensitive administration of classroom expectations that are consistent with developmental needs.

A second technique focuses on communication with the students. While each child will have some general ideas concerning the student role, each teacher has specific and often idiosyncratic rules. In this regard, the LD resource room or classroom is often quite different from the mainstream setting. Thus, it is important that teachers very clearly communicate the rules and expectations of the classroom to each child. Initially, this may entail frequent and comprehensive reviews of rules and routines that include accurate descriptions, careful explanations of their purposes, and specific demonstrations of expected academic and social performance; in short, informed self-control is the goal.

One should also allow the children some time to adjust to their classroom. During this period be sure to provide copious feedback concerning their behavior, both appropriate and inappropriate. When they act appropriately, they should be so informed and appreciated. When they misbehave, they should be told why their behavior was inappropriate and helped to determine how they could behave in that situation that would be consistent with the rules. Unless there is a particularly unruly group, punishment for rule infractions should not be given until the teacher is relatively sure that the students understand and can follow the rules. The teacher's behaviors for dealing with problems in self-concept therefore parallel those through which children naturally acquire role definitions—modeling and feedback.

Self-Regard

Children's self-regard or self-esteem is intimately linked with their self-concept, since for each role they play, they develop a sense of how well they are performing. This process encompasses interrelated steps (Harter, 1983). In the first step children evaluate or judge their role performance. They arrive at particular judgments primarily from feedback from important others or by comparison to others. In both cases, social interactions are crucial to affective development.

The second step in forming ideas of self-regard concerns children's values about the importance of each role. Children, for example, appear to vary greatly in how highly they value academic achievement. These differences may be linked to the family, culture, or earlier school experiences. It is this personal degree of importance accorded to schooling that leads to the final step in the process—developing feelings.

Children develop emotional reactions to their role performance based on both their judgments and their ideas of the importance of the role. Two examples can illustrate these processes. One LD student has been encouraged by his family to place a moderate value on school progress and to have a balanced view of himself. He has been taught that other parts of life, such as athletics and friendships, are also important. The feedback he receives as well as the social comparisons he makes to his classmates lead to essentially negative feelings: "I'm not a very good student." Based on the feedback and the degree to which he has learned to value school achievement, he is likely to develop emotional reactions that are reasonable—mild disappointment, perhaps some frustration, or even a positive reaction, if he feels challenged by the situation. Another student has been socialized to believe that school achievement is very important. Her self-regard is closely tied to this role. She receives the same type of feedback and draws the same comparisons as the first student—essentially negative—"I am a poor student." Her emotional reactions, however, are likely to be much more extreme than the first child's—depression, helplessness, or anger from frustration may result. Thus, these children's self-regard is a function of the feedback they are given as well as their own ideas about the importance of school achievement. Their different *feelings* about school and learning will be reflected in both their responsiveness to teaching and their classroom behavior.

Classroom Problems   Negative feelings about the self in the student role are often manifested in two areas—motivation on tasks and classroom misbehavior. Children who have developed negative feelings about their academic performance often will not be very task oriented—attending and peristing until tasks are completed (Butkowsky & Willows, 1980)—because they have formed an association between academic tasks and feelings of incompetence or embarrassment. Their history of school experiences tells them to anticipate failure. They often lack confidence in achievement situations; they may not start tasks without several reminders, may ask many questions about how they are doing (which can be very annoying to teachers), or may develop ways of looking busy without actually finishing tasks. Such behaviors are all aimed (probably unconsciously) at avoiding feelings of failure and incompetence.

Students' attempts to avoid humiliation and failure can become even more disruptive if their emotional reactions to failure are more extreme. For these students, avoidance behavior can take two forms—withdrawal or acting out. *Withdrawal* may be evidenced by excessive daydreaming, psychosomatic illnesses, truancy, or even fear of school. *Acting out* might include any standard classroom problems, such as excessive talking during work periods, out-of-seat behavior, aggression toward peers, and conflicts with the teacher concerning compliance with rules or assignments. In fact, many of these behaviors can even result in removal from the classroom, which may be precisely what the students want!

Avoidance behaviors are very powerful and resistant to change, because the students are escaping from situations that arouse extremely negative feelings about themselves. While to adults it may not appear to be fun to get into trouble constantly, to students such trouble may be less painful than failure. Furthermore, getting into trouble is an experience the children can essentially control. LD teachers report that substantial numbers of their students exhibit such problems (Pullis, 1983).

Teacher Sensitivity   Dealing with problems related to negative self-regard is a very real challenge for teachers of LD students. Such feelings develop over time, so it is reasonable to anticipate that it will take some time (and perhaps many efforts) to help the children develop new judgments and feelings about school achievement. Several studies do indicate that positive changes can be effected. Coleman (1983) has shown that LD students tend to score appreciably higher on measures of self-regard when these measures are completed by the students in their special education classrooms. As indicated earlier, children make some judgments about their performance by comparing themselves to others. Coleman showed that in the special education setting, LD children apparently see that they are in line with other students. In the regular classroom, on the other hand, they are likely to be somewhere near the bottom of the class in terms of achievement and therefore judge themselves more harshly. Thus, while there may be some negative social stigma concerning placement in special classes, LD students appear to feel somewhat better about themselves in such settings, where they make more positive predictions concerning their ability to achieve. Of course, smaller classes and more individualized attention may also help these students feel more comfortable.

One other point about group reference comparisons should be made. Children will naturally try to ascertain where they fit in the classroom hierarchies of achievement and social status. Teachers of LD children should probably not make additional comparisons that are known to the entire class. While competition and comparisons may be appropriate and even motivating in the regular classroom, these can be negative tactics in the LD setting because of problems of self-regard. It seems much more productive to challenge children to improve their classwork by referring only to their individual strengths and needs. Further, it is extremely beneficial for teachers to document improvement (see the charting procedures described in Chapter 3) and show students the progress they have made.

Research also indicates that aspects of children's self-concept and self-regard are multifaceted (Shavelson & Bolus, 1982). While children do have generalized positive or negative feelings about themselves as individuals, they also have feelings specifically related to various roles (Harter, 1983). Research also shows that students have feelings or attitudes associated with particular academic subjects. This knowledge can be used to the teacher's advantage. Ongoing assessment and systematic observation enable teachers to plan learning activities for children that will allow them both to be successful and to work on tasks that appeal to them. Assessment also allows a teacher to adjust factors like task length, accuracy expectations, and sequence of tasks to each child's capabilities and interests. Integrating carefully planned opportunities for success into the school day also facilitates students' development of more balanced views of themselves as learners. The anticipation of some success may in turn lead to more sustained efforts throughout the school day.

Success experiences need to be accompanied by a concerted effort to help these children deal with mistakes or errors. It is important for them to recognize that the process of learning includes making mistakes. Teachers can be helpful in two ways. First, they can be good "mistake-making" models. For example, the author was recently asked to help a resource room teacher who was having many behavior management problems. During a small group lesson the teacher made a mistake and was corrected by her students. She became embarrassed and responded quite sharply and negatively. Her discomfort and anxiety led to more mistakes, more corrections from students, and more negative encounters. The lesson was chaotic. Later, when helping one of the students with an assignment, the teacher was kind and supportive. The student appeared not only to be frustrated but also to recognize clearly the discrepancy between what the teacher was saying about making mistakes and how she had behaved earlier. Consequently, her attempts to help were basically ignored. Shortly thereafter the student initiated an argument with another student that resulted in expulsion from the room. Obviously, the teacher's feelings and behavior concerning mistakes set the tone for conflict and problems rather than acceptance and support.

Mistakes should be handled matter of factly to remind the children that the key is to take time to analyze their errors so they can learn from them. Moreover, it is important to show students specifically how to detect and analyze errors. It can be helpful to watch students as they work and to assist them to monitor and check their own work. Modeling appropriate responses to mistakes and offering supportive assistance during and after assignments has many benefits. It can help the student learn good work habits, facilitate a positive teacher-student relationship, and help the students learn to release some of their negative feelings and associations about academic tasks. Ultimately, these gains can positively influence a learner's self-concept and self-regard.

Self-Control

Self-control refers to the students' ability to regulate their own behavior in task situations. A variety of studies have demonstrated that LD children have problems in task orientation, or in persistence and strategic control of behavior. LD students have often been characterized as impulsively responding to task requirements and so making many errors. Responding too quickly is a problem in and of itself, but it also appears that LD children are not strategic, that is, they do not look over instructions and assignments carefully. This combination of problems in the area of self-control may be the result of motivational problems, developmental delays in these general skills areas (which are often implied neurological problems), or learning problems (which means that they never learned efficient ways of controlling and directing their behavior in task situations).

Classroom Problems The most obvious classroom problem related to self-control is that students make many errors on academic tasks. Interfaced with poor self-regard, this propensity produces even more deep-seated negative emotional reactions to learning. Making errors beyond guided instruction can also create teacher management problems, because assignments must be graded and returned again and again. Since one goal of special education instruction for many LD students is return to or be maintained in the mainstream classroom, where independent and self-directed behavior is expected, problems of task-related self-control must be directly addressed. For more seriously impaired students, error making must be ameliorated for progress to be seen.

Teacher Sensitivity Self-control problems, as indicated above, can stem from three areas—motivational problems, developmental delays, or learning deficiencies. Depending on the working hypothesis as to why these problems are occurring, teachers can apply one or some combination of the three corresponding remedies: If motivation appears to be the problem, teachers can manipulate incentives and expectations concerning task performance. In some classrooms, for example, students are given points for completed assignments. A task completed after guided learning, however, should not be considered complete until performance reaches some acceptable, prespecified level of accuracy. If students turn in assignments with lower accuracy levels, they should receive only a percentage of the points available. They should also go back and complete the assignment at an appropriate level of accuracy. These steps can help the children learn to slow down, ask for appropriate assistance, and work more accurately. The points students earn can be exchanged for a variety of reinforcers, usually special activities. The goal here is to help students see the benefits of controlling their behavior.

Although they can also be addressed by incentive manipulations, problems related to developmental level must also be accommodated by instructional modifications in both the length of assignments and the number of assignments expected in a given period. These adjustments help the child to develop an efficient working tempo and task-orientation strategies that lead to accuracy and therefore success. The teacher initially guides and directs and gradually increases expectations as the child learns to work at a reasonable rate, ask appropriate questions, and see the benefits associated with careful work.

Finally, students can profit from techniques to control and direct their behavior through the use of Cognitive Behavior Modification, or CBM. Recall that CBM is "self-talk" that provides the student with a verbal routine to follow in completing assignments. The University of Virginia research cited in Chapter 3, pp. 53–55, has shown that some students can learn to be more efficient and controlled in their task orientation when they become organized by saying to themselves, "Slow down, look at the instructions, . . ." The research indicates that students can improve their self-control by decreasing their impulsiveness and becoming more focused and independent in their approaches to tasks. Thus, modeling and demonstrating task-related strategies and having students incorporate these strategies through self-initiated verbal routines, manipulating task demands, and providing incentives are all approaches shown to help children correct task-related self-control problems in order to improve their academic performance, especially on independent seat work.

Social Dimension

In the past ten years, a variety of research reports have indicated that many LD children experience significant problems in social adjustment and acceptance (Bryan, 1982). *Social competence,* the ability to create and maintain appropriate interpersonal relationships, is a critical developmental area for children. LD children's social interaction problems may exacerbate their academic problems. If they are not able to interact effectively with their classmates or teachers, their school experiences (which may already be marked by severe academic failure) can become even more negative.

There are many factors to consider when attempting to determine why some children are socially competent and others are not. Two broad and interrelated factors that influence children's social functioning in school settings will be examined: social cognition and social tactics.[2] *Social cognition* generally refers to a child's ability to understand social interaction processes. Social cognition can involve a wide variety of cognitive processes such as perspective taking, empathy, and knowledge of social conventions of behavior. It is their knowledge base that helps direct children's social behavior or tactics. Thus, social cognition and social tactics are intimately related to one another. *Social tactics* can be viewed as children's strategies—communication and behavioral skills—in social situations. Bryan's synthesis of the research findings indicates that many LD children manifest deficits in both social cognition and social tactics. Thus, LD students as a group could be considered *at risk* for social interaction problems in school settings.

Classroom Problems   Problems interacting with classmates can result in classroom disruptions that lead to a negative and hostile classroom climate. During both individual tasks and group activities, a variety of social interaction skills are needed. Students must respect the rights of others to work and learn. For example, they must cooperate when necessary, take turns, listen to others, handle materials appropriately, share ideas, and respect others' feelings. Clearly, problems in task-related peer interactions can significantly limit productivity.

Social interaction problems with teachers can also interfere with learning and the smooth operation of a classroom. These problems are usually related to either academic or behavioral compliance. That is, many of these children do not follow instructions for completing assignments or adhering to class rules. Such difficulties can lead to inefficient learning for the individual child (and potentially for others) and create a negative teacher-child relationship. When students refuse to comply with instructions or requests, teachers often become angry and frustrated, which can lead to the use of coercive or punitive methods to control noncompliant behavior (Pullis, 1985b). Consequently, the focus for some students moves away from academic concerns and deteriorates into disruptive and draining power struggles.

Teacher Sensitivity   When confronted with students who exhibit social interaction problems, teachers need to consider four potential sources of such misbehavior. First, opportunities for peer interaction may be too infrequent or inappropriately structured. Students may not have been given enough direction and guided practice in task behaviors. If this appears to be true, teachers need to examine and manipulate the demands of class interactions through explicitly defined instructions or expectations. In this way, students will know precisely what is expected. Furthermore, they will have an adequate number of opportunities to analyze and practice effective social skills related to academic tasks. A caution is warranted here, however. Teachers have a tendency to limit peer interaction opportunities for students who have social skills deficits to avoid potential problems. Such decisions however, can prevent LD students from ever learning appropriate skills for interacting with their classmates in learning situations. *The key is to plan short, well-structured, and motivating learning activities that include productive peer interactions.*

Second, LD students may behave inappropriately because of social cognition problems. They may not clearly understand the demands of the situation and may, for example, misread others' behavior or fail to consider others' perspectives. Thus, the source of the problem lies in cognitive limitations or misunderstandings. Children experiencing these types of problems may need special assistance and practice in learning to examine and evaluate social situations critically. There are a variety of social cognition interventions to help teachers design these programs.[3]

Third, some children may have appropriate social cognition skills, that is, they may view and interpret social situations quite correctly but may not have learned how to behave in such situations. They may suffer from a lack of learning opportunities or they may have learned atypical or maladaptive methods of interacting.

Finally, some children are effective with respect to both social cognition and social tactics but may have few incentives to behave appropriately. Conversely, there may be external incentives for them to act inappropriately, such as peer reinforcement, gains in social status among atypical groups, teacher attention, and cloaking feelings of incompetence. If it appears that the child needs more incentives to behave appropriately, reinforcement for positive interactions with teachers and classmates must be determined and used. At the same time, sanctions (at first logical, such as loss of privileges, and then more directive, like isolation) that punish the undesirable behavior may need to be applied. By exerting pressure from both punishments and rewards, we can bring about the quickest and most durable changes in a child's consistent use of appropriate social skills.

Motivational Dimension

The motivational dimension of the affective domain involves LD students' academic achievement strivings in the classroom. It is critical for teachers to have some insight into why children do what they do or, sometimes more importantly, what they will *not* do. A teacher's sensitivity to students' motivational make-up along with their personal and social characteristics can be translated into healthy, supportive, and productive instructional and interpersonal approaches in the classroom learning environment.

Why some children put forth a great deal of effort to achieve and others do not, will not, or cannot is a question that teachers strive repeatedly to answer. Students' motivational characteristics represent a complex interplay of their learning history, their psychological understanding of learning and achievement, and their feelings about school performance. In this section, three areas that can help teachers understand students' motivation will be explored—attributions, anxiety, and interests.

Attributions

Attributions are children's explanations for their academic performance. Studies of children's explanations for their own success or failure on certain tasks have yielded a rather simple but powerful model that can help teachers. When asked to explain why they performed in a given way on a task, students typically give an answer that reflects a belief in one of four reasons for success or failure: (1) effort ("I tried very hard"), (2) ability ("I'm good at these types of tasks"), (3) luck ("I guessed and was lucky to get the correct answer"), and (4) task difficulty ("The test was easy"). The attribution model then has two major types of responses— internal (effort and ability) and external (luck and task difficulty). *Internal responses* reflect factors residing within children. *External responses* represent factors over which children perceive that they have little control. Research findings show that children who typically respond with internal attributions are more confident about achieving, actually achieve at higher levels, persist on tasks because they feel that they can score well, and feel like they have control over achievement outcomes (Weiner, 1979). This is yet another strong argument for teaching directed at informed, self-control.

Attributions are formed over time and result from experiences within learning contexts. They represent students' ideas about their control over learning as well as achievement. If, for example, students put forth a great deal of effort on a task of moderate difficulty and are not successful, they may have feelings of disappointment, frustration, or shame. Conversely, efforts that result in success can produce feelings of pride and confidence. Notice, however, that level of difficulty is an important consideration. Success on a task that the child perceives as quite easy will not likely yield very positive feelings, since the child believes that not much effort was required. Thus, it is not just the outcomes that are important but also students' perceptions of their control and the level of task difficulty. The attributions that children develop through their school history become powerful influences on their achievement strivings. Attributions are, in effect, predictions about: (1) the degree of children's control over their learning and (2) the feelings they develop about their performance.

The research on attributions with LD children affords a better picture of the motivational background they often bring to the classroom. Several findings have emerged from comparisons of LD students and normally achieving students. First, many LD children seem to have developed a very negative attributional pattern concerning their success or failure in school. Normally achieving children usually give internal explanations for success ("I'm smart at these things" or "I tried very hard") and tend to provide external explanations for failure ("The test was too difficult" or "It was tricky"). They can, however, also provide internal explanations for failure ("I didn't study as hard as I should have"). The general trend for normally achieving students, therefore, is a healthy one in which their responses reflect a good deal of control over and confidence in their learning. LD students, on the other hand, tend to internalize failure ("I'm not good at math") and externalize success ("It was an easy task" or "I was lucky"). The difference is clear and potentially quite negative: LD children do not have confidence about learning, and more importantly, they feel that they have little personal control over their learning outcomes. This perceived lack of control results in poor persistance on tasks. The reasons underlying this apparent poor motivation, of course, are that the students predict that they will not be successful and that they have little or no control over their achievement.

In addition to these negative ideas about achievement, LD children can develop extremely negative feelings about learning (Meyer, 1983; Thomas, 1979). Their history of academic failure becomes the source of many such feelings, which lead to a variety of classroom problems. *Learned helplessness* explains the frustration, disappointment, and depression that affects performance in this important arena of school adjustment. Most children, for example, begin their school experience motivated to learn and willing to put forth a good deal of effort to achieve. LD childrens' efforts, however, usually result in failure. They may be encouraged to "try harder," but often their increased efforts do not result in any different outcomes—they still fail. These children come to learn (or predict) that the degree of effort that they put forth does not really make any difference in their performance. They learn to feel helpless and without control over achievement. Depression can result, which can be even more devastating when these children also develop negative attributions about their ability ("I'm stupid" or "I'm dumb"). These feelings can cause further depression or embarrassment whenever the child is placed in a learning or achievement situation—every day.

Classroom Problems   Misbehavior or nonproductive behavior that emanates from the negative attributions that LD children develop can take many forms. Some LD students develop avoidance behaviors (they want to avoid the feelings of shame or embarrassment) that range from somatic problems and truancy to misbehavior. The latter is the surface expression of their underlying negative feelings, but it can put teacher and student into a cycle of interaction that focuses on discipline rather than on learning.

Nonproductive behavior usually takes one of two forms. First, studies have consistently shown that LD children with negative attributional characteristics will not persist very long on tasks (Hill, 1979). Any threat of making a mistake usually results in their just quitting. Rather quickly, of course, they find something else to do, which is usually distracting to others in the classroom.

Another tactic that these children develop is to appear to be working very hard. Casual monitoring of this type of behavior would lead the teacher to believe that the children are indeed working diligently. At the end of the work period, however, they have often accomplished little or nothing. The teacher becomes confused and very disappointed. The larger the classroom, the more likely it is that such children will literally hide among the others, seeking to avoid the embarrassment of not knowing what to do or how to do it. Until they learn to become active learners, progress for these children is painfully slow or even nonexistent. Prolonging the period of guided learning can often be extremely beneficial for such children.

Teacher Sensitivity   The most critical factor in dealing with the negative attributions of LD children is teacher empathy. It is very important that teachers try to put themselves in the students' place and feel what it must be like to be embarrassed or disappointed about a very important and daily aspect of life. Most teachers have had positive experiences in school and feel good about learning. In addition, as adults they can *choose* to try to master a challenging task or direct their attention to other areas. Schoolchildren, on the other hand, are a captive audience—they must attend school and try to cope. Thus, the first step in attempting to deal with these negative motivational characteristics is to try to develop a level of empathy, which can then be translated into both positive reactions to the children and instructional approaches that can help them develop more positive ideas and feelings about learning. Try to remember that the nonproductive surface behavior may reflect very real and negative feelings—feelings that most of us would probably have if we had had a similar set of failure experiences.

Motivational problems that result from negative attributions must, however, be dealt with during instructional planning. Three approaches appear to be useful. First, tasks must be developmentally appropriate for each child. The students should be capable of completing these tasks with some degree of success before they are asked to perform independently. This new attributional pattern will take some time to acquire, but it can result in increased student confidence and persistence.

Second, LD children must learn to deal with mistakes. Initially, this means that the teacher must work with them as they try to complete assignments. The teacher can model ways to analyze work, detect errors, and handle mistakes less emotionally. (Note the similarity to the approaches described in the section on self-regard).

Third, LD students must be assured that they are going to receive the assistance they need to complete tasks. Knowing one can depend on the teacher is an important part of the trust needed for a positive teacher-student relationship. While the long-range goal is to help the child become an independent learner, initially the child must feel safe in the classroom. Teachers are asking LD students to take daily risks concerning their feelings about themselves. Risk taking is *not* usually done unless there is a supportive atmosphere.

To summarize, teacher sensitivity (based on some attempt at empathy), effective instructional planning, and supportive assistance can help change LD students' attributions about achievement performance. As they come to know that they will be challenged by assignments in which success is possible and that they will be assisted and encouraged by their teacher, such students are more likely to develop predictions of self-control as well as feelings of both confidence and pride. Real accomplishments can then lead to more positive approaches to learning, less misbehavior, and a productive teacher-student relationship.

Anxiety

Another reaction that some LD children develop concerning school performance is *anxiety*, which is typically defined as the physiological and psychological reaction to environmental stress. While often characterized as negative, anxiety in and of itself is not a negative factor. Rather, it can be thought of as the *energy behind behavior*. Prolonged and extreme anxiety in students, however, can seriously affect their school performance, adjustment, and motivation.

Because school performance is considered important by many LD children, the stress associated with failure can produce anxiety that interferes with their ability to concentrate and consequently to master learning tasks. As they continue to fail, more tense and anxious feelings further impede their performance. Thus, a debilitating cycle can become established: The students are constantly nervous and worried about how well they are doing, but because of their anxiety, they continue to do poorly. This anxiety can meld with the feelings of helplessness and depression described above to produce LD students who are more motivated to avoid failure than to pursue learning actively and assertively (a key requirement of academic success).

Classroom Problems Anxious students can appear to be hyperactive, distractible, and irritable. These characteristics are often explained as being associated with some unspecifiable central nervous system problem but can also result from anxiety reactions. Anxious students can be difficult to interact with. They often avoid learning situations and ask questions constantly about how they are doing. Their nervousness is somewhat contagious. Just as it is difficult to relate with any person who is always on edge, these children can be frustrating and uncomfortable to be around. Their genuine problems with learning and their emotional reactions to their failure can be extremely draining for a teacher.

Teacher Sensitivity As with negative attributions, efforts to deal with anxious students should begin with empathy. Each of us confronts situations in which we feel nervous or tense, such as tests, speaking in front of a group, and certain social situations. It is important for us to try to *understand* and *feel* what those anxious children are feeling as they are continually bombarded with upsetting learning situations. Since they anticipate failure and the negative judgments of teachers, classmates, and parents, it is critical that they learn to see the teacher as someone who understands their feelings and is on their side. This does not mean that teachers are to coddle the students or make no demands on them. It does mean that teachers should try to create a safe and supportive emotional climate in the classroom.

Furthermore, instructional approaches should take into account the anxious feelings that some students may bring to the learning situation. Again, teachers should design appropriate tasks, offer encouragement and assistance through guided learning, and provide feedback that conveys their understanding and gives information concerning successful task completion. The importance of balancing interpersonal reactions with sound instructional techniques is paramount.

Interests

The final area of concern in the motivational dimension deals with *interests,* which can be thought of as areas of study (particular topics or subjects) or types of activities (such as individualized lessons, group projects, or peer tutoring) that appeal to the child. The value of these appealing subjects or activities is that they engage the students' intrinsic motivation. Similarly, children have preferences concerning how they like to learn, whether in group situations, alone, with certain types of materials, or the like. When teachers ask students to learn concepts or skills that have no meaning or types of activities that hold no appeal, they have failed to engage their motivation. Confronted with uninteresting experiences, children often complain that they are bored, that the material is useless or uninteresting, or that they "always" have to do the same activities. These reactions create unmotivated students who are often lethargic or resistant to otherwise well-developed instructional plans.

Classroom Problems   As mentioned above, the main problems resulting from lack of interest are lethargy and boredom. Since teachers are sometimes constrained by imposed curriculum content and teaching formats, many LD students have been exposed to the same content and materials year after year. Even though they have not mastered the content or skills, LD students often do resent having the same books, work sheets, and activities presented to them again and again. Even more serious problems arise when the assignments are neither interesting nor motivating.

Teacher Sensitivity   Dealing with difficulties in interests should also begin with teacher empathy. We can be empathic because each of us has been required to take courses that either were not directly related to our personal goals or were taught in ways that did not pique our interests or curiosity. It is important to remember that students are a captive group and that constant exposure to uninteresting topics and teaching methods, added to school failure, would likely lead most anyone to be unmotivated.

Trying to make school interesting and motivating to each student is a real and difficult task. Certain general guidelines may help. First, try to get to know what interests the students. Watch them during free time or recess, talk with their parents, or collect interest inventories from them. Using this information, integrate those interests into lessons by, for example, selecting appropriate reading materials or designing applied math problems. Second, try to look for relevant issues within academic subjects. Incorporating such topics and questions into regular lessons can personalize instruction and result in more motivated students. Third, observe how students respond to different types of learning activities and different classmates. If they appear to enjoy and perform better in certain types of activities, try to plan more of those lessons or groupings. Finally, it may be necessary to add external incentives for some students. It may not be feasible to try to manipulate either curriculum content or teaching methods continuously. When this is the case, teachers must acknowledge that they must begin to look for other types of rewards to elicit effort from students.[4]

Summary and Conclusions

In this chapter some of the affective needs and problems that many LD students bring into the special education classroom were explored. Research has shown that many of these students experience serious adjustment problems in addition to their learning deficiencies. Problems in personal, social, or motivational development significantly influence both their interpersonal relationships and responses to instructional approaches. The goal of this chapter was to familiarize teachers with these important affective concerns, to illustrate how affective problems can be manifested as classroom behavior problems, and to highlight some general areas of teacher sensitivity needed to deal with these problems (see Table 4.1). Subsequent chapters seek to build on these concepts and approaches and to present an organized framework to help teachers meet students' affective needs through effective decision making and utilization of specific management and instructional techniques.

Finally, affective concerns are significantly critical to effective instruction because social-emotional factors influence student activity. We need to view the child more holistically: A depressed student is seldom an active learner. A student trying to avoid shame is not likely to take risks in learning encounters. Affective and cognitive factors are clearly intimately related, especially in achievement settings in which personal, social, and motivational factors influence academic performance and interpersonal adjustment.

Table 4.1 The Relationship between Affective Dimension, Classroom Problems, and Teacher Strategies

Dimension	Key Ideas	Classroom Problems	Teacher Strategies
Personal			
Self-concept	Student role definition	Misbehavior, poor academic performance	Give clear rules and expectations, modeling and communication
Self-regard	Evaluations or judgments of personal importance, emotional reactions	Poor motivation on tasks, classroom misbehavior	Avoid comparisons, offer opportunities for success, help to handle mistakes
Self-control	Self-regulation of impulsivity, strategic responding	Errors on tasks, classroom distraction	Manipulate incentives for productivity, accommodate tasks, direct teaching of social control strategies
Social			
Social cognition	Understanding social interactions	Disruptions to peers or teacher, noncompliance with rules	Structure opportunities Use direct teaching of understanding and skills
Social tactics	Social skills (communication and behavioral)	Cannot participate in group activities	Manipulate incentives for appropriate behavior
Motivational			
Attributions	Ideas and feelings about control over achievement outcomes	Lack of persistance, avoidance withdrawal, looking busy	Empathy: offer appropriate instruction, supportive assistance
Anxiety	Nervousness or tension related to anticipated failure	Hyperactivity, distractibility, irritability	Challenges and success
Interests	Intrinsic motivation, relevance	Boredom, lethargy, resistance	Interesting and relevant content and methods

Endnotes

1. This is a good illustration of the interrelationships between the affective dimensions, for social relationships are critical to the child's development of self-concept.

2. See Greenspan (1979) for a comprehensive description of the social domain.

3. Examples will be covered in detail in chapters 5 and 6.

4. A variety of instructional approaches and incentive methods will be discussed in chapters 5 and 6.

Chapter 5

Using Affective and Motivational Factors as a Basis for Classroom Interventions

Michael E. Pullis

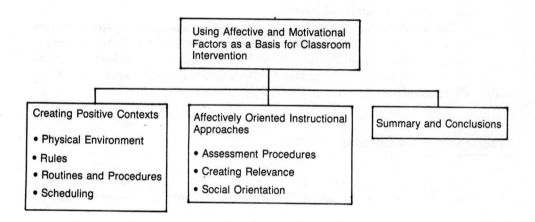

Questions to Consider

1. How can affective factors be addressed by instructional design?
2. What is proactive management and why is it important?
3. What are the two most important factors that enhance teacher decision making?

This chapter will focus on a wide range of techniques that have been shown to address the affective needs and problems of LD students. These approaches have been designed to focus simultaneously on three inter-related goals: (1) to meet the academic needs of LD students, (2) to accommodate to the wide range of affective problems that can manifest themselves in the classroom, and (3) to provide a sequence of procedures for teachers to follow in designing, implementing, and changing their classrooms. These techniques should be integrated into everyday classroom routines and interactions. Such *proactive* approaches attempt to (1) structure the classroom to invite positive and productive behavior and (2) eliminate potential problems by teaching in effective and supportive ways. Jones and Jones (1986) have shown that classroom behavior management is often tried only *after* problems arise, which puts the teacher in a reactive mode. While this tact can be somewhat effective, studies show that problems seldom arise in classrooms that are well organized, have clearly explained rules and routines, and have instructional activities that meet students' needs.

Box 5.1 shows that the standard sequence of decision-making steps depends on sound information derived from continuous assessment and evaluation. Effective decisions about the design, implementation, and modification of management and instructional approaches can only be made when teachers carefully observe and record the efficacy of their interventions.

Creating Positive Contexts

Many affective problems experienced by LD students result in disorganized, unproductive behavior. Some classroom learning problems, such as

---

Box 5.1   Decision-Making Procedures

Decision making, within the context of ongoing assessment, should:
1. create positive, structured contexts;
2. consistently use affectively oriented teaching activities and methods;
3. when problems arise, try to modify the existing structures and methods;
4. use problem-solving and incentive approaches to promote rule compliance and academic productivity; and
5. provide specific instruction for fostering independence in self-control and motivation.

hyperactivity, distractibility, poorly developed role definition, and anxiety, can be addressed through proactive approaches that produce a structured and supportive classroom environment. The teacher can manipulate several important aspects of classroom structure and design to eliminate disruptive or nonproductive behavior not through coercion or punitive, reactive methods but rather by creating an environment that invites positive, motivated, learning behaviors.

Physical Environment

The arrangement of the physical environment can profoundly influence students' behaviors. The arrangement of desks, materials, and decorations have been shown to affect a variety of behaviors and attitudes, including movement, communication frequency and direction, distractibility, and motivation. Movement, for example, is not a problem in and of itself, but the LD child's classroom movements often will be undirected and can distract both the teacher and other students. As a rule, the younger or more disordered the students, the more structure and organization should be imposed to invite orderly behavior and learning. The room arrangement should ensure that children move both under control and with clearly specified direction. Materials and activity areas should be placed so that the flow of traffic is productive but unintrusive.

Teacher movement is also important in managing the classroom. Desks must be positioned to optimize their view of students. Teachers must also move about the room to let children know that they will be assisted as soon as possible and to help structure student behavior through *proximity control*. Rather than waiting for problems to arise and then redirecting or reprimanding the students, moving in a nonthreatening way toward them can remind or prompt them to focus on the assigned activity. This nonverbal technique is not intrusive, eliminates the need for negative comments, and is more effective than attempts to control the students from across the room. Thus, both controlled student movement and purposeful teacher movement can foster orderly classroom interactions.

Communication patterns within the classroom are also controlled to a great extent by the physical arrangement of the classroom. While teachers have different ideas about how much talking should be allowed, they can use carefully planned seating arrangements to help establish the amount and direction of communication. The teacher needs to determine the various types of activities that will be used in the classroom and the amount and type of communication that will ensure their success. Such activities usually include independent seat work (accompanied by individualized teacher assistance); teacher-directed small-group instruction; individual, paired, or small-group work at learning centers or stations; whole class instruction or discussions; and peer tutoring. In each case, the teacher must decide where the activity should take place, who should be involved, how the desks and pupils should be arranged, and what materials will be needed. Such planning is likely to increase productivity and decrease unwanted or disruptive communication.

Two additional points deserve mention. First, assessment-based knowledge about who can and cannot function well in various activities or with certain other students is critical. Second, whenever possible, LD classroom arrangements should parallel those in regular classrooms. While at the beginning of the year it may be necessary to use highly structured and unique instructional arrangements, as the students gain more control over their communication and behavior, the teacher should gradually change the structures to replicate those in mainstream settings so that the children may practice appropriate task-oriented communication skills. If special educators continue to make the LD classroom or resource room different from the regular classroom, they may be unnecessarily and unintentionally impeding students' development of needed social and academic skills. In communication as in movement, the goal is to plan and arrange learning activities that invite goal-directed behavior rather than control students through reprimands or other disciplinary procedures.

The decorations in the classroom should be organized and directed whenever possible to academic goals and performance. There was a time when some special educators advocated that rooms be totally devoid of visually stimulating materials, but there is little evidence that this is of any real value. Rather, decorations or displays need to be linked to student achievements. Involving students or their work in the decorations of the room can be extremely motivating, for such involvement builds pride and a feeling that this is the students' room, one to which they can make important contributions.

One type of display uses procedure sheets to outline various task requirements of a reading or math operation. This can be accompanied by examples of student work that was accurately completed according to the steps shown in the display. Such outlines can serve as cognitive organizers that increase accuracy, provide direction, and free the teacher from having to remind students constantly of the proper procedures. They can also help students become more strategic and develop control over their achievement performance. Portable versions of these procedure sheets can be kept on student desks or in notebooks.

Another display that can be helpful is a sequential listing of assignments that represents the gradual acquisition of a new skill. This will reinforce the students' positive feelings and effort related to their performance as they see their progress. (Recall earlier discussions on self-regard, attributions, and anxiety.) It also fosters improved teacher-student relationships as both look for and appreciate the results of hard work and the careful analysis of errors. These assignments can also be sent home so that parents can share in the successes of their children. As a variation this type of display can be focused not on a particular academic skill but on a more general task or goal, such as neatness or effective use of time. Again, the purpose is to help students develop a sense of control over their learning, reduce their anxiety over mistakes, remind them of their success, and establish a pride in their efforts and accomplishments.

One final aspect of the physical environment needs to be discussed— the amount, level, and quality of teacher comments—which can distract or motivate students. Teachers serve as an important stimulus and model for classroom behavior both in terms of task orientation and interpersonal interactions. By modeling courteous and enthusiastic work behavior, teachers set the tone for the social and academic environment. It is helpful to tape-record the classroom occasionally to monitor the noise level, the quality of verbalizations, and the like to determine whether the teacher is helping or hindering students' performance. An example can illustrate. A high school teacher of LD students had had problems with students calling out for help during quiet seat work. She decided to reinforce students verbally when they remembered to raise their hands for assistance. When she noticed a raised hand, she moved quickly toward the compliant student saying, "I appreciate that you remembered to raise your hand." She hoped that this courtesy would reinforce the desired behavior and would provide a model for the others. Students of this age, however, dislike public praise. Furthermore, the other students stopped their work to attend to the commotion. They also began to yell to the teacher across the room in a covert plan designed to irritate her. The problem was solved when the teacher: (1) improved her instructions and clarified her expectations at the beginning of seat work time, (2) learned to move more slowly and quietly, (3) provided more personal praise, and (4) ignored the game intended to aggravate her.

The key point is that, in addition to manipulating physical factors, teachers themselves have a great deal to do with the emotional and work climate of their classroom. It can be important to try to ascertain how students feel about the class. Teachers need to ask themselves and their students: What does it feel like being in here? Is it safe? organized? fun? challenging? boring? fair? When teachers thus try to take into account the feelings and needs of the students, they are often able to see ways to change the classroom organization, methods of teaching, and approaches for interacting with students to produce more favorable outcomes in learning and affective development.

This means too that assessment should include teachers' self-evaluation of their own patterns of communication and teaching, as these can become automatic or routinized. Changing teaching methods is hard work that must begin with an accurate and ongoing assessment of current practices.

Rules

The establishment and administration of rules are critical steps in organizing an appropriate learning context in the classroom. Just as rules

---

Box 5.2 Guidelines for Effective Classroom Rules

---

1. Involve students in setting the rules and garner consensus.
2. Keep the rules short, behavior specific, and positively phrased.
3. Devise specific rules for different activities or times in the classroom to complement the more general rules.
4. Establish the rules through discussion, demonstration, posting, and reviews.

---

are important to the LD students' self-concept, self-control, and social interactions, they structure students' academic and social behaviors.

Setting rules is a process of defining, *in specific behavioral terms*, expectations concerning classroom behavior. Both general school rules and rules specific to the individual classroom should be incorporated. Creating a reasonable number of clearly defined rules is the first step in this process. These rules have to be linked to the goals or values of the classroom as defined by both the teacher and the students. Otherwise, they can appear to be attempts to control students and lead to power struggles, since students do not see their logic. Box 5.2 contains a set of guidelines for establishing classroom rules, which are discussed at length below.

1. *Involve students in setting the rules and garner consensus.* There are several advantages to this approach. First, students will feel more responsible and more motivated to follow rules that they have helped create. By starting with a discussion that focuses on the goals of the class, teachers can ask students how the classroom should operate to meet those goals. One teacher, for example, had a general rule that the classroom was a place of working and learning and that no one had the right to interfere with the work of other students or the teacher. The teacher then checked to see if all of the students agreed with this. Once this was established as a fair goal, inappropriate behavior became functionally defined as interfering with the work of the room and therefore was not to be allowed. The rule was neither capricious nor arbitrary, but rather linked to the goals of the room and to the concept of fairness. Because the students had been asked to create and agree to the rule, they did not think their teacher was trying to control them.

   Involving the students also assures that they know exactly what the rules mean, since they will not usually create rules that they do not understand. It is important to demonstrate specifically by giving several examples what compliance and noncompliance involves. Again, this discussion should link the rules to the goals and responsibilities of all involved in the classroom. It can also be helpful to discuss the importance of rules to other aspects of life, such as rules of the road, games, and various work places. Students need to see that rules function to organize people into cooperative groups so that work can be safely and productively accomplished. Comprehension of the purposes of rules can help assure that student misbehavior is not caused by a misunderstanding of what is expected and why. Remember too that the rules help shape the child's self-concept in the classroom.

2. *Keep the rules short, behavior specific, and positively phrased.* This guideline helps to create explicit rules and positive expectations for student behavior during classroom activities. Typical rules have a tendency to be vague ("Be nice to your classmates") or read like a litany of "don'ts" ("Don't talk during class,") ("Don't chew gum,") ("Don't interrupt the teacher"). Both sorts of rules have limited informational value for the student, which can lead to constant "negotiating" about their intent. A list of "don'ts" also creates a negative atmosphere and says little about what students actually should do: Even if they are not breaking any rules, they may not be completing any work.

   There needs to be a set of basic rules that focus on: (1) work or productivity, (2) treatment of property and materials, and (3) behavior toward others.[1] The bulk of the rules should specify positive expectations. By having positive rules, teachers inform the students of what is expected, not just what is not allowed. While there will be some need for prohibitions, these should be kept to a minimum. They should also be examined to determine if they can be phrased positively. In either case, the students need to know the specific rule as well as its intent and rationale. This can be most productively accomplished by exploring the effect of rule compliance and infraction on the classroom. Recall that many social problems of LD students result because they are not fully aware of the effect of their behavior on others. Having logical and positive rules can help students examine their own actions and realize their responsibilities for their own work, the classroom materials, and the work opportunities of others.

3. *Devise specific rules for different activities or times in the classroom to complement the more general rules.* If a variety of instructional activities are used, specific rules for those activities might be necessary to address such issues as behavior during transitions from activity to activity, amount of talking allowed, use of materials, and behavior during group activities. It is important to devise these rules *with* the students, cite the situations in which they are in effect, and review the applicable rules prior to the relevant activities. This helps students acquire specific expectations and establish orderly classroom behavior.

4. *Establish the rules through discussion, demonstration, posting, and reviews.* It will take some time for students to become fully aware of the classroom rules. Development of the rules through the techniques listed above can lead to their quick integration into everyday practice. Be sure to draw attention to the rules when the students are complying or as a way of reminding students about class expectations. The value of garnering consensus about the importance of rules is that you can then call on students to live up to their word. *Requesting* agreement is preferable to *demanding* compliance, because it forces the students to exercise some degree of self-control and underlines the importance of cooperative agreements in social relationships. Classroom interaction studies have shown that teachers tend to focus on rules only when they are not being followed—that is, they react to misbehavior. The goal, in contrast, is to be proactive and help establish an appropriate and productive classroom context.

Setting up effective rules is only the first step in classroom control and management. Teachers need to use rules consistently to invite positive behavior. This proactive approach can be thought of as establishing antecedent control—setting the conditions and cues for learning and social behavior. The ultimate effect of the rules, however, will be determined by the consequences for following or not following them. It is very important that *consequences be defined for both compliance and noncompliance.* It is often said that children need to learn that there are consequences for their behavior. This usually means that they should be punished for not following rules. Adults often fail to provide positive results of rule compliance, assuming that children will stay in line with expectations if they learn (fear) that rule infractions will result in swift and consistent punishment. It is critical, however, that both rule compliance and noncompliance are met with clear and motivating consequences. Teachers must offer rewards for following the rules if they want children to exercise control and put forth effort.

The provision of consequences should be integrated into the normal school day. Following the rules should result in accomplishments. Students should learn that the logical outcome of effort and appropriate social behavior will be a smooth, productive day. Furthermore, and this is especially true at the beginning of the year, teachers have to provide a great deal of social praise and appreciation for appropriate behavior. The opportunity to experience success through completed assignments as well as sincere appreciation and acknowledgment for rule compliance can go a long way in establishing the kind of work environment desired in the classroom. In addition, it can be helpful to work activity reinforcers, such as free reading time, academic games, and ongoing projects, into the day to give students natural incentives for completing assignments accurately and on time. Three incentives can thus help students complete their work and comply with classroom rules—social praise, successful assignments, and motivating activities.

Similarly, negative consequences need to be integrated into the typical day. Rule infractions are in violation of the students' agreement and should be met with disapproval from teachers and peers. The consequences should delay the student's completion of assignments and participation in the activity reinforcers discussed above. These logical and natural consequences should be thought of as initial attempts to help students become committed to positive behavior in the classroom.[2]

To summarize, the creation and administration of classroom rules are central to the establishment of a positive context for both learning and affective development. General guidelines for such rules include: (1) involve the students, (2) make sure they comprehend the logic and specifics of the expectations, and (3) provide clear and consistent consequences for *both* rule compliance and rule infractions.

Routines and Procedures

A key tactic for increasing efficiency in the classroom is establishing teaching routines and procedures. These approaches will be briefly discussed as management tactics in this chapter. In Chapter 6 they will be elaborated upon as a means of helping students become more independent in their classroom behavior.

Routines can be defined as a specified set of procedures that are used in a particular situation. The teacher, for example, may want to establish a routine for students entering the room and beginning their work. They may also want to establish a consistent way for grading assignments, checking homework, charting progress, and housekeeping. By thinking through and teaching efficient routines to the students early in the year, time can be more profitably devoted to instruction. Evertson and Emmer (1982) have found that particularly effective teachers were adept at increasing academically engaged time by routinizing many of the repetitive, business aspects of the class. This context manipulation helps organize everyone's behavior and can be particularly important for students who have self-control difficulties.

Scheduling

The scheduling of class time is another context variable that can be used to create an organized and productive classroom environment. Most LD students spend only part of their school day in a resource classroom. The coordination of instructional times for several students who are on different schedules and have a wide range of academic skill levels is a

---

Box 5.3   Guidelines for Effective Classroom Schedules

1. Plan and post (or distribute) schedules for students.
2. Alternate length and probability of tasks or activities.
3. Evolve from individual to group tasks.
4. Initially give work that can be finished that day and gradually stretch assignments. Give homework.

---

significant challenge to teachers. In this section, however, only scheduling issues within the resource room itself will be addressed.

Time-on-task studies have revealed a strong positive correlation between the amount of time engaged in task completion and achievement. Teachers should therefore try to maximize the amount of time spent on learning activities. A well-designed schedule can also help LD students with their self-control, social, and motivational difficulties. This integrated approach to meeting the academic and affective needs of students can guide teachers in the development and manipulation of classroom schedules to organize the learning environment so that both individuals and group needs can be met. Box 5.3 presents some approaches for creating effective schedules, which will be discussed below.

1. *Plan and post (or distribute) schedules for students.* Planning and posting schedules can help individual students know immediately what they are expected to do. Individual work folders or a classroom display can be used for this purpose. Many teachers prefer using the folder, because it can also be used to record completion and accuracy levels on each task. Many teachers likewise use a token economy or point system to increase incentives. A well-designed assignment sheet can also contain a section for keeping track of points and thus simultaneously foster self-control, independent work habits, and motivation.

2. *Alternate length and probability of tasks or activities.* After teachers have interacted with students for a few weeks, they will be able to assess how long each one can work on various tasks, such as individual seat work, peer tutoring, small group instruction, and whole class instruction, and in academic skills, such as math, reading, spelling, handwriting, and social studies. Teachers can then manipulate task length to keep students' attention at its highest throughout the day. Attention span across academic tasks is highly related to motivational level. If students enjoy and feel competent in a particular academic area, they will likely attend longer and put forth more effort. We use the term *probability* to describe this

relationship. A high probability task is one students believe they can tackle successfully and enjoy. They will typically work on such tasks for relatively long periods of time. A low probability task, conversely, is one that students perceive as either uninteresting or beyond their ability. They will therefore not be likely to put forth much effort. In some cases they may actively avoid the task, because they predict that they will fail.

The teacher can, through good record keeping and sensitive observation, arrange a sequence of activities that attempts to accommodate the learning and affective needs of students. Bill, for example, does not like math but loves reading. Further, he enjoys small group work and individual seat work, but does not respond well to whole class instruction. Armed with this information, the teacher can design Bill's work day to include a rather long individualized reading assignment, a short group lesson on reading, a relatively short math lesson with two or three children, and a short individual assignment to practice the math covered in the small group. This type of scheduling results in a series of learning tasks in which the type of activity, the academic area, and the length of the task are all manipulated to create the optimal motivational context. It should be apparent that this scheduling process can be very complicated. Total accommodation to each child is probably not possible, but it is critical to keep in mind that these types of manipulations are available and can go a long way in creating a productive learning setting for each student. Of course, they are most appropriate as *beginning* accommodations, for as the school year progresses, students should be required to conform increasingly to mainstream-like time frames and lessons.

3. *Evolve from individual to group tasks.* It may be most efficient to begin the school year with a majority of individual assignments to observe each child's academic strengths and weaknesses as well as their learning styles—length of attention span, work habits, and the like. Teachers can gradually introduce different types of activities such as peer work and small group instruction to determine how each child responds in the various structures. Shaping students' behavior over time will help them respond effectively to different types of teaching methods. Special attention should be given to those methods that are likely to be used in mainstream situations. This gradual evolution toward the mainstream can be most beneficial for students who are candidates for full integration into regular settings, for they will have the opportunity to learn and practice both the academic skills and social skills necessary for successful integration.

4. *Initially give work that can be finished that day and gradually stretch assignments. Give homework.* LD children usually lose a good deal

of their persistence toward a task because they do not feel competent or successful. By starting with a sequence of assignments that can reasonably be completed (and corrected) during the school day, the children can be given a sense of accomplishment and closure that can boost their feelings of competence and control. Once such feelings gradually lead to more persistence, the schedule can be stretched for longer assignments and goals. Again, skills and motivation levels should be shaped to meet those of the mainstream classroom.

Many teachers do not give homework, arguing that LD children often lack the independent work skills to complete such assignments. Further, they suggest that such children need to feel less pressure to complete assignments to develop more positive attitudes about learning. While this argument may have some merit, it may be just one more way that LD students are made to feel more different than is healthy. One critical aspect of learning is practice. Homework is a good opportunity for practice that can lead to the maintenance and generalization of an academic skill. Do not ask students to learn new material or skills at home. Rather, use homework (at least initially) for practicing or reviewing skills that are at least at levels of proficiency. Students will then know that homework is an expected part of school. Perhaps more importantly, homework assignments should be designed so that students are routinely successful in completing them, thereby bolstering their confidence. Parents, on the other hand, should not be expected to teach their children. Rather, homework can be an easy way of reporting to parents. It should afford them the opportunity to see their children working successfully and independently on school tasks and take pride in the learning that is taking place. It can also help the parents see that their children can learn and are not so very different from others.

Affectively Oriented Instructional Approaches

This section presents a framework for making decisions about instructional design. Assessment, creating relevance, and social orientation are all procedures that can be used with LD students in an integrated manner. A brief section on diagnosing problems is followed by a model for systematically examining and changing instructional practices.

Assessment Procedures

Effective teaching must begin by setting learning goals that are appropriate for each student. Some goals will be established within the process of creating the IEP. More specific, personalized goals, however, can be determined only after interacting with students for a few weeks, for systematic observations are needed to assess their current levels in each academic area and to determine how they learn best (their learning styles and preferences). Assessment determines what to teach, how to teach, and provides an indication of what an appropriate criterial task may be (e.g., tests, written reports, projects, or oral reports; see Part III for details about specific content areas).

Setting goals through effective assessment improves student cognitive and affective responses to instructional plans. In Chapter 4 several affective problems associated with school failure were examined—self-regard, attributions, and anxiety. These psychological and emotional responses resulted from students' interpretations of repeated failure and made them particularly resistant in learning situations. *Failure, however, may be just as much a function of inappropriate assessment and teaching* (Flavell, 1983), although it is typically attributed to some factor within the child (e.g., neurological or developmental problems). Some children experience failure because of regular-grade insistence that all children learn academic material at the same pace and by the same methods. This lack of flexibility inevitably ensures that a certain proportion of students will fail.

If teachers can accurately assess their students so that they know what the students can do alone and what they will need help with, many learning and affective difficulties can be ameliorated. Appropriate learning activities are those that students can do successfully with effort and that match their learning preferences (how they best learn different concepts and skills). Appropriate activities present students with opportunities to be successful on challenging tasks. They allow students to: (1) make healthy attributions ("I can do this work if I try hard"), (2) feel positive about themselves in the role of student, and (3) control some of their anxiety (e.g., by anticipating success and pride rather than failure and disappointment). Thus, the first step in teaching "affectively" is to determine students' characteristics and to observe their activities through systematic and sensitive assessments. Then plan developmentally appropriate activities and reassess.

Creating Relevance

Many students complain that academic tasks are boring or have no practical value. (See the section on motivational problems in Chapter 4). This perception usually results in lethargy or more direct and disruptive resistance to instruction. A key approach to dealing with these motivational problems is to create relevant activities that engage students' intrinsic motivation. Box 5.4 presents four such approaches, as discussed below.

Box 5.4   Guidelines for Enhancing Student Motivation

1. Personalize instruction by manipulating content choices.
2. Require students to be mentally active in the learning process.
3. Accent the similarity between traditional assignments and students' lives.
4. Include assignments based solely on student interests.

---

1. *Personalize instruction by manipulating content choices.* One approach involves manipulating *content choices,* that is what students are asked to learn or what skills they are asked to master. If teachers can affectively assess students' interests by asking them to complete interest inventories, speaking to students and their parents or other teachers, or watching students to see how they spend their free times, they can more likely choose content topics that are both developmentally appropriate and intrinsically motivating. When teachers personalize instructional content or apply skills to everyday situations, motivated student responses are more likely to result. While it is not always possible for an individual teacher to select topics or curriculum materials, the teacher should explain to students *why* they are required to learn certain subjects. Research has shown that children are much more purposeful and motivated when they have some understanding of the reason for their efforts (Wang, 1983). While some might argue that students should complete assignments simply because they are told to do (a compliance orientation), it is more desirable to engender informed, self-control with interesting and relevant lessons.

2. *Require students to be mentally active in the learning process.* Children are more motivated and show improved performance on tasks that demand active processing. Active involvement may be encouraged by the manipulation of learning materials or some of the instructional approaches discussed in previous and subsequent chapters of this book, such as estimation, story creation, and problem solving. Also, since LD students may not perform as actively during tasks as their normally achieving peers, teachers may require them to solve problems aloud. Manipulating objects may also help them realize that learning results from *their* activity, not someone else's. Furthermore, active participation enhances intrinsic motivation.

3. *Accent the similarity between traditional assignments and students' lives.* A recent classroom experiment will serve as an example of this method of creating relevance. The teacher was to present a social studies unit on American Indians of the Northeast to two

groups of middle-school LD students. Many of these students had significant affective problems along with their learning difficulties. For one group, she followed the lesson suggestions in the curriculum guide—read the unit together, present a supplementary lecture, watch a filmstrip, and give a test to evaluate mastery. The group activities were marked by many interruptions. Average performance was approximately 68 percent mastery.

For the next group she did two things differently. First, she discussed her expectations for appropriate group behavior during the activities. She reviewed these expectations with students at the beginning of each lesson, thus creating the appropriate context. Next, she looked through the reading and filmstrip and designed meaningful discussion questions. She asked students, for example, whether it was fair that the Indians lost their land to the settlers. Could they give examples of when someone took something from them? How did they feel? What did they do? In this way she not only required that students be mentally active, she also personalized the unit by helping the students see its relevance. The lessons ran more smoothly and retention of the information was facilitated. Test performance was almost 20 percent higher than for the other group.

4. *Include assignments based solely on student interest.* Students in LD resource programs usually have varied schedules ranging from three to twenty hours per week. Programing for these diverse needs and within the complicated time schedules can be very difficult. One method that simultaneously incorporates student interests and assists with scheduling is to assign ongoing projects based on students' expressed interests or hobbies at an apppropriate instructional level for independent functioning. Whenever students successfully complete their normal class work, they are allowed to spend time on these projects. Because the students helped design the activities, teachers can be assured that they are intrinsically motivated to behave appropriately while working on them. Students also learn that when their assignments are completed accurately (and this is key, because impulsive students will rush through tasks just to get to their projects), they will be able to move on to their own work.

Social Orientation

Because many LD students possess significant social skills problems, they invite teachers to keep them separated during most classroom activities. Most IEPs are strictly academic in nature, which, given time constraints, necessarily limits activities whose sole purpose is enhancing social interaction skills. But schools are supposed to address general socialization issues as well as academic gains. Several activity structures have an academic focus but utilize pairs or groups of students. Other activities, such as peer tutoring, cooperative or team learning, group projects, and learning center assignments, address academic and social concerns simultaneously. Indeed, the research on these approaches (especially as they compare to traditional whole class and individualized instructional methods) has been quite impressive. Findings suggest that activities that combine academic and social goals result in: (1) sound academic and cognitive gains, (2) improved task-related peer interaction skills, (3) social skills that generalize to other situations, (4) more reported feelings of acceptance within the group, and (5) higher scores on self-esteem measures (Johnson & Johnson, 1983; Slavin, 1983).

Teachers of LD students might use such lesson structures for a number of reasons. First, they retain their key focus on academic goals consistent with IEP mandates. Second, they address affective problems by helping children to develop and use task-related social interaction skills. Third, they require active cognitive involvement and appear to motivate many students. Finally, they underscore the importance of having classroom rules and expectations that focus both on academic productivity and social roles and responsibilities.

While there are many potential benefits to using socially structured activities, there are some cautions as well. The self-control, motivational, and social problems described in Chapter 4 often complicate LD students' participation, at least initially. These activity structures (like all learning activities) require careful planning, tight structure, and ongoing assessment and evaluation. Furthermore, they require some changes in the roles and responsibilities of the teacher. Because of space limitations each type of activity cannot be elaborated. Instead, general guidelines to follow in designing, implementing, and evaluating these approaches are presented in Figure 5.1.

It is easiest to conceptualize the process as three interrelated phases. The first phase, *preteaching,* involves design and planning procedures. The second phase, *implementation,* entails initiating and guiding the activity. The final phase, *evaluation,* analyzes the strengths and faults of the approach so that it can be improved.

In the initial step of the pre-teaching phase the teacher, using knowledge and assessment of the children, determines the specific academic and social goals of the activity. The teacher must be clear about the objectives and purpose of the activity. Several subsequent planning decisions must be made: the academic content of the activity, the number of students to be involved, the pairs or groups of students likely to work best together (both academically and socially), the length of the activity, the time of day the activity is possible and likely to be motivating, the area in the classroom where the activity should take place, the materials needed, and the rules that are to be followed during the activity. Once

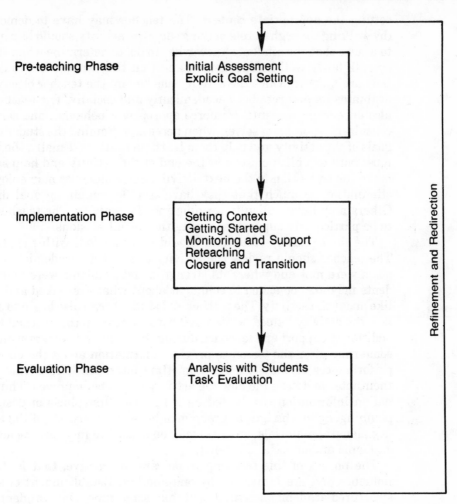

FIGURE 5.1 Teaching Cycle.

these decisions have been made (with student involvement wherever possible), the teacher can move to the implementation phase.

Carrying out the plan also involves several steps, many of which entail somewhat different responsibilities for teachers. Initially, the teacher must explain, model, or demonstrate the academic and social goals of the activity to the students. Remember that students respond better when they know what they are being asked to do, why they are being asked to do it, and how to go about it. The second step, therefore, is to outline the procedures. This step is especially important since many LD students are used to working alone or with only the teacher. Behavioral expectations can be set by specifying the rules for behavior during the activity, thus setting the appropriate context. The teacher may have to demonstrate (by walking through or role playing) how the activity should be conducted to assure that the students know what to do, to determine when they can operate fairly well independently, and that they know what to do when they are finished. Once the activity has begun, the teacher observes and evaluates its progress both academically and socially. The teacher must also encourage students, reinforce appropriate behavior, and serve as a consultant or problem solver, when necessary. Remind the students of the goals of the activity and help them learn its routines. Finally, the teacher must both establish closure at the end of the activity and help students make the transition to the next activity. Some students may enjoy social stimulation so much that they have trouble remaining goal directed. Others may have difficulty terminating the activity. The teacher needs to be particularly supportive during the initial sessions.

The final phase, evaluation, should be conducted with the students. The teacher should review the activity to see if its academic and social goals were met and where its strengths and problems were found. Students may also be asked to comment about what they liked and did not like about the activity. The teacher and students can also begin to analyze how the activity helped or hindered performance on the criterial task. In addition to support and feedback during the activity, teachers should take some time after the lesson to provide information about the efforts and performances of the students. Sometime later, teachers should review their notes to determine how the activity might be improved. Thus, evaluation information can be fed back into the first phase of design and planning. Some changes in group membership, or aspects of the activity (e.g., length, materials, or rules) may be needed to increase the activity's academic and/or social efficiency.

The phases of this teaching model are interactive, that is, they all influence and are influenced by one another. Establishment of socially structured academic activities will take some time. Once students learn how to behave effectively and independently within these structures, teachers can devote time to specific students, while being assured that the others are engaged in worthwhile activities.

This systematic approach to teaching can and should be used as a model for designing and changing all types of instructional activities. It incorporates many of the themes of Part II. First, it constitutes an organized approach to the design of learning activities. Second, it relies heavily on on-going assessment to make decisions both in the initial design and for subsequent changes. Third, it provides teachers with a tool for diagnosing problems at various points in the teaching-learning process by helping them focus systematically on the strengths and weaknesses of various activities to determine where modifications might be helpful. Finally, because it is aimed at increasing instructional efficiency, it meets teachers' needs while addressing affective problems in LD students. The model reinforces the idea that academic and affective factors are not separate or competing areas of concern but rather are significantly related and simultaneously addressable.

Summary and Conclusions

This chapter has focused on the need for teachers to use their knowledge about the affective needs and problems of LD students when making decisions about classroom structures and instructional options. In each section tactics were presented to design and modify activities. The discussions showed how affective factors were addressed in these decisions. Three other points were made. First, teachers must concentrate on proactive management by designing a positive and structured working context. Second, they need to be systematic in their decision making. Third, teachers should use on-going assessment data consistently to objectify their decision making. In the next chapter, strategies to deal with problematic students and foster independence will be presented.

Endnotes

1. As an exercise, try to develop three or four positively stated rules for each of these general areas.

2. Chapter 6 will discusss interventions that might be necessary for those students who are extremely disruptive despite these integrated consequences for rule compliance and infractions.

Chapter 6

Fostering Independence and Managing Behavior Problems

Michael E. Pullis

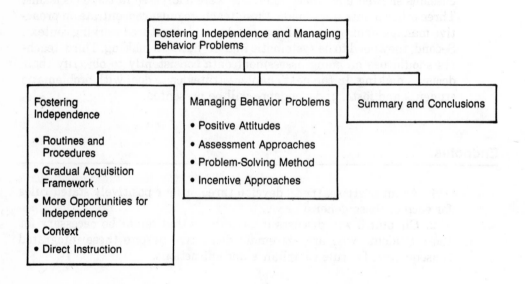

Fostering Independence and Managing Behavior Problems

Fostering Independence

- Routines and Procedures
- Gradual Acquisition Framework
- More Opportunities for Independence
- Context
- Direct Instruction

Managing Behavior Problems

- Positive Attitudes
- Assessment Approaches
- Problem-Solving Method
- Incentive Approaches

Summary and Conclusions

Questions to Consider

1. What knowledge and skills are integral to the social aspects of teaching?
2. Why is the integration of the cognitive and social demands of teaching so important?
3. In what sense are the social goals transparent (see Chapter 3)?

The content of this chapter builds on the ideas and strategies covered in the previous two chapters. Chapter 4 presented the key aspects and problems of the affective domain. Chapter 5 presented examples of how these affective needs and problems can be considered in the design of classroom structure and learning activities. The first part of this chapter presents a range of approaches that help students develop more independent functioning in the classroom, including the use of routines and procedures to create trust and foster independence, a decision-making framework for supporting the gradual acquisition of skills, and methods for fostering opportunities in which students have choices and display more positive and effortful behavior across learning situations. As in the previous chapter, these approaches represent aspects of the classroom that require sound initial planning and modifications based on ongoing assessment and evaluation. Together with the tactics covered in Chapter 5, these approaches represent basic classroom management—on-going assessment, structured context, well designed learning activities, and evaluation-based modifications.

Some LD students may, however, still present significant behavioral problems even within a good learning environment. Recall that most LD students have experienced a variety of affective and learning problems and some will take time to adjust to the learning situation and the teacher. Teachers must be cognizant, therefore, that behavioral difficulties can and will occur. The second section presents examples of techniques for dealing with particularly troubled children: assessment of affective and academic needs, positive attitudes for handling difficult children and disruptive behavior, problem-solving approaches to help children analyze and improve their behavior, and methods for adding incentives to compensate for problems in motivation.

Fostering Independence

Routines and Procedures

There are several advantages to establishing parts of the school day as classroom routines. First, routines promote responsible behavior. Organization and predictability create an atmosphere of structure and trust within which children feel confident. Self-control and anxiety are directly addressed within the course of daily interactions because routines lead to a feeling of safety, which frees children to focus on their academic tasks. Routines free teachers to focus on academic tasks too, for as they allow students to function more independently, much less supervision is required. One caution should be noted: A classroom that is overroutinized can become boring and repressive for both the students and the teacher.

The idea is first to establish control and support and then gradually to increase opportunities for the students to learn and practice the skills of self-control and self-management. Because many LD students are (or soon will be) involved in mainstreamed settings, routines should approximate regular classroom demands for both academic and affective behaviors.

Gradual Acquisition Framework

Fostering informed, independent functioning is at the heart of the cognitive developmental approach. While an organized classroom with established routines can be helpful, teachers still must decide when individual students can be expected to function increasingly independently. The key is for teachers to recognize when structure, direction, and support are needed and when students can be expected to be more on their own. A simple yet powerful framework for examining the gradual nature of learning will be presented here as an extension of the discussions of learning and teaching in Chapters 2 and 3. This framework provides a decision-making structure for helping teachers decide when and how to support student mastery of knowledge, strategies, and skills and when to step back and require independence.

Lovitt (1977) suggested that learning could be viewed as occurring in four phases ranging from initial exposure through solid mastery (see Table 6.1). He and his students have successfully used this framework to assess how and when to intervene.

Before the framework itself is discussed, some key ideas need to be presented. First, this framework has been successfully used to teach a wide range of knowledge, strategies, and skills, including math operations, strategies for reading comprehension, and cooperative work with other students. Second, students will move through the phases of acquisition at different rates, needing somewhat varying amounts of support. Third, the more complex the knowledge, strategy, or skill to be learned, the longer the process will likely take and the more support the child will need during the early phases of learning. Finally, the suggestions for instructional and interpersonal support are general; they serve only as guides. Teachers will need to tailor their specific interventions to individual children, based on their learning needs, the materials, the criterial task, and the nature of the ongoing teacher-student relationship.

In the initial stage of learning, *initial acquisition*, the criterial task is taught and made explicit. Depending on the nature of the task and how similar it is to previous learning, children will be more or less successful. Because there is often little probability of initial success, especially in the student's perception, the teacher needs to be particularly sensitive both instructionally and personally. The student cannot function independently and requires a good deal of guided instruction. The teacher

Table 6.1 Gradual Acquisition Framework

Stage	Student Needs/Abilities	Interpersonal Tactics	Instructional Approaches
Initial acquisition	Exposure to knowledge, strategy, or skill Small chance of success, detailed instruction, encouragement	Positive expectations, feedback for effort, direction and support	Well-designed lesson, precise instructions, demonstration and modeling, learning steps and tricks
Advanced acquisition	Continued instructional focus and support, guided learning	Feedback for effort and performance, reinforcement sandwich, slightly reduced direction	Guided practice, reteaching, error analysis
Initial proficiency	More independence, guided practice, reinforcement for performance	Remind or show success, focus on performance, internal attributions, minimized directions	Longer assignments, spot checks, error analysis, self-checking, homework
Proficiency	Adept and independent functioning, relevance, internal attributions (ability and effort)	Pride in accomplishment, task-relevant attribution, consultant role	Application activities, diverse assignments, student choices and challenges

Note. Adapted from *In Spite of All My Resistance I've Learned from Children*, p. 55 by T. Lovitt, 1977, Columbus: Merrill.

must focus on what students already know; give clear instructions, vivid demonstrations, expert modeling, and multiple examples; and explain how the knowledge, strategy, or skill can be either linked to earlier learning or used as the basis for future learning. If the knowledge, strategy, or skill requires a series of procedures that can be facilitated by memory devices (e.g., "procedure sheets"), the teacher needs to introduce them. Finally, the student must actively explore the knowledge, strategy, or skill. Because students cannot operate independently during this phase, teachers need to provide considerable support and guidance.

Since LD students are not likely to meet new tasks with feelings of confidence and success, teachers need to match intense instructional assistance with positive interpersonal feedback and encouragement. Judgments of student success should focus on the level of effort and engagement, not strictly performance. By anticipating the students' feelings of confusion, resistance, and perhaps even helplessness, teachers can challenge them in a way that communicates positive expectations, that is, so that they can learn the knowledge, strategy, or skill while receiving whatever support is necessary. As stated earlier, depending upon the complexity of the knowledge, strategy, or skill, this phase may last for only a brief period or a few sessions or may require intense assistance for a longer time. The key point is that the degree of the teacher's assistance must match the students' needs during this and each of the subsequent phases.

The next phase of learning is *advanced acquisition*. At this level, children have begun to grasp the concept, strategy, or skill but are inconsistent in their performance and may thus continue to experience anxiety or other negative feelings. Teachers need to continue to provide direction through guided practice, reteaching, and the like. They still must reward effort, but should also begin to shift emphasis gradually to providing positive feedback for correct performance. A *reinforcement sandwich* can be useful at this stage: The teacher should first note appropriate responses. When the child is incorrect, the teacher should reinforce the effort, provide correct information based on a mutual examination of the task, and offer reinforcement and encouragement as the child attempts to correct the mistakes.

Feedback and praise play important motivational and informational roles in helping students during learning. To accomplish these complementary goals, teachers should continually interact with students during these first two stages to: (1) continue teaching or modeling, (2) provide timely reinforcement and instructional feedback, (3) convey the message that students will be assisted, (4) offer feedback that helps them see their performance is improving, and (5) describe how students' own efforts and abilities (positive attributions) are leading to their improved performance (Anderson & Prawat, 1983; Brophy, 1981). While it is important for students to feel supported, they must not attribute their improvement to the teacher. They need to understand that their own efforts play a significant role in learning, for otherwise they will be ineffective learners who lack both pride and confidence—feelings essential to the self-esteem and achievement motivation that lead to increased independence.

The third phase of Lovitt's framework is *initial proficiency*. It is during this phase that students begin to perform accurately. Although their accuracy is fairly consistent, performances are typically still awkward (rather than smooth) and slow. Intense instructional assistance is no longer needed. Because the teacher can expect fairly independent functioning, opportunities to practice (perhaps with peers) with feedback become appropriate. The goal is to improve accuracy and increase speed. Homework practice is possible. Modifying the length and time requirements of assignments and framing these in challenging ways can be motivating. Allowing students to set personal goals concerning assignments is also possible during this phase.

While effort and positive attributions continue to be important, intrinsic motivation should develop as students observe their own progress. Continuing to reward effort or supervising too closely can undermine students' feelings of independence and pride. On the other hand, prolonged and delayed practice are necessary for firmly established mastery. The very real pressures for proceeding to new academic or social goals often lead to moving on too quickly, before the new learning is automatic, thus leaving students and teachers vulnerable to reciprocally directed feelings of frustration and disappointment.

The final phase in Lovitt's framework is *proficiency*. At this point, performance is stable, accurate, and fast. Students should use their new learning in applied or fairly novel situations. In the case of academic content such as math operations, students could begin to explore their application to problem solving. In the affective case, for example, cooperation skills, the teacher may help children transfer the skills to a variety of situations in the classroom and in mainstream or home settings. Helping students understand when and how the new learning can be applied creates relevance.

Interpersonally, students should be: (1) reminded of the progress they have made, (2) helped to maintain positive attributions about their improvement, and (3) assisted in generating novel or unique applications of their knowledge. Competence, success, and independence derive from interrelations among academic and affective factors. Explicitly teaching students about both the tetrahedral model and the phases leading to mastery can provide cognitive and motivational building blocks for future learning and positive student-teacher interactions.

This general acquisition framework can also be used as an assessment approach. The teacher can determine how each student is functioning with respect to a particular learning goal and, consequently, anticipate students' needs. Teachers can also examine student expectations to determine whether they are fair and appropriate. The framework can likewise help the teacher decide on the types of instructional interventions and the amount of support needed. Finally, determining the phase of learning can guide teachers' feedback or interpersonal approaches, such as whether to focus mainly on effort or push for better performance.

The second application of Lovitt's framework mentioned above is to metacognitive knowledge. In Chapter 4 we noted that many LD students are anxious about making mistakes. The framework shows very clearly that learning takes time and that mistakes are to be expected. The key is for students to feel supported throughout the process and to know that their mistakes will be handled in a productive and nonthreatening manner. By discussing both this framework and the tetrahedral model in preparation for classroom learning interactions, students can begin to understand their own learning processes as well as the logic behind the teacher's behavior. As a vehicle for communicating about learning-teaching interactions, the framework can be cast as a small display that illustrates the gradual acquisition of knowledge, strategy, or skill. Displaying assignments or other examples of improved performance helps students to learn about learning, see progress, and control negative feelings (since they can anticipate later positive outcomes).

In sum, Lovitt's framework and the tetrahedral model of learning can be useful tools for both teachers and students. With respect to the goal of fostering independence, they can help teachers determine the factors to manipulate to improve learning, the types and degree of support necessary, and when to expect students to function autonomously. In short, this approach enables teachers to coordinate their instructional and interpersonal tactics with the changing needs of students.

More Opportunities for Independence

Additional methods also foster both academic and affective independent functioning. Independence is an important and practical educational goal, particularly for LD students, who often demonstrate impulsive behavior or poor self-management skills. As highlighted in Chapter 4, managing impulsive feelings and displaying strategic behavior in task situations are the two basic goals related to self-control. Following is a brief discussion of means of helping students to develop more effective self-control skills.

Context

Teachers can focus their efforts in helping students improve their self-control in two ways (Pullis, 1985b): (1) creating appropriate context and (2) teaching of the requisite skills. Combining efforts in both areas will greatly enhance the possibility that students will be able to develop and use more efficient self-management skills.

First, in the area of context, four considerations help increase the occurrence of appropriately controlled and effectively managed behavior. First, teachers' expectations for self-control have to be reasonable with respect to the age, developmental level, learning experiences, emotional problems, and neurological integrity of students. Expectations set the tone and pace of interactions with students. Appropriate initial expectations and evolving expectations for gradual improvement create an accepting and challenging climate that directs children's growth.

Second, controlled behavior will emerge in those situations in which it is required. An overstructured learning environment that allows students few opportunities to make choices and exert self-discipline will not promote the development of these skills. Too much support, however positively intended, can actually retard students' development of such skills. Thus, the teacher's expectations and classroom demands must require some degree of self-control from students.

Third, controlled behavior is more likely to occur when teachers and peers demonstrate self-management skills. For example, teachers who are organized, prepared, and controlled provide important models for LD students, who need to see that controlled behavior yields benefits.

The fourth context factor, consequently, is that controlled behavior is more likely to be shown when it is reinforced. Students must learn the connections between controlled or strategic behaviors and positive outcomes. Teachers can reinforce controlled behavior in three ways: (1) appreciation (social reinforcement), (2) logical consequences (accomplishments lead to smooth movement through the day), and (3) tangible rewards (e.g., points, certificates, and privileges). Modeling and reinforcement must occur simultaneously for children to see the value of learning self-management skills clearly.

Direct Instruction

Teachers can also provide direct instruction in the specific skills of self-control (Coates & Thoreson, 1981). Instruction in such metacognitive skills should be transparent within the context of academic assignments and daily classroom demands. Special sessions devoted exclusively to the training of self-control skills seem to have little value, because students often do not recognize when and how to use these skills in actual situations. Thus, the skills should be addressed specifically, and in those task or social situations in which they will be useful; in other words, they need to be welded to appropriate activities.

The skills of self-management can be divided into two general categories: (1) managing impulsive feelings and (2) strategic behavior. LD students, who tend to be especially anxious and easily frustrated, must learn to monitor their feelings, to recognize when they are beginning to lose control, and to manage these difficult feelings. Students can be taught to identify feelings and physical signs (such as tense muscles and rapid heart rate) indicative of negative reactions to situational demands. Self-awareness is necessary to prevent students from becoming overwhelmed by their feelings and responding impulsively to stressful situations. In addition, students need to learn to deal with those feelings so that they can continue to work on the task at hand. Muscle relaxation, pleasant visual imagery, and deep breathing are among the techniques that have helped impulsive students relax when they began to feel upset. This author advocates that students be given "R & R" cards that can be displayed when students want to take a two-minute break or put their heads down to deal productively with anxiety or frustration (rather than impulsively acting it out). In sum, students must develop practical tools for recognizing and managing feelings if they are to behave in more controlled, independent ways.

Several types of strategic behavior can help students be more organized and controlled as they approach tasks or problem situations (see Box 6.1). First, students must learn to determine the expectations of a situation, that is, the criterial tasks. It is impossible to be strategic when one is not sure what the requirements are. Second, LD students must learn to set goals for themselves, as their more normally achieving peers do, to give their behavior limits and direction. Third, they must learn to create a plan of action to help them reach their own goals and meet the demands of the task or situation. Fourth, students need to monitor and evaluate their progress relative to their plan of action. They must determine if they are sticking to their plan and if the plan is indeed working. They must also check their work after it has been completed. Impulsive students often rush through assignments, seldom checking to see whether they have successfully finished. Finally, LD students must be able to engage in self-encouragement and self-reinforcement. Those who can think positively about their efforts and performances are more likely to persist in stressful situations. Pride in accomplishment, satisfaction in reaching goals, and realization of the importance of responsible behavior are values acquired as students recognize the benefits of managing their feelings and becoming more strategic. Evidence of the effectiveness of these approaches comes from research on the Adaptive Learning Environments Model (ALEM) conducted primarily by Wang and her colleagues at the University of Pittsburgh (Wang & Birch, 1984a, 1984b). The ALEM has two basic components. First, it has a highly structured instructional focus that emphasizes meeting students' individual learning needs through the use of precise assessment, teaching, and evaluation. Once students' levels of learning, types of assignments, and pace of learning have been determined, the second component is initiated: Students are given increasing

---

Box 6.1   Steps in Becoming a Strategic Learner

1. Learn to determine the requirements of criterial tasks.
2. Learn to set goals for oneself.
3. Learn to create a plan of action to reach goals.
4. Learn to monitor one's progress while implementing a plan of action.
5. Learn to evaluate one's work after completing the plan of action.
6. Learn to provide encouragement and positive reinforcement for oneself.

---

amounts of control and responsibility for their academic work. Specifically, they are taught how to set goals, plan work schedules, choose a variety of assignments, and evaluate their own work.

The ALEM has been used in a number of studies of LD students, in both resource rooms and mainstream classrooms. The results are positive and impressive. The program is consistently associated with significant academic gains. In addition, students report increased feelings of competence, higher ratings of self-confidence, and positive perceptions of personal control and responsibility. Along with these positive academic and affective gains is a concomitant decrease in the amount of observed behavioral difficulties.

In sum, LD students can and do improve their self-control when the appropriate conditions and opportunities for learning are provided. Independence is attainable when teachers take appropriate steps: (1) sound assessment, (2) effective instructional planning and implementation, (3) personal support, and (4) direct teaching of useful behaviors. Lovitt's framework and the ALEM studies were presented as guidelines for teachers to consider in designing instructional interventions that foster appropriate and effective self-management skills.

Managing Behavior Problems

The majority of LD children will positively respond to a well-designed classroom, appropriate instruction, and a firm, supportive teacher. Students with significant, longstanding affective problems, however, will probably continue to create some classroom disturbances. Teachers need to be prepared to work with these troubled students because they present a substantial challenge. Their behavior often interferes with the smooth operation of the classroom for both the teacher and other students. The four related issues presented in this section—(1) positive attitudes about classroom conflicts, (2) assessment techniques, (3) problem solving with students, and (4) incentive approaches—are designed to orient teachers positively to their responsibilities to help children grow. Furthermore, they provide specific approaches that have proved to be useful in understanding and managing difficult behavior.

Positive Attitudes

Few teachers relish the role of disciplinarian and the associated conflictual episodes that affectively disordered children introduce into the classroom. Consequently, teachers must realize that the feelings and attitudes they bring to difficult situations not only set the tone of the interactions but also influence the tactics they will choose to manage the situations and the children. Following are examples of positive attitudes that can lead to healthy resolution of classroom problems.

First, teachers need to understand that even normal development is characterized by certain adjustment problems. It has been argued that contemporary American life is significantly more stressful for children than at any previous period. Since LD children may be at risk for affective difficulties because of the failure associated with their learning, teachers must realistically expect some behavior problems.

Teachers also need to examine their own power and control needs. Many teachers (especially beginning teachers) think they have to control all situations and solve all classroom problems immediately. Because they often feel that behavior problems reflect on their competence as professionals, they can have a tendency to take the problems personally. Realizing that behavioral difficulties are to be expected among LD students can help teachers have more moderate and healthy reactions to problem situations.

Working through problems is not only the responsibility of teachers, but is also an important part of the interpersonal relationship that develops between the students and the teacher. Assisting students through difficult situations is a very real sign of caring. Sticking by them during hard times also conveys positive expectations that they *can* improve and change; that they can, with support, learn to behave more productively. The ability to be positive in troublesome situations can be improved when teachers can view conflict situations as opportunities for learning. Rather than fearing conflict, effective teachers see such situations as chances to help students learn to deal with affective difficulties, thus casting themselves into an instructional rather than a disciplinary role. Such perceptions and attitudes create a more healthy atmosphere and lead to more rational responses to affective problems.

In trying to help teachers orient themselves more positively to working with students with a long history of affective difficulties, the author has used *shaping* to conceptualize the processes of helping children change. Shaping implies four basic approaches to helping children develop new, more positive behavior (rather than just eliminating problem behavior): First, shaping requires that teachers know their students and accept them at their developmental level. Such knowledge comes from the observation and analysis of interactions and from careful assessment. Acceptance stems from this knowledge and requires sensitivity to the unique experiences and needs of each student. In contrast, the *wish approach* (in which the teacher wishes the children did not have the problems they do) not only leads to feelings of disappointment and frustration in both students and the teacher but also influences the management approaches employed by the teacher.

Second, shaping acknowledges that change is a gradual process. Helping children replace old patterns of maladaptive behavior with new, healthy behavior does not occur quickly or without extensive effort. Teachers must be realistic in their expectations—since negative patterns of behavior take a long time to develop, bringing about change will be a gradual, prolonged process. It is unreasonable to assume that if the teacher could say or do the exactly correct thing, the problem behaviors would quickly disappear. Unrealistic hopes for rapid change also lead to feelings of disappointment and frustration shared by the student and the teacher.

Third, shaping involves having positive goals, or trying to determine what types of behavior would represent positive responses to difficult situations. These goals help teachers to focus on and reinforce productive behavior. Often with disruptive students, teachers tend to concentrate on negative behavior because it captures their attention. Teachers sometimes characterize troubled students as "always" presenting problems or "never" responding appropriately. This negative orientation is clear and actually fuels continued disruptions.

Finally, shaping is an instructional process. Once teachers have begun to formulate positive goals, they determine the best ways to teach and reinforce approximations of appropriate behavior. In contrast, the disciplinarian role carries connotations of eliminating problem behaviors by using punishment. While aversive consequences for inappropriate behavior are sometimes desirable and helpful, they hardly ever teach the child new ways of behaving. For new behavior to emerge, teaching has to take place, an important concept that shaping emphasizes.

Assessment Approaches

Since managing behavior problems is conceptualized here as an instructional process, a systematic framework for decision making (similar to the one presented in Chapter 5 for designing group activities) provides a sequence of steps for teachers to follow (see Table 6.2).

Like all good teaching, this process should begin with adequate and on-going assessment. To work effectively with problematic behavior, the teacher must determine when and where the problems are occurring for each student. The teacher also has to explore the nature of the behaviors.

The first step represents careful assessment of problem situations for the entire day or for particularly problematic class periods. First, the teacher lists every facet of the normal activities for the day or period, including transitional phases and varying instructional activities. Second, a chart should be made with a column for each student so that individual problem behaviors can be tallied. All types of disruptive or nonproductive behavior should be entered on the chart. It can also be helpful to note when in the activity the problem occurs—at the beginning, middle, or end of the day or period. Base-line data should be collected for one or two weeks to get accurate information.

The second step involves a more detailed analysis of the nature of the problems. This analysis should be done after class, when the teacher has the time to reflect carefully about the situations. The first step is to examine each activity, noting the particularly problematic students (as indicated by the frequency of behavioral problems tallied under each name). Second, the teacher should describe the problems—for example, disturbing other students, not following directions, complaining, or not paying attention. The teacher should also determine if the problems occur early or late within the activity. Third, the teacher should establish the expected behavior for that activity. This very important step is a necessary component of shaping, for if teachers are going to help children develop appropriate behaviors for the activity rather than merely eliminate the problem through punishment, they need to have clear ideas of what they want children to do and share those ideas with the students. Finally, the teacher can attempt to determine which of the affective areas (self-esteem, social skills, motivation, etc.) might be related to the problem behavior.

At this point several important trends can be identified by a careful analysis. The teacher may notice, for example, that several students present behavior problems during a particular instructional period such as math. This might cue the teacher to look at the nature of that instruction. If the majority of the problems occur at the beginning of the activity, it may reflect students' anxiety or uneasiness about math. The teacher may want to examine more closely the amount or nature of the math being expected as well as the daily scores of the students. It may be that the students feel somewhat overwhelmed or particularly unsure of themselves in this subject and therefore need more instruction, support, or encouragement (phase 1 of Lovitt's framework). If problems are occurring at the end of the activity, the teacher may want to make the period shorter

Table 6.2 Managing Behavior Problems

Step

Step 1 Problem assessment (frequency and location)

	Activity			
Chart of Class activities	Mary	Jim	Sue	John
Transition to room	Bᵃ (directions)		B (complaint)	
Classroom business				
Transition to activity		E (inattentive)		
Math (group work)			B, M (disruptive)	
Math (independent work)			B (nonworking)	

Step 2 Nature of the problems

Class Activities	Problem Students	Type of Problem	Demands/Goals	Affective Area

Step 3 Organizational, instructional, or interpersonal strategies
Step 4 Problem solving with the student
Step 5 Incentive approaches
Step 6 Evaluation

ᵃTime of day or class period activity occurred: B = beginning; M = middle; E = end.

or add more instructional variation. The teacher may identify that several students have problems during a specific type of activity, for example, transitions, group work, or learning centers, regardless of the academic subject. Such a finding may signal teachers to modify that type of activity or establish a more secure routine. Group findings can thus help teachers clarify and restructure activities to align more closely with the needs of the group.

Individual student problems can also be analyzed at this stage of assessment. As with group trends, teachers can begin to determine academic subjects or particular types of activities in which an individual student consistently experiences problems. Tallying when in the activity the problems occur can help teachers add support at the appropriate time. Such information also cues them as to when to monitor students or have them monitor themselves carefully. Perhaps the data will suggest that some procedural or instructional modifications should be made. Thus, these two simple assessment steps help teachers pinpoint classroom situations in which general or individualized modifications might be needed.

By comparing the types of behavior problems students exhibit with expectations for that particular activity, the teacher may gain some insight into the affective difficulties that underlie the problems. Teachers may interpret, for example, bored or lethargic behavior during group reading as a problem in motivation. They may want to choose more relevant reading materials or make group reading a more exciting time. Some students may appear to be impulsive or inefficient when asked to work independently on tasks. In response, teachers may want to rethink the instructional plan using Lovitt's framework. Alternatively, teachers may decide to teach self-management skills to these children. Recall that examining task demands allows teachers to formulate clear and positive goals that can be shared with the student and become the basis for shaping new, more positive behavior.

Table 6.3 lists basic approaches to problems in the various affective areas. It summarizes the material covered in this and the previous two chapters. The first step in handling behavior problems is careful and ongoing assessment of children's behavior relative to activities designed by the teacher. The second step is to make modifications (based on the assessment information) in the organizational, instructional, or interpersonal interventions that the teacher is using. The vast majority of problems, however, can and should be addressed proactively with good organization, design, and planning. This philosophy and these approaches maintain a supportive, instructional teacher-student relationship and should constitute the major goal of managing behavioral difficulties. Only after these approaches have been tried, evaluated and modified should the more directive techniques of problem-solving and incentive modifications be employed. Finally, just as assessment provides information for decision making, evaluation allows teachers to determine whether and how their

Table 6.3 Affective Problem Interventions

Area	Needs[a]	Interventions
1. Self-concept	Expectations, instructions	Clear and approporiate rules and directions (see Chapters 4 and 5)
2. Self-esteem	Successful, competence	Appropriate assignment and positive expectations, salience
3. Self-control	Self-management skills, degree of self-control	Lovitt's (1977) framework of support
4. Social interactions	Feelings of acceptance, adequate peer skills and relationships, teacher-student relationship	Reasonable peer groupings, positive teacher feelings and communication
5. Attributions	Positive and internal attributions	Lovitt's framework/feedback
6. Interests/relevance	Intrinsic motivation	Creating relevance (see Chapter 5)
7. Anxiety	Feeling safe and confident	Lovitt's framework/support, handling mistakes
8. Learning style	Match with preferences	Environmental factors, type of assignment

[a]These are general need areas that can be explored as initial reactions to problem situations. Through assessment the teacher can begin to examine systematically the location and nature of the problem and formulate ideas for helping meet the affective needs through organizational, instructional, and interpersonal approaches. Only after these approaches have been tried should the teacher move on to the problem-solving and incentive tactics designed for more troubled students.

intervention approaches have been effective. The same methods illustrated in Steps 1 and 2 of Table 6.2 can help teachers evaluate their decisions and interventions. Thus, ongoing assessment and evaluation are crucial to effective management of behavior problems.

Problem-Solving Method

While most problematic behavior can be addressed using proactive instructional and interpersonal approaches, some students will need more support and instruction to learn more positive behavioral responses. In this section a problem-solving method based on Glasser's (1965) reality therapy will be presented. This method encompasses positive attitudes as well as specific steps for shaping new behaviors or handling problems. It is predicated on a positive teacher-student relationship and can be used after a problem occurs to capitalize on the event and turn it into an opportunity for learning.

The first step entails having students describe the problem from their own perspective. Teachers should encourage them to describe what happened, how they were feeling, and what they were trying to accomplish. This description allows teachers to understand the students' perspective as well as what led up to the problem. Encouraging students to share their feelings can help teachers understand the affective part of the interaction. It may be that teachers need to allow some ventilation of feelings or to let some time pass so that students are not upset during the discussion (or it could be the teacher who needs to cool down). Asking children what they were trying to accomplish provides teachers with some insight into the motivation for their behavior. Often, students were trying to accomplish something quite reasonable but went about it in an immature or unproductive way. Looking at it from this perspective lets teachers frame the issue in terms of helping children discover better ways to handle problems rather than deciding how to punish them.

The second step involves helping students make value judgments about their behavior. Was it fair? helpful? consistent with classroom rules? Children can thus be made to see the behavior as inappropriate or ineffective because it is not consistent with the rules or values of the classroom. Remind students that the classroom rules involve the values of productivity, socially cooperative behavior, and respect for materials. Also remind them that they were involved in the creation of the rules and agreed to abide by them. By evaluating the problem behavior relative to the classroom rules, teachers reinforce the importance of the rules as well as the value of keeping one's agreements. Discussing the rules also forces children to take responsibility for their behavior, rather than blaming teachers. Again, teachers can frame the problem in terms of learning a better way of behaving that is consistent with mutually determined classroom expectations. Student mistakes are acceptable, but, like mistakes on academic tasks, errors will continue until better ways of behaving are learned.

The third step involves helping students generate a variety of ways to handle the problem. Simply list a range of approaches that can help students reach their goals in more appropriate ways. By seeing three or four alternatives, students can learn that there are many ways to solve problems, not merely one perfect way to behave. The next step is to evaluate the alternatives by jointly anticipating possible outcomes of each. This fosters strategic thinking and forces students to analyze the possible results of their choices.

The fourth step involves three components. First, based on anticipated outcomes, teachers encourage students to choose the alternative that they think is going to work best, that is, the one that will help them reach their goals and is consistent with classroom rules. Second, teachers help students devise a plan for remembering and using the chosen approach.

Third, teachers secure a commitment from the children to try to use the chosen alternative by focusing on the importance of effort and the value of keeping one's promises. At this point teachers also make a commitment to try to help the children remember and use their plan. This promise signifies the cooperative nature of Glasser's approach. Note how different this approach is from the more adversarial discipline perspective.

The final step in the process requires generating a plan for evaluation. A meeting between the teacher and student to discuss the problem and the effectiveness of the student's chosen plan may be scheduled. More formal approaches such as self-monitoring by the student or systematic tallying by the teacher can also be used. The key is to continue to support the student and at the same time provide concrete evidence of progress. Also, the student needs to learn that the first effort may not necessarily be totally successful. If the problem situation occurs again and the plan is forgotten or does not appear to work, the teacher then helps the child analyze why it was not successful. It may be necessary (and profitable) to work through the steps of the problem-solving method again. There may be a flaw in the plan or the child may need more practice at the new skill. In addition, it may be that the plan sounded effective during discussions but just did not work out in a real situation. The teacher needs to deal with these possibilities in a very straightforward and supportive manner. It may be necessary to help the child through some of the disappointment and frustration and reanalyze the problem using the Glasser method. The teacher must *matter-of-factly* convey a "back to the drawing board" attitude to demonstrate that problem solving is an ongoing process.

Glasser recommends that no punishment for misbehavior be used while the problem-solving method is being applied, for this would undermine a process in which the goal is a productive relationship characterized by positive, nonthreatening interactions. Others have argued that the problem-solving method can be effectively used with punishment, especially if the contingencies for punishment are clearly specified in advance. Both positions seems reasonable. The teacher needs to decide in advance which approach is likely to be most beneficial to a specific child and seems fair to other students as well.

Many benefits are associated with the problem-solving approach. First, it is systematic and parallels methods for dealing with academic mistakes. It keeps the teacher in an instructional role, consistently reinforcing the idea that mistakes are part of learning. Second, its supportive nature promotes positive teacher-student relationships. Third, students can use this method to solve problems independently. One of the author's students, for example, taught the method to her students. Whenever there was an interpersonal conflict, the students had to work through the problem together, using a "procedure sheet" listing the steps of the method. The teacher became involved only by checking the agreement made by the students and then reminded them of their commitment to the solution.

Fourth, the method can be used for classwide problems as well. In fact, some teachers see it as an essential approach for modifying classroom rules, given that the students helped create the rules and agreed to abide by them. Finally, many of the author's students report that using this method keeps them from making snap judgments about how to intervene and creates a feeling of working with students rather than trying to control them.

Incentive Approaches

Some LD children really lack motivation to complete academic assignments or to behave in accordance with classroom rules. These students have likely had intense failure experiences and have poorly developed social interaction skills. It may be that they initially need more powerful incentives (both positive and negative) to help structure and shape their behavior. Several approaches to motivational problems have already been covered: (1) appropriate academic requirements based on sound assessment; (2) relevant tasks and a variety of types of learning activities; (3) logical, positive consequences associated with appropriate behavior, such as choice time and smooth movement through the day; and (4) logical negative consequences for inappropriate or nonproductive behavior, such as loss of privileges and uncertain progression through the day.

For particularly troubled students special rewards and somewhat more aversive negative consequences may need to be designed as a means of firmly establishing rules and academic expectations. Rewards should be reasonable in terms of expense as well as student response. It will take some time, and probably some trial and error, before effective rewards can be determined. They should be used for as brief a period as is possible, since these types of reinforcers are artificial. They should be thought of as a necessary *initial* source of motivation, used only to break through the resistance and poor motivation such children display. Relying on them for too long or making them too expensive puts a strain on both the teacher and other students. Ideally, children will become committed to positive behavior and the use of special rewards and punishments can end rather quickly.

Sometimes particularly strict penalties or punishments may appear to be necessary when an extremely troubled student will not make a reasonable adjustment to a classroom setting. The decision to use such procedures, however, should be very carefully made. Their implementation requires thorough knowledge of their effects, both direct and indirect. First, punishment procedures should never be used alone, because they do not teach children appropriate behaviors. Punishment is designed only to eliminate behavior. Instead punishment should be used in combination with reinforcement and teaching interventions. Second, loss of privileges is a preferable tactic to exclusion or the use of physical punishment. While short periods of "time out" may be warranted in some cases, it is more desirable to keep children in the classroom and help them work toward developing more adaptive behaviors. Third, the more extreme the punishment, the more potential it has for undesirable effects, such as increasing hostility, undermining the teacher-student relationship, or eliciting fear and anxiety. Fourth, teachers of LD students should not use extra academic work as punishment for misbehavior, for such assignments support (or maintain) a view that academic efforts are essentially negative and painful, thus creating more difficulties with motivation.

Summary and Conclusions

Two major themes characterize the three chapters of Part II: (1) the child-centered perspective of the cognitive developmental model and (2) the role of the teacher in child-centered education. To understand the academic and social performance of LD students, teachers must understand the nature of the interplay between cognition and affect. Implicit in this understanding is an appreciation for the complexity and uniqueness of each student. For too long the LD field has dealt almost exclusively with the intellectual capabilities of LD students.

The second major theme actually parallels the first but focuses on the role of the teacher, since with a more holistic view of the child comes a more complex perspective on teaching. Teaching is cognitive in that it requires knowledge and application of concepts and tactics from many areas of study—child development, curriculum, instructional approaches, classroom management, and assessment and evaluation procedures. Teaching is affective in that it involves significant social interactions. Throughout these chapters the importance of the teacher-student relationship was emphasized; terms like "sensitivity," "empathy," and "caring" pervade the text. The social part of teaching, however, requires knowledge and application of skills as well, including providing feedback, guiding instruction using the Lovitt framework, and solving problems with students. Integrating the cognitive and social demands of teaching allows teachers to support and challenge their students more effectively. Balance derives from being positive and realistic with affectively troubled LD students, which is no small challenge and very hard work! But it is also deeply satisfying.

PART III

A Cognitive Developmental Approach to Instruction in the Content Areas

At this point, it may be helpful to review information processing theory. Information processing assumes that there are three structural levels to the human mind—a sensory or intake register, a working memory (or a similar concept called short-term memory), and a long-term store. Although all information enters the system through the sensory register, it can be kept there only briefly. If it is to remain in the system, it must enter the working memory, where it can be combined with information from the long-term store. Information operations are carried out in working memory, where conscious thinking occurs. Working memory is often considered a bottleneck in the system, because it has a very limited capacity. Long-term memory, on the other hand, is essentially limitless and contains all the information, both factual and procedural, that one knows. The learning problem with long-term memory is accessing the information that is stored there. Furthermore, information processing theory postulates the presence of various executive control processes that regulate the operations of the system. These include general routines or strategies and heuristics for problem solving. LD students appear to have problems related to working memory, sometimes including the executive control processes. Very little evidence supports the existence of deficits related to the functioning of the sensory register or the structure of the long-term store. Problems accessing information from the long-term store have, however, been well documented.

Although it has frequently been assumed that descriptive theories of learning have little value in informing prescriptive instructional procedures (Glaser, 1976a, 1976b), in the last fews years considerable work has directly addressed relationships between the two. It is this work that is the foundation for the chapters to follow. Some academic domains have been well researched, while others seem to have been virtually neglected. While Case (1983; Case & Bereiter, 1982), Resnick (1982), and others have conducted research directed toward understanding children's mathematical learning, for example, very little intervention research has been done in mathematics teaching and even less with LD and other underachieving students or in the schools (Romberg & Carpenter, 1986). Consequently, the following chapters have uneven research foundations.

When a firm foundation does exist (for oral language, reading, handwriting and spelling, composition, and study skills), recommendations for instruction have generally followed those made in the first two parts of this text. Interestingly, the reader will notice that these writers recommend the use of covert, strategic processes; holistic rather than maximally segmented presentations, strategies that students must ultimately take responsibility for implementing, and suggestive rather than corrective feedback. In all cases, students are assisted in behaving more as experts behave either through traditional modes of direct instruction or the newer scaffolding techniques, depending on the nature of the criterial task and the specific materials to be learned.

When research evidence has not been available, the authors have admitted its absence and based their chapters on their own experiences instructing LD children (see, e.g., Chapters 10 and 16). Although the mathematics chapters have little direct support from instructional studies based on information processing theory, they were based on both research documenting problems LD children frequently exhibit and the author's field observations of LD students over several years and in several settings. Furthermore, they conform to the few criteria that have been established from the information processing studies of children's mathematical learning.

Each author was asked to address the following questions: What develops prior to schooling? What is an appropriate instructional model? And, within subtopics, what is to be learned? How will successful learning be demonstrated? What problems do LD students frequently have? What learner activities are appropriate? How will each student's strengths and weaknesses be assessed? What recovery procedures can be used for persistent problems? And finally, how should students be matched to tasks and performance monitored? Most authors answered these questions directly. In some chapters questions were grouped and in others answered in with other titles. The three sets of chapters that had little research support deviated from this structure, however, since many of the questions cannot be answered at this time.

The chapter sections on development prior to schooling were included for three reasons: First, in the cognitive developmental approach, it is important to build on students' strengths. Consequently, teachers must know what children know and do not know when they come to school. Second, since LD children exhibit slowed developmental patterns, teachers may need to provide experiences to help them acquire skills and concepts that they may have missed earlier. Third, recent interest in identifying and aiding the preschool LD child, coupled with the need to develop a life-span perspective for intervening with LD students and adults, demands such knowledge. Although our approach is not comprehensive in that it does not deal with adult living skills, it at least represents a theoretically sound, data-based approach to childhood and adolescent instruction with the emphasis on learning how to learn independently.

Chapter 7

Intervention Tactics for Learning Disabled Children with Oral Language Impairments

Sandy Friel-Patti

Gina Conti-Ramsden

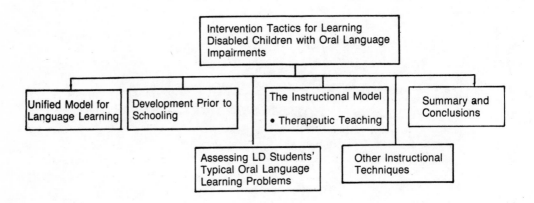

Questions to Consider

1. What is the unified model of language learning?
2. What is language impairment and which aspect of language functioning is most likely to be affected?
3. What needs to be considered in selecting intervention techniques and plans?
4. What assumptions underlie oral language interventions?

This chapter focuses on several aspects of LD children's development as effective communicators. The foundation of this discussion is *Communicative competence,* which includes the development of linguistic skill in language form (i.e., morphologic and syntactic structures) as well as the realization of the meaning of semantic expression of intention. *Morphology* is central to the study of the structure of words. A *morpheme* is a minimal unit of speech that is recurrent and meaningful. Word stems such as *gentle,* suffixes such as *-ly,* and prefixes such as *un-* are all morphemes. Morphologic learning, then, is learning how words are put together. *Syntactic* learning is the acquisition of the rules for organizing words into sentences and sentences into larger groups. *Semantics* is the study of the rules governing the meaning or context of words or grammatical units. The *semantic expression of intention* involves putting words together to convey intended meaning. Perhaps the central feature of communicative competence is the social utility of language: Children must learn to use language in a variety of environments in order to be effective communicators. This emphasis is relatively new in language intervention and reflects advances in the fields of developmental psycholinguistics, developmental psychology, and communication disorders.

The content of language intervention programs typically mirrors the prevailing theoretical assumptions. During the last two decades, the study of language development in children has expanded from an emphasis on syntactic form to a concern with communicative functions. Concurrently, analyses have shifted from the speaker alone to the communicative dyad of the speaker *and* listener. Reflecting this current view of language as communicative rather than simply linguistic behavior, the content of language intervention programs has changed considerably. Thus, the teaching of syntax through behavior modification schedules and tightly specified drills is rapidly giving way to therapy based on interpersonal experience and communicative needs.

Unified Model for Language Learning

The nature of the interaction among language, cognition, and social knowledge has been long debated. Currently, in the field of child language acquisition, some form of the unified model of language learning (Lewis & Cherry, 1977) is widely accepted. This model assumes that language, cognition, and social knowledge are interactive and interdependent since all are aspects of individual development. The point of intersection of the three domains is communicative competence (see Figure 7.1). Development is the gradual differentiation of these domains. Researchers working with the unified model are primarily concerned with understanding the common basis for behavior that gradually makes possible what some describe as separate language, social, and cognitive behaviors.

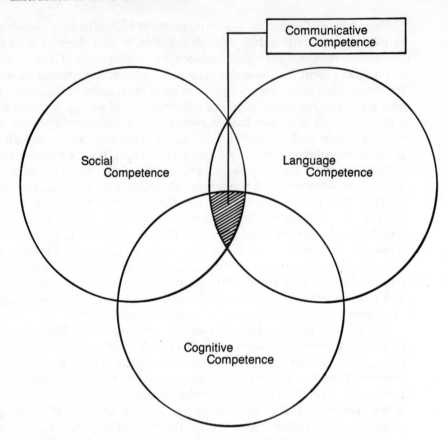

FIGURE 7.1 Unified Model of Communicative Competence.

Development Prior to Schooling

The past two decades of research have been marked by an increasing interest in the developmental period of infancy. As a result, the infant is currently described as an active learner from the very beginning of life (Bruner, 1982; Newhoff & Launer, 1984).The mutuality of the commitment of both caregivers and infants to social interaction is impressive: caregivers consistently approach newborns with the expectation that they will communicate. Consequently, there is a tendency to respond to the infants' behaviors as if they were intentional (Brazelton, Koslowski, & Main, 1974; Snow, 1977) and meaningful social communication (Owens, 1984; Harris, Jones, & Grant, 1983). The caregiver's responsiveness and sensitivity to the *pacing* of the interaction appear to be vital for the development of a successful communicative style. By eight to twelve weeks of age interactions are regulated by eye gaze and marked by alternating vocalizations. These early interactive exchanges provide a rich forum for the unfolding of the infant's communicative skills. The joint performance of the two participants seems to prefigure adult conversational exchanges:

> Here we see infants and mothers gazing at each other, as each smiles and vocalizes, apparently with pleasure and a sort of delighted courtesy. As with adult conversation, there is near-constant communication in one modality (visual) and intermittent, alternating communication in another (auditory). (Bateson, 1975, p. 101)

A common characteristic of these prototypal conversational exchanges is that the infant and caregiver take turns regulating the interchange (Bateson, 1975; Stern, 1974). Furthermore, both participants can and do initiate interactions.

These early protodialogues, however, do not fully explain the language development process. Bruner (1975) recognized language input within two common types of routines of parent-child interaction: joint action and joint reference. Within *joint action* routines, children learn to take turns and to predict and anticipate outcomes of behaviors. Within *joint reference* routines, children and parents establish a common focus of attention, which parents then talk about—a process Bruner (1975) views as the origin of semanticity and early syntactic learning. Parental speech directed to the child during these routines is systematically modified to reduce syntactic and semantic complexity while increasing redundancy and perceptual salience (Broen, 1972 and Snow, 1977). *Redundancy* is the built-in repetition of words or even whole phrases, which is thought to be motivated by the caregiver's desire to be understood. Sometimes the redundancy will involve repeating the idea but using different words. *Perceptual salience* means that some parts of the utterance stand out over others. Factors that contribute to perceptual salience include intonation, stress, and loudness on certain parts of words or the utterance. In speech directed to very young children, caregivers often use exaggerated intonation and high-pitched voices, thinking that such maneuvers increase perceptual salience and draw and hold the child's attention.

Although language input is important to language learning, viewing children as active learners necessitates consideration of what the children do with that input. Kuczaj (1982) emphasizes the importance of children's *use* of linguistic input—the interpretations they place on it, their organization of information, and their use of the information for subsequent interpretations. He distinguishes between *input*, or linguistic information to which children have been exposed, and *intake*, their selective use of the input. The basic assumption motivating such a distinction is that even simplified speech will not facilitate language learning if children do not attend to the information and organize the regularities. Children are thus active participants in the learning process and bring to it a set of behaviors and organizational strategies that allow them to benefit from the adults' facilitating behaviors.

Over time, children's language forms (sounds, words, and sentences) become more like those of the adults around them. As with some other important aspects of development, it is possible to describe a predictable sequence of language learning that virtually all children follow in the same order but at differing rates.

Brown (1973) and his colleagues at Harvard were the first to describe language learning based on stage rather than age. Brown has provided a general framework describing how children progress through the first five stages. He found that the length of children's utterances (spoken sentences) was the best way to group them into stages. He calculated the average length of morphemes in one hundred consecutive utterances, added the total morphemes per one hundred utterances, and then divided by one hundred to get the mean length of utterance (MLU). For each of the five stages, Brown described a range of MLU, a midpoint, and an upper bound (UB), or what would typically be the longest utterance produced in that stage (see Table 7.1). Up to Stage V, length reflects complexity—that is, the longer the utterance, the more complex.

The general sequence of development was also described by Brown. He noted that the order of appearance of fourteen morphemes was similar for different children (see Table 7.2). Each morpheme emerges by Stage II, but it is not mastered (or used correctly 90 percent of the time) until Stage V.

Other morphemes appear and develop within Brown's stages but were not studied in detail. The pronominal system in English is very complex, and thus while pronouns emerge in Stage II, they are not fully learned until many years later. The reflexive pronouns (e.g., *myself, yourself, herself*) are still not mastered by the time most children enter school.

Children also learn to use the auxiliary verb system, including *be, have,* and *do* and the modals *will, shall, can, may,* and *must* quite early.

Table 7.1   Developmental Levels of Mean Length of Utterance (MLU)

Stage	MLU Point	MLU Span	UB
I	1.75	1.5–2.0	5
II	2.25	2.0–2.5	7
III	2.75	2.5–3.0	9
IV	3.50	3.0–3.5	11
V	4.00	3.5–4.0	13

Note. Based on *A First Language: The Early Stages* (p. 56) by R. Brown, 1973, Cambridge, MA: Harvard University Press.

Table 7.2   The Fourteen Morphemes That Emerge by Stage II of Language Development

Morpheme	Example
Present progressive -*ing* (no auxiliary verb)	"Mommy eating."
In	*"Juice in cup."*
On	"Kitty on sofa."
Regular plural -*s*	"Cats drink milk."
Irregular past	Came, fell, went, sat, broke
Possessives	"Daddy's shirt."
Uncontractible copula (*to be* is main verb)	"Who is sick?" Response: "He is."
Articles	a, the,
Regular past -*ed*	Walked, pulled, etc.
Regular third person -*s*	"Tommy hits."
Irregular third person	Does, has
Uncontractible auxiliary	"Who's wearing your hat?" Response: "He is."
Contractible copula	"He's fat."
Contractible auxiliary	"She's drinking milk."

Note. Based on *A First Language: The Early Stages* (p. 274) by R. Brown, 1973, Cambridge, MA: Harvard University Press.

By the age of four, at least 50 percent of children will be correctly using these verbs in declarative sentences (Wells, 1979).

In Stage III children begin to use more adult forms such as negative statements and questions to express relationships. Some initial development may begin in Stage II, but most such learning occurs in Stage III. They use questioning to learn more about their world. Very young children can ask questions by simply raising the intonation of one word (e.g., "Horsie?"). As children develop in their use of language, they begin to use the question words (who, what, when, where, why, and how) to ask for more specific information. They also learn to use interrogative transformations to ask questions with auxiliary verbs ("Is this your house?," "Do you like ice cream?," "Will you play with me?").

Another hallmark of early language is expressing ideas with more than simple sentences. Ideas can be joined in compound sentences ("I went to the movies and I got some popcorn.") or embedded in complex sentences ("The boy who lives next door is a brat."). Brown found embedding to be a primary characteristic of Stage IV and conjoining typical of Stage V.

All of these morphologic and syntactic changes are accompanied by phonological changes. *Phonology* is the set of rules for speech sound patterns.

These rules govern the position of sounds and words in which sounds may appear together. Because of the phonological rules of English, for example, we cannot begin a word with the sound combination *nd,* although such a combination can occur in the middle of a word, as in *window.* In addition to learning the sounds of the language, children must learn the rules for their combination. As in other aspects of language development, children progress through a long period of hypothesis testing and rule building in developing the phonology of their language system. Again, there is an apparent orderly pattern of development related to stage rather than age. Children approximate the adult system by creating their own structures and then altering them as the adult forms become better known. Most children can produce all of the sounds of English by age seven, but many phonological rules are not mastered until later.

Children learn to associate sounds with meanings as they begin to decode what is said to them. They build their sound-meaning associations on the communicative context and their experience with the world. Semantic growth spans the full range of developing vocabulary words to describe objects and ideas, learning the meaning of abstract words, and learning how to interpret words with two meanings. Children become actively involved in learning their language by using the cognitive strategies available to them, strategies that serve them well in interpreting other aspects of the world.

The communicative context in which children learn language is the conversation. All conversational exchanges begun early in the first year between the child and caregiver are extended into well-developed conversations during the preschool years. *Pragmatics* refers to the use of language in a given context. Pragmatic rules for regulating taking turns in conversations must be learned. Children must also develop their skills in adjusting what they are saying to their listener's linguistic ability. The listeners' familiarity also determines how a topic can be introduced into the conversation. Children must learn to respond to requests for additional information or clarification ("Tell me more about that." or "Your brother went where?"). All of this pragmatic learning occurs simultaneously with morphologic, semantic, syntactic, and phonologic development.

Perhaps the most striking aspect of language development is that it is so complex yet appears to be effortless. From the children's perspective, language develops so that ideas can be exchanged, questions can be asked, friends can be made, games can be played, and so forth. Children learn to talk because they have a lot they want to say. They actively extract and organize information from the environment, building on past experience (Kuczaj, 1982). By age five, children use most of the major varieties of the English sentence. However, important syntactic, semantic, phonologic, and pragmatic advances are made during the school years. (For a more thorough presentation of language development, see Owens, 1984.)

Assessing LD Students' Typical Oral Language Learning Problems

The population of language-impaired LD children is a heterogenous one that is generally described as demonstrating a linguistic system that, in certain significant aspects, is different from that of their normal language-learning peers. *Language impairment* is a developmental disorder characterized by the late appearance and/or slow development of comprehension and/or expression of spoken language in children who do *not* have hearing loss, mental retardation, or emotional disorder (Leonard, 1979; Stark & Tallal, 1981). Various terms have been used to refer to this problem, including "congenital aphasia" (Eisenson, 1972), "delayed language" (Lee, 1966), "language disorder" (Rees, 1973), "deviant language" (Leonard, 1972), "specific language deficit" (Stark & Tallal, 1981). (For a review of the nomenclature, see Bloom and Lahey, 1978.) In keeping with the more recent work, the term "language impairment" will be used throughout this chapter.

Traditionally, the criterial attribute of language impairment has been a delay in the production of age-appropriate syntax, thereby defining the population on one aspect of expressive language skills. Recently, Rizzo and Stephens (1981) found that their subject group originally defined by expressive language delay also had varying degrees of delay in the comprehension of language. Leonard (1979) has proposed that language impairment "should no longer be viewed as a strictly linguistic deficit, but rather as a deficit associated with a delay in the development of a number of representational abilities." He based his recommendation upon findings that indicate that language-impaired children manifest deficits in *non-linguistic* representational skills, including a) symbolic play (Brown, Redmond, Bass, Liebergott, & Swope, 1975; Lovell, Hoyle, & Siddall, 1968) and b) imagery (deAjuriaguerra et al., 1965; Inhelder, 1966).

The content of language intervention programs for children has consistently been derived from the dominant language theory of the time. Shifts from behaviorism to syntax to semantics to pragmatics have had accompanying practical effects on which behaviors are considered important for assessment and intervention. It is apparent that over the last two decades, major new insights in psycholinguistics have led clinicians to reconsider the theoretical bases for language assessment. Ideally, this should be an economical and efficient procedure that allows the clinician to sample subsets of an individual's relevant cognitive, linguistic, and communicative behaviors, to use this information to predict the person's general communicative ability, and to plan appropriate intervention. Given the current pragmatic-interactive theoretical framework, what should assessment involve?

The assessment of oral language in children traditionally includes a carefully selected battery of both standardized and nonstandardized (often observational) measures of language production, comprehension, and articulation. Specifically, oral language assessment measures the individual's ability to comprehend and produce single vocabulary words (Ammons & Ammons, 1948; Kaplan, 1976), syntactic structures (Lee, 1971; Newcomer & Hammill, 1977; Wiig & Semel, 1980), morphological form and markers (Carrow, 1973, 1974), and relevant phonological distinctions (Goldman & Fristoe, 1969; Van Riper & Erickson, 1975). This seemingly comprehensive list of skills, however, does not include other critical language processing and production skills and communicative skills needed to interact successfully in a variety of spontaneous speaking situations. The speech-language pathologist is the one who assesses language to identify and describe any delay. Here our interest is in only those observational measures appropriate for classroom use.

The study of pragmatics developed as investigators began to recognize that language occurs within a social context and as such serves a variety of social functions. It has become increasingly apparent that to become competent communicators, children need to master not only the syntactic rules of their language but also the social and interactional aspects of discourse. Research on the pragmatic aspects of communication has revealed that two utterances may have similar grammatical forms but serve distinct functions, depending upon the context (Austin, 1962). The declarative utterance, "It is cold in here," for example, can be interpreted as a request for someone to close the window, as a statement about the general temperature of the room, or as a joking grumble about a heating system turned too high. Likewise, utterances may have different grammatical forms but perform similar functions. Directives, for example, can be made using imperative, interrogative, or declarative sentence forms: "Put the rest of the blocks away," "Would you put the rest of the blocks away?," and "The rest of the blocks must be put away." In addition, speakers and listeners appear to try to follow specific rules. In conversation they tell each other the truth, try to share relevant and sufficient information, and attempt to be clear (Clark & Clark, 1977; Grice, 1975). Children with normal language learning acquire these aspects of communicative competence at different rates. By their late preschool years most have developed large repertoires of the functions expressed by language (Dore, 1977, 1979; Ervin-Tripp, 1977); they continue to develop conversational skills, on the other hand, until middle to late childhood (Donahue, Pearl, & Bryan, 1980).

These pragmatic skills are critical to the assessment of communication in language-impaired LD children. There is mounting evidence that some LD children have significant problems using language functionally. The work of Donahue and her colleagues (Bryan, Donahue, & Pearl, 1981; Bryan, Donahue, Pearl, & Sturm, 1981; Donahue, 1981, 1983; Donahue, Pearl, & Bryan, 1980) strongly suggests that, although LD children may be active conversational partners, compared to their normal-language-learning peers they are less assertive, less able to respond to inadequate messages, and less able to produce appropriate requests. Furthermore, in situations that are either ambiguous or socially complex, LD children have greater difficulty with pragmatic skills—asking questions, responding to inadequate messages, disagreeing, supporting an argument, and monitoring a conversation (Bryan, Donahue, & Pearl, 1981).

Few standardized measures assess children's and adolescents' pragmatic skills. Instead, the speech-language clinician relies on informal, descriptive assessment tools derived from the literature. Dore (1977, 1979) and Coggins and Carpenter (1981) provide useful communicative intentions inventories for checking the preschool child's functional development. Chapman (1980) and Donahue (1981) offer suggestions for assessing school-age children's conversational competence. The Communicative Activities of Daily Living, or CADL (Holland, 1980), although developed to assess pragmatic aspects of adult language, provides assessment guidelines for measuring adolescents' communication.

The on-going observation of children's pragmatic behaviors in the classroom is especially revealing, because of the unique communicative demands of the setting. Classroom rules are not always taught explicitly, and children are expected to discover them on their own. LD children may have problems deducing these rules from everyday occurrences. For example, they may not be able to identify cues for being quiet in the class or going to recess. Because of oral language problems, being able to tell when the teacher is joking may likewise present a problem. It is thus important to observe children within the class setting to determine if they follow the conventional routine or have developed an idiosyncratic one.

Other pragmatic behaviors readily observed in the classroom include whether the children can follow verbal directions, presume too much, or follow instructions too explicitly. Because an important pragmatic behavior is learning to use language to learn, the frequency and appropriateness of requests for clarification should be noted. A partial check list for observation is presented in Box 7.1. (For more detailed suggestions, see Gallagher and Prutting, 1982, and Simon 1986a.)

Up to this point, the term *pragmatics* has been restrictively used to refer to an additional set of language rules (pragmatics would be one more level after phonology, syntax, and semantics). Children must acquire these rules to become proficient communicators, and the clinician has to assess them to include them among the goals of intervention. However, wider and more serious interpretation of the theory of pragmatics would consider the integration of structural, conversational, and social rules. Assessment would then have to include observations of the individual's skills *within* a variety of communicative contexts.

Box 7.1 Pragmatic Checklist for Classroom Observation

Speaker Behaviors:

1. Does the child check to see if the listener is attentive and if the directions are effective?
2. Does the child revise when necessary? Are the revisions appropriate?
3. Does the child give relevant and sufficient information for the listener?
4. Does the child get bogged down in too many details or irrelevant information?
5. Are gestures used effectively? Overused?
6. Is the vocabulary precise or too general?
7. Does the child introduce the topic and develop it systematically? Does the child jump from topic to topic?

Listener Behaviors:

1. Does the child attend to directions?
2. Does the child presume too much or follow too explicitly?
3. Does the child request additional information to clarify?
4. Does the child cue the speaker that the message is clear?
5. Does the child know how to indicate when he or she wishes to say something?

Note. Adapted from *Communication Skills and Classroom Success: Assessment of Language–Learning Disabled Students* (p. 116) by C. Simon (Ed.), 1985, San Diego: College-Hill Press.

Until recently, the language-impaired LD individual's primary partner in the assessment procedure was the clinician. All the information gathered on the individual's abilities was based on the interaction (natural or standardized) between the two in a specific situation (e.g., a clinic, playroom, or classroom). Now, the assessment procedure has to be *ecologically valid,* which means that the individual must be observed in several naturally occurring environments. The problem arises in defining the natural environment of language-impaired LD children.

Language-impaired LD children, like normal children, typically progress from interactions with the caregiver (who is traditionally the mother), to caregiver-mediated interactions with other adults and peers, to peer interactions representing same status alignments (Corsaro, 1981; Craig, 1983). It appears that in normal development, peer social skills are not the natural extension of the skills developed when interacting with adults.

Instead, individuals need opportunities to interact with their peers to become competent communicators in this context (Craig, 1983; Mueller & Brenner, 1977). Consequently, assessment of the individual's communicative abilities should be carried out within adult-child and peer-child conversations. In the early preschool years the role of the caregiver and adult-mediated interactions is emphasized. In the school years teacher-child and peer interactions take on more relevance. In adolescence, the peer becomes the friend, the classmate, and the boss as the domain of adult-adult interaction becomes more finely grained. But what should be assessed and under what conditions?

One concern that applies across the developmental continuum is the changes observed in an individual's language during communication with different partners. Some of the questions that should guide such an assessment procedure are: Is the individual sensitive to the characteristics of the listener? Does the individual experience more communicative success with a particular type of partner? What are the characteristics of the individual's most successful interaction? Is the child able to initiate and respond appropriately? Can the child maintain the topic of conversation? What are the characteristics of the least successful interaction?

The problem of deciding under which conditions the interactive episodes should be observed is intimately related to the issues of ecological validity and sampling variability (Muma, 1983). The more natural and spontaneous the assessment situation, the more likely that the evidence gathered is ecologically valid. The effects of sampling variability can be minimized if a representative sample of the individual's competencies is collected from several situations. The more contexts sampled, the greater the likelihood of representativeness. Nonetheless, the problem still remains of how many is "several." Some have suggested a minimum of three contexts (Crystal, Fletcher, & Garman, 1976). Muma (1983) gives a more appropriate rule:

> After sampling in three contexts, if a particular structure or function continues to be manifested in new ways, it is necessary to sample further; however, if the last sample replicated previous manifestations, the sample is sufficient. (p. 199)

Only after maximizing the chances for ecological validity and minimizing the problems involved in sampling behaviors can the leap from assessment to intervention be taken with confidence.

The Instructional Model

The greatest impact of the pragmatic-interactive theoretical perspective on intervention has probably been the realization that peer interaction significantly contributes to children's development (Cooper & Cooper, 1984; Muma & Pierce, 1981). Children help one another in their learning through play (Garvey, 1977), persuasion (Clark & Delia, 1976; Eisenberg & Garvey, 1981), tutoring (Allen, 1976), and collaborative work (Cooper, Marquis, & Ayers-Lopez, 1982). Peer interaction in the classrom is governed by a specific set of rules. Children who succeed in school have acquired these rules of discourse and thus can gain optimal access to resources (Mehan, 1979; Merritt, 1982).

Peers can be used as intervention agents in the classroom by serving as models to induce change in the behavior of LD children (Muma, 1983). Activities can be designed to encourage peer interactions. Cooper & Cooper (1984) described four prototypal peer learning forms in the classroom. First, in *parallel/coordinate* peer learning two or more children working on their own projects are encouraged to exchange comments and thus help each other accomplish their individual tasks. Second, in *didactic* peer learning one child acts as the teacher to help another learn. Cooper and Cooper observed that most didactic peer learning occurs after one child requests help from another. Fostering child-child interactions in the mainstream classroom would seem an important step in turning the LD child's peers into intervention agents. Third, in *collaborative* interaction children more equally share the power of directing the interaction through alternation. In this type of peer learning, there is not a clear leader-follower pattern. Finally, and of least interest, is *onlooker* peer interaction, which usually occurs in traditional classroom settings and involves one child looking at what another has done. The physical organization of the classroom as well as the teacher's intervention can encourage the first three types of interaction and reduce the fourth.

Peer interactions and learning do not undermine the importance of either teacher-child interactions or the teacher-therapist in the remediation process. Indeed, Craig (1983) advocates the use of as many intervention agents as possible, including parents, teachers, peers, and siblings. The role of the teacher-therapist [1] thus becomes that of a troubleshooter as they locate and guide the elimination of problems in LD children's communicative systems.

Therapeutic Teaching

Therapeutic teaching of language must be based on specific guidelines. The teacher-therapist is usually confronted with the tasks of discriminating and choosing among the many available language programs to fit the children's needs. To carry out each of these tasks it is necessary to have an idea of what therapeutic teaching entails, which should ideally include four principles: context, contrast, order, and consistency.

Context

The context in which language is taught is extremely important, because the child's reinforcement is inherent in the context. *Context* refers to the characteristics, verbal and nonverbal, of the communicative situation. *Natural context,* on the other hand, describes verbal and nonverbal behaviors known to occur spontaneously. When considering the principal of context, teachers should first ask, "What is the teaching context?" and second, "Is this context natural?" The more natural the context, the more likely it is that children will encounter similar situations in their everyday activities and thus have greater opportunities to practice. In addition, if the teaching context is natural, children will be reinforced by their successes in getting what they want, expressing their feelings and opinions, developing relationships, and the like. Further, a natural context supports children's existing communicative systems and complements and extends what is already available to them.

Therapeutic teaching programs do not always specify the nonverbal context in which instruction should occur. They usually do specify, in great detail, the verbal context; that is, what both the teacher-therapist and the child should say. The nonverbal context, however, is just as important, and its elements should be manipulated. For example, is the interaction going to take place in a one-to-one teacher-child situation, or a classroom situation? Will the teacher-therapist always function as the leader? Will the teacher-therapist maintain a neutral expression or change facial expressions depending on what the child says?

Therapeutic techniques can be described, criticized, and perhaps improved by considering the context principle. An imitation-based technique will serve as an example. The goal of the therapeutic session is to teach the child to use the carrier phrase, "It is a _____," when talking about picture objects. The teacher-therapist presents a picture of an object to the child and says, "What is it?" The child responds, "A clock." The teacher-therapist says, "No, *it is* a clock," and provides the child with the imitative model by saying "Say, 'It is a clock.'" The child then imitates the model, the teacher-therapist smiles and says, "Good." The same procedure is followed for a set of ten picture objects. The teacher-therapist will drop the imitative model as soon as the child is using the carrier phrase, "It is a _____," whenever talking about picture objects.

What is wrong with this technique? First, let us look at the verbal context. The teacher-therapist asks a question ("What is it?") to which the child needs to respond verbally. The child responds by saying, "A clock," which is perfectly adequate by adult standards but unfortunately does not fit the established training goal. What happens? The child is trained to ignore the adult ellipsis discourse rule (which says it is permissible to answer with just "A clock") and instead is taught, robotlike, that to answer completely is to answer correctly. In many ways we have made the task of language learning more difficult: The child will be receiving conflicting input at home, for everyone uses the ellipsis rule in normal conversation. This child will also have to "unlearn" the completeness rule and learn the ellipsis rule at a later time. Finally, incorrect hypotheses about language have been developed. The child has had to separate language for communication (the language used at home or with friends) from language as an exercise (the language carried out in a specific way in the therapeutic setting).

How can the verbal context of the above example be improved? First, the verbal context is not natural as it needs to be. One must therefore find out when the carrier phrase, "It is a _____," is used spontaneously. It precedes the noun when differentiating among objects using the negative. For example:

> *Mary* (looking at a new item in Sarah's kitchen): "Sarah, is this a coffeepot?"
> *Sarah:* "No, it is a teapot."

The verbal context that occurs in normal conversation has to be recreated in the therapeutic situation. In general, test therapeutic activities with adults, noticing how they behave verbally and nonverbally, and learn from their comments.

In the nonverbal context of the example, the teacher-therapist is in a one-to-one situation, always leading the interaction. Although the child realizes that the teacher-therapist knows what a clock looks like and what it is called, the child must identify the picture. There is nothing wrong with this kind of interaction except that it has its limitations. Children behave differently in one-to-one and other situations. If the desired verbal behaviors need to occur in the classroom, for example, it would probably be necessary to modify the therapeutic setting to a small group discussion and finally to a classroom activity. In the original plan, the participants' roles were very rigid. The teacher-therapist was always the leader and the child always the responder. However, this rarely occurs in normal interactions, and when it does, one does not particularly enjoy talking or playing a game with someone who is always the leader. Thus why not take turns in such assessments and let the child be the leader at times?

In sum, the contextual demands on the child in the sample technique were not natural. The child was asked to respond to an adult who was familiar with the intended answer, as both parties looked at the picture. Because the child knew that the adult knew the answer, this was not a real question, since real questions derive their force from the fact that the person posing them is not familiar with the answers. To provide a natural context in which a child can learn language, that force must be preserved. This can be done simply if the person asking the questions is not able to view the object picture. A game can be played in which the child picks up a card but does not show it to the teacher-therapist. The teacher-therapist then asks the child, "Is it a clock?". The child can answer positively ("Yes") or negatively ("No, it is a table"). Not only does this procedure allow the question to have its full force, but it also keeps the elements of surprise and challenge necessary to make a good game.

Contrast

Therapeutic teaching of language occurs bit by bit, step by step. Usually, the child is taught a small portion of the linguistic system and moves on only after achieving mastery. In many ways teaching language is like giving a child pieces of a puzzle and hoping they will be put together to form the entire picture.

The principle of contrast helps children assemble the puzzle in several ways. First, contrasts provide children with information that allows them to construct rules about language. By specifying what should and should not be included, the teacher-therapist offers children opportunities to observe the regularities and irregularities of language. These in turn give children raw information from which they can generalize and form rules. The task of the teacher-therapist is to find out what sorts of information are necessary before children can construct a rule. The teacher-therapist must draw hypotheses about what is important for children to know, carry these hypotheses out in therapy, and observe their outcomes. If there is evidence that the children derive rules and apply them to new but similar linguistic environments, the therapy has been successful. If children fail to acquire the rules or handle only the linguistic environments practiced in therapy, the therapy has not been successful. It will then be necessary to reconsider the type of contrastive information presented.

Second, linguistic information taught in contrast to other such information provides children with a focus. Linguistic information is complex. There are many aspects to the meaning of the word *horse,* for example, including: (1) a horse is an animal; (2) people do not eat its meat; and (3) although it is an animal, it is also a mode of transportation. By providing children with contrastive information about a cow, one is purposely focusing their attention on a limited set of properties, which helps them build the meaning of the word *horse* at a level they can handle and with a minimum of ambiguity.

Teaching language using contrasts, then, allows the teacher-therapist to give children a framework on which the pieces of the puzzle can be fit. Language is said to be a system of contrasts. Every aspect of language is related to other aspects of language in different ways. The use of contrast in teaching underlines the importance of relationships between the various relationships, whether they be between sounds, words, or sentences, to help children build or modify a language system.

Understanding the meaning of words and developing the sound system of the language are difficult for many LD students with language impairment. Each problem area will be examined to illustrate how the contrast principle can be applied. For these examples the technique of *focused stimulation* will be used. Focused stimulation provides children with concentrated exposure to certain linguistic forms, in this case, word meaning. The goal of the teacher-therapist is to teach the meaning of three verbs of locomotion: *drive, sail,* and *fly* (see Figure 7.2).[2] Learning occurs in play sessions with relevant toys in which the teacher-therapist produces appropriate utterances containing the target verbs. The child is encouraged to play but is not required to imitate what the teacher-therapist is saying.

The key to using contrasts lies in what the teacher-therapist says. The teacher-therapist can limit utterances, for example, to descriptions of actions ("The man is sailing; now he is driving the car."), the location of action ("The man is sailing on the river."), and so on. Or the teacher-therapist can include utterances that give contrastive information about the three verbs, which involves making comparisons, or, pointing out similarities and differences. Contrastive information specifies the meaning of the verbs in question with the minimum of ambiguity.

Focused stimulation can also be used with children who have difficulty developing the sound system of their language and consequently have problems being understood. Consider, for example, children who do not differentiate between /t/ and /k/—that is, who use /t/ for both /t/ and /k/ —and thus fail to distinguish between words such as *tick* and *kick, tea* and *key,* and *tap* and *cap.* Initial therapy takes the form of using words with the sound /k/ (or /t/). Children can practice simple sound combinations such as *key, koo,* and *kay* and then slowly more complex words. They have not yet been presented with anything to contrast with k. Instead, the sound has been learned in isolation. When the teacher-therapist establishes that both the /k/ and /t/ sounds are within the children's repertoire, the contrast principle can be incorporated by contrasting the target sound /k/ with the sound used in its place, the /t/ sound. This is done by focusing attention on the contrast the children are failing to make: the contrast between /t/ and /k/. Thus, the words used must point to this contrast. The teacher-therapist collects minimal pairs of words, identical except for one key sound, that include the sound contrasts children need to work on and represent concrete objects the children can identify. To teach children to hear the difference between two sounds, the teacher-therapist presents a pair of pictures (*tea* and *key*), says one of the words (*tea*), and asks the children to point to the correct picture. This procedure is repeated for all minimal pairs. As the children attempt to produce the sounds, the teacher-therapist helps them by explaining what they have to do. For example, the teacher-therapist explains that to produce /k/ the sound has to come from the back of the throat.

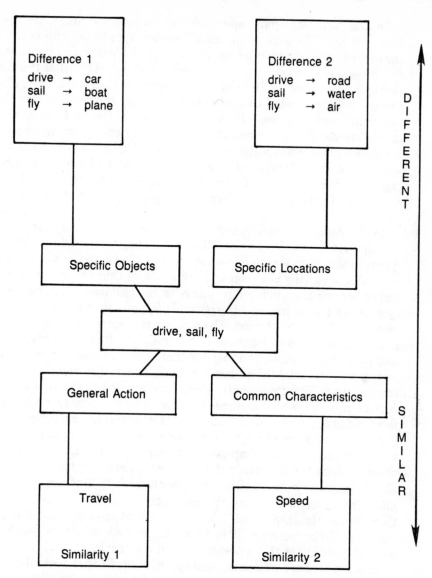

FIGURE 7.2 Schematic Teaching of the Concept of Contrast with Three Verbs.

Order

Because language is a complex, interrelated system that must be built systematically, the order in which language sounds, structures, and concepts are taught is important. All plans for teaching language have explicit or implicit assumptions about this order, which the teacher-therapist should recognize and understand.

In the "fill-in-the-gap" approach to teaching language, the teacher-therapist looks for gaps in the child's system and tries to fill them. Thus, the order is that of jumping from gap to gap. There is no inherent rationale for the sequence used. Instead, the order is dictated by what the teacher-therapist perceives as the child's deficiencies. If, for example, children respond with one-word utterances, the teacher-therapist trains them to use multiword responses. If they are not using the past tense, they are trained to use it. This approach relies heavily on the teacher-therapist's intuitions about what children should know. Unfortunately, what appears simple and straightforward to adults may indeed be linguistically and cognitively very complex for children. Consequently, there is likely to be a mismatch between what they are taught and what they are ready to learn.

In the developmental approach, which is widely recommended by clinicians and researchers alike (Bloom & Lahey, 1978; Winitz, 1983), language is taught to language-impaired LD children in the same order that normally achieving children acquire it. To do this, the teacher-therapist has to become thoroughly familiar with the children's existing language system to discover where in the normal sequence they are operating before planning what to teach next. The teacher-therapist must also understand normal language development. In teaching children the concepts of front and back, for example, the teacher-therapist has assessed one girl's language and has established her readiness to learn to use the concepts in conversation. The therapeutic technique applied is the *comprehension-based technique*, which assumes that the child's failure to use a linguistic form is due to a lack of understanding of its meaning and function. Training takes the form of games and conversations designed to clarify the meaning and function. Emphasis is on comprehension, not on having the child produce the linguistic items. After a period of training, the child should begin to produce the forms spontaneously. But how do we determine the order of teaching the concepts? Does the normal child learn them in relationship to self and then in relationship to other objects or vice versa? For answers, it is necessary to look at the research on the normal learning of the concepts of front and back.

In a series of experiments, Kuczaj (1975) found that normal-language-learning children acquire the notion that front and back are opposites before they understand each term independently. Children also acquire the meaning of these terms first with reference to the self (the child's own front and back), then with reference to objects with clear fronts (a teddy bear's front, a baker's back, a truck's front) and finally with reference to nonfronted objects (in front of or in back of a glass, a block, or a ball). It is thus clear that the acquisition of these concepts follows a specific sequence that does not necessarily fit one's intuitions of what is simplest or easiest for the child to learn. The teacher-therapist must therefore be guided by the developmental information in the literature.

Consistency

The last principle of therapeutic teaching to be addressed involves organizing the language input to the child in a predictable, consistent manner. The teacher-therapist, the classroom teacher, the child's parents, and as many others as possible need to be aware of the goals of language intervention so they can follow a consistent pattern when interacting with the child.

Let's return to our example of the children who are having difficulty developing a sound system. One boy goes to therapy once a week for an hour. During that hour he is receiving intensive input on the contrast between *t* and *k*. The rest of the week, however, he does not get any specific help with this contrast, even when he fails to make it. Because this child is receiving inconsistent input, the task of learning the sound contrasts will be prolonged. Collaboration with other professionals and parents may be useful in helping to ensure consistency.

Another example of the need for consistency comes from the therapeutic situation itself. The same child who is having difficulty with sounds is also learning to use the auxiliary verb *is* by describing what he sees in photographs of his family doing various activities ("Daddy is sleeping," "Mommy is reading."). In one session, the teacher-therapist praises him for different reasons at different times, but always uses the same word: "good." Sometimes the child omits the auxiliary but talks so clearly that the teacher-therapist praises him. Other times the child includes the auxiliary but speaks unclearly. The teacher-therapist praises him then as well. In this case it is the teacher-therapist who is being inconsistent. If criteria change from utterance to utterance or session to session, the child should be told. The child should know what is expected and what the "good" refers to during all tasks and at all times. Although 100 percent success is difficult to achieve, teacher-therapists must strive to have children participate as fully as possible in their own learning by keeping them informed about both the goals of instruction and the meaning of feedback.

Other Instructional Techniques

Three techniques of therapeutic teaching have been described: imitation, focused stimulation, and comprehension-based approaches. However, others can also be used to promote language development in LD children. One universally advocated approach is modeling, in which children observe someone else's behaviors but are not required to imitate them or produce similar behaviors. The teacher-therapist, parent, peer, or any other intervention agent can provide a model of how language is to be used and what gestures or nonverbal behaviors are appropriate. It is left to the child, however, to pick up on the model. This technique is widely used because it recognizes children as active problem-solvers.

The technique of general stimulation provides the child with exposure to language (or language-related skills) without regard to specific forms, unlike the focused stimulation discussed previously. The goal here is to immerse children in communication to address their specific language problems without having to work on them directly, one by one. With LD children with primarily phonological problems (on the phonological-syntactic continuum), for example, activities are centered on a variety of listening skills: attending to directions, discriminating among different sounds, associating sounds, and remembering sounds. With LD children with primarily semantic-cognitive problems, activities are centered on following simple directions, understanding the properties of objects, associating sequentially related actions, categorizing, and so on.

No one technique has been demonstrated to be more successful than others for *all children* (Bloom & Lahey, 1978; Leonard, 1981). (For a review of additional therapy approaches, see Fey, 1986, and Simon, 1986b.) The teacher-therapist must decide which technique fits best with: (1) the characteristics and activities of the learner, (2) the criterial task and nature of the materials to be learned, and (3) the teacher-therapist's own working style. Intervention should be evaluated and, if needed, corrected to adhere to the context, contrast, order, and consistency principles. Regardless of technique, however, effective language therapy accelerates the acquisition of linguistic forms beyond the rate seen in normal-language-learning children (Leonard, 1981).

Summary and Conclusions

The unified model of language learning views language, cognition, and social learning as interdependent aspects of development that differentiate increasingly with age. Children learn a great deal of what they know about oral language prior to attending school. They begin actively pursuing communicative interchanges with caregivers from birth. By the time they enter school most have acquired a rather extensive vocabulary, mastered much of the sound and syntactic systems, learned the uses to which language can be put, and learned to communicate both verbally and nonverbally.

Language impairment is a developmental disorder that describes a slowed rate of language learning. Language comprehension or expression or both may be affected. LD children with language impairments display a wide array of language difficulties, but most typically problems with pragmatics. Resources and suggestions for language assessment included formal (standardized tests), informal (check lists and inventories), and observational plans.

Several intervention principles—context, contrast, order, and consistency—were discussed while demonstrating three important instructional techniques—imitation, focused stimulation, and comprehension-based approaches. Two additional interventions, modeling and general stimulation, were described in the final section.

Perhaps the most important points from the perspective of a cognitive developmental model are:

1. Children are active language learners from birth.
2. Children learn language selectively as they are ready to attend to varied inputs.
3. Planning for teaching language requires both the systematic assessment of the LD child's language system and the comparison to the normal-language-learning child's system.
4. The validity of language intervention attempts rests on the results achieved.
5. Interventions, when effective, can increase the rate of the LD child's learning beyond the normal rate of acquisition of the same forms.

For all these reasons, the prognosis is optimistic.

Endnotes

1. Resource room or regular classroom teachers may plan or assist with oral language interventions, or they may be the exclusive domain of a speech-language pathologist or language therapist. Consequently, we will use the term *teacher-therapist* to include *both* roles.

2. For children with severe impairments, the teacher-therapist may choose to begin with just two contrasting verbs and gradually add others as the initial words are mastered.

Chapter 8

The Reading Process

Carol Sue Englert
Annemarie Sullivan Palincsar

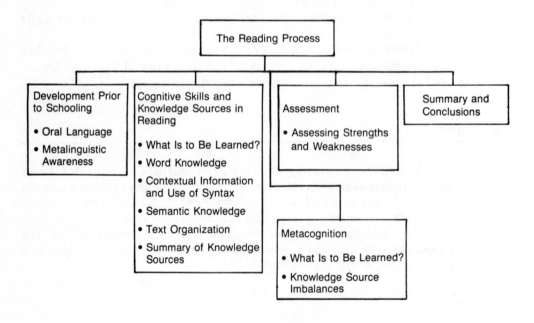

Questions to Consider

1. In what sense is the reading process interactive?
2. What knowledge sources are available during reading?
3. How can a child's ability to utilize knowledge sources be assessed?

Before discussing knowledge sources in reading and the problems LD students have using these sources successfully, it is important to understand how reading skills normally develop. Learning to read does not begin in school, for children bring a highly variable history of experiences to school that shapes subsequent learning (Brown, Palincsar, & Armbruster, 1984).

Development Prior to Schooling

Oral Language

One of the fundamental skills affecting early reading performance is oral language, which provides the context for the acquisition of grammar and a rapidly expanding vocabulary that children draw upon to make sense out of text. Furthermore, through oral language, children acquire critical ways of thinking about written language that advance their ability to comprehend.

Reading aloud to children may be the single most important activity for eventual reading success (Durkin, 1966; Heath, 1982; McCormick, 1977). When adults ask questions about background knowledge, they are teaching children to apply such knowledge in the comprehension process and to relate stories to real life. When adults ask questions that require children to apply specific strategies (e.g., predict what will happen next, summarize a story episode, or monitor comprehension), they are teaching children not only how but also when to apply specific comprehensions strategies (Anderson, Hiebert, Scott, & Wilkinson, 1985). When adults ask students to confirm their predictions with story information or to correct wrong answers, they are teaching key cognitive skills. In the preschool years, although adults do not conduct formal lessons in the use of specific strategies, children acquire tacit knowledge of strategies that can be applied to reading and other comprehension activities. Through these interactions, children internalize the inner dialogue that is important to later comprehension. Observations of parent-child interactions in instructional contexts (Deloache, 1983; Heath, 1982; Hodapp, Goldfield, & Boyatzis, 1984; Rogoff, Ellis, & Garner, 1984) suggest that some children (particularly those of middle-class parents) enter school with a better developed schema for teacher-student interaction because their parents have modeled these question-answering interactions.

Metalinguistic Awareness

Reading aloud to children also accomplishes other important reading outcomes, such as the development of metalinguistic awareness, or children's knowledge about language: its elements, conventions, form, and functions. Awareness of four metalinguistic abilities develop from frequent involvement in reading activities: word consciousness, language and conventions of print, functions of print, and emerging fluency.

Word Consciousness

Consciousness of words as discrete units does not develop until children are actively involved with printed materials, because words do not exist as separate units in oral language. The development of print awareness is fostered by the frequent reading of familiar books to the point of near-memorization. As children continually reread a book, they experience the phenomenon of "wholebooksuccess" (Martin & Brogan, 1971), meaning they can tell the entire story as they look at the pictures on the page. Gradually, children begin to connect the spoken words to the printed words as they realize that a printed word is identifiable because it is bounded by white space. As children begin to discern individual words, they also become aware of the features and letters that comprise the words.

Language and Conventions of Print

In addition to developing an awareness of printed words, through frequent interactions with print children acquire the language tools to talk about print and the vocabulary specific to later school instruction (Mason, 1984). They become cognizant of the specific actions that are performed with books—how to hold a book, how to turn the pages, where to direct their eyes, where to begin and continue reading across pages, and how to read from left to right.

Functions of Print

Through interactions with adult models and contacts with environmental print in television advertisements, logos, street signs, and so forth, children learn that print has multiple functions and properties. They also become aware that print can entertain, provide directions, and impart information. Because the purpose for reading influences the choice of specific reading strategies, this knowledge provides an important basis for later strategy selection.

Emerging Fluency

As children hear adult models reading fluently, they begin to imitate and practice the elements that make readers fluent. They begin to read in phrases and to use intonation. Chall (1979) suggests that some poor readers are disadvantaged in school because they have not been exposed to fluent reading models in their preschool years. Later schooling will not overcome this disadvantage if the only reading that poor readers hear modeled in school is the oral reading of other dysfluent readers in their reading group (Allington, 1983). Hence, young readers need to listen to stories and have opportunities to imitate fluent reading models.

Cognitive Skills and Knowledge Sources in Reading

What Is to Be Learned?

Skilled readers use at least four knowledge sources to construct meanings that go beyond the literal text. Figure 8.1 shows a pattern synthesizer integrating information from each source—word knowledge, syntactic (or contextual) knowledge, semantic (or background) knowledge, and text knowledge—during the process of reading. This is a modification of the interactive model of reading proposed by Rumelhart (1977). Although

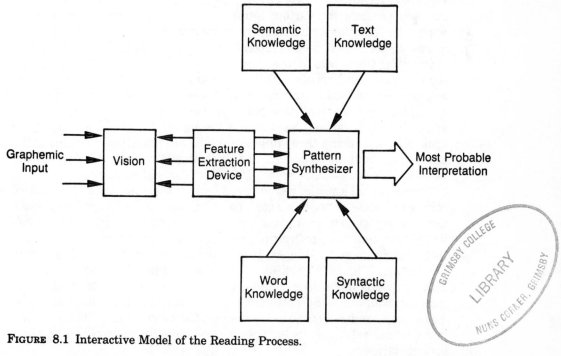

FIGURE 8.1 Interactive Model of the Reading Process.

readers have access to the four knowledge sources, the extent to which they rely on information from a particular source is determined by factors such as the criterial task, text quality, reader characteristics, and topic familiarity. Awareness of these sources is acquired developmentally. The extent to which this knowledge is refined in school depends on instructional practices, reading experiences, and learner characteristics. In the following section, we discuss LD readers' problems in using these sources strategically.

Word Knowledge

Word knowledge refers to readers' information about words and letters. There are two types of such knowledge—lexical and orthographic. *Lexical knowledge* is a mental dictionary of word meanings (Samuels & Kamil, 1984). There is a developmental tie between children's lexical knowledge and their initial acquisition of word recognition skills. According to Ehri (1978), the lexicon is initially composed of acoustic or phonetic representations of the words in their speaking vocabulary. Later, as children begin to match a spoken word to its printed equivalent, they amend the entry to include information about the distinctive features of its letters.

A second type of word information is *orthographic knowledge*. Through repeated exposures to letters in various combinations, children formulate rules for pronouncing various letter-sound correspondences that readers apply when they perform a component analysis of the letters in unfamiliar words. To perform this task successfully, readers must be skilled in both segmenting words into their elementary sounds (e.g., /c/-/a/-/t/), and blending these separate sounds rapidly into a single word (*cat*). When teachers ask students to "sound out" words they are actually asking them to perform phonemic segmentation and sound blending. These two skills are often difficult because the syllable is the smallest unit of sound heard in spoken language and these linguistic skills are not usually taught in the reading curriculum (Williams, 1984), although many argue they should be (see, for example, Liberman, 1985; Perfetti, 1985).

Orthographic knowledge, however, includes far more than the simple correspondences between single letters and sounds. With sufficient practice and exposure to words, readers begin to form the separate letters of words into common spelling patterns that are then processed as units (Samuels, LaBerge, & Bremer, 1978; Samuels, Miller, & Eisenberg, 1979). Orthographic knowledge thus takes into account that the sound of a letter depends upon its syllable context. The pronunciation of the *a* in *man* for example, is different from the pronunciation of the *a* in *mane, main, mall,* and *malt.* In sum, orthographic knowledge is the system of rules of the relationship between various spelling patterns and their pronunciations.

Typical Problems of LD Students

There is a strong relationship between orthographic knowledge and success in beginning reading (Gibson & Levin, 1975; Santa, 1977–78). By applying orthographic knowledge, readers can attempt to pronounce unknown words that can then be checked for meaning in their lexicon and with the ideas in sentence contexts. Even skilled readers sometimes rely on decoding skills for word recognition because there are too many words for the human mind to memorize successfully. The aspect of word recognition proficiency that most distinguishes good and poor readers is their level of automaticity in applying orthographic knowledge to identify words. Good readers recognize new words in the same amount of time that it takes them to recognize familiar words. Poor readers, on the other hand, are significantly slower (Golinkoff & Rosinski, 1976; Hogaboam & Perfetti, 1978; Perfetti & Hogaboam, 1975; Stanovich, 1980).

Many poor readers also have difficulties with phonemic segmentation and blending. When Williams (1979), for example, trained first-grade LD students to analyze and segment spoken words into phonemes, blend discrete phonemes into spoken words, and decode printed words through the twin processes of phonemic segmentation and sound blending, they made significant reading gains and even transferred their knowledge to new words. Without direct instruction, however, poor readers are left to figure out for themselves how to perform these complex linguistic processes.

LD students' success in applying word information is also hindered by their inflexibility in using variously sized units of information in words. Poor readers rely on a letter-by-letter processing strategy whether the word is presented in a sentence or in isolation (Patberg, Dewitz, and Samuels, 1981).

Finally, LD students have difficulty using their knowledge of familiar words patterns to recognize novel words, which is a problem of generalization by analogy. Cunningham (1979; Guthrie & Cunningham, 1982) studied mildly handicapped students who had been taught decoding skills but failed to make adequate progress. After they learned a pool of words with highly regular spelling patterns, a novel one- or two-syllable word was presented. Students were asked to: (1) find the word or words in the spelling bank that were spelled similarly and thus had rhyming parts, and (2) pronounce the rhyming parts the same way. Transfer to natural reading contexts was promoted weekly by presenting new words in passages and requiring students to apply the analogy strategy mentally. With this approach, students made significant gains in their ability to identify both trained and untrained transfer words. Specific *training* in how to extract familiar patterns and pronounce novel words by analogy to known words was thus necessary before LD students could generalize their knowledge.

In sum, the literature suggests that a successful program to develop word recognition skills would pursue the following goals:

1. development of phonemic segmentation and blending skills,
2. automatization of decoding skills until high fluency is obtained in reading novel words, most importantly, in story contexts,
3. mastery of flexible word recognition strategies, and
4. application of generalization strategies.

Although decoding skills may be introduced in isolation, priority should be given to extended practice with patterns in story contexts, even if this means less time is spent on worksheet activities (Anderson et al., 1985).

Contextual Information and Use of Syntax

A second knowledge source affecting reading performance is the sentence context of words. Most children begin reading able to comprehend and produce meaningful speech. Because of their linguistic knowledge, young readers rightly assume that reading will make sense in the same way that words and sentences in oral language make sense (Biemiller, 1970; Weber, 1970). Examination of the errors of beginning readers suggests that they usually substitute a word of the same syntactic class for an unknown word. If the word *brave* is unfamiliar, for example, many young readers would use contextual information to try to identify it by guessing a word that would make sense in that syntactic position in the sentence (e.g., "The _____ man ran back into the burning building."). Readers anticipate and even identify unknown words based on sentence information and their fund of syntactic knowledge. Many unfamiliar words that are not recognized in isolation are easily recognized in context (Dunn, 1970; Goodman, 1965; Levitt, 1970; Pearson & Studt, 1975). Thus, readers approach the process of learning to read with a "read for meaning" strategy. Oral language serves as a prominent source of information in reading, particularly for young and poor readers (Perfetti, 1986; Stanovich, 1980, 1985).

In word identification, readers process units ranging from individual letters to an entire word, depending on the quality of the text and the context. When the context is rich, readers may need very little information to identify unknown words (e.g., *br*_____ in *brave*). This example illustrates the interactive nature of word and contextual information in word recognition.

Typical Problems of LD Students

Readers are not uniformly successful in taking advantage of contextual information, probably because they have various levels of syntactic knowledge. (For a discussion of LD students' problems with syntax development, see Chapter 7.) Some do not use the redundant information in the sentence to aid word recognition (Patberg, Dewitz, and Samuels, 1981). Others fail to use contextual information to set up expectations and activate background knowledge. Bransford et al. (1982) found that less successful fifth graders were unable to use contextual information to write sentence continuations. They presented sentence stems containing attribute information about a person and a specific corresponding action (e.g., "The tall man bought some crackers."). When asked to write meaningful continuations (e.g., "The tall man bought some crackers from the top shelf."), they were unable to do so because they were not asking themselves, "Why does it have to be a tall man who bought some crackers?" Bransford et al. trained them to use such questions to stimulate their use of contextual and background information. The results showed significant improvement.

Wong and Sawatsky (1984) extended this research to LD children, training them to generate precise elaborations and check their accuracy. Their training procedure, which can be adapted for teachers, included five self-questions and answers taught by use of a modeling strategy:

1. What do I have to do? (Write a continuation of the sentence.)
2. What kind of continuation? (One that makes me understand why this kind of man did that action.)
3. How do I begin? (What do I know about being tall?)
4. Check my continuation. (Does it really make it clear why that kind of man did that action?)
5. I give myself a pat on the back. (I did it. I wrote a good continuation.)

The results showed that training was highly effective. The students had not been asking themselves questions about contextual information, nor did they use contextual information to create strong expectancies for succeeding text information. Since the intervention was short-term, the results suggested a production deficiency—LD students possessed the necessary questioning skills but did not use them to guide comprehension spontaneously.

Two additional skills are affected by readers' use of syntax. First, syntax influences how readers process text (Levin & Turner, 1968). Since most sentences are too long and complex for all units to be processed simultaneously, readers must have strategies for segmenting the text into meaningful units of information. Skilled readers look for meaningful word groups, such as phrases and clauses, and then treat them as single units. This strategy is absent in many LD readers, who instead process sentences word by word, resulting in too many isolated bits of information to remember successfully.

Second, syntax affects readers' ability to comprehend literal ideas. Readers can answer who, what, when, where, why, and how questions solely on the basis of syntactic relations. Given syntactically correct sentences containing semantically meaningful words (e.g., "The tarking pasher was stadding under the flishit because it was a blarmey parlin."), readers can answer many comprehension questions: (1) Who was stadding? (2) Where was the pasher stadding? (3) Why was the pasher stadding under the flishit? (Pearson, 1978). Syntax thus answers many of the questions that textbook authors classify as "literal *wh*- comprehension questions."

In sum, because the ability to use contextual information characterizes skilled reading performance, a successful reading program will:

1. teach word- and sentence-prediction strategies;
2. teach self-questioning and self-monitoring to predict and test predictions against preceding and succeeding text information;
3. develop fluent readers who read in meaningful phrases;
4. teach the use of *wh*-meaning units to predict, identify, and construct text meanings.

Semantic Knowledge

The third source, semantic knowledge, includes readers' background knowledge about people, places, and things. Readers actively construct semantic representations and interpretations that contain not only the literal or linguistic information from the text but also inferences suggested by their own store of world knowledge (Anderson, 1984; Blachowicz, 1977–78; Bransford, Barclay, & Franks, 1972). When information is missing, readers routinely make sense out of the text by inferring information from background knowledge. In addition to schemata for everyday experiences, readers also have abstract organizing schemata that contain lists of essential elements associated with specific concepts (see Chapter 2 for an explanation of schemata). When new information is encountered, skilled readers compare it to their schemata, and if the information is not represented, they modify the information structure to incorporate the new. What is recalled thus depends on the readers' background knowledge and information structures (Anderson & Pearson, 1984; Bransford & Johnson, 1974; Lipson, 1983).

Lipson (1983) presented two sets of passages about specific religious events, a Bar Mitzvah and a First Communion, to children of different faiths. When asked to recall the passages, children whose religious backgrounds matched the described event recalled more than those who were less familiar with the ceremony. Thus, prior knowledge of the topic is a good predicator of readers' comprehension (Alvermann, Smith, & Readence, 1985; Lipson, 1983).

Typical Problems of LD Students

For successful comprehension, readers must not only possess knowledge of the topic but also activate that knowledge. Several studies suggest that it is the activation that distinguishes good and poor readers (Bransford, et al., 1982; Owings, Peterson, Bransford, Morris, & Stein, 1980). LD students often fail to employ their background knowledge to infer cause and effect relationships, for example, when none are explicitly stated (Wong, 1980). Consequently, both their comprehension and recall suffer.

Text Organization

The fourth knowledge source that affects comprehension and recall is text organization, such as, story narratives, and exposition. Story narratives usually consist of: (1) setting (main characters, time, place); (2) problem (initiating event); (3) internal response and overt attempts to solve the problem; (4) outcomes of attempts; and (5) story conclusion. Exposition (sometimes called transactional writing) includes several categories of structures, such as description, compare-contrast, problem-solution, cause-effect, and time sequence (Meyer, 1975).

Readers' sensitivity to text organization affects what is comprehended and recalled. Englert and Heibert (1984), for example, found that when good readers confronted topic sentences that implied a specific text structure (e.g., "Birds build their nests in several steps."), they had strong expectancies for the information that followed and rapidly differentiated essential ideas (e.g., "Next, they gather nest-building materials, such as straw, string, and mud.") from intrusive or unessential ideas (e.g., "The swallow family builds nests."). Englert and Thomas (1987) later found that these expectancies seemed to be absent in LD readers. Since there are always more ideas in text than the reader can attend to and comprehend, the ability to distinguish major from minor ideas and to recognize the contribution of individual ideas to the overall structure is exceedingly important. Text structure provides an important framework that helps readers decide what is important and predict and identify what is relevant.

Typical Problems of LD Students

Although knowledge of text structure is important in comprehension, LD students often are insensitive to the organization of ideas in text and tend to: (1) focus on details rather than the most important ideas (Hansen, 1978), (2) lack awareness of potential confusions caused by inexplicable or irrelevant events (Bos & Filip, 1984; Englert & Thomas, 1987; Nodine, Newcomer, & Barenbaum, 1985); and (3) have difficulty using knowledge of text structures to create expectancies that help them identify and generate relevant details (Englert & Thomas, 1987; Thomas, Englert, & Gregg, in press). Nevertheless, studies suggest that teaching text structure skills can improve readers' comprehension and recall (Fitzgerald & Spiegel, 1983; Raphael & Kirschner, 1985; Taylor & Beach, 1984; Wong & Wilson, 1984). (Specific strategies will be elaborated in Chapter 9.)

Metacognition

What Is to Be Learned?

Metacognition can be thought of as the self-control mechanism that represents readers' awareness of the significance of a reading strategy and under what circumstances it should be utilized (Brown & Palincsar, 1982; Paris, Lipson, & Wixson, 1983). As explained in Chapter 2, metacognition refers to both the knowledge about cognition and the regulation of cognition. Metacognition distinguishes many good readers from poor readers: Poor readers acquire skills, but they seldom apply them independently in reading contexts. What these students lack are the self-management skills that help them regulate the flow among knowledge sources and know when to use a strategy and how to adapt it to ever-changing reading situations.

Box 8.1 contains a story and follow-up questions that illustrate the thinking processes that occur during reading. These should be responded to before proceeding to the next section. As you read the story, be conscious of your self-regulatory activities (i.e., self-questions and self-corrections) and the dialogue that you employ to help you make sense of the story. Read the story now.

As you attempted to comprehend the story, your thinking might have resembled the following:

> Hmmm. What's a havelock? Oh, well, the story will probably answer that question; I'll just read on. Now, who is Marianne? Well, obviously there's more information about Marianne than I have from this short passage. So she's staying at some hotel—at least the hotel can't be all that bad since it has bellhops. What's this? Why does it focus so much on such things as closing the door snugly, turning the deadbolt, and locking herself in the room? She also seems unusually concerned about pressing her clothes, as though she were trying to conceal her travel. I wonder if these things are significant? Oh, there is something odd going on here—this might be a mystery story. Let's see, it says, "her suspicions confirmed. . . ." This probably has something to do with the beginning part of the story that I'm missing. Here's that strange word—havelock. Let's see, what did it say back here? Some sort of hat with fabric and a bill? Hmm. I don't know exactly what a havelock means, but it's obvious that Marianne didn't put it there

Box 8.1   The Havelock

Marianne turned from the hotel bellhop who had helped her get her luggage into her room. She closed the door tightly, turned the deadbolt securely, and put the chain in the lock. Finally, feeling safe, she began the business of hanging up her dresses and coat, carefully pressing the clothes with her hand in attempts to remove any wrinkles that evidenced signs of her long journey. She hung up her blouses neatly and even began enjoying the rather tedious task of unpacking her belongings. Only when she turned to her largest suitcase were her suspicions confirmed that something was amiss. As she reached into the long compartment on the lid of her suitcase, her fingers brushed against a soft object with a hard bill. A havelock! Marianne hadn't seen a havelock since she packed up her father's army equipment after his death. In a pensive state, Marianne hurriedly finished unpacking. At last, she picked up the havelock and stared at it for a long moment. Then she secreted it back in its compartment and covered it with a scarf to hide its presence. Something was up and Marianne was becoming familiar with unusual happenings.

1. What is the plot of this story?
2. Where in the story would this passage appear (i.e., beginning, middle, or end)? Explain your reasoning.
3. Tell what the next part of the story is likely to be about. Tell what likely preceded this excerpt.
4. Write down everything you can remember of this story. (Do not look back at the passage.)

Note. Adapted from *A Reading Media Simulation: Teaching Special Needs Readers* by C. S. Englert, M.I. Semmel, & R. Perry, 1981, Santa Barbara, CA: University of California, Special Education Research Institute.

so I still have to find out how it got there. I'm going to finish this passage and then decide if I need to look up havelock.

As this dialogue indicates, people do a lot of thinking and questioning when they are reading. Although the dialogue is usually covert, data obtained by having readers think aloud reveal the strategic processes they apply. First, good readers seem to demand that stories make sense and thus are continually asking themselves questions, predicting information, and confirming hypotheses by relating each idea to what happened before and what will happen next. In doing so, readers are engaging in such self-regulatory activities as self-testing, self-instructing, self-questioning, and self-monitoring.

In addition, research shows that good readers are remarkably adept at understanding stories (Mandler & Johnson, 1977). In answering the questions that follow this story, for example, good readers know that this particular incident is not likely to be the first event, since Marianne undoubtedly has been previously introduced as a main character. Good readers also have strong expectancies for what is likely to follow. Given only thirteen sentences, they know that the next portion will shed light on the matter of the havelock. Similarly, they have strong expectancies for what preceded this excerpt (i.e., the introduction of Marianne and the reasons for her feeling that something is not quite right). Thus, good readers rely on their knowledge of story structure to predict, summarize, and determine what they know and what they need to know.

Second, this example illustrates the word recognition processes that might occur when skilled readers encounter unfamiliar words in text. Although most readers do not know the meaning of *havelock*, they use a variety of knowledge sources to form tentative hypotheses about its identity and meaning. Readers use sentence context and meaning and background knowledge to make a guess about its meaning. To attempt a pronunciation, readers would probably use an analogy strategy to compare and contrast it to similarly spelled words in their lexicon, such as *have* and *lock*. In so doing, they extract whole syllables and other parts from familiar words. The pronunciation of havelock, however, is less important to skilled readers than its meaning.

Third, this example shows that prior to and at the beginning of reading good readers engage in several strategic activities (Palincsar, Carr, Ogle, & Jones, 1986): comprehending the purpose for reading, developing associations and expectancies based on knowledge of the topic, constructing ideas about text content and its relation to prior knowledge, making predictions and hypotheses about content and structure, selecting a possible text structure, and choosing a reading strategy.

As they read, good readers continue to use context to decode and define words. They recall associations; confirm strategy selection; begin to confirm or reject predictions and hypotheses; search for links to prior knowledge; elaborate text by self-questioning, explaining, and visualizing; and predict what will happen next (Palincsar et al., 1986). Good readers also continually demand that the text makes sense by searching for answers to their questions, identifying important information, monitoring their comprehension, noting contradictions, and seeking clarification by rereading and other strategies. Throughout this phase, the questions good readers ask are an important basis of their anticipatory, monitoring, and confirmatory activities.

After reading, readers' strategies include: linking new information to old, confirming or rejecting predictions and hypotheses, adjusting their knowledge base to accommodate new information, identifying important data, integrating information from different sources, evaluating their comprehension, filling in gaps and confusions, and organizing information into superordinate and subordinate categories corresponding to their content schemata for the topic, which represents the relationships among the ideas (Palincsar, Ogle, Carr & Jones, 1986).

As this example illustrates, skilled readers realize that there are different strategies for various aspects of the reading process and that their use is determined by the nature of the material, the criterion task, the person, and the setting. However, such strategic reading occurs infrequently among poor readers. Compensatory reading strategies must therefore be explicitly taught to these students.

Typical Problems of LD Students

In an attempt to develop a theoretical basis for this discussion of reading problems we have borrowed from Stanovich's (1980, 1984) interactive-compensatory processing model. His conceptualization suggests that reading takes place "via the simultaneous amalgamation of information from many different knowledge sources" (1984, p. 14). Readers compensate for a deficiency in the processing capacity for a particular knowledge source by increasing their reliance upon other sources. For example, a reader with deficiencies in word recognition might depend more heavily on contextual and semantic information. Similarly, a reader with comprehension deficiencies might rely on word recognition strategies. According to this model of reading, several factors contribute to the problems of unsuccessful readers (see below).

Knowledge Source Imbalances

Overreliance on Contextual and Semantic Information

One reading problem results from an overreliance on contextual and semantic information to the near-exclusion of graphic data. Stanovich (1984) and Johnston (1985) suggest that such an overreliance is a compensatory strategy for students with word recognition difficulties. Readers with this problem predict words but do not test their predictions against the graphic information in printed words. This is most evident in oral reading errors. Such readers might substitute the word *garage* for *store* in the sentence, "John went into the store." When asked to answer comprehension questions, such readers may respond using their background knowledge instead of passage information.

Overreliance on Word Information

Another problem can result when readers attempt to read text containing a large number of unfamiliar words. Such readers become so focused on decoding words that they are unable to use other knowledge sources to comprehend the text. They might, for example, substitute the word *story* for *store* in the sentence, "John went into the store." Excessive reliance on graphic information enables readers to generate or predict words with high graphic correspondence to the original text, but these predictions do not make sense in the sentence and story context, for readers focused on decoding seldom stop to confirm their accuracy. At times, these readers may even produce nonsensical words, such as "John went into the stope."

Yet another problem results from excessive attention to word information when readers who have decoding difficulties become excessively attuned to identifying and sounding-out isolated words. Over time, they may become accurate decoders, but they are so focused on word calling that they lack fluency and read word by word. They have little capacity left for the all-important comprehension and text integration processes (Stanovich, 1984). They might be able to recall isolated facts or details that they gleaned during reading, but they are unable to interrelate the parts of the passage into a comprehensible whole.

Deficits in Content Knowledge, Background Knowledge, Text Structure, and Strategies

Another type of difficulty is associated with deficits in content knowledge, background knowledge, text structure or strategies. Some students come to reading lacking the knowledge or instructional experiences that would allow them to benefit maximally. The instruction most likely to improve their performance would strengthen the match between the learner and text by either teaching content-related knowledge or strategies or carefully selecting reading materials to match the learner's knowledge.

Metacognitive Deficits

Even readers who possess requisite background knowledge or information on reading strategies (e.g., summarizing, predicting, focusing, questioning, and confirming), relevant text structures, and self-control strategies may fail to activate that knowledge spontaneously. If questioned by the teacher, these readers are unaware of what should be done in a particular situation and why certain actions are important. In short, they lack metacognitive awareness about how to control and regulate their performance. They need self-control instructional programs that build their ability to self-regulate through teacher modeling of the thinking that directs strategy use.

Instructional Failures

Finally, reading problems can result from the failure of instruction to account for the interactive nature of the reading process. Not infrequently, teachers cause the development of incomplete reading strategies by placing excessive emphasis on one knowledge source, often to the exclusion of others. Such failures may be particularly problematic in special education because of the heavy emphasis on decoding and basic skills. Brown, Palincsar, and Armbruster (1984), for example, suggested that special education students receive less instruction and practice in strategies to foster and monitor comprehension than their normally achieving peers. Furthermore, special education teachers continually perform executive control functions by providing rigid step-by-step instruction. As a result, students gain poor control of strategy use and fail to become independent, self-regulating learners.

Assessment

Assessing Strengths and Weaknesses

Given the interactive nature of the reading process, assessment should be responsive to the relationships between the reader, criterial task, material, and strategies. Wixson and Lipson (1986) advocate this type of assessment and suggest that rather than looking for a pathology in the reader, teachers should search for patterns of interactions that can determine the conditions under which a reader can and will learn.

Based upon this model, reading assessment should include on-going testing across several materials and during classroom tasks to learn about students' reading strategies under various conditions and talking to students to gain insight into their thinking and awareness of strategy use in different situations.

Metalinguistic Awareness

With younger children, assessment should begin with an evaluation of metalinguistic awareness. Clay (1972) and Mason (1984) suggest several measures: (1) conventions of print, such as how to hold a book and turn the pages and the terminology applied to book parts and locations (e.g., front, page, top, and bottom) and sentence and word parts; (2) forms of print, such as lower-case letter recognition and spelling consonant-vowel-consonant words; (3) phonemic analysis of words, such as the segmentation into syllables and individual phonemes; and (4) beginning reading skills, such as the ability to read familiar logos and environmental print (e.g., Pepsi, stop, McDonald's), their own writing, and familiar stories (Hiebert, 1978; Sulzby, 1985).[1]

Informal Reading Inventories

With older readers, assessment can begin with the administration of an informal reading inventory, which consists of graded word lists and graded reading passages with comprehension questions. Traditionally, these measures are used to assess oral reading and comprehension performance. With minor modification (see below) they can effectively tap the knowledge and skills that reveal the instructional conditions under which students perform best.

Oral Reading

In interactive assessment, teachers attempt to determine which knowledge sources students use and how that use changes under various text and task conditions (Wixson & Lipson, 1986). Thus, teachers should determine how skillfully the reader can: (1) recognize words and use orthographic patterns to identify words, (2) use syntactic and contextual information to read words and phrases, and (3) comprehend semantic relationships in a passage.

To develop hypotheses about which knowledge sources readers are using, teachers should analyze oral reading performance by having the student read a set of graded passages while the teacher records all miscues,[2] such as omissions, insertions, nonwords, nonsense words, no attempts, substitutions, and self-corrections, on a second copy of the text. By summing the number of miscues and dividing by the total number of words read, teachers can calculate the student's overall percent accuracy, which provides some basis for making decisions about the appropriateness of the reading material: If the reader misses fewer than 10 percent of the words, reads at an acceptable rate, and answers 75 percent or more of the comprehension questions, the material is appropriate.

Teachers should also measure oral reading fluency by timing the student while the passage is read aloud and recording whether the student reads word by word or in phrases. Reading in phrases preserves the syntax and demonstrates that the child comprehends the relations among word meanings. These data can be recorded on a copy of the passage by marking the reader's pauses with a slash between words. A word-by-word reading would look like this: "His/father/seemed/tired/but/he/managed/to/stand/up/straight/and/say. . . ." Inconsistent use of phrasing might look like this: "His father/seemed/tired but/he managed to/stand/up straight/and/say. . . ."

Children who do not read words in meaningful groups need a specific instructional program to promote reading fluency. (Such programs will be discussed in Chapter 9.) It is important to measure fluency at least biweekly during the implementation of the fluency-building intervention until the child is reading in phrases with relatively high frequency. Mea-

---

Box 8.2   Basic Questions for Assessment of Knowledge Sources Used in Oral Reading

1. Does the child's miscue appear orthographically or visually similar to the original word (i.e., do 50 percent or more of the letters or sounds in the substituted word or error match those in the original word)?
2. Is the child's miscue syntactically or grammatically correct in the sentence read?
3. Does the child's miscue preserve the semantic meaning of the original text?

Note. Adapted from *A Reading Media Simulation: Teaching Special Needs Readers* by C. S. Englert, M. I. Semmel, & R. Perry, 1981, Santa Barbara, CA: University of California, Special Education Research Institute.

---

surement and recording procedures described above and in the remaining sections of this chapter should be used throughout the intervention.

In addition to the overall oral reading assessment, teachers should further analyze each reading miscue to determine which of the knowledge sources the student uses during reading. Englert, Semmel, & Perry (1981) suggest that teachers conducting this analysis should ask themselves the questions implied in Box 8.2 to discover whether the child is using orthographic, syntactic, and/or semantic information sources during reading.

As an example, let's examine Mrs. Drake's record of the oral reading miscues made by her student Mark Sullivan. To help her perform this analysis, she recorded her answers to each of the questions on a grid (see Table 8.1). To summarize Mark's performance, she calculated the percent accuracy in each knowledge source column (i.e., number of "yes" responses in a column divided by total number of "yes" and "no" responses). The results revealed that Mark consistently relied on orthographic information to a greater extent than syntactic or semantic information. Of his total miscues, those preserving the orthographic features of the text occurred 90 percent of the time, whereas those miscues that preserved the syntactic and semantic features of the text occurred only 50 percent and 20 percent of the time, respectively. Even more telling was that many of Mark's miscues were nonwords and that there were no self-corrections. Thus, Mark did not test his oral predictions against word knowledge or contextual information.

In an interactive assessment, an important goal is to test across passages at a single instructional level to determine whether students' strategies change as the nature of the material changes. Students may, for

Table 8.1   Initial Oral Reading Error Analysis of Mark Sullivan

Text/Miscue	Visually Similar	Syntactically Correct	Same meaning	Self-Corrected
plain/plan	yes	no	no	no
slid/slide	yes	yes	yes	no
jingled/jing	yes	no	no	no
front/from	yes	no	no	no
classroom/class	yes	yes	yes	no
believe/belif	yes	no	no	no
listen/speak	no	yes	no	no
excited/exited	yes	yes	no	no
blinded/blidded	yes	yes	no	no
temper/temple	yes	no	no	no
Percent accuracy	90	50	20	0

example, perform differently given narrative versus expository passages or prereading versus no prereading activities (cf. Hansen, 1981). Mrs. Drake tried to confirm her hypotheses about Mark by administering a second passage, this time on baseball—a topic she knew he was especially interested in. Table 8.2 shows that when Mark read this passage aloud, his oral reading strategies changed. This time Mark used orthographic cues only 40 percent of the time, but increased his use of syntactic and semantic cues to 100 percent and 80 percent, respectively. Furthermore, he self-corrected two times. Although the percent of oral reading accuracy was similar on the two passages, Mark displayed greater emphasis on making sense on the second passage, suggesting that he benefitted sub-

Table 8.2   Second Oral Reading Error Analysis of Mark Sullivan

Text/Miscue	Visually Similar	Syntactically Correct	Same Meaning	Self-Corrected
softball/ball	yes	yes	yes	no
third/second	no	yes	yes	yes
yesterday/today	no	yes	no	no
umpire/ump	yes	yes	yes	yes
next/then	no	yes	yes	no
plate/base	no	yes	yes	yes
batter/hitter	yes	yes	yes	no
cheered/clapped	no	yes	no	no
won/win	yes	yes	yes	no
champions/winners	no	yes	yes	no
Percent accuracy	40	100	80	20

stantially from prior knowledge of the topic. Motivation also cannot be dismissed as a possible factor since Mark's interest in the topic helped him activate prior knowledge, with substantial effects on comprehension. In short, he did show flexibility in using different knowledge sources based on topic familiarity, but he did not consistently activate his background knowledge about topics for all stories.

To verify what is suggested by analyses of oral reading miscues, teachers can follow-up with informal analyses, such as probe sheets to assess orthographic or word recognition skills and cloze passages to assess use of contextual and semantic information.

Probe Sheets   Probe sheets consist of lists of words correlated to particular phonic or orthographic patterns. For each of the curriculum subskills (see Box 8.3), a corresponding probe sheet with sixty to one hundred representative words is developed.

Teachers administer only those probe sheets for which there are suspected difficulties, based on an analysis of oral reading miscues. To perform the word recognition analysis, teachers examine oral reading miscues and formulate hypotheses about the nature of the difficulties (e.g., consonants, consonant clusters, or medial short vowels). For example, Mark's correct reading of many of the words suggested mastery of short vowel sounds (e.g., *band, stand, rut, pot*) and some common orthographic patterns (e.g., *wall, plank, wing*). On the other hand, reexamination of his miscues indicated that he had difficulties with long vowel sounds and structural analysis skills involving multisyllabic words (e.g., *classroom, believe, excited, blinded, temper, umpire*). Mrs. Drake's analysis of these word recognition problems is shown in Table 8.3.

After performing this initial word recognition analysis, teachers confirm suspected difficulties by administering the probe sheets that tap the respective subskills. In Mark's case, this meant administering the probe sheets that assessed his knowledge of long vowel patterns (CVCe, CVVC), compound words, and other multisyllabic word patterns (e.g., VC/CV, V/CV).[3] To confirm sight word deficiencies, teachers can administer lists of sight words.

When teachers administer probe sheets, students' reading rates should be timed with a stopwatch and miscues recorded on a second copy for later analysis using the diagnostic procedure described above. Oral reading accuracy as well as fluency (i.e., correct rates and miscue rates) should be calculated for each probe sheet. Use the following formulas to calculate:

Correct and miscue rates:

$$Correct\ rate = \frac{number\ of\ correct\ responses}{total\ time\ in\ minutes}$$

$$Error\ rate = \frac{number\ of\ incorrect\ responses}{total\ time\ in\ minutes}$$

Box 8.3   Skills That Can Be Measured with Probe Sheets

Phonics
1. Initial consonant sounds (in isolation and in spoken words)
2. Final consonant sounds (in isolation and in spoken words)
3. Short vowel sounds (in isolation and in spoken words)
4. Consonant-vowel-consonant words (CVC) with short vowels (*a, e, i, o, u*)
5. CCVC words with digraphs (*sh, ch, th, wh*)
6. CCVC words with consonant blends ("1'
7. CVCe words with final *e* (*pane, bite*)
8. CVVC words (*ai, ea, ee, oa, ay*)
9. R-controlling vowels (*ar, or, ir, er, ur*)
10. Vowel dipthongs (*oo, ou-ow, au-aw, al, ew, oi-oy*)
11. Variant sounds of *c* (*circle*) and *g* (*gist*)
12. Silent letters (*gh, gnt, gn, kn, mb, wr*)

Structural Analysis
1. Compound words
2. Noun plurals (*-s, -es*)
3. Variant forms of verbs (*-es, -ing*, double consonants before *-ing* or *-ed*)
4. Contractions (*it's, I'm, I'll, that's, let's, don't, didn't, isn't, we're, couldn't*)
5. Suffixes and basic word endings (*-s, -ing, -ed, -es, -er*)
6. Prefixes (*un-, dis-, in-, re-, de-, pre-, im-, mis-*)
7. Suffixes (*-ly, -ness, -less, -est, -ful, -tion, -ion, -ment, -ar, -or*)
8. Possessives
9. Syllabication between double consonants (VC/CV)
10. Syllabication between vowel and single consonants (V/CV)
11. Syllabication in words ending with *le* (*bubble, struggle*)

Sight Words
1. Mastery of basic sight vocabulary
2. Mastery of function words

Mark's performance on the VC/CV sheet confirmed suspected difficulties with this particular syllabic pattern since he read these multisyllabic words slowly and with low accuracy (i.e., 20 percent accuracy, with a correct rate of two words per minute and an error rate of eight per minute). When this analysis was repeated for other probe sheets, other hypothesized difficulties were likewise confirmed. By comparing performance across the oral read-

Table 8.3   Word Recognition Error Analysis of Mark Sullivan

Text	*Suspected Word Recognition Difficulty*
plain/plan	Double vowel (CVVC)
slide/slid	Final *e* (CVCe)
jingled/jing	Multisyllabic word (*-le* syllabic pattern)
classroom/class	Compound word
believe/belif	Sight word
listen/speak	Initial consonant and multisyllabic word (VC/CV)
excited/exited	Sight word and multisyllabic word
blinded/blidded	*-ind* word family
temper/temple	Multisyllabic word (VC/CV)
softball/ball	Compound word (synonyms)
third/second	Used syntax, not initial consonants
batter/hitter	Used syntax, not initial consonants

ing and word recognition measures, teachers can gain additional insight into students' performance if they apply the questions presented by Box 8.4. When preinstructional assessment is conducted in this fashion, it yields information about problem areas and instructional conditions that could affect a student's performance with particular material as well as base line data against which to measure future performance.

Cloze Measures Teachers could further assess students' use of contextual and semantic information during reading by developing and administering cloze measures. First the teacher selects a 250-word passage and deletes every fifth word. The student then reads the cloze aloud while supplying words to go in the blanks. If exact-word replacement criteria are used to make a placement decision, the instructional level is the highest level at which the student can supply 30 to 45 percent of the exact words from the original passage.

In informal assessment, a more useful diagnostic procedure is to delete systematically words that require use of contextual and semantic information and analyze the percentage of words supplied that are: syntactically acceptable. These data more accurately represent students' abilities to predict and confirm hypotheses using contextual information, word knowledge, and text structure. Mrs. Drake administered such a passage to Mark, who performed as follows:

> The *little* rabbit stopped dancing, and came quite close. The big rabbit came so *low* that his long *table* brushed the Velveteen Rabbit's *teeth,* and then he wrinkled his *shirt* suddenly and flattened his ears and *crawled* backwards.

Mark's cloze performance tended to confirm his suspected difficulties in activating prior knowledge to predict information. Because he did not

> **Box 8.4 Questions to Guide Assessment of Word Recognition Skills**
>
> 1. Does the student decode familiar sight words and novel words with equal facility?
> 2. Does the student recognize words more easily in passage contexts than in isolation?
> 3. How and why does the quality of miscues change across different testing conditions?

access his knowledge of rabbits, he supplied words that were syntactically acceptable (e.g., *table, shirt, crawled*) but unrelated to the other concepts in the passage. Moreover, Mark did not confirm his predictions with passage information, as indicated by his failure to complete successfully the first sentence using information from the second sentence (i.e., *big*) and vice versa (i.e., *close*). His failure to suspend judgment until he had more information or to self-correct in the face of contradictory evidence suggests that he was passively responding to information in single sentences instead of intersentential information. In sum, he was an inactive reader who did not actively ask questions based upon his own world knowledge or passage information.

Modifications of the cloze passage procedure found in the literature may also help assess contextual and semantic knowledge usage. Bransford et al. (1982) and Wong and Sawatsky (1984), for example, asked students to generate continuations for incomplete sentences. This assessment might be useful with a student like Mark to see if contextual information created expectancies that helped him meaningfully relate ideas.

Englert (Englert & Hiebert, 1984; Englert & Thomas, 1987) used a continuation task with a multiple-choice format to evaluate readers' ability to elaborate on a stimulus stem to identify relevant details consistent with specific expository text structures. In this set of studies, students were shown two stimulus sentences representing one of four text structures (description, enumeration, compare-contrast, and sequence). The stimulus sentences were carefully constructed to provide: (1) a topic of the paragraph; (2) a specific type of text structure (e.g., "The Mako shark looks frightening."); and (3) an exemplar detail sentence that met topic and text structure requirements (e.g., "The Mako shark's jaw has several rows of teeth."). Students then were asked to complete the paragraph with four sentences. Two of the four sentences were target sentences in that they were consistent with the established text structure (e.g., "The Mako's nose comes to a long, sharp point."); the remaining two were distractors that retained some of ideas introduced in the stimulus sentence but intruded on the text structure (e.g., "There are several steps to catching a shark."). The results showed that, for lower achieving and LD readers, initial text information did not activate text structure schemata that helped them predict and select relevant details. As a result, students could not distinguish relevant from intrusive passage information. The researchers suggested that expository text comprehension is often neglected in educational programs and that tasks like that used in the study might help identify those who need text structure instruction.

August, Flavell, and Clift (1984), Fitzgerald and Spiegel (1983), and Gordon and Braun (1985) used a macrocloze procedure to assess and develop knowledge of story structure. With this method, students are given information about all categories of story structure (e.g., setting, initiating event or problem, outcome, and conclusion) except attempt. Students then are asked to read the incomplete story and say whether anything is missing. If they think it is incomplete, they must say what information is missing and where it should be inserted. A modification of an incomplete story used by August et al. (1984, p. 57) is shown below:

> Kate lived with her parents by the railroad tracks. One day a terrible storm caused a flood. The flood washed away the wooden bridge near Kate's house. Kate knew that she had to stop the train before it was too late.
> She decided to warn the engineer. She was about 500 yards away when she fell. The train stopped safely before the bridge. Kate was glad that she had helped.

August et al.'s study showed that, compared to their normally achieving peers, less successful readers were not as aware of missing information and did not engage in comprehension-monitoring activities. These differences, however, were not attributable to intelligence or decoding ability. Thus, the assessment effectively distinguished readers who were using text structure to predict, infer, and comprehend. In the classroom, teachers should score macrocloze responses by asking:

(1) Does the child supply information that fits the missing story category?, and

(2) Does the supplied information fit the entire story, including information that follows the missing part? (Spiegel & Fitzgerald, 1986).

The cloze measures that have been discussed are considered informal assessment tools. Performance on these various elaborative tasks should be taken only as supporting evidence of whether students are aware of specific sources of information during reading and should be verified with on-going assessment during teaching. This can be accomplished by assessing comprehension and administering the metacognitive interview.

Comprehension   Teachers typically assess comprehension when they administer graded passages to students. These usually take the form of ten literal comprehension questions following oral and silent reading.

Comprehension assessment would be immeasureably strengthened, however, if it were more systematically based on the model of reading discussed in this chapter. As a first step, teachers should ask students to retell or summarize the passages orally, which provide important information about the structure of the reader's knowledge as well as what the reader considers important. To evaluate the quality of the summary, teachers should outline the passage in advance. If the passage is a story narrative, the outline should contain critical story information such as the setting, initiating event or problem, response to the event or attempt to solve the problem, outcome of the response or attempt, and conclusion. Students' retellings are then scored by the percentage of individual categories and general story ideas included. Their summaries can also be assigned a holistic rating that indicates their overall quality: A score of 4 means that all categories of story structure were present; 3 means that most categories were present but that one of three essential categories— problem, response, or outcome—was missing; 2 means that story information or characters but no real cause-effect relationships were described; and 1 means that isolated details or descriptions were listed.

Retelling of expository passages can be similarly scored. Teachers should outline the main ideas and supporting details of the passage. Students' summaries can then be scored according to the percentage of total ideas recalled, with weighted scores given to the recall of main ideas (2 points each) and related details (1 point each). In scoring both expository and story retellings, teachers should holistically analyze their structure to determine whether students are grouping information into structural units or simply listing isolated facts and details.

After a retelling, comprehension questions can be administered to tap students' understanding and recall of major story or expository ideas rather than insignificant details. These questions can be classified into one of three types based upon the sources of information students use in formulating answers (Pearson & Johnson, 1978): (1) *textually explicit*— information that is text based and explicit; (2) *textually implicit*—information that is not explicitly stated but can be inferred from information in several sentences; and (3) *scriptually implicit*—information that is based on prior knowledge. By classifying questions in this way, teachers are more likely to measure students' use of prior knowledge and inferential comprehension.

A final tool that may be useful in informal comprehension assessment is to ask students to read a passage, predict what will happen next, and formulate questions they would ask if they were the teacher. Asking questions is the basis of comprehension performance, yet teachers seldom evaluate the quality of students' questions. Palincsar and Brown (1984) found that students with reading difficulties had problems constructing questions that dealt with the major ideas in passages and instead focused on details. By measuring entry-level skills, teachers have some basis for evaluating the effects of instructional interventions on the nature and quality of questions that children ask.

Metacognitive Interview   As a final assessment technique, teachers could interview students about their reading strategies. The interview should contain questions that elicit information about what the student does while performing reading activities. The interview developed by Wixson, Bosky, Yochum, and Alvermann (1984) yields powerful information about students' reading knowledge and comprehension skill (see Box 8.5 for an adapted version). Their interview contains fifteen open-ended questions that explore the student's: (1) perception of the goal of reading activities in the context of different materials; (2) understanding of various reading task requirements; and (3) strategies for engaging in various reading activities.

Adaptations of the interview are particularly useful during on-going assessment in class. As students are reading, they should be stopped at various points and asked questions. After students read the title of the passage, for example, teachers can ask them to think out loud about the strategies they are using (e.g., "What are you thinking about when you read that title?" "What is something you should do when you read a title?") Teachers can evaluate the richness of students' background knowledge for topics in the story by asking them to tell all they know about the key story concepts. (For further information about evaluating the quality of background knowledge, see Chapter 9.) At the end of a page, students can be stopped again and asked if there is anything important they should do before reading the next page. Students also can be asked if they had any questions as they were reading the page. If students look back or pause while reading, teachers should stop them and ask, "I noticed you paused as you were reading. Why did you do that?" and "Why is that important to do?" Finally, at the end of reading, teachers can ask, "How would you remember this story if you knew that I was going to ask you questions about it?" "Why is that a good thing to do?" "Can you do anything else to help you study it?" "How do you do that?" "When should you do that?" Such questions can yield insight into children's strategies, for they tap children's declarative, procedural, and conditional knowledge as well as specific word recognition activities.

Box 8.5 Reading Knowledge and Comprehension Skill Interview

To gain information about student's perception of reading activities, teachers ask students:

1. What hobbies or interests do you have that you like to read about?
2. How often do you read in school and at home?
3. What school subjects do you like to read about?

To test a student's knowledge of strategies, Wixson et al. (1984) suggest that the teacher should have the student read passages from a basal reader and content area textbook and ask the following questions about each:

1. What is the most important reason for reading this kind of material? Why does your teacher want you to read this book?
2. Who's the best reader you know in _____ ? What makes that person a good reader?
3. How good are you at reading this kind of material? How do you know?
4. What do you have to do to get a good grade in _____ in your class?
5. What would be the best way to remember the information in this passage?
6. What would be the best way to find the answers to the questions in this book? Why?
7. What is the hardest part about answering questions like the ones in this book?

Note. Adapted from "An Interview for Assessing Student's Perceptions of Classroom Reading Tasks" by K. K. Wixson, A. B. Bosky, M. N. Yochum & D. E. Alvermann, 1984, *Reading Teacher, 37.*

Assessment should thus be designed to measure students' knowledge—the what, how, when, and why of strategy use. The search for and evaluation of LD readers' thinking is an unusual goal for teachers. Yet, if we are to change their thinking, we must have some understanding of their thinking processes. In sum, rather than focus on the results of reading performance, teachers must assess the processes by which children read and comprehend.

Summary and Conclusions

In this chapter, we have considered the interactive nature of the reading process. Readers with learning problems have difficulties applying one or more of their knowledge sources during reading. Metacognitive knowledge affects readers' abilities to self-activate, self-question, self-instruct, self-monitor, and self-correct. Assessment should allow teachers to examine the use of these sources under varying instructional conditions. This can be done by both observing and interviewing the students during different reading tasks. By continually considering students' understanding of the what, when, how, and why of reading, teachers can better design instructional programs to meet their evolving cognitive and metacognitive needs.

Endnotes

1. For a standardized measure, see Reid, Hresko, and Hammill, 1980.
2. A *miscue* is an oral reading that differs from what the text actually says. Sometimes it is an error. Sometimes, however, it may constitute an appropriate substitution, such as *house* for *home,* that even expert readers may make.
3. C = consonant; V = vowel.

Chapter 9

Teaching Learning Disabled Students to Read

Annemarie Sullivan Palincsar
Carol Sue Englert

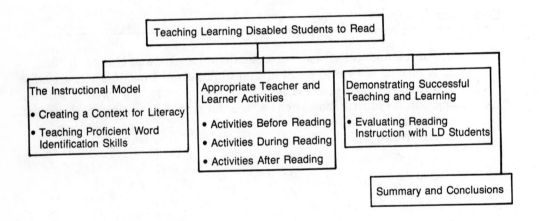

Questions to Consider

1. How is a context for literacy created and why is it important to do so?
2. How are word identification skills taught?
3. What opportunities for instruction exist before, during, and after reading?

In Chapter 8 we described reading as a constructive process designed to give meaning to the text. As we think about the reading activity, the metaphor of the art of juggling comes to mind. The demands on the juggler are the function of many variables: The number, weight, and configuration of the objects to be juggled; the confidence and expertise of the juggler; and the audience for whom the juggler is performing are but a few. As important to the act as smoothly initiating the routine is monitoring its rhythmical pattern, compensating for a miscalculation, gracefully resuming activity when the clubs come tumbling, and drawing the act to a clean, if not dazzling, conclusion. The reader must likewise juggle a number of variables, such as the structure, familiarity, and difficulty of the text and the purpose for reading. The skillful reader actively monitors progress, takes appropriate measures when reading falters, and can resume reading after there has been a breakdown in the process. The reading act comes to a successful conclusion when, to stretch the analogy, meaning falls into place.

The Instructional Model

In this chapter we describe the roles of both direct and scaffolded instruction in helping the reader independently apply decoding and comprehension skills to construct meaning. This independence is particularly crucial when discussing LD students, since they are notorious for their failure to transfer newly acquired skills spontaneously across settings or tasks. Teachers need to begin by creating a context for literacy. In recognition of the prevalent word recognition problems of LD students, instruction for word-identification proficiency is also important. Finally we address the instructional opportunities present before, during, and after reading.

Creating a Context for Literacy

In Ms. Key's classroom a group of students are engaged in a rather dynamic argument about what motivated the main character of the story they are reading to turn his friend in to the school counselor for using alcohol. In Mr. Dade's class, the children are given envelopes that contain a message updating them on their class performance and asking them to evaluate which of the recent reading activities they found most useful and why. Ms. Pope's class has been divided into teams and is playing a cooperative game of password (many of the words might be identified as "street talk"). Mr. Blare is sharing, by means of an overhead projector, a menu from a fancy restaurant he had the good fortune to find over the weekend. What do these classrooms have in common? We would suggest that in each a literacy event has been created.

As we discussed in the previous chapter, reading is not only a cognitive process but also a social and linguistic process. Children learn to read and write because they recognize the functions reading and writing serve. For some, the goal of performing successfully may be good grades and parental approval. For others the motivation may be quite different. A teacher recently told us about a high school student with whom she had struggled for three years to teach basic reading skills. Then suddenly, anticipating his sixteenth birthday, this student appeared to master the vocabulary necessary to pass the driver's exam through self-instruction!

As teachers, we may not be able to control the incentive to read, but we can certainly provide opportunities to participate in literacy events and facilitate our students' access to these events. It is not particularly tricky to create such situations. For many years, teachers have provided "print rich" environments: labels, bleached by sunlight and curled by heat, are taped to windows, closets, and doors; students' compositions decorate bulletin boards; whole schools engage in a solemn fifteen minutes of "sustained silent reading" following the principal's announcements. The difficult part is ensuring that these are not merely "displays of literacy" (Bloome & Greene 1983), but truly participatory events. How do we achieve this goal? A substantial body of ethnographic data would suggest that we do this by recognizing and building bridges between the context of literacy in the home and community and in the classroom and school. To illustrate this bridge building, we will describe one reading component of the language arts program of the Kamehameha Early Education Project (KEEP), designed for native Hawaiian children in primary grades (Au, 1980). These children participate in a traditional language experience called the *talk story,* during which the group constructs and conarrates personal experiences intermingled with folk material. In KEEP this rich experience is incorporated in language instruction. Groups of about five children meet with their teacher for twenty minutes of daily instruction on a story in their basal reader. The lessons are composed largely of rapid interactions between the teacher and children. The teacher first introduces the story and elicits students' experiences related to its topic. There is much interaction as the students complement and build upon one another's responses in a manner characteristic of the talk story. The teacher then assigns a page or two to be read silently for the purpose of answering questions. Following the silent reading, the teacher asks questions to assess comprehension and draw relationships between the text and the personal experiences of students. The teacher and students continue to contribute in this interweaving of text and personal experience, with frequent conarration. The result of this lesson form has been impressive: Hawaiian children from economically depressed rural areas have performed significantly higher on reading achievement measures than have their counterparts who have served as control students.

What features of this instruction illustrate the bridge building to which we referred? First, from a sociolinguistic perspective, a literacy experience from the home and community has been incorporated in a formal school setting. Second, general language usage was applied to reading activity to make the nature and function of reading more explicit. Third, the students can demonstrate the competence acquired through the talk story in a much less familiar context. From a cognitive perspective, this procedure provides ample opportunities for the students to interact with the text and link their schema about the topic and the new information provided in the text.

The interactive role of the teacher and students distinguishes this lesson from the more classic notion of a reading lesson in which students take orderly turns reading orally and then answer a series of teacher- or text-generated questions that generally elicit recall of story facts.

In sum, the teachers' first responsibility is to create an environment in which instruction can be implemented to nurture and cultivate reading processes, an environment that acknowledges the cultural and experiential heterogeneity of students.

Teaching Proficient Word Identification Skills

One need not look very far to find support for discussing the instruction of word identification in a text designed to help teachers work with LD students. The fact is that 85 percent to 90 percent of students referred to programs for those with mild learning impairments demonstrate problems in this area (Kaluger & Kolson, 1978), and the problems do not go away. Hagin (1971) determined that decoding continues to be a pervasive problem among LD adolescents. One could easily fill a volume discussing the research related to various approaches to instructing word identification. Consequently, we have had to be very selective in summarizing this work. Before doing so, however, three caveats must be mentioned.

First, we must not allow our students to lose sight of the goal of reading: comprehension of the material. Johns (1974) examined the relationship between readers' concepts of reading and their reading ability. He discerned that students reading a year or more below grade level seldom indicated comprehension as the purpose of reading; rather, they defined reading as "saying the words correctly." The observational research of Collins (1982), Allington (1980), and Hoffman et al. (1984), offers some understanding of why this might be the case. The teachers they observed tended to adopt different procedures when working with their high- and low-ability reading groups. The students in the high-ability groups were interrupted proportionately less often as they read aloud, they were permitted to finish a meaningful phrase before they were interrupted, and the teachers called attention to "reading with expression." Each of these instructional procedures reinforces the notion that reading must be a "meaningful" activity and permits the high-ability students to read more text, even though the reading lessons of the low-ability groups lasted the same amount of time.

The second caveat is born of our experience with students who are receiving multiple services. Illustrative of this is a third-grade student who was learning a phonetic approach to word identification in the classroom, a whole word approach using a familiar list of sight words in the resource room, and a language experience approach in a special program designed for underprivileged children. While an argument can admittedly be made for having a repertoire of strategies, this child was not given the opportunity to master any of these approaches.

The third caveat is that we are focusing on the instruction of one level of analysis of text. Recalling Rumelhart's (1977) model, this relates to the instruction of graphophonemic analysis of text. Our ultimate goal must be the instruction of all levels of analysis so that students can flexibly engage in them. Perhaps the most helpful way to describe and assess the various approaches to word identification instruction is to trace the history of research in this area. We will draw heavily from the comprehensive review of this history by Johnson and Baumann (1984).

The comparison of a phonetic with look-say approach to word identification stimulated decades of research. Proponents of a phonetic approach argued that the instruction of phonic skills as assessed by measures of phonics knowledge, word identification ability, and oral reading equipped students to engage independently in word attack; advocates of the whole-word approach suggested that their method focused more on comprehension and therefore enhanced the reading experience. In the end, the preponderance of evidence supported a phonetic approach.

Research next examined the most effective means of conducting phonics instruction. Two approaches were compared: the synthetic and the analytic. The *synthetic approach* first teaches letter sounds in isolation and then the blending of these sounds. The *analytic approach*, in contrast, analyzes learned sight words to deduce phonic rules. The evidence on this issue is far less conclusive, although a slight edge is given to the synthetic approach when the ability to read orally, identify unknown words, and accumulate a sight vocabulary are the criterial measures.

Comprehension ability has not been included as a measure in the two research questions we have addressed for two reasons: (1) Many of the early researchers did not include such measures, and (2) those who did reported mixed findings. We will return to this issue after describing more contemporary work on word identification instruction.

In keeping with the times, phonics research has become increasingly specialized. An important concern has become the extent to which students who are taught a phonetic approach can use this skill to decode unfamiliar words. Hence, students' ability to segment and blend word parts has received attention. This led to the development of an ordered set of skills, with the ability to (1) identify grapheme-phoneme correspondences prerequisite to the direct instruction of (2) phonemic analysis, which in turn is prerequisite to the (3) instruction of blending. The most effective blending instruction appears to be visually presenting and pronouncing a word (e.g., *make*). Consonants are then substituted (e.g., *flake*), and each word is pronounced. It should be emphasized that, while some children will apply blending skills to new words spontaneously, others require direct instruction across a number of patterns before they can do so successfully.

Other general approaches to word identification are structural and contextual analysis. *Structural analysis* includes the instruction in syllabication, base words, and affixes. *Contextual analysis* emphasizes the use of an unknown word in a sentence as a means of identifying it. While both approaches have intuitive appeal and are certainly components of a number of reading instructional programs, they have not received the same extensive investigation as phonics instruction, and the data that have been collected are inconclusive. One trend that is particularly worthy of note is that students with reading problems consistently seem to profit less from these instructional approaches than those without such difficulties. One reason for this may be that a certain level of proficiency with word identification is prerequisite to the use of these approaches.

To summarize, the evidence suggests that intensive programs of direct instruction on the use of phonics that follow an analysis-segmentation-blending sequence result in the acquisition of successful word identification skills. The data on structural and contextual analysis are less conclusive. And, importantly, the word identification instruction may not enhance and in fact may negatively affect comprehension skills. We would therefore propose using *a very careful balance between the direct instruction of word identification skills (beginning with phonetic analysis) and the direct instruction and monitoring of comprehension skills,* even if the comprehension skills were initially taught by listening to prose.

Another major objective in the instruction of students with reading difficulty is *fluency*, which is generally defined by both rate and accuracy. While formulas have been used to establish the most efficient reading rate (cf. Carver, 1982), we endorse a very ecological approach that argues that one must consider, at the very least, the purpose for reading, the material being read, the grade level of the reader, and the general expectancy of the classroom teacher (e.g., the fluency of the "best readers" at that grade level). Furthermore, it would seem counterproductive to stress fluency in oral reading without regard for comprehension. We will evaluate several instructional procedures that attend to these various features and can be incorporated in the classroom.

Lovitt and Hansen (1976), for example, investigated the "skip and drill" method used to enhance the oral reading and comprehension of primary and middle school LD students. For each student, data were collected on the correct rate per minute, incorrect rate per minute, and percent correct on comprehension questions. A criterion that represented a 20 percent increase over the current level was determined. Each student worked from a basal reader divided into four parts, with an equal number of stories in each. The students were told that if they achieved criterion performance on all three measures, they could skip that portion of the book and move to the next, an attractive proposition to these students, who were not performing at their grade level. They were also told that if they did not achieve criterion, they would be drilled. The oral reading drill involved repeated reading and direct instruction on error words. The comprehension drill was to return to the book to find the information to answer the comprehension questions correctly. The results indicated that (1) students' oral reading fluency often improved without drill; (2) practice in locating information improved comprehension; and (3) the students enjoyed the intervention because of the opportunity to advance in their texts.

Repeated reading, which was part of the above intervention, is frequently recommended as a means of increasing fluency, particularly for students who have reading difficulty. This procedure, which requires the student to reread a segment of text until a certain level of proficiency is achieved, is based on the rationale that repeated readings provide the opportunity for students to acquire automaticity with word attack skills. A number of studies have supported this notion (Gonzales & Elijah, 1984; Samuels, 1979). The most current research, however, suggests that increases in reading speed associated with the repeated reading method depend upon the amount of shared words among the stories. If the stories have few common words, repeated reading is no more effective for improving speed than an equivalent amount of time spent in nonrepetitive reading (Rashotte & Torgesen, 1985).

Pflaum and Pascarella (1980) designed and investigated an intervention not only to increase reading accuracy but also to instruct students in monitoring their own fluency. Their subjects were middle-school LD students. The first component of instruction used a tape recording of a student model making oral reading errors, which the students were to evaluate for their effects on comprehension. After achieving criterion performance in identifying and judging the errors, the students recorded and evaluated the significance of their own errors. In the second component, the model self-corrected serious errors. The students listened and read along, marking the self-corrections on their own copies of the passage. This exercise was followed by: (1) discussions of the purpose of self-correction, (2) practice in using context in a cloze task, and (3) recording and analyzing their own errors. The results indicated that those students who received both conditions *and* who were reading at least at the third-grade level benefitted most from the instruction. This intervention is effective in two respects: It teaches students that reading errors become problematic when they impede comprehension. Furthermore, the use of the model and the opportunity for guided feedback provided a means of gradually transferring control of self-monitoring (the cognitive developmental strategy) from the teacher to the student.

Since guided oral reading occupies a significant amount of time and attention in reading programs and since this activity is principally directed at improving fluency, we conclude this section with a discussion of the most effective of such procedures. Hoffman (1979) has suggested that teachers make at least three decisions during oral reading activities: (1) which miscues should be attended to, (2) when to respond to errors, and (3) how to respond to these mistakes. The decisions vary according to the abilities of the students. Hoffman and his colleagues (Hoffman et al., 1984) conducted a large-scale investigation of the effects of teacher-pupil interactions during oral reading. Their first significant finding was that there was a negative relationship between error rate and achievement, supporting *the need for students to practice reading with materials with which they achieve at least a 95 percent success rate.* At lower rates, they encounter frequent failure and frustration that leads to the constant disruption in their oral reading. In addition, low success rates minimize the opportunities for using such strategies as context cues to identify unknown words. There was also a negative relationship between immediately supplying the word when students hesitated and achievement. Delayed feedback, on the other hand, resulted in a greater number of self-corrections and also encouraged students to read on, thereby permitting the use of context cues.

Hansen (1975) investigated teachers' feedback to students when they made oral reading errors. When a student made a mistake, the teacher first said, "Try another way." Students were able to self-correct 40 percent of the time. If the alternative was not effective or if the students hesitated for three to five seconds, the teachers told the students to employ the following sequence of steps: (1) finish the sentence and guess the word to cue context clues; (2) break the word into parts and pronounce each one to cue the segmentation and analysis of words; (3) the teacher covers each part of the word and asks the students to decode each part; (4) the teacher asks, "What sound does ——— make?" (cueing the use of phonic clues); and (5) the teacher supplies the word.

In sum, instruction for fluency must attend to rate, accuracy, and comprehension. *Time spent reading is perhaps the single most important factor*

Table 9.1   Instructional Objectives of Activities Before, During, and After Reading

Before	During	After
Activate, assess, and provide relevant background information	Focus attention	Assess the extent to which the purpose has been met
Instruct in key vocabulary and concepts	Facilitate interaction with the text	Integrate the information that has been presented
Call attention to the structural features of the text	Evaluate comprehension	Consolidate the information read
Determine a purpose for reading		Apply the information to new learning situations
Generate a framework for student self-monitoring of comprehension		

Note. Adapted from *Teaching Reading as Thinking* by A. S. Palincsar, D. S. Ogle, B. F. Jones, and E. G. Carr, 1986, Alexandria, VA: Association for Supervision and Curriculum Development

in improving fluency. Such time is spent most efficiently when students are reading material written at a level at which they can successfully employ contextual clues and experience continuous rather than disjointed reading. Guided oral reading is particularly helpful when students are encouraged (and provided the means) to monitor their reading and correct their errors instead of being interrupted or given the missing words.

The next three sections address instructional opportunities before, during, and after reading text, emphasizing the motivation of the reader to engage in strategic reading and the role of the teacher in this activity (see Table 9.1).

Appropriate Teacher and Learner Activities

Activities Before Reading

It is helpful to begin by contemplating the purpose of instructional activity before students read the text. A comprehensive list of the instructional objectives of prereading are listed in Table 9–1.

Activating Relevant Background Knowledge

Recalling the role of schemata in understanding text from Chapter 2, one purpose of activating relevant background knowledge is to provide the opportunity for achieving an interface between the schemata already available to the learner and the new material in the text. In addition, it is important to *assess the quality* of the learner's background knowledge to help determine the extent to which (1) the student can independently achieve meaning, and (2) the teacher must assist in that process. In addition, research such as that by Anderson, Smith, and Ross (in press) and Alvermann, Smith, and Readance (1985) in science instruction shows that students who are naive or who possess partial or incorrect knowledge about concepts will recast the information they are reading so that it conforms to their existing knowledge. If that prior knowledge is incorrect, reading to learn becomes a very dysfunctional procedure.

We offer two examples of how to activate and assess background knowledge, one with primary school children and the other with older students. Hansen (1981) used metaphor to teach her second-grade students that we understand new information best when we "weave" that information into information that is already in our brains. To render this metaphor more concrete, she gave each child a sheet of gray paper (to represent the brain) and three strips of brightly colored paper to represent the new knowledge. Hansen then selected three important ideas from the story the children would read and introduced each in a two-step procedure: First, she asked a question related to possible previous experiences of the children. Second, she asked the children to speculate on something similar that might happen in the story. After the youngsters had orally responded to the first question, they recorded their own experiences on the gray paper. Following discussion of the second question, children wrote their own hypotheses on the colored strips. This process was repeated for each idea Hansen presented. The group discussed why it was important to relate new ideas to known ideas and then culminated the activity by weaving the strips into flaps of the gray paper. Comparing this procedure with a vocabulary instruction condition and a condition in which students were taught according to the plan proposed by the basal reader, Hansen found that those students who had activated their knowledge performed better on measures that assessed their ability to draw inferences from the material read.

Langer (1984a) has investigated a procedure she calls PReP (Pre-Reading Plan) with students in grade three through graduate school. The purpose of PReP is, once again, to draw upon students' existing knowledge about a topic during reading. The teacher prepares for the PReP by selecting central concepts from the passage to be read that can be represented by words, phrases, or pictures. The teacher then engages the

---

Box 9.1 Phases of PReP

1. Elicit initial associations by asking, "Tell me anything that comes to mind when you think of ———." The teacher non-judgmentally accepts all responses and records them on the board or an overhead projector.
2. Generate reflections on initial associations by asking, "What made you think of ———?" This helps the students become aware of what they know and judge whether this information is relevant to what they will read. Listening and interacting with the teacher and other students helps the students build on what they already know.
3. Lead the students in refining and reformulating their knowledge by asking, "Based on our discussion, do you have any new ideas about ———?"

Note. Adapted from "Examining Background Knowledge and Text Comprehension" by J. Langer, 1984, *Reading Research Quarterly, 19,* pp. 468–481.

---

students in the three phases presented in Box 9.1. Next, the students read, already aware of the knowledge they possess about the topic.

Langer also suggests how teachers can evaluate the quality of students' background knowledge while they are assessing the quantity. She advocates categorizing student-generated knowledge into three levels of organization: (1) When students provide definitions or analogies for concepts or draw links connecting the various concepts, they have fairly well-organized knowledge about the topic and will need minimal guidance in reading. (2) When students provide examples, describe attributes, or define aspects of concepts, their knowledge is somewhat organized. They may require additional assistance to understand the text. (3) When students make only very tangential or superficial remarks or recall firsthand experiences that may be only remotely relevant to the topic, their knowledge is diffusely organized, suggesting the need for considerable guidance in reading. PReP has been determined to increase the comprehension of average readers; however, while it improves the quality of knowledge of poor readers, they still need direct instruction to increase their comprehension.

Implementing Direct Instruction in Vocabulary and Concepts

Historically, vocabulary instruction has assumed a rather prominent role in reading instruction because it is frequently prescribed in basal reader manuals. Teachers are encouraged to list "difficult" or "new" words on the board, to elicit definitions from students or provide them if none are forthcoming, and perhaps to have the students use the word in a sentence. In addition, rather intensive vocabulary instruction programs have been investigated (Beck, McCaslin, & McKeown, 1980; Jenkins, Pany, & Schreck, 1978). Interestingly, these studies have yielded rather paltry results. Nagy and Anderson (1984) have suggested that "even the most ruthlessly systematic direct vocabulary instruction could neither account for a significant proportion of all words that children actually learn, nor cover more than a modest proportion of the words they will encounter in school reading materials" (p. 304). They came to this conclusion after an exhaustive and systematic analysis indicated that there are 88,500 word families in the English language! What's a teacher to do? Elaborating upon the recommendations of Nagy and Anderson, we suggest that any vocabulary instruction should be evaluated in terms of the extent to which it facilitates the students' ability to learn words on their own. Perhaps the first step is to stimulate interest in learning and using new vocabulary. The class can be challenged to use rich vocabulary in discussions, to find new words they have learned in the text in other contexts, and of course to enliven their own writing by increasing the diversity of words they use. Second, instructing students in procedures for inferring word meanings from word parts is a valuable activity. Such instruction focuses on word families, such as *real, realistic, realism,* and *reality*. This procedure helps students build bridges between the familiar and the new and calls attention to the processes used in word formation, which can then serve as a useful tool in attacking unfamiliar words. Finally, there is little question that word meanings are frequently derived from context. Thus, encouraging students to read for cues surrounding the unknown word is a constructive activity.

Because vocabulary words are frequently chosen to represent a concept to be presented in the text, both vocabulary and concepts can be taught using the "semantic mapping" procedure. Although semantic mapping can be used during and after reading, we will highlight its prereading use. Johnson and Pearson (1984) have suggested the steps of semantic mapping presented in Box 9.2. We will return to the use of mapping in our discussion of postreading activities. (Also see Chapter 17.)

The Importance of Text Structure

As the third prereading instructional objective, teachers should call attention to the *text structure,* or how the ideas are interrelated to convey a message to the reader (Meyer and Rice, 1984). When a text begins, "There are many ways in which the sequence of developments which led to the eruption of World War II parallel those which culminated in World War I," readers have been told of two probable features of the selection. First, we are likely to be reading about events that occurred chronologically. Second, this sequence will probably be compared and contrasted

---

Box 9.2   Semantic Mapping

---

1. Choose a word from the passage the students will read that represents the main idea.
2. Write the chosen word and ask the students to generate as many related words as they can.
3. Have the students share their word lists as the teacher records and charts them in broad categories.
4. Present additional words not generated by the students that will appear in the text and be important to comprehension.
5. Ask the students to assign names to the groups of words on the map (e.g., given the key word *desert* and the list *dry, hot, sandy,* and *windy,* the label might be *characteristics*).
6. Most importantly, lead the class in discussing and integrating the concepts. (Returning to desert example, the teacher might relate irrigation and modes of transportation to the characteristics of the desert).
7. Focus the students' attention on those portions of the map that will be particularly useful in reading the passage.

Note. Adapted from *Teaching Reading Comprehension* by P. D. Pearson & D. D. Johnson, 1978, New York: Rinehart & Winston.

---

with those that happened prior to World War I. This knowledge gives the reader a very specific purpose for reading as well as a map to guide that reading. The kind of student who is a teacher's pleasure might draw a line down a blank sheet of paper, labeling one half "W.W.I" and the second "W.W.II," without even reading another sentence. Furthermore, the map provides a means of monitoring comprehension, for if the expected parallels are not apparent, the reader will reread. Of course, it does sometimes happen that the author has, in a most "inconsiderate" (Armbruster & Anderson, 1984) fashion, set up the reader without following through. Authors, however, are generally more faithful to the structure portended than not. Awareness of this structure provides an excellent vehicle for summarizing and remembering what was read. Finally, a very valuable benefit of attending to text structure is that it can enhance writing (Gordon & Braun, 1983; Raphael, Englert, & Kirschner, 1985; Taylor & Beach, 1984).

Instructing Students in Text Structure

Initially, the teacher will most likely have to identify the text structure for the students. As they become more experienced with various forms of structure, they can preview the text, looking for cues that suggest the structure. One intervention for conducting text structure instruction used the following sequence of activities with sixth graders (Raphael & Kirschner, in press). First, the students were told they would be studying the way text is organized and why it is important to understand this organization. They were introduced to the characteristics of a specific type of text structure—compare-contrast—and asked to apply it very concretely. They were told that they had to choose between two puppies and could use the four questions to help them decide: (1) What is being compared/contrasted? (2) On what basis are they being compared/contrasted? (3) How are they alike? and (4) How are they different? After completing this activity, the students worked as a group with brief compare-contrast texts, filling in a chart with answers to these four questions. Each day, they reviewed the purpose for the activity, the form of the text, and the questions to be answered. Then they independently applied this knowledge to longer pieces of text, completing the chart as they read. In just four days, the students improved their ability to recall and organize text.

Several features of this procedure should be highlighted. First, the investigators gave the students the information about what they were learning and in which situations it would be helpful, which is equivalent to the declarative and conditional knowledge discussed in previous chapters. Second, they provided the procedural knowledge necessary to use text structure to enhance comprehension. They thus offered students not only this "how to" knowledge but also explicit guidance: After presenting the prerequisite concepts and vocabulary, the students were given the opportunity to apply this knowledge in a very familiar context. Following this practice, the students applied the knowledge to a short, highly structured piece of text in a group situation. This group work gave the teacher a chance to model the use of the question forms in the completion of the graph and the students an opportunity for guided practice.

Guiding Students' Choice of Reading Strategies

The final two purposes of prereading activity, setting a purpose for reading and generating a framework for monitoring understanding, are interrelated and therefore will be discussed together. When teachers set the purpose for reading, they are making the criterial task explicit. If the purpose is to answer the questions at the end of the chapter, this might suggest skimming to locate the needed information. Skimming will not be an effective strategy, however, if the task is to prepare for a multiple-choice or essay examination. Strategic readers will approach the reading activity in a manner reflective of the criterial task; less skillful readers need to be guided in this respect.

Determining the purpose also establishes the very large framework for monitoring understanding. While this framework may be sufficient for the skilled reader, the less proficient will require instruction on the specific steps. Perhaps the metaphor of a map will clarify the distinction being made. Some people seem to possess an uncanny sense of direction and, shown where they are in relationship to where they want to be, can make all the right decisions about where and when to turn, relying on what appear to be internal compasses. Others want to see their course plotted on a map that is clearly marked east, north, west, and south, with a few streets thrown in for good measure. There are also those who can reach a destination only if it is laid out in a list that indicates landmarks, left turns, and right turns. Students who have a history of reading difficulties fall into the third category as they maneuver their way through text. We will describe specific strategies they can use to monitor their reading comprehension.

Activities During Reading

The general criteria for evaluating the merits of a particular reading strategy were presented in Table 9.1. The proliferation of instructional studies in reading comprehension, however, forced us to use two additional criteria in selecting sample interventions: (1) their attempt to teach cognitive strategies, and (2) their successful implementation with problem readers. We will begin by describing interventions that address rather discrete skills, proceed to more general ones, and conclude with those that have an array of components.

Direct Strategy Instruction

Prompted by the important and pervasive nature of main idea identification in reading, Baumann (1984) investigated a procedure to instruct students to find main ideas presented both explicitly (as in a clear topic sentence) and implicitly (as in a dominant relationship among the details of a paragraph or passage). Baumann taught sixth-grade students to identify: (1) explicit main ideas and details in paragraphs; (2) implicit main ideas and details in paragraphs; (3) explicit main ideas and details in passages; and (4) implicit main ideas and details in passages. He concluded by teaching them to outline passages in which main ideas were presented either explicitly or implicitly.

Baumann followed five steps in teaching each of these skills. First, he provided a purpose for the lesson by explaining how the skill to be learned would enhance reading comprehension. Second, he gave an example of how understanding the relationship between the main idea and detail information would improve comprehension. Third, he engaged in direct instruction by leading the students through the process of identifying the main idea and the supporting details. Fourth, he made the students principally responsible for identifying the information, while he provided guidance and feedback. Finally, he had the students practice independently. Compared to their counterparts who used a basal reading program that covered the same skills but did not include the guided components, the students who received this direct instruction performed better on measures of ability to recognize implicit and explicit main ideas and to outline the main ideas in paragraphs and passages.

Adams, Carnine, and Gersten (1982) employed identical procedures to teach the following strategies: (1) preview the passage by reading headings and subheadings for an overall idea of the subject; (2) recite the subheadings until they are memorized; (3) indicate what each subheading suggests should be learned in that segment of text; (4) read to find the details needed to answer questions they posed and other important information; (5) reread the subheadings and recite the important information. This rereading and recitation was conducted cumulatively by way of a review. The instruction progressed from modeling each step to independently applying each step, while the teacher provided feedback. This procedure was found to be more effective than an independent study situation in which the students: (1) were told to study material until they were ready to be tested, (2) responded to a series of questions, and (3) received feedback regarding their responses.

Wong and Jones (1982) investigated the effects of teaching LD students how to generate their own questions to monitor their comprehension. The first step in their procedure was to teach main idea identification until the students achieved 80 percent accuracy. The students next received explanation, modeling, and guided practice in the following steps: (1) find and underline the main idea, (2) think of a question about that information, (3) answer that question, and (4) review the question and answer to evaluate the information they supplied. Students in a control group read the same materials,but were asked only to evaluate the quality of the writing. The students who received the intervention were more successful than the control students in predicting the kinds of information that would be included in a test of comprehension, answering comprehension questions, and recalling the material.

Each of the above studies has focused on the self-control of the instructed strategies by teaching those strategies to mastery or providing for independent practice and evaluation of strategy use. A study by Day (1980; Brown & Day, 1983) demonstrates the importance of self-control for students who have reading problems. While the students in Day's study were young adults, many had fifth-grade reading skills. The intervention was designed to teach the students to use basic rules of summarization: delete trivia and redundancy; identify superordinates of exemplars of a concept (e.g., name lists); select topic sentences when present; and invent topic sentences when they are not provided. Students were assigned to four instructional conditions. Students in the self-management condition received only the most general information about summaries, namely that they stated the main ideas and exercised economy with words. Students in the rules condition were taught the definition of a summary and the rules outlined above for completing a summary. Students in the rules plus self-management condition received the same instruction as those in the first two groups, but were not told how to integrate and apply these rules. Finally, a fourth group received not only the rule and self-management instruction but also *explicit directions* on when to use each rule and how to evaluate the effectiveness of their implementation. The results, measured by having the students write summaries, indicated that, at the very least, rules plus self-management instruction was necessary for students with no identified learning problems. Students with learning problems required the most explicit of the instructional conditions before they were able to show an improvement in their ability to summarize text. This finding was replicated by Kurtz and Borkowski (1985) in a study of middle-school students.

The value of calling students' attention to text structure has been discussed as a prereading activity. Taylor and Beach (1984), however, examined an intervention that integrates the use of text structure and summarization during reading. Their study was designed to determine whether summarizing text (based on its organization) improved middle-school students' writing and comprehension of expository passages. The students read social studies text by segments (as indicated by headings) and wrote a summary of the main ideas as well as three supporting details for each segment. The teacher provided feedback by comparing and discussing their writing with a teacher-generated summary. This instruction occurred for one hour a week for seven weeks. The results indicated that students receiving this instruction had better recall of text, gave more accurate responses to short-answer questions, and could write better opinion essays than students who did not receive the intervention.

The instructional procedures discussed thus far have all been investigated with the use of expository, or fact-telling, text. It is also possible, of course, to use strategies with narrative, or storytelling, materials. There has been particular interest in the instruction of story grammar as a strategy condition. Short and Ryan (1984), for example, conducted a study in which they taught skilled and unskilled fourth graders to underline the information that would answer five story grammar questions: (1) Who is the main character? (2) Where and when did the story take place? (3) What did the main character do? (4) How did the story end? (5) How did the main character feel? Once again a direct instruction procedure was employed. The strategy was first explained to the students as a game called "Clue." A storyteller provided clues that allowed the reader to make predictions. The readers looked for clues, asked questions about what was coming up in the story, and made predictions based upon their own experiences. The teacher then modeled how to use the story grammar questions to be a reader detective. Following this demonstration, the students and teacher practiced together.

The study by Short and Ryan is interesting not just for its examination of story grammar instruction but also for the instructional conditions that it compared. While one group received the strategy instruction, another received attribution training, which consisted of teaching the students the relationship between effort and outcome and five self-statements about effort: (1) Enjoy the story. (2) Praise yourself for a job well done. (3) Try hard. (4) Just think how happy you will be when it comes time for the test and you're doing well. (5) Give yourself a pat on the back. A third group received both attribution and strategy training. The effectiveness of the interventions was evaluated by having the students complete a recall measure and comparing the notes they took to use the story grammar strategy on a narrative passage that they read independently without any prompting. The results indicated that while the strategy training significantly enhanced performance, attribution training alone did not and only minimally augmented the effects of strategy training. Note, however, that in all of the above studies, reading comprehension is the goal and that strategies are taught as means of achieving that goal.

Reciprocal Teaching: Scaffolded Instruction

The teacher's role in strategy instruction is a unique one. We will elaborate upon this role by describing an intervention by Palincsar and Brown (1984, 1986) called *reciprocal teaching, which is a dialogue between the teacher and students regarding the text they are reading.* The teacher and students take turns leading the discussion. The dialogue is structured by the use of four strategies. First, the most important information is identified and integrated by summarizing across sentences, paragraphs, and the passage as a whole. When the students first begin the reciprocal teaching procedure, their efforts are generally focused at the sentence and paragraph levels. As they become more proficient, they are able to work at the paragraph and passage levels. Second, questions are generated to reinforce the summarizing and carry the reader one step further in the comprehension activity. When students generate questions, they must first identify the kind of information that has enough significance to provide the substance of a question. They then form it into a question and self-test to ascertain that they can indeed provide an answer. Question generating is a flexible strategy because students can be taught and encouraged to formulate questions at many levels. Some school situations, for example, require students to memorize supporting details; others demand that they infer or apply new information from the text. Third, students are taught the need for clarifying, which is particularly important when working with students with reading problems. As we discussed earlier, these students may believe that the purpose of reading is to pronounce the words correctly; they may not be particularly uneasy when the words and the passage do not make sense. When asked to clarify, however, they learn that there may be many reasons why text is difficult to understand (e.g., incomplete information, new concepts or vocabulary, or unclear referent words). They are thus taught to be alert to such impediments to comprehension and to take the necessary measures to restore meaning (e.g., reread, ask for help, or read on). Fourth, students must predict what the author will discuss next. To do this successfully, they must activate their relevant background knowledge on the topic. The students thus have a purpose for reading: to confirm or disprove their hypotheses. Furthermore, the opportunity has been created linking the new knowledge they will encounter in the text with their existing knowledge. The predicting strategy also facilitates the use of text structure as students learn that headings, subheadings, and questions embedded in the text are useful means of anticipating what might occur. Notice that this strategy enables readers to do much of the important prereading activities discussed earlier. The acquisition of these strategies is not the ultimate goal of instruction, however, for they are but a means to an end. They provide a vehicle for teaching students to read for meaning and to monitor their reading to ensure that they are understanding.

Method   When reciprocal teaching is first introduced, the teacher and students discuss the many reasons text may be difficult to understand, the importance of a strategic approach to reading, and when and how this particular activity will help them understand and monitor their comprehension as they read. In other words, the students are provided declarative and conditional knowledge. We know from the research of Duffy, Roehler, Meloth, Varrus, Book, Putnam, & Wesselman (1986) that students who are given this kind of explanation indicate greater awareness of which strategies they have been taught and when and how they should be used. This awareness is prerequisite to maintaining and applying the strategies. The students then learn the procedure that will be used to teach the strategies—taking turns as teacher.

Having provided this explanation, the teacher can begin teaching using the following components: instruction, modeling, guided practice, praise, and teacher judgment. *Instruction* is to define each strategy and ensure that the students have minimal competence with all before they begin the dialogue. The introduction of questioning starts with a discussion of the role that questions play in our lives, particularly in school. The students are asked to generate information-seeking questions about everyday events, which lets the teacher know that they do indeed know how to phrase a question. The students are then asked to form questions given simple sentences and are supplied words they might use to start their questions. Gradually, the question words are eliminated and the sentences become longer. After brief instruction with each of the strategies, the group begins the dialogue, and the major instructional component be-comes *modeling*. In this phase of reciprocal teaching, the adult teacher leads the dialogue, modeling the use of the four strategies by thinking aloud. The students are encouraged to comment on the teacher's sum-maries, add their own predictions and clarifications, and respond to the teacher-generated questions. As the instruction proceeds, however, more responsibility is transferred to the students through *guided practice*. The teacher is now monitoring the students' success in employing the strat-egies, *praising* their attempts, and providing further modeling and in-struction as *teacher judgment* indicates.

The hallmark of this type of instruction is its *interactive* nature, for there is on-going interplay between the teacher and students as well as among the students as they work cooperatively toward the goal of un-derstanding the text. Such instruction has been called scaffolded instruc-tion (Wood, Bruner, & Ross, 1976). This is an appropriate metaphor when one considers that a scaffold is an adjustable and temporary support. Here the teacher supports each student in the acquisition and mastery of the strategies by using explanation, instruction, and modeling, although this support is temporary since the student is challenged to use the strategy independently as comprehension increases. Recent work with first-grade students suggests that reciprocal teaching can also be used as a listening comprehension activity, with the students and teachers engaging in the same type of dialogue while the teacher reads the text aloud to the stu-dents (Brown and Palincsar, in press; Palincsar 1986).

Another Scaffolding Approach to Direct Instruction

Idol-Maestas (in press) taught third- and fourth-grade students with poor comprehension skills to use a story mapping strategy to enhance under-standing. She began the intervention by having the teacher model the use of a story map that required the students to identify the setting (character, time, and place), the problem posed in the story, the goal to be achieved, the action toward achieving this goal, and the outcome. In this phase, the students and teacher completed the story maps as a group, with the teacher completing it on an overhead projector while the students filled in their own copies. The students were then asked to complete the maps independently while reading or after reading the story (depending on student preference). The teacher next led the group in a discussion identifying the elements of the story map, once again filling it in on an overhead projector while the students compared their maps and made any necessary changes. The students then independently used the story maps without the group discussion and, finally, read passages and an-swered questions without completing the story maps. The effects of this intervention were measured by assessing: (1) the answers to comprehension questions that referred to the components of the story map, (2) the students' progress through the basal reader, (3) scores on a reading achievement test, and (4) the answers to comprehension questions after the students listened to stories. The results on each of these measures indicated that the story mapping procedure was a very successful intervention, particularly for LD and low-achieving students.

Each intervention described in this section represents a successful cognitive developmental approach to enhancing and monitoring text comprehension. The procedures shared many features, and they all gradually transferred the responsibility for applying the strategy from the teacher to the students. In this context, teacher modeling and guided practice (or scaffolding) figured prominently: the students were given the opportunity to acquire a degree of mastery of the strategies before they were expected to apply them independently. Finally, the level of difficulty of the material was controlled so that the students were working at an instructional reading level.

Activities After Reading

The instructional objectives of the activities conducted after reading text were presented in Table 9.1. When we pause to think about current practice with regard to postreading activities, among those that come quickly to mind are asking questions and completing worksheets. We will critically deal with each and propose others as well.

The prominent role of questioning in the classroom has stimulated a good deal of research on the use of *adjunct questions* before, during, and after reading. Questioning can serve many of the objectives identified throughout this chapter, including directing attention to the text, assisting with the integration of information presented in the text, and building relationships between the students' prior knowledge and new information. An exhaustive review of this research, conducted by Anderson and Biddle (1975), indicates that performance on measures of recall and understanding is better if adjunct questions appear after the text is read rather than before. Furthermore, there is a relationship between the type of question asked and the type of learning that occurs because students interact differentially with the text depending upon the information necessary to answer the question. Wixson (1983), for example, conducted a study in which fifth-grade students read expository passages. Afterward, they were asked to answer either textually explicit, textually implicit, or scriptually implicit questions (see Chapter 8). The students in the Wixson study read the assigned passages, answered the assigned questions, and were told that the investigator would return in a week and ask them to write about what they had read. The effect of answering the various question types was assessed using this recall measure. Wixson discerned that students assigned textually explicit questions indicated verbatim reproduction of text-based information in their recalls. In contrast, those assigned the textually implicit questions made more inferences from the text. As one might expect, those students given the scriptually implicit questions interpreted the text using prior knowledge to fill in the gaps. What is particularly salient about these results is the relationship between the type of question asked and the learning outcome. Question-asking activity (Guszak, 1972) should be guided by the purpose for which students are reading.

As described thus far, question asking in postreading instruction is a teacher-directed activity; however, it is possible to increase students' responsibility in this activity. In a series of studies by Raphael and her colleagues (Raphael & McKinney, 1983; Raphael & Wonnacott, 1985), the goal was to increase students' sensitivity to the relationships between comprehension questions and information sources. After first determining that sensitivity to sources of information distinguished the performance of good and poor readers on questions, the investigators successfully used modeling and guided practice to teach sixth-grade poor readers strategies for identifying and responding to textually explicit, textually implicit, and scriptually implicit questions. Instruction began by explaining and providing the following labels for the question. Textually explicit questions were called "right-there questions." Textually implicit questions were called "think-and-search questions," while scriptually implicit questions were entitled "on-my-own questions." The students were then given text samples, accompanying questions as well as their answers, and labels for each question-answer relationship, which they were asked to explain. Next the students were provided with text and questions and answers and had to apply the appropriate labels. Finally, the students were given text and questions and asked to supply the answers as well as the labels for the question-answer relationships. With each step the teachers gave the students feedback on their responses. The results of this research indicated that students who received instruction in question-answer relationships more accurately identified question types, answered questions, and matched the answer to the question type than those who merely received practice in answering the various question types.

As mentioned, in addition to asking questions, a typical postreading activity is the completion of skill sheets or workbooks. Unfortunately, *research suggests that the amount of time spent in such tasks is unrelated to gains in reading* (Leinhard, Zigmond, & Cooley, 1981).

Osborn (1984) has suggested certain valuable guidelines regarding the judicious use of workbook exercises. First, the workbook task should be evaluated to determine that a sufficient proportion is relevant to the instruction. Second, the language, vocabulary, and concepts presented in the task should also relate to those in the reading lesson. Third, the task should be substantial enough so that the students learn instead of simply being exposed to the material. Finally, the directions should be clear and briefly explain the purpose of the activity.

We conclude this section by discussing an instructional activity that integrates before, during, and after reading components: the procedure known as SPaRCS (Armbruster et al., 1986). The acronym stands for the three steps of the procedure: (1) Survey/Predict occurs before reading, (2) Read/Construct occurs during reading, and (3) Summarize occurs following reading. SPaRCS is distinguished by the use of graphic outlines that allow students to predict the categories of information they will be reading and present them in table form. This parallels semantic mapping, although that was described as a before reading activity and in SPaRCS the outline is used as an after reading activity. After the text is read, the students brainstorm to identify its key ideas and facts. They then question the teacher and one another to fill in any remaining gaps, and organize this information by using and revising the categories identified prior to reading. Finally, they construct a summary by integrating the information that has been presented in the graphic outline. The authors caution that while able readers can independently and quite creatively engage in this activity, students with reading difficulty should receive considerable guidance in the use of the graphic organizer and learn to apply it by first working with very clearly structured and presented materials.

Having examined an array of activities that can be conducted during reading instruction, we will now discuss guidelines for evaluating the success of such instruction.

Demonstrating Successful Teaching and Learning

Evaluating Reading Instruction with LD Students

In the previous chapter, we discussed a number of means by which teachers can evaluate the reading skills of their students. In this portion, we wish to discuss how teachers can evaluate their *own* instruction.

The Extent to Which Instruction Allows Students to Engage in Sustained Reading

Research has repeatedly suggested that there is a definite relationship between the time that students spend reading and reading achievement (Greany, 1980; Walberg & Tsai, 1984). The data indicate that *reading as little as ten minutes a day enhances reading proficiency.* To help students achieve this goal, teachers must select reading materials carefully, ensuring that decoding problems will not impede the flow and enjoyment of reading. A wide variety of materials should be available, with trade books assuming a prominent role. (See also Chapter 10 on using children's literature in the instructional program.) In fact, when Bruce (1984) compared the stories available in basal readers with those in trade books, he found that the latter had more intriguing plots and characters. Additionally, trade books have a richness of vocabulary, sentence structure, and text structure that is frequently absent in basal readers (Fielding, Wilson, & Anderson, 1986). Finally, we have spoken frequently of the role of modeling in instruction. Teachers have many opportunities to model an appreciation and hunger for literacy, sharing their enthusiasm for a new novel, the "I couldn't put it down" feeling that accompanies a good mystery, and the frustration of not feeling literate (e.g., at tax time). *A teacher whose students enjoy reading and read in their spare time is more successful than one whose students show two years' growth on a standardized test of word recognition but would not think to identify reading as something they do outside of school.*

The Extent to Which Instruction Enables Students to Function Independently

Whether the instructional aim is decoding skill, fluency, vocabulary knowledge, or comprehension, an important consideration is the extent to which instruction enables students to function independently. Students who have more perceived control of their learning activities express greater interest and enjoyment in those activities. Dweck and Elliott (1983) suggests that, rather than providing students with a series of success experiences and hoping that they will infer that they can be successful learners, it is more important to give them challenging tasks *and* the means of regulating their own activity as they complete those tasks. We have referred to these enabling activities as strategies. We have also spoken of the need to share with students the declarative, conditional, and procedural knowledge that accompanies these strategies so they can appropriately and flexibly employ them and monitor their success.

The Extent to Which the Reading Process Is Valued, Taught, and Evaluated

Teachers frequently feel constrained in their instruction by what tests will measure—usually discrete skills that may or may not enhance the reading process (e.g., sequencing a series of sentences, selecting the most appropriate title for a brief selection, or answering literal recall questions). The evaluation activities suggested in Chapter 8 are designed to call attention to the *process* of reading. When we evaluate instructional activities, we must ask the extent to which they communicate to students that the purpose of reading is to achieve meaning and offer students practice in reading for learning.

**The Frequency of Evaluating Instruction and Sharing the
Evaluations with Students**

Regardless of the instructional aim and procedure, it is important to
assess progress frequently to evaluate the appropriateness of the goals
and the effectiveness of the methods. Furthermore, it is imperative that
we share our evaluations with students. Graphs, for example, easily show
students how their oral reading rate and accuracy have improved. Samples of students' summaries or semantic maps can be saved and compared
over time to show change. Dialogues among students and teachers about
text can also be taped and shared to demonstrate changes in competency.
Sharing evaluations is an important step in increasing chances that students will maintain and apply the instructed skills independently.

Summary and Conclusions

We realize that the juggling metaphor used at the beginning of this chapter applies as readily to the teacher as to the reader. The teacher is
juggling time, behavior management, district and parent demands, heterogeneous students, and a myriad of other factors while trying to maintain a semblance of order, preserve mental health, and create opportunities
for learning. As with juggling, the misperception is frequently expressed
that "it looks so easy," but little could be farther from the truth.

Chapter 10

Using Children's Literature in the Instructional Program

Gaye McNutt

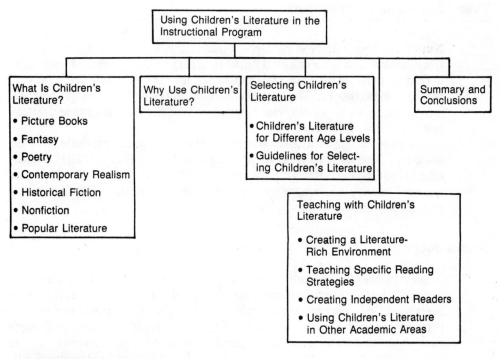

Questions to Consider

1. What is children's literature?
2. Why should children's literature be used in an instructional program for LD students?
3. How should children's literature be selected for use with LD students?
4. How should children's literature be used in an instructional program for LD students?

Although subjects covered in previous and subsequent chapters are obviously academic in nature, children's literature is not usually considered an academic subject, nor is it a content area in elementary schools, such as social studies and science. Instead, children's literature serves as a tool for teaching.

The format of this chapter will vary somewhat from that of other chapters, for there has been very little study of the effectiveness of using children's literature in teaching and even less of its effectiveness with the LD student. Much of this chapter is therefore based on the author's own experience teaching LD students or observing others work with them.

What Is Children's Literature?

Numerous books discuss children's literature (sometimes referred to as trade books) and offer many definitions. Perhaps the simplest definition is that it includes all materials published for children that are not basal readers or textbooks. The quality will therefore vary greatly. Teachers must try to choose wisely while remembering that the ultimate decision rests with the children.

A myriad of classification schemes exist for organizing children's literature. Those used in this chapter are based on Cullinan (1981), Hittleman (1983), Rose (1982), and Whitehead (1984), and include picture books, fantasy, poetry, contemporary realism, historical fiction, nonfiction and popular literature.

Picture Books

In picture books, the images play an important, if not predominant, role in conveying the author's meaning. Many children, once familiar with such books, can recognize particular illustrators' techniques even though they still cannot identify the writing styles of specific authors. Although such books are often considered appropriate only for young children, this is certainly not true, for they are especially useful for LD children with reading problems. Three subcategories of picture books are generally available: (1) naming or labeling books, (2) theme books, and (3) storybooks.

Fantasy

Fantasy is characterized by the use of imaginary places, events, things, or characters. In many of these books, the authors create imaginary worlds but make them believable. One popular type of fantasy is science fiction, which employs fantasy to project future events.

Poetry

Poetry often contains rhythm and rhyme, and may take many forms. It almost always requires a formal structure and the economical use of words. Mother Goose rhymes, nonsense rhymes, limericks, narrative poetry, free verse, quatrains, and couplets are often found in books of children's poetry. Although children are sometimes taught to write haiku, tanka (which has thirty-one syllables instead of the seventeen in haiku), and cinquain poetry, few examples are published.

Contemporary Realism

According to Cullinan (1981), "fiction set in modern times, with events that could occur, is called contemporary realism" (p. 28). Children can read these books to learn how other children handle certain problems or what the future may hold. Contemporary realism has characters who represent all types of humanity. In such books LD children can find children who have experienced problems similar to theirs (e.g., a divorce or death in the family).

Historical Fiction

Historical fiction is similar to contemporary realism except that the time frame is in the past. The language used in some of these books may actually reflect the historical period in which it is set. When chosen properly and used correctly, they can add a new dimension to teaching history and may help children bridge the gap between "now" and the more abstract "then."

Nonfiction

Nonfiction books include biographies, autobiographies, reference books, and informational books such as how-to manuals, photographic essays, and direct expository texts. The topics include history, mathematics, cooking, and arts and crafts. The books may document current or historical people, places, events, or cultures. While informational books are often useful in teaching social science, they also allow children to pursue their own interests. Biographies and autobiographies may also provide children with models of human behavior as well as inspiration.

Popular Literature

Popular literature includes posters, chants in children's games, slogans, jingles, jokes, graffitti, newspapers, magazines, and songs. While most of these items are not published as books and many are certainly not intended primarily for children, children are frequently interested in and influenced by popular literature.

Why Use Children's Literature?

Administrators and teachers can easily locate complete LD curricula in reading, language, math, and the like for kindergarten through grade six or even higher. Basal reading series, for example, typically contain readers, workbooks, duplicating masters, activity cards, filmstrips and/or audio tapes, picture and word cards, various tests for determining placement, progress, or mastery, and teacher's editions. While these materials are primarily used in regular education classes, there is usually ample information for adapting them for use with LD students. Furthermore, the market is replete with materials specifically designed for LD students. With so much material available, why should teachers use children's literature in their instructional program? The following vignette (see Box 10–1) illustrates the need for a program that uses material other than a "complete" published curriculum.

This example shows that basal readers often contain contrived, unnatural language that can seriously hamper comprehension. Gordon knew the words (i.e., he correctly read them aloud), but he did not understand what they meant. Furthermore, the fantasy in this story seemed to bother him and may have affected his ability to understand the text. If a selection from children's literature had been used, the teacher could have chosen one that contained language patterns similar to Gordon's that also avoided the use of fantasy.

Analyzing the language used in many basals (especially the beginning readers in grade one), Gourley (1984) determined that first graders make more reading miscues when the text does not adhere to common patterns of narration and discourse. That is, they find a text that digresses from good form more difficult to read, even though a readability formula might say it is at a "preprimer" level.

Although the above discussion shows why basal reading systems should not be used exclusively to teach reading to LD students, the question of why children's literature should be used remains. There are, however, four reasons. First, children's literature allows teachers to teach with the same type of material that children experience outside school. Second, by selecting children's literature that relates to the student's backgrounds, the children are more likely to perceive the learning as relevant. Third, because the supply of such literature is almost endless, teachers can choose several similar books to provide repeated instruction or practice as well as program for generalization. Fourth, and finally, children's literature can provide a natural language format, which, according to Smith (1983), can increase motivation and interest.

In sum, children's literature can help show that reading and writing

---

Box 10.1   Using Children's Literature: One Student's Experience

Gordon is an eight-year-old LD second grader. His teacher uses the HBJ Bookmark Reading Program (Early, Cooper, & Santeusanio, 1979), and also has him reading a story called "The Bug" in *Sun Up* (Mooser, 1979), the first preprimer. On the first page of the story, Mack, a talking rabbit, meets a bug who is wearing a sailor cap and collar. Gordon is asked to read the second page that pictures Mack in the water with a folded paper hat, which looks like a boat, talking to the bug, who is on the land. He flawlessly reads:

The hat went to the bug.
The bug went to the hat.
Mack said, "Up and in, Bug.
Up and in the hat!" (Mooser, 1979, p. 22)

Gordon's teacher asks him to tell the others about what he has just read. Instead of answering, Gordon seems quite concerned about the fact that the bug is standing up and, as he says, "Everybody knows bugs can't stand up." His teacher again asks him to tell the others about what he has read. Gordon looks at the words, frowns, fidgets, and finally shrugs his shoulders.

Teacher: Who is talking on this page?
Gordon: Mack, but rabbits aren't supposed to talk.
Teacher: That's right, Mack is talking. What does he want the bug to do:
[Gordon shrugs]
Teacher: Would you read only the words that Mack says?
Gordon: "Up and in, Bug. Up and in the hat!"
Teacher: That's very good. Now what does Mack want the bug to do?
Gordon: Wake up?
Teacher: No, he wants the bug to get in the boat.
Gordon (looking very surprised): If Mack wanted the bug to get in the boat, why didn't he say, "Get in the boat"? My dad always says, "Up and at 'em," when he wants us to wake up in the morning.

---

are meaningful and relevant, that learning is fun, that children are intelligent, that teachers are invaluable in the learning process, that schools are trustworthy, and that children's own interests, culture, and insights into language are valid, useful, and necessary.

Selecting Children's Literature

Few people would argue that many children have individual preferences for certain types of children's literature or even specific books. Some parents, for example, are fond of remembering that their youngster wanted to read a particular book over and over until it was memorized. Furthermore, educators are aware of such trends as intermediate-aged boys' preference for books on sports or action over fairy tales or alphabet books. Given this knowledge, are there specific guidelines to help select literature for an individual LD child or group of LD children? Unfortunately, no precise rules exist, although two bodies of general information may prove helpful. The first suggests types of children's literature that are appropriate for different age levels. The second focuses more specifically on how to choose children's literature.

Children's Literature for Different Age Levels

There are no unequivocal rules for specifying types of literature for certain chronological or developmental age levels, nor is there any definitive research about children's preferences at particular ages. Numerous authors (e.g., Butler, 1985; Cullinan, 1981; Glazer, 1980; Huck, 1979; Petty, Petty, & Becking, 1981; Trelease, 1985), however, have made such suggestions based on their own experiences and observations, as Table 10.1 presents.

Guidelines for Selecting Children's Literature

Space does not permit the discussion of comprehensive guidelines for selecting children's literature. Instead, Box 10.2 lists professional sources that can be helpful in such decisions, and Box 10.3 presents questions that may assist in making an appropriate selection.

In addition to using the preceding selection guidelines, teachers should become familiar with a wide variety of children's literature and, if possible, own their favorites. Teachers should also try to learn their students' likes and dislikes and reading preferences.

Teaching with Children's Literature

Any instructional activities that are used with LD students must: (1) guarantee a high rate of success for the students and (2) have a high degree of active student involvement. Selecting the appropriate children's literature to use in such activities can certainly help to assure the stu-

Table 10.1   Children's Literature for Various Ages

Ages	*Appropriate Literature*
Infants/toddlers: birth to 2 or 3 years old	Pop-up or movable books; scratch-and-sniff books; board or cloth books; books with single objects and the object's name on each page; books with short poems that rhyme, finger plays, Mother Goose rhymes, and songs; books that employ sounds (when an adult reads aloud) and bright, vivid colors.
Early childhood: 2 or 3 years old to 5 or 6 years old	Books from the preceding category; books on simple concepts (e.g., opposites, shapes, similarities and differences); alphabet and counting books; pattern books; poetry books that stress rhythm and rhyme, including nonsense rhymes; books with an obvious sequence; books with photographs; books about common childhood experiences; predictable books
Primary: 5 or 6 years old to 8 or 9 years old	Books from the preceding categories; believable and obvious fantasy books; books with different but easy to identify points of view, varying plots (including surprise endings), increasingly complex detail in narrative and/or illustrations, and realistic settings and events, including those that provide a sense of security, emphasize the self, and describe problems with which the children can identify; books with jokes, riddles, and obvious limericks; books of fairly short narrative poetry; books with "read-on-your-own" vocabulary; books with varying types of art (children at this age often select books primarily on this basis); nonfiction books; informational books with chapters or several stories
Intermediate: 8 or 9 years old to 11 or 12 years old	Books from the preceding categories; books that look like adult books (e.g., paperbacks with smaller print and greater length); action-filled and sports books; intrigue and mystery books; books on personal or social concerns; books with increasingly complex plots, language, or character development; books of nonsense, jokes, riddles, and subtle humor; books of all types of poetry; fewer picture books; more fantasy, contemporary realism, historical fiction, and nonfiction books that allow vicarious learning about the world

Box 10.2 Professional Sources to Assist in Selecting Children's Literature

Texts

Cullinan, B. E. (1981). *Literature and the child.* New York: Harcourt Brace Jovanovich. Contains separate criteria for various types of children's literature.

Huck, C. S. (1979). *Children's literature in the elementary school* (3rd ed., updated). New York: Holt, Rinehart & Winston.

Sutherland, Z., Monson, D. L., & Arbuthnot, M. H. (1985). *Children and books* (7th ed.). Glenview, IL: Scott, Foresman.

Journals

Bulletin of the Center for Children's Books, The University of Chicago Press, 5801 Ellis Avenue, Chicago, IL 60637.

Language Arts, National Council of Teachers of English, 1111 Kenyon Road, Urbana, IL 61801.

The Reading Teacher, International Reading Association, 800 Barksdale Road, P.O. Box 8139, Newark, DE 19714-8139.

School Library Journal, R. R. Bowker Co., P.O. Box 1426, Riverton, NJ 08077-9967.

Book Lists

The Children's Book Council, 67 Irving Place, New York, NY 10003.

Children's Choices, The Children's Book Council and the International Reading Association. Specialized lists (e.g., focusing on multi-ethnic literature) are available.

The Children's Services Division, American Library Association (ALA), 50 East Huron Street, Chicago, IL 60611.

ERIC, Clearinghouse on Reading and Communications Skills, 1111 Kenyon Road, Urbana, IL 61801.

Teacher's Choices, National Council of Teachers of English, Regional teams field test hundreds of children's books with classroom teachers and their students in kindergarten through grade eight.

Box 10.3   Questions to Ask When Choosing Children's Literature

Before Reading

What kind of book is this?

What does the reader anticipate from the:
    Title?
    Dust jacket illustrations?
    Size of print?
    Illustrations?
    Opening page?
    Chapter headings?
For what age range is this book appropriate?

Plot

Does the book tell a good story? Will children enjoy it?

Is there action? Does the story move?

Is the plot original and fresh?

Is it plausible and credible?

Is there preparation for the events?

Is there a logical series of happenings?

Is there a basis of cause and effect in the happenings?

Is there an identifiable climax?

How do events build to a climax?

Is the plot well constructed?

Setting

Where does the story take place?

How does the author indicate the time?

How does the setting affect the action, characters, or themes?

Does the story transcend the setting and have universal implications?

(continued)

Note. From *Children's Literature in the Elementary School,* 3/e (updated), by C. S. Huck (pp. 16–17). Copyright © 1979 by C. S. Huck. Reprinted by permission of CBS College Publishing.

Box 10.3   *(continued)*

Theme

Does the story have a theme?

Is the theme worth imparting to children?

Does the theme emerge naturally from the story, or is it stated too obviously?

Does the theme overpower the story?

Does it avoid moralizing?

Characterization

How does the author reveal characters?

   Through narration?

   In conversation?

   By thoughts of others?

   By thoughts of the characters?

   Through action?

Are the characters convincing and credible?

Do we see their strengths and their weaknesses?

Does the author avoid stereotyping?

Is the behavior of the characters consistent with their ages and background?

Is there any character development or growth?

Has the author shown the causes of character behavior or development?

Box 10.3 *(continued)*

Style

Is the style of writing appropriate to the subject?

Is the style straightforward or figurative?

Is the dialogue natural and suited to the characters?

Does the author balance narration and dialogue?

How did the author create a mood?

Is the overall impression one of mystery, gloom, evil, joy, security?

What symbols has the author used to intensify meaning?

Is the point of view from which the story is told appropriate to the purpose of the book?

Format

Do the illustrations enhance or extend the story?

Are the illustrations consistent with the story?

How is the format of the book related to the text?

What is the quality of the paper?

How sturdy is the binding?

Other Considerations

How does the book compare with other books on the subject?

How does the book compare with other books written by the same author?

How have other reviewers evaluated this book?

dents' success. How the material is used (i.e., the instructional activity itself), however, is most important in generating active student involvement and in influencing the rate of success. In this section, a variety of children's literature will be used as examples of instructional activities that meet these two basic criteria. Readers are encouraged to consider the preceding section on selecting children's literature and to substitute their own choices when using any of these activities. The instructional activities that follow are organized into four categories (with some overlap): (1) creating a literature-rich environment (also see Chapter 9), (2) teaching specific reading strategies, (3) creating independent readers, and (4) using children's literature in other academic areas.

Creating a Literature-Rich Environment

The first topic in this section on creating a literature-rich environment—the actual physical environment in which LD students will be instructed—is not specifically an instructional activity. The second topic involves teachers reading to students. The third and final topic focuses on extending children's literature after it has been read to the students (see Box 10.4).

The Physical Environment

Children's literature should be an integral part if not focal point of the classroom. The room must be physically conducive to reading, with a well-lighted display area (e.g., table or bookcase) and comfortable chairs

---

Box 10.4   Factors That Contribute to a Literature-Rich Environment

1. Physical Environment
     offer comfortable furniture
     provide a wide variety of children's literature
     place book jackets, posters, and illustrations on the wall
2. Reading to Students
     use books of interest to the reader (i.e., the teacher)
     select from a variety of books
     discuss books with the children
     question for comprehension
3. Extending Children's Literature
     follow oral reading with art projects that illustrate the book
     read favorite books in unison

(child-sized rocking chairs, loungers, or beanbag chairs are frequent favorites), pillows, or cushions. The area should contain a wide variety of children's literature with the students assisting in the selection whenever possible. A diversity of books as well as other materials (e.g.,comic books, magazines, greeting cards, books the children have written, listings of television programs, menus, coupons, and signs) should be included. While some favorites should be kept for months or longer, the material should generally be kept for only a few weeks, so that the students are constantly introduced to different materials.

Use book jackets, posters, and illustrations to decorate a bulletin board or blank wall. Add headings such as, "Have you met these wild things?" or "Which is your favorite?", that will create student interest. Choose one or two children each month or so to make a special display of favorite books by a favorite author.

Teachers and other adults in the classroom are also a part of the physical environment. They should make a point of sharing how they use literature in their own lives either by talking about their readings or actually reading when the students can observe.

Reading to Students

If possible, students should be read to daily regardless of their ages. This activity can take as little as five to ten minutes a day if time is at a premium. One of the major purposes of reading aloud is to help students learn to enjoy children's literature. A second goal is to help them develop listening comprehension skills that also can be applied to their own reading with only minor modifications. A third purpose is to create interest in a particular type of literature so the students will want to read independently.

The selection guidelines presented in Box 10.3 should be utilized as needed; perhaps most important in the selection process is choosing a book that the reader (i.e., the teacher) truly enjoys. Using a variety of books is also important; different types (e.g., fantasy and nonfiction) as well as different kinds (e.g., pop-up books, books with movable parts, and books with no pictures) should be used. Books that demonstrate that reading and writing are necessary parts of our lives should also be included.

The teacher should read the book several times before reading it to the students; questions to ask before, during, and after the reading also should be considered. While asking questions is one way to check comprehension, asking students to retell the story in their own words and extending the literature are other means.

Extending Children's Literature

Many books on children's literature, including those mentioned previously, have excellent and practical suggestions for extending children's literature. Two activities are presented here. Activity 1 involves creating art and dictating or writing by the students. Activity 2 involves reading in unison.

Combining Art and Writing (Activity 1)   Creating art of some kind after hearing a story is a common extension activity for students. Pucher (1985), for example, suggested that students, after reading and discussing *Alexander and the Terrible, Horrible, No Good, Very Bad Day* (Viorst, 1979), be asked to describe their own "terrible, horrible, no good, very bad days." (This serves as a prewriting time.) Depending on their abilities, they should then dictate or write drafts of their experiences (see Chapter 12). On their final copies, they are to illustrate their experiences. All of these pages can then be bound into a class book. Dwayne, one of my LD fourth graders, wrote of this activity, "I had a terrible, horrible, no good, very bad day when I ran to the bus stop, and the bus was gone." Cedric, an LD first grader, dictated: "I had a terrible, horrible, no good, very bad day when a car hit my bike and broke my tire." If the students enjoy this activity, they can next write about their wonderful, glorious, scrumptious, very good days.

Reading in Unison (Activity 2)   Reading in unison can also be used to extend children's literature and create independent readers—if the activity is repeated until students can read the selection by themselves. However reading in unison is used, three considerations should be kept in mind: (1) the written text should be clearly visible to all students; (2) as the text is read, the words should be pointed to in a flowing motion, not a word-by-word motion; and (3) the students should be encouraged but not forced to participate. In fact, LD students who tend toward impulsivity and saying random words that may not make sense should be urged to think about words they may not know and, instead of pronouncing them, listen to the group for verification of their understanding.

A predictable book with rhythm such as *A Monster Is Coming! A Monster Is Coming!* (Heide & Heide, 1980) or *Millions of Cats* (Gag, 1928), is easy for a student to read after the teacher has read it aloud. Songs, chants, poems, and jokes may also be used. Older students, who may not be interested in picture books, frequently have favorite popular songs that they would like to read. So students can see the text clearly, teachers could use an opaque projector to enlarge an entire page onto a screen or blank wall, write the text on chart paper, or create big books (see Activity 5).

This activity should begin with the teacher reading the material aloud. After the first reading, or part way through it, the students should be asked to join in. The text can be read several times during the first day (provided the students are interested and actively participating) or it can be reread one or two times each day for several days. As an added incentive, teachers may wish to award special reading certificates to students who eventually read the entire text by themselves. This would, of course, depend on the difficulty of the text and the students' ability.

Box 10.5   Specific Reading Strategies

---

1. Enhancing word recognition through mastery of basic, high-frequency sight words
2. Enhancing fluency through sequential exposure to and practice of independent oral reading
3. Enhancing comprehension by eliciting student feedback with book reports

---

Teaching Specific Reading Strategies

Most of the strategies for teaching reading described in previous chapters can be used with or adapted for use with children's literature. Consequently, only three specific approaches are presented here (see Box 10.5): (1) a basic sight word list, (2) a strategy for increasing fluency, and (3) book reports. For detailed plans for teaching reading strategies, such as how to deal with proper nouns that are hard to pronounce (sometimes referred to as the "blanking strategy"), see Goodman and Burke (1980).

A Basic Sight Word List for Children's Literature

Sight words are those high-frequency words students can immediately identify. These words are often presented and practiced in isolation. This procedure is *not* generally advocated in a cognitive developmental approach, and certainly should not be used with nonhandicapped students or with most LD students. Teachers will occasionally, however, have one or more LD students who appear to have severe difficulty in learning to read, despite their use of various cognitive developmental techniques. In such instances, teaches may wish to consider teaching a list of sight words.

Table 10–2 presents a list of words and their frequency of appearance as compiled by Eeds (1985) from over one thousand children's literature books that had been recommended by at least one authority. From this, she chose four hundred books that were suitable for teaching beginning reading. She entered the words in all of these books (120,000 running words) into a computer to derive a final list of the 227 used most often, which she labeled "Bookwords." Her guidelines, which may affect the teaching of this list, included:

1. Compound words were entered as two separate words.
2. Only the base of inflected forms was entered (e.g., *go* was entered for both *goes* and *going*).
3. Only the base of a word was entered if pronounciation was not affected (eg., *did* instead of *didn't*).

Table 10.2 High-Frequency Words in Children's Literature

the	1,334	at	122	back	67	school	43
and	985	have	121	now	66	house	42
a	831	your	121	friend	65	morning	42
I	757	mother	119	cry	64	*yes	41
to	746	come	118	oh	64	after	41
said	688	not	115	Mr.	63	never	41
you	638	like	112	*bed	63	or	40
he	488	then	108	an	62	*self	40
it	345	get	103	very	62	try	40
in	311	when	101	where	60	has	38
was	294	thing	100	play	59	*always	38
she	250	do	99	let	59	over	38
for	235	too	91	long	58	again	37
that	232	want	91	here	58	side	37
is	230	did	91	how	57	*thank	37
his	226	could	90	make	57	why	37
but	224	good	90	big	56	who	36
they	218	this	90	from	55	saw	36
my	214	don't	89	put	55	*mom	35
of	204	little	89	*read	55	*kid	35
on	192	if	87	them	55	give	35
me	187	just	87	as	54	around	34
all	179	*baby	86	*Miss	53	by	34
be	176	way	85	any	52	Mrs.	34
go	171	there	83	right	52	off	33
can	162	every	83	*nice	50	*sister	33
with	158	went	82	other	50	find	32
one	157	father	80	well	48	*fun	32
her	156	had	79	old	48	more	32
what	152	see	79	*night	48	while	32
we	151	dog	78	may	48	tell	32
him	144	home	77	about	47	*sleep	32
no	143	down	76	think	47	made	31
so	141	got	73	new	46	first	31
out	140	would	73	know	46	say	31
up	137	time	71	help	46	took	31
are	133	*love	70	grand	46	*dad	30
will	127	walk	70	boy	46	found	30
look	126	came	69	take	45	*lady	30
some	123	were	68	eat	44	soon	30
day	123	ask	67	*body	43	ran	30

(continued)

Table 10.2   (*continued*)

dear	29	*ride	27	gave	24	*blue	21
man	29	*pet	27	*does	24	*bath	21
*better	29	*hurry	26	*car	24	*mean	21
*through	29	hand	26	*ball	24	*sit	21
stop	29	hard	26	*sat	24	*together	21
still	29	*push	26	*stay	24	*best	20
*fast	28	our	26	*each	23	*brother	20
next	28	their	26	*ever	23	*feel	20
only	28	*watch	26	*until	23	*floor	20
*am	27	*because	25	*shout	23	wait	20
began	27	door	25	*mama	22	*tomorrow	20
head	27	us	25	*use	22	*surprise	20
keep	27	*should	25	turn	22	*shop	20
*teacher	27	*room	25	thought	22	run	20
*sure	27	*pull	25	*papa	22	*own	20
*says	27	*great	24	*lot	21		

*Indicates words *not* on Durr list.

Note. From "Bookwords: Using a Beginning Word list of High Frequency Words from Children's Literature K–3" by M. Eeds, 1985, *The Reading Teacher, 38,* p. 420. Reprinted by permission of M. Eeds and the International Reading Association.

The resulting list accounts "for an average of 73% of all running words and an average of 65% of all different words in that sample. The least common words on the list appeared 20 times" (Eeds, 1985, p. 421). Activity 3 offers alternatives for learning these words in isolation or sentences. Again, words should not be indiscriminately taught in isolation. Activity 4 describes a more meaningful approach for using the words.

Learning Sight Words (Activity 3) Students who need to learn these basic sight words should first be pretested to determine which words they already know. Unknown words and words they cannot quickly identify should be targeted for instruction and practiced. While flashcards can be used (e.g., in peer tutoring), teachers should be sure that the students are not rushed, are given ample time to study the words, and are provided with correct and prompt feedback. The Fernald (1943) approach, which includes saying each part of a word while tracing it with a finger, can also be used. A Language Master, a card with a strip of audio tape at the bottom that the child pushes through a machine to hear the recording, or a similar device may also be used. Each word can be written in isolation on the Language Master card and recorded or underlined and written in a sentence, with the entire sentence then recorded. If possible, LD students should be given several ways to practice the words independently, with each technique taking less than fifteen minutes. The teacher should also work with each student for only a few minutes each day on the sight words. Ideally, they will work on no more than ten or fifteen words, with new ones added as learned words are deleted. Periodically (once every week or so), the students should review all words they have learned. Likewise, they should periodically review the list once it is mastered.

Once the students know at least twenty Bookwords, teachers may want to write them on small cards so that the students can practice arranging them into meaningful sentences. These same cards can be used to create compound words, contractions (add cards with *n't, 's,* etc.), and inflected forms (add cards with *-s, -es, -ing,* etc.).

Reading Books to Learn Words (Activity 4)   Once the students know approximately half of the Bookwords and can create contractions, compound words, and inflected forms, they should begin to read books that contain the words. Eeds listed fifty for use with beginning readers. *There's a Nightmare in My Closet* (Mayer, 1968), for example, contains 142 running words but only 76 different words. Of the running words, 76 percent are on the Bookwords list; of the different words, 68 percent are on the list. The books on this list contain from 34 to 645 running words. The 645 running words are in *George and Martha* (Marshall, 1972); 75 percent are on the Bookwords list; there are 210 different words, with 68 percent on the Bookwords list.

A large portion of the words *not* on the Bookwords list are proper nouns or words that are unique to the story. For example, *nightmare* appears repeatedly in *There's a Nightmare in My Closet.* When Michelle, a five-year-old, read this book, she could not pronounce *nightmare* and did not understand what it meant, so she happily substituted *monster* (it made sense and fit the pictures) throughout.

A Strategy for Increasing Fluency

This strategy, designed to help students read in a natural tone with appropriate expression (i.e., fluently), involves combining and using several activities over a period of time, usually one to two weeks. Activity 5 deals with the use of "big books," Activity 6 suggests two follow-up activities, and Activity 7 briefly describes a culminating activity. In addition to increasing fluency, these activities may help students increase their sight-word vocabulary, make predictions, and create their own story based on the pattern of the book. All of these activities use *Brown Bear, Brown Bear, What Do You See?* (Martin, 1983), a predictable picture book. Similar books are suggested by Tompkins and Webeler (1983).

Using "Big Books" (Activity 5)   To create a "big book," write the words to *Brown Bear, Brown Bear,* as they appear on each page on large sheets of paper. On the page with the brown bear, write all of the words in brown except for *redbird,* which should be in red. (Also add a simple line drawing of a brown bear.) Each pair of pages (except the last) will follow the same pattern:

> Brown Bear,
> Brown Bear,
> What do you see?
> I see a redbird
> looking at me. (Martin, 1983, pp. 1–2)

The activity is started by reading the story from the actual book and discussing it. (For students with severe reading problems, teachers may wish to eliminate the last two pages, which list all the animals previously mentioned.) The students are then introduced to the "big book"and asked to help with the reading. After reading the first page, they are asked to predict what will be read on the next two pages. Once the page is turned, they should confirm or correct their predictions and identify that the redbird sees an animal that is yellow (the word should be written in yellow in the "big book") and that the name of the animal starts with *d*. If the students are unable to think of the animal, clues (e.g., "the animal has webbed feet") should be given by the teacher until they are successful. Continue until the book is finished or the students are no longer concentrating. Reread the story if time allows.

Over several days, reread the story, using the predicting strategies and helping clues as needed. Allow individual students to read pages (or the entire story) by themselves. Letting the students come to the "big book" to point to the words in a flowing motion as they read is one way to reinforce the concept of reading and writing from left to right and top to bottom. Teachers may also wish to point to various words (framing with both hands is helpful) and ask students to identify them. Additional activities with "big books" can be found in Holdaway (1979).

Creating Class Books and Individual Books (Activity 6)   After reading the "big book" a day or two, the students can be introduced to either or both of these activities. In one, the students work together to create a class book based on the *Brown Bear* pattern; in the other, they make their own *Brown Bear* books to take home.

To create a class book, for each student create one page that resembles Figure 10.1 (see Gammage, 1985). Each student thinks of one color word and one animal name to write on the blanks, with the teacher providing whatever help is needed. In the blank square, the student draws the animal, using primarily the selected color. Julian, a second-grade LD student, wrote the following:

> I see a pink lizard
> looking at me.

> Pink Lizard,
> Pink Lizard,
> What do you see?

His lizard was drawn in shades of pink. The students should then practice reading their own pages. When all can be read fluently, they should be tape-recorded as a unit. The teacher should begin the recording by reading: "Brown Bear, Brown Bear, What do you see?" (Martin, 1983, p. 1). Next, bind the pages in the order in which they were recorded (add a brown bear page and a final page with the necessary words) into a class book. The students can then listen to the tape and read the new book as a group or individually.

To create individual books, write the text from each two pages of *Brown Bear* on the bottom half of a standard-sized piece of paper (allow room on the left to staple into a book). Write large enough for the students to trace the words, and include a title page crediting Martin as the author. After duplicating the pages, have the students trace the words (in the appropriate colors if they need additional clues for predicting them) and add their own illustrations. These books can be used in the following culminating activity.

Reading Aloud (Activity 7) Using their own books, the "big book," or the actual *Brown Bear* book, the students should practice reading aloud as a group and individually. As they read, encourage them to "read like they talk." When necessary, exaggerate what word-by-word reading or reading with an unnatural rhythm sounds like. Repeated practice, encouragement, positive reinforcement, and good modeling are what most students need to read fluently, as long as the material is not too difficult.

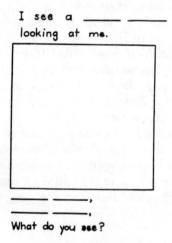

FIGURE 10.1 Sample page for a Class Book.

Once they can read the book aloud with a satisfactory degree of fluency, allow each student to record the entire book. All students should then listen to the recordings (see Box 10.6).

Book Reports

At some time during elementary or middle school, most LD students will be introduced to book reports, which usually require them to write on some type of children's literature they have read.

To be used for book reports, books do not have to be long. In fact, relatively short picture books are often best for LD students writing their first reports. Furthermore, book reports do not have to be lengthy or completely original. Evans and Moore (1984) created a set of reproducible book report forms that can provide structure and motivation for LD students. Of course, teachers can create "fill-in-the-blank" forms for reports on specific books. Finally, Szabos (1984) suggested a variety of means for extending activities with novels, many of which could be adapted for use with other types of children's literature and substituted for traditional book reports.

Just as traditional book report formats need not always be used, traditional children's literature should not always be read. For example, the Choose Your Own Adventure series of contemporary realism books published by Bantam and Bantam-Skylark (the latter at an easier reading level in larger print), has been gaining popularity. After reading a page or two, readers must choose between alternative actions. Depending on the choices, they are directed to different pages. This format is used throughout to involve the readers actively. *The Cave of Time* (Packard, 1979), listed for ages ten and up, is part of the Bantam series. *Your Very*

Box 10.6   Increasing Fluency: One Student's Experience

Preston is an eight-year-old first grader with a severe learning disability. He had successfully completed the activities with *Brown Bear* and seemed to enjoy them all. A few days after finishing activity 7, Preston was observed during his free time lying on a beanbag chair "reading" the book *Would You Like a Parrot?* (Barberis, 1967), although he was actually saying the words from *Brown Bear*. After reciting the entire *Brown Bear* book without an error while carefully turning the pages of *Would You Like a Parrot?*, Preston exclaimed, "Man! Reading is really easy now!"

Own Robot (Montgomery, 1982), from the Bantam-Skylark series, is listed for ages seven to nine, although this writer has used it successfully with LD students as old as thirteen. Popular literature should be used for book reports as well.

Creating Independent Readers

The major goal of any instructional program is to create independent learners (see Box 10.7). Certainly, the activities in Chapter 9 and this chapter are designed to help LD students read independently. Activities 8–10, however, are more specific and direct in their attempt to create independent readers. Activity 8 is an adaptation of the repeated readings concept. Activity 9 is a technique for teaching LD students to choose their own books for independent reading. Activity 10 presents the concept of Everyone Always Reads Silently (EARS).

Adapting the Repeated Readings Concept (Activity 8)   O'Shea, Sindelar, and O'Shea (1985) found that students' repeated readings increased if the students were cued to comprehension (e.g., "Try to remember as much as you can about the story you are about to read."). For students who have achieved some independence in reading, a variety of children's literature can be used for repeated readings. According to Samuels (1979), "the method consists of rereading a short, meaningful passage several times until a satisfactory level of fluency is reached. Then the procedure is repeated with a new passage" (p. 404).

The concept of repeated readings must be adapted for use with LD students who have minimal reading skills and strategies. One form of adaptation is to locate easy-to-read books with meaningful, naturally written text. They should be brief so that students can read the entire book at one time. The ten Start to Read books fit this description. One of these books, *Sue Likes Blue* (Gregorich, 1984), is a brief text (fifteen pages for the actual story) that uses limited vocabulary to tell a complete story. The major weakness of these books is that they are marked for ages four to seven. (Some LD students as old as thirteen, however, have asked to read them.)

Box 10.7   Means of Creating Independent Readers

1. Using recorded stories
2. Self-monitoring books for their reading difficulty
3. Scheduling silent reading periods

For students with extremely limited reading skills, teachers may wish to tape-record each book. Students are given both the book and the cassette and instructed to practice once or twice each day. The teacher should demonstrate that a bell or other tone indicates when to turn the page and should work with the students before expecting them to function independently. At first, the students may only listen to the tape and turn the pages. They should, however, be encouraged to say the words with the tape until they can "read" the whole book and answer oral comprehension questions. For some students, this may only take a day or so; for others, it may take several weeks.

Once students have finished or tried to finish (teachers *and* students can make mistakes) reading their books, they should record basic information about the selection on a book card (this is also a beginning step in writing book reports). Figure 10.2 shows a five-by-eight-inch card printed on heavy stock that is used with primary LD students; Figure 10.3 is used with intermediate LD students. The students file these cards behind their names (intermediate students subfile them alphabetically according to the author's name). The cards are used to keep track of which and how many books each individual has read, what preferences are evident, and the like. The cards are also used to introduce certain library skills (e.g., by dividing them into two groups—fiction and nonfiction).

Teaching Students to Choose Books (Activity 9)   Readability formulas are often used for determining the difficulty of particular books. In addition to being approximate and time consuming, such formulas do not consider individual interests and backgrounds. A technique that LD students can use independently (once it is thoroughly understood and practiced with the teacher) to select a book is called "one hand behind my back." Students are taught to choose a page near the middle of a book they think they want to read. With one hand in a fist behind their backs (or in their pockets), the students read the entire page, or several pages in picture books with few words on each page. Each time an unknown word is encountered, one finger is raised. At the end of the page, if all five fingers are raised, the book will in all likelihood be too difficult. If their hands are still in a fist, the book will probably be easy to read. The decision is still left to the students; that is, do they want to read a difficult or very easy book (sometimes they do because they are so interested in the topic) (see Box 10.8).

Obviously, this technique is not a scientific formula, but it does take into account individual interests and backgrounds. It also allows the students to assume responsibility for their own decisions while still providing them with some guidance. Students can learn to apply this technique quickly and surreptitiously to estimate the difficulty of a selection. (Barbara, a very exacting second grader, is still looking for a

Your name _____

Title of book _____

Author(s) _____

Date _____

Front

Did you read all of the book?

Yes ☐   No ☐

Did you like the book?

☺   😐   ☹

Yes ☐   Some ☐   No ☐

Back

FIGURE 10.2 Book Card for Primary Students.

Name _____

Title _____

_____

Author(s) _____

_____

Type of book _____

Front

What was the book about? _____

_____

Did you read the whole book? _____ If not, why not? _____

Would you recommend this book to anyone else? _____

To whom?   (Give their names) _____

Did you like the book?   ☐ Yes   ☐ Some   ☐ No

What would you like to read (about) next? _____

_____

Back

FIGURE 10.3 Book Card for Intermediate Students.

Box 10.8   Selecting Books with the "One Hand Behind My Back" Technique: One Student's Experience

---

Marvin, a much-improved LD third grader who has been in the program almost nine months, likes to check out "thick" books to see if he can read the entire text while his hand is still in a fist. He tallies the words he does not know on a bookmark, although he frequently comments that it did not really matter that a few words were unfamiliar because he had fun reading the book and could understand it anyway.

---

book that is "just right"; that is, one for which she will raise two and a half fingers!)

Everyone Always Reads Silently (Activity 10)   Everyone Always Reads Silently (EARS) is obviously not an accurate statement. It is, however, an acronym that students can remember and that can be used in bulletin boards and captions (a bookworm with ears serves as an appropriate mascot). EARS is similar to DEAR (Drop Everything and Read), SSR (Sustained Silent Reading), and other programs that advocate that time be set aside for silent reading by *everyone*. Depending on the students, the time may vary from five to twenty minutes and may occur everyday or only on certain days. Teachers should try to schedule silent reading for the same time and days. Naturally, the reading time should be increased as the students are able to read for longer periods. As a general guide, EARS should last only a minute or two after the first one or two students become restless.

When it is time for EARS, everyone in the room (including the teacher and any guests) must start reading silently. This can include reading independently, listening to a tape (with headphones) while following along in a text, or viewing a filmstrip and tape of a children's literature selection (with headphones). Usually, students are allowed to change books as often as they wish during the period, and their choices should not be limited (for example, comic books from home and newspapers are good candidates for silent reading). In most instances, the students should be allowed to select whatever they want to read, and no follow-up activities such as answering a series of questions should be required. However, teachers may want to allow students to discuss what they have read and share suggestions for future readings. Teachers may also wish to consider establishing certain rules (e.g., no changing places or going to the book table during EARS).

Box 10.9   Uses for Children's Literature in Other Academic Areas

1. To enhance creative writing by making student books and adding words to picture books
2. To enhance mathematics, social studies, and science by sharing nonfiction literature in these areas

---

Using Children's Literature in Other Academic Areas

The majority of this chapter has focused on using children's literature in teaching reading. Literature, however, can be used throughout the instructional program (see Box 10.9). Because of limited space, only a few general activities will be mentioned. Various books provide ideas for using children's literature with various subjects. Huck (1979), for example, suggests applications to art, sewing, cooking, music, movement and drama, and games, and Lamme (1981) provided short reference lists of children's literature for different curriculum areas along with some ideas for its use.

Writing Creatively (Activity 11)   Although only one basic activity is described in this section—using children's literature as a model for students' creative writing—the variations on this concept are almost endless.

In one such activity, *Dear Zoo* (Campbell, 1982), a picture book with a predictable (patterned) text and movable parts, is first read and discussed with the students. (McGee & Charlesworth, 1984, provided an annotated bibliography of such books.) Baker (1985) described how to use its pattern to help students create their own pop-up books either individually or as a group. For other types of books children can make (as well as writing suggestions and ideas), teachers may refer to Evans and Moore (1985).

Another way to use children's literature to help students with their own writing (especially for those who dread adding illustration) is to use wordless picture books. If possible, teachers should take the book apart and laminate it so that students can write directly on the pages (ink from a water-based felt-tipped pen comes off with water; permanent ink comes off with hairspray). As an alternative, the students can number sheets of paper to coincide with the pages in the book. *One Frog Too Many* (Mayer & Mayer, 1977) is one wordless book with richly detailed pictures that lend themselves to story writing (or storytelling). *Hiccup* (Mayer, 1976)

Box 10.10   Children's Literature Awards

The Caldecott Medal is an annual award to the artist of the most distinguished American picture book for children published in the United States during the preceding year. It is awarded by the Association for Library Services for Children of the American Library Association (ALA). The first award was given in 1938.

The Newberry Medal is also an annual award from the Association for Library Services for Children of the ALA. It is given to the author of the most distinguished contribution to children's literature published during the preceding year. The first award was given in 1922.

NCTE Award for Excellence in Poetry for Children is given each year by the National Council of Teachers of English to recognize and honor the aggregate work of a living American poet. The first award was made in 1977.

The Laura Ingalls Wilder Award is given every five years to an author or illustrator whose books have made a substantial contribution to children's literature. The Association for Library Services for Children of the ALA first made this award in 1954.

The Hans Christian Andersen Medal is given biennially to one living author (since 1956) and one illustrator (since 1966) for their entire body of work. It is given by the International Board on Books for Young People of Basel, Switzerland.

---

is an almost wordless (only *hiccup* and *boo* are used) picture book that tells a complete, humorous story that could be the basis for students' writings.

Teaching Mathematics, Social Studies, and Science

There are numerous counting books and concept books (e.g., those on geometric shapes or telling time) that can be used to introduce, illustrate, or reinforce mathematics instruction. Anno (1982) has written several picture books that explain and usually offer suggestions for helping the children understand various mathematical concepts.

There are an almost limitless number of books on history, geography, culture, customs, and the like that can be used in social studies programs.

Teachers are encouraged to include literature other than nonfiction, for picture books, contemporary realism, and historical fiction can also be particularly effective. Likewise, numerous books can be used in teaching science. One that is often considered a classic is *Bet You Can't: Science Impossibilities to Fool You* (Cobb & Darling, 1980). Picture books such as *Cloud Book* (De Paola, 1977) or *Animal Fact/Animal Fable* (Simon, 1979) can also be useful. LD students could use the latter to write a brief report or at least several statements about a particular animal. Their classmates then have to decide if the report is true (fact) or false (fable). Students could also be asked to locate the one false statement that was intentionally put in the report.

Summary and Conclusions

The first half of this chapter established the general background of children's literature by offering a definition and guidelines for its use. Box 10.10 lists children's book awards. Books and authors receiving such awards are usually good choices for selection. The second half discussed practical ideas and techniques for successfully using children's literature in the instructional programs for LD students in elementary and middle schools.

Chapter 11

Teaching Handwriting and Spelling

Paula C. Grinnell

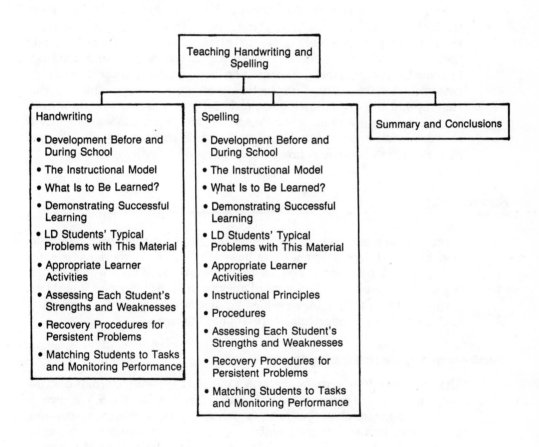

Teaching Handwriting and Spelling

Handwriting

- Development Before and During School
- The Instructional Model
- What Is to Be Learned?
- Demonstrating Successful Learning
- LD Students' Typical Problems with This Material
- Appropriate Learner Activities
- Assessing Each Student's Strengths and Weaknesses
- Recovery Procedures for Persistent Problems
- Matching Students to Tasks and Monitoring Performance

Spelling

- Development Before and During School
- The Instructional Model
- What Is to Be Learned?
- Demonstrating Successful Learning
- LD Students' Typical Problems with This Material
- Appropriate Learner Activities
- Instructional Principles
- Procedures
- Assessing Each Student's Strengths and Weaknesses
- Recovery Procedures for Persistent Problems
- Matching Students to Tasks and Monitoring Performance

Summary and Conclusions

Questions to Consider

1. How does the experience of learning handwriting and spelling compare in LD and normally achieving students?
2. What process is common to learning to write and spell?
3. What kind of atmosphere encourages the acquisition of handwriting and spelling skills?
4. What role does meaning play in learning handwriting and spelling?

Writing instruction for LD students has been historically limited to the technical skills—neat handwriting, accurate spelling, good punctuation, and proper grammar. Little attention has been paid to enhancing their ability to express themselves on paper. The need to increase their technical writing competence cannot be denied, although these skills are essentially useless without instruction in composition. Consequently, this chapter and the one following, on composition, must be seen as a unit. *Legible handwriting and accurate spelling are appropriate goals only if they are a means to communication.* Thus this chapter precedes the one on composition because it presents background knowledge.

Handwriting

Handwriting has been a, or sometimes the, main focus of writing instruction for LD children. It is not clear, however, that they experience greater difficulty with writing than do normally achieving children who are reading on a similar level (Tansley & Panckhurst, 1981). Since LD children progress through the same developmental sequence but at a slower pace, it is important to understand normal development.

Development Before and During School

That most children write on their own before they receive formal instruction has been well documented (Clay, 1975; Harste, Burke, & Woodward, 1981). It appears that spontaneous writers, like spontaneous readers, grow up in literate environments. Their parents make writing implements and paper easily accessible, thereby enabling these children to experiment with written language. In addition, books and other printed matter are available for them to examine. Parents model the functions of writing by making shopping lists, writing letters, jotting down notes, and the like. Furthermore, these parents read aloud to their children, which helps them understand writing as language written down and familiarizes them with correspondences between given letters and their sounds. Finally, people in the home answer the children's questions about letters, sounds, words, and other features of written language.

In literate environments, children do a lot of self-discovery about written language. Most learn written language in the same way that they learn oral language. They are surrounded by written language, create and test hypotheses about it, receive feedback on their accuracy, and revise their hypotheses based upon that feedback. Such children thus experiment or play with language. Their play, however, is purposeful in that it is motivated by a desire to communicate.

The steps in children's progress as writers parallels those in the historical development of writing: (1) tracemaking, (2) drawing and painting, and (3) writing (Kellogg, 1970). Children progress slowly as they gain experience with written language. As early as two, however, some children can differentiate writing from drawing (Grinnell & Burris, 1983). Phillip, for instance, at two and one-half years of age, used linear shapes to represent writing and circular shapes to represent drawing (see Figure 11.1) because his name is mainly linear (Harste et al., 1981).

Clay (1975) identified five principles of writing that children discover and produce on their own: (1) the recurring principle, (2) the generative principle, (3) the linear principle, (4) the flexibility principle, and (5) the sign principle. Children do not learn these in a specified order or at a given age, and for LD children, progress is slower and requires more instruction in school.

Recurring Principle

Generally the recurring principle—that the same marks appear repeatedly—emerges first. Writing resembles an EEG print-out, as seen in Figure 11.2. Here Phillip, age three years and four months, drew a jacket and then titled it. When asked what he wrote, he responded, "A jacket," which indicated his intent to communicate in writing.

FIGURE 11.1 Writing: Phillip at Age Two Years and Five Months.

FIGURE 11.2 Recurring Principle: Phillip at Age Three Years and Four Months.

Generative Principle

Knowledge of the generative principle—that writing is composed of a finite number of marks repeated in different sequences—gives children more variety. Their writing begins to look more like standard writing, and they often create books or pages with a few letters repeated often and randomly ordered. This can be seen in Figure 11.3, where Phillip, at age four years and eleven months, wrote a series of letters, which included his name and repetitions of some of those letters and others that he knew.

Linear Principle

Establishment of the linear principle involves directionality and continues to develop through second grade in normally achieving children. It includes knowledge that writing: (a) is organized horizontally on a page; (b) starts at the top left and moves to the right; (c) goes to the end of one line, moves down a line, and goes back to the left margin; and (d) goes from the end of one page to the top left margin of the next page.

Children who are in the process of mastering this principle will often reverse letters, do mirror writing, or start at the bottom of a page and then go up a line instead of down a line. Whether they move in the correct direction is often related to where on the page they start writing. Thus, if they happen to begin at the bottom right corner of the page, they will usually do mirror writing, whereas if the same children start at the top left, they would probably write normally.

At age five years and two months, Phillip began to discover the linearity principle, as seen in Figure 11.4. Here, since he started at the bottom left, the only place to go was up. He remembered to go to the left

FIGURE 11.3 Generative Principle: Phillip at Age Four Years and Eleven Months.

margin to write *day*. When he ran out of room for the *y* in *mommy*, however, it seemed more logical to put the letter near the rest of the word. Thus, he put the *y* in the right margin instead of the left.

Flexibility Principle

The flexibility principle is that some lines or curls can be added to letters to form new letters or stylistically change existing letters, while other additions cannot be made because they will create a nonexistent letter. Thus a line can be added to a capital *F* to make a capital *E*, and each letter can appear in numerous typographical styles. As with the linear principle, it can take many years for some children to master the alphabet.

At age four years, Phillip was discovering this principle (see Figure 11.5). He began by writing *ET* and ended by inventing a number of letters. Most of his inventions are embellishments of an *E* or a *T*, with numerous directional changes. He also signed his name in the bottom half of this display as *PHI*.

Sign Principle

The sign principle is that writing is done to communicate. As this principle takes hold, children strive for more complex forms of written com-

FIGURE 11.4 Linear Principle: Phillip at Age Five Years and Two Months.

munication and often combine drawing and writing. Furthermore, they like to ask, "What did I write?" As Figure 11.6 shows, at age five years and four months, Phillip drew a cat and labeled it. He could not read it back, however, because he did not know what *har* meant, although he did know that letters could be put together to label a drawing.

The Instructional Model

Handwriting instruction has traditionally ignored the learning that precedes formal schooling. With LD children, a medical model, which holds there is something wrong with these children that can be cured, has predominated. In particular, reversals and mirror writing have been singled out as problems thought to be peculiar to LD students. Velluntino (1979), however, casts doubt on this belief and on theories that have been used to explain the existence of mirror writing (e.g., spatial deficits and organic problems). He concluded that there is *no sound, objective evidence that reversals are caused by anything other than a lack of appropriate*

FIGURE 11.5 Flexibility Principle: Phillip at Age Four Years.

experience. To view reversals, then, as a spatial problem is inaccurate and will lead to inappropriate instruction.

Furner (1983) presents an alternative to the medical model that is in keeping with a cognitive developmental perspective. In a review of research, she concludes that learning handwriting is a perceptual task requiring cognitive processes (see Box 11.1). Children actively experiment with and make sense of their written environments. They are not passive recipients of information.

Furner's analysis relies on the three sequential, cognitive processes identified by Gibson (1969). First is the discrimination of distinctive features of letters, which eventually leads to the development of mental representations of the features. Distinctive features are those elements that differentiate one letter from another, such as circles; lines; number, direction, and size of strokes; and the starting and ending points of the letter. Thus *p* is distinguished from *b* by the single feature of a straight line that goes below the circle instead of above the circle, whereas *p* is distinguished from *q* by the orientation of the letter. Second in the hierarchy of cognitive processes is the recognition of a specific letter, and third is the production of that letter. Thus children cannot consistently write *p* correctly until they can distinguish *p* from *b, q,* and *o,* etc.

FIGURE 11.6 Sign Principle: Phillip at Age Five Years and Four Months.

What Is to Be Learned?

Graves (1983b) also believes that children must have appropriate experiences with writing. His work on composition has encouraged a rethinking of the purpose of handwriting instruction. For some time neatness was the major goal. However, when handwriting is seen as a means to communicate rather than as an end in itself, aesthetics becomes less critical as legibility (to enable the communication to be read) and physical ease of writing (to ensure willingness to write) become most important.

Since many adults vary the attractiveness of their writing depending upon how the finished product will be used, children should learn these same standards (e.g., a letter to a company must be neater than one to a friend). Understanding when and why a piece of writing must be neat releases children from the burden of having to make every letter pretty all of the time. Being able to relax as they write increases the desire to write and the quantity and quality of their writing.

Box 11.1   Cognitive Developmental Principles of Handwriting

1. Learning and development: Children's perceptual ability increases with appropriate experiences at their developmental level.
2. Discovery: Children form a mental representation of a letter through teacher-led discussion that helps them discover and describe distinctive features.
3. Motivation: Children's motivation and active problem solving enhance perceptual learning.
4. Exposure and attention: Numerous exposures to distinctive features help to focus children's attention.
5. Action modeling: Watching teachers who are simultaneously forming a letter and verbalizing the procedure helps children discover distinctive features and form mental representations.
6. Multiple modes: Using multiple sensory processing modes (visual, auditory, and kinesthetic) facilitates perceptual learning through a series of techniques. Children can: (a) see how the letter is formed as the teacher demonstrates; (b) describe and hear others describe the distinctive features of a letter as well as the steps in forming it; (c) verbalize the steps involved in forming the letter while writing the letter alone at their desk or with others in small groups or pairs; (d) compare their written letter with the model; and (e) revise and rewrite the letter to conform to the model.
7. Labels: Using labels to discuss letter formation and distinctive features aids children in developing mental representations. Teachers identify and define the most valuable terms (e.g., start, clockwise, and half-circle).
8. Verbalization: When children describe how a letter is formed, their attention is focused on the letter's distinctive features, thereby facilitating memory. After the class or small group discovers the critical distinctive features, each child verbalizes them on her own.
9. Mental activity: When children think through the motions needed to form a letter, they internalize the letter and the letter formation process, thereby creating a guide for continued practice and self-correction.
10. Reinforcement: Feedback, mainly through self-evaluation, helps children internalize the letter and develop accuracy through successive attempts and revisions.

(continued)

Box 11.1   *(continued)*

---

11. Grouping letters: Leading children to group letters according to common features (e.g., circles) facilitates both perceptual knowledge and formation of letters because their attention is drawn to the similarities and differences between letters. Which letters are grouped together depends upon the style of manuscript being used. With lower-case letters, the categories would probably be: circle letters (e.g., *o* and *c*); straight-line letters (e.g., *l* and *t*); point letters (e.g., *v* and *w*); hump letters (e.g., *m* and *u*) and tail letters (e.g., *y* and *g*).
12. Meaningful writing: Meaningful and functional writing experiences must precede, accompany, and follow writing instruction if children's desire to learn to write is to remain a priority.

Note. Adapted from "Developing Handwriting Ability: A Perceptual Learning Process" by B. A. Furner, 1983, *Topics in Learning and Learning Disabilities, 3.*

Demonstrating Successful Learning

Mastery of the above goals can be determined informally by observing daily work and formally by designating certain assignments to be evaluated. Writing for a variety of purposes should be assigned. Some should be a first draft and judged with criteria different from those applied to a final product. For children to take the time and effort to develop more than one draft, they must be highly motivated or else writing becomes an undesirable activity. Motivation can be kept high by having children do a final draft on something of their own choosing, especially if they know someone, in addition to the teacher, will read it (see Chapter 12). Computers can also be used to facilitate revisions (see Chapter 16).

LD Students' Typical Problems with This Material

Contrary to popular belief, *LD children are not guilty of reversals or mirror writing any more often than normally achieving children in the same stage of reading development* (e.g., Nelson, 1980). In determining who needs special assistance in handwriting, it is essential to remember that the goals of instruction are legibility and comfortableness. All adults do not write the same way, and neither do all children. Handwriting is a personal expression of self, and thus deviations from the style being taught are acceptable as long as the writing is legible and done with ease.

Disability, then, would be defined as writing that is illegible and/or laborious to produce. Illegibility is determined by poorly formed letters, irregularity of slant, lack of uniformity of size, and/or incorrect spacing between letters, words, or sentences. Discomfort with writing is manifested in extremely slow movements, tenseness, fatigue, lack of interest in writing, and/or putting too much or too little pressure on the writing implement (Tansley & Panckhurst, 1981).

Appropriate Learner Activities

When children are first learning to print, the teacher should create a literate environment and encourage them to: (1) draw pictures and dictate captions, (2) copy captions, (3) trace the teachers' print, (4) copy words, (5) write words that they remember, (6) invent words, and (7) obtain a printed model of unknown words from the teacher. In addition, the teacher can give a weekly formal group lesson coupled with daily individual instruction in letter formation (Clay, 1975).

Although copying and tracing are effective when children experiment with print, they are only minimally effective as formal instructional methods (Addy & Wylie, 1973; Herrick & Okada, 1963). Training children on discrimination tasks, for example, prepares them to do well on exercises requiring them to match letters but not on those asking them to write letters. What is most effective are the techniques described in Box 11.1 that complement cognitive and perceptual learning principles, such as demonstration and revision (Furner, 1983).

These techniques are most effective when handwriting activities are meaningful. In fact, children with writing disabilities often improve just by practicing writing as they compose daily (Graves, 1983b). Time spent in learning how to form letters, then, should be kept at a minimum, with children working only on those that are troublesome. The rest of the time should be spent practicing handwriting by using it to communicate by writing stories, journals, procedures for a science experiment, and "to do" lists (see Chapter 12).

Interest in developing legible handwriting can be increased through the study of the evolution of our alphabet and other writing systems, such as picture writing, smoke signals, and hieroglyphics. For most children, however, the desire to communicate suffices.

Assessing Each Student's Strengths and Weaknesses

Children should be observed both formally and informally while engaged in different kinds of writing tasks assigned as part of their regular classroom work. Such observations will yield information on the speed of movements, degree of tenseness, onset and frequency of fatigue, level of interest, amount of pressure exerted on writing implements, and procedures used for forming letters. Analyzing writing products will yield information regarding the regularity of letter slant and size, spacing between letters, words, and sentences, and overall legibility. It is important to vary the circumstances of observations to determine whether the behaviors are consistent or unique to certain tasks or situations. Some children, for instance, might produce better work under the pressure of doing a final draft, while others might have the opposite response.

Recovery Procedures for Persistent Problems

Causes of illegibility or discomfort with writing include the incomplete development of the prerequisite principles defined by Clay (1975), lack of knowledge on how to form letters, lack of practice, too much or too little concern for correctness, motor dysfunction, or poor vision. Each will be discussed below.

Clay's Principles

Since most children develop writing knowledge while living in literate home environments, it is advisable to duplicate these environments at school. In this way, children who either need additional practice or were never exposed to print in the home will have an opportunity to discover and assimilate the necessary knowledge. To do this, teachers must begin by filling the room with meaningful written language to offer models from which to extract distinctive features. The following items should be easily accessible: books; paper of different colors, sizes, and shapes; and writing implements of different colors and thicknesses. Because the children must also engage in literate activities, the teacher should read to them, allow them to read to each other, write down their dictated messages, let them dictate group or individual stories and read them back, and encourage them to write whatever and whenever they wish. Keep a classroom mailbox to encourage informal communications.

Let children guide instructional decisions. Some will choose to copy or trace, which is appropriate because it helps develop concepts about writing. Other children will want teachers to spell words for them to facilitate their learning and to ease their frustration.

When children can recognize a letter but have difficulty producing it consistently, help them to learn it by reminding them that it is just like the letter in a word that they can spell. For instance, Phillip knew how to write *Laura* but would often forget how to write an *L* in other words. When reminded that it was like the *L,* in *Laura,* he could write it. Eventually, Phillip no longer needed this prompting.

Encourage children in their self-discovery. Display their work prominently and emphasize their progress. Reinforce attempts to write regardless of accuracy or legibility. Convince children that they are capable learners, and most will live up to that expectation.

Letter Formation Knowledge

If children have difficulty forming certain letters, use Furner's (1983) procedure. It is effective even at the secondary level.

Practice

Many children do not write legibly or easily because they lack practice (Graves, 1983). This is especially true of LD students, because, unfortunately, outside of instruction in handwriting, very little writing is required of them. For handwriting to become both legible and comfortable, children must have *daily practice on meaningful materials*. No longer can writing rows of individual letters or copying sentences off the board pass as legitimate practice. Children must be engaged in creating written material for real purposes.

Correctness

For some children, *how* they write is more important than *what* they write. This inappropriate concern can lead to tenseness, slowness, and the application of too much or too little pressure on their writing implements. These children must realize that the attractiveness of a piece of writing should be determined by its purpose. Teaching them to draft, revise, and prepare a final copy is one method of instruction. Also let them write on scrap paper and paper without lines to help free their writing. Children also could do daily repeated writings, similar to repeated readings. First they choose something to write. On the first day a base-line timing of the activity is done. The next day, they try to beat their time, continuing until they have developed some automaticity. A chart should be kept to track progress.

Modeling legible handwriting that is not obsessively neat is also helpful. Show them hurriedly written shopping lists and reminder notes. Occasionally cross out when writing to them. Demonstrate that it is really acceptable to use different kinds of writing for different purposes.

Above all, do not mark up their papers with what they have done wrong. Emphasize the positive, and show them their progress by keeping samples of their work.

Some children, on the other hand, need to be motivated to pay attention to correctness and legibility. Again, an understanding of when legibility is necessary will be helpful. When students understand not everything must be neat, they are more willing to make selected items legible.

Help these children find a project they want to bring to completion. Identify the audience that is important to them, such as, parents, peers, or college admissions officers. Once they are committed to a project, they will usually work on making the finished product legible.

Motor Dysfunction

If children have a physical problem that interferes with the ability to write legibly, trying to improve handwriting will be a frustrating and fruitless endeavor. In such cases it makes more sense to look for alternatives to handwriting. Typewriters and computer word processing packages are excellent. There are even minicomputers that can be carried around and used in classes, the library, or the business office. Since handwriting is only a means to an end, mechanical devices should be used to ease the communication process whenever needed.

Poor Vision

One of the first things to check in a student with handwriting problems is whether a vision problem exists. Look for signs such as squinting, restlessness, neck craning, holding a book too close or too far away, headaches, and discrepancies between quality of work copied from far (the board) and near (a book). If a problem is suspected, talk with the school nurse and/or the parents.

If there is a vision problem, prescription glasses or contact lenses should alleviate the handwriting difficulty. At the very least, it can now be determined whether secondary factors, such as delayed letter knowledge due to poor eyesight, are interfering with progress.

Matching Students to Tasks and Monitoring Performance

With the goals of legibility and comfortableness in mind, learning how to write should be much less exacting than it has been in recent years. To facilitate the procedure further, formal instruction should begin only when children have the necessary prerequisites.

Initial Broad-Based Assessment

Determine childrens' readiness for handwriting instruction by observing whether their informal writing indicates an understanding of Clay's (1975) five principles (see p. 246). Evidence can be observed when they write notes, stories, or letters on their own.

Teachers should also observe children while they are writing to analyze how difficult the process is for them. If it is terribly painful, delay instruction until they become more relaxed. Observe how they hold writing implements such as pencils, pens, and markers and whether they prefer thick implements to thin ones and markers to pencils, since this can make a difference in the ease with which they write. Finally, watch how they form their letters to determine if they are doing so properly.

Management Plan

Children should have their own folder with dated samples of their writing compiled during the year. On the inside cover, put a mimeographed chart listing all of the points that are assessed. Keep the chart current by marking it every time a formal or informal observation is made. Thus, children (as well as their parents and teachers) can see their strengths and weaknesses, what has been worked on, and what still needs further work.

Summary

Handwriting is now being taught within the context of written communication. Of major concern are children's ability to write legibly (when necessary) and with ease. Since children do much learning on their own before formal instruction begins, this learning should be built upon in school. If Clay's (1975) five principles have not been mastered, developmental learning should continue in the classroom.

Formal instruction should be based upon cognitive and perceptual principles. Children need to have models, make discoveries, verbalize, visualize, practice, get feedback, and make revisions. It is essential, however, that handwriting does not become an end in itself. Children must know that it is only a tool to allow them to communicate, just as clear speech is a tool for oral communication. Thus they should be taught only the letters they make incorrectly and should always be engaged in meaningful writing.

Spelling

Spelling problems are very common among LD students, but until recently there has been little research in this area. Consequently, instruction has been based mainly on opinion. It is now known, however, that LD children's spelling errors do not differ dramatically from other children's (see, e.g., Gerber, 1984; Holmes & Peper, 1977). In fact, *their spelling development follows the same pattern as that of normally achieving children, except that it is delayed* (e.g., Gerber, 1985, 1986). An understanding, then, of how children learn to spell is critical in the instruction of LD children.

Development Before and During School

Before schooling, children's writing is often self-generated, and replete with nonstandard spellings. Sometimes the words can be deciphered by their relation to others, depending upon the level of the writers' conceptual and phonetic knowledge of the language. As children develop this essential knowledge, they move through five phases of spelling: prephonemic, early phonemic, letter name, transitional, and derivational (see Henderson, 1981).

Although the pace at which students acquire more sophisticated spelling knowledge varies, children obviously seek knowledge about their world. They act on their environment to try to make sense out of it, and in doing so develop strategies that they use consistently to spell new words. They, of course, need feedback, support, modeling, and guidance from those who know more than they do.

Prephonemic Spelling

At this phase of spelling, children have discovered that letters convey a message that can be read. They do not know, however, that there is a relationship between a word's spelling and its pronunciation. Even though they often can print their own name, they do not understand the concept of a word. Their writing may: (1) be a few squiggles on a page; (2) indiscriminately incorporate letters, numbers, and shapes that resemble letters; (3) appear randomly distributed on the page, horizontally from left to right or right to left; (4) begin at the top or bottom of the page; and (5) have spaces between words, words that run together, or no recognizable words at all. Since most children who use a prephonemic spelling strategy do not yet know how to read, they will usually ask the teacher to tell them what they wrote, read their own writing from memory, or make up a message. (See Figures 11.3–11.6 for examples of this stage.)

Early Phonemic Spelling

As children begin to understand that written letters represent certain sounds in spoken words, they adopt a new strategy, known as early phonemic spelling. They write at least one letter of a word, which is generally the beginning sound. When three or four sounds are written, they are typically consonants and long vowels. Interspersed is an occasional sight word spelled correctly.

Their writing can now be deciphered by patient and creative adults. These children are just beginning to read and sometimes can read back

FIGURE 11.7 Early Phonemic Spelling: Phillip at Age Five Years and Five Months.

what they wrote. Even though they spend a great deal of time sounding out the words as they write them, they easily lose their place in the word and repeat or omit sounds because of the complexity of the task.

An example of this stage can be seen in Figure 11.7. Here Phillip, at age five years and five months, began by drawing a rocket. He then labeled its parts. Starting at the top left, he wrote *PT* for *top*, but was dissatisfied and crossed it out. Next, he tried *POT* (a sight word) and asked for confirmation. He was given feedback that resulted in his writing *TOP*. Then he wrote another sight word, *hot*, and began experimenting with making words out of letters he knew—*PE* and *PC* (his cat's name). He then returned to his labeling and wrote: *DRO* (for *door*), *FIR* (for *fire*), *PNMET* (for *planet*), *RKET* (for *rocket*), *SDOR* (for *star*), and *PNET* (for *planet*).

Letter-Name Spelling

As children develop a firm beginning sight vocabulary, an awareness that a word is an entity surrounded by white space, and a stable understanding of letters as representing sounds, they switch to the letter-name strategy. At this stage of spelling some words are consistently spelled correctly. Unknown words are attempted by matching the name of a letter to the sound it represents in a word. Long vowels are generally used accurately, but silent letters are omitted. Short vowels are often used inaccurately, if at all, and some sounds are systematically left out, even though they can be heard as the word is pronounced.

These children are not fluent readers, but they usually can read back what they have written. Their spelling is also more easily discerned by others.

Laura's letter-name spelling strategy is seen in Figure 11.8. Some spellings are correct, others are based upon the name of the letter, and others are partially remembered spellings. The final *e* in *came, place,* and *sae,* represents *-ing* because the *i* sounds like a long *e*. *Are* is a sight word that sounds like *our*. The *h* and *s* are clearly heard in *house,* and she knows that some vowels go between the two letters. Finally, *Thk* exemplifies the difficulty with vowels and the letter *n*.

Transitional Spelling

In the transitional phase, children take a major step toward standard spelling. They master the short vowel sounds and understand some spelling rules, such as the use of the silent *e*. They are also more aware of

FIGURE 11.8 Letter-Name Spelling: Laura at Age Six Years and Five Months.

which spellings are correct and which are not, which sometimes leads to
a series of attempts to spell one word correctly.

LD students typically enter this phase in late elementary school and
stay in it for a number of years. Many rules and their exceptions must
be processed, which takes much experimentation and sensitive feedback
from teachers.

In Figure 11.9, Laura has spelled most words correctly with nonstandard spellings interspersed. The silent *e* and short vowels are now usually
correct. An occasional reversal is still made during a first draft, but these
do not appear in final drafts.

Derivational Spelling

LD children reach the derivational phase anywhere from high school to
adulthood, depending upon how much they have read, written, and studied word derivations. In this stage, people are on the verge of being correct
spellers. They have gained control over the spelling rules about marking
vowels, doubling consonants, and adding inflections, prefixes, and suffixes. They still must work, however, to obtain a more sophisticated un-

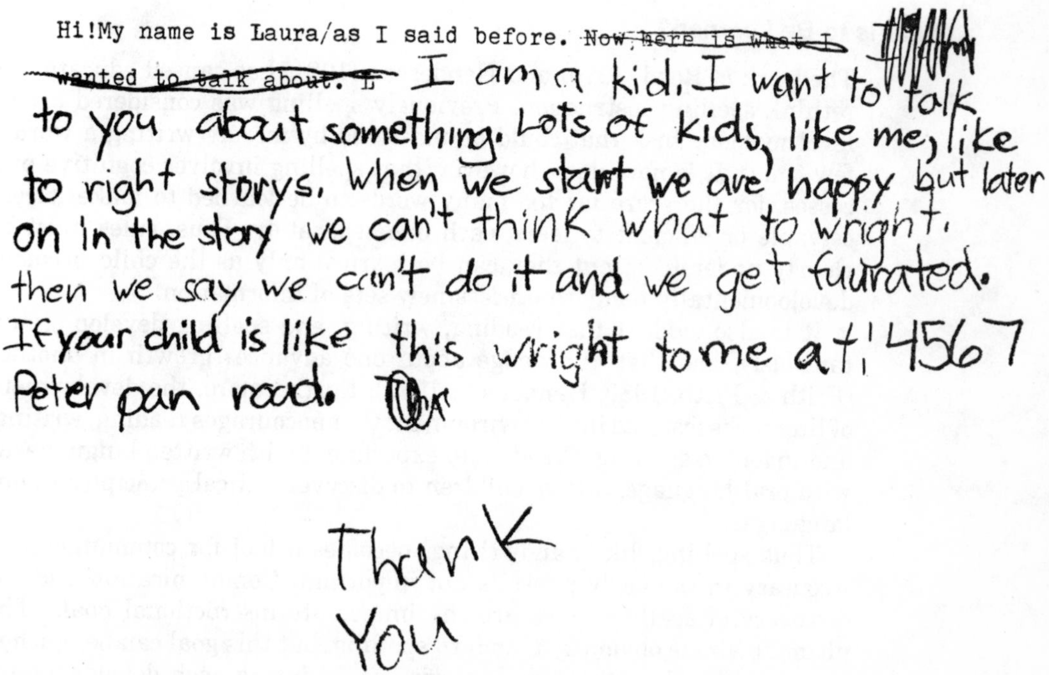

Hi!My name is Laura/as I said before. ~~Now, here is what I~~
~~wanted to talk about. I~~ I am a kid. I want to talk
to you about something. Lots of kids, like me, like
to right storys. When we start we are happy but later
on In the story we can't think what to wright.
then we say we can't do it and we get fuurated.
If your child is like this wright to me at 4567
Peter pan road. Or

Thank
You

FIGURE 11.9 Transitional Spelling: Laura at Age Nine Years and Seven Months.

derstanding of the English language through the study of word derivations—both the history of words and the relationships among words in the same family. At this stage, spelling is understood as a reflection of the meaning of words. Thus, *finance, financial,* and *financially* share spelling features because they have related meanings.

The Instructional Model

The research shows that learning to spell is a developmental and cognitive process. Consequently, *it is not very effective to have children memorize lists of spelling words* (Temple, Nathan, & Burris, 1982), for if they do not have their prerequisite knowledge to understand why the word is misspelled or what makes the correct spelling accurate, the instruction will not be retained much beyond the weekly test.

The responsibility for learning to spell rests largely with children. They must have plenty of opportunities to explore written language, invent spellings, and test and adjust hypotheses based upon feedback from teachers, peers, and reading material. The task of the teacher, then, is to provide the motivation, modeling, encouragement to guess, writing activities, and feedback (see Temple et al., 1982).

What Is to Be Learned?

The work of Read (1975) and Henderson (1981) has caused educators to rethink spelling instruction. Previously spelling was considered a low-level memory task that could be mastered by merely writing a word a few times. It is now clear, however, that spelling involves cognitive processes, for there are far too many words to be learned to make it conceivable or efficient to learn each one separately. Thus, rules must be clearly understood, but they can be learned only as the child becomes developmentally ready to process new sets of information.

It is also evident that reading, writing, and spelling develop simultaneously, and that knowledge about one advances growth in another (Frith & Frith, 1980; Henderson, 1981). Furthermore, the development of literacy is fostered in an environment that encourages reading, writing, and invented spelling. Freedom to experiment with written language, as with oral language, allows children to discover critical principles in our language.

Thus spelling, like handwriting, becomes a tool for communication. Accuracy in the early phase is not important. Communication and the discovery of spelling rules are the immediate instructional goals. The ultimate aim is obviously standard spelling, but this goal can be reached only by achieving a series of interim goals during each developmental phase. The teacher, then, must be able to adjust standards of accuracy to match students' current levels of spelling development.

Demonstrating Successful Learning

The only formal measure of spelling is tests on specific words. Small groups of words (three to twelve) are tested at a time to keep the task manageable. Students are expected to spell those words correctly in subsequent composing activities. Although early drafts may contain errors, they should be self-corrected on final drafts.

Students should also generalize their spelling knowledge through discussion of rules and other activities to promote word knowledge. Generalization will be apparent in final drafts of regular classroom writing. Finally, movement to the next phase of spelling development is a strong indication that learning is occurring.

LD Students' Typical Problems with This Material

Current research shows that the spelling errors made by LD children do not differ in quantity or quality from those made by normally achieving children who are in an equivalent phase of spelling development (Gerber, 1985). It was previously thought that LD children made more reversals, phonetic misspellings, and incorrect placement of letters. This, however, is not true (Nelson, 1980).

Appropriate Learner Activities

Although published spelling series are tempting because all of the planning is done for the teacher, they are instructionally inadequate in the way they group words for study and in the kinds of exercises they offer (Fitzsimmons & Loomer, 1980). Furthermore, they do not consider students' conceptual knowledge of spelling. Some students give the appearance of learning because they either knew the words before the lesson or could memorize them just long enough to pass the test. For these reasons, spelling textbooks are not advocated.

A complete spelling program needs to meet the needs of *individuals*. It should incorporate learning the words misspelled in daily writing, generalizing spelling knowledge, and mastering objectives in progressive phases of development.

Learning Individual Words

In practice many methods for learning to spell, such as writing misspelled words a few times, writing words in the air, breaking words into syllables, and learning rules are only minimally effective (Fitzsimmons & Loomer, 1980). These must be replaced with techniques that have been proven effective: (1) using self-corrected pretests followed by immediate study and retest; (2) developing flexible knowledge about spelling; (3) studying

---

Box 11.2 Learning to Spell Individual Words

1. Dictate the spelling words.
2. For those that are wrong:
    a. Write the incorrect spelling while saying something like, "This is incorrect. You spelled it this way."
    b. Write the word correctly while saying, "This is how to spell the word correctly."
    c. Have the child copy the correct spelling once.
3. Dictate the spelling words again.

Note. Based on "Techniques to Teach Generalizable Spelling Skills" by M. M. Gerber, 1984, *Academic Therapy, 20;* and "Spelling as Concept-Driven Problem Solving" by M. M. Gerber, 1985, in B. Hutson (Ed.), *Advances in Reading/Language Research,* vol. 3, Greenwich, CT: JAI Press.

---

whole words; and (4) writing often to maintain spelling competence (Fitzsimmons & Loomer, 1980). For LD students, three words chosen from daily work should be dictated and studied daily until mastery is shown on a dictation (Gettinger, 1984). These students need sufficient time to practice until mastery. Corrective feedback should focus their attention on the differences between their misspellings and standard ones (Gerber 1984, 1985, 1986). Box 11.2 describes a technique that incorporates these essential points.

Developing Generalizations

To develop independence in spelling, children must learn to predict spellings by using all potential sources of knowledge, including phonics, phonic rules, word structure, mnemonics, and analogy. Bookman (1984) uses group discussion to analyze errors. Children are led to discover rules, assuming more independence in the process.

In one technique, teachers use misspelled words to develop exercises. For example, if *missed* is spelled *mist,* children would be given sentences like: "Joe missed the ball"; "She missed her friend"; and "The mist was light." More sentences are added with words fitting the same pattern, (e.g., *find* and *fined*). Through discussion, children discover that: (1) phonics does not always work; and (2) *-ed* serves a specific, predictable function. In another technique, childen are given a few spellings of one word and asked to decide which shows the most spelling knowledge and which the least (e.g., *finly, finaly,* and *finele* are misspellings of *finally*).

Progressing through Spelling Phases

Students' levels of spelling development determine which activities are appropriate for further advancement. Since children function at many levels, these activities should be carried out individually or in small groups (see Boxes 11.3–11.7).

Instructional Principles

Establishing activities is only part of the teachers' role. They must also provide motivation, modeling, encouragement to invent spellings, meaningful writing activities, and feedback.

Box 11.3   Phase One of Spelling

Objectives (Temple & Gillet, 1984; Temple, Notha, & Burris, 1982)

1. Realizing that writing is a form of communication.
2. Discovering a word as a distinct entity, composed of letters, preceded and followed by blank spaces, written from left to right, and read from left to right.
3. Representing sounds in words with letters.

Activities

1. Reading daily to children. Use "Big Books" (e.g., *Scholastic Big Books,* 1980; *Story Box Big Books,* 1980) with groups or trade books with individuals. Move a finger or pointer across the line of print while reading. Read favorite books many times.
2. Making and repeatedly reading books that contain familiar logos (e.g., McDonald's, Crest, and Campbell's).
3. Writing captions to drawings and reading them.
4. Labeling items around the room and reading them.
5. Dictating stories, reading them, and playing word games that focus attention on beginning letters and sounds.
6. Asking parents to: read daily to their children, take them to the library, write notes to them, encourage them to write letters to relatives, let them help write the grocery list and shop for the items on the list, write birthday cards, and engage in other meaningful literacy activities (Grinnell, 1984).

Box 11.4   Phase Two of Spelling

Objectives

1. Continuing refinement of the objectives for prephonemic spelling.
2. Growing ability to segment the sounds within words into individual phonemes.

Activities

1. Continuing the activities for prephonemic spelling.
2. Focusing on individual words by pointing to each while reading from a "Big Book" or trade book.
3. Memorizing poetry, songs, or stories and pointing to the words as they are read individually or chorally. Especially useful for this procedure are "big books" and *Instant Readers* (Martin & Brogan, 1971).
4. Listening to tapes of a book and following with a finger.
5. Encouraging and reinforcing a large quantity of functional writing that can then be read by the child (e.g., notes to the teacher or classmates, thank you notes to friends, journals, and menus for playing restaurant).
6. Separating words from each other as they are written by putting a dot or a dash after each.
7. Pointing to a word in a memorized story and asking the children to identify it or, alternatively, asking them to find the word in the story.
8. Developing a word box containing words from dictated stories and other sources in the environment that the child wants to learn to read and spell as well as those that have already been mastered. These can be used as flash cards, references when writing, word games, and tools for building sentences.
9. Cutting sentences into individual words.
10. Writing first drafts and final drafts. Children should revise some of their spellings for the final draft, but it is too much to expect a perfect piece.

Box 11.5   Phase Three of Spelling

Objectives (Temple & Gillet, 1984)

1. Analyzing the spellings of words to learn about their structure.
2. Understanding the structure of words with
   a. common short vowel spellings,
   b. common long vowel spellings,
   c. common beginning consonant sound spellings, and
   d. common structures of one-syllable words.
3. Generalizing from the spellings of known words to similar novel words.
4. Experiencing reading and writing as communication.
5. Experimenting in an environment that encourages risk taking and invented spellings.

Activities

1. Developing word banks as described in Box 11.4.
2. Engaging in inductive or deductive word sorts. Children group their word bank cards according to common features, such as all words that rhyme with *boy* (Gillet & Kita, 1979). These features should then be reinforced through discussion and writing activities.
3. Engaging in word hunts through printed material for a specific word.
4. Developing personalized dictionaries of words children like to use in their writing.
5. Doing a lot of meaningful writing and invented spelling, such as writing stories and keeping journals.
6. Reading to children daily.
7. Discovering the common patterns in words through word sorts, word hunts, and discussions. Teach them in the order in which they most often appear in print: (a) consonant-vowel-consonant (e.g., *cat* and *red*); (b) consonant-vowel-consonant-silent *e* (e.g., *like* and *hope*); and (c) consonant-vowel-vowel-consonant (e.g., *read* and *coat*). Wait until these patterns are well established before introducing less common ones (Temple & Gillet, 1984).

Box 11.6   Phase Four of Spelling

Objectives

1. Understanding more advanced concepts, such as irregular vowel spellings, inflectional endings, and rules for doubling consonants.

Activities

1. Using word sorts.
2. Encouraging a wide range of reading.
3. Using the revision process to increase spelling competence. Do this by analyzing drafts to identify which patterns or rules the child is working to master. Then structure inductive and deductive activities to assist in the learning of those rules.
4. Using commercial spelling programs selectively to work on the rules identified for each child.
5. Engaging in meaningful writing activities to practice what is known and to learn more about what is yet unknown.
6. Playing word games (e.g., Boggle, Spill 'n Spell, and Hangman).

Motivation

As with handwriting, motivation to spell accurately can be established by having the students prepare final drafts. Spelling need not be perfect until it is ready for an audience. If students have a meaningful audience, they will be willing to correct their misspellings. Because the need to correct emphasizes the value of knowing how to spell, the tediousness of looking up correct spellings can be alleviated.

Additional motivators are seeing that others have similar problems learning how to spell, that it takes a long time for everyone to learn to spell, and that in the end they will be good spellers. This knowledge can be shared by showing students books containing invented spellings, like Temple et al. (1982), and compositions by their peers.

Modeling

In addition to modeling correct spelling, teachers need to model processes for finding the correct spellings. The misguided belief that teachers know

---

Box 11.7   Phase Five of Spelling

Objectives (Hodges, 1982)

1. Understanding that the meaning of a word affects its spelling.
2. Discovering the historical origins of words that are related through meaning.
3. Recognizing that words derived from the same root are spelled similarly even though they are pronounced differently.
4. Understanding that some combinations of letters are permissible and others are not.

Activities

1. Using dictionaries and other sources to explore etymologies.
2. Finding all words that are in the same family as a specific word. Discuss spelling and pronounciation similarities and differences.
3. Creating nonsense words and, based upon which letters are next to each other, discussing why some of the nonsense words could be actual English words and why others are not acceptable spelling patterns.
4. Studying prefixes and suffixes and their effect, if any, on the letters in the word to which they are affixed.
5. Playing word games (Boggle, Hangman, Perquackey, Password, anagrams, word-finds, and Scrabble).
6. Using meaningful writing activities to continue experimentation with both the meaning and spelling of words as well as the application of new information.
7. Reading widely and extensively.
8. Using the revision process to identify which conceptual knowledge the child is interested in mastering and is ready to assimilate. This provides motivation for the word learning activities.

---

everything must be altered. Children must hear teachers say, "I don't know. Let's look in the dictionary," or "I just read that word. Let me try to find it," to learn that knowledge is accessible to them just as it is to their teachers, that everyone has things they do not know, and that even adults use specific methods to gain information.

Encouraging Invented Spellings

Students must also be encouraged to experiment and make guesses as to how words are spelled. In an environment in which accuracy is demanded, children usually refuse to risk failures, thereby inhibiting new learning. They must know that their attempts to spell will be greeted with positive reinforcement and encouragement.

Not only must the atmosphere be risk free, but the teaching must be skilled. It is easier to ask the teacher or a friend how to spell a word than to figure it out. Children must understand, however, that they learn from their own mistakes and that *the absence of errors means the absence of learning*. When they invent spellings, they stretch their knowledge to find out what they know and do not know.

There are times, though, when teachers should provide the correct spelling, as when the struggle of figuring out the word interferes with the creative process (e.g., writing a composition) or when a speller in the early phases of development becomes discouraged by the laborious task of sounding out a word while writing it down.

Meaningful Writing Activities

Numerous meaningful writing activities are necessary to provide appropriate practice and transfer. They allow children to work on accurate spelling while engaging in the functional activities for which it is needed. The nature of these activities depends upon the developmental phase of the child. They may include writing captions on pictures, making menus for a fictional restaurant, keeping journals, composing poems, analyzing experiments, and writing research papers.

Feedback

Children need positive encouragement and specific feedback about invented spellings to refine their hypotheses. The exact form of the feedback depends upon a speller's level of knowledge. A prephonemic speller, for example, who is just beginning to attempt writing, should have every effort encouraged, regardless of accuracy. As the child gains both confidence and a more stable knowledge of the sound-symbol relationship, more information can be given.

Phillip, as a prephonemic speller, wrote his name as *PLIP* (Grinnell & Burris, 1983). He was highly praised for writing his name so well and was encouraged to write other things, sign his name to cards, and read his name as it was written by others. When he became an early phonemic speller, he was still given positive feedback but with more information. Around Halloween he labeled one picture *pmkn,* and upon finishing asked, "Is that right?" He was told,

You did a really good job of writing "pumpkin," and I can read what you wrote. You got most of the letters that you can hear in the word. Would you like to see how I spell "pumpkin?" O.K., the way I write it is "pumpkin." Now, you can see that the first letter, two of the middle letters, and the last letter are the same. Since you pronounce the word as "pumpkin," it makes sense that you left out the "p" because you don't say it. There's also a "u" and an "i" in the word. I'm really proud of the way you spelled "pumpkin"; and I know what you wrote even though it isn't spelled the same way as it looks in books. Soon you will be able to spell it that way too.

In this response to Phillip, the adult used positive reinforcement, modeled the correct spelling, and compared the similarities and differences between the two spellings, which gave him the encouragement and knowledge to help him move toward standard spelling.

Students can also obtain feedback from print. For example, if a child invents a spelling and later reads something that uses that word, the written word acts as data to help confirm, modify, or reject the invented spelling (Smith, 1982).

Procedures

Gerber (1984) devised a technique to build metacognitive awareness for the prediction and detection of spelling errors. In just two twenty-minute lessons, using words students can spell, they were taught to ask themselves questions like: "Have I seen this word before? Do I know any words that look/sound like this word? What part(s) of the word am I uncertain about? What are some different ways to write this word?" (p. 162). This procedure holds promise when used to help children eleven years and older access the information that they may have but do not use to improve their spelling.

Assessing Each Student's Strengths and Weaknesses

Improvement in spelling accuracy can be determined by analyzing the spelling students use in their regular writing activities. As they write, observe their level of independence, the strategies they use when they do not know how to spell a word, their level of confidence, and their freedom to invent spellings. In analyzing their writing products, note movement from one phase of development to another. Also look for subtle changes as children gradually master the conceptual knowledge necessary to move to a new level.

Recovery Procedures for Persistent Problems

LD students often believe they will never be able to spell correctly and/or are so self-conscious about their poor spelling that they will not even try to write words they do not know how to spell, if they are willing to write anything at all. Since experimenting with language is the cornerstone of learning to spell, the focus of recovery procedures is to free children to be willing to risk being wrong.

Numerous writing activities along with encouragement and positive reinforcement are essential. Among other things, this means not marking all over their papers. Emphasizing that they are doing certain tasks correctly and that they are communicating will bring faster results than focusing on mistakes.

Children need to know that their teachers believe in their ability to become accurate spellers. The first step toward this goal is valuing what they do produce. If they will not write anything, begin by letting them draw or dictate stories, then gradually move them toward writing their own. Writing in a daily journal is also helpful. If necessary, promise not to look at the journals, thereby allowing them to test their abilities secretly (see Chapter 12).

Varied and frequent opportunities to write are essential, for LD children need time and experience with written language to investigate the intricacies of spelling and to apply what they have learned. Keep expectations in line with their abilities so as not to demand too much too soon.

Matching Students to Tasks and Monitoring Performance

To match LD students to tasks, first identify their level of spelling development by analyzing their invented spellings to uncover the strategies used to spell unknown words. The two most useful ways to assess spelling are to evaluate the invented spellings that appear in the children's daily work, and to administer a specially designed test to elicit invented spellings. Either method produces a set of misspelled words to use to determine the child's developmental level. In some cases, both methods can be used for verification or clarification.

Initial Broad-Based Assessment

For an accurate assessment, ten to twenty-five invented spellings are needed (Temple & Gillet, 1984). Collect these over a two- or three-week period and from a variety of sources, such as journals, work sheets, and later drafts of compositions (use later drafts because on early drafts children occasionally misspell words they can spell correctly knowing they can be fixed).

Spelling Features Lists

Temple and Gillet (1984) suggest using two levels of lists to determine children's level of spelling development. One is a beginning features list

Box 11.8   Beginners' Features List

Part I: One session

Fish   I caught a fish.

Bend   Can you bend your arm?

Jumped   I jumped over a log.

Yell   We can yell all we want outside.

Learned   I learned to count in school.

Shove   Don't shove your neighbor in the lunch line.

Witch   Hansel and Gretel met a witch.

Piece   I want a piece of cake.

Part II: Another session

Late   I stayed up late.

Bench   We sat down on a bench.

Drive   I'm too young to drive a car.

Wet   Your hair is all wet.

Chirped   The cricket chirped in the yard last night.

Neck   She wore a gold chain around her neck.

Trained   I trained my dog to shake hands.

Tick   There was a tick on my dog.

Note. From Charles Temple and Jean Wallace Gillet, *Language Arts: Learning Processes and Teaching Practices*, p. 415. Copyright © 1984 by Charles Temple and Jean Wallace Gillet. Reprinted by permission of Little, Brown and Company.

for those reading through about the second-grade level (see Box 11.8). With LD children, however, this level may be extended upward. The other is for children functioning beyond that level (see Box 11.9). Either list can be given to groups or individuals. Before taking the test, children must understand that: (1) they probably will not know how to spell the words; (2) the test will not be graded; (3) the purpose of the test is to see how they think the words should be spelled; and (4) if they do not know how to spell a word, they should try to figure it out.

Box 11.9 Advanced Features List

Setter My dog is an Irish setter.

Shove Don't shove your neighbor in the lunch line.

Grocery I'm going to the grocery store.

Button A button popped off his jacket.

Sailor My cousin is a sailor.

Prison If you break the law, you may go to prison.

Nature We went for a hike on the nature trail.

Peeked The spy peeked out from his hiding place.

Special Birthdays are special days.

Preacher The preacher talked for an hour.

Slowed The truck slowed down for the curve.

Sail The boat had a torn sail.

Feature We went to see a double feature.

Batter The first batter struck out.

Note. From Charles Temple and Jean Wallace Gillet, *Language Arts: Learning Processes and Teaching Practices*, p. 415. Copyright © 1984 by Charles Temple and Jean Wallace Gillet. Reprinted by permission of Little, Brown and Company.

Administer the test by reading the word, the sentence in which it is used, and then the word two more times. If the children are overtaxed, the beginner's list can be administered in two or three sittings. Pronounce the word normally without exaggerating any of its parts. If a child scores 50 percent on the beginners' features list, administer the advanced test to get enough misspellings to score the test.

Scoring the Misspellings

Guidelines for determining students' phases of spelling development are shown in Box 11.10.

Management Plan

Children should choose three words at a time to study from their daily writing. They should keep track of words to study and words mastered

---

Box 11.10 Procedures for Scoring Features Lists

Use the following system to score from 1 to 5 points for each word spelled in the test:

1. *Prephonemic* (1 point): None of the letters represent sounds in the word (e.g., *DLD* for *once*).
2. *Early Phonemic* (2 points): Key sounds are omitted with the exception of *n* or *m* before a consonant or vowels before *m, n, r,* or *l* in unstressed syllables (e.g., *nd* for *wind*).
3. *Letter-Name* (3 points): Most of the letters represent the sound in their name. Often *i* is used for *o*, *e* for *i*, *a* for *e*, and *o* for *u* (e.g., *hek* for *chick*).
4. *Transitional* (4 points): Short vowels, digraphs, *y* and *w*, and the soft sounds of *c* and *g* are correct. These kinds of spellings are also allowable: *chr* for *tr*, *jr* for *dr*, *ch* for the *t* in nature, and *sh* for the *c* in *special*. Past-tense endings are spelled as they sound (e.g., *lurnd* for *learned*, *groshry* for *grocery*).
5. *Derivational* (5 points): Stems are spelled the same. Words like *nature* and *special* are spelled with *ti, si, ci, sy,* or *ty* (e.g., *sailer* for *sailor*, *natiur* for *nature*).

Note. From Charles Temple and Jean Wallace Gillet, *Language Arts: Learning Processes and Teaching Practices*, p. 416. Copyright © 1984 by Charles Temple and Jean Wallace Gillet. Adapted by permission of Little, Brown and Company.

---

using three-by-five-inch cards and a file box as they follow this procedure to mastery: test, get feedback, practice, and retest. Classmates, aides, or teachers can assist with dictation and corrective feedback. Progress is monitored by teachers and students with a chart to check mastery of the groups of three words and the generalization of given rules.

Summary and Conclusions

LD students' spelling is not dramatically different from that of normally achieving children of the same reading level. They learn to write and spell by going through the same phases of development and by being exposed to the same kinds of environments and activities. They can and must be engaged in cognitive activity for this learning to take place. The learning must occur in an environment that is rich with print and opportunities to experiment with language. They need to develop hypotheses, test them through experience with print, receive feedback, and make adjustments based upon that feedback. Teachers can establish a risk-free atmosphere for such experimenting by offering modeling, encouragement, and reinforcement and doing away with red pencils. Learning should be achieved by emphasizing what the students have done correctly, and grading should be a system of reward rather than punishment.

Above all, learning must take place within a meaningful context. Spelling and handwriting must be mastered because the child wants to communicate and not because it is an objective on an IEP. In short, students need a reason to learn. The best way to provide this is through functional writing, in which students communicate what they *want* to communicate. When this happens, LD students *will* write!

Chapter 12

Instruction in Composition

Paula C. Grinnell

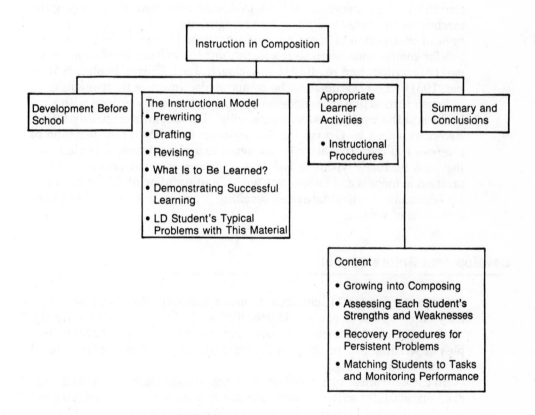

Questions to Consider

1. What does it mean to teach writing (composition) as a process?
2. What are the components of such a process? Why is it important to approach writing instruction in this way?
3. What is the relative importance of meaning and mechanics?
4. How should feedback be provided to writers?
5. How should specific composition objectives be introduced and managed?

LD students are rarely given opportunities to compose. Their instruction in writing is generally skills based, with emphasis on improving the mechanics that are thought to be prerequisites to composing. Since the bulk of instruction is spent on reading, there is very little if any time left for composition, despite the facts that: (1) writing is often more severely retarded than reading (e.g., Deloach, Earl, Brown, Poplin, & Warner, 1981), and (2) students who compose also improve their reading.

When instruction in composition is given, it usually is done with skill books and the very procedures with which LD students originally failed. Recent research by Graves (1983), however, has shown that learning to compose is a cognitive activity involving experimentation, question asking, and feedback within a risk-free environment that provides appropriate role models and encounters with meaningful print. Their work has led educators to reevaluate their teaching practices and in fact their very definition of writing.

Development Before School

As seen in Chapter 11, children do much learning about writing before they enter school (see, e.g., Harste, Burke, & Woodward, 1981). By the time they enter kindergarten, most have mastered Clay's (1975) principles of writing, are in the prephonemic phase, and have differentiated writing from drawing.

To the untrained eye, however, it is not always clear that young children are actually writing. Often one needs to observe them to determine whether literacy learning is occurring. For instance, in Figure 11.5 the writing to the right of the drawing of E.T. looks like scribbling. The adult present, however, interacted with Phillip and ascertained that he was trying to write *E.T.*

Once the differentiation between writing and drawing has occurred, children continue to use drawing to help them communicate graphically (Harste et al., 1981), moving back and forth between drawing and writing to put their complete message on paper. Since they do not have enough command of the writing system to relay their message adequately, they revert to drawing to fill in the gaps. Drawing can also serve to organize, plan, tell, embellish, decorate, or revise graphic communication (Grinnell & Burris, 1983). In Figures 11.2, 11.5, and 11.6, drawing is the center of the communication, with writing having mainly a labeling function. With Figure 11.7, however, a change occurs in the relationship between drawing and writing, for the picture of the rocket serves as both the stimulus for the writing and the center that gives all of the surrounding words meaning. Without the picture, the writing would be nothing more than a series of unrelated words. With the drawing, there is real communication. Although full sentences are not present, it is clear that Phillip was writing about a rocket that has a top and a door, expels fire, and travels near planets and stars.

In Figure 11.8 the drawing is more of a decoration than anything else. It came at the end of the main communication as an afterthought. Here, in fact, the phrase, "It's a Dog," serves to explain the drawing. This is the reverse of what was seen previously, when the picture was necessary to understand the writing.

Finally, drawings are often revised, just as writing is. In Figure 12.1, Phillip, at age four years and seven months began by making an *L*, which he discovered could also be a *7*. He then added two horizontal lines to make an *E*. The addition of a vertical line gave him a *B*, which he then revised by adding another vertical line down the center while saying, "Look what else I can make. It's a window" (Grinnell & Burris, 1983).

FIGURE 12.1 Revision in Drawing: Phillip at Age Four Years and Seven Months.

Most of the learning just described occurs spontaneously at home and is rarely displayed in school. Harste et al. (1981) hypothesize that in school children learn that there are right and wrong answers and that to avoid being wrong, they should write only what has been taught. Consequently their previous learning is not built upon, and they even may come to doubt its validity since the school does not offer legitimatization.

The Instructional Model

Of utmost importance is teaching writing as *process* rather than a product. Many go through school assuming that they do not know how to write because writing takes them a long time, and they are rarely satisfied with their first product. These people do not know the well-kept secret that professional writers have long known—writing is often slow, arduous, and even painful and requires much work before and after the first draft (Murray, 1968). The dissemination of the work of Graves (1983) and his associates (see, e.g., Calkins, 1983) is only now beginning to inform educators of this concept.

The writing process has three basic phases: prewriting, drafting, and revising. The time spent in each phase depends upon the writer and the piece of writing. These phases are recursive rather than linear. Thus, while drafting, the writer might stop to do more prewriting or some revising.

Prewriting

Prewriting is the planning phase of writing. It involves deciding on a purpose; finding and narrowing a topic; establishing an audience; collecting information; developing an organizational plan; and playing with ideas, mentally and on paper. The paper's content is researched, thought about, talked about, expanded, narrowed, and thoroughly examined as the writer attempts to make sense of the subject and decide how to treat it. This period of discovery and planning can be either exciting or overwhelming as the enormity of the task becomes apparent. Thus care must be taken to prevent the young writer from becoming immobilized.

Drafting

Drafting is the first writing of a paper during which ideas are developed and the full extent of the writer's message is realized. As they write, writers often discover the intricacies of their ideas and make connections between them that they had not made previously. Mechanics should be ignored at this stage to allow full concentration on the content. The draft should be done as quickly as possible to prevent the writer from ruminating and freezing. Drafting can be very threatening, because there is something about committing ideas to paper that makes one feel exposed and defenseless. It is almost as if the writer's ego is on the paper.

Revising

During the revising phase a piece becomes finalized as it is moved through a series of drafts and then edited for the mechanics of punctuation, spelling, grammar, and form. Drafts are rewritten to fill in gaps, develop ideas, add details, eliminate the unnecessary, reformulate concepts, and reorganize ideas. This is the point at which scissors, tape, and a wastebasket or a word processor are necessities. Whole sections and pages often are eliminated and/or moved. This phase also can pose problems, because authors feel an attachment to their writing and altering it is almost like self-violation. Children, then, must be carefully led to and through this phase. Only after the authors are satisfied with their writing should they work on the mechanics to make their final drafts accurate and presentable.

What Is to Be Learned?

It is critical for the teacher to establish the primary importance of content. Mechanics develop out of the need to communicate intelligibly (see, e.g., Graves, 1983). This approach allows students to become people who are capable of writing, will write, and understand the purposes for writing. With this perspective, Gaskins & Elliot (1983) have developed a hierarchy of writing objectives (see Box 12.1).

It is also important to establish an instructional environment that builds upon what children have learned prior to schooling to prevent the detrimental effects of the artificial yet overriding separation of home and school learning. Finally, teachers must help children develop the writing skills necessary for success in school, on the job, and at home. Many LD youngsters now go to college or to jobs requiring literacy skills. If they cannot perform according to the demands of the situation, their career options are limited. Since by definition LD students are of average or above average intelligence, schools should not constrict their futures.

Schools, then, must train children to write for different purposes. Britton (1970) classifies writing into three categories: (1) expressive, (2) transactional, and (3) poetic.

Expressive Writing

Expressive writing, stemming from personal experiences and feelings, is conversational and may leap from one subject to another. Children assume

---

Box 12.1   Check List of Writing Objectives

Content

Does it make sense?

Did I stay on topic?

Did I say enough to get the job done?

Did I express my ideas completely?

Organization

Does my work have an introduction and a conclusion?

Did I organize my ideas into paragraphs?

Did I support my ideas with details, examples, and comparisons?

Effectiveness

Did I use precise words and phrases?

Did I express my ideas interestingly and in new ways?

Did I use language that adds flavor and style?

Mechanics

Did I use complete sentences?

Did I write neatly?

Did I spell correctly?

Did I use appropriate capitals and end punctuation?

Note. Adapted from *Teaching for Success: Administrative and Classroom Practices at Benchmark School* (pp. 96–97) by I. W. Gaskins and T. T. Elliot, 1983, Media, PA: Benchmark Press.

---

that their audience knows them, is interested in their accounts, and is privy to details that may be left out of the text.

Transactional Writing

This writing is done to transact business and includes exposition, description, and persuasion. The reader must be engaged in this writing for the transaction to be completed.

Expository writing, which includes explaining a subject and delineating the steps in a procedure, is needed for success in writing science experiments, directions, technical reports, and the like. Descriptive writing, which helps readers visualize a subject, is needed for success in writing letters, essays, reports, and stories. Persuasive writing, which presents a thesis and supporting evidence, is needed for success in writing certain kinds of business letters, public relations materials, budget requests, and the like.

Poetic Writing

Poetic writing is an art form that represents formal literary style. Meant to be appreciated and enjoyed, it includes narratives, poetry, plays, fables, and fairy tales. Given the literary nature of poetic writing, it may seem unnecessary to expect LD children to master it. A number of successful writing programs, however, have shown this to be an illogical assumption (see, e.g., Rich & Nedboy, 1977).

Demonstrating Successful Learning

Teachers can determine students' mastery of composition objectives by observing their writing products and processes in a variety of informal and formal assignments, including first and final drafts.

Typical LD Students' Problems with This Material

Mykelbust (1973) found that LD children have more problems than normally achieving children with syntax, ideation (written expression of ideas, thoughts, and understandings), total number of words written, and number of words per sentence. Also problematic are spelling, grammar, capitalization, and punctuation, with the tendency being for older student's scores to deviate more from expected mean scores (Poplin, Gray, Larsen, Banikowski, & Mehring, 1980). It is noteworthy that LD third and fourth graders do not have problems with ideation. LD fifth and sixth graders are within one standard deviation of the norm (Poplin et al., 1980). Since LD children can convey meaning in writing, they have the main ingredient necessary for building good writing abilities.

Unfortunately, however, our expectations for writing success with LD children are often low. These children are not perceived as having the capacity to become real writers. The problem with this kind of thinking is that teacher expectations affect student performance (Anderson, 1982).

LD children can and do learn. It may be harder for them and will probably take them longer, but many can achieve the same proficiency as their similarly intelligent peers. Thus, they should be expected to perform all of the writing tasks that are required for success in school, business, and home environments.

Appropriate Learner Activities

In this section, appropriate learner activities for mastering the writing process will follow a discussion of instructional principles. The section ends with activities for teaching these procedures.

Instructional Procedures

To make instruction in writing effective, teachers can: (1) model writing behaviors, (2) provide a risk-free classroom climate, (3) give useful feedback, and (4) arrange and conduct conferences. They should also be cognizant of the need for (1) an audience, (2) sharing, and (3) respect for ownership.

Modeling

Modeling exposes both the affective and academic benefits that children derive from writing. Modeling shows when and why people write. In addition, by demonstrating that writers feel pain, frustration, uncertainty, and joy, thereby legitimatizes the children's same feelings.

When teachers share their writing, even more learning occurs. Children learn how good writing is shaped from beginning to end: the phases through which teachers pass, how they deal with each one, the changes they make and why, the questions they ask themselves, the feedback they receive, and the differences between the beginning and final drafts.

Children's literature (see Chapter 10), both fiction and nonfiction, also acts as a model for good writing (Smith, 1982). When children read and write, they read with an eye toward writing. They notice organizational patterns, sentence structure, word usage, style, grammar, and so on. Since they have been struggling with all of these in their own writing, it is of interest to them to see what others do.

Risk-Free Environment

Because writing involves self-disclosure, it is inherently a risk-taking activity. For children to be willing to write, they must be certain that neither their grades nor their egos will suffer for their attempts. They must also be allowed to invent spellings, make punctuation errors, write sloppily, have more problems with one piece than another, and the like. Writing is essentially a creative process. Until the final draft, freedom from concern over all of these ancillary issues will release creative energy for writing.

Feedback

Children need assistance during all phases of the writing process. Initially, they need help formulating topics and gathering information. Later, they need someone with whom to discuss their work—its progress, its problems, and its momentum. Finally, they need an audience to tell them if they are communicating what they intended to communicate. This point is crucial since accurate communication is the main reason for writing. Yet children have trouble deciding what the reader needs to know to understand the piece. Since they know what they are thinking, they mentally fill in any gaps that exist. Thus, children need feedback from teachers and peers to pinpoint inadequate or confusing information.

One of the most valuable ways to give feedback to writers is through conferences. These can take several forms: scheduled and unscheduled teacher-to-student conferences, informal student-to-student conferences, and regular peer group conferences. Unscheduled conferences can occur whenever a child wants informal feedback or a partner for brainstorming. Scheduled conferences differ by being structured. Conferences are valuable for both the writer and the listeners. The writer receives help with problems and begins to appreciate the importance of an audience. If the listeners/readers do not understand what is written, the purpose of writing is undermined. Listeners also benefit by becoming critics. Since they are emotionally distanced from the writing, they can see the pitfalls that emerge during writing. Thus children learn how to edit their own pieces by helping others.

Teacher Conferences   This process, described by Graves (1983), has been very successful in helping children mature as writers (cf. Calkins, 1983). Guidelines for conducting conferences are given in Box 12.2.

Group Conferences   When organizing peer group conferences, form groups of two or three children for the early grades and up to five students for grade five and above. The groups should be permanent to allow children to develop a high level of trust and composed of students with varying levels of competence to help them learn from each other through questioning and observing.

Calkins (1983) has offered several guidelines for conducting a peer conference (see Box 12.3). She also found that children who consistently participated in such sessions learned to ask questions that helped to develop good writing. In Box 12.4, these questions are categorized according to function.

Audience

Since writing is communication to someone for some purpose, children need legitimate audiences. They can reap the benefits of meaningful communication if, for example, they write a note to a friend or a book for the classroom library, and receive responses that are appropriate for its style and content.

Besides demonstrating purposeful writing, an audience provides immediate motivation: Writing to someone gives an inherent reason for

---

Box 12.2 Guidelines for Teacher Conferences

---

1. Children direct their own conference with the teacher following their lead.
2. Teachers first respond to the content of the piece; mechanics are discussed later.
3. Teachers only deal with one problem at a time.
4. When children have completed their conference agenda, teachers may discuss one content-related problem. When the final draft is submitted, teachers may identify one skill that needs work.
5. Conferences should be short, taking from one to six minutes, and only rarely as long as ten minutes.
6. Teachers should conduct informal conferences while walking around the room to monitor progress and help with problems that arise before the next scheduled conference. This also provides encouragement to keep writing.
7. Children should have scheduled conferences at least once a week and on the same day to enable them to plan.
8. Record keeping about the conference content and outcome should be very simple, taking only a few seconds. Forms can be put in a folder under each child's name. Graves (1983, p. 144) recommends recording the date, title of the piece, skill worked on, a quality rating of the conference, and a note on the conference content.

Box 12.3 Guidelines for Peer Group Conferences

---

1. Writers begin by stating where they are in the writing process and what kind of help they want.
2. They then read either the entire selection or only the pertinent parts aloud. (Sometimes this step can be omitted.)
3. Writers ask group members to retell what they heard or respond to the content.
4. Listeners ask questions or make suggestions pertinent to the writers' original concern.

Note. Adapted from *Lessons from a Child: On the Teaching and Learning of Writing* by L.L.M. Calkins, 1983, Exeter, NH: Heinemann Education Books.

Box 12.4   Kinds of Questions to Ask Peers

About the Opening

Is the opening so interesting that I want to read on? How does the author get me interested?

How is the opening like the ones I've been writing? How is it different?

What does the opening make me think will come later?

Does the author first tell the beginning of the story? If not, does it begin somewhere else, as in a flashback?

About the Characters

Which character seems most real? Why?

What particular sections helped me get to know the characters? What can I learn about writing from these sections?

Do some of the characters work better than others? Why?

In what paragraphs does the author tell me about the characters? How does the author show (rather than tell us) about other qualities of the characters?

Do the characters change from the beginning to the end of the story? How?

About the Point-of-View

Who is telling the story?

Why was it a good idea to have that particular character tell the story?

Who else might have told it? How would it have been different?

What can I learn from the way the author treated the point of view?

About the Plot

Can I map the events?

Is this story mostly about events or about characters?

How does the writer show that time has passed? Does time move backward?

How does the author show us that things are speeding up or slowing down?

(continued)

Box 12.4   *(continued)*

About the Ending

Does the end relate back to the opening?

Does the ending include a summary? Should it?

Do I feel as if the story is over? Does it feel like The End?

Note. Adapted from *Lessons from a Child: On the Teaching and Learning of Writing* by L.L.M. Calkins, 1983, Exeter, NH: Heinemann Education Books.

---

completing the assignment and putting forth a best effort. Writing only because the teacher assigned the task is not sufficient motivation for most students, especially LD children, who have had so many failures in school.

Sharing   Since an audience is essential to meaningful writing, organizing the classroom to allow continuous sharing makes the writing process real. Like conferencing, the Author's Chair (Graves & Hansen, 1983) provides an audience. This is literally a chair from which children read their books aloud. The listeners then offer their retelling of the content. This paraphrasing is followed by a question-and-answer session with the author. Each week a different child is chosen as Author of the Week and reads from the chair. Satellite chairs also can be informally established during reading time when children decide that they want to read their work to an audience.

Box 12.5 (Calkins, 1983) describes additional ways to share writing, both works in progress and final products.

Ownership

Writing is a very personal expression of self and should remain as such. Changes in a piece of writing should be decided upon and carried out by the author. Questioning and guidance from the teacher and peers is helpful, but the ultimate control must reside with the author, for only then can children experience a sense of pride in what they have accomplished. If someone else mutilates their composition, they are left with a feeling of violation that will detract from the energy needed to begin a new piece.

Content

The essential ingredient in composition instruction is that writing be meaningful. With this in mind, teachers can structure various activities

---

Box 12.5   Ways to Share Writing

1. Meetings. Children read their work one at a time. Listeners ask questions, attempting to follow one idea through their questions.
2. Writer's Circle. Children meet in groups of three or four. They take turns reading their writing aloud and answer questions and reactions from the listeners.
3. Quiet Sharing. Each child finds a reader who will make comments on the piece by writing on an index card.
4. Focused Sharing. Children share one aspect of their writing e.g., opening or ending, with the whole class.
5. Process Sharing. Children discuss the problems they encountered while writing and try to find strategies to overcome them. They also discuss the kinds of changes they made and why.

Note. Adapted from *Lessons from a Child: On the Teaching and Learning of Writing* by L.L.M. Calkins, 1983, Exeter, NH: Heinemann Education Books.

---

to facilitate growth in composition. Discussed here are ways to help children: (1) grow into composing, (2) progress through the writing process, and (3) write for different purposes.

Growing into Composing

What normally achieving children learned before school may not be indicative of what LD children learned (Barenbaum, 1983). Thus, it may be necessary to begin composition instruction by providing a literate environment and giving children ample time and encouragement to experience and experiment with print. Expect them to draw, make repetitive marks that resemble shorthand, write random letters and ask what they say, ask teachers to write words or sentences for them to copy, copy out of a book, ask teachers to spell words, and write notes and label pictures with invented spelling. All of this will, of course, parallel their exploration of reading manifested in the following kinds of activities: reading books from memory; reading books from pictures; making up a story as they flip through a book; and asking questions about letters, words, pictures and the meaning of a story.

To support these explorations, teachers must read daily to children. One-to-one work and "Big Books" enable the use of strategies such as assisted reading, oral cloze (filling in missing words), lap reading, and choral reading. Language Experience Activities (LEA), word banks, and listening to tapes while following along in the book are also valuable.

Experience with writing must be encouraged. Have a variety of paper and writing implements available at all times. Encourage students to write notes, label pictures, and keep journals that can be drawn and/or written in daily. By the time children have control of both the sound and the symbol of as few as six letters, they can engage in written communication that is comprehensible to the reader (Graves, 1983).

Progressing Through the Writing Process

Prewriting   No writing should be assigned to or expected from children without this step having been completed. Prewriting activities, such as those in Box 12.6, help children develop a topic, a reason for writing, an audience, and a structure.

Drafting   Now children are ready to commit their ideas to paper. They take what was garnered during the prewriting activities and develop it into a full piece. Content is more important than mechanics, with all of the children's energy focusing on what they want to say. Room for revisions should be left by writing on every other line and leaving wide margins.

One of the most valuable activities for promoting writing is keeping a daily journal. Less skilled writers should use unlined paper for drawing and/or writing, while more skilled writers use lined paper for writing. By writing daily, they learn to express themselves freely. They also increase their command of the conventions of print. Journals can be either private, public, or a combination. Children can keep a journal much like a diary in which they write anything, knowing that nobody will read it. The privacy agreement, however, must not be violated, because regaining trust once it is lost is very difficult, if possible at all. Alternatively, journals may be viewed as public property with anyone having access. Teachers should realize, however, that children often may have difficulty writing because what they want to say is not acceptable or because they are afraid of criticism. A compromise is to develop a signaling system whereby pages that are private are folded in half with no writing visible.

The purpose of journal writing is to create comfortable and fluent writing. Children should be encouraged to cross things out. They should not be concerned with mechanics or neatness, because concentration on these issues creates tenseness. This is true even though journal writing is a final draft, since it is never revised.

Furthermore, the journal should not be corrected or graded. Give credit based upon whether the journal entry was completed on a given day. Set a minimum time limit, and encourage children to write without stopping during that time. Start with five minutes for the youngest children, and increase the time as they get older.

Box 12.6 Prewriting Activity

1. Keep a list of potential writing topics.
2. Discuss topics thoroughly and from every angle possible.
3. Think about topics while going to and from school, just before going to bed, and while conducting normal activities.
4. Brainstorm ideas for topics with individuals, a group, or the class.
5. Use interest inventories to isolate topics.
6. Talk to friends about a topic before finalizing a decision.
7. Verbalize the story to a friend, in a tape recorder, or to yourself before writing it down.
8. Draw a picture or a series of pictures to develop and organize the story.
9. Read or listen to a story and then discuss it before writing.
10. Read or listen to poetry and then discuss it. Understand the form, purpose, and audience before writing. (Depending on the children, numerous examples may be needed.)
11. Participate in an activity (e.g., science experiment, field trip, or project). Take notes during the activity and discuss them with teachers and/or peers.
12. List elements to include in the piece. Think about, discuss, and organize the list.
13. Organize ideas by making a web or an outline. Webs are more fun, and it is easier to make additions and deletions on a web because it is not linear.
14. Conduct research by interviewing people, reading, watching a movie or filmstrip, or listening to music or radio talk shows.
15. Act out the story to develop the plot.
16. Do free writing (Elbow, 1976) to discover or narrow a topic. Begin by setting a timer for one to five minutes. Then write continuously until the timer rings. Write anything, even, "I don't know what to say," or "Why do I have to do this?" or a series of unrelated words. After the timer rings, read what has been written and decide on something that looks interesting, or else summarize what was written and again write for the same period of time on this new topic. Repeat this process once, concluding with three segments of writing. By the third segment, a topic should be chosen or be close to being chosen. This procedure can be adapted for different ages by having some children write only one segment or talk into a tape recorder.

(*continued*)

Box 12.6   *(continued)*

---

17. Conference with the teacher and/or peer.
18. Start writing. For a few, prewriting activities may take place covertly, without any apparent activity.
19. Develop prewriting guides (Beach, 1983). Using this five-step procedure, create and organize questions to guide information gathering for reports: (1) students list all of the questions they can think of related to their topics; (2) teachers write the questions on the board; (3) through discussion, the lists are revised with the audience and purpose in mind; (4) questions are listed in logical sequence, with paragraphing indicated; and (5) through discussion, the lists are reorganized.

Children should use their journals to relate events, feelings, thoughts, reactions, hopes, and observations. The content can be wide-ranging, as long as it is not offensive. Some teachers set aside time once a month for children to read their own journals and comment on their growth as either a person or writer or both (cf. Temple & Gillet, 1984).

Whether teachers respond in writing to journal entries is a matter of personal style and logistics (based upon class size). With a class of ten students, Gaskins and Elliot (1983) suggest making a short comment each day on all entries and an extended comment on one or two. With a larger class, modify this procedure by reading and commenting on one-half or one-third daily. (See Box 12.7 for more activities.)

Revising   It is during the revision process that the writing takes shape. The excess is removed, gaps are filled, paragraphs and ideas are rearranged, appropriate wording is found, and authors generally mold the piece into a crisp, clear, meaningful communication.

Not all writing warrants this arduous process. Since professional writers often abandon pieces that are not working, why should more be expected of children? Thus, some writing can be left in its original state, while others that hold promise are reworked. The decision about what to revise should be the author's. If ownership is to be maintained, children must make their own critical choices, including what they feel warrants their continued time and effort. If this principle is violated, quality and motivation will suffer.

It is essential, however, that children learn how to revise and that there be legitimate audiences for their finished pieces. Mounting displays on bulletin boards or in hallways, binding books for the classroom and

---

Box 12.7   Drafting Activity

---

1. Use a journal entry as a prewriting activity and develop it into a larger piece.
2. Reread the entire piece or the last few sentences to refocus and generate new ideas.
3. Use invented spellings to avoid interrupting a train of thought by looking up correct spellings.
4. Consult a dictionary or ask a peer or teacher for help if using invented spellings is disruptive.
5. Avoid asking questions about mechanics.
6. Do a prewriting activity if stuck at a difficult spot.
7. Talk into a tape recorder.
8. Remember not to worry about revision or deadlines but to focus just on getting ideas on paper.
9. Participate in positive self-talk. Repeat phrases like, "I am doing fine," "I have something worthwhile to say," and "I will be successful in completing this draft."
10. Ask for a conference during which the teachers can ask the following kinds of questions:
    a. How is it going?
    b. Tell me about your draft?
    c. What's happening now?
    d. What do you like about your piece?
    e. What's giving you trouble?
    f. Tell me more about _____ (fill in something from the draft that will get the children to verbalize information that may spark new ideas).

---

school library, and mailing letters are all good ways to share writing with real audiences. (See Box 12.8 for more activities.)

Final Draft   Once children are satisfied with their text, the mechanics must be addressed. To help children become independent, establish a classroom environment conducive to self-questioning and answer seeking. For some, the task of rewriting a paper is too arduous. Then teachers, aides, or volunteers can type the final product. (See Box 12.9 for activities.)

Writing for Different Purposes

Expressive Writing   Children need activities that emphasize practice with expressive writing, since it is the easiest for them. They have

Box 12.8 Revising Activity

1. Learning the technical aids to revising a paper:
   a. Using scissors and tape or a word processor to cut and eliminate or rearrange sections or paragraphs.
   b. Using a subordinate alphabetic system (e.g., page 1, page 1a, page 2) to add pages between existing pages.
   c. Using symbols to organize material, delete sections, or add parts: (a) an arrow going from the section that must be moved to the place where it will be inserted; (b) a caret (ˆ) between words with the material to be added written above; and (c) a numbering system in which both the material that must be moved from one page to another and the place where it will be inserted are given the same number.
   d. Photocopying a paper that has been cut and taped to give the children an easier surface on which to continue revising.
2. Focusing on content during teacher conferences until the final draft is finished. Teachers can make comments and ask questions to focus revision:
   a. How is it going?
   b. Tell me about your piece.
   c. What do you plan to do with the next draft?
   d. Tell me more about this part.
   e. What would be another way of saying this?
   f. I don't understand this part. Please explain it to me.
   g. Do you need to add or delete any information?
   h. Do you like the way you started this piece?
   i. Do you like the way you ended this piece?
   j. What's the main thing that you want to say?
   k. How did you choose your title?
   l. I like _____ (fill in something from the piece).
   m. Would you like my help with anything?
   n. What else do you want to say in your piece?
3. Reading the paper to classmates for feedback in a formal or informal conference.
4. Reading the paper silently and imagining the kinds of questions that your classmates would ask (Calkins, 1983).
5. Putting the paper aside for a day or two to get some distance.
6. Reading the paper aloud or into a tape recorder to see how it sounds.

(continued)

Box 12.8   (*continued*)

---

7. Doing prewriting or drafting activities to get more information or move beyond a difficult spot.
8. Making a clean copy of the draft to eliminate the frustration of trying to read a piece with many changes.
9. Thinking about the piece at bedtime to allow the subconscious to do some work.
10. Comparing the current draft with earlier ones to get a sense of progress and to find things that were eliminated but now belong in the piece.

---

difficulty taking the perspective of others, as is often expected of fiction or poetic writing. It is easier to write from their own experience, for a story line does not have to be invented; it already exists. The task of writing, then, becomes more manageable.

Topics for expressive writing can come from the home, school, or extracurricular activities. The experiences can be structured as for LEA (e.g., a field trip or a social studies unit) or children can determine their own topics (e.g., an activity with a favorite friend or trying to fall asleep alone in the dark). When children decide what they want to tell, the piece will be better written than when a topic is assigned.

Transactional Writing   Transactional writing is essential for success in school, but is rarely taught to LD children. Although public schools may make accommodations, universities and businesses generally will not.

Assignments for exposition or description could be natural outgrowths of student projects, growing plants, making objects, or conducting science experiments. The art of using persuasion also can be developed with real audiences; for example, letters can be written to the school principal about a policy that the student would like changed or to a local industry that is about to lay off employees.

With the exception of creative writing, most school- and business-related writing falls into the category of transactional writing (e.g., note taking, formal reports, subjective tests, and business letters and memos). The typical school assignments should serve as a guide for the areas emphasized (Walmsley, 1983). (See Box 12.10 for activities. For activities relating to text structure, see Chapter 9.)

Poetic Writing   Many LD children can write poetically and thus should be encouraged to do so. Even first graders can begin to learn this mode of writing with pattern books. (See Box 12.11 for activities.)

Box 12.9 Final Draft Activity

1. Read into a tape recorder and play it back while following along with the written copy. Listen for grammatical errors and pauses where punctuation belongs.
2. Read the paper, one sentence at a time, from the last sentence to the first. This eliminates interference from content to facilitate error detection and help identify sentence fragments. This procedure should be used only after the child has acquired a firm understanding of left-right, top-to-bottom processing.
3. Read the paper, one word at a time, from the last word to the first. This forces concentration on spelling but should only be used with children whose directionality is clearly established.
4. Identify one or two areas that are the most problematic and polish them. If a story is to be published, the teachers can polish the rest of the paper or it can be left as is. If the class norm is set such that developmental differences are acceptable, no one will ridicule the children for not having perfect papers.
5. Listen to teachers read the paper using only the punctuation that is present. Then discuss how it should sound and be read and how oral pauses relate to written punctuation.
6. Look through the paper and circle words thought to be misspelled. Use classmates, a dictionary, and other written sources to find the correct spellings.
7. Use a check list based upon the skills that should have been mastered. After preparing a final copy, respond to these types of items:
   a. I have checked the spelling of every word.
   b. I began every sentence with a capital letter.
   c. I read my paper aloud, and it makes sense.
   d. I used legible handwritng.
   e. I used a period, question mark, or exclamation mark at the end of every sentence.
   f. I used descriptive words and phrases.
   g. Each paragraph has a topic, and all sentences relate to the topic.
   h. I used a thesaurus to find just the right words to express my thoughts.

Box 12.10   Transactional Writing Activity

1. Making a classroom mailbox for each student and the teacher.
   a. Writing personal notes to the children and encouraging them to write notes to each other.
   b. Writing notes about class assignments, reminders about field trips, notes to take home to parents or to give to other teachers, and the like.
2. Publishing a class newsletter or magazine.
3. Conducting interviews about a specific topic and then writing about it.
5. Looking through catalogues and filling out order forms.
6. Writing a letter of complaint to a company regarding defective merchandise that the child has actually purchased.
7. Filling out forms that are meaningful to the children (e.g., magazine subscriptions).
8. Playing the role of executives who have to conduct formal business through correspondence.
9. Researching a subject of interest and writing a report on it.
10. Writing a report on a favorite book.
11. Composing essay and short-answer questions for a test and then answering them.
12. Taking notes during a lecture.
13. Taking notes from a textbook.

Since most LD children have had difficulties with composition, they are likely to expect to do poorly. When this happens, introducing the notion of self-talk is often effective. Every time children approach a writing task, they should repeat positively reinforcing statements such as, "I can write this story because I like telling stories, and writing them is almost the same," or "I can complete this assignment successfully if I take it one step at a time." Initially teachers model the phrases and have students repeat them every day. Later they monitor students periodically to ensure their continued usage of positive self-talk.

Check lists are also helpful for planning, monitoring results, and searching for alternatives. Questions for each stage can be established, such as, "What do I do first?"; "Does this section make sense?"; and "What can I do to fix this section?" (Torgesen, 1982).

In addition, metacognitive interviews can help students become effective writers. Teachers can ask students questions that will focus their

Box 12.11 Poetic Writing Activities

1. Pattern Books can be used individually, in small groups, or by the whole class. Children use the pattern from a published story to make their own story or poem. The pattern makes writing easier because it gives children a guiding form. *Brown Bear, Brown Bear, What Do You See?* is a good example (Martin, 1970):

   Brown bear,
   brown bear
   what do you see?
   I see a redbird
   looking at me.
   Redbird,
   redbird,
   what do you see?
   I see a yellow duck
   looking at me.

   This pattern is then used to create a new story:

   Smiling boy,
   smiling boy,
   what do you see?
   I see a happy clown
   looking at me.
   Happy clown,
   happy clown,
   what do you see?
   I see a dancing dog
   looking at me.

2. Just So Stories. Rudyard Kipling's (1978) stories such as, "How the Whale got his Throat" and "How the Rhinoceros got his Skin," give children another kind of guiding pattern.

3. Fables. Another kind of pattern to help structure their writing can be learned by reading and discussing fables.

4. Plays. Children can learn to write their own plays by first acting out stories. Then original plays can be written as a class, and then presented to other classes or groups. For variation, they can be also be presented as puppet shows.

5. Fictionalized Self. Children write about events in their own lives, but give the characters different names and add events they *wish* had occurred.

(continued)

Box 12.11   (*continued*)

---

6. Television. Children write about a television character or episode. These can be sent to the actor or producer of the program.
7. Music. Children write the words to songs as a class in small groups, or individually. The song could be sung at a school program.
8. Cinquain Poetry. Because it is highly structured, children find this kind of poetry easy to write. The poem must have a title and four lines of verse.
   a. A one word title stating the topic.
   b. A first line describing the topic and using two words.
   c. A second line expressing action and using three words.
   d. A third line expressing feelings and using four words.
   e. A last line expressing the essense of the topic in one word.
9. Unfinished Ending: Read only parts of a story and then have children write their own endings.
10. Group Story. Children can write a story with a partner, in a group, or with the whole class. Children can take turns writing sentences.

Note. Adapted from *Lessons from a Child: On the Teaching and Learning of Writing* by L.L.M. Calkins, 1983, Exeter, NH: Heinemann Education Books.

---

attention on the qualities of and strategies for good writing, such as, "What are the strengths (or weaknesses) in this piece? Explain your answer"; "What changes should be made and why?"; and "Why did you choose this opening paragraph over the other two that you wrote?"

Assessing Each Student's Strengths and Weaknesses

Assessment should be an outgrowth of regular classroom activities. Some takes place as part of the ongoing interactions between writers, teachers, and peers that occur throughout the writing process, i.e., both formal and informal conferences and sharing sessions. Another process—analysis—is also valuable if used once a month to monitor progress and determine areas that need work.

Analysis

Temple & Gillet (1984) have compiled a check list for analyzing the writing process, functions, qualities of style, fluency, mechanics, and enjoyment (see Box 12.12). The importance of the items listed should be self-evident, with the exception of the reference in number 16 to T-units. The term "T-unit," which was developed by Hunt (1965) and is widely used as a measure of writing maturity means minimum terminable unit, or the smallest segment of a sentence that can stand alone and still make sense. It is composed, then, of either a main clause or a main clause plus any subordinate clauses. As children's writing becomes more sophisticated, the number of T-units decreases and the number of words per T-unit increases. Thus teachers should monitor how these numbers change during the school year.

To exemplify this concept, in Box 12.13, the T-units in an excerpt from a child's story are marked.

Recovery Procedures for Persistent Problems

LD children often experience difficulties with writing, which are frequently exacerbated by lack of practice, confidence, and an inappropriate emphasis on mechanics. Teachers can help children deal with personal issues, such as anxiety, and skills issues, such as organization.

Personal Issues

When children experience continual failure, they and their teachers begin to assume that they will never become competent writers. These children develop a negative self-concept, which is reinforced through self-fulfilling prophecies and teachers' low expectations. When writing becomes associated with failure, it leads to an unwillingness to write, writing blocks, or writing anxiety. Activities to help children overcome these problems are listed in Box 12.14 (see also Chapter 4).

Skills Issues

Some children have greater deficiencies in skill development than others. The most critical ones should be remediated first. Using Gaskins and Elliot's (1983) objectives, a hierarchy emerges: content, organization, effectiveness, and mechanics. In Boxes 12.15 through 12.18, a few problem areas are identified with instructional strategies for helping LD children.

Matching Students to Tasks and Monitoring Performance

Both formal and informal assessment practices are valuable, depending upon their function. Formal tests identify global strengths and weaknesses, and informal measures provide ongoing knowledge about children's writing.

Box 12.12   A Writing Analysis Check List

The Writing Process

1. How often does the writer get ideas for writing
   —from the imagination?
   —from discussions with others?
   —by imitating a book, story, poem, TV show, and so on?
   —from the teacher's assignments?
   —from some other source? which?
2. When the writer means to rehearse what will be written, and narrow down the topic, does the writer
   —talk to classmates?
   —talk to the teacher?
   —draw a picture first?
   —think about it overnight?
   —start writing right away?
3. In drafting a paper, does the writer
   —write one draft only?
   —invent spellings, use a dictionary, or limit vocabulary to the words he or she can spell?
   —scratch out words and lines, and cut and paste?
   —seek comments from others about the way the drafting is going?
4. Does the writer revise a paper before it is considered finished? Do the drafts
   —all look like different papers, new beginnings?
   —look like mechanical refinements of earlier drafts?
   —interact with and build on the ideas of early drafts?
   —stop after one draft?

The Functions of Writing

5. What forms of writing has the writer produced?
   —stories?
   —poems?

(continued)

Box 12.12 *(continued)*

—expressive writing (personal experiences and opinions)?
—persuasive writing?
—descriptive writing?
—expository writing (that which explains or gives directions)?

6. What kinds of topics has the writer written about?
   —topics about which the writer was an expert?
   —topics about which the writer had to learn more before writing?
   —topics about things that were present?
   —topics about things that were past or absent?
   —topics about abstract ideas?

7. What audiences has the child written for?
   —the teacher?
   —classmates?
   —other people known to the child? Whom?
   —other people unknown to the child? Whom?

8. In trying to stick to the topic, did the writer
   —limit the focus of the topic before starting to write?
   —stick to one thing or ramble?
   —focus more on the object of the writing or on the writer?

9. In trying to stick with the purpose of writing, does the writer
   —keep expressing personal feelings, although the topic and purpose suggest doing otherwise?
   —declare one purpose but pursue another (such as "The story about ...," which is expository, not narrative)?
   —shift from one purpose to another?

10. In trying to meet the audience's need for information
    —does the writer appear to assume the audience knows and is interested in the author?
    —is he or she careful to tell the audience things they will need to know in order to understand what is talked about?
    —does the writer address the same audience throughout?

Qualities of Writing Style

11. Does the writer use exact, well-chosen words?
12. Does the writer "paint pictures with words"
    —make the reader see what the writer saw?
    —is the focus on immediate, "here-and-now" images?

(continued)

Box 12.12 (*continued*)

13. In regard to the organization of the papers:
    —does the writer keep the focus on one aspect of the topic at a time?
    —do the papers have identifiable openings?
    —are the details arranged in a reasonable order and do they relate reasonably to one another?
    —is there an identifiable ending to the papers?

Fluency of Writing

14. How long are the papers (in words or lines per paper)?
15. What is the average number of words per sentence?
16. What is the average number of words per T-unit?

Mechanics of Writing

17. In handwriting, does the writer
    —have problems forming letters? Which ones?
    —have problems spacing between letters?
    —keeping vertical lines parallel?
    —keeping the writing on the baseline?
    —write with uniform pressure?
    —in smooth or in jerky lines?
18. In regard to spelling:
    —does the writer misspell words in the first draft?
    —does the writer correct the spellings of many words between the first and later drafts?
    —what does the writer do when uncertain of how to spell a word?
19. Does the writer have trouble with standard English usuage?
    —does the writer write in complete sentences? If not, what are the units of writing like?
    —does the writer have problems with punctuation and capitalization? With which elements? In what circumstances?
    —are errors made in standard English grammar? If so, describe the errors.

Enjoying Writing

20. Does the writer take pleasure in writing?
    —how do you know?

Box 12.13   T-Units in a Child's Story*

I thought of a plan.|
I asked my cat to distract the peptiels.|
I would cross the lake safely and call to my cat.|
So the cat distracted the reptiels |
and I crossed the lake and called to my cat.|
My cat came |
and we went on our way. . . .|
"I think I hear morther calling us,"|
I said.|
We followed the sound.|
Our morther had been wread.|
We found our morther and went home.|
And HOME SWEET HOME it was.

Note. This is a child's story reproduced with the child's errors.

Box 12.14   Overcoming Writing Anxiety

1. Use free writing (Elbow, 1976). Have children write continually for a given period of time. Start with two minutes and build to ten as confidence increases and anxiety decreases. The rules to start children writing are simple but inflexible:
   a. Write continually for the time allotted.
   b. Do not consider neatness or mechanics.
   c. Write about anything within socially acceptable limits.
   d. Write page fillers, such as, "I don't know what to write," or repeat what has been written.
2. Be positive. Do not mark any errors until children are comfortable with writing. Consistently and frequently mark and discuss only what they are doing well, with special stress on content. Once children are consistently writing, teachers can gradually work on mechanics by tackling one targeted weakness at a time.
3. Emphasize the writing process. Discourage concern for mechanics until revision. Give positive reinforcement as children begin to understand and use a process approach.
4. Write on all subject areas. Make writing an integral part of the classroom environment. For example, have children:

Box 12.14   *(continued)*

---

    a. Write and solve story problems.
    b. Map the relationships between the various countries during World War II.
    c. Write a short research report on air pollution.

5. Use collaboration. Allow children to write with a partner. Pair children with different, but not too discrepant, abilities (e.g., a good with an average writer or an average with a poor writer) to enable them to learn from each other.

6. Make writing fun:
    a. Assign riddles, jokes, and comic strips.
    b. Cut pieces of paper into different shapes matched to topics (e.g., a tree, circle, or triangle) when working with younger children.

7. Share children's published writing. Show students drafts done by normally achieving children. Use a book with numerous writing samples (e.g., Harste et al., 1981; Temple, Nathan, & Burris, 1982), and emphasize that the work was sufficiently valued, even with "errors," to be published. Also point out that *all* children, not just LD children, go through the same writing process with misspelled words and lack of neatness.

8. Be a model. Talk about your own writing problems and ways of coping. Bring in samples of your writing and show how they evolved through many drafts.

9. Use scratch paper. Have children write on paper that gives the message, "This is only a working draft and neatness does not count," such as computer paper, scraps of paper, and the backs of discarded forms.

10. Use dictation. Initially have children dictate to someone. Try role-playing boss and secretary. Then transcribe the dictation, and gradually move children toward writing for themselves.

11. Use developmental activities. Pay special attention to pre-writing activities. Sometimes four or five of them are necessary to get a reluctant writer ready to put something on paper.

Initial Broad-Based Assessment

The Test of Written Language, or TOWL (Hammill & Larsen, 1983), is the most useful formal measure of written language performance for LD children. It can be administered to individuals or groups and gives information on handwriting, thought units, spelling style, word usage, vo-

Box 12.15 Supplying Incomplete Information

1. Identify the five *w*'s—who, what, when, why, and where—in the paper.
2. Read newspaper articles and underline the five *w*'s.
3. Write directions for an activity, such as making a peanut butter sandwich. Then have a classmate try to follow the directions.
4. Check referents to make sure that they have been clarified. Ask *who* every time a pronoun is seen and *which* every time *this, that, these,* or *those* appear. If the answers are not in the paper, add a clarifying statement or phrase.

Box 12.16 Remedying Inadequate Organization

1. Draw a web before and/or after writing. Before writing it can be a guide. After writing it can be a check on organizational clarity.
2. Arrange in proper sequence a story that has been cut into sentences. The story could be the child's, a classmate's, or from another source.
3. Repeat the same exercise with a story that has been cut into paragraphs or story elements (e.g., initiating event, goal, and outcome). This can also be done by putting two stories together and having the children separate and organize each one.
4. Arrange the segments of a cut-up comic strip into a logical sequence.
5. Use a word processing package to manipulate papers more easily during revision.

Box 12.17 Remedying Immature Sentence Structure

1. If the sentences are too short, try sentence combining. Take two sentences such as, "The ball is red," and "The boy threw the ball," and combine them into one sentence, "The boy threw the red ball." As children get better with this, use more sophisticated and/or more sentences.
2. If the sentences are too long, cross out every *and,* then read the paper aloud, and put back only those that are absolutely necessary.

Box 12.18   Supplying Missing Punctuation

1. Make a connection between oral and written pauses to develop an understanding of the role of punctuation. Discuss gestures, voice intonation, and pauses. Then note which punctuation marks match oral punctuation.
2. Have authors read their papers aloud. Read them back just as the written punctuation indicates. Ask if that sounds good. If not, discuss where the punctuation should go and what it should be.
3. Have children do choral reading with properly punctuated material and improperly punctuated material. Discuss the difference in ease of comprehension and reading.

---

cabulary, and thematic maturity. Since it provides both grade-equivalent and scaled scores, it is best used for establishing long-term instructional objectives at the beginning of the semester and measuring gross changes at the end of the semester.

Management Plan

Ongoing measures, then, are also needed to confirm the test results, monitor progress, determine emerging needs, and identify factors not measured by the TOWL. Temple & Gillet's (1984) check list (see Box 12.12) can be used about once a month to analyze children's writing products and behaviors while composing.

The purpose of evaluating children's compositions is to help them improve their writing. Students need to see their progress to prevent discouragement and to maintain a realistic understanding of their competencies. Keeping a folder with all their past work, in chronological order, helps children and teachers develop an historical and accurate perspective on current strengths and weaknesses.

Grading

If grades must be given, they should be rewards rather than punishments. Give children the greatest opportunity for success by allowing them to select the pieces that they want graded and to revise those pieces before grading. Some teachers use two grades, one for content and one for mechanics. Others isolate certain objectives and grade for mastery of those objectives, with children having more than one opportunity to attain

Students, please fill this in:

Your name: ____________________ Date: ______________

Class period: ____________

Title of your paper: ______________________________

This is your score: ________

Here is how you earned it —

___ / 25	1. Punch:	Right-sized topic Focused on one idea, one thing, one happening Made the reader see what the writer saw Used colorful, descriptive words
___ / 25	2. Plan:	Opening caught the reader's interest Details, events, arguments in sensible order Ending left the reader with a thought
___ / 25	3. Filling us in:	Seemed to have particular readers in mind Told the readers what they needed to know
___ / 25	4. Mechanics:	Spelling corrected before the paper was handed in Handwriting and paper neat Punctuation corrected before the paper was handed in Capitalization corrected before the paper was handed in
___ / 100	= Total	

FIGURE 12.2 Writing Score Sheet.

Note. From Charles Temple and Jean Wallace Gillet. *Language Arts: Learning Processes and Teaching Practices*, p. 296. Copyright © 1984 by Charles Temple and Jean Wallace Gillet. Reprinted by permission of Little, Brown and Company.

mastery. Still others give more weight to grades received at the end of the semester, thereby giving children credit for their progress. Regardless of how grades are assigned, if they are presented in a conference along with the rationale for the grade, students begin to view the experience as an opportunity for learning.

Temple & Gillet (1984) have also adapted a writing score sheet (see Figure 12.2) from one used by Kates. It should be shared with children during revision so they know the evaluation criteria.

Summary and Conclusions

Writing skills are a prerequisite to success in school and in employment. Schools must therefore include competency in writing as an essential goal for all children, including LD students. Teachers, however, must recognize that LD children progress more slowly and need more positive reinforcement and support.

The goal of writing competency can be accomplished by teaching writing as a process involving prewriting, drafting, and revising and by observing the other key instructional principles. Since writing is done chiefly to communicate, the content must be the main focus of instruction, with mechanics becoming important only during the final draft. Feedback on how well children have communicated should be: (1) ongoing, through formal and informal channels, and (2) from the teacher, classmates, and other legitimate audiences.

One problem at a time should be targeted for work, beginning with the key objective of writing content. LD students often have great anxiety about writing because of past failures. This anxiety must be dealt with before any progress can be made. Once the personal issues are under control, however, LD children will evidence a real capacity for becoming competent writers—given the proper instructional atmosphere, practices, and expectations.

Chapter 13

Composition Instruction in the Secondary School

Nancy Nelson Spivey

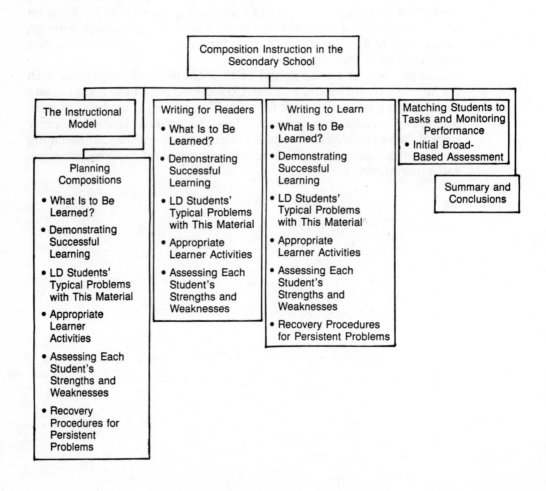

Questions to Consider

1. What must the teacher of high school LD students monitor to judge the effectiveness of the instructional program in writing?
2. How are composing and composition instruction recursive?
3. What is the goal of composition instruction in the cognitive developmental model?

Recently, high school students told me about the strategies they used when composing reports for their English classes. Some talked about their strategies for generating and selecting content. For instance, one student explained, "I decided that I would put in the important information from the articles that I read. I could tell what was important by the way things were emphasized." Another stated, "I decided to put in my report what was really essential. I put in enough so that the reader would know basically what I was talking about." The students also discussed their strategies for organizing their compositions. One "put it in chronological order and took it from there," and another "started with a broad subject and narrowed it down," the way she had seen other reports organized.

On composing tasks, students must not only decide what they want to accomplish through their writing but also generate and organize content, monitor their writing, and review and revise the written products. Writing is a complex cognitive process in which writers move back and forth among various subprocesses (Flower & Hayes, 1981a). Even an apparently simple assignment, such as a report, would present difficulties to an LD student who lacks the knowledge of strategies and the metacognitive skills that are required in writing. Many LD students have considerable difficulty with the writing tasks that they face in school (Roit & McKenzie, 1985; Walmsley, 1983b). This chapter emphasizes instructional approaches designed to help them develop effective strategies for composing.

The chapter follows the format of the other content area chapters. First, the instructional model for secondary composition is explained. Then three important aspects of writing in secondary schools are discussed: planning compositions, writing for readers, and writing to learn. The emphasis throughout is on strategies that students can learn initially with the support of the teacher but can apply *independently* to new composing situations. The chapter concludes with suggestions for the assessment of writing ability and the management of instruction.

The Instructional Model

In a cognitive developmental approach to instruction, the learner is an active participant, not a passive recipient, in teaching and learning activities. For writing, a cognitive developmental approach "essentially consists of working through various tasks on various topics and for various purposes, the consequence of which . . . is the development of new mental structures that allow the [student] to write more sophisticatedly" (Walmsley, 1983b, p. 280). Instruction is designed to foster metacognitive abilities, such as understanding what is required, knowing what strategies might work, and monitoring one's performance. This approach to teaching composition is consistent with approaches for developing metacognitive awareness and control of other processes, such as reading (Brown & Palincsar, 1982; Gaskins & Bacon, 1985; Johnston, 1984).

Applebee (1982), who has conducted a major study (Applebee, 1981, 1984a) of composition in American secondary schools, argues that the metacognitive knowledge essential to composition cannot be effectively developed with the "write-react" instructional pattern typical in schools today. In write-react teaching, students write and the teachers merely react to their writing. Students know when the process fails—because they receive unfavorable reactions—but they do not learn strategies to avoid such failures. An alternative model exists in Applebee and Langer's (1983) concept of *scaffolding,* based on the ideas of Bruner (1978). In the scaffolding model, the student learns new writing skills in a classroom in which the teacher provides the support, or scaffolding, necessary for students to carry out the language tasks. During the initial phases of instruction for a particular strategy, support takes the form of teacher modeling, student-teacher dialogue, and peer interactions. That support is gradually withdrawn as the learner gains proficiency in applying a particular strategy. A comprehensive review comparing various approaches to the teaching of composition (Hillocks, 1984) concluded that the most effective teaching mode is characterized by the teacher's clear objectives for writing tasks and by the students' active engagement in processes important to aspects of writing. The learning activities often have high levels of peer interaction.

Instruction that emphasizes strategies and fosters control of those strategies is essential for LD adolescents, who may have become passive in regard to learning (Wiens, 1983) or developed inappropriate learning strategies (McMillan, Keogh, & Jones, 1986). This chapter focuses on active composing strategies and metacognitive skills important for these students at the secondary level. Although the teacher provides the support, the goal of instruction is the students' independent use of effective strategies in their own writing.

Planning Compositions

What Is to Be Learned?

Writers, who set goals for their writing, must decide not only *what* to say but also *how* to say it. In addition to goal setting, then, planning involves both generating and organizing (Flower & Hayes, 1981a). Generating is drawing information from one's own knowledge or from other sources, and organizing is putting the information in some kind of order. Although some planning occurs before writing begins, much planning involving both generating and organizing takes place as the piece is written. According to Flower and Hayes (1984), planning is "the first, the necessary, and the continuing event of composing" (p. 126).

Writing plans constructed by writers are rarely formal, structured outlines (Emig, 1971; Flower & Hayes, 1980; Stallard, 1974). To be workable, a plan must be flexible enough to be modified and must be dispensable if it does not work (Flower & Hayes, 1980). Research into the phenomenon of "writer's block" (Rose, 1980, 1985) indicates that some students who experience difficulty in writing operate with "rigid rules and inflexible plans," such as a belief that they must always produce elaborate outlines before beginning to write. Nonblockers, on the other hand, have easily modified rules or plans, such as "I can throw things out" (Rose, 1980, p. 397).

One of the arts of classical rhetoric in the days of Aristotle and Cicero was *invention,* or the discovery of ways of developing a topic for an audience (for reviews see Young, 1976, 1987). Today students learn to develop topics by using various kinds of prewriting strategies to generate and organize content for the composition. Such strategies are an important component of process-oriented composition: "It is no accident that the shift in attention from composed product to the composing process is occurring at the same time as the reemergence of invention. . . . Invention requires a process view" (Young, 1978, p. 35).

Demonstrating Successful Learning

Students demonstrate their success in learning and applying strategies for generating and organizing content through their increased ability to manage composing tasks. Proficient writers have a repertoire of strategies with which to face the task of transforming blank pages into written texts. Even though the teacher provides scaffolding in initial instruction, successful learners flexibly use their own strategies. Learning is demonstrated through the product as well as the process, since, as students become more proficient in generating and organizing, they produce more effective compositions. The composition products can provide important insights into cognitive processes:

> There is a direct link between written products and the composing process. Whatever lawfulness is found in a text must reflect lawful behavior on the part of the writer because the physical properties of the text impose no requirements of lawfulness. (Bereiter & Scardamalia, 1983, p. 11).

LD Students' Typical Problems with This Material

Unskilled writers, who often have difficulties in planning, tend to perpetuate the tendencies of younger writers. Like young writers, many poor writers plan at the word level (Martlew, 1983) rather than on the whole-text level. They may also have a limited repertoire of strategies (Flower & Hayes, 1981b, Perl, 1979) that they can use in planning. Further, both poor writers and young writers, tend to use a knowledge-telling strategy (Scardamalia & Bereiter, 1986); that is, they turn a composing task into telling what they know about a topic. Although this strategy works sometimes, when the knowledge is well organized, it often results in writing that seems to lack planning and purpose. LD students' difficulties in organizing and classifying as well as their deficiencies in metacognitive skills (MacMillan et al., 1986) make planning difficult.

Appropriate Learner Activities

Analyzing the Writing Situation

A teacher can help students have a better conceptualization of a specific writing assignment—and of writing tasks in general—by discussing the various factors of the situation. To guide such a discussion, the teacher might use a communication triangle (cf. Kinneavy, 1971; Lindemann, 1982; Lloyd-Jones, 1977). The triangle illustrated in Figure 13.1 demonstrates that in a literacy event there is a *writer* who wants to accomplish a purpose by writing about some *subject* for an *audience* (readers) and the result is the *text*.

Any number of examples might be used to discuss writing situations: a parent's note to a teacher, the lyrics to a rock song, a prescription for cough syrup, a report for science class. Discussion can focus on the elements in the situation:

1. *Writer:* What is the writer's purpose? to inform? to persuade? to entertain? to express? What kind of image does the writer want to project?
2. *Audience:* What does the reader already know? What does the reader need to know? What are the readers' biases?

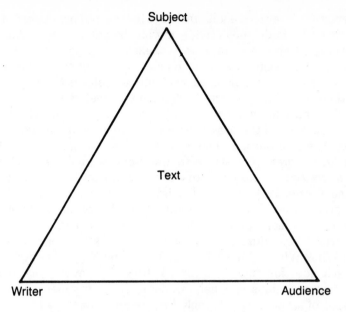

FIGURE 13.1 Communication Triangle for Writing.

3. *Subject:* What is important to include about the subject? Is there an ideal way to organize the content?
4. *Text:* What form should the text take? How long should it be?

Students are encouraged to consider these same aspects of the writing situation as they plan their own writing to clarify purpose and focus on the major content. A "nutshelling" technique (Flower, 1981), in which the writer briefly states the purpose, audience, and major ideas for the composition, can also be helpful in getting a student started on a composition.

Generating Content

Listing, Brainstorming, and Brainwriting   One strategy for generating content is to start listing what comes to mind about the topic after an assignment is given but before the actual drafting begins (Scardamalia & Bereiter, 1986). The emphasis at this point is on quantity of the ideas; selection can come later. Brainstorming (Adams, 1974) is a group problem-solving technique that can be used to generate content. Members of the group contribute ideas associated with the topic, and, in doing so, they follow four rules: (1) no evaluation is allowed; (2) participants are encouraged to think of unusual ideas; (3) emphasis is on the quantity of the ideas; and (4) participants build on the ideas of others.

An interesting interactive adaptation of listing and brainstorming has been suggested by Rodrigues (1983) in what he calls *brainwriting*. Students, working in groups of four or five, each write down several ideas on a topic that has been chosen by the class or assigned by the teacher. After recording three or four ideas, each student places the paper in the center of the group and gets another student's sheet. The student reads the other list and adds more ideas to it; this procedure continues until all in the group read all the lists. Students can then combine and organize ideas, select the best ones, and share them with the class.

Asking Questions   Questions that writers can ask themselves are known as *heuristics*, or explicit plans for searching one's memory to draw content (see Young, 1976, 1987). Heuristics, which were essential in the invention procedures of classical rhetoric, are also components of cognitive approaches to learning (e.g., Dansereau et al, 1979).

One heuristic procedure for exploring a topic is the reporter's set of questions: Who? What? When? Where? How? and Why? Asking and answering each question increases the likelihood of developing adequate content. These questions can help students as they generate ideas for various types of school writing, including essay tests.

Another heuristic is *cubing* (Cowan, 1980, pp. 244–245), which is a means of examining a topic in different ways:

1. *Describe it.* Look at the subject closely and describe what you see. Colors, shapes, sizes, and so forth.
2. *Compare it.* What is it similar to? Different from?
3. *Associate it.* What does it make you think of? Times, places, people?
4. *Analyze it.* Tell how it is made. If you don't know, make it up.
5. *Apply it.* Tell what you can do with it, how it can be used.
6. *Argue for or against it.* Take a stand.

The students first consider a topic from one perspective, write about it for three to five minutes, and then move to the next perspective and the next until they have examined the topic from all six. They then read what they have written to see which way of viewing is best for writing on that topic.

Sets of heuristics, such as these two, are eventually intended for spontaneous use as self-questioning techniques when students compose on their own. Because the computer too can ask questions, computer-assisted instruction has potential for helping students generate content for their writing. Burns (1984; cf. Burns & Culp, 1980), one of the first to study computer-assisted invention in writing, predicts that the new generation of computer invention programs will be relevant to specific writing tasks and will be recursive to allow for planning throughout composing.

Organizing Content

Clustering   An important follow-up to a procedure for generating content is organizing, perhaps by clustering the content into thematic groups. The term *clustering,* originally used by Bousfield (1953) in regard to free-recall list learning, is the grouping of items on the basis of shared characteristics. Figure 13.2 demonstrates how ideas generated through a listing procedure and/or selected from readings can be clustered and

Origin
  Roundup in Old West
  Entertainment for cowboys—fun, relaxation
  Competition in cowboy skills
        HISTORY

Evolution of rodeo   Rodeos today
  Spectators   Professional
  Prizes   Little Britches
  Cowboys' association   High School
                            Collegiate
                            All-women

U.S.—especially West Canada
        LOCATIONS

Australia
New Zealand

RODEO

EVENTS

Types
  Calf roping
  Steer wrestling—bulldogging
  Barrel racing
  Team roping
  Steer roping

    TIMED EVENTS
      Scoring
        Winner—shortest time
        Penalties for mistakes

Types
  Bullriding—favorite for many spectators
  Bareback bronc riding
  Saddle bronc riding

ROUGH STOCK EVENTS
  Scoring
    Must stay on 8 seconds
    Rider and animal both judged

FIGURE 13.2 Clustering of Content.

organized. These clusters may eventually lead to paragraphs or larger sections of composition.

Mapping. *Maps* are graphic representations of compositions. Because they are flexible, maps are strong alternatives to outlines. According to Buckley and Boyle (1983, p. 59), maps have the following additional advantages over outlines:

Mapping is easy to share.
Mapping illustrates relationships.
Mapping presents a whole structure.
Mapping is personal and idiosyncratic.
Mapping is easily learned.
Mapping moves students from fluency to form.

Like mapping for comprehension in reading (cf. Gold, 1971; Sinatra, Stahl-Gemake, & Berg, 1984; see also Chapter 17), mapping in composing involves organizing and relating concepts. Students can be introduced to this procedure through involvement in a group essay, perhaps on a topic that they have been studying and for which they have some source material. After receiving the assignment or deciding on a topic, the group begins generating ideas and selecting words for the map. Figure 13.3 illustrates a sample map. Students begin to organize the ideas as they decide where they should go on the map. Then, as they write, they may reorganize. After trying out the strategy in group writing, students should be able to use it in their own efforts.

A related graphic approach is *treeing* (Berkenkotter, 1982), which results in a hierarchical structure similar to a structured overview (Vacca & Vacca, 1986) in reading. Figure 13.4 shows a tree structure for the same content as that in Figure 13.3.

Using Text Patterns   For some types of writing, text patterns (cf. Dougherty, 1986; Horowitz, 1985a, 1985b; Vacca & Vacca, 1986) can assist students in the planning process. Although text patterns are visual representations similar to maps or trees, they are static patterns representing particular types of organization in writing. In various content areas, for example, writing assignments include the patterns illustrated in Figure 13.5; the comparison-contrast essay, which has an underlying matrix structure; the "how-to" essay, which has a time line (sequential) structure; and the argument, which has an assertion-support structure. To introduce a particular pattern, the teacher might present a topic and then lead students in a group generating session with the text pattern guiding the discussion. The matrix, for example, could be used to contrast living conditions in two countries. The time line could be used for giving an account of steps in a science experiment. The assertion-support pattern could be used for taking a position on a current issue in the community and giving reasons for the position.

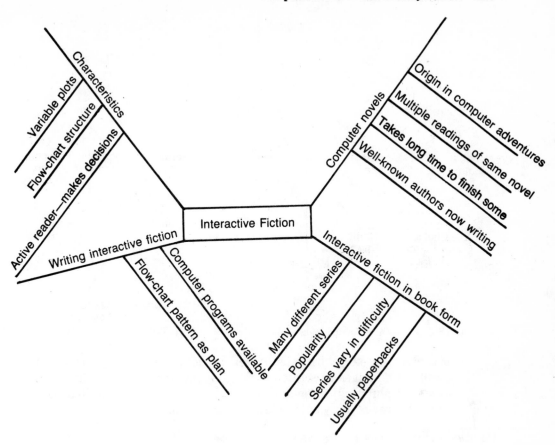

FIGURE 13.3 A Map As a Composition Plan.

Text patterns help organize other types of transactional writing (see Dougherty, 1986; Meyer, 1982) as well as stories and various forms of poetry, such as the cinquain and haiku.

Assessing Each Student's Strengths and Weaknesses

Students' strengths and weaknesses in planning can be assessed by observing the process, by interviewing the students, and by analyzing the products. The teacher, watching students as they begin writing particular pieces, notes the strategies they use (Jaggar, 1985). These observations are perhaps followed with retrospective interviews about composing processes in conferences. The composition products also reveal strengths and weaknesses in planning through their organization and development. Weaknesses include unclear or inappropriate structure and arrangement

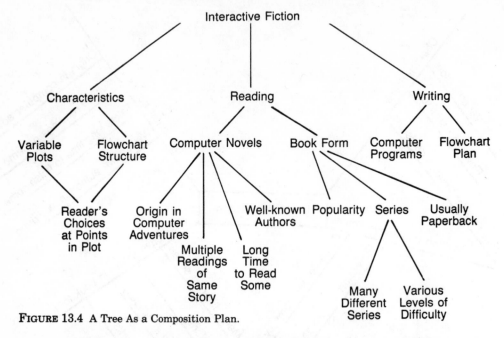

FIGURE 13.4 A Tree As a Composition Plan.

of content, possibly with gaps, as well as poor development of topics. Notes on planning pages or scratch paper also provide some insights into the extent of planning, although those insights are rather limited because the notes reveal only surface evidences of planning.

Recovery Procedures for Persistent Problems

The teacher can work individually with students experiencing difficulty in planning. Some students may need additional teacher support in the form of dialogue, explanation, or modeling as they conceptualize the writing situation, generate content, and organize the content. Teacher-student writing conferences (Freedman, 1984; Murray, 1978) should occur as needed. A conference can even come before actual writing, while the composition is still a "pre-text" (Witte, 1985), or the mental representation that is being constructed before any words are put down.

Another recovery procedure involves getting students to study their own cognitive processes. Canadian researchers Scardamalia and Bereiter (1986) have found that students learn by discovery when the teacher has individual students "think aloud," or say what they are thinking as they write.

Writing for Readers

What Is to Be Learned?

Critical to success in composing is the production of writing that communicates clearly because it meets the needs of the reader. Unlike oral

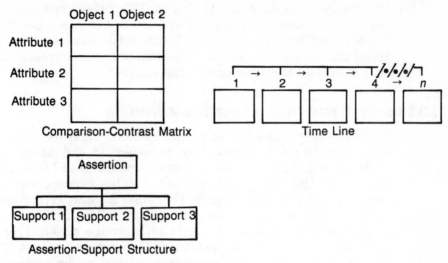

FIGURE 13.5 Sample Text Patterns.

communication, in which the hearer can ask questions if a point is not clear, the written text must stand on its own (Barritt & Kroll, 1978). The writer has to provide enough background and detail in a clear, coherent fashion for the reader to develop connections and structure. To do so, the writer must move back—"distance" (Myers, 1983)—from a composition, read it from another's perspective, and adapt it for the audience. Comprehension monitoring for a writer seems to be related to comprehension monitoring in reading (cf. Wagoner, 1983); however, in addition to monitoring for one's own comprehension, the writer must be aware of another's potential understanding. The writer must also test the actual message against a mental standard—the intended message. When the message fails this test, the writer experiences dissonance, "lack of congruence between what the work does and what the writer feels it should do" (Della-Piana, 1978, p. 106). Writers do not always produce in a first draft a piece that is ready for a reader. Murray (1978) argues that "writing is rewriting" (p. 85), and Flower (1979) has demonstrated that early efforts often result in writer-based prose, or "writing that is still to an important degree in the writer's head" (p. 30) and that needs to be transformed to meet the needs of a reader.

Demonstrating Successful Learning

Success in learning composition should be measured by the effectiveness of the final product in communicating the message to the intended readers. It would be inappropriate to measure success by counting numbers of revisions, for example, for even though revisions are often involved in transforming a text for a reader, the changes do not always result in an improved product (Bridwell, 1980; Perl, 1979). One important factor influencing revision is the level of dissonance between what the writer intended and what is written (cf. Witte, 1985). Successful learning involves an increased awareness of dissonance and an increased ability to change the text to eliminate that dissonance.

LD Students' Typical Problems with This Material

Writing ability appears to be related to social cognitive ability, or the ability to make inferences about the characteristics and qualities of others (Rubin, 1984). (To review social-cognitive problems in LD students, see Chapter 4.) Audience awareness and the ability to adapt writing to the reader are developmental abilities (Crowhurst & Piche, 1979; Kroll, 1985). Many writing problems arise from writers' failure to realize that the reader has different knowledge and beliefs about a subject. Poor writers often lack an awareness of the reader's requirements for understanding and do not know how to make composition more reader-based.

When rewriting a draft, many poor writers tend to limit changes to either mechanical aspects, such as spelling, or merely recopy the original draft, doing little or no revising for clarity of meaning (Bridwell, 1980; Perl, 1979). LD students often write unclearly (Morris & Crump, 1982). Their difficulties in monitoring the comprehensibility of their text are likely related to their difficulties in monitoring comprehension in reading (Roit & McKenzie, 1985).

Appropriate Learner Activities

Responses from the Teacher

Since writing is a social act involving communication between writer and reader, one way to increase the ability to read one's own writing from another's perspective is to interact with responding readers. In the secondary classroom emphasizing interactive approaches, the readers are most often the teacher and other students.

By becoming a responding reader, a teacher helps students who have difficulty imagining a reader (Freedman, 1984). Teachers can respond to student writing in conferences, preferably held while the paper is in draft form and can be changed. Through the conference, the teacher provides both *procedural facilitation,* or help in knowing what strategies to use, and *substantive facilitation,* or help in selecting and developing content (Scardamalia & Bereiter, 1986). An example of procedural facilitation would be the teacher's suggesting that the student map ideas to clarify relationships, and an example of substantive facilitation would be mentioning some related content. Various approaches to conferences can be taken. For instance, in the conference the teacher might offer an initial response to a draft by reading the composition for the first time and by thinking aloud when reading. Or the teacher and the student might just talk about the piece. The teacher's role as a responding reader is to be supportive and to ask questions that a reader would want answered by the composition. In the writing conference, according to Sowers (1982), the teacher's role is: (1) to reflect (to mirror the text by restating, paraphrasing, or summarizing what is said); (2) to expand (to encourage needed development and detail); and (3) to focus (to help the student decide what content should be emphasized). For conferences to succeed, the teacher should avoid taking too much of the initiative (Jacob, 1982) and instead should allow the student some control.

Another major way for the teacher to respond is through written comments on drafts. One examination of teachers' markings (Sommers, 1982) indicates that the stock phrases, such as "awkward," provide little help and may confuse students instead of helping them. Langer and Applebee (1983) propose that written comments that take the form of a dialogue, such as, "Did you mean to say . . . ?" or "I am confused about . . ." (p. 8).

Responses from Peers

Of course, peers can also act as responding readers when students work in pairs or groups. It is important for the interactive, collaborative response element to be present—for readers to respond to writers and writers to assist other writers. Members of the group should share, reflect, respond, and help (Mayher, Lester, & Pradl, 1983).

Self-Evaluating

As writers compose drafts, they do much rereading, which has been called *retrospective structuring* because, while reading, the writer is seeing if the piece is being shaped into what was intended. The writer is mentally asking, "Are these words right for me?", "Do they capture what I am trying to say?", and "If not, what's missing?" (Perl, 1980, p 367). The writer must also do another kind of reading before the piece is ready for an audience—*projective structuring*—or projecting oneself into the role of reader and imagining how someone else would respond.

To help student writers read and revise their drafts, teachers can provide guides such as the one in Box 13.1, which is designed to assist students in distancing from their compositions and measruing them against internal standards.

Responses from the Computer

Text feedback programs on the computer can provide response to writers. Although current programs, such as Writer's Workbench (Frase, 1980),

---

Box 13.1 Self-Evaluation Scale

1. How much time did you spend on this paper?
2. [After the first evaluation] What did you try to improve, or experiment with, on this paper? How successful were you? If you have questions about what you are trying to do, what are they?
3. What are the strengths of your paper? Place a squiggly line beside those passages you feel are very good.
4. What are the weaknesses, if any, of your paper? Place an *X* beside passages you would like your teacher to correct or revise. Place an *X* over any punctuation, spelling, usage, etc., where you need help or clarification.
5. What one thing will you do to improve your next piece of writing? Or what kind of experimentation in writing would you like to try? If you would like some information related to what you want to do, write down your questions.
6. (Optional) What grade would you give yourself on this composition? Justify it.

Note. From "Individual Goal Setting, Self-Evaluation, and Peer Evaluation" in *Evaluating Writing: Describing, Measuring, Judging* (p. 143) by C. R. Cooper and L. Odell (Eds.), 1977, Urbana, IL: National Council of Teachers of English. Copyright 1977 by National Council of Teachers of English. Reprinted by permission.

---

are intended mainly for business and technical writers, they demonstrate the sort of response that computers can give. Their feedback typically takes the form of statistical information, such as number of passive sentences and average number of words per sentence (see Bridwell, Nancarrow, & Ross, 1984).

Assessing Each Student's Strengths and Weaknesses

As in assessing for strengths and weaknesses in planning, the teacher can observe the process, question, and look at the products of composing to evaluate students' abilities to prepare compositions for readers. Observations of students as they write can reveal whether they are reading to improve content or simply hunting errors. These observations can be clarified by interviewing students during conferences to see whether they are aware of the requirements of the reader and of ways to make their writing more reader-based. The teacher may even occasionally have students read their compositions aloud during a conference to see if they are aware of dissonance between what they have produced and what they intended to produce and if they offer any fix-up strategies. Some studies (e.g., Perl, 1979) reveal that students spontaneously make changes as they orally read their written compositions. The products themselves also provide insights into characteristics of writer-based prose, such as abbreviated wording, incomplete context, sentence fragments, and unclear connections between ideas (Flower, 1979).

Recovery Procedures for Persistent Problems

Problems in writing for readers can be individually addressed during the writing conference. The teacher may also focus on particular problems in lessons on various aspects of composing. For instance, a group of students may be consistently producing brief, unconnected sentences that leave to the reader the task of connecting ideas. For these students, the teacher can design a lesson on sentence combining (O'Hare, 1973; Simms, 1984), perhaps using sentences from the students' compositions.

Writing to Learn

What Is to Be Learned?

During the elementary school years, most writing tends to be expressive and poetic (see Chapter 11), taking the forms of personal writing and stories. In secondary school, however, writing is necessarily directed to transactional functions, such as presenting information or arguing a point. Langer and Applebee (1985) provide the following categories for writing in secondary school:

> notetaking—from class lectures and discussions as well as from text sources;
> reporting—describing the here and now of what happened, as in lab reports and accounts of field trips;
> summarizing—requiring generalizing or synthesizing in that the information conveyed is selected and shaped by the writer;
> analyzing—examining the reasons, causes, or motivations underlying ideas, actions, or relationships;
> journal writing—writing for self discovery and expression;
> writing of stories and poems—literary writing that provides a unique way of sharing experience and understanding ideas. (p. 37)

All fit into the transactional category, except journal writing, which is typically expressive, and the writing of stories and poems, which is poetic.

Influenced by the work in Great Britain of such people as Britton (1970) and Martin (Martin, D'Arcy, Newton, & Parker, 1976), the "writing to learn" and "writing across the curriculum" movements are gaining momentum in the United States (see Fulwiler & Young, 1982; Mayher et al., 1983). The potential of writing to enhance the learning of content is beginning to be acknowledged (Emig, 1977), and writing is viewed as a way of elaborating information and integrating new information with prior knowledge (Applebee, 1984b; Weinstein & Mayer, 1986). Composing requires "joining bits of information into relationships, many of which have never existed until the composer utters them" (Van Nostrand, 1979, p. 178). Studies (e.g., Newell, 1984) comparing writing with other learning activities demonstrate that writing does increase learning and that the nature of the writing task does affect the nature of the learning that results. Teachers successfully using writing-to-learn assignments know that the assignments must be keyed to the learning objectives for students.

Unfortunately, the schools have not fully recognized the potential of writing for learning. Applebee's (1981, 1984a) extensive research in secondary schools indicates that school-sponsored writing is typically intended to demonstrate learning rather than to develop it.

Demonstrating Successful Learning

Successful use of the writing-to-learn approach is evident in increased understanding of content as well as the strategies to use in writing. Writing and learning can take various forms. If the writing involves summarizing a text, perhaps a section of a textbook chapter, the resulting content knowledge is very closely related to what is in the text. If the writing involves reasoning and reflecting, as in essays, the new content becomes more integrated with previous knowledge and is more influenced by individual perspectives. If the writing is more expressive, as in keeping notes in a content-area log, the knowledge is directed toward learners' awareness of such factors as what they know, how they came to know it, and how they feel about it.

Some writing in content classes, such as that done on essay tests, is writing to demonstrate learning instead of writing to learn. Success in writing responses on essay tests is measured by the students' use of strategies for taking such tests along with the content knowledge demonstrated on the test.

LD Students' Typical Problems with This Material

Since writing to learn often involves reading an assignment and then doing some related writing, LD students' reading problems (see Chapters 8 and 9) influence their writing and learning. One important reading-writing ability is summarizing, which is based on the metacognitive awareness of what is important in a text (Brown & Day, 1983; also see Chapters 2 and 9). This awareness guides the selections that are made for the summary. Other writing-to-learn tasks, such as essay writing, require a high degree of reflective processes in verbal reasoning (Birnbaum, 1986). Some LD students' tendencies to select solutions to problems impulsively rather than reflectively can create difficulties. Finally, in writing responses for essay tests, LD students can have special problems because this task requires them not only to generate and organize knowledge that comes, at least in part, from reading but also to apply composing strategies within a constrained time frame (cf. Herbert & Czerniejewski, 1976).

Appropriate Learner Activities

Keeping Learning Logs

One way that teachers can help students gain control of their learning is by using *learning logs,* or informal records of learning in a particular course (Martin et al., 1976; Mayher et al., 1983). Through these logs teachers can also gain insights into students' learning. In their logs, students record and question information, relate the course content to their knowledge, and make predictions. The following is a log entry from a student who had been studying sleep patterns:

> The book says that a person who is waked up often during REM will be irritable. But how would someone else know if the person is in REM just by eye movements? It's interesting that someone who wakes up during the REM cycle will usually remember the dream. I used to remember dreams better than I do now.

Students need directions before they start on these logs. Box 13.2 is a list of Rudrud's ideas (see Mayher et al., 1983) for students to use as they keep track of their own learning.

A dialectics strategy has been suggested by Berthoff (1982) to help students develop new ideas about a subject. She has students divide pages in half. On the left side they record notes from their reading, and on the right side they write comments or questions.

Teachers can write responses in dialogue fashion to students' writing in the logs. Although they should not grade the entries, they can encourage students to review their notes periodically to analyze them for such aspects as recurring ideas to develop their awareness of their own learning.

Summarizing

Summarizing is a predominant type of secondary school writing, in assignments from teachers and in textbooks (Applebee, 1981, 1984a). Read-

---

Box 13.2 Learning Log Ideas
_____

1. React to class activities—what did you think of a lab, a movie, test, etc.? Was it valuable?
2. Describe yourself as a science, math, social studies, etc., student.
3. Explain new concepts and ideas. How does new information fit in with what you already know? (Audience is yourself in this case.)
4. Explain new concepts to another student. Identify various audiences—a younger student, a student who has been absent, for example.
5. Question the significance of what you've learned.
6. Question what you don't understand. Try to get material straight when you're confused.
7. Explain assignments in your own words.
8. Describe what has been said about the subject during class.
9. Explain why assignments aren't done on time.
10. Evaluate the teacher and the course content.

Note. From *Learning to Write/Writing to Learn* (p. 82) by J. S. Mayher, N. Lester, and G. M. Pradl, 1983, Upper Montclair, NJ: Boynton/Cook. Copyright 1983 by Boynton/Cook Publishers, Inc. Reprinted by permission.

---

ing research (see, e.g., Brown & Day, 1983; Kintsch & van Dijk, 1978) has revealed a set of mental rules that skilled readers use as they summarize a passage. Although summaries are often ways to demonstrate learning, summary writing is also a means of enhancing the learning of content because it helps students understand and remember important ideas. Since poor readers tend to have difficulty summarizing (Winograd, 1984), methods have been developed for explicitly teaching the summary rules. Box 13.3 lists those rules (cf. Brown & Day, 1983) taught to poor readers in one study (Hare & Borchardt, 1984). Training in summarizing can have beneficial effects on both reading and writing. Getting the gist of a passage is an important part of reading comprehension, and writing summaries is an important writing skill. Training in summarizing also has been found to improve the quality of other kinds of writing (Taylor & Beach, 1984).

Summarizing activities need not be limited to textual material. Gere (1985) suggests using exit slips as a summarizing activity to improve learning in a course. On these slips students summarize at the end of a class period what has occurred in class that day. This helps them perceive closure and practice determining what is important. Additionally, it provides the teacher with insights into what the students are learning.

Box 13.3   Summarizing Rules

1. *Make sure you understand the text.* Ask yourself, "What was this text about?" "What did the writer say?" Try to say the general theme to yourself.
2. *Look back.* Reread the text to make sure you understand the theme. Also read to make sure that you really understand what the important parts of the text are. Star important points.
3. *Collapse Lists.* If you see a list of things, try to think of a word or phrase name for the whole list. For example, if you saw a list like, "eyes, ears, neck, arms, and legs," you could say "body parts." Or, if you saw a list like, "ice skating, skiing, and sledding," you could say "winter sports."
4. *Use topic sentences.* Often authors write a sentence that summarizes a whole paragraph. It is called a topic sentence. If the author gives you one, you can use it in your summary (in paraphrased form). Unfortunately, not all paragraphs contain topic sentences. That means you may have to make one up for yourself. . . .
5. *Get rid of unnecessary detail.* Some text information can be repeated in a passage. . . . [The] same thing can be said in a number of different ways, all in one passage. Other text information can be unimportant or trivial. Since summaries are meant to be short, get rid of repetitions or trivial information.
6. *Collapse paragraphs.* Paragraphs are often related to one another. Some paragraphs explain one or more other paragraphs. Some paragraphs just expand on the information presented in other paragraphs. Some paragraphs are more necessary than other paragraphs. Decide which paragraphs should be kept or eliminated, and which might be joined together.
7. *Rethink.* Reread a paragraph of the text. Try to say the theme of that paragraph to yourself. Is there a topic sentence? Have you underlined it? Or is the topic sentence missing? If it is missing, have you written one in the margin?
8. *Check and double-check.* Did you leave in any lists? Make sure you don't list anything out in the summary. Did you repeat yourself? Make sure you didn't. Did you skip anything? Is all the important information in the summary?

(continued)

Note. Adapted from "Direct Introduction of Summarization Skills" by V. C. Hare and K. M. Borchardt, 1984, *Reading Research Quarterly, 20,* p. 66. Copyright 1984 by International Reading Association. Adapted with permission of Victoria C. Hare and the International Reading Association.

Box 13.3   *(continued)*

A Final Suggestion

Polish the summary. When a lot of information is reduced from an original passage, the resulting concentrated information often sounds very unnatural. Fix this problem and create a more natural-sounding summary. Adjustments may include but are not limited to: paraphrasing, the insertion of connecting words like "and" or "because," and the insertion of introductory or closing statements. Paraphrasing is especially useful here for two reasons: one, because it improves your ability to remember the material, and two, it avoids using the author's words, otherwise known as plagiarism.

Writing Essays

In two comparisons (Langer, 1986; Newell, 1984) of various writing-to-learn tasks in secondary schools (taking notes, answering short questions, and writing essays), the writing of analytic essays was found to have the strongest impact on knowledge growth. The essay topics used in both studies had the students take their own perspectives on content that they had read. According to Langer (1986), when writing essays, "students seem to step back from the text after reading—they reconceptualize the content in ways that cut across ideas, focusing on larger issues or topics. In doing this, they integrate information and engage in more complex thought" (p. 40). An assignment suggested by Bleich (1975) that asks the students to complete the statement, "The most important word in the story is. . . ," requires the students to do some analytic reasoning, to make a choice, and to support that choice.

To begin to teach essay writing to LD students, the teacher can model strategies selected from those discussed in the first part of this chapter. The writing situation, for example, can be analyzed and a focus formed. Planning might involve listing ideas and then organizing them into a map or using the assertion-support text pattern.

Taking Essay Tests

When writing is used to demonstrate learning, the composing task is quite often an essay test. However, students are rarely taught skills for taking such tests, even though they are frequently expected to produce written responses under such conditions. They are thus left to their own resources in learning how to do this kind of writing. Box 13.4 suggests some strategies for taking essay tests that teachers can help students learn.

Assessing Each Student's Strengths and Weaknesses

By looking at students' written work, the teacher can get an idea of their abilities to perform the various writing-to-learn tasks. Students are likely to be writing summaries in many content classrooms and some analytic essays in English classes (Applebee, 1984a). Learning logs can reveal their perceptions of their own strengths and weaknesses. Insights may also be gained by asking students questions about how they approach writing assignments in content-area classes and how they write their answers on essay tests.

Recovery Procedures for Persistent Problems

With the new emphasis on process, a somewhat artificial dichotomy has been set up between "process" and "product" approaches to composition instruction. In actuality, both process *and* product should receive attention. Processes develop when people strive to produce adequate compositions. By becoming aware of the characteristics of an effective product, students have a clearer idea of what they should try to achieve (Perkins, 1985; Scardamalia & Bereiter, 1986). Students learn much about writing quality, for example, from reading pieces that other students have written (Hilgers, 1984). Recovery procedures for students experiencing difficulty in producing various forms of writing-to-learn tasks should include having them read and discuss good examples of the types of writing that they are attempting.

Matching Students to Tasks and Monitoring Performance

Initial Broad-Based Assessment

Tests of writing ability indicate level of performance and often the strengths and weaknesses in writing. Many of the instruments that are called writing tests, however, do not actually measure compositional factors; instead they attempt to measure writing ability indirectly by presenting multiple-choice items that emphasize transcription factors, such as mechanics and usage (for a review, see Walmsley, 1983b). Some tests, however, *do* measure writing ability directly by eliciting writing samples

Box 13.4 Strategies for Taking Essay Tests

Prewriting

1. Make certain to read the examination question carefully. Know exactly what is being asked of you. Underline key words and phrases in the assignment to remind yourself of what you must do.
2. If options are presented, think about the choices of topics or approaches that will best enable you to display what you know. (Also, if you think you would *enjoy* writing one option more than another, choose it, because your writing will probably be more natural.)
3. Write down the audience for this paper. For whom are you writing? What are you trying to show that person? Try to visualize your audience in your mind.
4. Take time—maybe only five minutes—to jot down some notes and plans for yourself. Don't just start writing the first thing that comes into your head.
5. Look for an angle or plan of attack on your topic, some way to get into it that lets you write from your own perspective.
6. Let your knowledge of the topic structure your paper. You know the material. Think about what you know, how you want to write about it, and the audience for whom you are writing. In that way, you'll discover your angle of organization.

Writing

1. Take time, but not too much time. Write fairly rapidly, but don't let panic or nervousness make you write too quickly.
2. If you get stuck, keep on going. Don't waste time worrying about how to get around a writing block. Just move to the next item in your notes and come back to patch up the stuck place later.
3. Don't worry too much about "correctness," but be certain to leave yourself time to check your work later. If you get stuck trying to spell a word, choose another word with similar meaning that you can spell.
4. Once or twice as you write, look back at the examination ques-

(continued)

Note. From *Teaching Writing in Content Areas: Senior High School* (pp. 72–73) by S. Tchudi and J. Yates, 1983, Washington, DC: National Educational Association. Copyright 1983 by the National Educational Association. Reprinted by permission.

Box 13.4 *(continued)*

---

tion to make certain you are answering it and haven't drifted away from your purpose.

5. Once or twice as you write, look back at the audience you have chosen for the paper and visualize your reader(s) again.

Revision

1. At all costs, leave time for revision, even if it's only five minutes. People write strange things under the pressure of examinations, and they need to go back over their writing.
2. Ask yourself if you have answered the question. If not, look for places to insert a few lines to improve your answer.
3. Ask yourself whether any places sound awkward. (A good way to do this is to read the examination silently, mouthing the words.)
4. With two minutes or more to go, look over the paper with spelling, punctuation, and usage in mind. Correct anything obviously wrong or change it to something that seems right.

---

from the students, including the Diagnostic Evaluation of Writing Skills (DEWS) (Weiner, 1980), the Test of Written Language (TOWL) (Hammill & Larsen, 1978), and the Picture Story Language Test (PSLT) (Myklebust, 1965). Although these three include evaluations of an actual writing sample, the range of writing measured is limited. The DEWS sample is an autobiography, and the TOWL and PSLT samples are stories. Some authorities on composition (e.g., Lloyd-Jones, 1977; Walmsley, 1983) maintain that writing ability should be judged on the basis of the writer's success in accomplishing various purposes of writing. A relatively new test, the Stanford Writing Assessment Program (SWAP) (Gardner, Rudman, Karlsen, & Merwin, 1982) is a normed test measuring performance on four different types of writing tasks (Describing, Narrating, Explaining, and Reasoning). Each of the four compositions is evaluated for five qualities of writing. In addition to scores from such tests, the teacher may have access to scores from a state competency test, many of which include direct measures of writing, or from a district-wide assessment.

Most frequently, teachers conduct writing evaluations with their own assignments, which can be similar to the types of tasks expected of the students. These writing samples can be collected and scored at the beginning of the year and at various points throughout the program. For scoring essays, teachers can use holistic methods (see Brown, 1986; Cooper

	Low		Middle		High
Ideas	2	4	6	8	10
Organization	2	4	6	8	10
Wording	1	2	3	4	5
Flavor	1	2	3	4	5
Usage	1	2	3	4	5
Punctuation	1	2	3	4	5
Spelling	1	2	3	4	5
Handwriting	1	2	3	4	5
				Sum	_____

FIGURE 13.6 Diederich's Analytic Scale.

Note. From *Measuring Growth in English* by P. B. Diederich, 1974, Urbana, IL: National Council of Teachers of English. Copyright 1974 by the National Council of Teachers of English. Reprinted by permission.

& Odell, 1977), although when assessing for instructional purposes, it is probably best to select procedures that provide some indication of relative strengths and weaknesses. Two examples are included here. Figure 13.6 is Diederich's (1974) analytic scale, which is based on research into the rating of college students' essays. This sort of scale is called *analytic* because it gives a profile of strengths and weaknesses. Figure 13.7 is a rubric based on the generic scale used by the Texas Education Agency (Greenhalgh & Townsend, 1981) for evaluating compositions in its student competency tests. If that rubric is used, the scorer can circle the holistic numerical score and underline the descriptors that helped determine the score. In both of these scoring methods, content factors receive more weight than mechanical factors.

In any evaluation of writing, the teacher of composition should maintain the cognitive developmental perspective on error. Because errors are natural in the active learning of a language, a teacher of disabled writers should view errors as clues—"windows"—to "organized rules and intelligent strategies that a student draws on to perform a composing task" (Barritt & Kroll, 1978, p. 54). Active composing strategies often result in error when something new is attempted.

Summary and Conclusions

In managing a composition program, the teacher keeps track of students' progress in learning and applying strategies, such as planning, monitoring, and elaborating. This information can be obtained from observations

0

Appropriateness?
  It does not respond to the assignment.
    It is on a different topic.
    It is a copy or paraphrase of the assignment.
Organization, Clarity, Coherence?
  It is incoherent.
Elaboration?
  It is a brief phrase.

1

Appropriateness?
  It is an attempt to respond, but the attempt is inappropriate to the
    purpose and/or audience.
Organization, Clarity, Coherence?
  It is poorly organized and contains gaps.
  It is unclear and incoherent because of lack of control of written
    language.
Elaboration?
  It is skeletal and brief.

2

Appropriateness?
  It is somewhat appropriate for purpose and/or audience.
Organization, Clarity, Coherence?
  Although it shows some organization, it has gaps and inconsistencies.
  It shows limited control of written language.
Elaboration?
  It is somewhat elaborated.

3

Appropriateness?
  It is appropriate for purpose and/or audience.
Organization, Clarity, Coherence?
  Overall, it is clear, coherent, and organized.
  It may contain some brief digressions, but they don't intefere too
    much.
Elaboration?
  It is moderately well elaborated (e.g., details, examples).

4

Appropriateness?
  It is appropriate for purpose, mode, and audience.
Organization, Clarity, Coherence?
  It is well organized into a unified whole.
  It contains no gaps or inconsistencies.
  The sentence structure and word choice are sophisticated.
Elaboration?
  It is well elaborated and contains rich details.

FIGURE 13.7 Holistic Scoring Rubric Based on Focused Holistic Scoring Procedure for Texas Assesment of Minimum Skills.

Note. Adapted from "Evaluating Students Writing Holistically: An Alternative Approach" by C. Greenhalgh and D. Townsend, 1981, *Language Arts, 58.*

of the process, dialogues with students, and study of the compositions themselves. Instruction succeeds when the students actively and independently apply the composing strategies first taught with teacher support. The teacher can also record evaluations of the students' progress in writing for different functions, including various forms of transactional writing. The students' expressive writing in their learning logs can be examined for the development of their awareness of their own cognition.

The teaching of composition, like composing processes, is recursive. Composition instruction is directed to processes that reoccur as a new composition is conceived and produced. Yet in the teaching of composition, as in composing itself, there should be noticeable movement toward goals. As emphasized throughout this chapter, the educational goal in a cognitive developmental approach is the independent and successful use of strategies to produce effective compositions.

Chapter 14

Mathematics Instruction in the Elementary Grades

George W. Fair

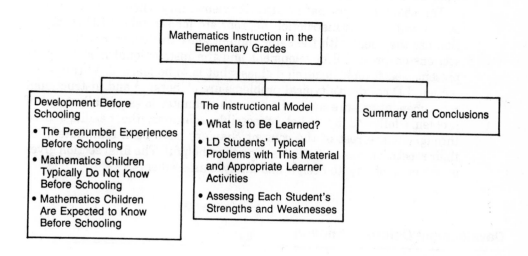

Questions to Consider

1. How does arithmetic differ from mathematics?
2. What are likely to be the most troublesome aspects of mathematics learning for LD children?
3. What are recommended guidelines for mathematics instruction?
4. How can these guidelines be met in the instruction of place value, addition, subtraction, multiplication, division, fractions, and problem solving?

The demand for mathematics knowledge and competence in both personal and professional life continues to increase. LD students, if they are to be successful, must achieve mathematics levels approximately commensurate with those of their average, nondisabled peers. This chapter and the next are designed to provide teachers with tactics and activities for helping the LD student who is failing in this area. *Arithmetic* applies primarily to the skills of computation. *Mathematics,* on the other hand, applies to the study of the properties of and relationships among quantities. Mathematics is the broader term, and is the concern of these chapters.

These chapters differ from the preceding chapters in one important way—they address only those areas of learning that have proven to cause problems for LD students. Because nearly all states or school districts specify both the mathematics curriculum and the specific objectives to be accomplished at each grade level, teachers generally have a well-structured plan of instruction. These chapters, therefore, concentrate on what to do when LD students fail to achieve within a regular instructional program.

This chapter covers mathematics for elementary school children. Chapter 15 will address instruction appropriate for secondary LD students. Because they deal with the same content, only this chapter will contain sections on preschool development and the instructional model. By its presence, each topic heading defines what is to be learned. Within each section, LD children's typical problems are elaborated and instructional recommendations are made. Because this chapter is essentially a list of problems followed by a list of possible solutions, the headings used throughout the rest of the content chapters have been eliminated, for their repetition was more distracting than helpful. The final section gives an example of how to design and analyze assessments.

Development Before Schooling

Mathematics has been defined as the study of relationships. The early development of mathematical concepts is concerned with activities in the home, preschool, or community that facilitate an understanding and awareness of these relationships. Developmental instruction should be related to, and grow from, what a student already knows. It is essential, therefore, for teachers to understand the early development of mathematical concepts if they are to make instructional decisions for students. Some LD students will come to school without a firm foundation in mathematics. These students may benefit from immersion in a developmental instructional environment that will enable them to derive these basic concepts. Because it is the teacher's task to plan experiences that help children understand mathematical concepts, relationships, skills, and problem solving, the remainder of this section will answer three questions: (1) What are the prenumber experiences children have before entering school? (2) What mathematics do children typically not know before school? (3) What mathematics are children expected to know as they enter school?

The Prenumber Experiences Before Schooling

Early development includes the emergence of logical thinking and not only the mastery of narrow academic skills. Abstract symbols, number names, and numerals can be meaningful only to the extent that children have accumulated prior knowledge about their relevance to the world. Before entering school, most young children engage in informal experiences that provide an initial understanding of mathematical relationships and later assist in the formation of abstract mathematical ideas and models (see Box 14.1).

Four processes directly related to the meaningful development of number are describing, classifying, comparing, and ordering. *Describing* is the process of characterizing an object, set, or event in terms of its attributes. Children, for example, describe dolls and cars and other toys they own. *Classifying* is the process of sorting objects, sets, or events on the basis of one or more criteria. Young children, for example, often sort jelly beans according to color. *Comparing* is the process of determining whether two objects, sets, or events are the same or different on a specified attribute. Children, for example, compare their height to that of a sister or brother to determine who is the taller. *Ordering* is an extension of

---

Box 14.1 Prenumber Experiences

1. Describing: characterizing an object, set, or event in terms of its attributes
2. Classifying: sorting objects, sets, or events on the basis of one or more criteria
3. Comparing: determining whether two objects, sets, or events are the same or different on a specified attribute
4. Ordering: ordering story events temporally and toys by size
5. Equalizing: making two objects or sets the same on an attribute
6. Joining: putting together two objects or sets with a common attribute to form a single object or set
7. Separating: distributing a single object or set into two or more objects or sets
8. Patterning: recognizing, developing, and repeating a series of related objects or sets

comparing in which more than two objects, sets, or events are compared. Children may order story events temporally and toys by size. Describing, classifying, comparing, and ordering provide the necessary background for the higher degree of abstraction that is required for an operational understanding of number.

Other processes, such as equalizing, joining, and separating, are directly related to number operations and also occur spontaneously before schooling. *Equalizing* is the process of making two objects or sets the same on an attribute. If, for example, a young child is given three jelly beans and a sibling is given one, the first child will request that the distribution be equalized. *Joining* is the process of putting together two objects or sets with a common attribute to form a single object or set, as when two children place their dolls together to form a family. *Separating* is the opposite of joining, or the division of an object or set into two or more objects or sets. A child may separate a group of toys to share them with playmates. Equalizing, joining, and separating are precursors to the equality relation and the addition and subtraction operations.

Children take part in activities related to measuring and patterning prior to school entrance. Children *measure* when they attach numbers to specified attributes. A girl may measure the amount of sand in different buckets by remembering that she put two shovels in one bucket and four in the other. Young children also have many experiences with *patterns*. Children repeat patterns, for example, when they listen to or say a nursery rhyme. The ability to recognize, develop, and repeat a pattern is basic to future mathematics ability. All equations or open sentences, for example, can be considered incomplete patterns. That is, $2 + ? = 5$, and $3x - 4 = 2x$ may be considered puzzles to be completed. The prenumber relationships identified in this section are all important as activities that enable the child to have meaningful experiences with numbers.

Mathematics Children Typically Do Not Know Before Schooling

The identification of tasks that young children typically do not know as they enter school is helpful in understanding the development of mathematical concepts (see Box 14.2). However, in general, meaningful activities with numbers in the teens or larger are extremely difficult for young children who have not begun school. It is not unusual to find young children who can count to 100, but who cannot tell whether fifty is larger or smaller than seventy. Such children are easily confused by questions such as, "What is more, twenty-five or fifteen?"

The part-whole concept is another major area of difficulty for preschoolers. Understanding this relationship makes it possible for children to begin to think about numbers as compositions of other numbers, which

---

Box 14.2   Mathematics Typically Not Known at School Entrance

1. Operations on numbers larger than twelve
2. The part-whole concept
3. The Hindu-Arabic system of graphonumeric notation:
   a. the additive system
   b. the place value system
   c. the zero symbol

---

in turn enables the beginning of addition and subtraction and the other number operations. A young child, however, will tell you how many brothers he has but find it very difficult to say how many brothers his sister has.

The third area of difficulty for young children is numerical notation. The Hindu-Arabic system is superior to other numeration systems because of its (1) additive system, (2) place value system, and (3) zero symbol. These same properties make it extremely difficult for young children to comprehend. They also cause the most difficulty for LD children after school entrance, because they are developing more slowly than their normally achieving peers and have not acquired some of the more basic ideas that are usually learned spontaneously. This discussion of the material that children typically do not know as they start school was provided to present a more complete picture of young children. However, from a cognitive developmental perspective, it is far more important to focus instructional planning on what students *have* learned.

Mathematics Children Are Expected to Know Before Schooling

Various surveys (Bjonerud, 1960; Brownell, 1941; Ilg and Ames, 1951; Rea and Reys, 1970) have assessed the mathematical knowledge acquired by children during their first five or six years. This information has been useful for determining the content of instruction for kindergarten and first-grade students, but the generalizations that can be made from them are limited with respect to individual students (Brownell, 1941), for what teachers need to know is not what other children know but what their students know. The research does, however, provide a context in which the early development of mathematical concepts can be placed. A summary (Suydam and Weaver, 1975, p. 49) of data from several of these surveys is presented in Box 14.3.

Prior to entering school the typical child has already constructed a representation of number that can be characterized as a mental number line (Res-

---

Box 14.3 Mathematics Typically Known at School Entrance

Five year olds without prior school knowledge usually:

1. can count and find number of objects to ten. Some are able to count to at least twenty.
2. can say the number names for tens in order. Far fewer can say the names when counting by twos or fives.
3. know the meaning of "first." Many can identify ordinal positions through "fifth."
4. can recognize the numerals from one to ten. Some can write them.
5. can give correct answers to simple addition and subtraction combinations presented verbally either with or without manipulative materials.
6. have some knowledge about coins, time, and other measures, simple fractional concepts, and geometric shapes.

Note. Adapted from "Research on Learning Mathematics" by M. Suydam and F. Weaver in *Mathematics Learning in Early Childhood, 37th Yearbook* (p. 49) by J. N. Payne (Ed.), 1975, Reston, VA: National Council of Teachers of Mathematics.

---

nick, 1983), which is used to establish quantities by counting to compare quantities directly. Children may think about numbers as corresponding to positions on a string with individual positions linked by a "one more than" relationship and positions to the right being larger than those to the left. A considerable amount of arithmetic problem solving can be accomplished with this concept. Other researchers have identified other techniques of early mathematical competence, but there is the most consensus on the six operations and skills reported by Suydam and Weaver (1975).

The Instructional Model

Very little research has been conducted on mathematics instruction using an information processing framework. Romberg and Carpenter (1986), in their review of research on teaching and learning mathematics during the last decade, lament that the teaching of mathematics has not changed much. It still typically consists of having the teacher give explanations and ask questions, followed by student seat work. Difficult problems are sometimes worked by the teacher or students at the board. The flavor of their review is apparent in their comment that "students spend their time absorbing what other people have done, rather than in having experiences of their own" (p. 851).

In summarizing what the few cognitive developmental studies have revealed about children's functioning in mathematics, Romberg and Carpenter (1986) listed the following:

1. Children actively construct knowledge from interacting with the environment and reorganizing their own mental constructs.
2. Although instruction affects what children learn, it does not determine it.
3. There are three basic levels of problem solving:
   a. problem schemata for joining, separating, and comparing;
   b. action schemata that relate the information stored in the semantic network for the problem schemata to the actual problem-solving procedures; and
   c. strategic knowledge for planning problem solutions.

Their implications indicated that current practices in mathematics fail to capitalize on the rich fund of mathematical knowledge that children bring to school. Moreover, research suggests that it is not necessary to delay word problem instruction until computational skills have been mastered. Conversely, these higher level problems can function as a context to facilitate the acquisition of computational skills. Finally, they have suggested that it is not sufficient to build on the concepts and skills with which children start school, for instruction should move children through successive stages in the development of those concepts and skills. The reader is encouraged to consult the new journal, *Cognition and Instruction*, for forthcoming reports on a cognitive developmental approach to mathematics learning.

Perhaps the only systematic attempt to study LD students' skills using a cognitive perspective has been the work on arithmetic by the Institute for the Study of Learning Disabilities at Teachers College, Columbia University, New York. Their findings (Conner, 1983) indicate that:

1. LD students evidence a general delay or disability in the development and use of age-appropriate strategies. Even those students identified for special education because of reading problems demonstrated delays in arithmetic computation.
2. Although LD students attempted fewer problems in timed tests in addition, subtraction, and multiplication, they performed as well on an index of proficiency (percent correct of the number attempted) as their nondisabled peers. This finding is further testimony to the slow speed of processing in LD students generally reported in the literature
3. LD students relied on overt counting procedures more than their normally achieving peers and were much more apt to use recon-

structive (working out problems using various strategies) rather than reproductive (responses retrieved automatically from memory) strategies. This finding is consonant with differences typically associated with the distinction between novices and experts (Chi & Glaser, 1980).

Furthermore, what work has been done in mathematics using an information processing perspective has most often addressed the order in which facts should be sequenced (Romberg & Carpenter, 1986). When the Columbia Institute attempted to determine whether fact sequencing influenced LD students' achievement, they found that neither of two sequences they devised more strongly affected gains, although LD students did significantly progress with both sequences when direct instructional methods were used.

The Columbia team also used direct instruction methods to teach LD students that they should have a plan for approaching problems and what the steps in the plan should be. The students were taught to state the relevant information in the problem and to restate the question asked. Because steady and significant improvement occurred when such strategic behaviors were utilized, the Columbia researchers concluded that LD students are lacking in the ability to devise and implement spontaneously adequate cognitive plans for solving complex tasks. It may well be, however, that the students had the ability to plan but were not encouraged under normal circumstances to be mentally active and thus did not demonstrate their knowledge.

The instrucuctional model used in this chapter follows the tetrahedral model detailed in Chapter 2. There are, however, several points that need to be highlighted with respect to its application to mathematics learning.

First, teachers will be more effective if they view mathematics as an activity or a way of thinking rather than as body of knowledge or a collection of computational skills. The teacher must: (1) gain facility with the mathematics the child is expected to learn, (2) know diverse and functional instructional interventions, and (3) be informed and reflective about the unique learning characteristics of individual LD students.

The characteristics and activities of LD students mentioned in earlier chapters are relevant to mathematics learning. Their learning strategies, previous knowledge, metacognition, capacity, and, more generally, learning style, are important considerations for instructional planning. Assessment and evaluation of these learner characteristics must take place individually and with reference to specific tasks in mathematics. An example of such an evaluation is provided in the section on multiplication below. Therefore, as activities are presented, some of the characteristics and needs of the learner for which each is appropriate will be stated.

Instructional interventions attempt to teach LD students both to master content and to operate strategically. They are discovery and activity oriented, related to what the students already know, and relevant to the students' environment.

Content involves four levels of mathematical learning and encompasses the material to be learned and the criterial tasks of the tetrahedral model. The levels of mathematical learning that are important for LD students are presented in Box 14.4. Correspondence between the level of mathematical learning and the criterial tasks for each instructional activity is imperative. Furthermore, understanding is an important goal of instruction for LD students. Content that promotes meaningfulness and facilitates understanding should be selected.

The learning environment, which includes instructional materials, should be inviting and interesting to the LD students and include continua of learning materials, such as real objects, representative objects such as plastic disks, pictorial displays, diagrammatic prototypes such as number lines, and symbols of concepts. The environment should encourage the student to observe, explore, and discover mathematical relationships. Manipulation of the teacher's role and attitude, the characteristics and activities of the learner, instructional tactics, content, and the learning environment defines a cognitive developmental approach to instruction in mathematics for LD students.

The instructional interventions described below also require students to be mentally active. Instruction takes the form of puzzles and problems and relies heavily on revealing the structure of the mathematical operation so that meaningful learning can occur. This is accomplished through the presentation of prototypes, which enable students to select among various conceptions of a problem. Given that these students appear to process information so slowly and to continue to use reconstructive strat-

---

Box 14.4   Mathematical Content for LD Students

1. Development of mathematics concepts such as the understanding of fiveness, three-fourths, and the term *square*.
2. Development of mathematics relationships. An example is finding the solution of the number statement, $2 \times 3 = ?$. Solving the problem requires knowledge of the concepts of two, three, six, product, and equality and the relationships among them implied in the statement.
3. Development of mathematical skills such as computation efficiency, measuring, and the tasks performed by calculators.
4. Development of the ability to solve problems, including those from the environment and textbooks and from nonroutine problems.

egies even after their peers have progressed to reproductive ones, initial comprehension of the problem schema should be followed with opportunities for guided practice until a level of automatic functioning is achieved. Of course, process sheets that outline problem procedures and other methods of increasing functional capacity can be employed as well.

Cawley's (1984) interactive unit methodology can be utilized to promote active participation and meaningful understanding. This method prescribes four instructor-learner combinations that require oral responses from students. In the first, manipulate-state, the teacher manipulates materials and asks the students to state what has been done. The teacher might, for example, join sets and ask the students to describe the activity. The second unit, display-state, asks the students to describe a display, such as parallel lines. Using the third unit, state-state, the teacher might give a definition and ask students to state its meaning in their own words. Finally in the write-state unit, the teacher may show the plus sign on a card and ask the students to name it aloud. This simple response requirement ensures that the student is actively participating in the instructional interaction. For a variety of other instructional ideas, see Cawley (1985).

In sum, the activities described here adhere to the guidelines for instruction recommended by Greenwood and Anderson (1983): (1) provide an environment that stimulates communication between the instructor and the students; (2) require students to demonstrate conceptual understanding before skills are emphasized; (3) define computational proficiency in terms of both speed and accuracy; (4) focus on students' ability to observe both patterns and relationships; (5) encourage novel ways of approaching problems and skills; and (6) promote self-diagnosis, self-evaluation, and self-awareness among students. The latter can be accomplished by keeping charts of progress, by giving immediate and appropriate feedback, by asking students to "debug" incorrect solutions, by making cognitive strategies an explicit part of the instructional program, and by teaching students to manipulate factors within the tetrahedral model and to chart their learning progress using Lovitt's (1977) framework.

What Is to Be Learned?

Place Value

The systematic study of numbers greater than nine involves the basic concepts of place value. Since the decimal system employs only the symbols 0, 1, 2, 3, 4, 5, 6, 7, 8, and 9, it is important for children to understand that the position of a given digit determines its relative value. Whenever more than nine objects are symbolically represented, the representation must utilize place value and it must contain more than one symbol.

As soon as students are expected to write numerals larger than nine, therefore, it is important to teach them the basic concepts of place value. Early work should stress this utilizing a variety of manipulative materials in active learning situations. Teachers should be well equipped with structured materials, which may be either purchased or teacher made. Cuisenaire rods, flats, and blocks, Dienes multibase arithmetic blocks, and Unifix cubes are commercially prepared materials useful for these activities. A teacher-made place value chart is illustrated in Figure 14.1.

LD Students' Typical Problems with This Material and Appropriate Learner Activities

Four problems LD students frequently encounter in learning place value are discussed: (1) understanding the grouping process, (2) understanding that each position to the left represents another multiple of ten, (3) understanding the placement of one digit per position, and (4) understanding the relationship between the order of the digits and the value of the numeral. Appropriate instructional activities are presented for each. The initial area of difficulty is related to the understanding of the process of grouping upon which the place value system of notation is based. Units are first grouped according to some number, these groups are then grouped

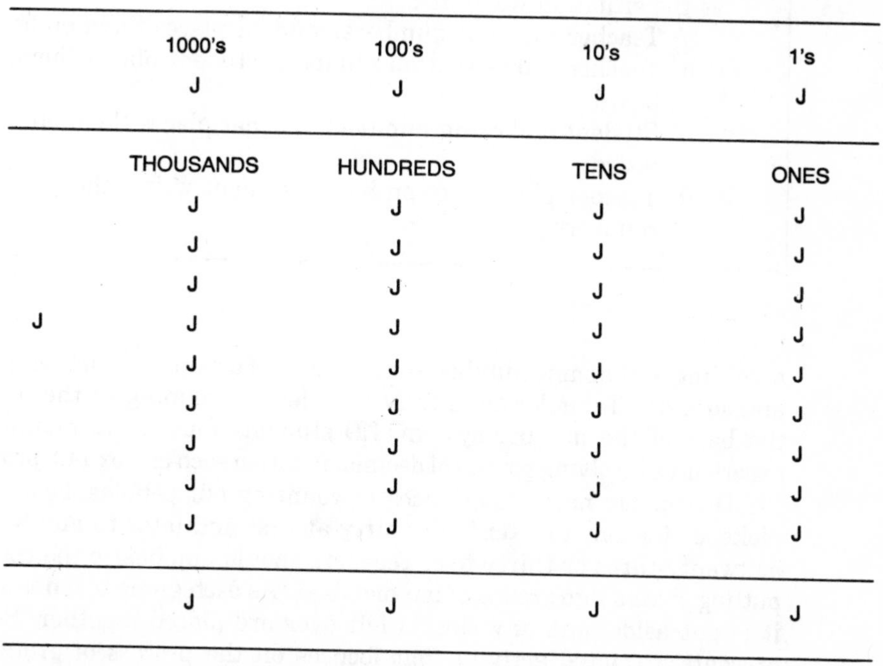

	1000's	100's	10's	1's
	J	J	J	J
	THOUSANDS	HUNDREDS	TENS	ONES
	J	J	J	J
	J	J	J	J
	J	J	J	J
J	J	J	J	J
	J	J	J	J
	J	J	J	J
	J	J	J	J
	J	J	J	J
	J	J	J	J
	J	J	J	J

FIGURE 14.1 Place Value Board.

Box 14.5   Place Value Grouping A

Materials Needed

1. Place value board (see Figure 14.1)
2. Fifty or more blank tags
3. Ten twist ties
4. Two sets of tags numbered from 0 to 9

Procedure

1. The teacher and/or student place tags on the place value board in the ones column as the student counts.
2. The student labels the number by placing numbered tags on the bottom of the ones column.
3. When working with numbers larger than nine, the student removes each set of ten tags from the ones column, ties them together, and places the group in the tens column.
4. Repeat this procedure using numbers less than forty, varying it as the situation warrants:
   a. Teacher calls out numbers, student places them on board.
   b. Teacher shows written numbers, student places them on board.
   c. Student makes up numbers, teacher places them on board.
   d. Teacher places tags on board, student writes the numbers.

---

according to the same number, these groups of groups are further grouped, and so forth. To understand fully the idea of grouping in the powers of the base of the number system, LD students must have manipulative experiences involving powers of decimal notation such as Box 14.5 provides.

LD students need experiences in counting out pebbles, beads, toothpicks, or buttons to twenty or thirty at first and later to numbers such as twenty-three or thirty-five. Teachers should emphasize the concept of putting objects into groups of ten members. As each group of ten is counted, it is put aside, and any objects left over are placed together. Box 14.6 presents a related activity that focuses on the process of grouping by utilizing different sized groups.

Box 14.6 Circle That Dot

Materials Needed

1. Three pieces of paper divided into fourths with different groupings of randomly spaced dots on each section.

Procedure

1. Ask the student to circle a group of dots of a specific size.
2. Have the student write a statement about the groups circled,
such as, "There are _____ groups and _____ units."
3. If appropriate, ask the student to represent the grouping more
abstractly, for example, 4(3) + 1.
4. Continue the procedure with variously sized groupings.

LD students also have difficulty understanding that each position or place
to the left represents a higher multiple of ten. Students often confuse these
values and are not able to state that 139 represents one group of one hundred
plus three groups of ten plus nine ones. After students demonstrate a mastery of place value concepts through thirty-nine, they should continue to
work with place value devices and structured materials to learn place value
through ninety-nine. As they progress to larger numbers, structured materials should continue to be used and adapted appropriately. Box 14.7 is
an activity designed for students who are working with numbers between
99 and 999. For activities with numbers of this magnitude, it is not necessary to continue counting objects or using proportional instructional aids.
Box 14.8 is a group activity that can be used to develop an understanding
of appropriate representations for numerals less than 10,000. It is integral
to this activity that the students arrange themselves in an order that correctly represents the numeral that is written or stated by the teacher. Two
versions of this activity are described. LD students often demonstrate difficulty reading numbers of this magnitude because of their lack of a thorough understanding of the placement of one digit per position and the
relationship of the order of the digits to the value of the numeral. They also
have problems in the regrouping process in addition and subtraction and
in sequencing numbers by magnitude.

Most of the previously stated activities are more appropriate for elementary school students who need representative or diagrammatic experiences with place value concepts. Box 14.9 is more mature in its

---

Box 14.7   Place Value Grouping B

Materials Needed

1. Place value board (see Figure 14.1)
2. Two hundred or more blank tags
3. Fifteen or more twist ties
4. Four sets of tags numbered from 0 to 9

Procedure

1. The student and teacher make ten groups of ten tags with twist ties.
2. The procedure is similar to that described in Box 14.5, except the student does not count individual tags because of the size of the numbers.
3. Have the student make a group of 100 out of the groups of ten. Hang it in the hundreds column.
4. Discuss the awkward representation in the hundreds column, seek an alternative, and direct the student to transfer using one tag to represent 100.
5. Begin using one tag to represent groups of ten.
6. Proceed with various numbers through 999, using similar variations as those in Step 4 of Box 14.5. (Note: If appropriate, different colored tags may be used to represent each column.)

---

appearance and has been used very successfully with high school LD students although it is useful for students of all ages.

As LD students progress through elementary and high school, they will need to use both compact and expanded forms of numerals. The compact form is the one that is normally used when the number two hundred forty-three is written as "243." There are several forms of expanded notation, and each is appropriately used in different circumstances. When students are learning about place value, for example, the expanded form "2 hundreds + 4 tens + 3 ones" emphasizes place value in our numeration system. As students begin to add and subtract numbers, the expanded notation "200 + 40 + 3" can be used to emphasize the development of the addition and subtraction algorithms. After students can multiply by ten and powers of ten they are ready to express numbers in two other forms: $(2 \times 100) + (4 \times 10) + (3 \times 1)$ and $[2(10 \times 10)] + [4 \times 10] + [3 \times 1]$. When LD students un-

Box 14.8   Team Grouping

Materials Needed

1. Large white bed sheet marked to show place value columns up to 10,000
2. Eight sets of small number cards (each set contains single digit number from 0 to 9)
3. Large number cards that include a variety of numbers from 10 to 9,999
4. Place value tags and pins (single digit numbers from 0 to 9 to be pinned on students; tags are color coded; for example, ones = red, tens = yellow, etc.)

Procedure: Game 1

1. Divide the class into two teams. Each team is given four sets of the small number cards, and captains are chosen to organize team members.
2. The teacher holds up a large number card and reads the number aloud. Each team must find the appropriate small number cards and arrange them in the correct order to duplicate teacher's number.
3. The first team to produce the correct number wins the point.
4. The teacher may also choose just to call out a number between 10 and 9,999 to make the game more challenging.

Procedure: Game 2

1. Divide the class into five groups, representing ones, tens, hundreds, thousands, and ten thousands. Each child pins on an appropriate place value tag.
2. The teacher places the place value bed sheet on the floor, shows a large number card to the class, and calls out the number.
3. Each group must send the correct number of children to their appropriate place on the sheet. For example, if the teacher called out thirty-four, the tens group would send three people to the tens column on the sheet, and the ones group would send four people to the ones column on the sheet.
4. The teams that have the correct number of people in their column get a point.
5. To make the game more difficult, the teacher calls out the number (without showing the card), and the children have to picture the number in their minds.

Box 14.9   Grouping with Graph Paper Squares

Materials Needed

1. Graph paper
2. Scissors
3. Number cards with numbers 9 to 999

Procedure

1. Give each student a sheet of graph paper.
2. All students cut out shapes to represent ones (one square), tens (ten squares in a row), and hundreds (one large square containing 100 squares). One sheet of graph paper should be enough to allow the student to count out ten ones, ten tens, and ten hundreds.
3. After cutting out the shapes, the students use them to represent the numbers from 9 to 999, which are written on the number cards. They may work with the teacher, in groups, or individually. The suggestions found in Step 4 of Box 14.5 may also be used with this activity.

---

derstand the meanings of all of these forms of expanded notation, they will have little difficulty learning how to express numbers in exponential notation for more advanced mathematics exercises.

Addition and Subtraction

The first "real" mathematics that LD students are expected to learn is addition and subtraction. They will increase their probability of success in these operations if they have some understanding of place value concepts and relationships. Instruction should begin with manipulative activities that explore addition and subtraction. After they are adequately understood, LD students must practice to achieve the immediate recall of basic addition and subtraction facts which often poses major difficulties. Metacognitive strategies for learning these facts must also be mastered. LD students should progress to algorithm skills after understanding place value, addition, and subtraction concepts and their relationships.

Addition can be conceptualized as the union of two disjoint sets or as jumps on a number line. Conceptualization is aided by activities with manipulative materials, which in turn complement and facilitate the

---

Box 14.10   Beginning Addition

Materials Needed

1. Five dolls
2. Objects such as toy cars, dishes, blocks, or books (in sets of eight or less)

Procedure

1. Divide the dolls into two groups (sets).
2. Ask the children to state the number of dolls in each set.
3. Join the two sets and have the children determine the total number.
4. Repeat the procedure with the other objects. Ask the students to describe the addition operations by statements such as, "A set of two dolls joined with a set of three dolls makes a set of five dolls"; "Two dolls and three dolls make five dolls"; "Two plus three is five"; or "Two and three equal five."

---

learning of basic facts and the development of algorithms. For the union of disjoint sets, for example, the teacher might ask the students wearing red shirts or those wearing green shirts to stand up. Box 14.10 is an example of using disjoint sets in beginning addition, and Box 14.11 is an example of the use of the number line.

After many manipulative and representative experiences with addition, students may begin work on the basic facts. The number facts that a student needs to learn are reduced by an understanding of the commutative and associative property and the identity element of addition. Box 14.12 offers several metacognitive strategies to help students construct and evaluate the accuracy of basic sums (see also Figure 14.2).

Another metacognitive approach to mastering the basic addition facts utilizes fact families. Attention is focused on number patterns that assist in understanding. Two fact families are:

$$0 + 5 = 5 \qquad 2 + 3 = 5$$
$$1 + 4 = 5 \qquad 5 - 2 = 3$$
$$2 + 3 = 5 \qquad 3 + 2 = 5$$
$$3 + 2 = 5 \qquad 5 - 3 = 2$$
$$4 + 1 = 5$$
$$5 + 0 = 5$$

Box 14.11   Addition Jump

Materials Needed

1. Roll of masking tape
2. Marker
3. Flash cards of addition facts of ten or less

Procedure

1. Place a long strip (at least ten feet long) of masking tape on the floor.
2. Mark the tape from 0 to 10 in one-foot intervals to form a number line.
3. Show the flash card and call out the addition fact.
4. Ask the student to jump the number of spaces indicated by the first addend and stop. Then ask the student to jump the second addend and discover the answer.
5. Ask the student to verbalize the problem by stating, "Two plus four is six."

Box 14.12   Addition Facts

Materials Needed

1. Addition fact chart (see Figure 14.2)
2. Map colors (colored pencils)

Procedure

1. Give each student an addition fact chart.
2. The teacher shows a completed chart to motivate the students.
3. The students color their own charts, with a different color for each letter, as they learn their facts.

(continued)

Box 14.12   *(continued)*

4. The teacher may incorporate the following steps as the addition facts are introduced:
   a. When zero is an addend, the sum is the other addend. (Zero is the identity element for addition.) This knowledge eliminates the need to memorize nineteen facts and is indicated by the letter *A* on Figure 14.2.
   b. When one is an addend, the sum is one more than the other addend. This knowledge eliminates the need to memorize another seventeen facts and is indicated by the letter *B* on Figure 14.2.
   c. The order in which the addition is performed does not change the sum (commutative property of addition). This knowledge eliminates the need to memorize twenty-eight more facts and is indicated by the letter *C* on Figure 14.2.
   d. The eight doubles (both factors are the same) indicated by the letter *D* on Figure 14.2 are relatively easy to master.
   e. Three facts with sums less than ten $(2 + 3, 3 + 4,$ and $4 + 5)$ can be worked around the doubles: if $3 + 3 = 6$, then $3 + 4 = 7$ and $3 + 2 = 5$. These facts are indicated by the letter *E* on Figure 14.2
   f. The nines are relatively easy to learn after demonstrating the pattern that when nine is an addend, the sum is ten plus the other addend less one. These are indicated by the letter *F* on Figure 14.2.
   g. This leaves nine facts with sums of ten or less to master. These are indicated by the letter *G* on Figure 14.2.
   h. Six facts with sums greater than ten can be mastered using the associative property of addition. These are indicated by the letter *H* on Figure 14.2.
   i. Three more, those lettered *I* on Figure 14.2, can be worked around the doubles as before, that is, if $6 + 6 = 12$, then $6 + 5 = 11$ and $6 + 7 = 13$; if $7 + 7 = 14$, then $7 + 8 = 15$.
5. Continue this activity as long as necessary to help students learn the addition facts.

+	0	1	2	3	4	5	6	7	8	9
0	A 0	A 1	A 2	A 3	A 4	A 5	A 6	A 7	A 8	A 9
1	A 1	B 2	B 3	B 4	B 5	B 6	B 7	B 8	B 9	B 10
2	A 2	B 3	D 4	E 5	G 6	G 7	G 8	G 9	G 10	F 11
3	A 3	B 4	C 5	D 6	E 7	G 8	G 9	G 10	H 11	F 12
4	A 4	B 5	C 6	C 7	D 8	E 9	G 10	H 11	H 12	F 13
5	A 5	B 6	C 7	C 8	C 9	D 10	I 11	H 12	H 13	F 14
6	A 6	B 7	C 8	C 9	C 10	C 11	D 12	I 13	H 14	F 15
7	A 7	B 8	C 9	C 10	C 11	C 12	C 13	D 14	I 15	F 16
8	A 8	B 9	C 10	C 11	C 12	C 13	C 14	C 15	D 16	F 17
9	A 9	B 10	C 11	C 12	C 13	C 14	C 15	C 16	C 17	D 18

FIGURE 14.2 Addition Fact Chart.

As some understanding of place value and the basic addition facts is achieved, activities that involve the addition algorithm and regrouping can be used. Box 14.13 shows the use of the place board in beginning addition algorithm activities.

Expanded notation can also be used to develop mastery of the algorithm. As students acquire an understanding of the process represented by expanded notation, the expanded form of writing the algorithms should be shortened to the conventional form, as follows:

Box 14.13   Place Value Board Addition

Material Needed

1. Place value board (see Figure 14.1)
2. Fifteen blank tags
3. Nine bundles of ten tags each
4. Twist ties
5. Two sets of numbered tags with digits from 0 to 9

Procedure

1. Write a problem on the chalkboard that involves regrouping in the units column, such as 25 + 37.
2. Ask the student to place tags to represent the joining of the two numbers from the units column on the place value board (5 + 7). As the student is counting and reaches ten, have the student remove the ten tags from the board, bundle with a twist tie, and place the bundle at the top of the tens column.
3. Ask the student to finish counting the remaining single tags and place them in the units column.
4. Ask the student to place bundles on the place value board to represent the joining of two tens and three tens.
5. Add the previously grouped bundle to the other bundles.
6. Place the numbered tags at the bottom of the columns to represent the answer.
7. Repeat same procedure with at least two or more problems.

$$2 \text{ tens} + \ 9 \text{ ones} = 20 + \ 9 = 29$$
$$3 \text{ tens} + \ 5 \text{ ones} = 30 + \ 5 = 35$$
$$5 \text{ tens} + 14 \text{ ones} = 50 + 14 = 64$$
$$5 \text{ tens} + 1 \text{ ten} + 4 \text{ ones} = 50 + 10 + 4$$

Subtraction can be conceptualized as an operation applying to three different situations, which are diagrammed in Figure 14.3. Each can be easily explained by the use of word problems. Box 14.14 presents an excellent activity to assist students in understanding these three interpretations of subtraction.

The basic subtraction facts are generally more difficult for students to master than the addition facts. Mastery is assisted by relating subtraction

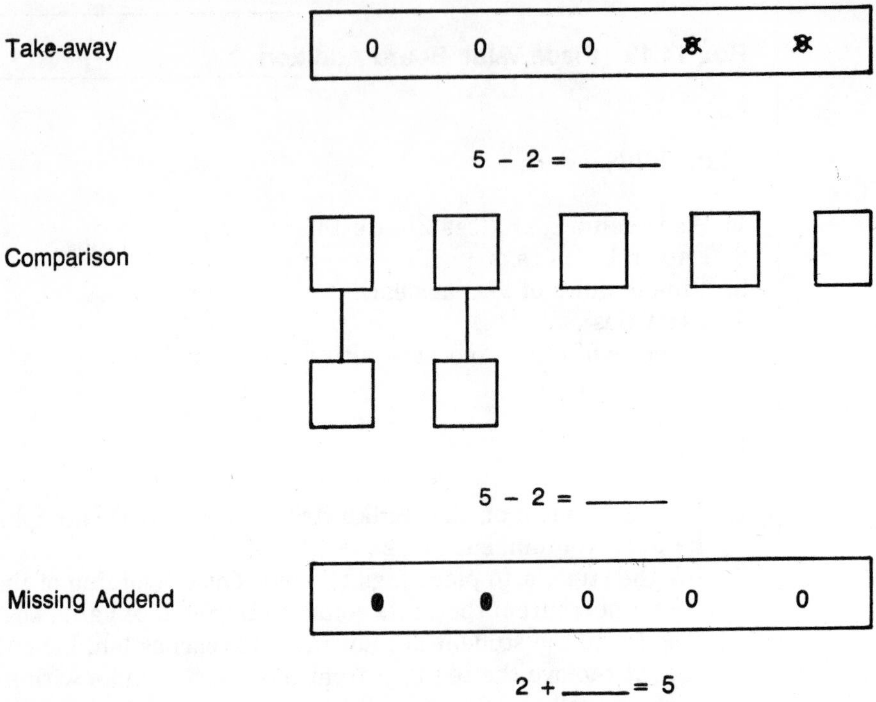

Take-away

| 0 | 0 | 0 | X | X |

5 − 2 = _____

Comparison

5 − 2 = _____

Missing Addend

| ● | ● | 0 | 0 | 0 |

2 + _____ = 5

FIGURE 14.3 Conceptualizations of Subtraction.

facts to the appropriate inverse addition facts and by utilizing metacognitive patterns that are already available to the student. Three metacognitive patterns that use the number ten as a pivotal point may provide assistance for facts with minuends of eleven to eighteen. See Table 14.1 for an example. Many persons use similar metacognitive patterns or in-

Table 14.1   Metacognitive Patterns for Subtraction of 14 − 6

Step	Metacognitive Pattern 1	Metacognitive Pattern 2	Metacognitive Pattern 3
Step 1	Because $6=4+2$ and	Because $6+4=10$ and	Because $14=10+4$ and
Step 2	$14-4=10$ and	$(14+4)-(6+4)=14-6$ and	$(10+4)-6=14-6$ and
Step 3	$10-2=8$ then	$18-10=8$ then	$(10-6)+4=(10+4)-6$ then
Step 4	$14-6=8$	$14-6=8$	$4+4=8$ or $14-6=8$

Box 14.14   Subtraction Word Problems

Materials Needed

1. Poster board
2. Chart illustrating the diagrams in Figure 14.3
3. Twelve sample word problems (four of each of the three
   interpretations)

Procedure

1. Write the following problems on the poster board:
   a. John's dog had six puppies. Four were given away. How
      many did he have left?
   b. Jill had six cookies in her lunch sack. Jessica had four
      cookies in hers. How many more cookies did Jill have
      than Jessica?
   c. Jack had six friends at his birthday party. He had only
      four favors. How many more favors does he need?
2. Read the problems aloud and discuss what needs to be done to
   solve each.
3. Diagram the problems on board and ask the student to identify
   the type of problem by looking at the chart.
4. Proceed through the sample problems, and ask the student to
   identify the types of problems.
5. Ask the student to suggest problems to diagram.
6. Ask the students to draw diagrams.

---

vent their own. LD students need to be assisted in identifying and utilizing such patterns.

Multibase or base ten blocks are very useful in teaching the subtraction algorithm with regrouping. Box 14.15 shows a detailed example.

Finally, mastery of both the addition and subtraction facts requires considerable, consistent practice.

Multiplication and Division

Like their normally achieving peers, LD students, have more difficulties with multiplication and division than with addition and subtraction.[1] It is essential that LD students be told at the beginning of instruction that several

---

Box 14.15 Subtraction Algorithm with Regrouping

Materials Needed

1. Multibase blocks (units, tens, and hundreds only)
2. Paper (graph paper may be substituted for multibase blocks)
3. Pencil

Procedure

1. Present problem involving regrouping in the units column only, such as, 321 − 213.
2. Ask the student to set out blocks to represent the minuend.
3. Before three units can be removed from one unit, one long rod must be exchanged for ten unit blocks.
4. The three units may be taken away from the eleven unit blocks, leaving eight unit blocks.
5. Remove one long rod and two flat blocks.
6. The result is 108 and should be represented as one flat block, no long rods, and eight units blocks.
7. Repeat the procedure using problems of increasing difficulty.
8. Ask the student to transfer to paper and pencil activities, first using the paper and pencil with the blocks and then only the paper and pencil.
9. This activity is easily extended by asking the student to represent both the minuend and subtrahend with blocks and use the comparison model for subtraction.

---

conceptualizations of multiplication and division exist. Their relationship to conceptualizations of addition and subtraction must also be made clear for several reasons. First, conceptualizations of multiplication and division are derived from the operations of addition and subtraction, respectively. Second, multiplication and division may be interpreted in ways that are related to, but not intuitively dependent upon, addition and subtraction. Finally, individual LD students conceptualize multiplication and division differently, that is, one student finds it easier to understand the linear prototype while another finds the arrays interpretation easier.

Multiplication can be conceptualized as five different yet equally valid operations: repeated addition, arrays, Cartesian product of two sets, linear prototypes, and multiple sets (for diagrams, see Figure 14.4).

Repeated Addition

$$3 + \underbrace{3 + 3 + 3}_{4 \times 3} = 12$$

Four times three

Arrays

$4 \times 3 = 12$

Four times three

$3 \times 4 = 12$

Three times four

Cartesian Product

		Shirts			
		White	Blue	Green	Red
Pants	Brown	0	0	0	0
	Black	0	0	0	0
	Grey	0	0	0	0
		0	0	0	0

12 Possible Combinations
4 Shirts × 3 Pants = 12 Outfits

Linear Prototype

$4 \times 3 = 12$

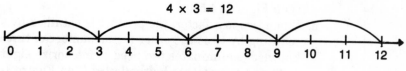

Cuisenaire rods may also be used.

Multiple Sets

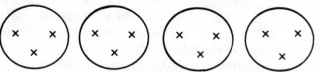

Four sets of three
$4 \times 3 = 12$

FIGURE 14.4 Conceptualizations of Multiplication.

Box 14.16   Multiplication Facts

Materials Needed

1. Multiplication fact chart (see Figure 14.5)
2. Map colors (colored pencils)

Procedure

1. Give each student a multiplication fact chart.
2. The teacher shows a completed chart to motivate the students.
3. The students color their own charts with a different color for each letter, as they learn their facts.
4. The teacher may incorporate the following steps as the multiplication facts are introduced:
   a. When zero is a factor, the product is zero. This knowledge eliminates the need to memorize nineteen facts and is indicated by the letter A on Figure 14.5.
   b. When one is a factor, the product is the other factor. (One is the identity element for multiplication.) This knowledge eliminates the need to memorize another seventeen facts and is indicated by the letter B on Figure 14.5.
   c. The order in which the multiplication is performed does not change the product (commutative property of multiplication). This knowledge eliminates the need to memorize twenty-eight more facts and is indicated by the letter C on Figure 14.5.
   d. When two is a factor, the product is obtained by skip counting by twos the other factor number of times. This knowledge eliminates the need to memorize eight more facts and is indicated by the letter D on Figure 14.5.
   e. When five is a factor, the product is obtained by skip counting by fives the other factor number of times. This knowledge eliminates the need to memorize six more facts and is indicated by the letter E on Figure 14.5.
   f. When nine is a factor, the product is obtained by using one of the following patterns: (1) As the products are written vertically, the ones digit decreases and the tens digit increases; (2) the sum of the ones digit plus the tens

(continued)

Box 14.16   *(continued)*

---

digit equals nine; (3) the tens digit is one less than the other factor. This knowledge eliminates the need to memorize six more facts and is indicated by the letter *F* on Figure 14.5.

  g. When three is a factor, the product is obtained by skip counting by threes the other factor number of times. This knowledge eliminates the need to memorize six more facts and is indicated by the letter *G* on Figure 14.5.

  h. The four doubles (both factors are the same), indicated by the letter *H* on Figure 14.5, are relatively easy to master.

  i. Six facts for which there is no simple pattern are the most difficult to master. These should be worked using successive addition. That is, if $4 \times 5 = 20$, then $4 \times 6 = 20 + 4 = 24$ and $4 \times 7 = 24 + 4 = 28$. These are indicated by the letter *I* on Figure 14.5.

5. Continue this activity as long as necessary to help students learn the multiplication facts.

By manipulating physical objects LD students can discover many of these patterns for themselves. They should first be assisted to work with the conceptualization that is most comfortable for them and, as familiarity increases, explore other prototypes.

There are one hundred basic multiplication facts that should be mastered, to the extent possible, by all LD students. As with addition, the number of facts to be mastered may be reduced considerably through the application of the properties of multiplication. Many LD students have numerous difficulties acquiring automatic responses for these facts. With continued and appropriate practice, however, most can achieve this goal. Box 14.16 utilizes a multiplication fact chart (Figure 14.5) and provides suggestions and metacognitive strategies to assist LD students who may have problems memorizing facts.

The standard multiplication algorithm is very complex for students who are not familiar with it. Success in understanding the algorithm is based on knowledge of place value and the distributive property. An excellent extended discussion of the algorithm is presented by Schminke, Maertens, and Arnold (1973).

Division can be conceptualized as two operations: measurement and partition (for diagrams, see Figure 14.6). In the measurement situation the total number of objects in each group is given and the solution is the number of groups that can be made. In the partition situation the total number of objects and the number of groups to be made are given and

×	0	1	2	3	4	5	6	7	8	9
0	A 0	A 0	A 0	A 0	A 0	A 0	A 0	A 0	A 0	A 0
1	A 0	B 1	B 2	B 3	B 4	B 5	B 6	B 7	B 8	B 9
2	A 0	B 2	D 4	D 6	D 8	D 10	D 12	D 14	D 16	D 18
3	A 0	B 3	C 6	G 9	G 12	G 15	G 18	G 21	G 24	F 27
4	A 0	B 4	C 8	C 12	H 16	E 20	I 24	I 28	I 32	F 36
5	A 0	B 5	C 10	C 15	C 20	C 25	E 30	E 35	E 40	E 45
6	A 0	B 6	C 12	C 18	C 24	C 30	H 36	I 42	I 48	F 54
7	A 0	B 7	C 14	C 21	C 28	C 35	C 42	H 49	I 56	F 63
8	A 0	B 8	C 16	C 24	C 32	C 40	C 48	C 56	H 64	F 72
9	A 0	B 9	C 18	C 27	C 34	C 45	C 54	C 63	C 72	F 81

FIGURE 14.5 Multiplication Fact Chart.

the solution is the number of objects to be placed into each group. Box 14.17 will help students understand these two conceptualizations of division.

The one hundred possible division facts are easily reduced to ninety because division by zero is not possible. Teachers can help students understand this by asking, "How many zeros are in eight?" There is no correct answer: Division by zero is undefined. If division is appropriately

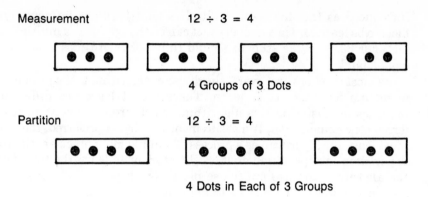

Measurement $12 \div 3 = 4$

4 Groups of 3 Dots

Partition $12 \div 3 = 4$

4 Dots in Each of 3 Groups

FIGURE 14.6 Conceptualizations of Division.

Box 14.17   Division Word Problems

Materials Needed

1. Poster board
2. Chart illustrating the diagrams in Figure 14.6
3. Eight sample word problems (four of each of the two interpretations)

Procedure

1. Write the following word problems on the poster board:
   a. Jim had eight lawns to mow. He cut two each day. How many days did he work to cut all eight?
   b. Mrs. Taylor had eight pieces of candy to give to her two children. How many did each child get?
2. Read the problems aloud and discuss what needs to be done to solve each.
3. Diagram the problems on the board and ask the student to identify the type of problem by looking at the chart.
4. Proceed through the sample problems, and ask the student to identify the type of problems.
5. Ask the student to suggest problems to diagram.
6. Ask the student to draw diagrams.

introduced as the inverse of multiplication, there are no new division facts to be learned. That is, every fact can be thought of as a multiplication fact. For 63 ÷ 7, the student should think, "Seven times what number equals 63?"

As most teachers are aware, the division algorithm is the most difficult algorithm for students to learn. There are at least two different approaches to mastering this algorithm, which are dependent on the preferred conceptualization. If measurement division is preferred, the student must learn the algorithm as a process of making more precise estimations. A partition interpretation enables the student to learn the final form of the algorithm and use multibase blocks or graph paper to reflect each step in the process, as Box 14.18 demonstrates.

Box 14.18   Division Algorithm

Materials Needed

1. Multibase blocks or graph paper cut into units (one square), tens (one row of ten), and hundreds (ten-by-ten square); approximately fifty of each
2. Four sheets of paper
3. Paper and pencil

Procedure

1. Write down a problem, such as $4\overline{)342}$. Keep the divisor below five for simplicity.
2. Place the four sheets of paper on the table.
3. Explain that the number 342 will be divided into four equal parts.
4. Pick up the three flat blocks (hundreds) and try to distribute equally on the four sheets of paper. Help the student realize this cannot be done, and write 0 on the problem:

$$\frac{0}{4\overline{)342}}$$

5. Trade three hundreds for thirty tens. Now there are thirty-four tens. Distribute the thirty-four tens equally among the four sheets of paper. There will be two left over.

(continued)

Box 14.18   *(continued)*

6. Ask the student to count the number of tens on each sheet of paper. There are eight. Therefore, $4 \times 8 = 32$:

$$\begin{array}{r} 08 \\ 4\overline{)342} \\ -\underline{32} \\ 2 \end{array}$$

7. The two tens cannot be distributed equally, so exchange the two tens for twenty units and add to the two units in the problem. Explain that this is why the two is brought down in the division algorithm. There are twenty-two units:

$$\begin{array}{r} 08 \\ 4\overline{)342} \\ -\underline{32} \\ 22 \end{array}$$

8. Distribute the twenty-two units equally on the four sheets of paper. There will be two left over.

9. Ask the student to count the number of units that are on each sheet of paper. There will be five. Therefore, $5 \times 4 = 20$:

$$\begin{array}{r} 085 \\ 4\overline{)342} \\ -\underline{32} \\ 22 \\ -\underline{20} \\ 2 \end{array}$$

10. Ask the student to count the amount on each sheet of paper and realize that it is the same as the answer written down. The two remaining units are the remainder:

$$\begin{array}{r} 085r2 \\ 4\overline{)342} \\ -\underline{32} \\ 22 \\ -\underline{20} \\ 2 \end{array}$$

11. Continue with other problems.

Fractions

Understanding fractional numbers is usually difficult and confusing for LD students. Learning to use fractions is initially frustrating for nearly all students, but the several relationships that are true for whole numbers, which are modified for fractional numbers, are especially frustrating for LD students. If two fractions have the same numerator, for example, the fraction with the larger denominator is less than the other fraction. The opposite will be predicted by most LD students. There are many important concepts, relationships, skills, and problem-solving abilities on which attention should be focused for LD students that cannot be included in such a short discussion. The reader is referred to Marks, Hiatt, and Neufeld (1985) for a more comprehensive examination, including instructional techniques for the following concepts, which consistently present problems for LD students: (1) common fractions, (2) inequality and equality of fractions, (3) multiplication of fractions, and (4) prototypes for decimal fractions.

Students should have working knowledge of fractions and refer to them orally before they are expected to understand the concepts or notation involved. A *fraction* can be interpreted as a part of the whole, a subset of a parent set, or as a ratio. The "part of the whole" interpretation is the conceptualization that is most familiar to LD students. Fraction bars (see Figure 14.7) can help students master the basic fraction concepts and answer the following questions:

1. How many pieces are there in the whole? (four)
2. Are the pieces all the same size? (yes)
3. How much is each piece? (one-fourth)
4. How many pieces are shaded? (three)
5. How much is shaded? (three-fourths)

Box 14.19 is a game that provides additional work with these concepts.

The addition and subtraction of fractions with unlike denominators is a complex operation that often creates difficulties. For LD students to be successful at this task, they must understand the concepts and relationships of whole number addition and multiplication, the equality of fractions, and the physical representations of these ideas. Furthermore, by using equivalent fractions, LD students can discover that fractional numbers can be renamed (in an infinite number of ways) so that any two

x x x x x x x x x x	x x x x x x x x x x	x x x x x x x x x x	
x x x x x x x x x x	x x x x x x x x x x	x x x x x x x x x x	
x x x x x x x x x x	x x x x x x x x x x	x x x x x x x x x x	
x x x x x x x x x x	x x x x x x x x x x	x x x x x x x x x x	

FIGURE 14.7 Fraction Box.

Box 14.19   Fraction Bar War

Materials Needed

1. Set of fraction bars
   (⁰⁄₂, ½, ²⁄₂) (⁰⁄₃ . . . ³⁄₃), (⁰⁄₄ . . . ⁴⁄₄), (⁰⁄₆ . . . ⁶⁄₆), (⁰⁄₈ . . . ⁸⁄₈),
   (⁰⁄₁₂ . . . ¹²⁄₁₂)

Procedure

1. This game is for two students.
2. Shuffle the fraction bars and distribute equally to each player.
3. Each player places bars face down on the table.
4. Each player turns the top card on the stack over and the players determine which fraction (shaded area) is larger. If they do not know, they can compare the bars side by side.
5. The player with the larger fraction takes both bars.
6. If the fractions are equal, each player places the next three bars face down on the pile. They compare the fourth bar, and the player with the larger one receives the six bars used in battle. Battle must be repeated if the fourth bar is the same.
7. The player with all the bars is the winner, or the teacher may want to set a time limit with the player with the most bars at the end of the time winning.

---

fractions can be made to have common denominators. Several processes can be used to find the least common denominator or least common multiple of two or three numbers (Kennedy, 1984). The factorization process is recommended for LD students, because it generalizes to many other mathematical situations. An example of this process is demonstrated in Box 14.20.

Although the multiplication and division of fractional numbers are relatively easy for LD students, their understanding of the meanings of these operations may not be complete. LD students are often confused by the fact that the product of multiplying a fraction by a fraction is less than either factor. This confusion comes about because the students interpret the multiplication sign to mean "times," which with whole numbers always produces a larger product. Interpreting the multiplication sign as "set(s) of" helps to alleviate this problem.

Box 14.20   Factor Trees

Materials Needed

1. Paper and pencil
2. Flash cards with digits from 1 to 50

Procedure

1. Ask students to identify numbers as prime or composite as the teacher holds up flash cards.
2. The teacher demonstrates factoring using factor trees.
3. Demonstrate and practice with other numbers.
4. Present fractions such as ¹⁄₁₂ and ¹⁄₁₅. Explain the use of factor trees for finding the least common denominator (LCD).
5. The factors from the first denominator are written down first. The factors from the second denominator that do not appear as factors of the first denominator are included in the expression. Multiply these factors for the LCD.
6. Repeat using other pairs of numbers.

The array concept of multiplication extended to fractions provides a meaningful interpretation of fraction multiplication. This approach is illustrated in Box 14.21 and can be used for multiplying two proper fractions, two improper fractions, or a proper and an improper fraction.

Decimal fractions are the logical extension of both the place value system and common fractions. As the use of calculators, computers, and the metric system increases, the need for knowledge of the decimal system will also grow. As with other concepts, LD students should begin by working with manipulatives. Initially, decimals may be interpreted as common fractions with denominators of ten, one hundred, and one thousand, and so on, so students understand that common fractions and decimal fractions both represent fractional numbers. They should be encouraged to understand the notation system used as a generalization of the place value system of whole numbers. Figure 14.8 will help students

Name	Hundreds	Tens	Ones	Tenths	Hundredths	Thousandths
Value	100	10	1	¹⁄₁₀ = .1	¹⁄₁₀₀ = .01	¹⁄₁₀₀₀ = .001

FIGURE 14.8 Decimal Place Values.

Box 14.21   Multiplication of Fractions

Materials Needed

1. Graph paper
2. Pencil
3. Blue and yellow map pencils
4. Colored chalk

Procedure

1. Write the problem $\frac{3}{5} \times \frac{2}{4}$ on the board.
2. Draw a rectangle on the board.
3. Divide the rectangle horizontally into five equal parts and mark each with $\frac{1}{5}$.
4. Divide the rectangle vertically into four equal parts and mark each with $\frac{1}{4}$.
5. Count the total number of squares to get the denominator for the problem.
6. Shade in the area representing $\frac{3}{5}$ in blue. Shade in the area representing $\frac{2}{4}$ in yellow.
7. The area where the blue and yellow overlap represents the numerator, to make the answer $\frac{6}{20}$.
8. Ask the student to continue with other simple fractions, using their graph paper to draw the arrays.

---

reach this level of understanding. Box 14.22 is typical of the type of exercise that will enable students to master decimal concepts.

Problem Solving

Problem solving is an integral part of a good mathematics program, especially for LD students. These students can solve problems in everyday life if they have a solid instructional base, which also improves their skills in logical and quantitative thinking.

Because teaching LD students to solve problems skillfully has been especially difficult, both teachers and their students often avoid such activities. Consequently, LD students typically learn fewer useful problem-solving techniques than their normally achieving peers. A mathematics program for LD students designed to teach such techniques should sys-

---

Box 14.22   Decimals

Materials Needed

1. Graph paper cut out in one square, one vertical row of ten squares, and a piece of ten by ten squares.
2. Small circle of construction paper to represent a decimal point.
3. Flash cards of numbers to the thousandths.

Procedure

1. The teacher designates what decimal place is represented by each graph paper cutout.
2. After demonstrating the use of the cutouts, the teacher holds up a flash card and calls out a number using tenths. It is important to call out 1.2 as "one and two-tenths" rather than "one point two" and to continue in this manner throughout. The student represents the number using the cutouts.
3. As the teacher extends the numbers to include more decimal places, a designation of which decimal place is represented by each cutout is made. (The teacher may add larger cutouts and move each cutout one place to the right. However, the cutouts must be sequenced in decreasing size.)

---

tematically address the skills of analysis and interpretation. Overholt, Rincon, and Ryan (1984) have articulated eight steps in the problem solving process, which are identified in Box 14.23. Each step should be modified according to needs of individual students. LD students often resist using all eight steps in this procedure. It does, however, provide a global structure that can be pared down and adjusted. Once this procedure has been mastered, it will help LD students become more efficient problem solvers in the classroom and in other applied situations. Many excellent activities incorporating this approach are found in Overholt, Rincon, and Ryan (1984).

Assessing Each Student's Strengths and Weaknesses

The assessment and evaluation of LD students for the purposes of instruction should be task specific. An example can detail appropriate as-

---

Box 14.23   Eight Steps of Problem Solving

---

1. Main idea: What is the problem about?
2. Question: What is being asked in the problem?
3. Important facts: What are the important facts to be used to find a solution?
4. Relationship sentence: State verbally (preferably without using numbers) how to solve the problem. This helps the student to organize thoughts about the problem and select the computational operations to use.
5. Equation: Write a number statement based upon the relationship sentence.
6. Estimation: Estimate the solution.
7. Computation: Compute the answer.
8. Answer sentence: State the computed answer orally in a statement that answers the question in the problem.

Note. Adapted from *Math Problem Solving for Grades 4 through 8* (p. 4) by J. L. Overholt, J. B. Rincon, and C. A. Ryan, 1984, Newton, MA: Allyn and Bacon.

---

sessment strategies better than a description. This activity, demonstrated in Box 14.24, should be used prior to beginning instruction on the multiplication algorithm. The results of the evaluation will enable the teacher to build instruction on the student's previous knowledge. Solution A shown in Box 14.24 indicates that: (1) the student used repeated addition and (2) additional experiences are needed before this problem type is seen as appropriate for multiplication. The student will have to be helped to write a horizontal multiplication sentence that is equivalent to the addition sentence. It is essential for the student to write, $5 \times 16 = ?$ for the multiplication algorithm to be meaningful.

Students who have responded with Solutions B and C appear to have used similar processes. Solution B, however, may actually be more advanced. The student who used Solution C probably recognized that an application of the distributive property could solve the problem. This student simply used two multiplication facts and summed the partial products. This is also the case for Solution B, except that this answer shows more knowledge of place value. This student summed $9 + 7$ and subsequently renamed the sum to $10 + 6$. This is a more advanced approach involving knowledge of both place value and the distributive property.

The teacher should proceed differently depending on which solution the student used. That is, students who understand Solution B demon-

---

Box 14.24   The Assessment and Evaluation Process

---

1. Give the student an index card bearing the following problem: "Five students stop at a convenience store on their way home from school. They decide to combine their left over lunch money to buy candy. The students want to buy five pieces of bubble gun at seven cents each and five chocolates at nine cents each. How much money must they have all together?"
2. Ask the student to compute the answer on the back of the card. Encourage the student to use multiplication to solve the problem.
3. Collect the card and analyze the computations according to the following examples:
     a. Solution A: $16 + 16 + 16 + 16 + 16 = 80$
     b. Solution B: $5 \times 16 = 5 \times (10 + 6)$
     $$= (5 \times 10) + (5 \times 6)$$
     $$= 50 + 30$$
     $$= 80$$
     c. Solution C: $(5 \times 9) + (5 \times 7) = 45 + 35$
     $$= 80$$

---

strate mastery of the concepts of place value, the distributive property, the place value and distributive property relationship, selected computation skills, and problem-solving techniques. Although many teachers do not develop task-specific evaluation activities similar to the example, this procedure is recommended to obtain the precise data that is needed for effective instruction of LD students.

Summary and Conclusions

This chapter first examined the early development of mathematics concepts and concluded with a discussion of the importance of problem-solving instruction for LD students. An instructional model based on the tetrahedral model but expanded to include instructional interventions and the learning environment was presented. This model was utilized in sections on place value, addition and subtraction, multiplication and division, and fractions. No one instructional intervention is effective for all LD students: the teacher must adopt an instructional approach that is most consistent with the information and experience that the student brings to the learning negotiation. Several learning activities have been suggested and demonstrate that a cognitive developmental approach is meaningful and activity oriented. Finally, it has been argued that problem solving should permeate all content areas.

Endnote

1. There is no definitive evidence to explain why multiplication and division are more difficult. Some logical reasons are the complexity of the algorithm and the dependence of the division algorithm on multiplication and subtraction.

Chapter 15

Mathematics Instruction in Junior and Senior High School

George W. Fair

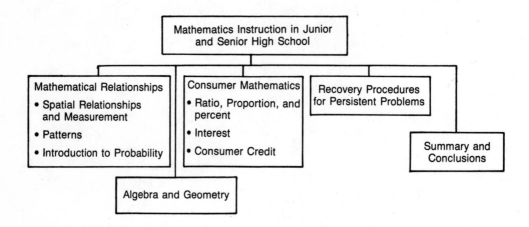

Questions to Consider

1. What are the important areas of mathematics that are frequently absent from the curriculum offered secondary LD students?
2. How should geometry and algebra and consumer mathematics be taught to LD students?
3. Why is it so important that mathematics instruction be meaningful and comprehensible?

Mathematics instruction for secondary LD students can serve as either the foundation for future instruction in higher education or the final formal instructional experience. Many LD students are denied an opportunity to learn the broad array of mathematical relationships studied by their normally achieving peers. Because teachers place undue emphasis on computation during the elementary school years, other topics of interest and importance (e.g., spatial relationships, measurement, patterns, and probability) receive little or no attention. For this reason, the first section of this chapter will highlight these other topics utilizing techniques that have proved successful with secondary LD students.

The second section will address algebra and geometry, because increasing numbers of LD students attend higher education institutions after high school. High school algebra and geometry are among the minimum requirements for entrance. Important areas of competence prerequisite to the study of algebra are identified and examples of instructional techniques that have been successfully used with LD students are provided.

The third section is concerned with consumer mathematics for those high school students who are not planning to continue their education. Instructional recommendations related to ratio and percent, interest, and consumer credit are presented using an interesting, meaningful, and environmentally based approach.

Finally, the chapter discusses recovery procedures for LD students with persistent mathematics problems. The processes and techniques that are described require an experienced teacher who is willing to focus on the needs of individual students.

Mathematical Relationships

Spatial Relationships and Measurement

All students should be provided the opportunity to participate in the entire mathematics program, including the study of spatial relationships and measurement, for these concepts are fundamental to understanding and describing the environment. Consumers, for example, are often presented with directions and explanations about their appliances that use diagrams and geometrical language. There are also pedagogical reasons for study in this area. Spatial relationships and measurement are ideal for developing self-reliance: Because LD students can often determine the correct answer by manipulating pictures or other materials, they may discover "what always happens" and "what never happens," which fosters the expectation that mathematics makes sense.

Since three-dimensional objects are familiar, less abstract, and more interesting, they should be studied before working with Euclidean shapes. Working with real objects, such as balls, boxes, and drink cans, students are encouraged to identify points, corners, edges, size, roundness, flatness,

---

Box 15.1   Faces, Vertices, and Edges

Materials Needed

1. The following geometric solids: sphere, cylinder, cube, rectangular prism, triangular pyramid, square pyramid, pentagonal pyramid, and cone
2. A geometric solid chart (see Table 15.1)

Procedure

1. Ask the student to manipulate several solids and record the number of faces, edges, and vertices on the chart.
2. Ask the student to lay the solid on paper and trace it.
3. Ask the student to identify those solids having similar characteristics.
4. Ask the student to discover Euler's Theorem:

$$\text{Faces} + \text{Vertices} = \text{Edges} + \text{Two}$$
$$F + V = E + 2$$

5. Each student will need a unique amount of direction.
6. Students will enjoy testing this formula by examining other shapes, such as boxes, books, and desks.

Table 15.1   Geometric Solid Chart

Geometric Solid	Faces	Vertices	Edges
Sphere			
Cylinder			
Cube			
Rectangular Prism			
Triangular Pyramid			
Square Pyramid			
Pentagonal Pyramid			
Cone			

---

and the ability of solids to roll, stack, and slide. The activity presented in Box 15.1 can be used as soon as students can identify faces, vertices, and edges.

As a natural outgrowth of work with solid figures and as a development from early experiences with curves, students may be encouraged to investigate special closed curves known as polygons. By describing various shapes with words such as "straight," "sides," "corners," and "round," they will learn the names for triangles, rectangles, squares, and circles.

Geoboards allow students to engage in a wide range of investigations. A geoboard is a square piece of wood or plastic in which pegs are arranged in some orderly fashion. A commonly used geoboard has twenty-five pegs arranged in five rows and five columns on which rubber bands can be stretched to outline shapes. Box 15.2 includes geoboard activities that should challenge and be enjoyable for students.

Box 15.2   Geoboards

Materials Needed

1. A five-by-five geoboard
2. Five rubber bands

Procedure

1. Ask the student to use the rubber bands to make as many different quadrilaterals as possible on the geoboard. The student should be assisted in forming at least a square, rectangle, parallelogram, and trapezoid. The student should discuss each figure, noting similarities and differences with others and between models of the same figure. This information can be organized in a table that includes the name of the figure, the number of angles, and the number of sides.
2. Ask the students to make three-, four-, five-, six-, and seven-sided figures. For each of these figures the student should stretch diagonals. Ask the student to record the number of diagonals that can be drawn for each of these figures and to discover a pattern that can be used to predict the number of diagonals for figures as they increase in the number of sides. (The number of diagonals increase according to the following sequence: two, three, four, five, etc.) A table helps the student organize this information.
3. Ask the student to form both concave and convex figures (see Figure 15.1). A figure is concave when a line segment that connects two points on or inside the figure does not necessarily lie

(*continued*)

Box 15.2 (*continued*)

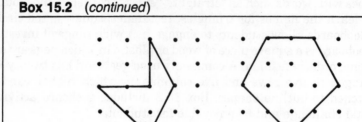

Concave   Convex

FIGURE 15.1   Concave and Convex Figures.

entirely within the figure. If a line segment that connects any
two points on or inside the figure lies entirely within the figure, then the figure is convex.
4. Ask the student to sketch eight three-by-three geoboards. Then
   have the student sketch one noncongruent triangle that can be
   formed on each geoboard. Ask the student to identify the triangles as isosceles, right, or scalene.
5. Ask the student to sketch sixteen three-by-three geoboards and
   the sixteen noncongruent quadrilaterals that can be formed on
   each geoboard. Have the student identify the shapes as
   squares, rectangles, parallelograms, trapezoids, convex, or
   concave.

Tangrams are an old and popular Chinese puzzle game. The seven pieces
of a tangram are cut from a square, as indicated in Figure 15.2. Box 15.3 is
a tangram activity that will challenge both students and adults.

Measurement is the process by which numbers are assigned to properties of objects. Relationships between objects are defined by comparisons, and objects having more of some property are given a larger number.
Measuring in school is limited to specific attributes such as length, area,
volume and capacity, weight and mass, time, and temperature. The process of measurement of any property is specific to that property, but
generally either counting, reading a scale on a calibrated instrument,
computation, or a combination of these are used. In counting, an object
is taken as a unit and physically iterated against the object being measured. A calibrated instrument is used when the temperature is read or
the weight of a person is determined.

Measurement experiences for students usually begin with exploratory
activities such as pouring, matching, balancing, ordering, sorting, and

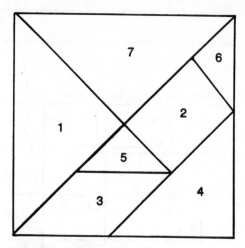

FIGURE 15.2 Tangram.

comparing. Work with many of these processes should continue with nonstandard units of measure for length, weight, capacity, volume, time, area, and temperature. For example, the students may measure the teacher's desk using their hands as a nonstandard unit of measure. The purpose of this sort of activity is to demonstrate the reason for standard units, as each student will get a different measurement for the size of the desk because of the size differences among their hands. Finally, students should be provided with experiences that include measuring, estimating, converting, and describing properties utilizing standard units of measurement for the same attributes used with nonstandard units of measure.

Box 15.3   Tangrams

Materials Needed

1. A square piece of paper
2. Pencil
3. Scissors

Procedure

1. Ask the student to cut the square piece of paper into the seven pieces indicated in Figure 15.2 and number them.
2. Ask the student to draw a table as shown in Figure 15.3.

(continued)

Box 15.3 (*continued*)

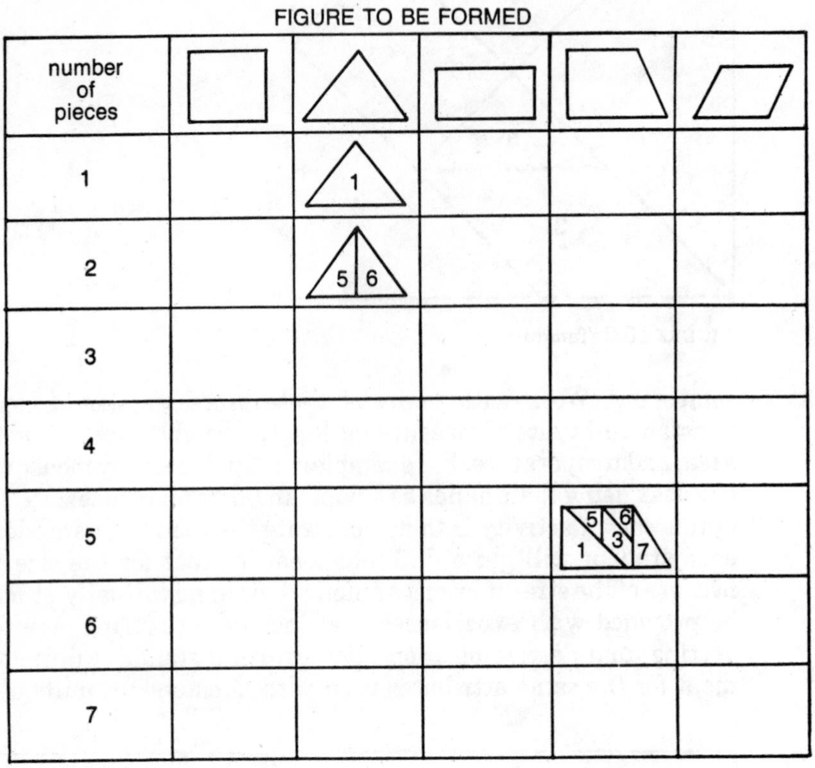

FIGURE TO BE FORMED

FIGURE 15.3 Tangram Table.

3. The student should try to complete as many of the figures as possible and record each solution on the table.
4. Ask the student to discuss the name of the figure and describe the pieces that were used to complete it.

Patterns

The study of patterns helps students realize that mathematics is a logical and predictable process. Problems become more meaningful and easier to solve when they are organized into workable frameworks. Success in mathematics is directly related to the student's ability to sort out relationships and patterns. When working with patterns, students need not always be concerned with concise, formalized conclusions. They do need to be aware, however, of developing logical strategies for finding solutions instead of depending on random guesses or luck.

Various approaches are effective for introducing patterns to students. Problems may deal with the logical sequence of numbers, clever arrangements of numbers, or number computations that follow unusual patterns. Word problems that are fun for students involve people, places, and events. As students work with patterns, they must develop strategies for arriving at logical conclusions, including using charts, arrays, sketches, and other orderly arrangements of information. The teacher should, of course, model thinking processes to help the students initially structure the problems and organize information so that the solution appears simple. As students grow in skill and confidence and realize that they too can develop workable strategies, they will experience satisfaction in thinking mathematically independently.

Complex problems involving patterns should be introduced only after students can solve a variety of simple problems using appropriate strategies. Those students who have developed confidence in their own predictions and conjectures should be challenged with more complicated ways to generate and use procedures and concepts of elementary mathematics. A geoboard is a useful tool for visualizing patterns and complex mathematical ideas (see Box 15.2). Students work with rubber bands to form shapes such as triangles and squares, compute areas, and determine relationships. It is helpful to use finite systems when working with geoboards so that students can more easily examine complete mathematical systems. Through a variety of manipulative experiences, students become aware of many mathematical relations or properties.

Examples of activities that encourage generating mathematical patterns from real and abstract situations and more complex problems using a structural model, the geoboard, are presented below. Box 15.4 focuses on number series. Determining patterns for number sequences is a very old form of mathematical recreation. The triangular array of numbers indicated in Box 15.5 is a famous number pattern known as Pascal's Triangle. There are many relationships between the various rows, columns, and diagonals.

Solving a seemingly complex problem in mathematics has psychological implications. Many adults still have phobias about mathematics that developed from school experiences. Box 15.6 presents two puzzles known as magic squares, one more complex than the other. Concentrate on discovering a procedure for finding the solution, rather than depending on trial and error. Success in making sense out of mathematics is directly related to the ability to sort out relationships and patterns. An approach that works very effectively is to set up a record-keeping system to identify

Box 15.4 Number Series

Determining patterns for number sequences is a very old form of mathematical recreation. The following number series have patterns that can be described with words or formulas:

1. Continue this pattern. Then write a general description of how it will continue.
   $1 = 1$
   $1 + 3 = 4$
   $1 + 3 + 5 = 9$
   $1 + 3 + 5 + 7 =$
   $1 + 3 \cdots =$
   $1 + \quad \cdots =$
   $1 = 1$
   $3 + 5 = 8$
   $7 + 9 + 11 = 27$
   $13 + 15 + 17 + 19 =$
   $21 + 23 + 25 + 27 + 29 =$
   $31 + 33 + 35 + 37 + 39 + 41 =$
   $43 + \cdots =$

2. Continue this pattern. Then write a general description of how it will continue.
   $1 = 1$
   $1 + 1 = 2$
   $1 + 1 + 2 = 4$
   $1 + 1 + 2 + 3 = 7$
   $1 + 1 + 2 + 3 + 5 = 12$
   $1 + 1 + 2 + 3 + 5 + 8 = 20$
   $1 + 1 + 2 + 3 + 5 + 8 + 13 = 33$
   $1 + 2 + \cdots =$
   $1 = 1$
   $1 + 4 = 5$
   $1 + 4 + 9 = 14$
   $1 + 4 + 9 + 16 = 30$
   $1 + 4 + 9 + 16 + 25 = 55$
   $1 + 4 + \cdots =$

what is known. Box 15.7 presents two examples of how such a system can make a seemingly impossible puzzle quite manageable. All of the above-mentioned activities have been used with LD students and, because

Box 15.5   Number Triangle

The triangular array of numbers shown in Figure 15.4 is a famous number pattern known as Pascal's Triangle. There are many relationships between the various rows, columns, and diagonals. Continue this pattern for several more rows:

1. Describe two ways in which this pattern generates itself.
2. What is the relationship between two adjacent numbers in one row and the number below them?
3. Explore other patterns in the triangle, such as the sums of the numbers in each horizontal row or the sequence of numbers in the diagonal columns, and make a conjecture about each of the patterns discovered.

```
              1

           1     1

        1     2     1

     1     3     3     1

  1     4     6     4     1

  □  □   □    □   □  □

 □   □   □    □    □    □   □
```

FIGURE 15.4 Pascal's Triangle.

Box 15.6 Magic Squares

1. In the 3 × 3 array (see Figure 15.5), arrange the digits 1, 2, 3, 4, 5, 6, 7, 8, and 9 so that the sum of each column, row, and diagonal is 15. Write each number on one of the little squares so that they can be conveniently arranged. Describe the method used to find a solution.

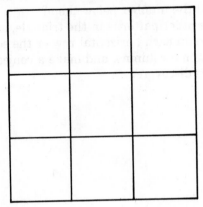

FIGURE 15.5 3 × 3 Array.

2. In the 4 × 4 array (see Figure 15.6), arrange the digits 1, 2, 3, 4, 5, 6, 7, 8, 9, 10, 11, 12, 13, 14, 15, and 16 so that the sum of each main diagonal is 34. Describe the method used to find a solution. Find other arrangements that are clever.

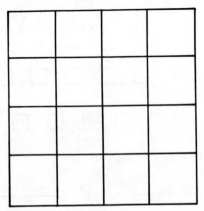

FIGURE 15.6 4 × 4 Array.

Box 15.7   People Puzzles

1. In the Jones Grocery Store, the positions of cashier, manager, and clerk are held by Williams, Smith, and Miller, although not necessarily respectively (see Table 15.2). The clerk, who is an only child, earns the least. Miller, who married Williams's sister, earns more than the manager. Determine which position each employee fills. (Place Xs or Os in the appropriate boxes.)

Table 15.2   The Jones Grocery Store

Employee	Cashier	Manager	Clerk
Williams			
Smith			
Miller			

2. An engineer, a first mate, a radio operator, and a cook are all members of the same ship's crew that has crossed the equator many times (see Table 15.3). Their names are Bill, Carol, Sam, and Joan. Carol is taller than the radio operator or the cook. Bill eats lunch by himself. The tallest of the four likes to work logic problems. Sam meets the engineer and the first mate each day for lunch. Bill is older than the cook. Carol plays card games with the engineer. What job does each person hold?

Table 15.3   A Ship's Crew

Position	Bill	Carol	Sam	Joan
Engineer				
First mate				
Radio operator				
Cook				

they clarify procedures and relationships, assist in developing their understanding and feelings of success with mathematics.

Introduction to Probability

The ideas that are commonly grouped under the heading of probability are an enjoyable and important application of the use of fractions. LD students do not have many opportunities to explore these concepts, although probability is encountered daily when reading, watching, or listening to news reports. Statements such as, "There is a 70 percent chance of rain," "The probability of winning the lottery is one in ten thousand," and "The odds of the Cowboys beating the Bears in football on Sunday are 5 to 3," are encountered by all of us, including LD students. In this section, probability, counting techniques, odds, and mathematical expectation will be presented by using activities in which LD students have demonstrated success.

To introduce the concept of the probability of a given event, the student is asked to toss a coin fifty times and record the results. The probability of obtaining heads (H) when a coin is tossed, denoted by $P(H)$, is one out of two. That is, $P(H) = 1/2$. The probability may be defined as:

$$\frac{\text{Number of Favorable Outcomes}}{\text{Total Number of Outcomes}}$$

Another excellent activity for teaching the operational definition of probability is rolling of a die or a pair of dice while asking questions such as, "What is the probability of rolling a five?", "What is the probability of rolling an even number?", and "What is the probability of rolling a seven?" The $P(5) = 1/6$, $P(2, 4, \text{ or } 6) = 3/6$, and $P(7) = 0$, because on an ordinary die any one of the six faces has an equally likely chance of turning up. For the rolling of two dice, students will enjoy making a diagram similar to Figure 15.7. Questions such as, "What is the probability of rolling a seven?", "What is the probability of rolling snake eyes?", and "What is the probability of rolling a double?", should be asked when a pair of dice

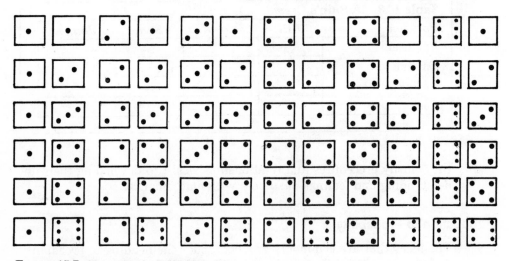

Figure 15.7 Outcomes of a Roll of Two Dice.

Table 15.4   Possible Responses to Two Test Questions

First Question	Second Question	Possible Responses
T	T	T T
	F	T F
F	T	F T
	F	F F

is used. The P(sum of 7) = 6/36 = 1/6, P(faces of both dice being 1) = 1/36, and P (faces of both dice being the same) = (1/36 + 1/36 + 1/36 + 1/36 + 1/36 + 1/36) = 1/6, because there are thirty-six equally likely outcomes when two dice are rolled.

Counting techniques are used to determine the number of outcomes when more than one event is considered. How many different ways can two questions be answered, for example, on a true-false test? Table 15.4 is a diagram of this situation. By tracing each path from left to right, we find that there are four end points, which correspond to the $2 \times 2 = 4$ ways in which the two questions can be answered. LD students should be asked to solve the following problem by drawing a similar diagram:

> "A person wants to purchase a car. Two body styles (two door or four door) and three colors (red, white, or blue) are available. Find how many choices the person has."

The responses should be similar to those in Table 15.5. By tracing each path we find that there are six end points, which correspond to the 2×3 ways of making the two decisions in succession in the stated order. This example illustrates a basic relationship: If one thing can occur in m ways and a second thing can then occur in n ways, the sequence of two things can occur in $m \times n$ ways.

Table 15.5   Choices of Cars to Purchase

Body Style	Color	Possible
Two-door (T)	Red (R)	T R
	White (W)	T W
	Blue (B)	T B
Four-door (F)	Red (R)	F R
	White (W)	F W
	Blue (B)	F B

This counting relationship has a natural extension to probability that will be discovered by asking, "What is the probability of rolling a six twice on two successive rolls of a die?" That is, $P(6, 6) = 1/6 \times 1/6 = 1/36$. Also, "What is the probability of rolling an even number on the first roll and the same number on the second roll?" That is, $P(\text{even, same}) = 1/2 \times 1/6 = 1/12$. These responses are direct extensions of the basic counting relationship for two events that occur in succession, which is easily understood by LD students. The counting technique discussed above, in which an ordered arrangement of objects or events is considered, is called a *permutation* of the objects. An arrangement of objects or events in which the order is disregarded is called a *combination* of the objects. Combinations also lead to very interesting applications for LD students, but because of space limitations, they will not be discussed here.

Games of chance and the probabilities of sporting events are often discussed in terms of odds. At the race track it may be announced that, "The odds of Red Mane winning are four to one." This *racetrack statement* means that for every dollar bet on Red Mane, the management will put up four dollars. If the horse wins, the bettor will receive the amount of money bet plus the money matched by the race track; for a one dollar bet, the bettor receives five dollars, and for a two dollar bet, the bettor receives ten dollars. The relationship between odds and probability is easily illustrated with the fraction bar (see Figure 14.7). The twelve to one odds *against* picking an ace from a deck of cards is illustrated in Figure 15.8. This is an example for one suit, such as spades, but easily extends to a full deck of cards with four suits. To summarize, the *probability* of an event is the ratio of the number of favorable outcomes to the total number of outcomes, and the *odds* of an event is the ratio of the number of favorable outcomes to the number of unfavorable outcomes. Students should be asked to solve the problem presented in Box 15.8 using the strategy described above.

To evaluate the fairness of a game that involves a monetary gain as well as the probability of winning, mathematical expectation is used. Here is another example of how a sophisticated mathematical concept

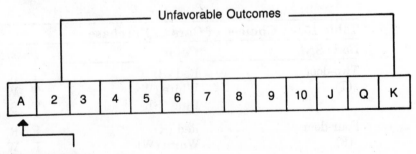

FIGURE 15.8 Odds of Picking an Ace from a Suit of Cards.

Box 15.8 Probability and Odds with a Deck of Cards

A deck of fifty-two cards contains 13 cards in each of the four suits: spades, hearts, clubs, and diamonds. The clubs and spades are black, and the diamonds and hearts are red. Each suit has three face cards: jack, queen, and king. Compute the probabilities and odds of drawing each of the following cards: an ace, a face card, a diamond, and a black face card.

---

has been used with LD students to provide interesting and educationally enriching activities. The probability of rolling a sum of seven on two dice, for example, is 1/6. This means, that on the average, a sum of seven will come up once on every six rolls. If it costs $1.20 to roll the dice and the payoff is six dollars for rolling a seven, over a period of time, the game is fair, or the player will break even. The probability of winning multiplied by the value of the prize is called *mathematical expectation* in equation form: (See Figure 15.7).

$$\text{Expectation } (E) = P(\text{win}) \times \text{Prize} + P(\text{loss}) \times \text{Cost}$$
$$= 1/6 \times \$6 + 5/6 \times (-\$1.20) = \$1.00 - \$1.00 = 0$$

When the expectation (E) equals zero, the game is fair (see Box 15.9).

Box 15.9 Game Condition Choices

Ask students under which of the following conditions a person would choose to play a game in which a single die is thrown:

1. When a 1 is thrown, win $6 and lose $12 for any other number.
2. When a 1 is thrown, win $6 and lose $6 for any other number.
3. When a 1 is thrown, win $30 and lose $6 for any other number.
4. When a 1 is thrown, win $36 and lose $6 for any other number.

The expectation for each condition is:

1. $E = 1/6\ (\$6\ ) + 5/6\ (-\$12) = -\$9$
2. $E = 1/6\ (\$6\ ) + 5/6\ (-\$6\ ) = -\$4$
3. $E = 1/6\ (\$30) + 5/6\ (-\$6\ ) = \quad 0$
4. $E = 1/6\ (\$36) + 5/6\ (-\$6\ ) = \quad \$1$

This section has discussed mathematical topics in which most LD students do not receive instruction, yet another case of how they are frequently denied access to the fair and appropriate education they deserve. These examples have been successfully used by this author with such students, who have reported that these areas are interesting and enjoyable. Tests and daily records indicate that LD students do master such material.

Algebra and Geometry

Many LD high school students (often with the support of their families) plan to complete the college preparatory mathematics courses in algebra and geometry. This section offers examples of the content and instructional techniques that are necessary.

Areas that are important to the study of algebra are integers, prime numbers and factoring, exponents, fractions, set theory, and equations. LD students may have difficulty in one or more of these areas, because: (1) they lack instruction, (2) earlier instruction emphasized computation rather than understanding, and/or (3) they may experience problems with the relatively large amount of new vocabulary and symbolism. Each of these topics, however, can be presented with a focus on understanding. Viewing mathematics as an *activity* rather than a body of knowledge offers instructional approaches that are intuitive and inductive. In this cognitive developmental approach, mathematical ideas are initially presented through prototypes. Extensions are gradually introduced that model the thinking involved in the progression to abstractions, always with a strong emphasis on understanding.

Since human beings first began to count, the concept of number has been extended and refined. The extension that is important in the study of algebra is the extension to the negative number. A prototype for sets of numbers is the number line. The correspondence of numbers with points has far-reaching consequences and is often not completely understood for either fractions or negative numbers. Subzero temperatures and deficit finance serve as sources of examples, because these are illustrations of negative numbers familiar to LD students.

As discussed earlier, the concept of addition can be conceptualized as the union of two disjoint sets. If there are N objects in one group and M in another, putting the two piles together yields a new pile with $N + M$ objects. Unfortunately, this conceptualization provides no information when adding negative numbers, because no pile can contain a negative number of objects. A helpful instructional device that can be used with LD students is a modified slide rule. Figure 15.9 depicts this device and shows how easily it can be made from graph paper. This device can be

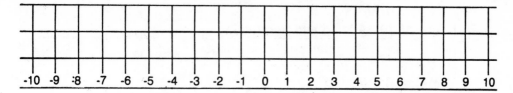

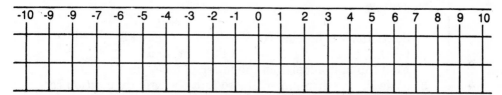

FIGURE 15.9 Device for Computing Negative Numbers.

made by all students and used for both addition and subtraction. Box 15.10 offers instruction for its use.

The multiplication of integers can be shown as repeated addition, provided that at least one of the two factors is positive. There is a problem, however, when both factors are negative. The story of the incompetent mail carrier helps students understand the multiplication of integers even when both factors are negative. The mail carrier delivers both bills and dividends—often to the wrong addresses. A dividend delivered is $(+)(+)$, a dividend picked up because of an incorrect address is $(-)(+)$, a bill delivered is $(+)(-)$, a bill picked up is $(-)(-)$. Picking up two bills for five dollars that were mistakenly delivered would be, for example, (-2) (-5), or $(+10)$, for the resident.

Prime numbers are fundamental building blocks of the number system and an absolutely necessary concept for simplifying and working with algebraic expressions. These concepts are first introduced in early elementary school. Often, however, they are not mastered and cannot be easily extended to algebra. Any composite number may be expressed as a product of prime numbers. Figure 15.10 shows two examples of the factorization of 36. The difference in order of final prime factors is unimportant, because multiplication is commutative and associative. A graphic representation of factoring such as Figure 15.10 is often helpful to LD students in understanding the process.

Exponential notation is also a part of the elementary school curriculum, but operations with numbers in exponential form is usually reserved for algebra. Exponents are especially helpful for working with very large and very small numbers and have important applications in physics and

---

Box 15.10   Adding and Subtracting

Materials Needed

1. Two pieces of graph paper numbered as in Figure 15.9

Procedure

1. Select random number combinations such as $(+3) + (+2) = x$; $(+3) + (-2) = x$; $(-3) + (+2) = x$; and $(-3) + (-2) = x$.
2. Find the first addend on the lower number line.
3. Slide the upper number line so that the zero (0) position corresponds with the first addend on the lower number line.
4. Find the second addend on the upper number line.
5. The sum is the position on the lower number line that corresponds to the second addend on the upper number line.
6. Select random number combinations such as $(+3) - (+2) = x$; $(+3) - (-2) = x$; $(-3) - (+2) = x$; and $(-3) - (-2) = x$.
7. Find the minuend on the lower number line.
8. Slide the upper number line so that the zero (0) position corresponds with the minuend on the lower number line.
9. Find the additive inverse (opposite) of the subtrahend on the upper number line.
10. The difference is the position on the lower number line that corresponds to the additive inverse of the subtrahend on the upper number line.

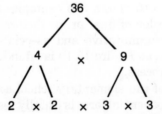 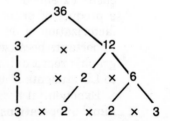

FIGURE 15.10 Prime Factors.

chemistry. A basic constant in chemistry, for example, is Avogadro's number, which is 602,000,000,000,000,000,000,000. In scientific notation this is simply 6.02×10^{23}. The natural extension of exponents exists in logarithms and trigonometry. The development of computers and calculators has made some hand computations with logarithms obsolete, but the underlying theory of exponents remains fundamental to algebra and calculus. Special attention should be focused on exponential notation prior to the study of algebra for many LD students.

Thorough competence in operations with common fractions is necessary for success in algebra. Although it takes most students years to attain such a level, limitations in their preparation will be especially apparent in the study of algebra. The study of algebra, however, can help students identify these limitations and provides motivation for their improvement. If such an approach is attempted for LD students, the instructor must select instructional activities that are appropriate for the backgrounds of the students.

The theory of sets and set notation involves a relatively large amount of vocabulary and symbolism, but sets permeate instructional approaches to both algebra and geometry. The study of set theory begins in elementary school, but the understanding attained by most students, and especially LD students, is not sufficient for the study of algebra. A problem-solving approach with the use of Venn diagrams (see Box 15.11) is an informal tactic that has been productive with LD students.

An *equation* is a mathematical statement that two objects or quantities are the same or equal. Equations are one of the main tools of algebra, but LD students have often had insufficient work with them. Begin by asking students to find the answer to simple equations such as $x + 5 = 7$. This approach can be supplemented by asking students to manipulate pictures of bags of objects and units to represent statements such as $2b + 5$, $4b + 7$, or $3b + 2$. Word problems such as, "If I subtract from the double of my present age the treble of my age six years ago, the result is my present age (e.g., $2x - 3(x - 6) = ?$). What is my age?" (Chrystal, 1961), *sound* confusing, but can be solved simply with an equation (see Box 15.12). This type of problem helps students understand the importance and value of equation-solving skills and consequently motivates them for this work. A natural extension of this study is inequalities, which can be represented by using a number line.

Instruction in graphs, square roots, area, angles, and polygons offers the kind of experiences that are beneficial to LD students who plan to study geometry as well. Students are helped in locating points in space by using a coordinate system. Activities similar to that in Box 15.13 relate geometry to algebra, and may also be extended to the important mathematical concept of a function.

The square root concept is often confusing for LD students as the study of algebra is begun. An interesting and very logical way of computing

Box 15.11   Venn Diagrams

1. Discuss the following problem and use a Venn diagram to find
   the solution (use Figure 15.11):
   a. There are forty people at a political meeting. Twenty-five
      are men and twenty people are less than thirty-five years
      old. How many women are over thirty-five, if ten of the
      men are under thirty-five?

People at Meeting

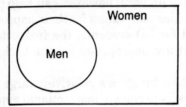

People at Meeting

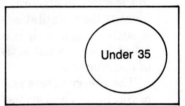

People at Meeting

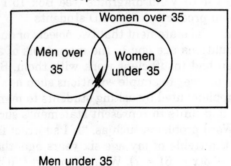

Men under 35

FIGURE 15.11 Venn Diagrams.

2. Use Venn diagrams to solve the following problems:
   a. The number of people in a town is approximately twenty-
      five thousand. There are nine thousand men and fifteen
      thousand registered voters. Only five thousand men are
      registered voters. How many women are not registered?
   b. When 400 sixth-grade students were tested in reading
      and math, 250 scored at or above grade level in reading
      and 120 were at or above grade level in math. Only 90
      scored at or above in both subjects. How many scored be-
      low grade level in both subjects?

Box 15.12   Age Problem Equation

---

1. Let x = present age
2. Express the problem in terms of x, for example, "The double of my present age equals $2x$."
3. Write and solve the equation:

$$2x - 3(x-6) = x$$
$$2x - 3x + 18 = x$$
$$-x + 18 = x$$
$$18 = 2x$$
$$9 = x$$

Box 15.13   Analytic Geometry

Materials Needed

1. Graph paper

Procedure

1. Demonstrate the process of drawing x and y axes at right angles on graph paper and label each.
2. Ask the student to draw two axes meeting at right angles near the center of a piece of graph paper and to plot the following points: $(1, 2)$, $(3, 5)$, $(-2, 4)$, $(-1, 5)$, $(-3, -5)$, $(-5, -2)$, $(3, -5)$, $(4, -5)$.
3. Ask the student to draw another set of axes and to find five points that satisfy the equation, $y = 2x$.
4. Ask the student to find five points that satisfy the equation, $y = 2x + 5$.
5. Ask the student to draw lines through the five points that satisfied each of the two equations above.
6. Ask the student to draw another set of axes and to draw a line through the five points that satisfy the equation, $y = x + 1$. Ask the student to find five other points that satisfy this equation using only positive and negative fractional numbers.

square roots of numbers that are not perfect squares is by successive approximations. Clearly the square root of 12 lies between 3 and 4, since $3^2 = 9$ and $4^2 = 16$. A good guess is 3 1/2, therefore, $(7/2)^2 = (49/4) = 12\ 1/4 > \sqrt{12}$. It is now assumed to be between 3 and 3 1/2. A good guess is 3 1/4; therefore, $(13/4)^2 = (169/16) = 10\ 9/16 < \sqrt{12}$. It is now assumed to be between 3 1/4 and 3 1/2. Using decimals $3.25^2 < 12 < 3.5^2$. A good guess is 3.35; therefore, $3.35^2 = 11.22 < \sqrt{12}$. It is now assumed that $3.35^2 < 12 < 3.5^2$. A good guess is 3.40; therefore, $3.40^2 = 11.56 < 12$. A good estimate of $\sqrt{12}$ is 3.4. This method is relatively slow but it focuses attention on the nature of the problem at hand.

Area is a measure of how much ground something covers. Box 15.14 is concerned with areas and content, and Box 15.15 deals with congruency using geoboards. Both activities have been used successfully with LD students to discover formulas to compute the area of polygons and to develop the concepts of area and congruency informally.

Intuitively, angles can be thought of as rotations. This approach to angles is made clear to students if angles are initially pictured as in Figure 15.20.

Box 15.14   Areas and Content of Polygons

Materials Needed

1. Geoboard
2. Rubber bands

Procedure

1. Using rubber bands and the geoboard, construct and record several closed shapes with different numbers of sides. Classify and label them as follows: triangle, quadrilateral, pentagon, hexagon, and octagon.
2. Construct and record the following triangles: equilateral (all sides equal), isosceles (two sides equal), scalene (no sides equal), right (one 90° angle), acute (all acute angles), and obtuse (one obtuse angle). Is it possible to construct an equilateral triangle on the geoboard? Why?
3. An equilateral triangle is also an isosceles triangle, and an isosceles triangle is a type of triangle. Determine a similar sequence of the following four shapes: parallelograms, quadri-

(continued)

Box 15.14 *(continued)*

laterals, rectangles, and squares. The length between two nails on the geoboard, vertically and horizontally, is *one unit*. (The diagonal length between two nails is *not* one unit. The unit of area is a square with one unit on each side. The unit of area is referred to as *one square unit*. See Figure 15.12.)

One Unit of Length

FIGURE 15.12 One Unit.

4. Using Figure 15.13, compare the areas of shapes A and B, and shapes C and D. Determine a conjecture about how the diagonal divides the area of a square or rectangle. Based on the conjecture, determine the area of shape E.

    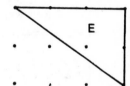

FIGURE 15.13 Areas of Simple Shapes.

5. Study the two following techniques for finding the areas of more complex shapes:

a. The area of a shape can be found by adding the areas of the parts into which the shape is subdivided (see Figure 15.14).

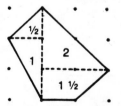

$\frac{1}{2} + 1 + 1\frac{1}{2} + 2 = 5$

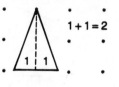

$1 + 1 = 2$

FIGURE 15.14 Areas of Complex Shapes (Method A).

b. It may be more convenient to find an area by subtracting the area of some small part from the known area of a larger part (see Figure 15.15).

(continued)

Box 15.14 *(continued)*

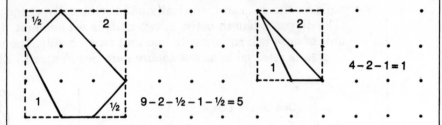

$$9 - 2 - \frac{1}{2} - 1 - \frac{1}{2} = 5$$

$$4 - 2 - 1 = 1$$

FIGURE 15.15 Areas of Complex Shapes (Method B).

6. On the geoboard construct the shapes in Figure 15.16, using additional rubber bands as needed. Determine their areas, and write the number of units in each:
A: _____ B: _____ C: _____ D: _____ E: _____ F: _____ G: _____

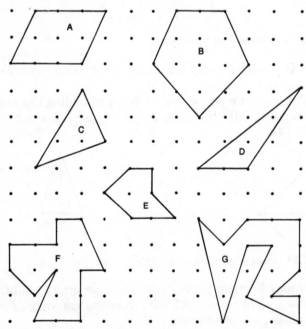

FIGURE 15.16

(continued)

Box 15.14 *(continued)*

7. On the geoboard construct a five-sided shape with an area of four units and record it.
8. Construct and record a square with an area of two. (Hint: A square does not have to be vertical and horizontal on the geoboard.)
9. Construct and record a three-sided shape with the least possible area.
10. Construct several polygons that touch eight nails and have two interior nails. Make a conjecture about the area of all such figures. Record their areas.

Box 15.15 Congruent Shapes

Materials Needed

1. Geoboard
2. Rubber bands

Procedure

1. Using the geoboard, construct triangles A and B shown in Figure 15.17.
   a. What is the sequence of lengths of the sides from shortest to longest for each triangle?
   b. How are the sequences of sides related?
   c. Find the area of each triangle.

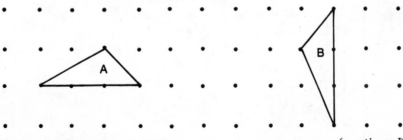

FIGURE 15.17 Triangles *A* and *B*.
(continued)

Box 15.15 *(continued)*

2. Construct Shapes C and D shown in Figure 15.18.
   a. What is the sequence of lengths of adjacent sides for each shape?
   b. How are the sequences of sides related?
   c. Find the areas of each shape.

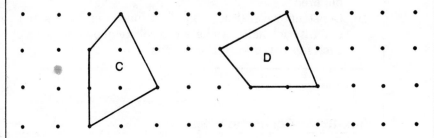

FIGURE 15.18 Shapes *C* and *D*.

3. Triangles A and B are *congruent,* and shapes C and D are *congruent.* Write a definition for congruent shapes.
4. Construct the shapes shown in Figure 15.19 and find five pairs of congruent shapes:
   a. _____ and _____   d. _____ and _____
   b. _____ and _____   e. _____ and _____
   c. _____ and _____

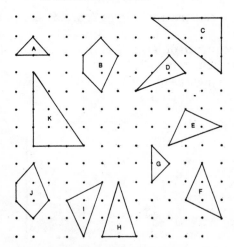

FIGURE 15.19 Congruent Shapes.

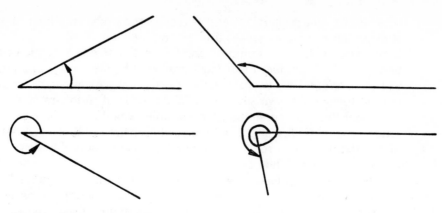

Figure 15.20 Angles.

The basic tool for measuring angles is a protractor. Activities in which students measure and draw specified angles and intuitively identify congruent, noncongruent, and similar polygons without the use of theorems are useful in concept development.

The study of polygons is closely related to the study of angles. A construction activity assists in the development of understanding. For LD students, such an approach is facilitated by the use of a protractor in addition to the traditional compass and straight edge. Activities that students will find enjoyable are the construction of scalene, isosceles, equilateral, acute, right, and obtuse triangles; quadrilaterals such as parallelograms, rectangles, rhombuses, squares, and trapezoids; and other polygons. Informal activities, such as paper folding, which focus attention on symmetry, can also facilitate understanding of geometrical concepts.

Consumer Mathematics

Ratio, Proportion, and Percent

LD students come face to face with consumer problems every day of their lives. Advertisements and other media appeals are constantly made to all of us. Calculating best buys, checking credit account statements, comparing interest rates, using credit cards, and buying or leasing a place to live are all potential sources of difficulty. It is very difficult to teach skills such as balancing a checkbook, however, because most LD students do not have a fundamental understanding of adding and subtracting decimals (Fair, 1974). LD students need to have a basic understanding of the concept of percent in order, for example, to be successful in comparing interest rates. Consequently, this section will begin with a discussion of ratio, proportion, and percent—the areas in which many LD students need more complete understanding.

"A nationwide survey names cereal X, by two to one over the next best brand, as the breakfast meal most preferred by students." The phrase 2 to 1 is a *ratio,* a very useful concept in which a pair of positive numbers is used to compare two sets. In 1976 the ratio of numbers of Air Force personnel to Army personnel, for example, was 3 to 4. The common notation for ratio is 3:4 or 3/4, and is read as "three to four." Ask students to report the ratio of males to females and conversely females to males in their classes and homes.

"The EPA rating for a new Ford is nineteen miles per gallon." A *rate* is a special kind of ratio in which the two sets being compared have different units. Other examples are pay per hour, speed, and exchange rates. Ask students to provide others.

"Sale: 3 cucumbers for $1." At this rate, six cucumbers cost two dollars and nine cucumbers cost three dollars. An equality of two ratios is called a *proportion.* In the previous example, three for one dollar and six for two dollars are equal ratios, and 3/1 = 6/2 is an example of proportion. Proportions are very useful for solving problems and, in this author's experience, very helpful for LD students. Typically, three of the four numbers in a proportion are given and only the fourth is to be found. Historically, the rule that is used has been called the "rule of three" or the "golden rule." That is, when two ratios form a proportion, the cross products are equal:

$$2/3 = 4/6 \qquad\qquad 3/4 = 9/12$$

$$2 \times 6 = 3 \times 4 \qquad 9 \times 4 = 3 \times 12$$

$$12 = 12 \qquad\qquad 36 = 36$$

(Example ratio problems can be seen in Box 15.16).

An understanding of ratio leads directly to the most important ratio concept for consumers: *percent.* The word *percent* comes from the Latin *per centum,* meaning *out of a hundred.* Percent is simply a ratio in which the denominator is 100. Ask students to find advertisements using percent in the daily newspaper. All percents can be written as a fraction or a decimal for computation. The recommended procedure is to write percents as fractions with a denominator of 100, as follows:

$$32\% = 32/100 \qquad 5.4\% = 5.4/100 \qquad 125\% = 125/100$$

Most computations with percents are of two kinds. In one case, a percent is given to determine a part of the whole. An ad may state, for example, that an article is reduced for sale by 15 percent. The original price was

---

Box 15.16   Ratios

---

1. One can has three tennis balls. How many will be in four cans?
2. There were five hot dogs for every three people at the party. If there were thirty-six people at the party, how many hot dogs were needed?
3. Three lemons are used with two quarts of water for lemonade. If six quarts of water are used, how many lemons are needed?
4. Which is the better buy: a fifteen-ounce can of soup for fifty-nine cents, or an eight-ounce can of soup for twenty-eight cents?

---

sixty dollars. What is the amount that is discounted? The solution is found by using proportions:

$$15/100 = x/\$60$$
$$100x = \$900x$$
$$x = \$9 \text{ discounted}$$

In the second case, a percent is determined by comparing a part to the whole. A certain well-known cereal, for example, sells for $1.20 a box. A coupon, however, can be used to reduce the price by fifteen cents. What percent savings does the coupon offer? The solution is found by using proportions:

$$x/100 = 15/120$$
$$120x = 1,500$$
$$x = 12.5, \text{ or } 12.5\%, \text{ savings}$$

This approach can be generalized for all percent problems:

$$percent/100 = part/whole$$

Applying the "golden rule" of proportions is the recommended approach for LD students to use to solve all percent problems. Box 15.7 offers additional practice.

Interest

How much interest will be received for two years on $10,000 in a bank account that pays 8 percent interest? The answer depends on how this interest is calculated. In any event, the answer will involve three factors:

1. The principle (*P*), or the amount of money lent or deposited in the transaction ($10,000 in the above example).
2. The rate (*r*), or the amount of interest per period (8 percent in the example).
3. The time (*t*), or the term during which the principle is used (two years in the example).

The annual percentage rate (*APR*) is based on a one-year period. It is important for LD students to have a thorough understanding of these three parts of all interest problems. The formula for calculating the simple interest (*I*) is:

$$I = P \times r \times t$$

For the above example:

$$I = \$10,000 \times 8/100 \times 2 = \$1,600$$

As a consumer the most commonly encountered problems concerning *simple interest* are loans and deposits. For example, a finance company may charge 20 percent simple interest for a three-year, $600 loan. What is the total interest on this loan? What is the amount that must be paid to the loan company at the end of three years?

$$I = P \times r \times t$$
$$I = 600 \times 20/100 \times 3$$
$$= \quad \$360 \text{ interest}$$
$$\underline{+600} \text{ principle}$$
$$\$960 \text{ to be repaid}$$

Interest is said to be *compounded* when it is calculated not only on the original principle but also on the earned interest. If $1,000 is deposited

---

Box 15.17   Percent

1. Chrysler Corporation has offered rebates to spur sales. The rebate on a certain model was $800. If the price of the car was $12,000, what percent of the price is the rebate?
2. If the sales tax on the above car purchase is 6 percent, how much tax will be paid?
3. To obtain a loan to purchase a car, the credit union requires a 20 percent down payment in cash. What is the maximum price of a car for which a loan can be obtained if the purchaser has $1,000 in cash?

in a savings account that pays 6 percent interest compounded annually, for example, in the first year the account will earn interest calculated as:

$$I = \$1,000 \times 6/100 \times 1 = \$60$$

If no withdrawals are made, at the beginning of the second year the accumulated amount will be $1,060, which is the new principle. In the second year this new principle will earn interest calculated as:

$$I = \$1,060 \times 6/100 \times 1 = \$63.60$$

Thus, at the beginning of the third year, the accumulated amount will be:

$$\$1,060 + \$63.60 = \$1,123.60$$

When interest is compounded, the earned interest increases each year. Piecewise calculation of the accumulated amount is a very time-consuming procedure and is usually done with computers or tables. Table 15.6 is a portion of such a table. Box 15.18 offers practice with this table. It is important for LD students to receive instruction in both compound and simple interest, because all consumers encounter these concepts. From a pedagogical viewpoint, these applications of mathematics provide evidence that there are real, everyday uses for what is learned in school. These applications to consumer affairs increase LD students' motivation and willingness to study.

Consumer Credit

Credit cards are used by the vast majority of consumers. One of the costs associated with credit cards is the finance charge that is collected when payments for purchases are made later than the allowed payment period. Figure 15.21 is a sample monthly statement issued by a department store for a credit card holder. The periodic (monthly) rate is 1.5 percent. This

---

Box 15.18   Compound Interest

Use Table 15.6 to find the accumulated amount and the interest earned for:

1. $100 at 8% compounded annually for five years.
2. $500 at 10% compounded annually for ten years.
3. $1,000 at 7% compounded annually for eight years.

Table 15.6   Compound Interest

Years	7%	8%	9%	10%	11%
1	1.0700	1.0800	1.0900	1.1000	1.1100
2	1.1449	1.1664	1.1881	1.2100	1.2321
3	1.2250	1.2597	1.2950	1.3310	1.3676
4	1.3108	1.3605	1.4116	1.4641	1.5181
5	1.4026	1.4693	1.5386	1.6105	1.6851
6	1.5007	1.5869	1.6771	1.7716	1.8704
7	1.6058	1.7138	1.8280	1.9487	2.0762
8	1.7182	1.8509	1.9926	2.1436	2.3045
9	1.8385	1.9990	2.1719	2.3579	2.5580
10	1.9672	2.1589	2.3674	2.5937	2.8394

Note. Each entry is the amount (in dollars) to which $1 will accumulate in n periods under compound interest.

rate is used to calculate the charge on $286.51. Where does the $286.51 come from? The back of the statement indicates that, "To get the Average Daily Balance we add up all the daily balances for the billing period and divide the total by the number of days in the billing period." The computer calculates this amount. Box 15.19 asks for verification of some of the entries on the statement. This problem is another example of the everyday

▲ **DETACH HERE AND KEEP LOWER PART FOR YOUR RECORDS** ▲

If you telephone us with a billing inquiry, you do not protect your rights under Federal law. To do so, write to us as explained on the reverse side.

ACCOUNT NUMBER	CLOSING DATE	DUE DATE			
	6-27-87	7-22-87			

STORE & REFERENCE NO.	CHARGES	PAYMENTS & CREDITS	DEPT. NO.	DESCRIPTION	DATE
1125-0090		50.00		PAYMENT - THANK YOU	6-3

PREVIOUS BALANCE	TOTAL CHARGES	TOTAL PAYMENTS AND CREDITS	AVERAGE DAILY BALANCE	FINANCE CHARGE	NEW BALANCE	MINIMUM PAYMENT (INCLUDES PAST DUE)
303.26	.00	50.00	264.20	3.96	257.22	26.00

Your credit card identifies you as a member of our family of customers. It will be welcomed with pleasure at any of our stores.

	PERIODIC RATE	APPLIED TO FOLLOWING PORTION OF AVERAGE DAILY BALANCE	ANNUAL PERCENTAGE RATE
	1.50 %	264.20	18.0 %
	%		%
	%		%

To avoid **FINANCE CHARGE** next month, payment of New Balance must reach us by Due Date shown above.

NOTICE: See reverse side for important information.

FIGURE 15.21   Credit Card Statement.

Box 15.19   Consumer Credit

---

1. Verify the "finance charge" (interest) to be paid on the statement shown in Figure 15.21 by multiplying the "periodic rate" by the "average daily balance."
2. Verify the "new balance" by subtracting the payment and adding the "finance charge."
3. Verify the "minimum payment." The back of the statement indicates that a 10 percent minimum payment is required.

---

application of mathematics that is of interest to LD students. Another involves buying a house. One of the first decisions that must be made before deciding to buy a house is how much to spend. Certain guidelines are sometimes used to help a family decide what price home to buy. Three such rules are:

1. Spend no more than two to two and a half times annual income.
2. Limit housing expenses to one week's pay.
3. The amount of the monthly payment for principal, interest, taxes, and insurance must not exceed one-quarter of take-home pay.

For example, Mary and John Smith earn $30,000 annually. Their take-home pay is $26,000. Can they afford a $60,000 home with a $40,000 mortgage that requires monthly payments of $570, including principal, interest, taxes, and insurance? The solution can be computed as follows:

1. $30,000 × 2.5 = $75,000
2. $30,000 annually is $576.92 weekly ($30,000 ÷ 52 = $576.92)
3. The take-home pay is $26,000 annually, which is $2166.67 monthly times 25%, which is $541.67 (26,000 ÷ 12 = $2166.67; $2166.67 × 25/100 = $541.67)

Therefore, the Smiths qualify under the first and second criteria.

An infinite number of consumer mathematics activities can be developed for LD students. The examples in this section are not intended to be comprehensive, but they have been used *successfully* and *enjoyably* by LD students.

Recovery Procedures for Persistent Problems

In junior and senior high school, many LD students have difficulties in mathematics that have persisted since elementary school. This section provides techniques for examining these problem areas and developing recovery procedures. Each student must be viewed as possessing a relatively unique set of learning characteristics that need to be understood by both the teacher and the student. Evaluation of individual LD students' mathematical strengths and weaknesses involves assessing their performances in reference to a given set of objectives or tasks, and *not with respect to the performance of others*. The teacher attempts to find out: (1) what the student has already learned, (2) how the student typically attacks problems, and (3) how the student likes to learn.

The first focus for inquiry is what the student has already learned in the specific problem area. Four levels of mathematics learning—concepts, relationships, skills, and problem-solving ability—should be addressed. The development of appreciation and favorable attitudes toward mathematics should also be examined. Several questions that should be answered are:

1. What is the student's level of performance in reference to the concepts, relationships, skills, and problem-solving ability in the area of persistent difficulty?
2. What are the concerns expressed by the student?
3. How does the student's evaluation compare with the kind of work that is presently required in school?
4. Does the student have any suggestions for improving performance in the identified area?
5. Does the student primarily need more practice in skill areas?
6. Does the student attempt to check for accuracy to find mistakes in completed work?
7. How does the student's performance compare across mathematics areas?

The second focus for inquiry are the strategies that help the student learn and attack problems. Questions that should be answered are:

1. What are the student's metacognitive patterns in the problem areas?
2. Does the student appear to be motivated for increased competence development?
3. Does the student systematically attack problems?
4. Does the student primarily use trial and error strategies for problem solution?
5. Does the student become easily frustrated when an immediate answer is not apparent?
6. When the student is not immediately successful, is an alternative strategy readily available?

Another teacher, parent, the student, or the results of an achievement test may indicate areas in which an LD student has persistent problems. The student's math teacher can then design learning objectives and finally tasks that are to be performed by the student. Many school districts, textbooks, study groups, and publications (e.g., Flanagan, Mager, & Shanner, 1971) provide detailed lists of learning objectives. The teacher should select the list that is most appropriate for the particular student. An example of a detailed list of curriculum area objectives is shown in Box 15.20. For each enabling objective, tasks are presented. The teacher ascertains whether the student has mastered the objective, is making progress, or needs considerable help before achieving mastery. In addition to utilizing a rating system, the teacher should try to determine why the student performed as she did. This can be partially obtained by designing tasks to identify specific areas of competence. The teacher should attempt

---

Box 15.20   Curriculum Area Objectives

Terminal Objective

Show that you can use subtraction to perform operations with 4-digit numbers.

Enabling Objectives

Using a picture of two sets of objects or a number line, subtract a 1-digit number from a larger 1-digit number.

Subtract a 1-digit numeral from a larger 1-digit numeral vertically and/or horizontally.

Subtract numerals where the minuend is not greater than 18.

Subtract 2-digit numerals without regrouping.

Subtract 2-digit numerals with regrouping.

Subtract a 2- or 3-digit numeral from a 3-digit numeral without regrouping.

Subtract a 2- or 3-digit numeral from a 3-digit numeral with regrouping.

Subtract 4-digit numerals without regrouping.

Find the missing number in an addition or subtraction problem with 2-digit numerals.

Note. Adapted from *Behavioral Objectives: A Guide to Individualizing Objectives*, Vol. 2 by J. C. Flanagan, R. F. Mager, and W. M. Shanner, 1971, Palo Alto, CA: Westinghouse Learning Press.

to determine how the student's level of performance compares with problem-solving abilities in this area.

Informal clinical observation should be utilized throughout the evaluation process. A task is presented to the student while the teacher tries to analyze the student's learning characteristics. Observations are made of the student's performance on all of the components of the evaluation process. The teacher may ask the student questions such as, "How do you know?", "Are you sure?", "Why did that happen?", and "Why are you trying that?" The teacher attempts to get the student to verbalize her own thinking during and after the solution of a problem. Probing questions are necessary to enable the teacher to detail the student's understanding of a particular concept. The teacher should form open-ended questions to permit the student to respond to the task individually. An attempt must be made to avoid biasing responses.

The above data must then be collected and analyzed to develop a sufficiently precise theory of the LD student's mathematical thinking to use in formulating recovery procedures. The appropriate synthesis and analysis of the evaluation information are dependent upon the expertise and experience of the teacher. Because there is little agreement on a taxonomy of general mathematical abilities or disabilities, each LD student has a relatively unique set of evaluation information to be interpreted. The process described above should enable the teacher to answer the two important questions:

1. What processes does this student use to learn mathematics?
2. What processes should be used in teaching this student mathematics?

Summary and Conclusions

Learning disabilities research investigating mathematics instruction is almost nonexistent (Cawley, 1981). Recent publications continue to state that this is one of the most neglected areas of study (Bryan & Bryan, 1986; Gearheart, 1985). The purpose of this chapter was to focus on mathematics instruction at the secondary level and to provide instructional recommendations for teachers of LD students. The instructional recommendations are the result of years of clinical experience of the author and other teachers who have developed and implemented a cognitive developmental approach to mathematics instruction.

Spatial relationships, measurement, patterns, and probability were included because of the lack of attention they receive in conventional programs for LD students. Probability receives the least attention, but activities and instructional techniques were presented that make it interesting and enjoyable for most secondary-level LD students. A large proportion of probability computations involve fractions, and thus, probability is a meaningful application of adding, subtracting, multiplying, and dividing fractions. The question of the tetrahedral model, "What is to be learned?" was the focus of this section.

Algebra, geometry, and the prerequisite mathematics skills necessary for success in these areas were the subject of the second part of this chapter. The minimum admission requirements of all postsecondary academic institutions require high school algebra and geometry. The LD student's typical problems with this material were discussed, and learner activities were provided for integers, factoring, exponents, fractions, set theory, and equations that offer instructional prototypes that facilitate understanding.

All students who are not planning to continue formal education beyond high school enroll in a course equivalent to consumer mathematics. For LD students, the quantity of topics in such courses should be reduced, and a thorough study of those areas selected is recommended. Calculators should be used for computations, and learner activities should use real materials such as newspapers and credit card statements. Examples of such activities were presented.

Finally, the chapter dealt with recovery procedures for persistent problems. Questions were identified that focus on what the student has already learned and which strategies the student uses to learn and attack problems. Clinical observation was described, and its importance was emphasized.

Ausubel (1968) has said meaningful learning occurs when a learner wants to relate new material to the existing repertoire of knowledge. Fitzmaurice-Hayes (1985) emphasizes the importance of mathematics instruction that promotes conceptual understanding in LD students. *Meaningfulness* and *understanding* are the two words that best characterize the instructional approach that has been presented both here and in Chapter 14.

Chapter 16

Teaching Learning Disabled Students to Use Computers

Evelyn B. Block

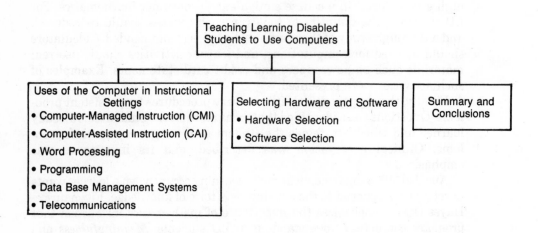

Questions to Consider

1. What are the main educational uses of computers?
2. What concerns affect the quality of hardware and software?
3. What are the advantages of some of the new "intelligent" software packages, especially for LD students?

The need to prepare LD students to function in a computer-literate society is increasingly accepted by both educators and laypersons, for ignorance of computers could render many otherwise well-trained LD students functionally illiterate. Educational applications of computer technology are among the most frequently discussed topics in instructional magazines, educational journals, and professional meetings. State and national conferences on educational computing are being sponsored at a prolific rate. Since more than three-fourths of all occupations deal with sharing of information in some way (Molnar, 1981), it is essential for persons concerned with the education of LD students to articulate a philosophy for the use of new technologies and to establish criteria for the anticipated benefits to students.

This chapter prepares teachers to use computers with LD children by describing the six main uses of computers in education and some guidelines for selecting hardware and software. Due to the paucity of research into the effects of computers on LD students' learning, the reader is urged to evaluate the value of computer instruction in light of forthcoming research and ongoing assessments with children. (See Box 16.1 for a list

---

Box 16.1   Computer Periodicals

Byte, 70 Main Street, Peterborough, NH 03458

The Computing Teacher, Department of Computer Science, University of Oregon, Eugene, OR 97403

Electronic Learning, Scholastic, Inc., 902 Sylvan Avenue, Englewood Cliffs, NJ 07632

Infoworld, 530 Lytton Avenue, Palo Alto, CA 94301

Journal of Computer-Based Instruction, ADCIS, 409 Miller Hall, Western Washington University, Bellingham, VA 98225

Journal of Learning Disabilities, PRO-ED, 5341 Industrial Oaks Blvd., Austin, Texas 78735–8898

Journal of Special Education Technology, Exceptional Child Center, Utah State University, UMC68, Logan, VT 84322

Learning Disabilities Quarterly, Council for Learning Disabilities, P.O. Box 40303, Overland Park, KS 66204

Microcomputers in Education, QUEUE, 5 Chapel Hill Drive, Fairfield, CT 06432

The National LOGO Exchange, P.O. Box 5341, Charlottesville, VA

Personal Computing, P.O. Box 1408, Riverton, NJ 08077

Teaching, Learning, Computing, Seldin Publishing, Inc., 1061 South Melrose, Suite D, Placentia, CA 92670

Young Peoples' LOGO Association, P.O. Box 855067, Richardson, TX 75085

of periodicals that publish such research.) Furthermore, the reader is urged to apply the interactive frameworks for teaching described in the preceding chapters. For, as those chapters point out, the benefit of any instructional material will not be realized fully until the students' characteristics, the criterial task, and the learning activities are taken into account.

Uses of the Computer in Instructional Settings

Six major uses of computers that are frequently employed with LD students will be addressed: computer-managed instruction, computer-assisted instruction, word processing, programming, data base management systems, and telecommunications.

Computer-Managed Instruction

School districts have used the data processing capabilities of computers for years for administrative purposes. Large computer-managed instruction (CMI) systems can maintain records on up to ten thousand students. Good CMI offers diagnosis, prescription, and data collection and reporting.

With the advent of the competency based education movement and the call for a return to basics, the management of instruction has become a routine part of teachers' responsibility. CMI systems help teachers organize and manage teaching and record keeping for classes. In addition to testing and prescribing, new CMI programs are linked to tutorial programs in which students' test results are used by the computer as the basis for computerized lessons.

Some CMI programs are strictly for record keeping. They can store all relevant information about students and allow for its constant updating. CMI programs are being used to prepare report cards, Title I evaluations, IEPs, and other periodic reports. The danger, however, is that CMI will be used even when the data base for prescription is obsolete or with children for whom it was not intended. For schools with limited resources, a basic question is whether this should be a priority use of the computer. Box 16.2 highlights issues pertaining to evaluation of CMI programs.

Although CMI is still in its infancy, computers are already successfully used in the assessment of special needs students (Hasselbring & Crossland, 1982). While the programs currently in use are only precursors to the more elaborate and powerful expert systems under development, it is conceivable that within a decade we will have expert systems that contain much of the knowledge and skill of our nation's foremost educators. A recent United States Department of Education conference on

---

Box 16.2   Evaluating CMI Programs

Is the program sensitive to the learning styles of different children?

Does the program reflect a sound understanding and clear conception of the curriculum?

Does the program have a research base? How recent is it?

Does the program reflect excellent test construction?

Are the directions clear and concise?

Is the program more than generally diagnostic?

Are parallel tests available for retakes?

Do the tests demand more than simple recall of information?

Is the record keeping accurate for both individuals and groups?

Does the program print hard copies of progress for both individuals and groups?

---

the future of computers in education resulted in the recommendation that more time and effort be spent on determining how computers can be used in the assessment and diagnosis of student learning problems (Hasselbring, 1984). One potential danger, however, is that such a system might reemphasize the characteristics of the learner as the central concern in the definition and treatment of disability rather than more instructionally relevant concerns such as learners' activities, the criterial tasks, and the nature of the materials (see Chapter 1).

Computer-Assisted Instruction

Computer-assisted instruction, or CAI, refers to software packages that attempt to teach new academic skills or review existing skills. The available packages cover the spectrum of the curriculum, including mathematics, reading, writing, science, social studies, art, music, and vocational education. What sets CAI software apart from applications software, such as word processing packages, is that CAI instructs the user in more than just using the package. A CAI program is designed to teach a skill or provide practice on skills. The format of the programs, like curriculum materials, varies in quality. Some of the packages present material in an interesting, sound educational format, while others appear to be no more than a poorly reproduced workbook page. Although animation is used with many programs and makes the software appealing, it may not render it pedagogically sound. In fact, for some LD students the pace of the activity, especially with animation, can be quite overwhelming. Other animation, however, may be clear, concise, and highly motivational. Teachers need to evaluate CAI materials with the same care that they would a text, film, or workbook.

Teachers can use CAI programs to review skills already taught. For example, several excellent programs review arithmetic facts. Students can review multiplication tables in an interesting and varied format for as long as needed. The computer will not get bored, and, if the program is good, neither will the student. Many of these programs are not specifically designed for LD students but prove effective when used by them. Drill and practice programs come in two formats: workbook and game. Computerizing the workbook adds feedback and, potentially, the ability to adapt to individual needs, although many of these programs are of poor quality. Students generally prefer the game formats of drill and practice. Sometimes, however, the feedback can actually interfere with learning the targeted skill. Thus, although many game programs are effective teaching tools, a teacher must always carefully monitor their use.

Problem-solving games are potentially a much more powerful type of CAI. LD students can benefit from programs that encourage logical thinking, problem solving, and strategy development. Because problem-solving games teach a process or strategy rather than specific content, they can be used in a variety of subject areas. Simulations, for example, require the student to make decisions that affect the outcome. Existing programs allow a student to fly an airplane, drive a car, or run a business; they are ideal for vocational training. The student is allocated a variety of resources (money, tools, etc), and how they are used determines the success or failure of the mission. The student is given several different options and learns their consequences in a safe environment. Simulations thus allow LD students to have experiences and make decisions that they would not normally encounter in a classroom.

Recent studies have shown that CAI works effectively as a *supplement* to instruction by teachers (Torgesen, 1984). Computers can offer the extensive practice that LD students often require to master skills in areas such as reading and math (Lesgold & Reif, 1983; Torgesen & Young, 1983). CAI is by far the easiest use of the computer for both students and teachers. It is an excellent way to begin work with computers, for it requires no technical knowledge and gives affirmative feedback. Our experience indicates that adults as well as children feel more positive toward the computer after using CAI. LD students appear to be highly motivated by a masterable, computer-based instructional program (Cartwright & Dervensky, 1976). Teachers with no computer experience are often willing to bring a computer into the classroom if several good CAI programs are provided. For many, this is the first—and very important—step.

Success using the computer opens endless possibilities for classroom applications. Before long, teachers discover that, rather than replacing them in the classroom, the computer can teach, review, and drill certain topics with infinite patience and perseverance, freeing the teacher to function even more effectively.

The ultimate effectiveness of CAI in helping LD students will depend a great deal on the quality of teacher training in computer usage, the regular availability of computers, and further developments in the field. One must keep in mind, however, that computers are uniquely suited to delivering large amounts of closely monitored and individualized practice in basic skills in formats that will maintain interest and motivation.

Word Processing

Computers can also make reading and writing easier and more rewarding (Collins, 1984) through the word processing equipment that is generally available as a software package. Packages exist for every type of hardware; the text is stored on a disk and then transferred to a computer that is attached to a compatible printer, where it is quickly made into a hard (i.e., paper) copy. Often several computers will share a printer.

Word processing programs are now being successfully used by students as early as first grade. These programs, such as Bank Street Writer, Paper Clip, and Writing Assistant, are user friendly (i.e., they require no technical knowledge) and can perform various activities: correcting spelling or grammar, revising or inserting sentences, moving paragraphs, and printing a draft or final copy of the work with just a few commands. Students are more inclined to correct their written work when revision means more than just neatly copying a paper or fixing misspelled words and misplaced commas. With such a word package, the teacher can both edit and reproduce student-generated stories and compositions in a fraction of the time.

Psychologists studying the development of writing skills are starting to work with those who design computer writing environments, so we may expect exciting developments in this area within the next several years (Pea, 1984; Pea & Kurland, 1984). Box 16.3 offers suggestions for using existing word processing programs to teach writing.

Word processing programs also provide students with a good opportunity to learn how computers work: The user gives the computer information, in this case a story, report, or letter; the computer stores and manipulates that information on command; and the information is then called back in "processed" form by the user. The user is required, as with any computer program, to be precise and logical. The problem of poor

---

Box 16.3   Uses for Word Processing Programs in Teaching Writing

The following suggestions include those developed at Bank Street College, which began using word processing with students in 1979.

1. Give the students a time limit for their writing, such as:
   a. writing until the screen is full
   b. writing for fifteen minutes
   c. writing until there is nothing left to say
2. Type several sentences out of order. Have the students rearrange them sequentially.
3. Give the students the beginning and ending of a story and ask them to supply the middle.
4. Have the student retell a folk tale in an original style.
5. Develop a classroom newspaper. Have different journalists contribute various articles and have the students edit the paper.
6. Type a passage with exposition or action words in one verb tense. Have the student change the tense of the passage.
7. Type a long passage and merge the paragraphs into one. Have the students break the passage into appropriate paragraphs.
8. Type a passage with a few words capitalized. Have the students replace each capitalized word with a lower-case synonym.
9. Type the instructions and skeleton of a business letter. Have the students use this form letter to request information about their projects.
10. Have students send letters developed on their word processing program to electronic "pen pals" in different parts of the country.
11. Type a passage with repetitious words and sentences. Have the students edit the writing.
12. Team pairs of students to work on a project and edit one another's work.

---

typing skills is rapidly being ameliorated by software packages (such as Kids on Keys, MasterType, and Typing Tutor) designed to teach touch typing in a pleasurable format.

Furthermore, when the physical act of writing is difficult, the word processor can facilitate the production of text. Many LD students in high school and college are also using portable word processing equipment for daily note taking. While word processing is attractive for its ease of correction and modification, there is also a likely cognitive efficiency (less demand on processing capacity) when the individual does not have to think at a "meta level," that is, continuously perceiving printed texts in their unique orthographic forms and then having to transpose their responses into a cursive form (Weisgerber & Blake, 1984). Furthermore, software manufacturers are experimenting with alternatives to the "QWERTY" keyboard as well as with direct speech to print processes. Students will soon be able to choose among handwriting, typing, and speaking as methods of transferring their ideas to print.

Students must perceive a continuous and immediate sense of purpose for all writing. Accordingly, just as computer programming transforms a learner's problem-solving strategies, word processing transforms how students view the creation of text. How liberating it is to experiment with ideas on a screen, move them around, try different words and phrases, and not stop until one is totally satisfied with the product!

LD students have a tendency to "downslide," that is, to focus on lower level task components such as capitalization or spelling when they write. Recently developed computer interactive writing and reading activities enable students to initiate and to control their writing as they plan, compose, and revise text. One example is, the Story Maker (Collins, 1984; Rubin, 1980, 1982), which helps children concentrate on the structure and content rather than the mechanical aspects of narratives (Liebling, 1984).

Programming

The computer can be most effectively exploited through programming. Students and teachers, however, need to feel comfortable using the computer before venturing into this area, for it represents totally new learning for all. Those who have used packaged software or word processing equipment are most likely to feel comfortable with the machine and its workings and thus want to know how to "make the computer do what you want it to do," as a three year old said at the Callier Center for Communication Disorders in Dallas.

Software games and animation often motivate middle and high school students to invent games of their own. Teachers can actually be intimidated by the enthusiasm and speed of learning exhibited by such students. My experience teaching both adults and children indicates that young people often learn to program more quickly than adults. For this reason, many school systems postpone teaching programming until their teachers have been sufficiently trained.

Programming has no ceiling; there is always more to learn. Once students have learned basic programming skills, they are free to explore many other "languages." Some of the most frequently taught languages,

from preschool through college, include LOGO, PILOT, BASIC, FOR-
TRAN, COBOL, and ASSEMBLER.

The development of programming expertise can lead to a chain of
cognitive consequences for students. Skilled programmers, for example,
use strategic planning and "debugging" skills extensively. While it is
possible to generalize these skills to noncomputer learning environments
(Linn, 1983), the research in this area is still inconclusive (Dalbey &
Linn, 1985). Because "top-down" processing seems to relate to achievement (Bradley, 1985), LD students may benefit from training that helps
them develop and utilize strategies in computer environments. Programming is generally highly motivating to students and allows teachers and
students to observe and discuss how they think about problems. This
knowledge of how the LD student processes information may help the
teacher plan learning activities for that student.

A recent study by Coombs, Gibson, and Alty (1982) related the level
of success in a first programming course with learning style. It was found
that learners were more successful when they understood the logical
relations between structures in the programming language. This indicates that the student's learning style may significantly determine the
amount of benefit derived from programming instruction. Teachers need
to be cognizant of the student's learning style and provide alternative
modes of instruction geared to individual needs. Clearly, much more research is needed before we understand the interactions between the demands of the programming task, the individual learning style of the
student, and the role of the teacher. The Educational Technology Center,
a consortium headed by the Harvard Graduate School of Education, is
one of several groups currently examining more effective ways of providing instruction in programming skills.

Using LOGO

It is the author's opinion that LOGO is the computer language to teach
first, for it invites students and teachers alike to take initiative in a world
that provides unique possibilities for exploration and discovery, a world
of instructional feedback that all learners can make their own. Adults
can use LOGO effectively, although most school curricula introduce children to LOGO in the early grades and teach additional programming
languages to middle and high school students. Developed by Papert (1980)
and the staff of the Artificial Intelligence Laboratory at the Massachusetts
Institute of Technology in Cambridge, LOGO encourages learning by
discovery, which is the natural way a child finds out about the world.
Papert claims the skills a child develops using LOGO are life skills:
problem solving, logical sequencing, decision making, self-direction, planning, and exploration.

Two fundamental principles of problem solving include subdividing the problem into smaller parts and relating the problem to existing knowledge. LD children who write LOGO procedures are constantly involved in these fundamental aspects of problem solving. Experience in teaching LOGO to students aged three through adult has led proponents to claim several other positive results, including:

1. the development of logical thinking and a sense of command. Students learn to divide a problem into a series of steps. Only when they proceed logically will the computer respond to their commands. Corrective messages from the computer assist their thinking and help them proceed (Solomon, 1982).
2. the understanding of powerful ideas (Papert, 1980).
3. the lowering of frustration levels due to the nonjudgmental quality of the language (Maddux, 1984).
4. improved self-image and sense of control and power (Hagen, 1984).
5. a growth in analytic thinking (Papert, 1980).
6. the construction of new knowledge based on existing knowledge (Papert, 1980).
7. breaking the LD student's cyclical view of school as a failure environment (Torgesen, 1984).
8. assisting children in monitoring their own errors through self-corrective features (Papert, 1980).
9. teaching a student that impulsive acts can result in failure and illustrating the importance of planning (Maddux, 1984).
10. giving LD students who are deficient in math a chance to use numbers and mathematics in an interesting setting that is novel and free from past associations (Maddux, 1984).

While the claims for LOGO's potential are noteworthy, there is a great need for their empirical substantiation, especially regarding LD students. LOGO can be most effective when used by trained teachers using well-developed curriculum materials (for a list of resources, see Box 16.5). Some of the activities in which LOGO can be used are exploring geometric concepts from a simple square to complex recursive designs, inventing games, writing poems and stories, creating animation, and exploring the world of mathematical thinking (angles, degree, etc.).

Notwithstanding the possible value of LOGO, a caveat is necessary. Because programming is a relatively new discipline, it has not been studied in depth. Also, because it is a complex skill, it is difficult to analyze and understand. Additional research is necessary to determine exactly what effects programming has on the student, how students actually behave in programming environments, what they find difficult about programming, which models of programming they utilize, and how they resolve some of the formal demands of programming. These studies will need to evaluate large populations over long periods of time to answer these questions definitively.

Data Base Management Systems

Data Base management systems are programs that allow users to create large files of information on any topic. Unlike typical note cards, the information, once it has been entered into the computer, can be sorted, edited, reorganized, updated, summarized, or printed. These systems make large amounts of information available for reports, graphs, and other purposes. Students can search for particular data and manipulate it according to their needs. Middle and high school students can use such data bases in social studies, science, and language arts classes.

Telecommunications

By attaching modems (devices used to send information to and from a computer using telephone lines) to computers, one can receive and send information on a variety of topics, including news, stock market reports,

---

Box 16.4   On-Line Networks and Data Bases for LD Students

Assistive Device Database System (ADDS), American International Data Search, Inc., 2326 Fair Oaks Boulevard, Suite C, Sacramento, CA 95825 (916) 925-4554

DEAFNET, Deaf Communications Institute, Deaf Community Center, Farmington, MA 91701 (617) 875-3617

Educational Research Information Center (ERIC), The Council for Exceptional Children, 1920 Association Drive, Reston, VA 22091 (703) 620-3660

Handicapped Education Exchange (HEX), 11523 Charleton Drive, Silver Spring, MD 20902 (301) 681-7372

Microcomputer Education Applications Network (MEAN), 256 North Washington Street, Falls Church, VA 22046-4544 (703) 536-2310

Special Education Computer Technology On Line Resources (SECTOR), Utah State University, Logan, UT 84322 (801) 750-3243

SpecialNet, National Association of State Directors of Special Education, 1201 Sixteenth Street NW, Suite 610, Washington, D. C. 20036 (201) 296-1800

and entertainment. (See Box 16.4 for a list of networks relevant to LD students.) Many commercial information sources provide electronic mail systems (computer-to-computer messages via telephone lines) that enable communication anywhere in the world. Nonprofit educational systems are also used, for example, by students living on Indian reservations to communicate with students in the city. High schoolers studying the stock market retrieve hourly quotes. LD students in different parts of the country communicate with each other, sending and receiving electronic mail. Teachers at home can connect to the computer at work, designing and planning for their classes. Parents in some cities can call the school computer and gather information about their child's attendance, grades, and activities. Because telecommunications will likely increase in importance; it is important to help students become familiar with its applications and opportunities.

Selecting Hardware and Software

One of the most important concerns facing administrators and teachers interested in initiating computer instruction for LD students is the selection of appropriate materials. The machines and all of their mechanical additions are referred to as *hardware*. The programs used to run those machines constitute *software*. Software is usually developed by experts and is sold on discs or tapes. The following discussion presents guidelines and considerations for purchasing both.

Hardware Selection

With the large number of brands of computers presently on the market and over 1,800 firms handling software, educators can easily become overwhelmed by the choices. Market changes, instant obsolescence, and machine incompatibility all contribute to the general confusion. Today's marketplace leader could easily be obsolete within five years. Consequently, hardware purchases should be based on immediate needs with an eye toward the future.

Some difficult questions need to be addressed. How will the hardware be utilized and by whom? A large system that both manages a school district's financial and internal affairs and serves students' learning needs will necessarily be more expensive and extensive than a system that is used only by students. Will there by networking? That is, does the system need to "talk to" other machines? Once these questions are answered, consumers must consider the ease of having the system repaired. Repair needs to be both rapid and convenient, preferably on site.

One needs to consider the types and cost of additional equipment—such as a printer, communication links, additional disk drives, "joy sticks," or a "mouse"—that are necessary. Most classrooms will require a printer, "joy sticks" or "track balls," and the option of additional disk drives. The system should be expandable, but there is a tendency to overbuy. Decisions about peripherals also appear more complex than they actually are. If a printer, for example, provides graphic capabilities but is being used exclusively for second-grade word processing, it is likely that one has paid more for that printer than was necessary.

It is safest to purchase from a well-known company that has a local office with a staff trained to understand educational needs. Some schools have elected to use different computers at different levels, adding sophistication as the students' needs grow. An advantage to this procedure is that students become familiar with a variety of machines as they proceed through the grades. A possible disadvantage is that the cost of purchasing and maintaining a variety of machines could be higher. Many of the major computer corporations are offering incentives to schools, including a free computer with a minimal purchase, free training for the staff, free peripherals, and contracts for on-site servicing. Shop around for a good deal.

Additionally, purchasers should find out how others in similar positions are using their computers. What recommendations can they make? Is the school willing to give up quality to be able to purchase more machines? Is a luxury model required or will a solid, dependable version do the job? While these choices seem overwhelming, the fact remains that many of the available computers are likely to meet most needs, and the final choice becomes one of personal taste.

Planning for effective hardware selection requires ongoing information gathering and flexible adaptation to new and constantly changing situations. While the general professional literature is replete with testimonials lauding microcomputer applications for LD students, at this time it appears reasonable to conclude that the ultimate success or demise of microcomputer education is dependent upon the degree to which the technology is used by those appropriately closest to its intended applications (Semmel, Cosden, Semmel, & Keleman, 1984). If microcomputer applications are to fulfill their potential for LD students, all aspects of the tetahedral model must be taken into account in planning instructional programs. Furthermore, teachers must be computer literate and prepare to integrate the hardware and software into their educational programs.

Software Selection

Software selection is intertwined with hardware selection, since educational software is often hardware dependent. Software is available for every curriculum user, from preschooler through adult. Educators' reviews of software found in most major computing magazines are often good sources for evaluation. Additionally, almost every major journal has

---

Box 16.5   Educational Software Reviews and Exchanges

The Apple Journal of Courseware Review, P.O. Box 28426, San Jose, CA 95159

Educator's Handbook and Software Directory, Vital Information Inc., 350 Union Station, Kansas City, MO 64108

Educational Products Information Exchange (EPIE), EPIE Institute, 1018 Keith Ave., Berkeley, CA 94708

Microcomputer Courseware for the Classroom: Selecting, Organizing and Using Instructional Software, Addison-Wesley, 1982

Microcomputer Resource Center, Teachers College, Columbia University, P.O. Box 18, New York, NY 10027

Microform Review, Inc., 520 Riverside Avenue, Westport, CT 06880

MicroSIFT, Northwest Regional Educational Laboratory, 300 SW Sixth Street, Portland, OR 97204

Reference Manual for Instructional Use of Microcomputers, Jem Research, Discovery Park, University of Victoria, P.O. Box 1700, Victoria, BC V8W 2Y2

School Microware Reviews, Evaluations of Educational Software, Dresden Associates, P.O. Box 246, Dresden, ME 04342

Sourceware Report Card, 150 West Carob Street, Comptom, CA 90220

---

devoted at least one issue to a review of available software for its targeted population. All quality software stores will permit the previewing of a software package, and many public and university libraries carry a large selection of educational software. (See Box 16.5 for a list of software reviews and exchanges.)

Good software characteristically allows a student to participate in a lesson without fear of failure by providing hints, cues, and alternative paths to minimize frustration and assure success. Immediate feedback that is both nonjudgmental and supportive often encourages LD students to assume a less passive stance with respect to learning (Torgesen, 1984). Good software also flexibly adjusts to the way an individual best learns. LD students, for example, should be able to slow the rate of text presentations. The ability of a program to branch to a learner's ability level is another indication of its flexibility. The rationale for branching is that if the student repeatedly gives an incorrect reponse, the program will adjust the level of instruction. Only when the student has mastered the content will the program move on to a more difficult level. In addition, a well-designed program will motivate students to try more difficult problems without fear of failure. Motivated learners will repeat a task over and over again. Cognitive curiosity can be enhanced by programs that allow users to perceive that they have an incomplete understanding of the structure or pattern of the program by motivating them to acquire more information to complete the task.

Good software also allows the teacher to modify the program to create individualized lessons without requiring programming knowledge. For the LD student, the teacher could design a quiz, present additional material for drill and practice, or create individualized vocabulary or spelling lists. In this way, students with a wide range of abilities can share the same program, drawing from it according to their individual needs. The dynamic quality of some software is likewise beneficial to the LD student. Simulations enable students to view driving a car, for example, from a more realistic perspective than a static text or chalkboard would permit. Research indicates that successful learning is a function of active strategic engagement with the material in order to make sense of it in terms of what is already known (Sheingold, Hawkins, & Kurland, 1983). Quality software makes explicit some of these important learning strategies.

In addition to providing instruction, software can perform tasks that relate to instructional planning, such as keeping records of individual students' strengths and weaknesses, building profiles for diagnostic or evaluative purposes, and storing and updating IEPs.

Given the diversity of software materials and the unevenness of their quality, it is obvious that carefully delineated evaluation procedures are needed. Box 16.6 provides some of these guidelines.

Much more interesting and cognitively demanding software is still needed for schools to capitalize on the computer learning environments (Linn & Fisher, 1983). In the interim, teachers must evaluate and adapt the available material to the needs of their students. Commercially available programs designed for general populations can easily be adapted and used effectively with LD students. Special education teachers should also be involved with other teachers in the selection of software. While little software directly addresses cognitive processes, existing programs can be adapted to build these skills.

Summary and Conclusions

Many people believe that the impact of computer technology on modern society will parallel the effect of the invention of printing in the fifteenth century. LD students must take part in such a technological revolution

Box 16.6   Guide to Software Review

Product Title: _____   Computer: _____
Author/Publisher: _____
Publishing/Copyright Date: __   Cost: _____
Purpose or Objective: _____

Input Mode: Output Mode:
_____ Cassette   _____ Color Monitor
_____ Diskette   _____ B/W Monitor
_____ Cartridge   _____ Printer
_____ Other   _____ Plotter
                                    _____ Trackball
                                    _____ Joy Stick
                                    _____ Other

Type of Program: (check all that apply)
   A. Administrative Aid ____   F. Simulation ____
   B. Drill and Practice ____   G. Testing ____
   C. Educational Game ____   H. Tutorial ____
   D. Entertainment ____   I. Word Processing ____
   E. Problem Solving ____   J. Other ____
                                             (Describe: ____)

Format of Instruction:
   Does the format fit the instructional goal?
   ____ Drill and Practice   ____ Tutorial
   ____ Informational   ____ Game
   ____ Other

Target Population: (check appropriate description)

   A. Students ____ Grade Level ____ Ability Level ____
   B. Teachers ____
   C. Administrators ____
   D. Other ____   (Describe: _____)

Appropriateness:
   A. Are the stated objectives of the course   Yes __ No __
      being met by this product?
   B. Can materials be used with other than   Yes __ No __
      the stated population?
   C. Can materials be used to accomplish   Yes __ No __
      other than the stated goals?

(continued)

Box 16.6 *(continued)*

D. Is the product adaptable to various   Yes __ No __
   teachers or situations?
E. Are alternative learning opportunities Yes __ No __
   suggested/provided for?
F. Is there a definite need for this particular Yes __ No __
   product in teaching the course?

Content:
   Does the content focus on a specific objective? (yes / no)
   Is the content accurate? (yes / no)
   Is it appropriate for the learner's age and ability? Are reading
      selections interesting for the student? (yes / no)
   Is the content free of racial, ethnic, sexual, and religious bias?
      (yes / no)
   Is the content sufficient in quantity to cover the topic as presented
      in the syllabus adequately? (yes / no)
   Is the content sufficient in quality to cover the topic as presented
      in the syllabus adequately? (yes / no)
   Does the instructional material provide adequate quantity and
      quality of additional content to provide for remedial instruction?
      (yes / no)
   Does the instructional material provide adequate quantity and
      quality of additional content to provide for enrichment exercises
      for individuals? (yes / no)

Content Bank:
   Is there a bank of items? (yes / no)
   Can the teacher add to the bank of items? (yes / no)

Organizational and Technical Components: (rate each item)
A. Instructions are clear,   Exc. Good Fair Poor
   concise, understandable.   __   __   __   __
B. Content is accurate.   __   __   __   __
C. Presentation of matrial is
   consistent with accepted
   practices.   __   __   __   __
D. Reading level is appropriate
   for intended users.   __   __   __   __
E. Program motivates learner.   __   __   __   __
F. Program employs positive
   feedback and reinforcement.   __   __   __   __
G. Program handles learner
   input errors effectively.   __   __   __   __

(continued)

Box 16.6 *(continued)*

	Exc.	Good	Fair	Poor
H. Program helps student develop correct response.	___	___	___	___

I. Program employs the following techniques: (rate each that applies; leave others blank)

	Exc.	Good	Fair	Poor
1. Graphics	___	___	___	___
2. Color	___	___	___	___
3. Sound/Music	___	___	___	___
4. Voice	___	___	___	___
5. Time Display	___	___	___	___
6. Score Display	___	___	___	___
7. Personalized Responses	___	___	___	___

Screen Format:

Are print size and space between lines acceptable? (yes / no)

Are special text features (such as flashing words, underlining, or inverse printing) used to attract attention? (yes / no)

Do graphics enhance the program content? (yes / no)

Rate of Presentation:

Can the learner adjust the reading rate? (yes / no)

Can the learner exit and reenter the program at various points? (yes / no)

Learner Interaction with the Program:

Is required input easy to enter? (yes / no)

Is positive feedback present and appropriate? (yes / no)

Is negative feedback present and appropriate? (yes / no)

Documentation:

Is a teacher's manual available? (yes / no)

Are directions clear and complete? (yes / no)

Is the lesson content shown in detail? (vocabulary lists, reading selections, etc.) (yes / no)

Are needed forms included? (yes / no)

Has the program been field tested? (yes / no)

Record Keeping:

Can records be kept for an ample number of students? (yes / no)

Are responses and progress reported in a usable form? (yes / no)

Can records be printed on paper? (yes / no)

Time:

Does the time required for the lesson fit the schedule? (yes / no)

Instructional Support:

Is the program easy for the teacher to use? (yes / no)

Note. Adapted from a similar guide distributed for public use by the Region 11 School District, Fort Worth, Texas.

if they are to be prepared to compete in the work place. Computers are becoming increasingly important in nearly all major businesses and industries. Researchers have demonstrated that computers can work in the schools as untiring drill masters, infinitely patient tutors, demanding testers, and astute diagnosticians of educational problems (Kulik, Kulik, & Bangert-Drowns, 1985). Moreover, the development of quick, inexpensive microcomputers has lowered costs considerably and made a computer revolution in education a real possibility. The question that remains unanswered, however, is whether such a revolution will ultimately benefit students' learning. This is not yet directly answerable by comparing the performances of students who have learned on the computer and students who have learned without computer assistance, for as Clark (1985) argues, apparent effects of the computer may be novelty effects or even selection effects produced by journal editors who are unwilling to publish nonsignificant or negative findings. The question of whether we should make a large-scale commitment to use computers for their presumed benefit to LD students must be answered by individual school districts as they make decisions regarding hardware and software and determine when and how computers will be used in the instruction of LD students. Of course, individualizing such instruction will complicate the process of assessing the usefulness of the computer across its different dimensions, but it will also likely most positively affect the students' learning.

CAI is a more "conversational" model of instruction. The computer interacts with the learners in intelligent ways, enabling them to build the cognitive capacities of reasoning and understanding. The most recent cognitively oriented work on CAI has been called I-CAI (Intelligent CAI) because it uses techiques of artificial intelligence and cognitive science to solve instructional problems. The goal is to have the computer build and continuously update a model of the students' activities vis-à-vis the criterion tasks. That model is then used to determine what is presented to the student next. The program attempts to detect errors in thinking and to analyze the nature of those errors. It then provides appropriate information to help the student correct the errors. I-CAI, while still highly experimental, will adapt on line to different learning styles and performance levels, making it ideal for use with LD students. Similar exciting innovations in software are emerging in word processing, data base management, and telecommunications. There is still much more work to be done in curriculum design for LD students. Research is needed to determine what is being learned from computer usage, what LD students seem to find especially easy or taxing, what skills and other characteristics are mandatory, and which conditions best assure that the LD student selects appropriate strategies and "debugging" activities. Students and teachers must work together to create more effective learning environments for the future.

Chapter 17

Independent Study Skills

D. Kim Reid
Wayne P. Hresko

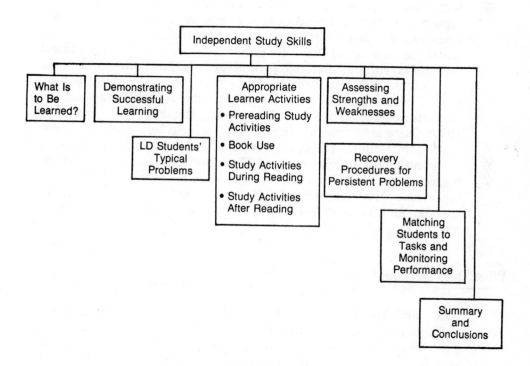

Questions to Consider

1. What skills are required for independent studying?
2. Which study behaviors must students engage in before, during, and after reading?
3. Why should even quite demanding study skills be taught to LD students? Under what circumstances should difficult tasks be avoided?

One of the most difficult tasks facing teachers is helping their LD students develop competent, independent study skills. Most LD students have never been taught how to study. Left to their own devices, proficient readers usually figure out how to study; LD students seldom do. As they advance through the grades, their dependence on teacher direction becomes increasingly obvious. Responsive teachers provide short, carefully controlled assignments. The students in turn are reinforced in their perception that they are dependent learners and the cycle of dependency leads to continued verification of the self-fulfilling prophecy. By high school the cumulative deficit (in comparison to their normally achieving peers) is substantial, and high percentages of LD and other underachieving students drop out of school. The problem is so severe in New York State, for example, that as many as 25 percent of the sixth-grade suburban students failed to meet *minimal* competency standards (New York Times, 1980). There is no evidence to suggest that New York State is unique in this regard: Griffiths (1980) reported that the latest National Assessment of Educational Progress survey (1979–80) showed that reading comprehension among seventeen year olds had declined since the 1970–71 testing period. Although most all of these students receive instruction in "reading for meaning," few are explicitly taught "reading for remembering" skills.

What Is to Be Learned?

Baker and Brown (1984), in their review of research on metacognitive skills and reading, argue that reading for remembering includes all the skills necessary to read for meaning: comprehension failures seriously impede efforts to study. But to study, the reader must ensure that the text is not only comprehensible but also "rememberable." Initial efforts to understand must be followed by additional attempts at selecting and retaining the important information. Studying requires a split mental focus: Students must both concentrate on the material itself to make certain that it is understood and at the same time ensure that they are performing the mental operations necessary to learn (Locke, 1975, cited in Baker and Brown, 1984). Study monitoring requires: (1) the appropriate allocation of time; (2) the ability to concentrate on the main ideas; (3) the decision to use some deliberate tactic to aid learning; and (4) the ability to determine concurrently that the tactic is indeed working.

Demonstrating Successful Learning

The ultimate criterion for studying is grade-appropriate achievement in academic domains. LD students, however, will need significant amounts of guided instruction in both cognitive and metacognitive aspects of studying to achieve that goal. Addressing the requirements of studying in three phases—before, during, and after reading—the instructional task becomes somewhat less complex because it enables us to specify manageable instructional units.

Prestudying is a planning stage that includes making decisions about the allocation of time and resources and selecting a technique for systematically dealing with the material. Since one way of determining what LD students need to learn is to find out what experts do in the same situation, Anderson's (1978) survey of skilled readers' studying performances is instructive. Skilled readers ask themselves three implicit questions: First, "What do I already know about this topic?" Second, "How interested am I?" Third, "How much effort and time is this going to take?"

What information do the skilled readers use to answer these questions? First, they focus on the nonsentence parts of the text that are rich in information (e.g., titles, headings, charts, and graphs). Second, they look to introductory and summary sentences, paragraphs, and subsections. Third, they read longer sections of text *only* when deemed necessary. By analyzing the skilled readers' responses it becomes clear that their knowledge of the structural components of the text guided their surveying.

Particularly important to LD teachers is Anderson's finding that the process was likely to break down if, during surveying, the students found that their interest in the text was low or the difficulty level too high. Studying was successful only if the student was at least partially informed about the content, was interested, and did not perceive that the work would take an inordinate amount of time to complete.

If a student is able to gather enough information during prestudying, the during study phase may never be entered. If and when they do enter this phase, skilled readers become actively engaged in gathering information. Their manner of reading changes depending on the nature of the text. They spend more time, for example, on sections that are needed to answer their implicit questions (Reynolds, Standiford, & Anderson, 1978). Further, they spend more time on paragraphs containing contradictions in supporting detail, which they usually attempt to resolve—sometimes with serious misinterpretation as a result. What most strongly influences the way skilled readers study, however, is their knowledge of the criterial task, that is, whether they have been asked to respond to adjunct questions, to construct their own questions, to answer the questions of other students, to take notes, to underline, to outline, or to paraphrase. They continuously self-monitor, asking themselves such questions as whether the text is making sense and whether they have enough information to answer the questions.

Some researchers have begun studying the "automatic monitoring mechanism," or AAM (Anderson, 1978). The AAM is thought to be a subawareness mechanism that intrudes upon the reading process when the student becomes confused. The research is only in its infancy, but has already yielded important implications for teaching students to study. It appears beneficial, for example, to teach students to recognize when their process of reading has changed—slowed down or become hesitating—because that signals confusion in comprehending. More attention must then be given to that section of the text by rereading, looking up unknown words, rereading prior sections, and so forth.

Poststudying is characterized by activities that further enhance comprehension—note taking, outlining, rehearsal, repetition, elaboration, question generating, writing, mapping, and other such techniques. One of the most important learning problems associated with this phase is determining the response demands and matching them with an appropriate response.

LD Students' Typical Problems

The first, and certainly one of the most significant, problems LD students have with study skills is their low level of reading functioning. These are typically the lowest scoring of the underachieving students, with average achievement at the third-grade reading level in seventh grade that plateaus at the fifth-grade level in high school (Deshler, Lowry, & Alley, 1979). Eighty-five percent of these students demonstrate retardation in the acquisition of test-taking and study skills (Alley, Deshler, & Warner, 1979). Specific problems have been documented with respect to note taking, checking for writing errors, test taking, scanning behaviors, listening comprehension, and to creating and applying cognitive strategies (Carlson & Alley, 1981; Schumaker, Sheldon-Wildgen, & Sherman, 1980).

Appropriate Learner Activities

Because LD students have difficulties with all phases of the studying process, we will address each phase in turn. It is important to note, however, that it is not inappropriate to begin study skills instruction before students have mastered reading for meaning. There is no evidence to indicate that study skills cannot be taught in tandem with other reading behaviors. Anderson's survey would suggest, however, that the materials used for study skills instruction should be at the student's independent reading level, even if scaffolding techniques are consistently used. Furthermore, the materials must be interesting and the assignments short. Gradual lengthening of the assignments as students gain confidence is, of course, appropriate. The reader may wish to review suggestions in Chapter 6 for supporting LD students in independent learning efforts and the descriptions of direct instruction and scaffolding techniques in Chapter 9 for research-based approaches to instructional programs for teaching informed, self-control skills to LD readers.

Prereading Study Activities

Our review of expert readers' study behaviors has suggested the following topics as important aspects of the prereading phase of studying. First, the acquisition of appropriate work habits will be described. Second, flexible reading rates will be addressed. Finally, the topics to be included in the nonsentence information surveyed during prestudying will be delineated. Instructional research related to teaching children about text structure has been presented in Chapter 9.

Independent Work Habits

As with many other important aspects of learning how to learn in school, good work habits are very rarely taught directly. The assumption of at least some teachers is that such habits will be spontaneously learned. Many LD students, however, have little or no conception of the kinds of work habits that can help them become efficient and effective learners. Some leave for school without their homework or textbooks. Often they study at haphazard times and under conditions and in places that impede rather than promote learning. They also frequently fail to understand that *learning depends on the intent to remember. Reading a passage is not equivalent to studying it!*

For younger students, these types of problems can often be rectified by asking them, together with their parents, to designate a specific time for studying every evening. The work area should be quiet and well organized, with pencils, paper, and other materials stored conveniently. All assignments and materials that must be taken the next day should be put into the child's back pack or schoolbag in the evening, when assignments are completed, to eliminate the need to look for them in the morning. Each study session should end with the student sharpening pencils and putting materials back into storage to be ready for the next evening's work.

Helping older students is somewhat more complicated, because many have sports activities or favorite television programs in the evenings. Nevertheless, a consistent study period must be found and an appropriate work area maintained. Frequently, a self-analysis of scheduling will help students identify a time when they are both willing and able to study. Sometimes, when such an analysis is carried out, students are amazed at how much time they waste. The place of study should be neither too comfortable nor too uncomfortable. It is also helpful if that place is not used for other activities. Most frequently, a desk or table in the bedroom or another room is appropriate. Study should certainly occur in a place in which the need for quiet neither disturbs nor is disturbed by other family members. Again, collecting all the papers and materials needed for school the next day and preparing materials in the study center for the next evening's homework are integral components of the study session. The study skills inventory in Table 17.1 may prove useful.

Flexible Reading Rate

Research supports the hypothesis that the more specific the learner's knowledge of the criterial task, the greater the effectiveness of studying, as long as the learner modifies study strategies accordingly (Anderson & Armbruster, 1984). One way to begin informed, self-controlled instruction of study skills that highlights the need to vary the approach to reading is to teach flexible reading rates. Such instruction alerts LD students to the need to match encoding processes during the study session with the demands of the criterial task, that is, the purpose for reading.

There are two types of reading rates that help students focus on important information in the text: skimming and scanning. *Skimming* requires rapidly reading the titles and headings of a text to get some sense of both the content and its structure. It is useful, for example, to determine whether the text is interesting or important to the reader. Skimming is used quite often to determine whether the reader wants to address the text more slowly and carefully. *Scanning* is used to locate information quickly by looking for key words or phrases, once the purpose for reading has been established.

Locating Information

Other than the most rudimentary texts, the complexity of information requires authors to use methods to indicate the location of topics. Students need to be given explicit instruction regarding how information is organized both within and between texts. They should be taught to use tables of contents, indexes, glossaries, and appendices; almanacs and reference books; and the library card catalogue.

In the primary grades students can be taught to alphabetize, to use dictionaries appropriate to their reading levels, to consult tables of content, and to develop some general understanding of the arrangement of books in a library. Emphasis should be given to hypothesizing about how words are spelled, how material can be organized, and how certain information might be found. In the intermediate grades emphases should be placed on the extended use of books (indexes, glossaries, appendixes, and dictionaries) and library skills. The use of flexible reading rates, especially skimming and scanning, should also be stressed. In junior and senior high school, in-depth usage of all of these skills is required.

Book Use

Once students are introduced to the parts of books, one at a time, and are told what to expect from each, they should be guided through activities that require them to answer questions. Content area readers may be used to ask students such questions as:

Table of Contents

1. On what page does the author begin writing about mammals?
2. If your assignment were to read a story about fish, where could you find one in this book?
3. What are the important topics in this book?

Index

1. On what page does the poem "I Saw A Little Star" appear?
2. Where would I turn to read about canaries?

Glossary

1. What is a reptile?
2. Where could I find the definition of a simile?

Appendix

1. Where does the author give extra information about whales?

Other book parts that should be introduced are the *preface* and *foreword*. It is sufficient if students are aware that the preface contains the author's description of the purpose and plan for the book and that the foreword is written by another person who comments on its strengths. Students should also be told that the first chapter of a book serves as an introduction to the major topic and that the final chapter usually serves as a summary. Read the first and last chapters of a book and the table of contents, and then ask the students to predict what information might

Table 17.1 Study Skills Inventory

Student _____

course/period _____

date _____

Directions:

Study skills will be important to your success in this course and this inventory is designed to find out what your strengths and weaknesses may be in these areas. Think carefully about each of the following statements and then *answer as honestly as you can.* This is NOT a test!!

Circle 1, 2, 3, or 4 next to each statement to indicate whether the statement could be true for you usually, sometimes, seldom, or never.

	USUALLY	SOMETIMES	SELDOM	NEVER
Use of Time				
1. I spend about forty-five minutes each day studying for each of my courses.	1	2	3	4
2. When I study, I can stick with it until I am finished.	1	2	3	4
3. I study where I will not be interrupted.	1	2	3	4
Using a Textbook				
4. I use the table of contents to help me understand how topics are related.	1	2	3	4
5. I use the index in my studying.	1	2	3	4
6. I use the glossary to find meanings of unfamiliar words.	1	2	3	4
Underlining				
7. I underline all important ideas as I read.	1	2	3	4
8. I underline only key words and phrases, not whole sentences.	1	2	3	4
9. I underline details and examples.	1	2	3	4
10. I underline almost everything.	1	2	3	4
Notetaking				
11. When I study, I take notes from my reading.	1	2	3	4
12. When I take notes from my reading, they are clear enough to make sense several weeks later.	1	2	3	4
13. When I take notes from my reading, I put down the page numbers where I got the information.	1	2	3	4

442

	USUALLY	SOMETIMES	SELDOM	NEVER
14. When a teacher is lecturing in class, I take clear notes of what is said.	1	2	3	4
15. In my lecture notes, I make sure to write down the main ideas.	1	2	3	4
16. In my lecture notes, I include details and examples that help me clarify ideas.	1	2	3	4

Outlining

	USUALLY	SOMETIMES	SELDOM	NEVER
17. I outline the major things I learn when I study.	1	2	3	4
18. In my outlines, I include main ideas in the primary headings.	1	2	3	4
19. In my outlines, I include details as subheadings that clarify the main ideas.	1	2	3	4

Using Maps

	USUALLY	SOMETIMES	SELDOM	NEVER
20. I can use the keys and legends when reading maps.	1	2	3	4
21. I can interpret what the maps suggest about historical trends.	1	2	3	4

Taking Essay Tests

	USUALLY	SOMETIMES	SELDOM	NEVER
22. When taking essay tests, I read the directions and all the questions before beginning to answer any of the questions.	1	2	3	4
23. When taking essay tests, I think about what I want to write before beginning.	1	2	3	4
24. When taking essay tests, I organize my answer so my ideas will be clear to the instructor.	1	2	3	4
25. I proofread my answers when I am finished and before I turn in my paper.	1	2	3	4

Taking Objective Tests

	USUALLY	SOMETIMES	SELDOM	NEVER
26. When answering a multiple choice question, I try to eliminate first the obviously incorrect choices.	1	2	3	4
27. I trust my first guest when unsure of an answer.	1	2	3	4
28. I proofread to make sure no question is left unanswered, even if the answer is a wild guess.	1	2	3	4
29. I read through all of the choices given before marking an answer, even if the first or second one seems correct.	1	2	3	4
30. I look for clues in other questions that can help in answering questions of which I am unsure.	1	2	3	4

Note. From *Reading and Learning in the Content Classroom* (pp. 112–113) by T. H. Estes and J. L. Vaughan, Jr., 1979, Boston: Allyn & Bacon, Inc. Reprinted by permission.

be contained in each of the intervening chapters. Keep a list of their predictions to be checked after they have read each chapter.

Dictionary Use

Dictionary skills include finding words, learning to use the pronunciation and syllabication guides, and understanding word meanings. Students need to be taught that dictionaries have specific structure and functions, that is, they list words in alphabetical order, have guide words on the top of the page to help the reader locate words rapidly, and explain what words mean. Most intermediate grade reading texts provide extensive coverage of teaching methods for dictionary skills. In the junior high school, the thesaurus is generally introduced. Both of these resources should be taught and utilized as they are needed. When the student confronts an unknown word or needs a synonym to make a composition more interesting, the motivation for meaningful and exciting learning will be present.

Library Skills

Students are often introduced to libraries during free reading periods. Libraries perform many functions, which continue to grow, and should be approached as a source of both pleasure and knowledge. Currently, then can offer videotapes, computer software, and seminars. Many also have access to on-line data banks, which can provide information without laborious catalogue searches. Although their functions are expanding, their basic use is to gain information. Thus, understanding their organization is very important.

Students must be taught that the card catalogue works just like a book index to allow people to locate material. Books and materials are catalogued in three ways: by author, subject, and title. Exercises can be generated asking students to find books using first one and then the other systems. Begin by presenting at least one set of author, subject, and title cards in the classroom so that students understand what they look like and what information they contain. It is best to introduce these skills in conjunction with report writing to make their value apparent. Particular attention should be paid to the meaning of the numbers and letters in the upper left. It is often helpful to walk students through the library several times to help them develop efficient procedures for locating books.

Macrorules for Comprehending and Remembering

Determining they know enough to be tested, that is, that they can stop studying, is one of the most important decisions LD students need to learn to make. Knowledge of the criterial task is crucial. If the test is as easy as studying pictures until they are remembered, third graders (Flavell, Friedrichs, & Hoyt, 1970) and even mentally retarded children (Brown & Campione, 1979) can perform well. Remembering lists is only moderately difficult when children are taught to engage in simple strategies, such as rehearsal or anticipation, because engaging in such tasks provides immediate and intrinsic feedback.

Knowing you are ready to be tested on a prose passage is a considerably more difficult task because the criteria are less precise: Knowing that you've grasped the main idea is a far more subjective judgment than testing list recall. Furthermore, as common sense would dictate, learning to make I-know-the-list decisions does not prepare children to make the latter determination. One very useful strategy is to summarize the text—a very complex, but effective task. LD students will, of course, need to be taught to summarize. (These rules were presented in Chapters 9 and 13, pp. 321–322.) Other rules for monitoring readiness for testing may also be necessary and effective—check to make certain the entire assignment was read, and all the study questions were answered.

Study Activities During Reading

Widely used traditional study techniques, such as Robinson's (1941) SQ3R (Survey, Question, Read, Recite, Review) method, have focused on what to do before and after reading. Emphases on what to do *during* reading to ensure appropriate encoding have grown out of the current interest in metacognition. Baker and Brown's (1984) review of the research identified several components of study activity that occur during reading: selecting the main idea, using logical structure, self-interrogating, and self-testing the results of studying. The results relevant to each topic are summarized below.

Selecting and Studying the Main Idea

The ability to identify the main idea of a text is a skill that gradually develops. It appears that information such as the main character of a story may be easily remembered, whereas determining the important elements of more complex passages requires active processing of those aspects of the text that are not automatically retained.

Brown and Smiley (1978) found that only after the seventh grade do children actually benefit from extended study time. Although both younger and older students remembered the important elements of text, recall of less important details did not improve even among the older students. When they observed the students, Brown and Smiley learned that the youngest children interpreted studying as rereading, while the older students spontaneously underlined or took notes, thereby selectively attending to the most important elements. Poor readers appear to respond more like the younger normally achieving students in the Brown and Smiley study. Although they know that increasing the amount of study time improves performance, when given an opportunity to study, they do not choose to work longer. Furthermore, they do not allocate extra time to processing the ideas not likely to be remembered automatically.

Pearson and Johnson (1978) have recommended the use of a free association technique to help students access prior knowledge that can be used to teach them to evaluate ideas to determine the most important ones. This technique can be expanded to order those ideas to facilitate paragraph (or theme) writing—a common criterion task.

Once children have learned to categorize, they can be taught to identify the main idea. In the *free association* technique, the teacher introduces a topic and asks students to tell everything they know about it. Their ideas are listed on the board, unedited. Once the list is complete, that is, when the students have no more ideas to offer, the teacher asks them to review the list to select what they consider to be the most important idea. Several nominations should be elicited. The students can then be asked to explain their choices. After each nomination has been justified, students should vote by a show of hands for the most preferred idea. If no one chooses to support one of the ideas nominated, it can be dropped, as long as the teacher asks them to explain why they think no one chose that idea. In this way, the process of selection can be modeled to demonstrate the kinds of considerations that go into making a decision. This same nominating-justifying-voting procedure can be used when the information is derived from first a paragraph, then several paragraphs, gradually increasing segments of text, and finally entire selections.

Intermediate grade students are taught more advanced categorizing skills and techniques for evaluating the relevance of information. Using free association, they can be asked to rank those ideas that were not selected as "most important." Ideas that do not fit any of the categories can be discarded as irrelevant or, if the students agree that they are important, new labels can be generated for additional "most important ideas." These lists can then be used as the basis for composing compositions.

Students should be shown how authors use one "most important" idea and several other ideas that can be categorized as "most supporting ideas." The concept of main and supporting ideas will be very useful for students when they write their own compositions, for they will discover ways to combine subordinate ideas within a paragraph to compose one of the most useful expository formats, generalization supported by examples (Devine, 1981).

The next step, which can be begun in the elementary school and continued throughout schooling, is to coordinate information from a variety of sources, which is one of the main library activities to be taught. Students can read several passages about, for example, whales. A story, a magazine article, and an encyclopedia description would allow students to see how whales are represented in different genre and would help them make decisions about the most likely sources for the type of information they need. A group lesson using the free association technique or just brain storming at their desks will help students to draw upon both their readings and background knowledge. Once the ideas are down on paper, they can be arranged according to most important and supporting ideas. These lists can then become the basis for other activities, such as writing reports, making books, or developing media presentations.

The teacher should vary the length of such assignments to force students to decide what to include. Information must be grouped according to several levels. The length of the paper will determine how many levels should be used. If they have only one paragraph to write, their selections will necessarily be different than if a ten-page report is assigned.

After students have had several opportunities to practice selecting information from texts and arranging it into "most important" and "supporting" ideas, they should be taught to develop a simple outline to perform additional selection activities. They should work first in small groups with teacher direction, then in small peer groups with teacher feedback, and finally individually. Sample outline forms are presented in Boxes 17.1 and 17.2.

Using Logical Structure

Familiarity with the types of activities described will also help students become aware of the structure of expository text. Bransford, Stein, Shelton, and Owings (1981) gave good and poor (bottom quartile) students passages that varied as to the precision with which character descriptions

---

Box 17.1   Simple Outline Form for Paragraph Writing

Most important idea:_____

Supporting idea:_____

_____

Supporting idea:_____

_____

Supporting idea:_____

_____

Box 17.2 Simple Outline Form for Composition Writing

Central idea of composition (intro.) : _____

Supporting idea of paragraph 2: _____

Supporting idea of paragraph 3: _____

Supporting idea of paragraph 4: _____

Most important idea (for each paragraph): _____

Supporting idea: _____

Supporting idea: _____

Supporting idea: _____

Most important conclusion to be drawn: _____

Supporting idea of paragraph 2: _____

Supporting idea of paragraph 3: _____

Supporting idea of paragraph 4: _____

---

were congruent with their behaviors, for example, "The hungry boy ate a hamburger," versus, "The tall boy ate a hamburger." Better students spent more time studying the imprecise passages and knew why they needed to. Poor readers, on the other hand, were able to do as well when instructed specifically to do so. Wong found very similar results, including responsiveness to training, with children labeled LD.

Self-Interrogation During Study

LD students cannot become independent learners without acquiring both the ability and the inclination to ask themselves questions to guide their reading and thinking. The research evidence indicates that self-questioning can be taught using direct instruction, modeling, imitation, reinforcement, and reciprocal questioning (students ask each other in turn). Furthermore, self-questioning strategies have been taught successfully to LD students (see, for example, Hori, 1977; Palincsar, 1982; Wong & Jones, 1982), who in some cases maintained use of the strategy after instruction stopped and even transferred use of the strategy to somewhat different tasks. The implications are that students should be instructed in the types of questions to ask both to succeed on particular tasks and to monitor their performances ("procedure sheets" can be useful as temporary guides).

Furthermore, they must understand the rationale for likely payoff of the use of a strategy.

LD students can be successfully trained to ask themselves higher order questions (e.g., evaluation, comparison, problem solving, and cause and effect), which lead to better reading comprehension than do lower order (e.g., literal) questions. Andre and Anderson (1978–79) also found that junior high school students who asked themselves good questions (i.e., related to the main idea or paraphrasing a text statement) correctly answered post-test questions 78 percent of the time. The accuracy rate dropped to 39 percent when inadequate questions had been generated. The effectiveness of self-questioning was also reduced when students lacked background or metacognitive knowledge, for to ask a question, one must know something about the topic. Miyake and Norman (1979), for example, found that college students using a difficult manual to learn word processing asked fewer questions than their peers who were given a more simplified version. Because they often have limited prior knowledge, LD students too tend to ask fewer questions than their academically competent peers. Furthermore, their failure to understand the benefits of asking questions and the task demands asssociated with their purpose for reading hamper their ability to generate useful, on-target questions. Consequently, if classroom instruction in self-questioning is to be effective, teachers must give clear and careful directions (perhaps providing continued reminders through "procedure sheets" and other structuring devices), allow sufficient time, and teach to mastery.

Determining Relations Between Paragraphs

Often an author will use clue words to signal the relations between paragraphs. Clue words indicate that: (1) there will be more to say about a particular topic (e.g., *in addition, another, since, furthermore, moreover*); (2) a previously stated idea will be reversed or modified (e.g., *nevertheless, on the other hand, however*); or (3) a summary statement is forthcoming (e.g., *finally, in sum, in brief, in conclusion*). Students should be taught to look for these words and others used to describe the topic or conceptual relations in terms of cause and effect, time, space, or degree.

Authors also indicate relations through sources not directly attributable to paragraph or sentence structure. A review of chapter titles, heading, and subheadings, for example, will also offer cues to the relations among paragraphs. If essays are well formed, certain assumptions can be made. All paragraphs within a section, for example, should deal with a single topic. When the topic is changed, it can be assumed that a new heading is inserted. It can also be assumed that certain rules are followed within a paragraph. There might be a topic sentence, for example, with supporting details and a brief summary statement.

Self-Testing the Results of Study

It is not easy to judge whether one has acquired and retained enough information during studying to pass a test. One strategy that experts typically use is summarizing. Because Brown and Day's (1983) work in summarizing was reviewed in both Chapters 9 and 13, no further discussion will be offered here.

Study Activities After Reading

Anderson and Armbruster (1984) reached several conclusions from their review of the research on study techniques. First, nearly any technique can be effective if it is accompanied by focused attention and encoding that is appropriate to the criterial task. This suggests the use of "process sheets" to focus studying attempts during the initial stages of learning and explicit instruction in the interactions of the tetrahedral model to make students aware of the need to match their procedures to the criterial task. Second, some techniques, such as outlining, mapping, and visual displays, have more power than others, especially when the criterial task requires in-depth comprehension, because they force students to discover the relationships among elements of the text. Not surprisingly, however, the most effective techniques are also the most costly in terms of student time and effort.

Note Taking

Note taking requires the extraction of main ideas from information either presented orally or in print. Primary grade students are not taught these skills, for they must still concentrate on letter formation and generally write quite slowly. They also have difficulty deciding what is important to take down in any sufficiently rapid way. Note-taking skills are, however, introduced in the intermediate grades. Brown and Day (1983) suggest that by about the fourth grade, students can successfully profit from such instruction. Students should first be taught to review paragraphs to extract the few words in each sentence that convey its meaning. Otherwise, note taking becomes the lifting of entire passages (Lapp & Flood, 1978). Instruction should continue throughout high school and into college as students' ability increases. Hints that can help students develop these skills are: (1) pick out the most important and supporting ideas, listen, and then summarize; (2) write notes in your own words or in some abbreviated code that you will be able to read later, and (3) use words that give structure clues, such as *first* and *because*. Again a posted "procedure sheet" can be helpful.

To teach beginning note taking, read a selection aloud while the students follow along. Make sure that the text is well formed. At first, avoid texts that contain ambiguous or otherwise confusing passages. Ask the students to put a check by the important ideas. Remind them to search for those that tell who, what, when, where, how, and how many. Ask the students to list the items they chose as important on the board. Use the notes to organize the information into an outline, list, chart, or time line, which can serve as checks to ensure that it all relates. Extraneous information can be discarded. (It is important for students to learn that they do not have to include everything from the passage). Once the notes are taken, students should be required to use them to study, prepare a report, or complete an activity.

Another tactic for teaching note taking (at any age) is to read a story aloud to students. Their sensitivity to the various aspects of grammar increases with age. The complexity of the stories can therefore also be increased with age. To use this technique, stop reading after each story element (i.e., the introduction of the protagonist, the initiating event, etc.). During each pause, have the students write a single statement that expresses the main point(s) of that part. Continually stress that note taking is not a verbatim transcription but rather the extraction and reorganization of the content in their own words.

When teaching note taking, it is important to remember that these are the students' *personal* notes. They need not be neat nor readable by others. Notes are not written for an audience. The best way to check note-taking skills is by reading the follow-up activity. If a teacher suspects that the student is having difficulty and needs intervention, a conference in which the student reads the notes to the teacher is probably the best format. Since note taking is a personal activity, changes must be suggested in a sensitive way that respects the attempts and achievements of the student. There is nothing worse than having students put forth their best effort in some personal endeavor and then rebuking them for the inadequacy of their attempts.

Outlining

Perhaps the most widely used organizational technique is outlining, which is the self-generation of concise representations (usually summaries) of text for use in later study or writing. Although if any outlining technique is taught, it is usually formal outlining, it is probably not the most useful method for LD students or anyone with problems in reading, regardless of age or reading level (Poplin, Gray, Larsen, Banikowski, & Mehring, 1980). The rule, for example, "Never an A without a B," poses potential problems for unskilled readers. Students with problems in written language will suffer from being constrained not by their ability to think but by their ability to write. Consequently, visual arrays, which require minimum written language competence, may be more effective with problem learners.

Formal Outlining

Formal outlining is the preferred method of text organization of some (i.e., Emans & Fisher, 1967) because it theoretically: (1) makes the organization of the material apparent, (2) focuses on the essential aspects of the text, and (3) contributes significantly to easing the requirements of later study. Furthermore, outlines can be useful for reviewing the relations among topics and encouraging discussion. Examples of formal outlines are given in Boxes 17.3 and 17.4.

There are two very important considerations to keep in mind when suggesting formal outlining to students. First, formal outlining is effective only if the writing is well formed. Otherwise, there is not implicit structure for students to follow. Second, this technique is effective only if students have reached a level of written language understanding sufficient to work within such specific constraints. The restrictions placed on students by the structure of formal outlines may have an inhibiting effect, especially if problem readers (Vacca, 1981) are required to use sentence or certain phrase structures. Because these students frequently do not have facility with written expression (Poplin et al., 1980), their productions become less spontaneous, more restricted, and very constrained. The possibility of creating an outline (structure) that is personally meaningful becomes remote.

When teaching outlining, it is beneficial to provide the students with a partially completed sample, perhaps of the first few pages of a passage. Read the passage with the students to explain where you got the information and why you made the choices you did. Students should then attempt to complete the outline: A group outline can be generated. As students suggest outline topics, they can be evaluated, retained, or eliminated through discussion, which is another good way to have more competent students model appropriate behaviors and provide feedback for those who are more seriously impaired.

Visual Organizers

Visual techniques require the student to represent information according to some logical system without the restriction of having to use well formed written language structures. Although a myriad of such techniques can be used or developed, only a representative few will be discussed here. For additional ideas, the interested reader is directed to Anderson (1979) and Vacca (1981).

An example of array outlining (Stevenson, 1978) is presented in Figure 17.1; it is a variant of mapping (see Figures 17.2 and 17.3). These techniques require the student to organize ideas by writing key word concepts and connecting them through meaningful visual patterns. In the arrays, the arrows indicate either one-way or reciprocal relationships. These tech-

Box 17.3   Formal Outline

The Crystals of Earth

I. Identifying Minerals
   A. Investigating Physical Properties
      1. Physical properties
         a. Color
         b. Luster
         c. Streak
         d. Hardness
         e. Specific gravity
   B. Investigating Chemical Properties
   C. Other Tests

II. Crystals
   A. Crystal Structure of Minerals
   B. The Structure of Crystals
   C. Crystal Properties

III. Mineral Groups
   A. A Rock-Forming Mineral: Quartz
   B. Other Rock-Forming Minerals
      1. Silicate
      2. Calcite and Magnetite
   C. Metal-Bearing Minerals
      1. Hematite, bauxite, and sphalerite
   D. Nonmetallic Minerals
      1. Sulphur
      2. Graphite
      3. Halite
      4. Gypsum
      5. Diamond
      6. Corundum
      7. Beryl

Note. From "Squeezing Study Skills (Into, Out of) Content Area" by James Walker. In *Reading Through Content* by R. T. Vacca and J. A. Meagher (Eds.), 1979, pp. 77–92, Storrs, CT: University Publications and the Reading-Language Arts Center, University of Connecticut. Used with permission of the author.

Box 17.4   More Detailed Formal Outline

I. Origins of the universe
   A. What is the Big Bang theory?
      1. Countless galaxies created when a single original mass of matter exploded (10 billion years ago).
      2. Galaxies now rushing outwards at high speed.
      3. Elements formed at time of "bang."
   B. How did the solar system develop?
      1. Condensation of cloud and dust particles (4.5 billion years ago).
      2. Formation of central and satellite masses.
      3. Contraction and rising of temperature of central mass.
      4. Surrounding masses became dependent planets.
   C. What is the impact of scientific theories?
      Great—most people accept them. Most religions find scientific theory compatible with their beliefs.

II. Beginnings of life and man
   A. How did Darwin believe life evolved? (Key ideas)
      1. *Struggle for existence:* Animals must compete for limited food supply.
      2. *Survival of fittest:* The strongest are able to stay alive and bear young.
      3. *Natural selection:* Animals with particular characteristics that help them in their environments will be the ones to survive and reproduce.
      4. *New species:* Over millions of years, animals of a species become so different because of different environments they are no longer the same species. That's how new species come into being.
   B. What did scientists find out about early man?
      Raymond Dart and Robert Leakey, anthropologists:
      1. *Australopithecus*—S & E Africa, 2 million years ago.
      2. *Homo erectus*—500,000 years ago, more advanced, used fire, hunted big animals.

Note. Reprinted from *Teaching Reading in Secondary Schools—Content Subjects, a Book Thinking Process* by Carl B. Smith, 1978, New York: Holt, Rinehart, & Winston. Used by permission of the author, Carl B. Smith.

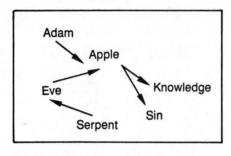 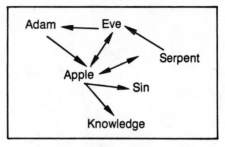

FIGURE 17.1 Array Outlines.

Note. From "Stepping Up to Outlining" by T. S. Hansell, 1978, *Journal of Reading,*
22, pp. 248–252. Reprinted with permission of T. S. Hansell and the International Reading Association.

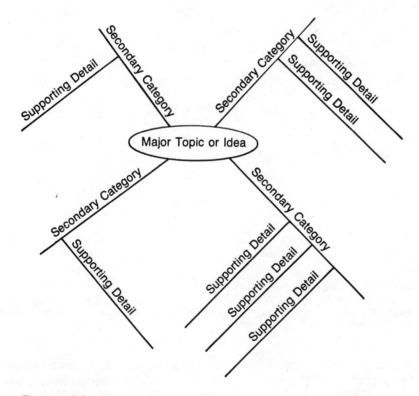

FIGURE 17.2 Mapping.

Note. From *A Practical Approach to Content Area Reading* (p. 252) by Richard P. Santeusanio, 1983, Menlo Park, CA: Addison-Wesley Publishing Company, Inc. Reprinted by
permission.

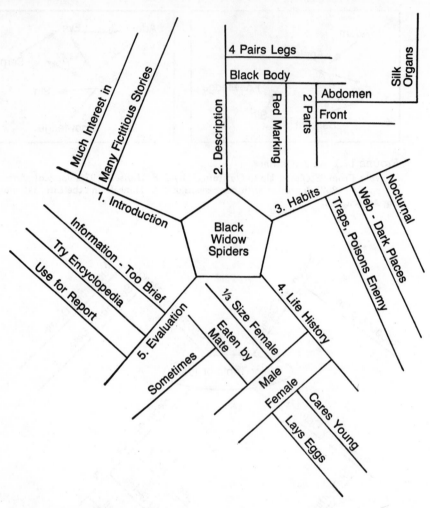

FIGURE 17.3 Mapping.

Note. From "Mapping: A Technique for Translating Reading Into Thinking" by M. B. Hanf, 1971, *Journal of Reading, 14,* p. 228. Reprinted with permission of M. B. Hanf and the International Reading Association.

niques can be introduced by: (1) dividing the class into groups, (2) having the groups write the most important words and phrases from a passage on a strip of paper, (3) discussing the relations among the words and phrases with the groups, (4) having each group construct an array, (5) pasting each array on a sheet of paper, and (6) having groups share their arrays (Vacca, 1981).

In pyramid outlining (see Figure 17.4), the major topics are written across the top of the paper with the supporting details listed under them.

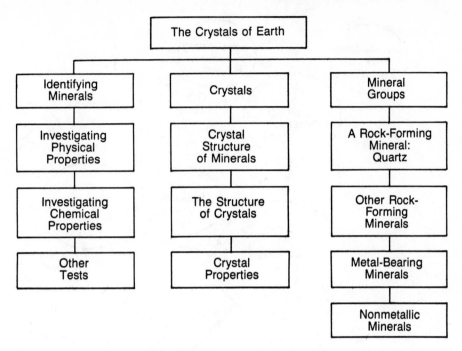

FIGURE 17.4 Pyramid Outline.

Note. From "Squeezing Study Skills (Into, Out of) Content Area" by James Walker. In *Reading Through Content* by R. T. Vacca and J. A. Meagher (Eds.), 1979, pp. 77-92, Storrs, CT: University Publications and the Reading-Language Arts Center, University of Connecticut. Used with permission of the author.

Radial outlines (see Figure 17.5) place the central theme or topic in the center of the paper. Double spokes are drawn from the central topic to the supporting details. Single spokes are drawn from the supporting details to their own supporting ideas. Another variant of the radial outline is the web, which was introduced by Huck (1979) for use in organizing information from stories. See Figure 17.6 for a web of "Little Red Riding Hood." The herringbone technique of outlining (see Figure 17.7) uses questions whose answers are listed in the appropriate box. These techniques may be introduced in the same ways as the arrays.

Despite their effectiveness, visual techniques are an alternative, not a panacea. They may be easier for LD students to produce than formal outlines. They serve much the same function, however, and may be taught prior to or in lieu of outlining.

Other Visual Displays

Teaching students to use graphs, tables, charts, maps, cartoons, and diagrams is generally best begun by having them make their own examples

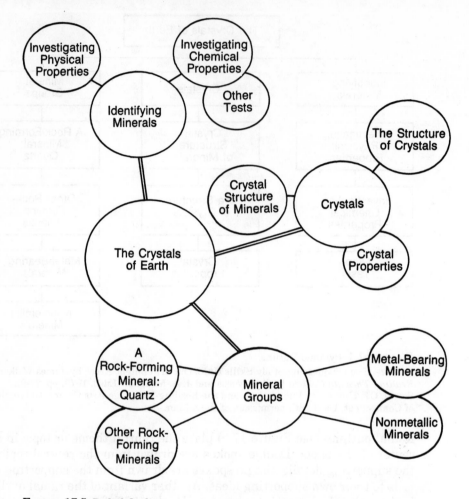

FIGURE 17.5 Radial Outline.

Note. From "Squeezing Study Skills (Into, Out of) Content Area" by James Walker. In *Reading Through Content* by R. T. Vacca and J. A. Meagher (Eds.), 1979, pp. 77–92, Storrs, CT: University Publications and the Reading-Language Arts Center, University of Connecticut. Used with permission of the author.

after seeing several samples that are related to their actual work. Because the complexity or subtlety of such aids changes throughout schooling, ongoing instruction is needed.

Answering a Variety of Question Types

Students at all levels need to be introduced to various types of questions for two very important reasons. First, they must understand the kinds

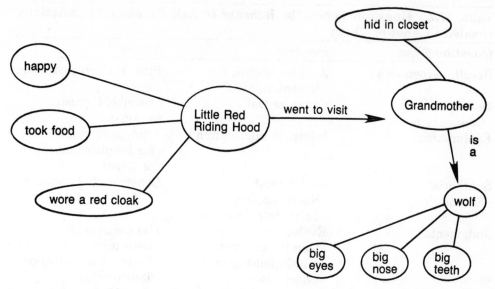

FIGURE 17.6 Web of "Little Red Riding Hood."

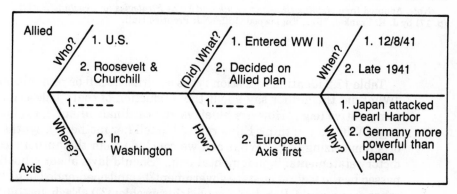

FIGURE 17.7 Herringbone Outline.

Note. Adapted from *Reading Strategies and Practices* (p. 85) by R. J. Tierney, J. E. Readence, and E. K. Dishner, 1985, Rockleigh, NJ: Allyn & Bacon. Reprinted by permission.

of questions being asked of them. Second, students need to know how to ask appropriate questions for gathering information. Most LD students fail to ask questions, probably because they have never been taught how to do so and do not understand how asking questions can help them. The content of the materials about which questions are asked will control the difficulty level. Even young students can make judgments if the topic is familiar.

Table 17.2   Question Types, the Reasons to Ask Them, and the Actions Needed to Answer Them

Question Type	Purpose	Action
Recall, Recognition	Acquire Specific Information	Provide Correct Answer
Descriptive, Comparison	Organize Data	Describe, Compare, Contrast
Explanation	Interpret Information	Analyze Reasons for People's Behavior or Events
Synthesis, Summary	Understand Relationships, Formulate Conclusions	Construct Relationships
Judgmental	Evaluation of the Quality/Truth of a Relationship or Conclusion	Use Criteria to Determine Better Alternative or Truth Value
Open-Ended	Divergent Thinking	Give-Many Possibilities

Note. Adapted from *Helping Students Think and Value Strategies for Teaching Social Studies* (p. 17) by J. R. Frankel, 1973, Englewood Cliffs, NJ: Prentice Hall.

Table 17.2 identifies question types as either recall or recognition (e.g., "What did the author say about the production of coal?"), descriptive or comparative (e.g., "How are bluejays and cardinals alike?"), explanatory (e.g., "Why do you think Ellen refused to tell her mother?"), synthesizing or summarizing (e.g., "What can we conclude from the author's contradictory statements?"), judgmental (e.g., "Should laws about schooling be passed by the federal or state government?"), and open-ended (e.g., "What other ways could Bob have solved his problem?"). Each has different response demands. Students need to be taught to read questions carefully to determine whether they are expected to give a correct answer, suggest as many ideas as possible, state a relationship, or give reasons why. Teaching the use of clue words, such as *what, when, where, why, how,* and *how many,* will help them to understand what is expected of them and to match their responses to question types.

Of course, the implicit assumption is that teachers (and textbook authors) develop questions that are well formed, accurate, and can be solved through either direct references to or inferences from the text. But this is not always the case. Goodstein (1981), for example, lamented that most questions in mathematical word problems contain irrelevant information, are ambiguous, or require inferences that go beyond the information given. Clearly, instruction in understanding questions must also include experience in dealing with ambiguity. First, students must learn to recognize ambiguity in questions, to rephrase those questions so they make sense, and to anticipate what the author or teacher actually means. Second, if students are taught to ask questions about what they are reading, as some suggest (i.e., Wong & Jones, 1982), they should be taught how to evaluate their questions to assure that they are related to the reading.

Following Directions

Instruction in following directions takes place from the first day of schooling until the last. The youngest students need to be taught to follow one-step directions, while older ones must be taught to follow complex directions in sequence. It is important to teach students how to monitor their work to know when one step is completed and they are ready to begin working on another. The discussion of question types above will help to provide some awareness of how responses to questions must be constructed. There are three steps to teaching students to follow directions: First, tell them *what* has to be done. Second, explain *why* it is important. Third, help them plan *how* to work through the steps required (Brown & Palincsar, 1982).

Teaching students to follow directions has the benefit of allowing them to use established study sequences to guide their interactions with material. Several authors have developed sequences for studying that are best known by their acronyms, such as PQRST: Preview, Question, Read, State, Test (Staton, 1954), Triple S: Scan, Search, Summarize (Farquhar, Krumboltz, & Wrenn, 1960), OK5R: Overview, Key Idea, Read, Record, Recite, Review, Reflect (Pauk, 1974), and PQ4R: Preview, Question, Read, Reflect, Recite, Review (Thomas & Robinson, 1972). Although all are valuable techniques, perhaps the most well known of these study systems is SQ3R: Survey, Question, Read, Recite, Review (Robinson, 1970). (For variations useful for studying the physical sciences and mathematics, see Forgan & Mangrum, 1981). This system is appropriate for students in the intermediate grades and beyond. The following is a description of each phase of the SQ3R technique.

Survey   Surveying means reading quickly through the major headings, and introductory and summarizing chapter or paragraph(s). Students should also be taught to skim the preparatory material in a book as well as headings and subheadings, charts, pictures, graphs, and other illustrations. Once the survey is complete, the materials can be evaluated to determine whether they are appropriate to the reader's needs.

Question   Based on the survey, questions are developed to predict what may be included in the reading material. Teach students to derive questions from the headings and chapter titles. As they become adept at studying, the questions will become implicit and will not need to be written out.

Read   Reading is directed toward locating the answers to the question generated after surveying. This type of reading is a very active process and needs to be done slowly and carefully to grasp the main ideas and important details. Students should focus on reading introductory paragraphs carefully to test their basic assumptions. Questions should be revised or added if necessary. If minor ideas can be sorted from the main ideas, these should be skimmed rather than read in-depth.

Recite   Reciting is the process of answering the questions. Both outlining and visual techniques may be helpful formats for this step. Answering the questions in writing provides notes for further study. All work should be in the student's own words to ensure that it is meaningful.

Review   Reviewing is the process of memorizing the information. The questions developed earlier should be the basis for the review. If the recitation step is done in the student's own words and if both the main idea and supporting details were clearly understood, the notes rather than the original material are the best source to study.

To teach the SQ3R method, select well-written textbooks. If the chapter titles and headings are not well designed, for example, the questions the students generate may be trivial or inappropriate. However, this or any other study system cannot be learned without both instruction and practice. But, once they have been mastered, they provide students with endless possibilities for independent functioning.

Assessing Strengths and Weaknesses

One of the most productive methods for assessing students' ability to study is to have them evaluate the effects of their own learning. One group method for carrying out such an evaluation is Herber's (1978) Triangular Review. Students may also use this procedure to prepare for tests or to estimate prestudying knowledge. First, a list of key words and concepts is generated (initially by the teacher and later by the students themselves). Second, the learner states everything remembered about the topic, while another student puts a check next to each item on the list that the students discusses adequately. Once the learner has provided all the information remembered, each topic that was not addressed is introduced by a third student using a prompt (e.g., "What do you know about the Civil Rights Movement?"). The second student puts a plus sign next to each item the learner recalls with prompts. When the prompting is finished, the learner has a record of what is already well known (the items with checks), what needs to be reviewed (the items with plus signs), and what needs considerable study (the items with no marks).

Recovery Procedures for Persistent Problems

Probably the most powerful method of addressing student problems with study skills is to use the scaffolding approaches mentioned repeatedly throughout earlier chapters. First, direct instruction should be used to make declarative, procedural, and conditional knowledge all explicit. Then guided practice using scaffolding approaches can be used until students begin to acquire proficiency. Although it has not been tested for this purpose, reciprocal teaching may be especially effective.

Matching Students to Tasks and Monitoring Performance

Most school districts, basal reader series, and the like have a schedule for introducing study skills. What is selected for instruction should directly relate to the requirements for learning held for the students. Nearly all techniques described in this chapter can be taught at a variety of levels of complexity and of teacher support. Certainly, however, outcome data should be collected and charted continuously to determine their effectiveness.

Summary and Conclusions

It is no longer sufficient for teachers to teach content alone. Unlike their more academically successful peers, LD students fail to mobilize their behavior for a variety of reasons, including limited prior knowledge, failure to access existing knowledge, and poor metacognitive skills. This chapter has focused on rather global strategies for fostering independent study behaviors. More specific strategies must necessarily be tied to particular content areas and were presented earlier.

Three phases of studying were addressed—before, during, and after reading. The first and last have been traditionally considered in discussions of study skills, while the second is an outgrowth of the current interest in metacognition. The most demanding approaches in studying tend to be the most effective, as long as the structural requirements (e.g., of formal outlining) do not interfere with responding among LD students. Of paramount importance, however, is that the material to be learned is at an appropriate reading level, is interesting, and is perceived by the students as "doable" in a reasonable amount of time. Finally, it is important to remember a point addressed repeatedly throughout this text: teach strategies within the context of tasks. Or, put another way, *TEACH STUDENTS HOW TO PERFORM THE TASKS ASSIGNED*.

References

Adams, A., Carnine, D., & Gersten, R. (1982). Instructional strategies for studying content area texts in the intermediate grades. *Reading Research Quarterly, 18,* 27–55.

Adams, J. L. (1974). *Conceptual blockbusting.* Stanford, CA: The Stanford Alumni Association.

Adams, M. J., & Collins, A. A. (1977). *A schema-theoretic view of reading* (Tech. Rep. No. 23). Urbana: University of Illinois, Center for the Study of Reading.

Addy, P., & Wylie, R. E. (1973). The "right" way to write. *Childhood Education, 49,* 253–254.

Adler, M. J. (1982). *The Paideia proposal: An educational manifest.* New York: MacMillan.

Airasian, P. W., & Madaus, G. F. (1983). Linking testing and instruction: Policy issues. *Journal of Educational Measurement, 20,* 103–118.

Allen, V. L. (1976). *Children as teachers.* New York: Academic Press.

Alley, G. R., Deshler, D. D., & Warner, M. M. (1979). Identification of learning disabled adolescents: A Bayesian approach. *Learning Disability Quarterly, 2*(2), 77–83.

Allington, R. L. (1977). If they don't read, how they ever gonna get good? *Journal of Reading, 21*(1), 57–62.

Allington, R. L. (1980). Teacher interruption behaviors during primary grade oral reading. *Journal of Educational Psychology, 72,* 371–377.

Allington, R. L. (1983). Fluency: The neglected reading goal. *Reading Teacher, 36,* 556–561.

Allington, R. L. (1984). So what is the problem? Whose problem is it? *Topics in Learning and Learning Disabilities, 3*(4), 91–99.

Alvermann, D. E., Smith, L. C., & Readence, J. E. (1985). Prior knowledge activation and the comprehension of compatible and incompatible text. *Reading Quarterly, 20,* 420–436.

Ammons, R. B., & Ammons, H. S. (1948). *Full-range picture vocabulary test.* Palo Alto, CA: Psychological Test Specialists.

Anderson, C. S. (1982). The search for school climate: A review of the research. *Review of Educational Research, 52,* 369–420.

Anderson, C. W., Smith, E. L., & Ross, K. (in press). Teaching science. In V. Koehler (Ed.), *The educator's handbook: A research perspective*. New York: Longman.

Anderson, L., & Prawat, R. (1983). Responsibility in the classroom: A synthesis of research on teaching self-control. *Educational Leadership, 40,* 62–66.

Anderson, R. C. (1977). The notion of schemata and the educational enterprise: General discussion of the conference. In R. C. Anderson, R. J. Spiro, & W. E. Montague, (Eds.), *Schooling and the acquisition of knowledge* (pp. 415–431). New York: Erlbaum.

Anderson, R. C. (1984). Some reflections on the acquisition of knowledge. *Educational Researcher, 13*(9), 5–10.

Anderson, R. C., & Biddle, W. B. (1975). On asking people questions about the way they are reading. In G. H. Bower (Ed.), *The Psychology of learning and motivation* (Vol. 9, pp. 90–132). New York: Academic Press.

Anderson, R. C., Hiebert, E. H., Scott, J. A., & Wilkinson, I.A.G. (1985). *Becoming a nation of readers*. Washington, DC: National Institute of Education.

Anderson, R. C., & Pearson, P. D. (1984). A schema-theoretic view of basic processes in reading comprehension. In P. D. Pearson (Ed.), *Handbook of reading research* (pp. 255–251). New York: Longman.

Anderson, T. H. (1978). *Study skills and learning strategies* (Tech. Rep. No. 104). Urbana: University of Illinois, Center for the Study of Reading.

Anderson, T. H. (1979). Study skills and learning strategies. In H. F. O'Neil & C. D. Speilberger (Eds.), *Cognitive and affective learning strategies* (pp. 77–98). New York: Academic Press.

Anderson, T. H., & Armbruster, B. B. (1984). Studying. In P. D. Pearson (Ed.), *Handbook of reading research* (pp. 657–680). New York: Longman.

Andre, M., & Anderson, T. H. (1978–1979). Development and evaluation of self-questioning technique. *Reading Research Quarterly, 14,* 615–623.

Anno, M. (1982). *Anno's counting house*. New York: Philomel Books.

Applebee, A. N. (1981). *Writing in the secondary school* (Research Monograph No. 21). Urbana, IL: National Council of Teachers of English.

Applebee, A. N. (1982). Writing and learning in school settings. In M. Nystrand (Ed.), *What writers know: The language, process, and structure of written language* (pp. 365–381). New York: Academic Press.

Applebee, A. N. (1984a). *Contexts for learning to write: Studies of secondary school instruction*. Norwood, NJ: Ablex.

Applebee, A. N. (1984b). Writing and reasoning. *Review of Educational Research, 54,* 577–596.

Applebee, A. N., & Langer, J. A. (1983). Instructional scaffolding: Reading and writing as natural language activities. *Language Arts, 60,* 168–175.

Armbruster, B. B., & Anderson, T. H. (1984). *Producing "considerate" expository text: Or easy reading is damned hard writing* (Reading Education Rep. No. 46). Urbana: University of Illinois, Center for the Study of Reading.

Armbruster, B. B., Anderson, T. H., Cox, B. E., Friedman, L. B., Jones, B. F., Karlin, S., Kazarian, M., Martin, B., Osborn, J., & Walter, B. J. (1986). *The collaboration to improve reading in the content area (The CIRCA Project): A description* (Reading Education Rep. 65). Urbana: University of Illinois, Center for the Study of Reading.

Athey, I. (1974). *Essential skills and skills hierarchies in reading comprehension and decoding instruction.* Paper presented at the conference of the National Institute of Education.

Athey, I. (1976). Reading research in the affective domain. In H. Singer & R. Ruddell (Eds.), *Theoretical models and processes of reading* (pp. 352–380). Newark, NJ: International Reading Association.

Au, K. H. (1980). Participation structures in a reading lesson with Hawaiian children: Analysis of a culturally appropriate instructional event. *Anthropology and Education Quarterly, 11*(2), 91–115.

August, D. L., Flavell, J. H., & Clift, R. (1984). Comparison of comprehension monitoring of skilled and less skilled readers. *Reading Research Quarterly, 20,* 39–53.

Aulls, M. W. (1982). *Developing readers in today's schools.* Boston: Allyn & Bacon.

Austin, J. (1962). *How to do things with words.* Oxford: Oxford University Press.

Ausubel, D. P., (1968). *Educational psychology—A cognitive view.* New York: Holt, Rinehart & Winston.

Ausubel, D. P., Novak, J. D., & Hanesian, H. (1978). *Educational psychology.* NY: Holt, Rinehart & Winston.

Baker, F. (1985). Pop-up books. *LD Forum, 11*(1), 1–2.

Baker, L. (1978). Processing temporal relationships in simple stories: Effects of input sequences. *Journal of Verbal Learning and Verbal Behavior, 17,* 559–572.

Baker, L., & Brown, A. L. (1984). Metacognitive skills and reading. In R. Barr, M. L. Kamil, and P. Mosenthal (Eds.), *Handbook of reading research* (pp. 353–394). NY: Longman.

Bandura, A. (1977). Self-efficacy: Toward a unifying theory of behavioral change. *Psychological Review, 84,* 191–215.

Barbe, W. (1961). *Educator's guide to personalized reading instruction.* Englewood Cliffs, NJ: Prentice-Hall.

Barberis, F. (1967). *Would you like a parrot?* New York: Scroll Press.

Barenbaum, E. M. (1983). Writing in the special class. *Topics in Learning and Learning Disabilities, 3*(3), 12–20.

Barritt, L. S., & Kroll, B. M. (1978). Some implications of cognitive developmental psychology for research in composing. In C. R. Cooper &

L. Odell (Eds.), *Research on composing: Points of departure* (pp. 49–57). Urbana, IL: National Council of Teachers of English.

Bates, E. (1976). *Language and context: Studies in the acquisition of pragmatics.* New York: Academic Press.

Bateson, M. (1975). Mother-infant exchanges: The epigenesis of conversational interaction. In D. Aaronson & R. Rieber (Eds.), Developmental Psycholinguistics and Communication Disorders. *Annals of New York Academy of Sciences* (Vol. 263, pp. 101–113). New York: Academy of Sciences.

Bauer, R. H. (1977). Memory processes in children with learning disabilities: Evidence for deficient rehearsal. *Journal of Experimental Child Psychology, 24,* 415–430.

Bauer, R. H. (1979). Memory, acquisition, and category clustering in learning disabled children. *Journal of Experimental Child Psychology, 27,* 365–383.

Baumann, J. F. (1984). The effectiveness of a direct instruction paradigm for teaching main idea comprehension. *Reading Research Quarterly, 20,* 93–108.

Beach, J. D. (1983). Teaching students to write informational reports. *Elementary School Journal, 84,* 213–220.

Beaven, M. H. (1977). Individualized goal setting, self-evaluation, and peer evaluation. In C. R. Cooper & L. Odell (Eds.), *Evaluating writing: Describing, measuring, judging* (pp. 135–156). Urbana, IL: National Council of Teachers of English.

Beck, I., McCaslin, E., & McKeown, M. (1980). *The rationale and design of a program to teach vocabulary to fourth grade students.* Pittsburg, PA: University of Pittsburgh Learning, Research, and Development Center.

Beck, I., Perfetti, C., & McKeown, M. (1982). The effects of long-term vocabulary instruction on lexical access and reading comprehension. *Journal of Educational Psychology, 74,* 506–521.

Belmont, J. M., & Butterfield, E. C. (1977). The instructional approach to developmental cognitive research. In R. V. Kail, Jr., & J. W. Hagen (Eds.), *Perspectives on the development of memory and cognition* (pp. 437–481). Hillsdale, NJ: Lawrence Erlbaum.

Bennett, R. E. (1982). Applications of microcomputer technology to special education. *Exceptional Children, 49*(2), 106–113.

Bereiter, C., & Scardamalia, M. (1983). Levels of inquiry in writing research. In P. Mosenthal, L. Tamor, & S. A. Walmsley (Eds.), *Research on writing: Principles and methods* (pp. 3–25). New York: Longman.

Berkenkotter, C. (1982). Writing and problem solving. In T. Fulwiler & A. Young (Eds.), *Language connections: Reading and writing across the curriculum* (pp. 33–44). Urbana, IL: National Council of Teachers of English.

Berthoff, A. (1982). *Forming thinking writing: The composing imagination.* Upper Montclair, NJ: Boynton/Cook.

Biemiller, A. (1970). The development of the use of graphic and contextual information as children learn to read. *Reading Research Quarterly, 6,* 75–96.

Birnbaum, J. C. (1986). Reflective thought: The connection between reading and writing. In B. T. Petersen (Ed.), *Convergences: Transactions in reading and writing* (pp. 30–45). Urbana, IL: National Council of Teachers of English.

Bjonerud, C. E. (1960). Arithmetic concepts possessed by the preschool child. *Arithmetic Teacher, 7,* 347–350.

Blachowicz, C. (1977–1978). Factors affecting semantic constructivity in children's comprehension. *Reading Research Quarterly, 12,* 188–189.

Bleich, D. (1975). *Readings and feelings: An introduction to subjective criticism.* Urbana, IL: National Council of Teachers of English.

Block, E., & Reid, D. K. (1984a). *Computer curriculum for Solomon Schechter Academy.* Unpublished manuscript. NTD: Richardson, TX.

Block, E., & Reid, D. K. (1984b). *Effects of word processing on second graders' story writing.* Unpublished manuscript.

Bloom, L. (1970). *Language development: Form and function in emerging grammars.* Cambridge, MA: MIT Press.

Bloom, L., & Lahey, M. (1978). *Language development and language disorders.* New York: Wiley & Sons.

Bloome, D., & Greene, J. (1984). Directions in the sociolinguistic study of reading. In P. D. Pearson (Ed.), *Handbook of reading research* (pp. 395–422). New York: Longman.

Bookman, M. O. (1984). Spelling as a cognitive-developmental linguistic process. *Academic Therapy, 20,* 21–32.

Bos, C. S. (1982). Getting past decoding: Assisted and repeated readings as remedial methods for learning disabled students. *Topics in Learning and Learning Disabilities, 14,* 51–58.

Bos, C. S., & Filip, D. (1984). Comprehension monitoring in learning disabled and average students. *Journal of Learning Disabilities, 17,* 229–233.

Bousfield, W. A. (1953). The occurrence of clustering in the recall of randomly arranged associates. *Journal of General Psychology, 49,* 229–240.

Bradley, C. (1985) The relationship between students' information-processing styles and LOGO programming. *Educational Computing Research, 1*(4), 427–435.

Bransford, J. D. (1979). *Human cognition: Learning, understanding, and remembering.* Belmont, CA: Wadsworth.

Bransford, J. D., Barclay, J., & Franks, J. (1972). Sentence memory: A constructive versus interpretive approach. *Cognitive Psychology,* 193–209.

Bransford, J. D., & Johnson, M. K. (1972). Contextual prerequisites for understanding: Some investigations of comprehension and recall. *Journal of Verbal Learning and Verbal Behavior, 11,* 717–726.

Bransford, J. D., Stein, B. S., Nye, M. J., Franks, J. F., Auble, P. M., Mezynski, K. J., & Perfetto, G. A. (1982). Differences in approach to learning: An overview. *Journal of Experimental Psychology: General, 3,* 390–398.

Bransford, J. D., Stein, B. S., Shelton, T. S., & Owings, R. A. (1981). Cognition and adaptation: The importance of learning to learn. In J. Harvey (Ed.), *Cognition, social behavior and the environment* (pp. 93–109). Hillsdale, NJ: Lawrence Erlbaum.

Brazelton, T., Koslowski, B., & Main, M. (1974). The origins of reciprocity: The early mother-infant interaction. In M. Lewis & L. Rosenblum (Eds.), *The effect of the infant on its caregiver* (pp. 49–76). New York: John Wiley & Sons.

Bridwell, L. (1980). Revising strategies in twelfth-grade students' transactional writing. *Research in the Teaching of English, 14,* 197–222.

Bridwell, L. S., Nancarrow, P. R., & Ross, D. (1984). The writing process and the writing machine: Current research on word processors relevant to the teaching of composition. In R. Beach & L. S. Bridwell (Eds.), *New directions in composition research* (pp. 381–398). New York: Guilford.

Britton, J. (1970). *Language and learning.* Harmondsworth, Middlesex, England: Penguin.

Broen, D. A. (1972). *The Verbal Environment of the Language-Learning Child.* ASHA Monograph No. 17. Washington, DC: American Speech-Language-Hearing Association.

Brophy, J. (1979). Teacher behavior and student learning. *Educational Leadership. 37* (October), 33–38.

Brophy, J. (1981). Teacher praise: A functional analysis. *Review of Educational Research, 51,* 301–318.

Brophy, J., & Good, T. L. (1986). Teacher behavior and student achievement. In M. L. Wittrock (Ed.), *Third handbook of research on teaching* (pp. 328–375). New York: Macmillan.

Brown, A. L. (1974). The role of strategic behavior in retardate memory. In N. R. Ellis (Ed.), *International review of research in mental retardation* (Vol. 7, pp. 55–113). New York: Academic Press.

Brown, A. L., Bransford, J. D., Ferrara, R. A., & Campione, J. C. (1983). Learning, remembering, and understanding. In J. H. Flavell & E. M. Markman (Eds.), *Handbook of child psychology: Cognitive development* (Vol. 3, pp. 77–167). New York: Wiley.

Brown, A. L., & Campione, J. C. (1986). Psychological theory and the study of learning disabilities. *American Psychologist, 41,* 1059–1068.

Brown, A. L., & Day, J. D. (1983). Macrorules for summarizing texts: The development of expertise. *Journal of Verbal Learning and Verbal Behavior, 22*(1), 1–14.

Brown, A. L., & Palincsar, A. S. (1982). Inducing strategic learning from texts by means of informed self-control training. In B.Y.L. Wong (Ed.), Metacognition and leaning disabilities. *Topics in Learning and Learning Disabilities,* 2(1), 1–18.

Brown, A. L., & Palincsar, A. S. (in press). Reciprocal teaching of comprehension strategies: A natural history of one program for enhancing learning. In J. D. Day & J. G. Borkowski (Eds.). *Intelligence and exceptionality: New directions for theory, assessment, and instructional practices.* New York: Ablex.

Brown, A. L., Palincsar, A. S., & Armbruster, B. B. (1984). Instructing comprehension-fostering activities in interactive learning situations. In H. Mandl, N. Stein, & T. Trabasso (Eds.), *Learning and comprehension of text* (pp. 255–286). Hillsdale, NJ: Lawrence Erlbaum.

Brown, A. L., & Smiley, S. S. (1977). Rating the importance of structural units of prose passages: A problem of metacognitive development. *Child Development, 48,* 1–8.

Brown. A. L., & Smiley, S. S. (1978). The development of strategies for studying texts. *Child Development, 49,* 1076–1088.

Brown, J., Redmond, A., Bass, K., Liebergott, J., & Swope, S. (1975). *Symbolic play in normal and language-impaired children.* Paper presented to American Speech-Language-Hearing Association Convention, Washington, D.C.

Brown, R. (1973). *A first language: The early stages.* Cambridge, MA: Harvard University Press.

Brown, R. (1986). Evaluation and learning. In A. R. Petrosky & D. Bartholomae (Eds.), *The teaching of writing* (pp. 114–130). Chicago: The National Society for the Study of Education.

Brownell, W. A. (1941). *Arithmetic in grades I and II: A critical summary of new and previously reported research* (Duke University Research Studies in Education, No. 6). Durham, NC: Duke University Press.

Bruce, B. (1983) *Computers and the writing Process.* Unpublished manuscript. Harvard School of Education, Cambridge, MA.

Bruce, B. (1984). A new point of view on children's stories. In R. C. Anderson, J. Osborn, & R. J. Tierney (Eds.), *Learning to read in American schools* (pp. 153–174). Hillsdale, NJ: Erlbaum.

Bruner, J. S. (1975). The ontogenesis of speech acts. *Journal Child Language, 2,* 1–19.

Bruner, J. S. (1978). The role of dialogue in language acquisition. In A. Sinclair, R. J. Jarvelle, & W.J.M. Levelt (Eds.), *The child's conception of language* (pp. 241–256). New York: Springer.

Bruner, J. S. (1982). The organization of action and the nature of the adult-infant transaction. In E. Tronick (Ed.), *Social interchange in in-*

fancy: Affect, cognition, and communication (pp. 23–35). Baltimore: University.

Bruner, J. S., Goodnow, J. J., & Austin, G. A. (1956). Programming alternatives for learning disabled adolescents. *Academic Therapy, 14,* 2–12.

Bryan, T. H. (1982). Social skills of learning disabled children and youth: An overview. *Learning Disability Quarterly, 5,* 332–334.

Bryan, T. H., Donahue, M., & Pearl, R. (1981). Learning disabled children's peer interaction during small-group problem-solving tasks. *Learning Disability Quarterly, 4,* 13–22.

Bryan, T. H., Donahue, M., Pearl, R., & Sturm, C. (1981). Learning disabled children's conversational skills: "The TV talk show". . . . *Learning Disability Quarterly, 4,* 250–259.

Bryan, T. H., & Bryan, J. H. (1986). *Understanding learning disabilities* (3rd ed.). Palo Alto, CA: Mayfield.

Bryant, N. D., Fayne, H., & Gettinger, M. (1980). *"LD efficient" instruction in phonics: Applying sound learning principles to remedial teaching* (Teaching Rep. No. 1). New York: Columbia University, Teachers College, Research Institute for the Study of Learning Disabilities.

Buckley, M. H., & Boyle, O. (1983). Mapping and composing. In M. Meyers & J. Gray (Eds.), *Theory and practice in the teaching of composition: Processing, distancing, and modeling* (pp. 59–66). Urbana, IL: National Council of Teachers of English.

Burns, H. (1984). Recollections of first-generation computer-assisted prewriting. In W. Wresch (Ed.), *The computer in composition instruction* (pp. 15–33). Urbana, IL: National Council of Teachers of English.

Burns, H., & Culp, G. (1980). Stimulating invention in English composition through computer-assisted instruction. *Educational Technology, 20,* 5–10.

Butkowsky, I., & Willows, M. (1980). Cognitive-motivational characteristics of children varying in reading ability: Evidence for learned helplessness in poor readers. *Journal of Educational Psychology, 72,* 408–422.

Butler, D. (1985). *Babies need books: How books can help your child become a happy and involved human being.* New York: Atheneum.

Calkins, L.L.M. (1983). *Lessons from a child: On the teaching and learning of writing.* Exeter, NH: Heinemann Educational Books.

Campbell, R. (1982). *Dear zoo.* New York: Four Winds Press.

Campione, J. C., & Armbruster, B. B. (1985). Acquiring information from texts: An analysis of four approaches. In J. W. Segal, S. Chipman, & R. Glaser (Eds.), *Thinking and learning skills* (Vol. 1, pp. 297–317). Hillsdale, NJ: Erlbaum.

Campos, J., Barrett, K., Lamb, M., Goldsmith, H., & Sternberg, C. (1983). Socioemotional development. In P. Mussen (Ed.), *Handbook of child psychology: Vol. 2. Socialization, personality and social development* (pp. 783–915). New York: Wiley.

Carlson, S. A., & Alley, G. R. (1981). *Performance and competence of learning disabled and high achieving high school students on essential cognitive skills.* (Research Report No. 53). Lawrence, KS: University of Kansas Institute for Research in Learning Disability.

Carpenter, T., & Moser, J. (1976). *"Using the microcomputer to teach problem-solving skills."* Unpublished manuscript. Wisconsin Center for Education Research, Madison.

Carrow, E. (1973). *Test of auditory comprehension of language.* Austin, TX: Learning Concepts.

Carrow, E. (1974). *Carrow elicited language inventory.* Austin, TX: Learning Concepts.

Cartwright, P., & Dervensky, J. (1976). An attitudinal study of computer assisted testing as a learning method. *Psychology in the Schools, 13*(3), 317–321.

Carver, R. (1982). Optimal rate of reading prose. *Reading Research Quarterly, 28,* 56–88.

Case, R. (1983). *Intellectual development: A systematic reinterpretation.* New York: Academic Press.

Case, R. & Bereiter, C. (1982). *From behaviorism to cognitive development: Steps in the evolution of instructional design.* Paper presented at the Conference for Educational Technology in the 80s, Caracas, Venezula.

Case, R., Kurland, D. M., & Goldberg, J. (1982). Operational efficiency and the growth of short-term memory span. *Journal of Experimental Child Psychology, 33,* 386–404.

Cawley, J. (1981). Commentary. *Topics in Learning and Learning Disabilities, 1*(3), 89–94.

Cawley, J. F. (1984). An integrative approach to needs of learning-disabled children: Expanded use of mathematics. In J. F. Cawley. (Ed.), *Developmental teaching of mathematics for the learning disabled.* Rockville, MD: Aspen.

Cawley, J. F. (1985). *Cognitive strategies and mathematics for the learning disabled.* Rockville, MD: Aspen Systems.

Ceci, S. J. (1982). Extracting meaning from stimuli: Automatic and purposive processing of the language based learning disabled. *Topics in Learning and Learning Disabilities, 2*(2), 46–53.

Chall, J. S. (1979). The great debate: Ten years later, with a modest proposal for reading stages. In L. B. Resnick & P. A. Weaver (Eds.), *Theory and practice of early reading* (Vol. 1, pp. 29–55). Hillsdale, NJ: Erlbaum.

Chapman, R. S. (1980). Exploring children's communicative intents. In J. F. Miller (Ed.), *Assessing language production in children* (pp. 111–136). Baltimore: University Park Press.

Chi, M.T.H. (1976). Short-term memory limitations in children: Capacity or processing deficits? *Memory & Cognition, 4,* 559–572.

Chi, M.T.H., & Gallagher, J. D. (1982). Speed of processing: A developmental source of limitation. *Topics in Learning and Learning Disabilities, 2*(2), 23–32.

Chi, M.T.H., & Glaser, R. (1980). The measurement of expertise: Analysis of the development of knowledge and skill as a basis for assessing achievement. In E. L. Baker & E. S. Quillmalz (Eds.), *Educational testing and evaluation: Design, analysis, and policy* (pp. 37–48). Beverly Hills: Sage.

Chomsky, N. (1957). *Syntactic structures.* The Hague: Mouton.

Chomsky, N. (1965). *Aspects of the theory of syntax.* Cambridge, MA: MIT Press.

Chrystal, G. (1961). *Textbook of algebra* (Vol. 1). New York: Dover.

Clark, H., & Clark, E. (1977). *Psychology and language.* New York: Harcourt Brace Jovanovich.

Clark, R. A., & Delia, J. G. (1976). The development of functional persuasive skills in childhood and early adolescence. *Child Development, 47,* 1008–1014.

Clark, R. E. (1985). Confounding in educational computing research. *Journal of Educational Computing Research, 1*(3), 129–139.

Clarke, B. K. (1985). Bibliotherapy through puppetry: Socializing the young child can be fun. *Early Child Development and Care, 19,* 338–344.

Clay, M. (1972). *SAND: The concepts about print test.* Auckland, NZ: Heinemann.

Clay, M. M. (1975). *What did I write?* Exeter, NH: Heinemann Educational Books.

Cleary, A., Mayes, T., & Packham, D. (1976). *Educational technology: Implications for early and special education.* London: John Wiley & Sons.

Coates, T., & Thoreson, C. (1981). Behavioral self-control and educational practice, or do we really need self-control? *Review of Research in Education, 7,* 3–45.

Cobb, V., & Darling, K. (1980). *Bet you can't: Science impossibilities to fool you.* New York: Lothrop.

Coburn, P., Kelman, P., Roberts, N., Snyder, T., Watt, D., & Weiner, C. (1982). *Practical guide to computers in education.* Reading MA: Addison-Wesley.

Coggins, T. E., & Carpenter, R. L. (1981). The communicative intention inventory: A system for observing and coding children's early intentional communication. *Applied Psycholinguistics, 2,* 235–252.

Coleman, J. M. (1983). Handicapped labels and instructional segregation: Influences on children's self-concepts vs. the perceptions of others. *Learning Disability Quarterly, 6,* 3–11.

Collins, A. (1986). Teaching reading and writing with personal computers. In J. Orasanu (Ed.), *Reading Comprehension: From research to practice* (pp. 171–187). New York: Erlbaum.

Collins, J. L. (1982). Discourse style, classroom interaction and differential treatment. *Journal of Reading Behavior, 14,* 429–437.

Collins, J. L., & Williamson, M. M. (1981). Spoken language and semantic abbreviation in writing. *Research in the Teaching of English, 15,* 23–95.

Conner, F. P. (1983). Improving school instruction for learning disabled children: The teachers college institute. *Exceptional Education Quarterly, 4*(1), 45–74.

Coombs, M. J., Gibson, R., & Alty, J. L. (1982). Learning a first computer language: Strategies for making sense. *International Journal of Man-Made Machines Studies, 16,* 449–486.

Cooper, C. R., & Cooper, R. G. (1984). Skill in peer learning discourse: What develops? In S. A. Kuczaj II (Ed.), *Discourse development* (pp. 77–98). New York: Springer.

Cooper, C. R., Marquis, A., & Ayers-Lopez, S. (1982). Peer learning in the classroom: Tracing developmental patterns and consequences of children's spontaneous interactions. In L. C. Wilkinson (Ed.), *Communicating in the classroom* (pp. 69–84). New York: Academic Press.

Cooper, C. R., & Odell, L. (Eds.). (1977). *Evaluating writing: Describing, measuring, judging.* Urbana, IL: National Council of Teachers of English.

Corsaro, W. A. (1981). The development of social cognition in preschool children: Implications for language learning. *Topics in Language Disorders, 1,* 77–95.

Cowan, E. (1980). Student-centered teaching and industrial management theory. In B. J. Mandel (Ed.), *Three language arts curriculum models: Pre-kindergarten through college* (pp. 235–252). Urbana, IL: National Council of Teachers of English.

Cowan, P. (1978). *Piaget with feeling: Cognitive, social and emotional dimensions.* New York: Holt, Rinehart & Winston.

Craig, H. K. (1983). Applications of pragmatic language models for intervention. In T. M. Gallagher & C. A. Prutting (Eds.), *Pragmatic assessment and intervention issues in language* (pp. 101–127). San Diego: College-Hill Press.

Crowhurst, N., & Piche, G. L. (1979). Audience and mode of discourse effects on syntactic complexity at two grade levels. *Research in the Teaching of English, 13,* 101–109.

Crystal, D., Fletcher, P., & Garman, M. (1976). *The grammatical analysis of language disability.* London: Edward Arnold.

Cullinan, B. E. (1981). *Literature and the child.* New York: Harcourt Brace Jovanovich.

Cunningham, P. M. (1979). A compare/contrast theory of mediated word identification. *The Reading Teacher, 32,* 774–778.

Dalbey, J., & Linn, M. C. (1985). The demands and requirements of computer programming: A review of the literature. *Educational Computing Research 1*(3), 253–275.

Dansereau, D. F., McDonald, B. A., Collins, K. W., Garland, J., Holley, C. D., Diekoff, G. M., & Evans, S. H. (1979). Evaluation of a learning strategy system. In H. F. O'Neil, Jr., & C. D. Spielberger (Eds.), *Cognitive and affective learning strategies* (pp. 3–44). New York: Academic Press.

Davison, M. M. (1983). Classroom bibliotherapy: Why and how. *Reading World, 23*(2), 103–107.

Day, J. (1980). *Training summarization skills: A comparison of teaching methods.* Unpublished doctoral dissertation, University of Illinois, Urbana.

de Ajuriaguerra, J., Jaeggi, A., Guignard, F., Kocher, F., Marquard, M., Roth, S., & Schmid, E. (1965). Evolution et prognostic de la dysphasie chex l'enfant. *La Psychiattrie de L'Enfant, 8,* 291–352.

Della-Piana, G. M. (1978). Research strategies for the study of revision in writing poetry. In C. R. Cooper & L. Odell (Eds.), *Research on composing: Points of departure* (pp. 105–134). Urbana, IL: National Council of Teachers of English.

Deloach, T., Earl, J., Brown, B., Poplin, M., & Warner, M. (1981). LD teachers' perception of severely learning disabled students. *Learning Disability Quarterly, 4,* 343–358.

Deloache, J. S. (1983, April). *Mother-child picture book reading as a context for memory training.* Paper presented at the Society for Research in Child Development. Detroit, MI.

De Paola, T. (1977). *Cloud book.* New York: Scholastic Book Services.

De Paola, T. (1980). *The knight and the dragon.* New York: G. P. Putnam's Sons.

Derry, S. J., & Murphy, D. A. (1986). Designing systems that train learning ability: From theory to practice. *Review of Educational Research, 56,* 1–39.

Deshler, D. D., Lowry, N. J., & Alley, G. R. (1979). Programming alternatives for learning disabled adolescents: A nationwide survey. *Academic Therapy, 14,* 54–63.

Deshler, D. D., & Schumaker, J. B. (in press). Learning strategies: An instructional alternative for learning disabled adolescents. *Exceptional Children.*

Deshler, D. D., Schumaker, J. B., Lenz, B. K., & Ellis, E. (1984a). Academic and cognitive interventions for LD adolescents: Part I. *Journal of Learning Disabilities, 17*(2), 108–117.

Deshler, D. D., Schumaker, J. B., Lenz, B. K., & Ellis, E. (1984b). Academic and cognitive interventions for LD adolescents: Part II. *Journal of Learning Disabilities, 17*(3), 170–179.

Devine, T. G. (1981). *Teaching study skills*. Boston: Allyn & Bacon.

Diederich, P. B. (1974). *Measuring growth in English*. Urbana, IL: National Council of Teachers of English.

Donahue, M. L. (1981). Requesting strategies of learning disabled children. *Applied Psycholinguistics, 2,* 213–234.

Donahue, M. L. (1983). Learning-disabled children as conversational partners. *Topics in Language Disorders, 4,* 15–27.

Donahue, M. L., Pearl, R., & Bryan, T. (1980). Learning disabled children's conversational competence: Responses in inadequate messages. *Applied Psycholinguistics, 1,* 387–403.

Dore, J. (1975). Holophrases, speech acts and language universals. *Journal of Child Language, 2,* 21–40.

Dore, J. (1977). "Oh them sheriff": A pragmatic analysis of children's responses to questions. In S. Ervin-Tripp & C. Mitchell-Kernan (Eds.), *Child discourse* (pp. 139–164). New York: Academic Press.

Dore, J. (1979). What's so conceptual about the acquisition of linguistic structures? *Journal of Child Language, 6,* 129–138.

Dougherty, B. (1986). Writing plans as strategies for reading, writing, and revising. In B. T. Petersen (Ed.), *Convergences: Transactions in reading and writing* (pp. 82–96). Urbana, IL: National Council of Teachers of English.

Douglas, V. I., & Peters, K. G. (1979). Toward a clearer definition of the attentional deficit of hyperactive children. In G. A. Hale & M. Lewis (Eds.), *Attention and cognitive development* (pp. 173–174). New York: Plenum.

Doyle, W. (1979). Making managerial decisions in the classroom. In D. L. Duke (Ed.), Classroom management. *The 78th Yearbook of the National Society for the Study of Education* (Pt. 2, pp. 42–74). Chicago: University of Chicago Press.

Duffy, G. G., Roehler, L. R., Meloth, M. S., Vavrus, L. G., Book, C., Putnam, J., & Wesselman, R. (1986). The relationship between explicit verbal explanations during reading skill instruction and student awareness and achievement: A study of reading teacher effects. *Reading Research Quarterly, 21,* 238–252.

Dunn, J. (1970). *A study of the techniques of word identification*. Doctoral dissertation, Brigham Young University.

Dunn, L. M. (1959). *Peabody picture vocabulary test*. Circle Pines, MN: American Guidance Service.

Durkin, D. (1966). *Children who read early: Two longitudinal studies*. NY: Teachers' College Press.

Durkin, D. (1978–1979). Reading comprehension instruction. *Reading Research Quarterly, 14*(4), 481–527.

Dweck, C. S., & Elliot, E. S. (1983). Achievement motivation. In P. Mussen & E. M. Hetherinton (Eds.), *Handbook of Child Psychology* (Vol. 4, pp. 643–691). New York: Wiley.

Eanet, M. G., & Manzo, A. V. (1976) REAP—A strategy for improving reading/writing/study skills. *Journal of Reading, 19* (May 1976), 647–652.

Early, M. J., Cooper, E. K., & Santeusanio, N. (1979). *HBJ bookmark reading program.* New York: Harcourt Brace Jovanovich.

Eeds, M. (1985). Bookwords: Using a beginning word list of high frequency words from children's literature K–3. *Reading Teacher, 38,* 418–423.

Ehri, L. C. (1978). Beginning reading from a psycholinguistic perspective: Amalgamation of word identities. In L. C. Ehri, R. W. Barron, & J. M. Feldman (Eds.), *The recognition of words.* Newark, DE: International Reading Association.

Eisenberg, A. R., & Garvey, C. (1981). Children's use of verbal strategies in resolving conflicts. *Discourse Processes, 4,* 149–170.

Eisenson, J. (1972). *Aphasia in Children.* New York: Harper Row.

Ekwall, E. E. (1981). *Locating and correcting reading difficulties.* Columbus, OH: Charles E. Merrill.

Elbow, P. (1976). *Writing without teachers.* New York: Oxford University Press.

Elliot, A. J. (1981). *Child language.* Cambridge: Cambridge University Press.

Emans, R., & Fisher, G. M. (1967). Teaching the use of context clues. *Elementary English, 44,* 243–246.

Emig, J. (1971). *The composing processes of twelfth graders* (Research Rep. No. 13). Urbana, IL: National Council of English Teachers.

Emig, J. (1977). Writing as a mode of learning. *College Composition and Communication, 28,* 122–128.

Englert, C. S., & Hiebert, E. H. (1984). Children's developing awareness of text structures in expository materials. *Journal of Educational Psychology, 76,* 65–75.

Englert, C. S., Semmel, M. I., & Perry, R. (1981). *A reading media simulation: Teaching special needs readers.* Santa Barbara, CA: University of California, Special Education Research Institute.

Englert, C. S., & Thomas, C. C. (1987). Sensitivity to text structure in reading and writing: A comparison of learning disabled and nondisabled students. *Learning Disabilities Quarterly, 10,* 93–105.

Ervin-Tripp, S. (1977). Wait for me, Roller Skate. In S. Ervin-Tripp & C. Mitchell-Kernan (Eds.), *Child discourse* (pp. 165–188). New York: Academic Press.

Estes, T. H., & Vaughan, J. L., Jr. (1978). *Reading and learning in the content classroom.* Boston: Allyn & Bacon.

Evans, J., & Moore, J. E. (1984). *Book report forms.* Carmel, CA: Evan-Moor.

Evans, J., Moore, J. E. (1985). *How to make books with children: Teacher's resource book.* Carmel, CA: Evan-Moor.

Evertson, C., & Emmer, E. (1982). Preventive classroom management. In D. Duke (Ed.), *Helping teachers manage classrooms* (pp. 2–31). Alexandria, VA: Association for Supervision and Curriculum Development.

Fair, G. W. (1974). *The development of sequential competencies and an instructional device for counting money for adults classified as mentally retarded.* Unpublished doctoral dissertation, University of Pittsburgh.

Farnham-Diggory, S. (1977). The cognitive point of view. In D. J. Trefinger, J. K. Davis, & R. E. Ripple (Eds.), *Handbook of teaching educational psychology.* New York: Academic Press.

Farquhar, W. W., Krumboltz, J. D. (1959). A checklist for evaluating experimental research in psychology and education. *Journal of Educational Research, 52,* 353—354.

Federal Register, August 23, 1977, *42* Pt. B, Education of the Handicapped Act.

Fernald, G. M. (1943). *Remedial techniques in basic school subjects.* New York: McGraw-Hill.

Fey, M. (1986). *Language intervention with young children.* San Diego: College-Hill Press.

Fielding, L. G., Wilson, P. T., & Anderson, R. C. (1986). A new focus on free reading: The role of trade books in reading instruction. In T. E. Raphael (Ed.), *Contexts of school-based literacy* (pp. 149–180). New York: Random House.

Finley, C. W. (1921). Some studies of children's interests in science materials. *School Science and Mathematics, 11,* 1–24.

Fitzgerald, G., & Spiegel, D. L. (1983). Enhancing children's reading comprehension through instruction in narrative structure. *Journal of Reading Behavior, 15* (2), 1–18.

Fitzmaurice-Hayes, A. M. (1985). Classroom implications. In J. F. Cawley (Ed.), *Cognitive strategies and mathematics for the learning disabled* (pp. 209–236). Rockville, MD: Aspen Systems Corporation.

Fitzsimmons, R. J., & Loomer, B. M. (1980). *Spelling: The research basis.* Iowa City: University of Iowa.

Flanagan, J. C., Mager, R. F., & Shanner, W. M. (1971). *Behavioral objectives: A guide to individualizing learning mathematics* (Vol. 2). Palo Alto, CA: Westinghouse Learning Press.

Flavell, J. H. (1983). The curriculum disabled child. *Topics in Learning and Learning Disabilities, 3,* 37–48.

Flavell, J. H. (1985). *Cognitive development* (2nd ed.). Englewood Cliffs, NJ: Prentice-Hall.

Flavell, J. H., Beach, D. H., & Chinsky, J. M. (1966). Spontaneous verbal rehearsal in memory tasks as a function of age. *Child Development, 37,* 283–299.

Flower, L. (1979). Writer-based prose: A cognitive basis for problems in writing. *College English, 41,* 19–37.

Flower, L. (1981). *Problem-solving strategies for writing.* New York: Harcourt Brace Jovanovich.

Flower, L., & Hayes, J. R. (1977). Problem-solving strategies and the writing process. *College English, 39,* 449–461.

Flower, L., & Hayes, J. R. (1980). The dynamics of composing: Making plans and juggling constraints. In L. W. Gregg & E. R. Steinberg (Eds.), *Cognitive processes in writing* (pp. 31–50). Hillsdale, NJ: Erlbaum.

Flower, L., & Hayes, J. R. (1981a). A cognitive process theory of writing. *College Composition and Communication, 32,* 367–387.

Flower, L., & Hayes, J. R. (1981b). The pregnant pause: An inquiry into the nature of planning. *Research in the Teaching of English, 15,* 220–243.

Flower, L., & Hayes, J. R. (1984). Images, plans, and prose: The representation of meaning in writing. *Written Communication, 1,* 120–160.

Forgan, H. W., & Mangrum, C. T., III. (1981). *Teaching content area reading skills.* Columbus, OH: Charles E. Merrill.

Forrest-Pressley, D. L., & Waller, T. G. (1984). Knowledge and monitoring abilities of poor readers. *Topics in Learning and Learning Disabilities 3*(4), 73–80.

Frase, L. T. (1980). *Writer's workbench: Computer supports for components of the writing process* (Tech. Rep.). Murray Hills, NJ: Bell Labs.

Freedman, S. W. (1984). *Teaching and learning in the independent writing conference* (Research Foundation Final Rep.). Urbana, IL: National Council of Teachers of English.

Frith, U. (1980). *Cognitive processes in spelling.* London: Academic Press.

Fulwiler, T., & Young, A. (Eds.). (1982). *Language connections: Reading and writing across the curriculum.* Urbana, IL: National Council of Teachers of English.

Furner, B. A. (1983). Developing handwriting ability: A perceptual learning process. *Topics in Learning and Learning Disabilities, 3*(3), 41–54.

Gag, W. (1928). *Millions of cats.* New York: Coward, McCann & Geoghehan.

Gallagher, J. M., & Reid, D. K. (1983). *The learning theory of Piaget and Inhelder.* Austin, TX: PRO-ED.

Gallagher, Y., & Prutting, C. (Eds.). (1982). *Pragmatic assessment and intervention issues in language.* San Diego: College-Hill Press.

Gammage, S. (1985). *Creating class books based on children's literature.* Unpublished manuscript.

Gardner, E. F., Rudman, H., Karlsen, B., & Merwin, J. C. (1982). *Stanford writing assessment program.* New York: Psychological Corporation.

Garvey, C. (1975). Requests and responses on children's speech. *Journal of Child Language, 2,* 41–59.

Garvey, C. (1977). *Play.* Cambridge, MA: Cambridge University Press.

Gaskins, I. W., & Bacon, J. (1985). Teaching poor readers to cope with maladaptive cognitive styles: A teaching program. *Journal of Learning Disabilities, 18,* 390–394.

Gaskins, I. W., & Elliot, T. T. (1983). *Teaching for success: Administrative and classroom practices at Benchmark School.* Media, PA: Benchmark Press.

Gearheart, B. R. (1985). *Learning disabilities: Educational strategies* (4th ed.). St. Louis: Times Mirror/Mosby College.

Gerber A. (1981). Problems in the processing and use of language in education. In A. Gerber & D. N. Bryen (Eds.), *Language and learning disabilities.* Baltimore: University Park Press.

Gerber, M. M. (1984). Techniques to teach generalizable spelling skills. *Academic Therapy, 20,* 49–58.

Gerber, M. M. (1985). Spelling as concept-driven problem solving. In B. Hutson (Ed.). *Advances in reading/language research* (Vol. 3, pp. 39–75). Greenwich, CT: JAI Press.

Gerber, M. M. (1986). Generalization of spelling strategies by LD students as a result of contingent imitation/modeling and mastery criteria. *Journal of Learning Disabilities, 19,* 530–537.

Gerber, P. J. & Harris, K. B. (1983). Using juvenile literature to develop social skills in learning disabled children. *Pointer, 27*(4), 29–32.

Gere, A. R. (1985). Introduction. In A. R. Gere (Ed.), *Roots in the sawdust: Writing to learn across the disciplines* (pp. 1–8). Urbana, IL: National Council of Teachers of English.

Gettinger, M. (1984). Applying learning principles to remedial spelling instruction. *Academic Therapy, 20,* 41–48.

Gibson, E. J. (1969). *Principles of perceptual learning and development.* New York: Appleton-Century-Crofts

Gibson, E. J., & Levin, H. (1975). *The psychology of reading.* Cambridge, MA: The MIT Press.

Gillet, J. W., & Kita, M. J. (1979). Words, kids and categories. *Reading Teacher, 32,* 538–542.

Glaser, R. (1976a). Cognitive psychology and instructional design. In D. Klahr (Ed.), *Cognition and instruction* (pp. 303–316). Hillsdale, NJ: Erlbaum.

Glaser, R. (1976b). Components of a psychology of instruction: Toward a science of design. *Review of Educational Research, 46,* 1–24.

Glaser, R., & Takanishi, R. (1986). Psychological science and education. *American Psychologist, 41,* 1025–1028.

Glassner, W. (1965). *Reality therapy.* New York: Harper Row.

Glazer J. I. (1981). Reading aloud with young children. In L. L. Lamme (Ed.), *Learning to love literature* (pp. 37–46). Urbana, IL: National Council of Teachers of English.

Glazer, S. M. (1980). *Getting ready to read: Creating readers from birth through six.* Englewood Cliffs, NJ: Prentice-Hall.

Gold, P. C. (1984). Cognitive mapping. *Academic Therapy, 19,* 277–284.

Goldenberg, E. P. (1979). *Special technology for special children: Computers as protheses to serve communication and autonomy in the education of handicapped children.* Baltimore: University Park Press.

Goldman, R., & Fristoe, M. (1969). *Goldman-Fristoe test of articulation.* Circle Pines, MN: American Guidance Service.

Golinkoff, R. M. (1975–1976). A comparison of reading comprehension processes in good and poor comprehenders. *Reading Research Quarterly, 11*(4), 623–659.

Golinkoff, R. M. & Rosinski, R. R. (1976). Decoding, semantic processing, and reading comprehension skill. *Child Development, 47,* 252–258.

Gonzales, P. C., & Elijah, D. V. (1984). Rereading: Effect on error patterns and performance levels of the Informal Reading Inventory. *Reading Teacher, 28,* 647–652.

Goodman, K. (1965). A linguisitic study of cues and miscues in reading. *Elementary English, 6,* 126–135.

Goodman, K. S. (1976). Reading: A psycholinguistic guessing game. In H. Singer & R. B. Ruddel (Eds.), *Theoretical models and processes of reading* (pp. 497–508). Newark, DE: International Reading Association.

Goodman, Y. M., & Burke, C. (1980). *Reading strategies: Focus on comprehension.* New York: Holt, Rinehart & Winston.

Goodstein, H. A. (1981). Are the errors we see the true errors? Error analysis in veral problem solving. *Topics in Learning and Learning Disabilities, 1*(3), 31–45.

Gordon, C. J., & Braun, C. (1983). Using story schema as an aid to reading and writing. *Reading Teacher, 37,* 116–121.

Gordon, C. J., & Braun, C. (1985). Metacognitive processes: Reading and writing narrative discourse. In D. L. Forrest-Pressley, G. E. Mackinnon, & T. G. Waller (Eds.), *Metacognition, cognition, and human performance: Vol. 2. Instructional Practices* (pp. 1–75). New York: Academic Press.

Gourley, J. W. (1984). Discourse structure: expectations of beginning readers and readability of text. *Journal of Reading Behavior, 16,* 169–188.

Graves, D. H. (1981). Pattern of child control of the writing process. In R. D. Walsh (Ed.), *Children want to write* (pp. 17–28). Exeter, NH: Heinemann Educational Books.

Graves, D. H. (1983a). The author's chair. *Language Arts, 60,* 176–183.

Graves, D. H. (1983b). *Writing: Teachers & children at work.* Exeter, NH: Heinemann.

Graves, D. H., & Hansen, J. (1983). The author's chair. *Language Arts, 60,* 176–183.

Gray, L. (1984). LOGO helps remove children's handicaps. *Educational Computer 4.*

Gray, L. (1986, January 5). When a computer joins child's building blocks: Guidelines for choosing a program that is geared to the nursery. *New York Times*.

Greany, V. (1980). Factors related to amount and type of leisure reading. *Reading Research Quarterly, 15*, 337–357.

Greenhalgh, C., & Townsend, D. (1981). Evaluating student's writing holistically: An alternative approach. *Language Arts, 58*, 811–822.

Greenspan, S. (1979). Social intelligence in the retarded. In N. R. Ellis (Ed.), *Handbook of mental deficiency: Psychological theory and research* (pp. 483–531). Hillsdale, NJ: Lawrence Erlbaum.

Greenwood, J., & Anderson, R. (1983). Some thoughts on teaching and learning mathematics. *Arithmetic Teacher, 3*, 42–49.

Gregorich, B. (1984). *Sue likes blue*. Grand Have, MI: School Zone Publishing.

Grice, H. P. (1975). Logic and conversation. In P. Cole & J. L. Morgan (Eds.), *Syntax and semantics: Speech acts*. New York: Academic Press.

Griffiths, D. E. (1980). Beyond the basics. *New York University Quarterly, 12*, 5–6.

Grinnell, P. C., (1984). *How can I prepare my young child for reading?* Newark, DE: International Reading Association.

Grinnell, P. C., & Burris, N. A. (1983). Drawing and writing: The emerging graphic communication process. *Topics in Learning and Learning Disabilities, 3*(3), 21–32.

Guszak, F. J. (1972). *Diagnostic reading instruction in the elementary school*. New York: Harper & Row.

Guthrie, F. M., & Cunningham, P. M. (1982). Teaching decoding skills to educable mentally handicapped children. *Reading Teacher 35*, 554–559.

Hagen, D. (1984). *Microcomputer resource book for special education*. Reston, VA: Reston Publishing.

Hagin, R. (1971). How do we find him? In E. Schloss (Ed.), *The educator's enigma: The adolescent with learning disabilities* (pp. 13–22). San Raphael, CA: Academic Therapy Publications.

Haines, D. J., & Torgesen, J. K. (1979). The effects of incentives on rehearsal and short-term memory in children with reading problems. *Learning Disabilities Quarterly, 2*, 48–55.

Hall, R. J. (1980). An information processing approach to the study of exceptional children. In B. K. Keogh (Ed.), *Advances in special education* (Vol. 2, pp. 79–110). Greenwich, CT: JAI Press.

Hallahan, D. P., Hall, R. J., Ianna, S. O., Kneedler, R. D., Lloyd, J. W., Loper, A. B., & Reeve, R. E. (1983). Summary of research findings at the University of Virginia Learning Disabilities Research Institute. *Exceptional Education Quarterly, 4*(1), 95–114.

Hallahan, D. P., & Reeve, R. E. (1980). Selective attention and distractability. In B. K. Keogh (Ed.), *Advances in special education* (Vol. 1, pp. 141–182). Greenwich, CT: JAI Press.

Hallworth, H. J., Brebner, A. (1980). *CAI for the developmentally handicapped: Nine years of progress.* Paper presented at the Association for the Development of the Computer-Based Instructional Systems, Washington, DC: (ERIC Document Reproduction Service No. 198–792).

Hammill, D. D., & Bartel, N. R. (1978). *Teaching children with learning and behavior problems.* Boston: Allyn & Bacon.

Hammill, D. D., & Larsen, S. C. (1978). *Test of written language.* Austin, TX: Pro-Ed.

Hammill, D. D., & Larsen, S. C. (1983). *Test of written language* (rev. ed.). Austin, TX: Pro-Ed.

Hammill, D. D., Leigh, J. E., McNutt, G., & Larsen, S. C. (1981). A new definition of learning disabilities. *Learning Disability Quarterly, 4*(4), 336–342.

Hanf, M. B. (1971). Mapping: A technique for translating reading into thinking. *Journal of Reading, 14*, 225–230.

Hansen, C. L. (1975). *Corrective cues vs. aided oral feedback in word attack strategies.* Unpublished manuscript, Experimental Education Unit, Child Development and Mental Retardation Center, University of Washington, Seattle.

Hansen, C. L. (1978). Story retelling used with average and learning disabled readers as a measure of reading comprehension. *Learning Disabilities Quarterly, 1*, 62–69.

Hansen, J. (1981). The effects of inference training and practice on young children's reading comprehension. *Reading Research Quarterly, 26*, 391–417.

Hare, V. C., & Borchardt, K. M. (1984). Direct instruction of summarization skills. *Reading Research Quarterly, 20*, 62–78.

Harris, M., Jones, D., & Grant, J. (1983). The nonverbal context of mother's speech to infants. *First Language, 4*, 21–30.

Harste, J. C., Burke, C. L., & Woodward, V. A. (1981). *Children, their language and world: Initial encounters with print.* Bloomington: Indiana University.

Harter, S. (1983). Developmental perspectives on the self system. In P. Mussen (Ed.), *Handbook of Child Psychology* (Vol. 4, pp. 275–385). New York: Wiley.

Hasselbring, T. (1984). Computer-based assessment for special needs students. *Special Services in the Schools: Microcomputers and Exceptional Children, 1*, 7–19.

Hasselbring, T., & Crossland, C. (1982). Application of microcomputer technology to spelling assessment of learning disabled students. *Learning Disability Quarterly, 5*, 80–82

Haugo, J. E. (1981). Management applications of the microcomputer: Promised and pitfalls. *AEDS Journal, 14,* 182–188.

Hazel, J. S., Schumaker, J. B., Sherman, J. A., & Shelton, J. (1982). Application of a group training program in social skills and problem solving to learning disabled and non-learning disabled youth. *Learning Disability Quarterly, 5*(4), 398–408.

Heath, S. (1982). Questioning at home and at school: A comparison study. In G. Spindler (Ed.), *Doing the ethnography of schooling.* NY: Holt, Rinehart & Winston.

Heide, F. P., & Heide, R. (1980). *A monster is coming! A monster is coming!* New York: Franklin Watts.

Henderson, E. H. (1981). *Learning to read and spell: The child's knowledge of words.* De Kalb: Northern Illinois University.

Herber, H. L. (1978). *Teaching reading in content areas.* Englewood Cliffs, NJ: Prentice-Hall.

Herbert., M. A., & Czerniejewski, C. (1976). Language and learning therapy in a community college. *Bulletin of the Orton Society, 26,* 96–100.

Herrick, V. E., & Okada, N. (1963). The present scene: Practices in the teaching of handwriting in the United States. In V. E. Herrick (Ed.), *New horizons for research in handwriting* (pp. 17–32). Madison: University of Wisconsin Press.

Hilgers, T. L. (1984). Toward a taxonomy of beginning writers' evaluative statements on written compositions. *Written Communication, 1,* 365–384.

Hill, C. L. (1979). *Attributional profiles on the IAR and susceptibility to learned helplessness in learning disabled boys.* Bloomington, IN: Indiana University Press.

Hillocks, G. (1984). What works in teaching composition: A meta-analysis of experimental treatment studies. *American Journal of Education, 93,* 133–170.

Hittleman, D. R. (1983). *Developmental reading, K–8: Teaching from a psycholinguistic perspective* (2nd ed.). Boston: Houghton Mifflin.

Hodapp, R. M., Goldfield, E. C., & Boyatzis, C. J. (1984). The use and effectiveness of maternal scaffolding in mother-infant games. *Child Development, 55,* 772–781.

Hodges, R. E. (1982). *Improving spelling and vocabulary in the secondary school.* Urbana, IL: National Council of Teachers of English.

Hoffman, J., O'Neal, S., Kastler, L., Clements, R., Segal, K., & Nash, M. (1984). Guided oral reading and miscue focused verbal feedback in second grade classrooms. *Reading Research Quarterly, 19,* 367–384.

Hoffman, J. V. (1979). On providing feedback to reading miscues. *Reading World, 18,* 342–350.

Hogaboam, T. W., & Perfetti, C. A. (1978). Reading skill and the role of verbal experience in decoding. *Journal of Educational Psychology, 70,* 717–729.

Holdaway, D. (1979). *The foundations of literacy.* New York: Ashton Scholastic.

Holland, A. L. (1980). *Communicative activities of daily living.* Baltimore: University Park Press.

Holmes, D. L., & Peper, R. J. (1977). An evaluation of the use of spelling error analysis in the diagnosis of reading disabilities. *Child Development, 48,* 1708–1711.

Hori, (1977). *An investigation of the efficacy of a questioning training procedure on increasing the comprehension performance of jr. high school learning disabled students.* Unpublished master's thesis. University of Kansas.

Horowitz, R. (1985a). Text patterns: Part I. *Journal of Reading, 28,* 448–454.

Horowitz, R. (1985b). Text patterns: Part II. *Journal of Reading, 28,* 534–541.

Huck, C. S. (1979). *Children's literature in the elementary school* (3rd rev. ed.). New York: Holt, Rinehart & Winston.

Hunt, K. W. (1965). *Grammatical structures written at three grade levels* (Research Rep. No. 3). Champaign, IL: National Council of Teachers of English.

Huntgate, H. (1982). Computers in the kindergarten. *Computing Teacher,* 5–18.

Huttenlocher, J., & Burke, D. (1976). Why does memory span increase with age? *Cognitive Psychology, 8,* 1–31.

Hymes, D. (1972). *Towards communicative competence.* Philadelphia: University of Pennsylvania Press.

Idol-Maestas, L. (1987). Group story mapping: A comprehension strategy for both skilled and unskilled readers. *Journal for Learning Disabilities, 20(4),* 196–205.

Ilg, F., & Ames, L. B. (1951). Developmental trends in arithmetic. *Journal of Genetic Psychology, 79,* 3–28.

Inhelder, B. (1976). Cognitive develoment and its contribution to the diagnosis of some phenomena of mental deficiency. *Merrill-Palmer Quarterly, 12,* 299–319.

Jacob, G. P. (1982). An ethnographic study of the writing conference: The degree of student involvement in the writing process. *Dissertation Abtracts International, 43,* 386A. (University Microfilms No. DA 821 6050).

Jaggar, A. M. (1985). On observing the language learner: Introduction and overview. In A. M. Jaggar & M. T. Smith-Burke (Eds.), *Observing the language learner* (pp. 1–18).Newark, DE: International Reading Association.

Jenkins, J. J. (1979). Four points to remember: A tetrahedral model and memory experiments. In L. S. Cermak & F.I.M. Craik (Eds.), *Levels of processing in human memory,* pp. (429–446). Hillsdale, NJ: Lawrence Erlbaum.

Jenkins, J. J., Pany, D., & Schreck. J. (1978). *Vocabulary and reading comprehension: Instructional effects* (Tech. Rep. No. 11). Urbana: University of Illinois, Center for the Study of Reading. (ERIC Document Reproduction Service No. 160–999).

Johns, J. (1974). Concepts of reading among good and poor readers. *Education, 95,* 58–60.

Johnson, D., & Baumann, J. (1984). Word identification. In P. D. Pearson (Ed.), *Handbook of reading research* (pp. 583–608). New York: Longman.

Johnson, D., & Pearson, P. D. (1984). *Teaching reading vocabulary* (2nd. ed.). New York: CBS College Publishing.

Johnson, J., & Pearson, D. (1984). *Teaching reading vocabulary* (2nd. ed.). New York: Holt, Rinehart & Winston.

Johnson, R., & Johnson, D. (1983). Effects of cooperative, competive, and individualistic learning experiences on social development. *Exceptional Children, 49,* 323–329.

Johnston, C. L. (1984). The learning disabled adolescent and young adult: An overview and critique of current practices. *Journal of Learning Disabilities, 17,* 386–391.

Johnston, P. H. (1985). Understanding reading disability. *Harvard Educational Review, 55,* 153–177.

Jones, V., & Jones, L. (1986). *Comprehensive classroom management: Creating positive learning environments.* Boston: Allyn & Bacon.

Kaluger, G., & Kolson, C. J. (1978). *Reading and learning disabilities* (2nd. ed.). Columbus, OH: Charles E. Merrill.

Karlin, R. (1984). *Teaching reading in high school: Improving reading in the content areas.* Cambridge, MA: Harper & Row.

Kauffman, J. M., & Hallahan, D. P. (1979). Learning disability and hyperactivity (with comments on minimal brain dysfunction). In B. B. Lahey & A. E. Kazdin (Eds.), *Advances in clinical child psychology* (Vol. 2, pp. 72–105). New York: Plenum.

Kaufman, A., Baron, A., & Kopp, R. (1966). Some effects of instruction on human operant behavior. *Psychonomic Monograph Supplement, 1,* 243–250.

Kavale, K. A., & Glass, G. V. (1984). Meta-analysis and policy decisions in special education. In B. K. Keogh (Ed.), *Advances in special education* (Vol. 4, pp. 195–247). Greenwich, CT: JAI Press.

Kavale, K., & Mattson, P. D. (1983). One jumped off the balance beam: Motor training. *Journal of Learning Disabilities, 16,* 165–173.

Kellogg, R. (1970). *Analyzing children's art.* Palo Alto, CA: National Press Books.

Kennedy, L. M. (1984). *Guiding children's learning of mathematics.* Belmont, CA: Wadsworth Publishing.

Keogh, B. K., & Glover, A. T. (1980). The generality and durability of cognitive training effects. *Exceptional Education Quarterly, 1,* 75–82.

Keogh, B. K., & Hall, R. J. (1983). Cognitive training with learning disabled pupils, In A. Meyers & W. Craighead (Eds.), *Cognitive behavior therapy with children* (pp. 163–191). New York: Plenum.

Keogh, B. K., & Pelland, M. (1985). Vision training revisited. *Journal of Learning Disabilities, 18,* 228–236.

Kinneavy, J. L. (1971). *A theory of discourse.* Englewood Cliffs, NJ: Prentice-Hall.

Kintsch, W., & van Dijk, T. A. (1978). Toward a model of discourse comprehension and production. *Psychological Review, 85,* 363–394.

Kipling, R. (1978). *Just so stories.* New York: Weathervane Books.

Kirk, S., McCarthy, J., & Kirk, W. (1968). *The Illinois test of psycholinguistic abilities.* Urbana: University of Illinois Press.

Kroll, B. M. (1985). Rewriting a complex story for a young reader: The development of audience-adapted writing skills. *Research in the Teaching of English, 19,* 120–139.

Kuczaj, S. (1975). On the acquisition of a semantic system. *Journal of Verbal Learning and Verbal Behavior, 14,* 340–358.

Kuczaj, S. (1982). On the nature of syntactic development. In S. Kuczaj (Ed.), *Language develoment: Syntax and semantics* (pp. 37–71). Hillsdale, NJ: Lawrence Erlbaum.

Kulick, J. A., Kulick, C.L.C., & Bangert-Drowns, R. L. (1985). The importance of outcome studies: A reply to Clark. *Journal of Educational Computing Research, 1*(4), 381–387.

Kurtz, B. E., & Borkowski, J. G. (1984). *Metacognition and the development of strategic skills in impulsive and reflective children.* Dissertation. University of Notre Dame.

LaBerge, D., & Samuels, S. J. (1974). Toward a theory of automatic information processing in reading. *Cognitive Psychology, 6,* 293–323.

Lachman, R., Lachman, J. L., & Butterfield, E. C. (1979). *Cognitive Psychology and information processing: An introduction.* Hillsdale, NJ: Lawrence Erlbaum.

Lamme, L. L. (1981). Literature throughout the curriculum. In L. L. Lamme (Ed.), *Learning to love literature* (pp. 47–54). Urbana, IL: National Council of Teachers of English.

Langer, J. A. (1984a). Examining background knowledge and text comprehension. *Reading Research Quarterly, 19,* 468–481.

Langer, J. A. (1984b). Literacy instruction in American schools: Problems and perspectives. *American Journal of Education, 93,* 107–132.

Langer J. A. (1986). Learning through writing: Study skills in the content areas. *Journal of Reading, 29,* 400–407.

Langer, J. A., & Applebee, A. N. (1983). *Learning to manage the writing process: Tasks and strategies.* Urbana, IL: ERIC Document Reproduction Service No. ED 243–420.

Langer, J. A., & Applebee, A. N. (1985). Learning to write: Learning to think. *Educational Horizons, 64,* 35–38.

Lapp, D., & Flood, J. (1978). *Reaching reading to every child.* New York: Macmillan.

Launey, R. D. (1981). The motor-handicapped support system. *Proceedings of the John Hopkins First National Search for Applications of Personal Computing to Aid the Handicapped* (pp. 104–109). New York: Institute of Electrical and Electronic Engineers.

Lawler, R. W. (1982). *Designing computer-based microworlds.* Byte Publications.

Lee, L. (1966). Developmental sentence types: A method for comparing normal and deviant syntactic development. *Journal of Speech and Hearing Disorders, 31,* 311–330.

Lee, L. (1971). *Northwestern syntax screening test.* Evanston: Northwestern University Press.

Leinhardt, G., Zigmond, N., & Cooley, W. W. (1981). Reading instruction and its effects. *American Educational Research Journal, 18,* 343–361.

Leonard, L. (1972). What is deviant language? *Journal Speech Hearing Disorders, 37,* 427–447.

Leonard, L. (1979). Language impairment in children. *Merrill-Palmer Quarterly, 25,* 205–232.

Leonard, L. (1981). Facilitating linguistic skills in children with specific language impairments. *Applied Psycholinquistics, 3,* 89–119.

Leonard, L., Bolders, J., Millers, J. (1976). An examination of the semantic relations reflected in the language usage of normal and language disordered children. *Journal of Speech and Hearing Research, 19,* 371–392.

Lerner, J. W. (1977). *Children with learning disabilities.* Boston: Houghton Mifflin.

Lesgold, A., & Reif, F. (1983). *Computer in education: Realizing the potential.* Washington, DC: U.S. Government Printing Office.

Levin, H., & Turner, A. (1968). Sentence structure and the eye-voice span. In H. Levin, E. J. Gibson, & J. J. Gibson (Eds.), *The analysis of reading skill.* (Project No. 5-1213). Washington, DC: U. S. Office of Education.

Levitt, E. (1970). The effect of context on the reading of mentally retarded children at the first grade level. *Journal of Special Education, 4,* 425–429.

Lewis, M., & Cherry, L. (1977). Social behavior and language acquisition. In M. Lewis & L. Rosenblum (Eds.), *Interaction, conversation and development of language* (pp. 227–245). New York: John Wiley & Sons.

Lewis, M., & Freedle, R. (1973). Mother-infant dyad: The cradle of meaning. In P. Pliner, L. Krames, & T. Alloway (Eds.), *Communication and affect: Language and thought* (pp. 127–155). New York: Academic Press.

Liberman, I. Y., & Shankweiler, D. (1985). Phonology and the problems of learning to read and write. *Remedial and Special Education, 6*(6), 8–17.

Liebling, C. (1984). *Creating the classroom's communicative context: How parents, teachers and microcomputers can help* (Center for the Study of Reading, Reading Education Rep. No. 47). Cambridge, MA: Bolt, Beranek & Newman.

Lindemann, E. (1982). *A rhetoric for writing teachers.* New York: Oxford University Press.

Linn, M. C., & Fisher, C. W. (1983, December). *The gap between promise and reality in computer education: Planning a response.* Paper presented at Making Our Schools More Effective: A Conference for California Educators, San Francisco.

Lipson, M. (1983). The influence of religious affiliation on children's memory for text information. *Reading Research Quarterly, 18,*448–457.

Lloyd, J. W., & de Bettencourt, L.J.U. (1982). *Academic strategy training: A manual for teachers.* Charlottesville: University of Virginia Learning Disabilities Research Institute.

Lloyd-Jones, R. (1977). Primary trait scoring. In C. R. Cooper & L. Odell (Eds.), *Evaluating writing: Describing, measuring, judging* (pp. 33–66). Urbana, IL: National Council of Teachers of English.

Lovell, K., Hoyle, H., & Siddall, S. (1968). A study of some aspects of the play and language of young children with delayed speech. *Journal of Child Psychology and Psychiatry,* 41–50.

Lovitt, T. (1977). *In spite of my resistance I've learned from children.* Columbus, OH: Merrill.

Lovitt, T., & Hansen, C. (1976). The use of contingent skipping and drilling to improve oral reading and comprehension. *Journal of Learning Disabilities, 9,* 481–487.

MacMillan, D. L., Keogh, B. K., & Jones, R. L. (1986). Special educational research on mildly handicapped learners. In W. C. Wittrock (Ed.), *Handbook of research on teaching* (3rd ed., pp. 686–724). New York: Macmillan.

Maddux, C. D. (1984). Using microcomputers with the learning disabled: Will the potential be realized? *Educational Computer, 31–32.*

Mandler, J. M., & Johnson, M. S. (1977). Remembrance of things parsed: Story structure and recall. *Cognitive Psychology, 9,* 111–151.

Marks, J. L., Hiatt, A. A., & Neufeld, E. M. (1985). *Teaching elementary school mathematics for understanding.* New York: McGraw-Hill.

Marlew, M. (1983). Problems and difficulties: Cognitive and communicative aspects of writing. In M. Marlew (Ed.), *The psychology of written language* (pp. 295–333). London: John Wiley & Sons.

Marshall, J. (1972). *George and Martha.* New York: Scholastic Book Services.

Martin, B., Jr. (1970, 1983). *Brown bear, brown bear, what do you see?* New York: Holt, Rinehart & Winston.

Martin, B., Jr., & Brogan, P. (1971). *Instant readers.* New York: Holt, Rinehart & Winston.

Martin, N., D'Arcy, P., Newton, B., & Parker, R. (1976). *Writing and learning across the curriculum, 11–16*. London: Ward Lock Educational.

Mason, J. M. (1984). Early reading from a developmental perspective. In P. D. Pearson (Ed.), *Handbook of reading research* (pp. 505–543). New York: Longman.

Mason, J. M., & Au, K. H. (1986). *Reading instruction for today*. Glenview, IL: Scott, Foresman and Co.

Mayer, M. (1968). *There's a nightmare in my closet*. New York: Dial Press.

Mayer, M. (1976). *Hiccup*. New York: Dial Press.

Mayer, M., & Mayer, M. (1977). *One frog too many*. New York: Dial Press.

Mayher, J. S., Lester, N., & Pradl, G. M. (1983). *Learning to write/writing to learn*. Upper Montclair, NJ: Boynton/Cook.

McCormick, S. (1977). Should you read aloud to your children? *Language Arts, 54*, 139–143.

McDonald, F. J., & Elias, P. (1976). *Beginning teacher evaluation study: Phase II* [Executive summary rep.]. Urbana, IL: ERIC Document Reproduction Service No. ED 142-592.

McFarland, W. D. (1981). A communications aid for the non-oral severely disabled. *Proceedings of the John Hopkins First National Search for Applications of Personal Computing to Aid the Handicapped* (pp. 19–20). New York: Institute of Electrical and Electronic Engineers.

McGee, L. M., & Charlesworth, R. (1984). Books with movables: More than just novelties. *Reading Teacher, 37*, 853–859.

McNutt, G. (1986). The status of learning disabilities in the states: Concensus or controversy? *Journal of Learning Disabilities, 19*, 12–16.

Mehan, H. (1979). *Learning lessons*. Cambridge, MA: Harvard University Press.

Meichenbaum, D. (1977). *Cognitive-behavior modification*. New York: Plenum.

Meichenbaum, D. (1979). Teaching children self-control. In B. B. Lahey & A. E. Kazdin (Eds.), *Advances in clinical child psychology* (Vol. 2, pp. 1–33). New York: Plenum.

Meichenbaum, D. (1980). Cognitive-behavior modification: A promise yet unfulfilled. *Exceptional Children Quarterly, 1*(1), 83–88.

Meichenbaum, D., & Goodman, J. (1969). Reflection-impulsivity and verbal control of motor behavior. *Child Development, 40*, 785–797.

Meichenbaum, D., & Goodman, J. (1971). Training impulsive children to talk to themselves: A means of developing self-control. *Journal of Abnormal Psychology, 77*, 115–126.

Menyuk, P. (1964). Comparison of grammar of children with functionally deviant and normal speech. *Journal of Speech and Hearing Research, 7*, 109–121.

Menyuk, P. (1982). Language development. In C. Kopp & J. Krabow (Eds.), *The child: Development in a social context* (pp. 282–331). Reading, MA: Addison-Wesley.

Merritt, M. (1982). Distributions and directing attention in primary classrooms. In L. C. Wilkinson (Ed.), *Communicating in the classroom* (pp. 223–244). New York: Academic Press.

Meyer, A. (1983). Origins and prevention of emotional disturbances among learning disabled children. *Topics in Learning and Learning Disabilities, 3*, 59–70.

Meyer, B. (1975), *The organization of prose and its effects on memory.* Amsterdam: North-Holland.

Meyer, B.J.F. (1982). Reading research and the composition teacher: The importance of plans. *College Composition and Communication, 33*, 37–49.

Meyer, B.J.F., & Rice, G. E. (1984). The structure of text. In P. D. Pearson (Ed.), *Handbook of reading research* (pp. 315–352). New York: Longman.

Miyake, N., & Norman, D. A. (1979). To ask a question, one must know enough to know what is not known. *Journal of Learning and Verbal Behavior, 18*, 357–364.

Molnar, A. (1981). The coming of computer literacy: Are we prepared for it? *Educational Technology, 21*(1), 26–28.

Montgomery, R. A. (1982). *Your very own robot.* Toronto: Bantam-Skylark.

Mooser, S. (1979). *Sun up.* New York: Harcourt Brace Jovanovitch.

Morris, N., & Crump, D. (1982) Syntactic and vocabulary development in the written language of learning disabled and non-learning disabled students at four age levels. *Learning Disabilities Quarterly, 5*, 163–172.

Morrison, F. J., Giordani, B., & Nagy, J. (1977). Reading disabilities: An information processing analysis. *Science, 196*, 77–79.

Morse, W., Ardizzone, J., Macdonald, C., & Pasick, P. (1980). *Affective education for special children and youth.* Reston, VA: Council for Exceptional Children.

Moss, J. F. (1984). *Focus units in literature: A handbook for elementary school teachers.* Urbana, IL: National Council of Teachers of English.

Mueller, E., & Brenner, J. (1977). The origins of social skills and interaction among playgroup toddlers. *Child Development, 48*, 854–861.

Muma, J. R. (1983). Speech-language pathology: Emerging expertise in language. In T. M. Gallagher & C. A. Prutting (Eds.), *Pragmatic assessment and intervention issues in language.* San Diego: College-Hill Press.

Muma, J. R., & Pierce, S. (1981). Language intervention: Data or evidence? *Topics in Learning and Learning Disabilities, 1*, 1–11.

Murray, D. M. (1968). *A writer teaches writing.* Boston: Houghton Mifflin.

Murray, D. M. (1978). Internal revision: A process of discovery. In C. R. Cooper & L. Odell (Eds.), *Research on composing: Points of departure* (pp. 85–103). Urbana, IL: National Council of Teachers of English.

Myers, M. (1983). Approaches to the teaching of composition. In M. Myers & J. Gray (Eds.), *Theory and practice in the teaching of composition:*

Processing, distancing, and modeling. Urbana, IL: National Council of Teachers of English.

Myklebust, H. R. (1965). *Development and disorders of written language* (Vols. 1 and 2). New York: Grune & Stratton.

Nagy, W., & Anderson, R. C. (1984). How many words are there in printed school English? *Reading Research Quarterly, 19,* 304–330.

National Advisory Committee on Handicapped Children. (1968). *First annual report.* Washington, DC: U.S. Department of Health, Education and Welfare.

The National Joint Committee on Learning Disabilities. (1985, February). *Adults with learning disabilities: A call to action.* Paper presented at the meeting of the Orton Dyslexia Society, Baltimore.

The National Joint Committee on Learning Disabilities. (1986, February). *Learning disabilities and the preschool child.* Paper presented at the meeting of the Orton Dyslexia Society, Baltimore.

Nelson, H. E. (1980). Analysis of spelling errors in normal and dyslexic children. In U. Frith (Ed.), *Cognitive processes in spelling* (pp. 475–493). London: Academic Press.

Nelson, K. (1974). Concept, word and sentence: Interrelations in acquisition and development. *Psychological Review, 81,* 267–285.

Newcomer, P., & Hammill, D. D. (1977). *Test of language development.* Austin, TX: Empiric Press.

Newell, G. E. (1984). Learning from writing in two content areas: A case study/protocol analysis. *Research in the Teaching of English, 18,* 265–287.

Newhoff, M., & Launer, P. (1984). Input as interaction: Shall we dance? In R. Naremore (Ed.), *Language science: Recent advances.* San Diego: College-Hill Press.

New York Times. (1980) March 21.

Nitsch, K. E. (1977). *Structuring decontextualized forms of knowledge.* Unpublished doctoral dissertation, Vanderbilt University.

Nodine, B. F., Barenbaum, & Newcomer, P. (1985). Story composition by learning disabled and normal children. *Learning Disability Quarterly, 8,* 167–179.

Norman, D. A. (1982). *Learning and memory.* New York: W. H. Freeman.

O'Hare, F. (1973) *Sentence combining: Improving student writing without formal grammar instruction* (Research Rep. No. 15). Urbana, IL: National Council of Teachers of English.

Oka, E. R., & Paris, S. G. (in press). Patterns of motivation and reading skills in underachieving children. In S. K. Ceci (Ed.), *Handbook of cognitive social and neuropsychological aspects of learning disabilities.* Hillsdale, NJ: Erlbaum.

Osborn, J. (1984). Workbooks that accompany basal reading programs. In G. Duffy, L. R. Roehler, & J. Mason (Eds.), *Comprehension instruction: Perspectives and suggestions.* New York: Longman.

O'Shea, L. J., Sindelar, P. T., & O'Shea, D. J. (1985). The effects of repeated reading and attentional cues on reading fluency and comprehension. *Journal of Reading Behavior, 17,* 129–142.

Ouzts, D. T. (1984). Breaking the emotional barrier through the bibliotherapeutic process. *Reading Horizons, 24*(3), 153–157.

Overholt, J. L., Rincon, J. B., & Ryan, C. A. (1984). *Math problem solving for grades 4 through 8.* Newton, MA: Allyn & Bacon.

Owens, R. (1984). *Language development: An introduction.* Columbus, OH: Charles Merrill.

Owings, R. A., Peterson, G. A., Bransford, J. D., Morris, C. D., & Stein, B. S. (1980). Spontaneous monitoring and regulation of learning: A comparison of successful and less successful fifth graders. *Journal of Educational Psychology, 72,* 117–175.

Packard, E. (1979). *The cave of time.* New York: Bantam Books.

Palincsar, A. S. (1982). *Improving reading comprehension of jr. high school students through reciprocal teaching of comprehension-monitoring strategies.* Unpublished doctoral dissertation. University of Illinois.

Palincsar, A. S. (1986). The role of dialogue in scaffolded instruction. *Educational Psychologist, 21* (1, 2), 73–98.

Palincsar, A. S., & Brown, A. L. (1984). Reciprocal teaching of comprehension fostering and monitoring activities. *Cognition and Instruction, 1,* 117–175.

Palincsar, A. S., & Brown, A. L. (1986). Interactive teaching to promote independent reading from text. *Reading Teacher, 39*(8) 771–777.

Palincsar, A. S., Ogle, D. C., Carr, E. G., & Jones, B. S. (1986). *Teaching reading as thinking.* Washington, DC: Association for Supervision and Curriculum Development.

Papert, S. (1980). *Mindstorms: Children, computers and powerful ideas.* New York: Basic Books.

Papert, S., Abelson, H., diSessa, A., Watt, D., & Weir, S. (1979). *The final report of the Brookline LOGO project: Assessment and documentation of a children's computer laboratory* (MIT LOGO Memo No. 53 and 54). Cambridge, MA: MIT LOGO Group.

Paris, S. G. (1986). Teaching children to guide their reading and learning. In T. E. Raphael (Ed.), *Contexts of school-based literacy* (pp. 115–130). New York: Random House.

Paris, S. G., Lipson, M. Y., & Wixson, K. K. (1983). Becoming a strategic readers. *Contemporary Educational Psychology, 8,* 293–316.

Patberg, J., Dewitz, P., & Samuels, S. J. (1981). The effect of context on the size of the perceptual unit used in word recognition. *Journal of Reading Behavior, 13,* 33–48.

Pauk, W. (1974). *How to study in college* (2nd ed.). Boston: Houghton Mifflin.

Pea, R. D. (1982). What is planning development the development of? In D. Forbes & M. T. Greenberg (Eds.), *New directions for child develop-*

ment: Children's planning strategies (No. 18). San Francisco: Jossey-Bass.

Pea, R. D. (1984). *Prospects and challenges for using microcomputers in school* (Tech. Rep. No. 7). New York: Bank Street College of Education, Center for Children and Technology.

Pea, R. D., & Kurland, D. M. (1984). *On the cognitive and educational benefits of teaching children computer programming: A critical look* (Tech. Rep. No. 17). New York: Bank Street College of Education, Center for Children and Technology.

Pearson, P. D. (1978). Some practical applications of a psycholinguistic model of reading. In S. J. Samuels (Ed.), *What research has to say about reading instruction* (pp. 84–99). Newark, DE: International Reading Association.

Pearson, P. D. (1984). A context for instructional research on reading comprehension. In J. Flood (Ed.), *Promoting reading comprehension* (pp. 1–15). Newark, DE: International Reading Association.

Pearson, P. D., & Gallagher, M. C. (1983). The instruction of reading comprehension. *Contemporary Educational Psychology, 8,* 317–344.

Pearson, P. D., & Johnson, D. D. (1978). *Teaching reading comprehension.* New York: Rinehart, & Winston.

Pearson, P. D., & Studt, A. (1975). Effects of word frequency and contextual richness on children's word identification abilities. *Journal of Educational Psychology, 67,* 135–139.

Pelham, W. E. (1979). Selective attention deficits in poor readers? Dichotic listening, speeded-classification, and auditory and visual central and incidental learning tasks. *Child Development, 50,* 1050–1061.

Penty, R. (1956). *Reading ability and high school dropouts.* New York: Teachers College Press.

Perfetti, C. A. (1985). *Reading Ability.* NY: Oxford University Press.

Perfetti, C. A. (1986). Continuities in reading acquisition, reading skill, and reading disability. *Remedial and Special Education, 7,* 11–21.

Perfetti, C. A., & Hogaboam, T. (1975). Relationship between single word decoding and reading comprehension skill. *Journal of Educational Psychology, 67,* 461–469.

Perkins, D. N. (1985). General cognitive skills: Why not? In S. S. Chipman, J. W. Segal, & R. Glaser (Eds.), *Thinking and learning skills: Current research and open issues* (Vol. 2, pp. 339–363). Hillsdale, NJ: Erlbaum.

Perl, S. (1979). The composing processes of unskilled college writers. *Research in the Teaching of English, 13,* 317–336.

Perl, S. (1980). Understanding composing. *College Composition and Communication, 31,* 363–369.

Petty, W. T., Petty, D. C., & Becking, M. F. (1981). *Experiences in language: Tools and techniques for language arts methods* (4th ed.). Boston: Allyn & Bacon.

Pflaum, S. W., & Bryan, T. H. (1980). Oral reading behaviors in the learning disabled. *Journal of Educational Research, 73*(5), 252–257.

Pflaum, S. W., & Pascarella, E. T. (1980). Interactive effects of prior reading achievement and training in context on the reading of learning disabled children. *Reading Research Quarterly, 16,* 138–158.

Piaget, J. (1965). *The child's conception of number.* New York: W. W. Norton.

Piaget, J. (1970). *Genetic epistemology.* New York: Columbia University Press.

Piaget, J. (1976). *The grasp of consciousness: Action and concept in the young child.* Cambridge, MA: Harvard University Press.

Poplin, M. S. (Ed.). (1981). The severely learning disabled: Neglected or forgotten? *Learning Disability Quarterly, 4,* 330–335.

Poplin, M., Gray, R., Larsen, S., Banikowski, A., & Mehring, T. (1980). A comparison of components of written expression abilities in learning disabled and non-learning disabled children at three grade levels. *Learning Disability Quarterly, 3,* 46–53.

Prutting, C. A. (1982). Pragmatics as social competence. *Journal of Speech and Hearing Disorders, 47,* 123–124.

Pucher, J. (1985). Our terrible, horrible, no good, very bad day book. *LD Forum, 11*(1), 5.

Pullis, M. (1983). Stress as a way of life: Special challenges for the LD resource teacher. *Topics in Learning and Learning Disabilities, 3,* 24–36.

Pullis, M. (1985a). LD students' temperament characteristics and their impact on decisions by resource and mainstream teachers. *Learning Disability Quarterly, 8,* 109–122.

Pullis, M. (1985b). Teaching self-management skills to E.D. adolescents. In J. Gilliam & B. Scott (Eds.), *Topics in emotional disturbance.* Austin, TX: Behavior Learning Center.

Raphael, T. E., Englert, C. S., & Kirschner, B. M. (1985, December). *The impact of text structure instruction and social context on student's knowledge about the writing process.* Paper presented at the National Reading Conference, San Deigo.

Raphael, T. E., & Kirschner, B. M. (1985). *The effects of instruction in compare/contrast text structure on sixth grade students' reading comprehension and writing production* (Research Series No. 161). East Lansing, MI: Michigan.

Raphael, T. E., & McKinney, J. (1983). An examination of fifth and eighth grade students' question answering behavior: An instructional study in metacognition. *Journal of Reading Behavior, 15*(3), 67–86.

Raphael, T. E., & Wonnacot, C. A. (1985). Heightening fourth grade students' sensitivity to sources of information for answering comprehension question. *Reading Research Quarterly, 20,* 282–296.

Raschotte, C. A., & Torgenson, J. K. (1985). Repeated reading and reading fluency in learning disabled children. *Reading Research Quarterly, 20,* 180–188.

Rea, R. E., & Reys, R. E. (1970). Mathematical competencies of entering kindergarteners. *Arithmetic Teacher, 17,* 65–74.

Read, C. (1975). *Children's categorization of speech sounds in English.* Urbana, IL: National Council of Teachers of English.

Rees, N. (1973). Auditory processing factors in language disorders: The view from Procausters' bed. *Journal Speech Hearing Disorders,* 304–315.

Reid, D. K., & Hresko, W. P. (1981). *A cognitive approach to learning disabilities.* New York: McGraw-Hill.

Reid, D. K., Hresko, W. P., & Hammill, D. D. (1988). *The test of early reading ability: II.* Austin, TX: Pro-Ed.

Research in learning disabilities [special issue]. (1983). *Exceptional Education Quarterly, 4*(1).

Resnick, L. B. (1982). Syntax and semantics in learning to subtract. In T. P. Carpenter, J. M. Moser, & T. A. Romberg (Eds.), *Addition and subtraction: A cognitive perspective,* (pp. 136–155). Hillsdale, NJ: Erlbaum.

Resnick, L. B. (1983). A developmental theory of number understanding. In H. P. Ginsberg (Ed.), *The development of mathematical thinking* (pp. 109–151). New York: Academic Press.

Reynolds, R. E., Standiford, S. N., & Anderson, R. C. (1978). Distribution of reading time when questions are asked about a restricted category of text information. *Journal of Educational Psychology, 71*(27), 183–198.

Rich, A., & Nedboy, R. (1977). Hey man . . . we're writing a poem. *Teaching Exceptional Children, 9,* 90–92.

Rico, G. L. (1983). *Writing the natural way.* Los Angeles: Tarcher.

Rizzo, J., & Stephens, M. I. (1981). Performance of children with normal and impaired oral language production on a set of auditory comprehension tests. *Journal Speech Hearing Disorders, 46,* 150–159.

Robinson, F. P. (1962). *Effective reading.* New York: Harper & Row.

Robinson, R. P. (1941). *Effective study.* New York: Harper & Row.

Rodrigues, R. J. (1983). Tools for developing prewriting skills. *English Journal, 72,* 58–60.

Rogoff, B. (1986). Adult assistance of children's learning. In T. E. Raphael (Ed.), *Contexts of school-based literacy* (pp. 27–42). New York: Random House.

Rogoff, B., Ellis, S., & Gardner, W. (1984). Adjustment of adult-child instruction according to child's age and task. *Developmental Psychology, 20,* 193–199.

Rogoff, B., & Gardner, W. (in press). Guidance in cognitive development; An examination of mother-child instruction. In B. Rogoff & J. Lave

(Eds.), *Everyday cognition: Its development in social context.* Cambridge, MA: Harvard University Press.

Roit, M. L., & McKenzie, R. G. (1985). Disorders of written communication: An instructional priority for LD students. *Journal of Learning Disabilities, 18,* 258–260.

Romberg, T. A., & Carpenter, T. P. (1986). Research on teaching and learning mathematics: Two disciplines of scientific inquiry. In M. C. Wittrock (Ed.), *Handbook of research on teaching* (3rd. Ed.) (pp. 850–873). New York: Macmillan.

Rose, K. (1982). *Teaching language arts to children.* New York: Harcourt Brace Jovanovitch.

Rose, M. (1980). Rigid rules, inflexible plans, and the stifling of language: A cognitivist analysis of writer's block. *College Composition and Communication, 31,* 389–401.

Rose, M. (Ed.). (1985). *When a writer can't write.* New York: Guilford.

Rosenshine, B. (1979). Content, time and direct instruction. In P. Peterson & H. Walberg (Eds), *Research on teaching: Concepts, findings, and implications* (pp. 28–56). Berkeley: McCutchan.

Rosenshine, B., & Stevens, R. (1984). Classroom instruction in reading. In P. D. Pearson (Ed.), *Handbook of reading research* (pp. 745–798). New York: Longman.

Rosenshine, B., & Stevens, R. (1986). Teaching functions. In M. C. Wittrock (Ed.), *Handbook of research on teaching.* (3rd ed., pp. 376–391). New York: Macmillan.

Roth, K. J. (1985). *Conceptual change learning and student processing of science text.* Paper presented at the Annual Conference of the American Educational Research Association. Chicago, IL.

Rowley, T., & Leckrone, R. (1984). *The big trak book.* Reston, VA: Reston.

Rozin, P. (1976). The evolution of intelligence and access to the cognitive unconscious. *Progress in Psychobiology and Physiological Psychology, 6,* 245–280.

Rubin, A. D. (1980). Making stories, making sense. *Language Arts, 57,* 285–293.

Rubin, A. D. (1982). The computer confronts language arts: Cans and shoulds for education. In A. C. Wilkinson (Ed.), *Classroom computers and cognitive science* (pp. 201–217). New York: Academic Press.

Rubin, D. L. (1984). Social cognition and written communication. *Written Communication, 1,* 211–245.

Rumelhart, D. E. (1977). Toward an interactive model of reading. In S. Dornic (Ed.), *Attention and performance* (Vol. 6, pp. 573–603). Hillsdale, NJ: Erlbaum.

Rumelhart, D. E. (1976). *Toward an interactive model of reading* (Tech. Rep. No. 56). La Jolla, CA: Center for Human Information Processing.

Rutter, M., Maughm, B., Martimore, P., Ouston, J., & Smith, A. (1979). *Fifteen thousand hours: Secondary schools and their effects on children.* Cambridge, MA: Harvard University Press.

Ryan, M. C., Miller, C. D., & Witt, J. C. (1984). A comparison of orthographic structure in word discrimination by learning disabled and normal children. *Journal of Learning Disabilities, 17,* 38–40.

Sachs, A. (1984). Assessing scripts before reading the story. *Learning Disability Quarterly, 7,* 226–228.

Samuels, S. J. (1979). The methods of repeated readings. *Reading Teacher, 32,* 403–408.

Samuels, S. J., & Kamil, M. L. (1984). Models of the reading process. In P. D. Pearson (Ed.), *Handbook of reading research* (pp. 185–229). New York: Longman.

Samuels, S. J., LaBerge, D., & Bremer, D. (1978). Units of word recognition: Evidence for developmental change. *Journal of Verbal Learning and Verbal Behavior, 17,* 715–720.

Santa, C. L. (1977–78). Spelling patterns and the development of flexible word recognition strategies. *Reading Research Quarterly, 12,* 125–144.

Santeusanio, R. P. *A practical approach to content area reading.* Menlo Park, CA: Addison-Wesley.

Scardamalia, M., & Bereiter, C. (1986). Research on written composition. In M. C. Wittrock (Ed.), *Handbook of research on teaching* (3rd ed., pp. 778–803). New York: Macmillan.

Schank, R. C., & Abelson, R. P. (1977). *Scripts, plans, goals, and understanding.* Hillsdale, NJ: Lawrence Erlbaum.

Schminke, C. W., Maertens, N., & Arnold, W. (1973). *Teaching the child mathematics.* Hinsdale, IL: Dryden Press.

Schneider, W., & Shiffrin, R. M. (1977). Controlled and automatic human information processing: Vol. 1, Direction, search, and attention. *Psychological Review, 84,* 1–66.

Scholastic Big Books. (1980). Auckland: Ashton Scholastic.

Schumaker, J. B., Denton, P. H., & Deshler, D. D. (1984). *The paraphrasing strategy.* Lawrence, KS: University of Kansas.

Schumaker, J. B., Deshler, D. D., Alley, G. R., Clark, F. L., Warner, M. M., & Nolan, S. (1982). Error monitoring: A learning strategy for improving adolescent academic performance. In W. K. Cruickshank & J. L. Lerner (Eds.), Vol. 3. *Coming of Age: Best of ACLD* (pp. 170–183). Syracuse, NY: Syracuse University Press.

Schumaker, J. B., Deshler, D. D., Alley, G. R., & Warner, M. M. (1983). Toward the development of an intervention model for learning disabled adolescents. *Exceptional Education Quarterly, 4*(1), 45–74.

Schumaker, J. B., Deshler, D. D., Alley, G. R., Warner, M. M., & Denton, P. H. (1982). Multipass: A learning strategy for improving reading comprehension. *Learning Disability Quarterly, 5*(3), 295–304.

Schumaker, J. B., Sheldon-Wildglen, J., & Sherman, J. A. (1980). *An observational study of the academic and social behaviors of learning disabled adolescents in the regular classroom* (Research Rep. No. 22). Lawrence: University of Kansas Institute for Research in Learning Disabilities.

Semmel, M., Cosden, M., Semmel, D., & Keleman, E. (1984). Training special education personnel for effective use of microcomputer technology: Critical needs and direction. *Special Services in the Schools: Microcomputers and Exceptional Children, 1,* 63–82.

Shaughnessy, M. P. (1977). *Errors and expectations: A guide for the teacher of basic writing.* New York: Oxford University Press.

Shavelson, R., & Bolus, R. (1982). Self-concept: The interplay of theory and methods. *Journal of Educational Psychology, 74,* 3–17.

Sheingold, K., Hawkins, J., & Kurland, D. M. (1983). *Classroom software for children and technology.* New York: Bank Street College.

Shiffrin, R. M., & Schneider, W. (1977). Controlled and automatic human information processing: II. Perceptual learning, automatic attending, and a general theory. *Psychological Review, 84,* 127–190.

Short, E. J., & Ryan, E. B. (1984). Metacognitive differences between skilled and less skilled readers: Remediating deficits through story grammar and attribution. *Journal of Educational Psychology, 76,* 225–235.

Siegler, R. S. (1983) Information processing approaches to cognitive development. In W. Kesson (Ed.), *Handbook of child psychology: History, theory, and methods* (Vol. 1, pp. 129–211). New York: Wiley.

Simms, R. B. (1984). Techniques for improving student writing. *Academic Therapy, 19,* 579–584.

Simon, C. (Ed.). (1986a). *Communication skills and classroom success: Assessment of language-learning disabled students.* San Diego: College-Hill Press.

Simon, C. (Ed.). (1986b). *Communication skills and classroom success: Therapy methodologies for language-learning disabled students.* San Diego: College-Hill Press.

Simon, S. (1979). *Animal fact/animal fable.* New York: Crown Publishers.

Sinatra, R. C., Stahl-Gemake, J., & Berg, D. N. (1984). Improving reading comprehension of disabled readers through semantic mapping. *Reading Teacher, 38,* 22–29.

Skinner, B. F. (1954). The science of learning and the art of teaching. *Harvard Educational Review, 24,* 86–97.

Skinner, B. F. (1957). *Verbal behavior.* New York: Appleton-Century-Crofts.

Skinner, B. F. (1968). *The technology of teaching.* New York: Appleton-Century-Crofts.

Slavin, R. (1983). *Cooperative learning.* New York: Longman.

Smith, D. D. (1981). *Teaching the learning disabled.* Englewood Cliffs, NJ: Prentice-Hall.

Smith, F. (1971) *Understanding reading: A psycholinguistic analysis of reading and learning to read.* New York: Holt, Rinehart & Winston.

Smith, F. (1982). *Writing and the writer.* New York: Holt, Reinhart & Winston.

Smith, F. (1983). *Essays into literacy.* Exeter, NH: Heinemann Educational Books.

Snow, C. (1977). The development of conversation between mothers and babies. *Journal of Child Language, 4,* 1–22.

Solomon, C. (1982). *Introducing LOGO to children.* Byte Publications.

Somers, A. B., & Worthington, J. E. (1979). *Response guides for teaching children's books.* Urbana, IL: National Council of Teachers of English.

Sommers, N. (1982). Responding to student writing. *College Composition and Communication, 33,* 148–156.

Sowers, S. (1982). Reflect, expand, select: Three responses in the writing conference. In T. Newkirk & N. Atwell (Eds.), *Understanding writing: Way of observing, learning and teaching* (pp. 76–90). Chelsford, MA: Northeast Regional Exchange.

Spiegle, D. L., & Fitzgerald, J. (1986). Improving reading comprehension through instruction about story parts. *Reading Teacher, 39,* 676–682.

Stallard, C. K. (1974). An analysis of the writing behavior of good student writers. *Research in the Teaching of English, 8,* 206–218.

Stanovich, K. E. (1980). Toward an interactive-compensatory model of individual differences in the development of reading fluency. *Reading Research Quarterly, 16,* 32–71.

Stanovich, K. E. (1984). The interactive-compensatory model of reading: A confluence of developmental, experimental and educational psychology. *Remedial and Special Education, 5,* 11–19.

Stark, R., & Tallal, P. (1981). Selection of children with specific language deficits. *Journal of Speech Hearing Disorders, 46,* 114–122.

Staton, T. F. (1954). *How to study.* Nashville, TN: McQuiddey Printing Company.

Stern, D. N. (1974). The goal and structure of mother-infant play. *Journal of American Academy Child Psychiatry,* 402–421.

Sternberg, R. J. (1987). A unified theory of intellectual exceptionality. In J. G. Borkowski and J. Day (Eds.), *Cognition and intelligence in special children: Comparative approaches to retardation, learning disabilities and giftedness.* Norwood, NJ: Ablex.

Sternberg, R. J., & Wagner, R. K. (1982). Automatization failure in learning disabilities. In H. L. Swanson (Ed.), Controversy: Strategy or capacity deficit. *Topics in Learning and Learning Disabilities, 2(2),* 1–11.

Stevenson, H. T. (1978). Stepping up to outlining. *Journal of Reading, 22,* 248–252.

Story box big books. (1980). Auckland: Shortland Publications.

Sutherland, Z., Monson, D. L., & Arbuthnot, M. H. (1985). *Children and books* (7th ed.). Glenview, IL: Scott Foresman.

Suydam, M., & Weaver, F. (1975). Research on learning mathematics. In J. N. Payne (Ed.), *Mathematics learning in early childhood, 37th yearbook* (pp. 43–67). Reston, VA: National Council of Teachers of Mathematics.

Swanson, H. L. (Ed.). (1982). Controversy: Strategy or capacity deficit. *Topics in Learning and Learning Disabilities, 2*(2).

Swanson, L. (1978). Verbal encoding effects on the visual short-term memory of learning-disabled and normal readers. *Journal of Educational Psychology, 70,* 439–444.

Szabos, J. (1984). *Reading—A novel approach.* Carthage, IL: Good Apple.

Tadlock, D. F. (1978). SQ3R–Why it works, based on information processing theory. *Journal of Reading, 22,* 110–116.

Taenzer, S., Cermak, C., & Hanlon, R. (1981). Outside the therapy room: A naturalistic approach to language intervention. *Topics in Learning and Learning Disabilities, 1,* 41–46.

Tansley, P., & Panckhurst, J. (1981). *Children with specific learning difficulties.* Windsor, England: NFER-Nelson Publishing.

Tarver, S. G. (1981). Underselective attention in learning-disabled children: Some reconceptualizations of old hypotheses. *Exceptional Education Quarterly, 2,* 25–35.

Taylor, B., & Beach, R. (1984). The effects of text structure instruction on middle grade students' comprehension and production of expository text. *Reading Research Quarterly, 19,* 134–146.

Taylor, B. M., & Samuels, S. J. (1983). Children's use of text structure in the recall of expository material. *American Educational Research Journal, 20,* 517–528.

Taylor, R. (Ed.). (1981). *The computer in the school: Tutor, tool, tutee.* New York: Teachers College Press.

Tchudi, S. N., & Yates, J. (1983). *Teaching writing in the content areas: Senior high school.* Washington, DC: National Education Association.

Temple, C. A., Nathan, R. G., & Burris, N. A. (1982). *The beginnings of writing.* Boston: Allyn & Bacon.

Temple, C. H., & Gillet, J. W. (1984). *Language arts: Learning processes and teaching practices.* Boston: Little Brown.

Templin, M. (1957). *Certain language skills in children* (Institute of Child Welfare Monograph Series No. 26). Minneapolis: University of Minnesota Press.

Terry, P., Samuels, S. J., & LaBerge, D. (1976). The effects of letter degradation and letter spacing on word recognition. *Journal of Verbal Learning and Verbal Behavior, 15,* 577–585.

Thomas, A. (1979). Learned helplessness and expectancy factors: Implications for research in learning disabilities. *Review of Educational Research, 49,* 208–221.

Tierney, R. J., & Cunningham, J. W. (1984). Research on teaching comprehension. In P. D. Pearson (Ed.), *Handbook of reading research* (pp. 609–655). New York: Longman.

Tierney, R. J., Readence, J. E., and Dishner, E. K. (1985). *Reading strategies and practices* (2nd ed.). Rockleigh, NJ: Allyn & Bacon.

Tobias, S. (1982). When do instructional methods make a difference? *Educational Researcher, 11,* 4–10.

Tompkins, G. E., & Webeler, M. (1983). What will happen next? Using predictable books with young children. *Reading Teacher, 36,* 498–502.

Torgesen, J. K. (1977). The role of nonspecific factors in the task performance of learning disabled children: A theoretical assessment. *Journal of Learning Disabilities, 2,* 45–52.

Torgesen, J. K. (1980). Conceptual and educational implications of the use of efficient task strategies by learning disabled children. *Journal of Learning Disabilities, 13,* 19–26.

Torgesen, J. K. (1982a). The learning disabled child as an inactive: Educational implications. *Topics in Learning and Learning Disabilities, 2*(1), 45–52.

Torgesen, J. K. (1982b). The use of rationally defined subgroups in research on learning disabilities. In J. P. Das, R. F. Mulcahy, & A. E. Wall (Eds.), *Theory and research in learning disabilities* (pp. 111–132). New York: Plenum.

Torgesen, J. K. (1984). Instructional uses of microcomputers with elementary aged mildly handicapped children. *Special Services in the Schools: Microcomputers and Exceptional Children, 1,* 37–48.

Torgesen, J. K., & Houck, G. (1980). Processing deficiencies in learning disabled children who perform poorly on the digit span test. *Journal of Educational Psychology, 72,* 141–160.

Torgesen, J. K., & Kail, R. V., Jr. (1980). Memory processes in exceptional children. In B. K. Keogh (Ed.), *Advances in special education* (Vol. 1, pp. 55–110). Greenwich, CT: JAI Press.

Torgesen, J. K., & Young, K. (1983). Priorities for the use of microcomputers with learning disabled children. *Journal of Learning Disabilities, 16*(4), 234–237.

Trelease, J. (1985). *The read-aloud handbook*. New York: Penguin Books.

Turkell, S. B., & Podell, D. M. (1984). Computer-assisted learning for mildly handicapped students. *Teaching Exceptional Children, 16*(4), 258–262.

Vacca, R. T. (1981). *Content area reading*. Boston: Little, Brown.

Vacca, R. T., & Vacca, J.A.L. (1986). *Content area reading* (2nd ed.). Boston: Little Brown.

Van Nostrand, A. D. (1979). Writing and the generation of knowledge. *Social Education, 43,* 178–180.

Van Riper, C., & Erickson, R. L. (1975). *Predictive screening test of articulation*. Michigan: Western Michigan University, Continuing Education Office.

Veatch, J. (1959). *Individualizing your reading program.* New York: G. P. Putnam's Sons.

Vellutino, F. R. (1979). *Dyslexia: Theory and research.* Cambridge, MA: MIT Press.

Viorst, J. (1979). *Alexander and the terrible, horrible, no good, very bad day.* New York: Atheneum.

von Bertalanffy, L. (1981). *A systems view of man.* In P. A. Violette (Ed.). Boulder, CO: Westview Press.

Vygotsky, L. S. (1978). *Mind in society: The development of higher psychological processes* (M. Cole, V. John-Steiner, S. Scribner, & E. Souberman, Eds. and trans.). Cambridge, MA: Harvard University Press.

Wagoner, S. A. (1983). Comprehension monitoring: What it is and what we know about it. *Reading Research Quarterly, 18,* 328–346.

Walberg, H. J. (1984). Improving the productivity of America's schools. *Educational Leadership, 41,* 19–30.

Walberg, H. J., & Tsai, S. (1984). Reading achievement and diminishing returns to time. *Journal of Educational Psychology, 76,* 442–451.

Walmsley, S. A. (1983a). Helping the learning-disabled child overcome writing disabilities in the classroom.

Walmsley, S. A. (1983b). Writing disability. In P. Mosenthal, L. Tamor, & S. A. Walmsley (Eds.), *Research on writing: Principles and methods* (pp. 267–286). New York: Longman.

Wang, M. (1983). Development and consequences of students' sense of personal control. In J. Levine & M. Wang (Eds.). *Teacher and student perceptions: Implications for learning* (pp. 213–247). Hillsdale, NJ: Erlbaum.

Wang, M., & Birch, J. (1984a). Effective special education in regular classes. *Exceptional Children, 50*(5), 391–398.

Wang, M. & Birch, J. (1984b). Comparison of a full-time mainstreaming program and a resource room approach. *Exceptional Children, 51*(1), 33–40.

Wang, M. C. (1987). Toward achieving educational excellence for all students: Program design and student outcomes. *Remedial and Special Education, 8,* 25–34.

Wang, M. C., & Baker, E. T. (1985–1986). Mainstreaming programs: Design features and effects. *The Journal of Special Education, 19,* 503–521.

Watt, D. (1981). Computer literacy: What should schools do about it? *Instructor, 91,* 85–87.

Waxman, J. C., Wang, M. C., Anderson, K. A., & Walberg, H. J. (1985). Adaptive education and student outcomes: A quantative synthesis. *Journal of Educational Research, 78,* 228–236.

Weaver, P. A. (1979). Improving reading comprehension: Effects of sentence organization instruction. *Reading Research Quarterly, 15,* 129–146.

Weber, R. M. (1970). A linguistic analysis of first-grade reading errors. *Reading Research Quarterly, 5,* 427–451.

Weiner, B. (1979). A theory of motivation for some classroom experiences. *Journal of Educational Psychology, 71,* 3–25.

Weiner, E. S. (1980). Diagnostic evaluation of writing skills. *Journal of Learning Disabilities, 13,* 48–53.

Weinstein, C. E., & Mayer, R. E. (1986). The teaching of learning strategies. In M. C. Wittrock (Ed.), *Handbook of research on teaching* (3rd ed., pp. 315–327). New York: MacMillan.

Weir, S., & Watt, D. (1981). LOGO: A computer environment for learning disabled students. *Computing Teacher, 8*(5), 11–19.

Weisgerber, R. A., & Blake, P. L. (1984). *The evaluation and selection of instructional software for use with the learning disabled.* Palo Alto, CA: American Institutes for Research in the Behavioral Sciences, Center for Research and Evaluation.

Wells, G. (1979). Learning and using the auxilliary verb in English. In V. Lee (Ed.), *Language development* (pp. 250–270). New York: John Wiley.

Werner, E. E., & Smith, R. S. (1980). An epidemiological perspective on some antecedents and consequences of childhood mental health problems and learning disabilities. *Journal of American Academy of Child Psychiatry, 18,* 292–306.

Wertsch, J. V., & Stone, C. A. (1979, February). *A social interactional analysis of learning disabilities remediation.* Paper presented at the International Conference of the Association for Children with Learning Disabilities. San Francisco, CA.

White, C. V., Pascarella, E. T., & Pflaum, S. W. (1981). Effects of training in sentence construction on the comprehension of learning disabled children. *Journal of Educational Psychology, 73,* 697–704.

White, S. H. (1970). The learning theory tradition for child psychology. In P. H. Mussen (Ed.), *Carmichael's manual of child psychology* (Vol. 1, pp. 657–701). New York: Wiley.

Whitehead, R. J. (1984). *A guide to selecting books for children.* Metuchen, NJ: Scarecrow Press.

Wiederholt, J. L. (1974). Historical perspectives on the education of the learning disabled. In L. Mann & D. A. Sabatino (Eds.), *The second review of special education.* Philadelphia: JSE Press.

Wiederholt, J. L. (Ed.). (1982). Lifespan instruction for the learning disabled. *Topics in Learning and Learning Disabilities, 2*(3).

Wiens, J. (1983). Metacognition and the adolescent passive learner. *Journal of Learning Disabilities, 16,* 404–425.

Wiig, E. H., & Semel, E. M. (1980). *Clinical evaluation of language function.* Columbus, OH: Charles E. Merrill.

Williams, J. (1979). The ABD's of reading: A program for the learning disabled. In L. B. Resnick & P. A. Weaver (Eds.), *Theory and practice of early reading* (Vol. 3, pp. 179–196). Hillsdale, NJ: Erlbaum.

Williams, J. P. (1984). Phonemic analysis and how it relates to reading. *Journal of Learning Disabilities, 17,* 240–245.

Winitz, H. (Ed.). (1983). *Treating language disorders: For clinicians by clinicians.* Baltimore: University Park Press.

Winograd, P. N. (1984). Strategic difficulties in summarizing texts. *Reading Research Quarterly, 4,* 404–425.

Winograd, P. N., & Hare, V. C. (1984, October). *Direct instruction of reading comprehension strategies: The nature of teacher explanation.* Paper presented at the conference on Learning and Study Strategies: Issues in Assessment, Instruction and Evaluation, College Station, TX.

Witte, S. P. (1985). Revising, composing theory, and research design. In S. W. Freedman (Ed.), *The acquisition of written language: Response and revision,* (pp. 250–284). Norwood, NJ: Ablex.

Wixson, K. K. (1983) Postreading question-answer interactions and children's learning from text. *Journal of Educational Psychology, 75,* 413–423.

Wixson, K. K., Bosky, A. B., Yochum, M. N., & Alvermann, D. E. (1984). An interview for assessing student's perceptions of classroom reading tasks. *Reading Teacher, 37,* 346–353.

Wixson, K. K., & Lipson, M. Y. (1986). Reading (dis)ability: An interactionist perspective. In T. E. Raphael (Ed.), *Contexts of school-based literacy* (pp. 131–148). New York: Random House.

Wong, B.Y.L. (1979). Increasing retention of main ideas through questioning strategies. *Learning Disability Quarterly, 2,* 42–47.

Wong, B.Y.L. (1980). Activating the inactive learner: Use of question/ prompts to enhance comprehension and retention of implied information in disabled children. *Learning Disabled Quarterly, 3,* 29–37.

Wong, B.Y.L. (Ed.). (1982). Metacognition and learning disabilities. *Topics in Learning and Learning Disabilities, 2*(1).

Wong, B.Y.L. (1985). Self-questioning instructional research. *Review of Education Research, 55*(2), 227–268.

Wong, B.Y.L. (in press). Metacognition and learning disabilities. In T. G. Waller, D. Forrest, & E. MacKinnan (Eds.), *Metacognition, cognition, and human performance.* New York: Academic Press.

Wong, B.Y.L., & Jones, W. (1982). Increasing metacomprehension in learning disabled and normally achieving students through self-questioning training. *Learning Disabilities Quarterly, 5,* 228–238.

Wong, B.Y.L., & Sawatsky, D. (1984). Sentence elaboration and retention of good, average and poor readers. *Learning Disability Quarterly, 7,* 229–236.

Wong, B.Y.L., & Wilson, M. (1984). Investigating awareness of and teaching passage organization in learning disabled children. *Journal of Learning Disabilities, 17,* 447–482.

Wong, B.Y.L., Wong, R., & Foth, D. (1977). Recall and clustering of verbal materials among normal and poor readers. *Bulletin of the Psychonomic Society, 10,* 375–378.

Wong, B.Y.L., Wong, R., & LeMare, L. J. (1982). The effects of knowledge of criterion tasks on the comprehension and recall of normally-achieving and learning disabled children. *Journal of Educational Research, 76,* 119–126.

Wood, P., Bruner, J., & Ross, G. (1976). The role of tutoring in problem solving. *Journal of Child Psychology and Psychiatry, 17,* 89–100.

Worden, P. E. (1983). Memory strategy instruction with the learning disabled. In M. Pressley & J. R. Levin (Eds.), *Cognitive strategy research* (pp. 129–153). New York: Springer.

Worden, P. E., Malgren, I., & Gabourie, P. (1982). Memory for stories in learning disabled adults. *Journal of Learning Disabilities, 15,* 145–152.

Young, K., Torgesen, J. K., Rashotte, C. A., & Jones, K. M. (1983). *Microcomputers in the resource room: A handbook for teachers.* Tallahassee, FL: Leon County Public Schools.

Young, R. E. (1976). Invention: A topographical survey. In G. Tate (Ed.), *Teaching composition: Ten bibliographical essays* (pp. 1–43). Fort Worth: Christian University Press.

Young, R. E. (1978). Paradigms and problems: Needed research in rhetorical invention. In C. R. Cooper & L. Odell (Eds.), *Research on composing: Points of departure* (pp. 29–47). Urbana, IL: National Council of Teachers of English.

Young, R. E. (1987). Recent development in rhetorical invention. In G. Tate (Ed.), *Teaching composition: Twelve bibliographical essays* (pp. 1–38). Fort Worth: Texas Christian University Press.

Ysseldyke, J. E., & Algozzine, J. (1981). *Critical issues in social and remedial education.* Boston: Houghton Mifflin.

Ysseldyke, J. E., Thurlow, M., Graden, J., Wesson, C., Algozzine, B., & Deno, S. (1983). Generalizations from five years of research on assessment and decision making: The University of Minnesota Institute. *Exceptional Education Quarterly, 4*(1), 75–93.

Index